Paths to Peace:
Is Democracy
the Answer?

CSIA Studies in International Security

Michael E. Brown, Sean M. Lynn-Jones, and Steven E. Miller, series editors
Karen Motley, executive editor
Center for Science and International Affairs (CSIA)
John F. Kennedy School of Government, Harvard University

Published by The MIT Press:

Allison, Graham T., Owen R. Coté, Jr., Richard A. Falkenrath, and Steven E. Miller, *Avoiding Nuclear Anarchy: Containing the Threat of Loose Russian Nuclear Weapons and Fissile Material* (1996)

Allison, Graham T., and Kalypso Nicolaïdis, eds., *The Greek Paradox: Promise vs. Performance* (1996)

Brown, Michael E., ed., *The International Dimensions of Internal Conflict* (1996)

Falkenrath, Richard A., *Shaping Europe's Military Order: The Origins and Consequences of the CFE Treaty* (1994)

Feldman, Shai, *Nuclear Weapons and Arms Control in the Middle East* (1996)

Forsberg, Randall, ed., *The Arms Production Dilemma: Contraction and Restraint in the World Combat Aircraft Industry* (1994)

Shields, John M., and William C. Potter, eds., *Dismantling the Cold War: U.S. and NIS Perspectives on the Nunn-Lugar Cooperative Threat Reduction Program* (1997)

Published by Brassey's, Inc.:

Blackwill, Robert D., and Sergei A. Karaganov, eds., *Damage Limitation or Crisis? Russia and the Outside World* (1994)

Johnson, Teresa Pelton, and Steven E. Miller, eds., *Russian Security After the Cold War: Seven Views from Moscow* (1994)

Mussington, David, *Areas Unbound: The Globalization of Defense Production* (1994)

Published by CSIA:

Allison, Graham, Ashton B. Carter, Steven E. Miller, and Philip Zelikow, eds., *Cooperative Denuclearization: From Pledges to Deeds* (1993)

Campbell, Kurt M., Ashton B. Carter, Steven E. Miller, and Charles A. Zraket, *Soviet Nuclear Fission: Control of the Nuclear Arsenal in a Disintegrating Soviet Union* (1991)

Paths to Peace:
Is Democracy the Answer?

Editor
Miriam Fendius Elman

CSIA Studies in International Security

The MIT Press
Cambridge, Massachusetts
London, England

Library of Congress Cataloging-in-Publication Data

Paths to peace: is democracy the answer? / Miriam Fendius Elman, editor.
p.   cm.—(CSIA studies in international security)
Includes bibliographical references and index.
ISBN 0-262-55029-6 (pbk.: alk. paper)
1. Peace. 2. Democracy. 3. Pacific settlement of international disputes.
I. Elman, Miriam Fendius.
II. Series.
JZ5548.P38 1997

321.8—dc21   97-21782
                                                                              CIP

10 9 8 7 6 5 4 3 2 1
Printed in the United States of America

Contents

Preface

This book critically examines two of the most important propositions to emerge from studies of international security in recent decades: the idea that democracies almost never go to war with each other, and the notion that democracies are more pacific in general than are other types of states. Known as "democratic peace theory," these arguments have become widely accepted explanations for international war and peace. The claim that democracies do not wage war on each other *because* they are democracies has captured the imagination of scholars and policy makers alike, and proponents of the theory hold that a certain domestic political structure—democracy—is the best way to ensure international cooperation and the absence of war. Thus, enlarging the zone of democratic governance has replaced containment as the optimal solution for maintaining a peaceful international order.

In this book we are gate-crashers at the democratic peace party. We argue that democratic peace proponents have overstated their case. Democratic peace theorists overemphasize domestic regime type and political ideology in explaining war and peace outcomes and underestimate the capacity for other domestic- and international-level factors to promote international cooperation and conflict. Focusing on international crises between democratic, democratic-nondemocratic, and nondemocratic pairs of states, we show that domestic political structure frequently is not the most important domestic-level variable to influence war and peace decisions; that liberal norms and democratic institutions may not always prevent wars among democracies; that the democratic process does not always generate benign foreign policies; that geopolitical factors and strategic calculations can often explain peace among democracies and wars among nondemocracies and mixed regimes; and that the internal characteristics of nondemocratic states do not invariably increase the likelihood of war.

This book, which includes contributions from both proponents and critics of the democratic peace theory, advances the debate in three ways. First, using the comparative case study method, we test dyadic and monadic versions of the democratic peace theory; institutional versus normative explanations for the democratic peace phenomenon; and democratic peace theorists' claims regarding the behavior of nondemocracies. While a number of the chapters find support for the democratic peace thesis, our cumulative findings suggest that some variants of the democratic peace theory are more robust than others and that certain claims frequently voiced by democratic peace proponents cannot be logically deduced from the theory.

Second, we assess the extent to which domestic norms and institutions influence threat perceptions and the foreign policy making process. We find that although domestic politics influences war and peace decision making, democratic peace proponents should abandon zealous claims, and focus more on the complex phenomenon of war and peace and less on the single cause of domestic political structure. We find that other internal characteristics often better account for war and peace decisions, and that normative principles other than political ideology often explain war-proneness. Together, we show that regime type is not the only—nor typically the most important — variable that influences foreign policy decision making. We warn that a research agenda aimed at deepening our understanding of war and peace by studying only the impact of one domestic-level variable is doomed to failure, and provides a dangerous blueprint on which to base policy. We must learn how domestic regime type—democracy versus nondemocracy—interacts with a variety of other factors at both the domestic and international levels.

Third, we analyze the causes of democratic-democratic conflict and the sources of peace among democracies. Democratic peace proponents insist that wars among democracies are unlikely; democratically governed states have rarely—or at least hardly ever—waged war against one another. But rather than dismiss the democratic peace theory in its entirety or proclaim its universal validity, democratic peace proponents and their critics should specify the conditions that contribute to democratic peace, and the conditions that are likely to undermine it. Our joint effort identifies several such contingencies.

This is the first book to provide a qualitative, case-based assessment of the various arguments that might account for a democratic peace. Case studies are important because they can help to identify the reasons why democracy generates pacific international outcomes, specify the circumstances under which a liberal peace might break down, and assess the extent to which foreign policy makers act in ways that are consistent with the theory's propositions. Such analysis requires a firm grasp of the theoretical propositions to be tested, and an in-depth knowledge of numerous countries, historical periods, and events. Consequently, some of the best research utilizing the comparative case research design has been published by groups of scholars who pool their case-specific knowledge into a joint assessment of a theoretical proposition. I was fortunate to find nine authors who were willing to share their expertise on a diverse range of cases, and expend the time and energy to investigate the causal arguments underlying the democratic peace finding. I thank the contributors to this volume for their enthusiasm, for their extraordinary efforts to focus on a common theoretical framework, and for patiently cooperating in three rounds of revision.

This book was launched in September 1995, when Steven E. Miller, Director of the International Security Program at Harvard University's Center for Science and International Affairs (CSIA) and Editor-in-Chief of *International Security*; Michael E. Brown, Associate Director of the International Security Program and Managing Editor of *International Security*; and Sean M. Lynn-Jones, Editor of *International Security*; and Research Associate at CSIA, encouraged me to write a book proposal for the CSIA Studies in International Security based on my idea that the democratic peace theory should be tested using the comparative case study method. After numerous rewrites, the book prospectus was approved in February 1996.

The fact that a junior scholar, who had barely finished with her doctoral dissertation, could undertake this project and complete it in such a short period is due to the guidance and support of a great number of people. I would like to thank Graham Allison, Director of CSIA, for inviting me to spend the 1995–96 academic year as a postdoctoral research fellow at CSIA, for supporting this project, and for insisting on perfection. CSIA was an ideal intellectual home, and I am grateful to its staff and fellows, especially the members of the Working Group on Preventing Deadly Conflict, for their comments and constructive criticism on the book prospectus and early drafts.

I also thank the CSIA fellows and the fellows from Harvard's John M. Olin Institute for Strategic Studies for attending my presentation of the book prospectus in May 1996, and for the good advice in the project's initial stages. I am also indebted to Mike Brown, Chris Gelpi, Joe Hagan, Sean Lynn-Jones, and Randy Schweller, who graciously interrupted their own work for several days to take part in a June 1996 workshop held at CSIA, where we met to review first drafts of chapters and discuss the book's contribution to the debate. These colleagues sharpened our arguments and our understanding of the democratic peace theory, corrected several errors, and helped generate spirited debates at our workshop meetings. I am grateful to them, and to the authors of this book, whose comments, criticism, and suggestions at the workshop made the task of revising our draft chapters much easier. We have also profited enormously from many colleagues, too numerous to list here, who read our draft chapters and gave valuable feedback. These scholars are thanked individually by each author. We are grateful to all of them.

I speak for all the authors in thanking our exceptional copyeditor, Miriam Avins. She far exceeded the efforts of normal copyediting, and greatly improved the quality of our chapters. Her insightful suggestions for revision and her rapid work allowed us to meet our production deadlines without sacrificing conceptual or organizational clarity. At Arizona State University, junior fellows Elisa Ringlen, Gabriel Torres, and Zachary Porianda helped with proofreading. My special thanks to my graduate research assistant, Kevin Ellsworth, for expertly preparing our index.

I would like to thank the staff at CSIA for carrying out the administrative burden of getting this book into print. I thank Graceann Todaro for helping me to organize our June 1996 workshop, and Marie Allitto and Peggy Scannell for handling the financial record keeping. Karen Motley, Executive Editor of the CSIA Studies in International Security, orchestrated the production of this book with her usual good cheer, patience, and efficiency. Dawn Opstad, Ann Callahan, and Deborah Kamen helped with proofreading, a task made much easier by Puritan Press's expert type-setting job completed in record time.

Three others deserve my deepest thanks. Colin Elman contributed suggestions and valuable insights from the start, cheerfully adjusted to deadlines, and provided comic relief. This book could not have been carried out without Mike Brown and Sean Lynn-Jones's unflagging enthusiasm for the project, and their confidence in my ability to pull it off. I am grateful to them for reading numerous drafts, for providing detailed comments and constructive criticism throughout, and for teaching me the dos and don'ts of editing.

Finally, generous financial support was provided by a number of institutions. I thank the Center for Science and International Affairs and Arizona State University for supporting my year at Harvard in 1995–96. Steve Walker, Chair of the Department of Political Science at ASU, graciously agreed to my leave of absence and made sure that ASU financial support ran smoothly. I also thank the Carnegie Corporation of New York for providing a generous grant, administered by CSIA, that enabled us to undertake this project. I am especially grateful to David Hamburg, David Speedie, and Astrid Tuminez of the Carnegie Corporation and to Jane Holl, Esther Brimmer, and Thomas Leney of the Carnegie Commission on Preventing Deadly Conflict for supporting our endeavor.

Miriam Fendius Elman
Tempe, Arizona, April 1997

Paths to Peace: Is Democracy the Answer?

Introduction

The Need for a Qualitative Test of the Democratic Peace Theory

Miriam Fendius Elman

This book is about democracy and its impact on war and peace. In it, we ask five central questions. First, do democratic states remain at peace because of democratic norms and institutions? Second, under what circumstances and conditions might democracies become enemies? Third, are democracies predisposed to peaceful methods of international conflict resolution? Fourth, do democratic states base their foreign policy choices on the regime type of their adversaries? Finally, are nondemocratic norms and institutions obstacles to international peace?

In answering these questions, this book examines one of the most important empirical findings and theories to emerge from studies of international relations in recent decades—the absence of war between democracies and the theory that explains this "democratic peace."[1] According to the democratic peace thesis, the best explanation of a state's behavior lies in the nature of the state. Factors internal to the

The author thanks the participants in the project, and Michael Brown, Raymond Cohen, Renée de Nevers, Colin Elman, Christopher Gelpi, Joe Hagan, Arie Kacowicz, Alexander Kozhemiakin, Sean Lynn-Jones, Susan Peterson, James Lee Ray, Steve Rock, Randy Schweller, Sheldon Simon, Jack Snyder, Jeff Taliaferro, Brian Taylor, and Brad Thayer for their helpful comments and contructive criticism.

1. Strictly speaking, the democratic peace is an empirical finding and not a theory. The empirical finding includes both evidence that democracies have rarely waged war on each other (the dyadic finding) and evidence that they are less likely to use force in general (the monadic finding). While I use the term "democratic peace theory" for convenience, readers should be aware that there are multiple democratic peace theories that attempt to explain these curious empirical findings. These two different empirical findings and the various arguments explaining the democratic peace are discussed below.

state affect how those who make foreign policy decisions are likely to interpret the external environment. Political ideologies, culture, and institutions determine decision makers' threat perceptions, and thus influence the state's propensity to wage war. Democracy exerts a pacifying force: according to some proponents of the theory, democracies are more peaceful in their relations with all other countries; according to others, democratic states are likely to exhibit less conflict among themselves than other types of states.

In the 1990s, U.S. foreign policy makers have also increasingly linked the spread of democracy to international peace. The apparent absence of war between democracies has prompted policy makers to make democratization the cornerstone of U.S. foreign policy in the post–Cold War era. President Bill Clinton has relied on the idea that democracies do not go to war with each other to justify aid to Russia and intervention in Bosnia and Haiti. Both President Clinton and former National Security Adviser Anthony Lake have suggested that building a community of democratic states would serve U.S. strategic purposes, since "democracies rarely wage war on one another." President Clinton has made the enlargement of the world's roster of democracies one of the top U.S. foreign policy priorities for his administration's second term in office.[2] In 1993, President Clinton created new posts in the State Department and National Security Council for the purpose of spreading democracy, and proposed a 60 percent increase in funds for the National Endowment for Democracy's programs to encourage elections overseas.[3] In short, many policy makers are convinced that a democratic world will be a world with less war because shared democratic institutions and values decrease war-propensities. How other states manage their internal affairs is now considered of direct consequence to U.S. national security.

Events in the 1980s and 1990s appear to reinforce the idea that democracy dampens international conflict. For example, since 1991, democratic Argentina and Chile have reduced their military expenditures and have amicably settled twenty-two border disputes.[4]

---

2. See "Transcript of Clinton's Address," *New York Times*, January 26, 1994; and Anthony Lake, "The Reach of Democracy," *New York Times*, September 23, 1994.

3. See Les Aspin, *Report on the Bottom-Up Review* (Washington, D.C.: U.S. Department of Defense, October 1993), pp. 1–31; and Judith Miller, "At Hour of Triumph, Democracy Recedes as Global Ideal," *New York Times*, February 18, 1996.

4. Bruce Russett and James Lee Ray, "Why the Democratic-Peace Proposition Lives," *Review of International Studies*, Vol. 21, No. 3 (July 1995), p. 321, n. 8.

Similarly, long-term disputes between India and Pakistan have been resolved short of war in recent years, coinciding with increased democratization in Pakistan in the early 1990s. Finally, since the collapse of the Soviet empire, democratization of the post-communist countries seems to have lowered their likelihood for war involvement—of the fourteen states that made rapid progress towards democracy between 1988 and 1993, none took part in an interstate war.[5] In all these cases, the end to bitter and violent conflict has coincided with the emergence of democratic norms and institutions.

Yet the premise of a democratic peace has recently come under increasing attack. Critics insist that the democratic peace is a myth, and that arbitrary definitions of both democracy and war have allowed the theory's proponents to exclude numerous cases of democratic war. Others argue that peace among democracies has less to do with shared norms and institutions than with alliances against common enemies or insufficient military power; that is, decision makers base policies on the risks that will be incurred by challenging other states and using force. According to this view, all states' foreign policy decisions are primarily motivated by the external constraints and opportunities of relative power. Even democratic states will take their cues more from the international security environment than from the nature of domestic politics.

Some U.S. policy makers are also becoming less sanguine about the democratic peace. Many warn that U.S. national security will be threatened if democratic Germany or Japan carries out independent foreign policies or joins the ranks of nuclearized states. Others warn that a democratization crusade will over-stretch U.S. resources and mire the United States in the domestic politics of other countries. According to this view, the U.S. government should concentrate more on the foreign policies of other countries and less on their form of government.[6]

Events in the mid-1990s suggest that democratic countries may still threaten international peace. For example, during the 1996 crisis between Turkey and Greece, Clinton found it necessary to remind

---

5. Reinhold Wolf, "Correspondence: Democratization and the Danger of War," *International Security*, Vol. 20, No. 4 (Spring 1996), p. 177.

6. Strobe Talbott, "Democracy and the National Interest," *Foreign Affairs*, Vol. 75, No. 6 (November/December 1996), p. 48. See also Christopher Layne and Sean M. Lynn-Jones, *Should the U.S. Try to Export Democracy? A Debate* (Cambridge, Mass.: MIT Press, forthcoming).

the leaders of both countries that democratic members of the Atlantic Alliance cannot go to war with each other. That Greece and Turkey nearly came to the brink of military confrontation suggests that democratic institutions may not always be sufficient to keep the peace between democratic states. Geopolitical considerations may often trump norms and ideology as determinants of national security policy, and democratic states may not automatically settle overlapping territorial claims by negotiation or mediation.[7] Moreover, it appears that in this case democratic politics made matters worse; the leaders of both countries adopted hard-line foreign policy positions to shore up their fragile new coalition governments.[8]

While the state of peace between South Korea and Japan—the only two adjacent states in East Asia that can be classified as "free"— appears to support the rule of democratic peace, there are signs that rivalry and threats of force will outlast joint democracy.[9] South Korea expects to fight Japan in the near future, and is preparing to do so. It is investing billions of dollars to enhance its readiness for war—primarily against its nondemocratic neighbor to the north, but also in anticipation of possible aggression from its democratic neighbor to the east.[10] Japan's "democraticness" has not alleviated South Korea's perception of Japan as potentially aggressive and untrustworthy. With territorial disputes in the Sea of Japan unresolved, what matters to South Korea is Japan's latent power and past reputation for aggression, not its domestic political structure.

Finally, the foreign policies of post-Soviet Russia also appear inconsistent with the democratic peace argument. Russia has tended to cultivate relations with neighboring states that support close ties with Russia, whether or not they have initiated democratic reform. It appears that what is critical for Russian policy in Central Asia is whether local regimes respect Russia's sphere of influence.[11]

7. See the chapters by Christopher Layne, Stephen R. Rock, John M. Owen, and Šumit Ganguly.

8. "Ancient Rivalry in the Aegean," *Boston Globe*, February 1, 1996, p. 8.

9. Donald K. Emmerson, "Realism or Evangelism? Security Through Democratization as a National Strategy," *NBR Analysis*, Vol. 7, No. 2 (September 1996), p. 40.

10. "America's Key Allies in East Asia Unleash Their Ancient Animosities," *Wall Street Journal*, February 21, 1996, p. 1.

11. Rajan Menon, "In the Shadow of the Bear: Security in Post-Soviet Central Asia," *International Security*, Vol. 20, No. 1 (Summer 1995), p. 168.

Democratization in Russia is also increasing the likelihood of interstate conflict. For example, President Boris Yeltsin's willingness to use force in Russia's near abroad allows his administration to deflect attacks from a powerful reactionary majority in Parliament.[12]

This book addresses the heart of the debate between proponents and critics of the democratic peace theory: its purpose is to determine whether domestic regime type significantly affects the calculations of decision makers involved in interstate crises, and to assess whether proponents or critics of the theory are vindicated. The chapters focus on international conflicts involving democratic, nondemocratic, and democratic-nondemocratic pairs of states. While war was a real possibility in each case, some of the crises ended in armed combat and others were resolved peacefully. Our aim is to see whether domestic institutions and norms made a difference in these outcomes, and whether the cases confirm or refute the democratic peace thesis. Each chapter investigates the decision making process and the domestic and international factors that determined the decision to escalate and use force, or solve the crisis by peaceful methods.

---

12. Russian military intervention in the Caucasus is the most pronounced. In 1991–92, Russia provided covert military support to the ethnic Armenian majority in the Nagorno-Karabakh Autonomous Region of Azerbaijan. By 1993, Armenian gains in the war prompted the Azeri government to forge closer ties with Russia and apply for membership in the Commonwealth of Independent States (CIS). Similarly, Russian troop assistance and military aid to the small secessionist Abkhazian army was instrumental in defeating Georgia's substantial counterforces. Abkhazia's successes in its war for independence compelled Georgian president Eduard Shevardnadze to request an indefinite Russian military presence in the area and membership in the CIS. For more on Russian military intervention in the Soviet successor states, see Thomas Goltz, "The Hidden Russian Hand," *Foreign Policy*, No. 92 (Fall 1993), pp. 92–116; Fiona Hill and Pamela Jewett, *Back in the USSR: Russia's Intervention in the Internal Affairs of the Former Soviet Republics and the Implications for United States Policy Toward Russia*, (Strengthening Democratic Institutions Project, John F. Kennedy School of Government, Harvard University, January 1994); Edward D. Mansfield and Jack Snyder, "Democratization and the Danger of War," *International Security*, Vol. 20, No. 1 (Summer 1995), pp. 5–38. See also "Mr. Yeltsin's Conversion," *New York Times*, January 17, 1996; and Stefan Halper, "While We Weren't Watching Russia," *Washington Times*, January 25, 1996, p. 17. Several students of contemporary Russian politics suggest that international conflict was less likely during the Gorbachev era because a centralized, nondemocratic regime increased Gorbachev's capacity to determine the state's foreign policy agenda. See, for example, Thomas Risse-Kappen, "Ideas Do Not Float Freely: Transnational Coalitions, Domestic Structures, and the End of the Cold War," *International Organization*, Vol. 48, No. 2 (Spring 1994), p. 210; and Janice Gross Stein, "Political Learning By Doing: Gorbachev as Uncommitted Thinker and Motivated Learner," *International Organization*, Vol. 48, No. 2 (Spring 1994), pp. 161, 163.

This book offers a qualitative, case-based assessment of the democratic peace argument. While there are many studies that determine the rarity of wars involving democracies by examining many cases at once, only a handful of works test the theory against particular historical episodes.[13] These qualitative studies present mixed reviews for the democratic peace proposition; however, taken as a whole they are not an adequate body of evidence. Researchers have repeatedly examined particular cases and countries—such as the Fashoda crisis and U.S. foreign policy making. Scholars have also focused primarily on democratic pairs of states; there are few in-depth case studies of war and peace decision making involving nondemocratic dyads and mixed pairs of states. In short, more case study analysis—particularly of a comparative nature—is needed.

The case studies that follow compare the democratic peace theory with the validity of alternative theories, seeking to delineate the circumstances under which the democratic peace theory is likely to have the greatest and least explanatory power. We argue that both international and domestic factors influence state behavior, often in ways that are inconsistent with the claims of democratic peace proponents *and* their critics. First, several chapters suggest that the balance of material capabilities explains state behavior in crisis, even among democracies. These chapters show that war and peace decision making is not always based on normative frameworks or hampered by domestic politics; sometimes it is a response to international pressures. Second, a number of chapters suggest that a state's foreign policy may often be inconsistent with prevailing external conditions and can only be understood by examining domestic politics. These chapters suggest that the behavior of democracies may be consistent with some theories of the democratic peace, but inconsistent with others. Third, some of the domestic-level arguments presented here are inconsistent with the democratic peace proposition. For example, some chapters argue that democratic politics is not a benign force.

---

13. The main qualitative studies are James Lee Ray, *Democracy and International Conflict: An Evaluation of the Democratic Peace Proposition* (Columbia: University of South Carolina Press, 1995), pp. 158–200; Christopher Layne, "Kant or Cant: The Myth of the Democratic Peace," *International Security*, Vol. 19, No. 4 (Fall 1994), pp. 5–49; John M. Owen, "How Liberalism Produces the Democratic Peace," *International Security*, Vol. 19, No. 2 (Fall 1994), pp. 87–125; Susan Peterson, "How Democracies Differ: Public Opinion, State Structure, and the Lessons of the Fashoda Crisis," *Security Studies*, Vol. 5, No. 1 (Autumn 1995), pp. 3–37; and Ido Oren, "The Subjectivity of the 'Democratic Peace': Changing U.S. Perceptions of Imperial Germany," *International Security*, Vol. 20, No. 2 (Fall 1995), pp. 147–184.

Others argue that rules and structures in nondemocratic countries influence the policy process, but do not invariably increase the likelihood of war. Many of the authors suggest that a country's regime type is not the most important domestic source of its foreign policy.

The first section of this introduction discusses the importance of the democratic peace theory and reviews its main variants. The second section summarizes the main critiques of the theory. The third section discusses the limitations of the recent debate, suggests the need for a fresh look, and highlights how this book contributes to the debate. The fourth section details our approach and method. Finally, I provide a summary of the chapters.

Democracy and Peace: Explaining the Link

A long political tradition regards democratic governance as the path to peace. Two centuries ago, Immanuel Kant predicted that republican states would enjoy a "perpetual peace" with other republics. In the twentieth century, U.S. President Woodrow Wilson expounded the belief that the expansion of democracy abroad would have a positive effect on U.S. national security. However, throughout the 1960s and 1970s—the heyday of the development of international relations as a sub-field of political science—the linkage between democracy and war was of interest to only a handful of scholars.[14] Today, the idea of a democratic zone of peace is routinely voiced in both academic and policy making circles, and there is widespread support for making the promotion of democracy the centerpiece of U.S. post–Cold War foreign policy.

THE IMPORTANCE OF THE DEMOCRATIC PEACE THEORY

In the social sciences, theories often thrive not necessarily because of their scientific superiority, but because they are consistent with the academic community's prevailing values. In particular, dramatic events encourage us to question established theories and reconsider neglected approaches.[15] Thus, while students of international relations

---

14. For an excellent overview of this literature and the recent reemergence of the democratic peace theory, see Ray, *Democracy and International Conflict,* chap. 1.

15. Keith L. Shimko, "Realism, Neorealism, and American Liberalism," *The Review of Politics,* Vol. 54, No. 2 (Spring 1992), p. 283; Peter J. Katzenstein, "Introduction: Alternative Perspectives on National Security," in Peter J. Katzenstein, ed., *The Culture of National Security* (New York: Columbia University Press, 1996), pp. 1–37. See also Thomas S. Kuhn, *The Structure of Scientific Revolutions* (Chicago: University of Chicago Press, 1962).

have long argued that democratic norms and institutions play a role in keeping states at peace, the forceful reemergence of this thesis in recent years can be considered a reaction to neorealism, the prevailing theoretical perspective in the postwar period. The idea of a separate peace among democracies seemed "too soft" for the post–World War II academic and policy making community, which felt more comfortable with concepts such as deterrence, bipolarity, and the balance of material capabilities for war.[16] In the post–Cold War era, however, idealism is once again more compelling. The new international order beckons us to pay greater attention to the domestic factors that shaped the foreign policy decisions that affected the contemporary sea change in the international system.[17] This sea change—the end of bipolarity and the Cold War and the break-up of the Soviet Union—has provided a hospitable environment for theoretical perspectives like the democratic peace proposition, which emphasizes normative and institutional variables. The evident causes of these dramatic events highlight the importance of domestic politics, and leadership values and ideas.[18] In fact, some have gone so far as to suggest that we are witnessing the end of competition between opposing political ideologies—that the notion that free government is the best means of organizing state and societal activities has triumphed.[19]

The renewed debate over the democratic peace has important ramifications for both theory and policy. Theoretically the debate is important because it undermines the neorealist viewpoint.[20] The

---

16. Nils Petter Gleditsch, "Democracy and Peace," *Journal of Peace Research*, Vol. 29, No. 4 (November 1992), p. 373.

17. Michael D. Yaffe, "Realism in Retreat? The New World Order and the Return of the Individual in International Relations Studies," *Perspectives on Political Science*, Vol. 23, No. 2 (Spring 1994), p. 79.

18. Charles W. Kegley, Jr., "How Did the Cold War Die? Principles For an Autopsy," *Mershon International Studies Review*, Vol. 38, No. 1 (April 1994), pp. 11–41; Risse-Kappen, "Ideas Do Not Float Freely"; Stein, "Political Learning By Doing."

19. See, for example, Francis Fukuyama, "The End of History?" *The National Interest*, No. 16 (Summer 1989), pp. 3–18.

20. For more on this debate, see, for example, Ethan B. Kapstein, "Is Realism Dead? The Domestic Sources of International Politics," *International Organization*, Vol. 49, No. 4 (Autumn 1995), pp. 751–774; and Fareed Zakaria, "Is Realism Finished?" *The National Interest*, No. 30 (Winter 1992/93), pp. 21–32. In this book, I prefer to use the term neorealism rather than realism. Realists acknowledge that both domestic and international factors play a role in determining state behavior. By contrast, neorealists insist that the external environment matters more.

apparent existence of a democratic peace challenges neorealism's pessimism about the long-term prospects for international peace and emphasis on the external, material factors that influence states' behavior. According to neorealists, war is always a possibility in the absence of world government. Consequently, all states must prepare for war, and must expect that even current allies may become enemies in the future: no pair of states can count on peaceful relations indefinitely. The existence of both a separate and permanent peace between democracies challenges this pessimistic outlook.[21]

Neorealists also argue that the distribution of military capabilities among states and their shared security interests are far more important determinants of state behavior than are domestic institutional features or political norms. In determining foreign policies, leaders are most attentive to strategic concerns, the national interest, and the relative distribution of material capabilities.[22] Consequently, states that are similarly situated in the international system and face similar external constraints and opportunities will act similarly regardless of their particular political institutions or values.[23] By contrast, democratic peace proponents claim that the attributes of a state's political system largely determine which states will and will not go to war with each other. In contrast to neorealism, the theory posits

21. Like neorealism, the dyadic version of the democratic peace theory (discussed below) relies on the notion of strategic interaction—states behave based on their expectations of how other states are likely to act. The key difference is that for neorealists, strategic interaction renders peace a temporary and fleeting condition borne out of joint need, while the democratic peace theory insists that strategic interaction among democracies will be characterized by a separate and lasting peace.

22. Neorealists do not discount the impact of unit-level variables on state behavior, but they claim that the pressures of international competition "weigh more heavily than ideological preferences or internal political pressures." Kenneth N. Waltz, "Reflections on *Theory of International Politics*: A Response to My Critics," in Robert O. Keohane, ed., *Neorealism and Its Critics* (New York: Columbia University Press, 1986), p. 329. Most neorealists agree that both in crises and in the long run, structural factors tend to dominate other factors. Because the stakes in the realm of international security are so high, in a crisis states usually respond to the strategic environment rather than in a way that is consistent with their ideological preferences. For more on the tenets of neorealism, see Colin Elman and Miriam Fendius Elman, "History vs. Neo-realism: A Second Look," *International Security*, Vol. 20, No. 1 (Summer 1995), pp. 182–193; and Colin Elman, "Horses for Courses: Why *Not* Neo-realist Theories of Foreign Policy?" *Security Studies*, Vol. 6, No. 1 (Autumn 1996), pp. 18–21.

23. Kenneth N. Waltz, *Theory of International Politics* (Reading, Mass.: Addison-Wesley, 1979).

that threat perceptions and foreign policy choices are determined by domestic political regimes and ideologies rather than the balance of power. That is, domestic regime type is the key to international cooperation and conflict. In short, acceptance of the democratic peace theory therefore undermines neorealism's pessimism about the prospects for international peace, as well as its claim that much of international politics can be explained without reference to domestic political features.[24]

Aside from its implications for theory, the debate over the democratic peace is important for policy. If democracies never go to war with each other and if they exhibit pacific tendencies in general, then encouraging the spread of democracy is the path to peace. The democratic peace theory thus provides direct support for a U.S. policy mission of promoting democracy abroad. It also suggests strategies for deciding which states should be considered current and potential U.S. enemies, and which can be considered fast friends. By contrast, if democracy does not cause peace between democracies and if democratic wars are possible, then U.S. policy makers should more vigilantly monitor the military potential of current democratic allies. Nor can the United States afford to ignore domestic political developments in fellow democratic countries; since new leaders with new world views may come to power, critics suggest that efficient deterrence (rather than stable democracy) is the path to peace.

THE DEMOCRATIC PEACE: THEORETICAL FOUNDATIONS
There are as many versions of the democratic peace thesis as there are advocates of its central premise that there is a linkage between democracy and peace. This section reviews the main variants of the theory.

THE DYADIC PROPOSITION. The most familiar version of the democratic peace theory asserts that democracies create *a separate and joint peace*—they do not fight wars against each other, but they are no less conflict-prone than nondemocracies.[25] Most scholars agree that the

24. For more on the theoretical implications of the democratic peace debate, see Sean M. Lynn-Jones, "Preface," in Michael E. Brown, Sean M. Lynn-Jones, and Steven E. Miller, eds., *Debating the Democratic Peace* (Cambridge, Mass.: MIT Press, 1996), pp. ix–xiii.

25. See, for example, Bruce Russett, *Grasping the Democratic Peace: Principles for a Post-Cold War World* (Princeton, N.J.: Princeton University Press, 1993), pp. 11, 30–31; Owen, "How Liberalism Produces the Democratic Peace"; Michael W. Doyle, "Liberalism and World Politics," *American Political Science Review*, Vol. 80, No. 4 (December 1986), pp. 1151–1169; and Erich Weede, "Some Simple Calculations on Democracy and War Involvement," *Journal of Peace Research*, Vol. 29, No. 4 (November 1992), pp. 377–383.

democratic peace is necessarily dyadic—it takes two democracies to make peace.[26] That is, the dyadic empirical finding asserts that war ceases to be a possibility *only* among democracies. Democracies are as belligerent as nondemocracies and may even have incentives to fight nondemocracies because of their competing political ideologies.

Proponents of the dyadic finding usually attribute this curious empirical finding to a shared culture and shared democratic norms among democracies, or to the institutional constraints on a leader's actions; that is, the structure of a democratic government makes it difficult for leaders to make war.[27] The "normative" or "cultural" argument, which is supported by a substantial body of quantitative research, is that shared democratic and liberal values foster peace between democratic states. According to this argument, democratic political culture encourages peaceful means of internal conflict resolution, which "come to apply across national boundaries toward other democratic states."[28] Political ideology solves the problem of how to distinguish potential adversaries from allies: liberal states, with domestic structures that encourage the peaceful resolution of

---

26. Harvey Starr, "Why Don't Democracies Fight One Another? Evaluating the Theory-Findings Feedback Loop," *Jerusalem Journal of International Relations*, Vol. 14, No. 4 (December 1992), p. 43.

27. For attempts to group explanations for the democratic peace into "institutional" and "normative" models, see Russett, *Grasping the Democratic Peace*; Ray, *Democracy and International Conflict*; T. Clifton Morgan and Sally H. Campbell, "Domestic Structure, Decisional Constraints and War: So Why Kant Democracies Fight?" *Journal of Conflict Resolution*, Vol. 35, No. 2 (June 1991), pp. 187–211; T. Clifton Morgan and Valerie L. Schwebach, "Take Two Democracies and Call Me in the Morning: A Prescription for Peace?" *International Interactions*, Vol. 17, No. 4 (Summer 1992), pp. 305–320; Scott Gates et al., "Democracy and Peace: a More Skeptical View," *Journal of Peace Research*, Vol. 33, No. 1 (1996), pp. 1–10; and David L. Rousseau et al., "Assessing the Dyadic Nature of the Democratic Peace, 1918-88," *American Political Science Review*, Vol. 90, No. 3 (September 1996), pp. 512–533. Since the normative and institutional models are the most common explanations for the democratic peace phenomenon, this book focuses on these two variants. It excludes the hypothesized relationship between economic interdependence and democratic peace. For more on this linkage, see John R. Oneal et al., "The Liberal Peace, Interdependence, Democracy, and International Conflict, 1950-85," *Journal of Peace Research*, Vol. 33, No. 1 (1996), pp. 11-28. For more skeptical views, see Barry Buzan, "Economic Structure and International Security: the Limits of the Liberal Case," *International Organization*, Vol. 38, No. 4 (Autumn 1984), pp. 597–624; and Dale C. Copeland, "Economic Interdependence and War: A Theory of Trade Expectations," *International Security*, Vol. 20, No. 4 (Spring 1996), pp. 5–41.

28. Russett, *Grasping the Democratic Peace*, p. 31.

domestic conflict, are treated with respect and consideration; nonliberal states, which have domestic structures of violence and oppression, are approached with suspicion.

Thus, war is avoided because democratic decision makers expect the leaders of other democracies to follow the norms of conflict resolution that characterize their own domestic political processes: "if a norm mandates the peaceful resolution of disputes within two states, it will also mandate the peaceful resolution of disputes between them."[29] Disputes between democratic states do not escalate to war because leaders expect, on the basis of a common political ideology, to be able to work out their differences peacefully. As Bruce Russett puts it, *"to use or to threaten to use force is not usually normatively acceptable behavior in disputes between democracies . . .* [democratic] states not only do not fight each other, they do not expect to fight each other, or significantly prepare to fight each other."[30] In short, because leaders of contending democracies are accustomed to mutual accommodation in domestic politics, they trust that their democratic counterparts will also be faithful to that game.[31]

Other advocates of the dyadic democratic peace thesis insist that the empirical finding can be attributed to domestic constraints that prevent leaders from choosing war as a foreign policy option; this is the "institutional" or "structural" argument. Since democratically elected leaders cannot easily commit the state to war, democratic institutions serve as a useful indicator of a state's trustworthiness, legitimacy, and reliability: "Some political institutions help foster beliefs . . . about the dovish inclinations of certain states. Democratic institutions are visible signs that the state in question is likely to face high political costs for using force in its diplomacy."[32] Thus, foreign

29. Joanne Gowa, "Democratic States and International Disputes," *International Organization*, Vol. 49, No. 3 (Summer 1995), p. 514. For an extended discussion, see Russett, *Grasping the Democratic Peace*, pp. 31–35; and Thomas Risse-Kappen, "Democratic Peace—Warlike Democracies: A Social Constructivist Interpretation of the Democratic Peace," *European Journal of International Relations*, Vol. 1, No. 4 (December 1995), pp. 491–517.

30. Russett, *Grasping the Democratic Peace*, p. 42, emphasis in the original.

31. Joe D. Hagan, "Domestic Political Systems and War Proneness," *Mershon International Studies Review*, Vol. 38 (October 1994), p. 186.

32. Bruce Bueno de Mesquita and David Lalman, *War and Reason: Domestic and International Imperatives* (New Haven, Conn.: Yale University Press, 1992), p. 272; see also pp. 156–157. For the argument that democratic states avoid wars with each other because fighting democracies harms leaders' chances to stay in power, see Ray, *Democracy and International Conflict*, pp. 40–41; and David A. Lake, "Powerful Pacifists: Democratic States and War," *American Political Science Review*, Vol. 86, No. 1 (March 1992), pp. 24–37.

policy makers' degree of autonomy from oversight by the public and other branches of government provides a barometer for whether states should be treated as friends or foes.

According to the institutional argument, democratically elected leaders are unable to act quickly, and this cautious foreign policy behavior reduces the likelihood that a conflict will escalate to war.[33] Democratic leaders will consider other democracies reluctant and slow to fight because institutional constraints require that elected leaders first mobilize the support of the voting public: "If another nation's leaders regard a state as democratic, they will anticipate a difficult and lengthy process before the democracy is likely to use significant military force against them. They will expect an opportunity to reach a negotiated settlement."[34] In short, institutional arrangements that curtail the discretionary behavior of leaders produce the greatest impediments to decisions for war—such constraints will be the greatest within democracies where public debate is expected and is a ready outlet for opposition to leaders' actions.

A number of democratic peace proponents have suggested that normative-cultural arguments are more robust than the competing institutional-structural explanations.[35] The shortcomings of institutional-structural arguments is that they cannot account for a democratic public's willingness to fight wars against nondemocracies: "If citizens are reticent to employ their blood and taxes for fighting wars, why should they care if the opponent is a democracy or an autocracy?"[36] Yet, for several reasons the institutional argument should not be jettisoned.

First, normative and institutional arguments are not mutually exclusive. As John Owen notes, both are necessary components for explaining peace between democracies. Democratic structure and norms work in tandem—liberal norms proscribe wars among democracies,

---

33. Margaret G. Hermann and Charles W. Kegley, Jr., "Rethinking Democracy and International Peace: Perspectives from Political Psychology," *International Studies Quarterly*, Vol. 39, No. 4 (December 1995), p. 514. See also Russett, *Grasping the Democratic Peace*, pp. 38–40.

34. Russett, *Grasping the Democratic Peace*, p. 39.

35. Ibid., pp. 90–93, 117; and Zeev Maoz and Bruce Russett, "Normative and Structural Causes of Democratic Peace, 1946-1986," *American Political Science Review*, Vol. 87, No. 3 (September 1993), pp. 624–638.

36. Gates et al., "Democracy and Peace," p. 4; see also Risse-Kappen, "Democratic Peace—Warlike Democracies," pp. 498–499.

and democratic institutions ensure that this proscription is followed.[37]

Second, normative arguments do not explain well why democracies often *do* engage in militarized disputes with other democratic states. The finding that democratic states threaten to use force against each other is inconsistent with the prediction that democratic states will not contemplate the use of force against each other, much less go to war. Indeed, if democratic states are supposed to view each other as holding similar values, and if shared cultural norms preclude war, why would democratic states fight each other in ways short of open warfare?[38] In short, democracies' tendency to use covert action against elected democratic governments is inconsistent with the normative model but fully compatible with the institutional argument. Institutional arguments can explain why such militarized conflicts might occur, but do not escalate to war. Since checks and balances on leaders account for war and peace outcomes, shared normative convictions about how political conflicts ought to be resolved are not necessary in order for democracy to exert a pacifying effect. Democratic leaders might initiate low-level hostilities against democratic counterparts because they can; since decisions for war do require the consent of the public or other decision making bodies, leaders will not escalate these low-level conflicts without first receiving wide-spread public approval.[39]

These caveats suggest that normative explanations for the dyadic democratic peace phenomenon may not be superior in their predictive power, and the authors in this book subject both explanations to empirical tests.

THE MONADIC PROPOSITION. Are democracies more peaceful? Or do they merely maintain peaceful relations among themselves? While

---

37. Owen, "How Liberalism Produces the Democratic Peace," p. 119; see also p. 124. For other explanations of the dyadic democratic peace phenomenon that combine institutional and normative models see Alex Mintz and Nehemia Geva, "Why Don't Democracies Fight Each Other? An Experimental Assessment of the 'Political Incentive' Explanation," *Journal of Conflict Resolution*, Vol. 37, No. 3 (September 1993), pp. 484–503; and Rousseau et al., "Assessing the Dyadic Nature of the Democratic Peace."

38. Patrick James and Glenn E. Mitchell, "Targets of Covert Pressure: The Hidden Victims of the Democratic Peace," *International Interactions*, Vol. 21, No. 1 (July 1995), p. 91.

39. Ray, *Democracy and International Conflict*, p. 37. For an extended argument that the normative model may be less persuasive than we have recently been led to believe, see ibid., pp. 34–37.

there is almost general agreement that the democratic peace effect applies only among democracies, and does not extend to relations between democracies and nondemocracies, many proponents of the democratic peace assert that democratic states are less prone to use force regardless of the regime type of their opponents. According to this monadic empirical finding, the more democratic the state, the less violent its behavior toward other states.[40]

In quantitative analyses carried out in the 1960s and 1970s, numerous researchers found support for the notion that democracies are inherently pacific.[41] Similarly, in recent studies on the democratic peace, not all proponents agree that it takes two to make peace. For example, R.J. Rummel argues that "democracies are in fact the most pacific of regimes." Since costly and unsuccessful wars can increase a leader's chances of losing his or her position, leaders in democracies are less likely to initiate wars that are expected to be severely violent or that are likely to have high overall costs.[42] Bruce Bueno de Mesquita and David Lalman suggest that disputes will end in negotiations if either the initiator or the target state is democratic. They argue that the pacifying effects of democracy do not require that both states in a conflict be democratic.[43] Similarly, Russell Leng argues that in international crises, democratic states are more likely to use reciprocating bargaining strategies, largely because reciprocation is an ingrained value of democratic political processes. Behavior such as bullying or stonewalling is not normatively acceptable.[44] Zeev Maoz and Nasrin Abdolai find that democratic states are less likely to escalate disputes

40. Both institutional and normative arguments are also employed to account for this empirical finding. According to the normative argument, the foreign policies of democratically elected leaders are likely to reflect domestic norms of nonviolent resolution of political conflicts. Coercion and violence will be considered less legitimate means for resolving international disputes with all other states. According to the institutional argument, democratically elected decision makers will have to be sensitive to the domestic costs of using force regardless of the regime type of the opposing regime.

41. For a review of these studies, see Ray, *Democracy and International Conflict*, chap. 1. See also Rousseau et al., "Assessing the Dyadic Nature of the Democratic Peace."

42. R.J. Rummel, "Democracies ARE Less Warlike Than Other Regimes," *European Journal of International Relations*, Vol. 1, No. 4 (December 1995), pp. 457–479. See also Randolf M. Siverson, "Democracies and War Participation: In Defense of the Institutional Constraints Argument," *European Journal of International Relations*, Vol. 1, No. 4 (December 1995), pp. 481–489.

43. Bueno de Mesquita and Lalman, *War and Reason*, p. 158.

44. Russell J. Leng, "Reciprocating Influence Strategies in International Crisis Bargaining," *Journal of Conflict Resolution*, Vol. 37 (March 1993), pp. 3–41.

into wars. As James Lee Ray notes, their finding "covering the years from 1816 to 1976 is not dependent upon the kinds of states with which democracies become involved."[45] Clifton Morgan and Valerie Schwebach also suggest that domestic political structures constrain democratic leaders from choosing war as a foreign policy option regardless of the "domestic structure of the opponent." They argue that domestic political structures can curb the belligerent impulses of state leaders by forcing them to pass through substantial barriers before deciding to go to war, and they insist that this effect is not dependent on the regime type of the opponent.[46] Finally, David Rousseau and his coauthors find that democracies are less likely than nondemocracies to initiate crises with all other types of states.[47] Thus, much of the aggregate data on the democratic peace phenomenon suggests that democracies are less war prone in general, and that it is not only in their relations with each other that the pacifying effects of democracy emerge.[48]

Qualitative analyses of democratic state behavior also support this monadic finding. For example, Randall Schweller shows that declining democratic states do not wage war against rising challengers, regardless of their regime type. While declining nondemocracies do wage preventive wars, declining democracies have been more likely to opt for peaceful methods of conflict resolution—either accommodation or defensive alliances. Similarly, Jack Snyder argues that democratic states are less likely to extend their commitments beyond their capabilities. Snyder suggests that democratic institutions assert an identifiable pacifying effect, regardless of the domestic regime type of other states. In short, for both Schweller and Snyder, democratic states are more prudent—they are quicker to abandon and are less likely to take on strategic overcommitments, and they do not fight preventive wars.[49]

---

45. Ray, *Democracy and International Conflict*, p. 19. See also Zeev Maoz and Nasrin Abdolai, "Regime Types and International Conflict, 1817-1976," *Journal of Conflict Resolution*, Vol. 33, No. 1 (March 1989), pp. 3–35; and Rousseau et al., "Assessing the Dyadic Nature of Democratic Peace."

46. Morgan and Schwebach, "Take Two Democracies and Call Me in the Morning," p. 318.

47. Rousseau et al., "Assessing the Dyadic Nature of the Democratic Peace."

48. Ray, *Democracy and International Conflict*, p. 20; see also pp. 18, 33.

49. Randall L. Schweller, "Domestic Structure and Preventive War: Are Democracies More Pacific?" *World Politics*, Vol. 44, No. 2 (January 1992), pp.

The monadic variant of the democratic peace theory makes two central propositions. First, democratic states are less likely to see war as a viable foreign policy option. Force is not seen as a legitimate tool of foreign policy, but rather as an option of last resort. Second, the regime type of the opponent is not likely to play a crucial role in democratic states' decisions to go to war.

Both claims stand in sharp contrast to the dyadic argument. According to proponents of the dyadic model, democracies are no less war-prone than other types of states, and the regime type of the opponent will crucially affect war decisions—democratic states will be especially war-prone when facing nondemocratic counterparts. Hostility toward nondemocratic states is more likely because it is easier to mobilize public support for military actions. As Michael Doyle states, "Because non-liberal governments are in a state of aggression with their own people, their foreign relations become for liberal governments deeply suspect . . . fellow liberals benefit from a presumption of amity; nonliberals suffer from a presumption of enmity."[50] Thus, the dyadic argument suggests that democracies carefully identify the type of state with which they are interacting, and adjust their behavior accordingly. This implies that even if a democratic state builds its offensive capabilities, fellow democracies will not find this threatening. Conversely, even if a nondemocratic state's military capabilities are quite weak, democracies will be likely to code the state as an enemy.[51]

235–269; and Jack Snyder, *Myths of Empire: Domestic Politics and International Ambition* (Ithaca, N.Y.: Cornell University Press, 1991). Edward D. Mansfield and Jack Snyder's discussion of war propensity among democratizing states also presents a monadic argument. Democratizing states are likely to be more war-prone than states experiencing no democratic regime transitions. Nothing in Mansfield and Snyder's argument requires that this be dependent on the regime type of potential opponents. See "Democratization and the Danger of War."

50. Doyle, "Liberalism and World Politics," p. 1161. See also Owen, "How Liberalism Produces the Democratic Peace," pp. 96, 102–103; and John M. Owen, "How Do Liberal States Identify One Another: Perceptions and Liberal Peace," paper presented at the annual meeting of the American Political Science Association, Chicago, September 1995.

51. Some proponents of the dyadic democratic peace theory suggest that nondemocracies are at fault for conflict between democratic-nondemocratic pairs. For example, Russett argues that leaders in nondemocracies anticipate that democracies will be slow to go to war—they exploit democracies' structural constraints by threatening or bullying a democracy to make concessions, thus decreasing the democratic state's initial inhibition against fighting. See Russett, *Grasping the Democratic Peace*, p. 39. For more on this point see Rousseau et al., "Assessing the Dyadic Nature of the Democratic Peace."

In short, monadic and dyadic interpretations of the democratic peace differ in the extent to which the regime type of the target state is considered important. According to the dyadic version, the regime type of the opponent matters a great deal in calculations of whether or not to go to war. In deciding whether continued negotiation is warranted, democracies assess the political regime type of their adversary and infer from the nature of its domestic institutions whether force should be used. According to the monadic version, the foreign policies of democratic states should not be significantly affected by whether they are in disputes with fellow democracies or nondemocracies. Factors internal to the democratic decision making process and democratic cultures determine the foreign policies of democratic states; explanations for war and peace do not require that we know whether a state carefully pays attention to the regime type of its opponent.

DYADIC AND MONADIC VERSIONS AND PROPOSITIONS ABOUT NON-DEMOCRACIES. In asserting that democracies will be less likely to use force—either in general or only against each other—the democratic peace theory contrasts democracies with nondemocracies. Both the dyadic and the monadic variants of the democratic peace theory rest on a counterfactual claim: outcomes that occurred because states were democratic would have been different if the states were nondemocratic.[52] Both versions imply that democracies will have foreign policies strikingly different from those of nondemocratic states because of differences in institutional constraints on decision making and normative frameworks that regulate the use of force.

Thus, the democratic peace theory implies that features common to nondemocratic states increase their war propensity. For example, according to Ernst-Otto Czempiel: "autocratic systems of rule . . . are the main causes of threat and military violence in the international system."[53] Similarly, according to Russett, nondemocratic states tend to externalize their norms of domestic political competition; that is, just as nondemocracies use force and try to eliminate the adversary

52. On counterfactual analysis, see Stephen Van Evera, *Guide to Methodology for Students of Political Science* (Cambridge, Mass.: Defense and Arms Control Studies Program [DACS] and Massachusetts Institute of Technology [MIT], 1996), p. 12; and James Fearon, "Counterfactual and Hypothesis Testing in Political Science," *World Politics*, Vol. 43, No. 2 (January 1991), pp. 169–195.

53. Ernst-Otto Czempiel, "Governance and Democratization," in James N. Rosenau and Ernst-Otto Czempiel, eds., *Governance Without Government: Order and Change in World Politics* (New York: Cambridge University Press, 1992), p. 263.

at home, we can expect them to do so abroad as well. Moreover, because nondemocracies are not "encumbered by powerful structural constraints," they will be more likely to escalate disputes to war.[54]

Nevertheless, the democratic peace theory says little about the causes of nondemocratic war or peace; the dyadic version of the theory merely asserts that democracies share a joint and separate peace. Presumably, peace can be maintained by a partnership of nondemocratic nations. As Bruce Russett and James Lee Ray claim, "Even in its strongest form the democratic-peace proposition contends 'only' that democracy is sufficient for states to be at peace with one another, not that everyone else is at war."[55] Furthermore, since anarchy reigns outside of the democratic circle, wars between nondemocracies may result from either international, balance-of-power reasons or from internal, domestic reasons.

The democratic peace theory makes no explicit claims about the sources of nondemocratic war or peace, but democratic peace proponents generally imply that wars among nondemocracies can be attributed to their flawed systems of government. According to the writings of democratic peace proponents, if nondemocracies are at war it must be because of their flawed regimes. Nondemocracies are aggressive because of features associated with their domestic institutions and cultural norms of conduct. By contrast, instances of peace between nondemocratic states tend to be attributed to external strategic considerations and the balance of power; rarely do democratic peace proponents acknowledge that peace among nondemocracies could be the result of influences internal to their regime types.[56] In

---

54. Russett, *Grasping the Democratic Peace,* pp. 33, 39, 81. In the conclusion to his book, Russett argues that the democratic peace theory should not be interpreted as encouragement to make wars against authoritarian states, or overturn them. He insists that nondemocracies may not be aggressive (p. 134). This stands in contrast to his earlier claims that autocracy and dictatorship cause war.

55. Russett and Ray, "Why the Democratic-Peace Proposition Lives," p. 323.

56. Proponents of the democratic peace theory would be the first to agree that regions comprising nondemocratic states are not necessarily zones of war. South America is a good example. South American states fought numerous wars during the nineteenth century, but since 1941 there have been no wars in this region. Moreover, only two wars have occurred in South America since 1903—the Chaco War between Bolivia and Paraguay and the war between Ecuador and Peru in 1941. At first glance, this evidence appears inconsistent with the democratic peace hypothesis: until the 1980s, most governments in South America were not democratic. If this nondemocratic peace was determined by geopolitical factors, the democratic peace theory is not seriously compromised. Since benevolent

short, regardless of what can be correctly deduced from the theory, proponents of the democratic peace theory typically assert that democracy has the potential to ameliorate international conflict, while nondemocracy is an important cause of war.

Debating the Democratic Peace: Critiques of the Theory

The recent flurry of studies on the democratic peace theory has generated a substantial backlash against both the empirically established generalization and the explanations purported to account for it.

THE DEMOCRATIC PEACE DOES NOT EXIST

Some critics claim that the number of wars between democracies is higher than claimed by democratic peace proponents. These critics are skeptical about the existence of a democratic peace. They claim that the democratic peace may be the result of mere chance; that shifting definitions of democracy and war make the democratic peace appear more significant than it really is; and that democracies often use force against each other, even if short of full-scale war.

INSUFFICIENT DATA. A number of critics suggest that the aggregate data provides insufficient support for the theory, since democracy is a relatively new phenomenon and interstate wars are generally rare occurrences. Because the statistical evidence is too sparse to provide decisive proof of the democratic peace hypothesis, the "democratic peace" may be merely a statistical fluke.[57] Others suggest that the

---

regional hegemons, great power deterrence and intervention, and the lack of military capabilities to fight wars have kept the peace in South America, the democratic peace proposition remains unscathed. Only if nondemocracy in South America—and other domestic political variables—were the sources of this nondemocratic peace would we have cause to question the theory. See Arie M. Kacowicz, "South America as a Zone of Peace: Democratic Peace Refuted or Revindicated?" paper presented at the annual meeting of the International Studies Association, San Diego, April 16–20, 1996, and his chapter in this volume. See also Kalevi J. Holsti, *The State, War and the State of War* (New York: Cambridge University Press, 1996), pp. 150–182.

57. Henry S. Farber and Joanne Gowa, "Polities and Peace," *International Security*, Vol. 20, No. 2 (Fall 1995), pp. 137–138; David E. Spiro, "The Insignificance of the Liberal Peace," *International Security*, Vol. 19, No. 2 (Fall 1994), pp. 50–86; and Raymond Cohen, "Needed: A Disaggregate Approach to the Democratic-Peace Theory," *Review of International Studies*, Vol. 21, No. 3 (July 1995), p. 324. Even proponents of the theory recognize the limitations of the aggregate data. Indeed, a good part of James Lee Ray's evaluation of the democratic peace proposition is devoted to challenging the statistical evidence. See Ray, *Democracy and*

empirical findings are suspect because much of the aggregate data is from the post–World War II period, when most scholars agree that factors other than domestic regime type worked to produce peace between democracies.[58]

SHIFTING DEFINITIONS. A related critique is that scholars with different definitions of democracy and war have omitted cases that provide evidence against the democratic peace phenomenon. According to this argument, democracies have fought each other, but democratic peace proponents quickly dismiss this anomalous evidence by showing that one of the states in question was not an independent state or a democracy, or that the conflict in question was not a war.[59]

For example, defining democracy as a regime in an independent state that ensures full civil and economic liberties; voting rights for virtually all the adult population; and peaceful transfers of power between competing political groups makes it fairly easy to exclude numerous cases of warring democracies.[60] A good example is Israel's war of independence, where democratic Lebanon was a cobelligerent with other Arab states. Bruce Russett dismisses the case by arguing that Israel was not previously independent and had not yet held a national election.[61] This is crucial in Russett's view, since democratic peace can only emerge if citizens in both countries regard one another as governed by democratic principles. If little time has elapsed for

---

International Conflict. Nevertheless, most advocates have countered that while history may not provide substantial evidence to support the theory, recent developments in world politics, where numerous states are becoming democratic, will provide the raw data to support the correlation. See, for example, Russett, *Grasping the Democratic Peace,* p. 73.

58. Farber and Gowa, "Polities and Peace." For a discussion of the multiple causes of the "long peace" among the western democracies since 1945, see John Lewis Gaddis, "The Long Peace: Elements of Stability in the Postwar International System," in Sean M. Lynn-Jones, ed., *The Cold War and After: Prospects for Peace: An International Security Reader* (Cambridge, Mass.: MIT Press, 1991), pp. 1–44. Gaddis does not discount the role of democracy and mutually shared liberal values in preventing a great power war, but he does suggest that this non-event is largely overdetermined.

59. See, in particular, Spiro, "The Insignificance of the Liberal Peace."

60. Bruce Russett is well aware that such restrictive definitions safeguard the theory and appear to "cook the books." He suggests that by lowering the standards, some events will indeed be labeled as wars between democracies. Russett, *Grasping the Democratic Peace,* p. 16. See also Gleditsch, "Democracy and Peace," p. 370.

61. Russett, *Grasping the Democratic Peace,* p. 18. See also Ray, *Democracy and International Conflict,* p. 120.

democratic institutions to become established, then democratic states might very well go to war because "newness and instability cloud others' perceptions."[62] In this case, however, Lebanese decision makers had over twenty-five years to see Israeli democracy at work. National elections, peaceful transfers of power between opposing political groups, and civil rights were all well entrenched long before Israel's independence. Researchers of the period agree that Israel can be considered a democracy prior to its independence—there was little reason for Lebanese leaders to think that Israel would cease to practice the democratic processes that it had instituted since the 1920s. In short, by including in the definition of democracy the assumption of statehood, democratic peace proponents are able to hide major anomalies and discrepant evidence.

Other instances of democratic wars are excluded by overemphasizing states' autocratic features while ignoring their democratic ones; that is, democracy is treated as a discrete rather than a continuous attribute. For example, democratic peace proponents omit the Spanish-American War as an instance of warring democracies by pointing to the nondemocratic aspects of Spain's foreign policy making process. By contrast, critics contend that since Spain had already instituted some democratic procedures, the case counts as disconfirming evidence. Similarly, critics of the democratic peace theory point to Germany's democratic features and thus conclude that World War I was an important instance of democratic war, while proponents of the theory point to the autocratic aspects of Imperial Germany and insist that World War I was not a conflict between democratic states.[63]

A conservative definition of war as a conflict with 1,000 battle deaths also allows democratic peace proponents to exclude some troublesome cases. For example, although democratic peace proponents code Finland as a democracy, Finland's alliance with Germany in World War II is summarily dismissed because fewer than 1,000

---

62. Russett, *Grasping the Democratic Peace*, p. 16; see also p. 34. James Lee Ray excludes other instances of democratic wars on the same grounds—one of the countries in question was newly independent and, consequently, did not yet have the chance to exhibit a peaceful transfer of power. These cases include the U.S. Civil War, the Second Philippines War, and Peru's war with Ecuador in 1981. See *Democracy and International Conflict*, pp. 110–115, 122.

63. See Layne, "Kant or Cant," pp. 41–42; John J. Mearsheimer, "Back to the Future: Instability in Europe After the Cold War," in Lynn-Jones, *The Cold War and After: Prospects for Peace*, pp. 186–187; Russett, *Grasping the Democratic Peace*, pp. 18–19; and Ray, *Democracy and International Conflict*, pp. 118–119.

Finns were killed in armed combat.[64] According to critics, defining war in this way allows democratic peace proponents to omit the case despite the fact that Finland allied itself to the nondemocratic Nazi regime, aided and abetted the enemy of a liberal democratic alliance, and absorbed British bombing of its territory.[65] According to critics, the fact that Finland and Great Britain were officially on opposite sides of a wartime alliance is disconfirming evidence for the democratic peace theory, even if their military forces did not engage in full-scale armed combat. Although no Finnish troops died as a result of this conflict, it would be erroneous to assert that the state of relations was peaceful in any "positive" sense.[66]

In sum, critics contend that democratic peace proponents tinker with definitions of democracy and war to dismiss important cases that the theory fails to account for. Skeptics insist that analyses of the relationship between war and democracy should consider alternative definitions of both variables, and assess the extent to which the relationship breaks down as we extend the definitional boundaries of each concept.[67]

DEMOCRACIES DO USE FORCE AGAINST EACH OTHER. A third methodological critique undermines the argument that joint democratic institutions and norms have not prevented democracies from threatening each other with force and engaging in militarized disputes. Critics insist that democracies do sometimes prepare and expect to fight each other, and often threaten each other with force.[68] Specifically, critics maintain that democratic peace researchers overlook instances of coercive actions short of formal war. Skeptics point out that military intervention does occur between pairs of democratic states: since 1975 there were at least fifteen incidents of unequivocally free states inter-

---

64. Russett, *Grasping the Democratic Peace*, p. 18. See also Bruce Russett, "And Yet it Moves: Correspondence on the Democratic Peace," *International Security*, Vol. 19, No. 4 (Spring 1995), p. 168.

65. Spiro, "The Insignificance of the Liberal Peace."

66. The 1967 Six Day War is another example of how semantic labeling can hide anomalous evidence; whether the conflict between Israel and Lebanon during the war is treated as an instance of warring democracies is highly sensitive to the way war is defined. Russett notes that Lebanon was a democracy, but rules out the incident as a disconfirming case because Lebanon only sent a few aircraft into Israeli air space and sustained no casualties. See *Grasping the Democratic Peace*, p. 18.

67. Gates et al., "Democracy and Peace."

68. Layne, "Kant or Cant."

vening with military force against other mature democracies.[69] Critics also point to past U.S. attempts to subvert popularly elected regimes through covert means. During the Cold War, a Third World country's increased respect for civil and political rights did not automatically lead to an improvement in its relations with the United States. For the United States, the question of democracy was at best secondary to the national interest. Furthermore, national security and economic concerns prompted the United States to engage in covert international action to end regimes that were partially democratic, and were certainly far more democratic than the regimes that followed. U.S. leaders favored democracy only when democracies supported U.S. policies; otherwise they bolstered the power of local anti-democratic forces. In short, critics contend that the United States undermined democracies in the past when this suited its interest, and that today the democratic peace theory allows the United States to support democratization as the newest tool of intervention. Kalevi Holsti puts it well: "Western democracies may not war against each other, but Western democracies also seem to hold a veto over the politics and policies of democracies elsewhere."[70]

DEMOCRACY DOES NOT ACCOUNT FOR THE DEMOCRATIC PEACE

Another group of critics does not argue with the aggregate data, but questions whether *democracy* causes the observed peace between democratic states. These researchers accept the empirical finding of a dyadic democratic peace, but reject the explanation for its cause; that is, they challenge the theories that purport to explain the democratic peace. For example, some suggest that neorealist variables are more important than regime type in explaining war and peace—that while democracies have avoided wars with each other, there is little reason to believe that they did so because of shared democratic norms or institutional features. Others suggest only mature democracies are likely to behave in ways consistent with the dyadic and monadic democratic peace hypotheses, and that new democracies and democratizing states are more belligerent than the democratic peace theory would lead us to expect.

---

69. Charles W. Kegley, Jr. and Margaret G. Hermann, "Military Intervention and the Democratic Peace," *International Interactions*, Vol. 21, No. 1 (July 1995), p. 9. For example, the authors note that from 1974–1988, the United States intervened militarily in eight free states. See also David P. Forsythe, "Democracy, War, and Covert Action," *Journal of Peace Research*, Vol. 29, No. 4 (1992), pp. 385–395.

70. Holsti, *The State, War, and the State of War*, p. 180.

NEOREALISM. Critics maintain that since factors other than democratic norms and institutions can often account for peace between democratic states, instances of nonwarring democracies do not necessarily confirm the theory. In particular, these critics insist that neorealist theories can explain the same empirical patterns. For example, peace among democracies has often occurred when cooperation is required in response to third-party threats, or when neither state can envision victory in war. Adverse distributions of military capabilities often account for why democracies have avoided war in the past.[71] Similarly, a common interest for security—rather than shared norms and institutions—has worked to keep the peace between democracies since World War II.[72] Indeed, according to skeptics, geopolitical considerations are so important that when allies become enemies, their domestic political systems are often recoded by their new enemies. Contrary to the expectations of democratic peace proponents, rather than domestic regime type driving the differentiation of friends from foes, quite the reverse is often the case.[73] In short, neorealists claim that the clash of national interests remains a central tool for understanding war and peace outcomes, even among jointly democratic states.[74] The upshot is that even the most benign democratic state cannot be trusted if it has excessive power: despite good intentions and good values, states will behave with moderation only if checked by the power of others.[75]

---

71. Layne, "Kant or Cant"; and Raymond Cohen, "Pacific Unions: A Reappraisal of the Theory that 'Democracies Do Not Go to War with Each Other'," *Review of International Studies*, Vol. 20, No. 3 (July 1994), pp. 207–223.

72. Farber and Gowa, "Polities and Peace"; and Mearsheimer, "Back to the Future."

73. Oren, "The Subjectivity of the 'Democratic Peace'."

74. Spiro, "The Insignificance of the Liberal Peace," p. 59; and Cohen, "Pacific Unions," pp. 219, 222.

75. This critique draws on methodological issues of how theories are tested within the social sciences. As one scholar notes, "Theory confirmation involves much more than merely finding true predictions (positive instances) of the theory. A genuinely confirming evidence not only must favor the theory at hand, but must simultaneously disconfirm its plausible rival theories." See Bahman Fozouni, "Confutation of Political Realism," *International Studies Quarterly*, Vol. 39, No. 4 (December 1995), p. 487. Thus, to make the claim that peace between two democracies is the result of democratic norms or institutions, proponents must eliminate other possible alternative theories that might equally predict democratic peace as a logical consequence. Critics contend that democratic peace proponents have merely accumulated positive instances that accord well with the predictions

PEACE PRODUCES DEMOCRACY. A related critique is that democracy breaks down or is consolidated because of a state's security environment. Critics insist that if states become democratic *because* their external environments are not characterized by high conflict in the first place, then it is misleading to conclude that democracy creates the possibility of peace.[76]

These critics draw on a long tradition in comparative politics emphasizing that a state's need to fight wars prevents it from developing democratic institutions, while peaceful interstate environments facilitate the democratization process. Frequent war-making requires a centralized state with concentrated and extensive powers in order to mobilize national resources for battle. In these situations, the decentralized domestic political structures that characterize democracy are likely to appear inefficient and undesirable.[77] In other words, while malign international environments and war limit incentives for democratization, the diminished probability of war contributes to democratic development. Thus, democratic states do not go to war with each other because they tend to become nondemocracies *before* fighting.

DEMOCRATIC BREAKDOWN. According to other critics, the fact that even mature democracies can revert to authoritarianism suggests that democracies cannot afford to ignore other democracies' relative gains, the balance of military power, and the possibility of future war.

---

deduced from it, but have not disconfirmed competing plausible explanations for these events. In particular, critics insist that because balance-of-power theory can account for the same behavior for which the democratic peace theory claims explanatory monopoly, most examples of the democratic peace cannot count as supportive evidence of the theory.

76. Layne, "Kant or Cant," pp. 44–45; William R. Thompson, "Democracy and Peace: Putting the Cart Before the Horse?" *International Organization*, Vol. 50, No. 1 (Winter 1996), p. 142; and Gates et al., "Democracy and Peace," p. 5. This criticism highlights the problem of endogeneity, where dependent variables (peace) can be a cause, as well as a consequence, of independent variables (regime type). For more on this problem, see Gary King, Robert O. Keohane, and Sidney Verba, *Designing Social Inquiry: Scientific Inference in Qualitative Research* (Princeton, N.J.: Princeton University Press, 1994), pp. 185–196.

77. Thompson, "Democracy and Peace"; Robert G. Kaufman, "A Two-Level Interaction: Structure, Stable Liberal Democracy, and U.S. Grand Strategy," *Security Studies*, Vol. 3, No. 4 (Summer 1994), pp. 678–717; and Bruce D. Porter, "Is the Zone of Peace Stable? Sources of Stress and Conflict in the Industrial Democracies of Post-Cold War Europe," *Security Studies*, Vol. 4, No. 3 (Spring 1995), pp. 520–551.

These critics contend that democratic peace proponents incorrectly omit a number of anomalous cases of democratic war by arguing that, by the time war was fought, at least one state in the dyad had experienced democratic breakdown. For example, Bruce Russett discounts instances of U.S. intervention against democratically elected governments by arguing that the target state was no longer democratic when covert operations took place.[78] World War II is also excluded for similar reasons. Critics contend that the case refutes the theory because Adolf Hitler established Nazi rule following elections.[79] Proponents counter that Germany was no longer a democracy when Hitler began to adopt aggressive foreign policies: "Adolf Hitler was democratically elected and, of course, extremely belligerent toward democratic states . . . [but] by the time Hitler became involved in war against democratic states in World War II he had expressly, overtly, and officially terminated Germany's democratic system. Thus the conflicts between Germany and several democratic opponents were not wars between democratic states."[80] Yet, while critics agree that Germany was nondemocratic when it fought the Allies, they emphasize that democracy cannot guarantee peace. If the possibility always exists that democracies will revert to authoritarian rules, then liberal democracies must continue to be concerned with the balance of military power among themselves.

THE DEMOCRATIC PROCESS DOES NOT FOSTER BENIGN INTERNATIONAL BEHAVIOR. A number of critics cast doubt on the claim that democracy decreases the likelihood of aggressive foreign policies. They suggest that the democratic process can *increase* the chances for war, particularly because public opinion is often not pacific. The democratic peace hypothesis suggests that democracies will initiate fewer wars—either in general or merely with each other—because the voting public must pay the price: "The fear of electoral punishment makes democratic leaders as sensitive to public opinion as public opinion is to the costs of war."[81] By contrast, critics insist that public pressures within democracies have frequently pushed leaders toward war, even against other

---

78. Russett, *Grasping the Democratic Peace*, pp. 121–122.

79. Spiro, "The Insignificance of the Liberal Peace." Spiro suggests that World War II is an instance of warring democracies precisely because Hitler and his party were elected to the German Parliament.

80. Ray, *Democracy and International Conflict*, p. 119; see also p. 10.

81. Peterson, "How Democracies Differ," pp. 10–11. For more on this claim, see Mintz and Geva, "Why Don't Democracies Fight Each Other?"

democracies. Public opinion may constrain war-prone leaders from choosing war, but it can also prevent moderate leaders from pursuing peace.[82] In addition, mass publics are rarely unified; while some societal groups may not favor war, leaders who advocate belligerent foreign policies can almost always find concentrated interest groups to support their policies. Since democratic institutions allow diverse interest groups access to the decision making arena, democratic politics can facilitate logrolling among more militaristic parochial groups.[83] Finally, critics contend that it is questionable whether public opinion drives leaders' military strategy or vice versa. For example, pro-imperial leaders often mobilize public opinion on behalf of these policies. And while public opinion can influence whether leaders will end costly wars, the voting public is usually not significantly involved in war-initiation.[84] According to critics, the frequency with which democratically elected leaders pursue belligerent foreign policies before consulting public representatives, and even after misleading the public, should make us question the extent to which foreign policy is driven by the demands and reactions of public opinion.

In addition to questioning the pacific nature of public option, critics argue that in democracies, groups organize into narrow, parochial lobbies. These specialized interest groups will have strong incentives to control the policy making process and will often support war in exchange for securing support for their own issues. Indeed, critics contend that the benefits of war, military preparations, and imperial conquest are often concentrated among a few parochial interest groups even in fully consolidated democracies.[85] Similarly, critics contend that because democracies have trouble forming governing

---

82. Mearsheimer, "Back to the Future," p. 185; and Layne, "Kant or Cant," p. 12. Michael Doyle also acknowledges this point, reminding proponents of the democratic peace theory that Kant offers no support for the claim that participatory, representative states—democracies—should be peaceful either in general or with fellow democracies. Democracies that are nonliberal (that is, motivated by racism or ethnic purity) should not be included in the list of pacific Kantian republics. Democracies can be quite aggressive abroad if the preferences of the median voter condone war. See "Michael Doyle on the Democratic Peace—Again," in Brown, Lynn-Jones, and Miller, *Debating the Democratic Peace*, p. 367. For more on the distinction between democracy and liberalism, see Owen, "How Liberalism Produces the Democratic Peace."

83. Farber and Gowa, "Polities and Peace," p. 127.

84. Menon, "In the Shadow of the Bear," p. 156, n. 13.

85. Farber and Gowa, "Polities and Peace," p. 127.

coalitions that integrate a wide spectrum of interests, political stale-mates will often result. Alternatively, tough foreign policy trade-offs will be avoided in order to maintain fragile coalitions made up of diverse and contradictory bases of support. Such weak governments are particularly prone to using military force in order to secure legit-imacy for the ruling elite.[86]

DEMOCRATIZING STATES. A number of critics who do not reject the democratic peace finding suggest that democratization gives vent to nationalism, which is an important cause of war. For example, Edward D. Mansfield and Jack Snyder argue that the democratic peace theory is confined to the relations between mature, stable democracies.[87] States in the process of democratization are more like-ly to engage in war. These new democracies are characterized by weakly institutionalized democratic procedures, and they often con-front illiberal, radicalized societal groups. Furthermore, elites in democratizing states cannot easily form stable coalitions or pursue coherent policies, so that appeals to nationalism and risky foreign policies become attractive ways to shore up domestic political power.

---

86. For more on how democratic leaders may use force abroad in order to divert attention from domestic problems and shore up legitimacy for the incumbent leadership, see, for example, C.W. Ostrom, Jr. and B.L. Job, "The President and the Political Use of Force," *American Political Science Review*, Vol. 80, No. 2 (1986), pp. 541–566. Since the monadic version of the democratic peace theory asserts that democracies choose force only as an option of last resort, such behavior under-mines this democratic peace argument. By contrast, proponents of the dyadic ver-sion of the democratic peace theory argue that such diversionary activity is not inconsistent with the theory if the force is directed against nondemocracies. Yet, at the heart of the democratic peace thesis is the notion that democratic politics decreases the incentives for leaders to go to war. Finding that the "electoral con-nection" increases the incentives for leaders to use force and that democratic gov-ernments are particularly prone to using force to secure legitimacy strongly undermines the usefulness of foreign policies that encourage democratization, even if force is directed at nondemocratic states.

87. Mansfield and Snyder, "Democratization and the Danger of War." See also Emmerson, "Realism or Evangelism?"; V.P. Gagnon, Jr., "Ethnic Nationalism and International Conflict: The Case of Serbia," *International Security*, Vol. 19, No. 3 (Winter 1994/95), pp. 130–166; and Alexander V. Kozhemiakin, "Expanding the 'Pacific Union'? The Impact of the Process of Democratization on International Security," paper presented at the National Security Seminar, John M. Olin Institute of Strategic Studies, Harvard University, February 12, 1996. Note that democratic peace researchers use the terms "mature," "developed," "consolidated," and "sta-ble" interchangeably to distinguish older democracies where cultural norms and institutional procedures are well embedded, from newer democracies where these features are not yet established rules.

In short, immature democracies are a force for war, not peace. Compared to states that remain autocracies, states that make the transition from autocracy to democracy are more than twice as likely to be in a war during the decade after democratization.[88]

JOINT CULTURE. According to some critics, common cultures, not common political institutions or ideologies, tend to keep the peace between democracies. For example, according to Samuel Huntington, cultural differences and similarities are far more important in explaining international peace and conflict than are differences among political ideologies and regime types. Democracies that belong to the same Western culture will maintain peaceful relations; war is more likely to be viewed as a legitimate option among democracies that share common political ideologies and institutions but have cultures that clash. Thus, enlarging the zone of democracy will not necessarily enlarge the zone of peace if democracies with different cultural traits are compelled to interact with each other.[89]

NONDEMOCRACIES ARE NOT SO DIFFERENT FROM DEMOCRACIES. A final group of critics points out that some of the same features said to influence the calculations of democratic leaders also affect the motivations of decision makers in nondemocracies. For example, critics point out that leaders in nondemocracies are also subject to decision making constraints. Proponents of the democratic peace thesis claim that nondemocracies are war-prone because leaders in nondemocracies are not

---

88. While Mansfield and Snyder's argument helps to delineate the conditions under which the democratic peace theory is applicable, their notion of "democratization" renders the democratic peace theory nonfalsifiable. Because the democratization process can last for years, "democratization" provides a convenient way to explain wars between democracies. For example, if India and Pakistan do not fight a war in the next few decades, democratic peace supporters will hail the theory as vindicated. But if these two states do wind up at war, the theory will not be seriously compromised; proponents can maintain that Pakistan is not yet a mature democracy.

89. Samuel P. Huntington, "The Clash of Civilizations?" *Foreign Affairs*, Vol. 72, No. 3 (Summer 1993), pp. 22–49; Samuel P. Huntington, "The West: Unique, Not Universal," *Foreign Affairs*, Vol. 75, No. 6 (November/December 1996), pp. 28–45. This critique minimizes the alleged differences between democracies and nondemocracies. According to the normative version of the democratic peace proposition, nondemocracies go to war with each other because they lack shared cultural norms that sanction the use of force, and are likely to export these norms of domestic conflict resolution. By contrast, this critique implies that nondemocracies may also avoid war because of the psychological need to support states with similar cultural beliefs. For empirical examples of how shared common cultures and normative consenses—not merely democratic ideologies or institutions—can prevent the recourse to war, see the chapters by Stephen R. Rock, Arie M. Kacowicz, and Martin Malin.

constrained from initiating costly and reckless foreign policies. By contrast, democratically elected leaders are more constrained from going to war because they first need to ensure the support of the voting public. Yet, critics contend that nondemocratic leaders are also subject to the approval of those groups which brought them to power; they must heed the policy preferences of coalition partners and other influential groups. William Thompson phrases it well: "the contrasting image of capricious autocrats with nothing to lose in going to war is no doubt exaggerated . . . Authoritarian leaders rarely are free of all constraints on their own behavior; nor are they always highly risk-acceptant."[90]

Critics also contend that nondemocratic states often pursue pacific foreign policies and that democratic peace proponents expect non-democracies to be far more aggressive abroad than they usually are. Nondemocratic leaders do sometimes adopt aggressive foreign policies to shore up their political power and limit the influence of domestic resistance movements.[91] But critics contend that they will often respond to domestic instability by pursuing more moderate policy agendas; political elites confronted by internal opposition usually prefer to eliminate the sources of internal problems, or perhaps co-opt the opposition.

In fact, critics maintain that it is often the very weakness of nondemocratic states that deflects their attention from the international arena and prevents them from mobilizing national capabilities for war. States that expend time and energy in employing force internally are less capable of waging international wars.[92] Nondemocracies

---

90. Thompson, "Democracy and Peace," p. 149. See also Hagan, "Domestic Political Systems and War Proneness," pp. 192–193; and Farber and Gowa, "Polities and Peace," p. 128. In fact, the risks of waging war without sufficient domestic support might often be higher for leaders in nondemocracies. In democracies, losing a war means that one might be replaced at the polls. It is this risk which makes democratic leaders more cautious in their foreign policy behavior. But nondemocratic leaders also frequently risk their lives. As a result, nondemocratic leaders may have greater incentives to fight until victory is achieved, but they also will have more reason to think twice about waging war in the first place.

91. Michael E. Brown, "The Causes and Regional Dimensions of Internal Conflict," in Michael E. Brown, ed., *The International Dimensions of Internal Conflict* (Cambridge, Mass.: MIT Press, 1996), pp. 571–601; Jack S. Levy, "Diversionary Action by Authoritarian Regimes: Argentina in the Falklands/Malvinas Case," in Manus I. Midlarsky, ed., *The Internationalization of Communal Strife* (London: Routledge, 1992), pp. 118–146; and Czempiel, "Governance and Democratization," p. 262.

92. Stanislav Andreski, "On the Peaceful Disposition of Military Dictatorships," *Journal of Strategic Studies*, Vol. 3, No. 3 (December 1980), pp. 3–10.

will not necessarily prefer diversion and scapegoating—and they certainly do not have more to gain from such strategies. A more profitable means of dealing with domestic opposition is to seek support from other states, including resources to quell internal unrest.[93] In addition, states that are divided and whose leaders lack legitimacy generally do not develop armies worthy of battle on an international scale: "the more support an army enjoys from the masses of citizens, the greater is the likelihood that it will fight well . . . The armed forces' role as an engine of coercion has the opposite effect and tends to weaken their strength for war."[94]

Furthermore, critics contend that nondemocratic procedures may also increase the state's ability to carry out rational foreign and security policies. That democratically elected leaders are compelled to heed the demands of a fickle public limits the possibility of devising a coherent and rational foreign security policy based on external exigencies. By contrast, leaders in nondemocracies can often fashion more rational military strategies precisely because domestic considerations are less limiting, and decision makers can respond primarily to the demands of the international system. Thus, nondemocracies are often able to bargain and negotiate more effectively because leaders can bypass domestic political constraints.[95]

In short, critics maintain that nondemocratic states do not invariably act aggressively and do not necessarily export the norms of

---

93. Michael N. Barnett and Jack S. Levy, "Domestic Sources of Alliances and Alignments: The Case of Egypt, 1962-73," *International Organization*, Vol. 45, No. 3 (Summer 1991), pp. 369–395.

94. Andreski, "On the Peaceful Disposition of Military Dictatorships," p. 4. See also Stephen Peter Rosen, "Military Effectiveness: Why Society Matters," *International Security*, Vol. 19, No. 4 (Spring 1995), pp. 5–31. For more on the claim that nondemocratic institutions can be forces for peace, see section four of this book.

95. In foreign policy analysis, it is a truism that rational foreign policy and democracy are inherently at odds. The view that democracy distorts, impedes, and confuses national security policy can be traced to Alexis de Tocqueville and more recently to George Kennan, Walter Lippman, and Hans Morgenthau. For a review of these arguments, see Kjell Goldmann, "'Democracy Is Incompatible With International Politics': Reconsideration of a Hypothesis," in Kjell Goldmann, Sten Berglund, and Gunnar Sjostedt, eds., *Democracy and Foreign Policy: The Case of Sweden* (Brookfield, Vermont: Gower, 1986); and Hans-Henrik Holm, "The Democratic Victory: What Will Happen to Foreign Policy," *Cooperation and Conflict*, Vol. 25, No. 4 (1990), pp. 195–206. For a critique, see James D. Fearon, "Domestic Political Audiences and the Escalation of International Disputes," *American Political Science Review*, Vol. 88 (September 1994), pp. 577–592.

domestic conflict resolution. In many regions where nondemocracies are the prevailing regime type, there have been widespread domestic violence, military coups, and civil conflicts—but no international wars. Contrary to the expectations of democratic peace theorists, governments that kill their own people are not necessarily more likely to kill the citizens of other countries.

Shortcomings of the Debate and the Need for a Fresh Look

Since the mid-1990s, critics of the democratic peace theory have called on the scholarly and policy making community to revisit the democratic peace theory's prescription for preventing international conflict. The debate has raised a number of important questions: Are shared democratic values or constraints on leaders the reason that democratic states have refrained from fighting each other? What are the circumstances that have sometimes led democracies to become increasingly hostile and belligerent toward one another? To what extent has the regime type of the opposing state been the basis for decisions to go to war or back down from the brink? Are certain democratic institutions likely to increase the state's war propensity, even against fellow democracies? Are democracies predisposed to choose negotiation over war? Have internally repressive governments ever been a source of interstate peace? Are wars between nondemocracies linked primarily to nondemocratic rules and norms?

These questions have important implications for policy and the study of international relations. In this book we aim to provide some answers. Shortcomings on both sides of the debate suggest a need for a new approach.

A SHORTAGE OF CASE STUDIES

The quantitative empirical analyses that find that democracy is associated with peace are correlational studies, and provide no evidence that leaders actually consider the opponent's regime type in deciding between war and peace. These studies focus primarily on foreign policy outcomes and ignore the decision making process. If we want to move beyond correlation to causation, we need to reveal the decision making processes of aggressive and pacific states. We need to see if leaders took their nations to war, or remained at peace, for the reasons hypothesized by the democratic peace theory. In short, the challenge now facing democratic peace proponents and skeptics alike is to put the general theory to the test of detailed historical analysis: have leaders tended to act and think in ways consistent with the theory?

To date, qualitative tests of the democratic peace proposition have examined a small handful of case studies—for example, the Fashoda crisis and the Spanish-American War. Other case studies focus on the foreign policy decisions of the United States, and few have tested the theory's claims about the behavior of mixed or nondemocratic dyads. Moreover, many of these qualitative analyses have not posed strong enough tests for either competing arguments or the democratic peace thesis. In particular, many of the case studies are overdetermined and thus do not provide conclusive corroboration for either the democratic peace argument or its neorealist rival.

For example, the outcome of the Fashoda crisis between France and Britain in 1898 is consistent with what both the democratic peace theory and neorealist balance-of-power theory would lead us to expect. Critics contend that the crisis was resolved peacefully because of the balance of power—France was far too weak to contemplate military action against the British. By contrast, democratic peace proponents maintain that even though the military balance of power goes far in explaining why the crisis was resolved short of war, shared democratic values did play a part in moderating the conflict.[96] Since both the democratic peace theory and its rival predict similar outcomes—that France would back down from the brink of war—the Fashoda case is not a particularly useful test of either theory.

By contrast, in many of the cases discussed in this book, the democratic peace theory and competing perspectives lead us to expect opposite outcomes. We can then look at the empirical evidence and see which theory predicts outcomes more accurately.[97] In some of the chapters that follow, the historical evidence presents an easy case for the democratic peace theory and a hard case for neorealism; these cases favor the democratic peace theory either because during the course of the crisis, democratic states were becoming more democratic or because democratic norms and institutions were firmly in place. If the predictions of the democratic peace theory do not hold, these cases are particularly damaging to the theory, since we would expect

96. Layne, "Kant or Cant"; Russett, *Grasping the Democratic Peace*, pp. 7–8; and Ray, *Democracy and International Conflict*, chap. 5.

97. For more on hard tests, see King, Keohane, and Verba, *Designing Social Inquiry*, pp. 209–212. For an empirical example, see Miriam Fendius Elman, "The Foreign Policies of Small States: Challenging Neorealism in Its Own Backyard," *British Journal of Political Science*, Vol. 25, No. 2 (April 1995), pp. 171–217.

the theory to work well in these situations. In other chapters, the crises present a hard case for the democratic peace theory—the balance of power or external threats should easily account for the decision making process and the foreign policy outcome. If the democratic peace theory can explain these cases where we do not expect it to succeed, then it should be more deserving of our confidence.

CRITICS THROW THE BABY OUT WITH THE BATHWATER

Critics who refocus our attention on geopolitical considerations ignore how domestic politics in general, and democratic politics in particular, can affect state behavior—albeit not necessarily in the benign manner assumed by the democratic peace thesis. Certainly, the finding that states define their interests, and choose their allies and enemies based on external threats and the distribution of material capabilities, is a powerful indictment of a theory that asserts that the degree of ideological solidarity between states determines their threat perceptions and their propensity to wage war.[98] But examining the international determinants of a state's foreign policy is not the only way to critique the democratic peace theory. Indeed, since the theory posits that a *particular* domestic level variable (regime type) matters more than others, a comprehensive test would also ask whether the democratic peace theory adequately depicts the nature of domestic politics in both democratic and nondemocratic regimes.

Critics of the democratic peace theory who focus on the international level of analysis are likely to prove easy targets for democratic peace proponents; it is difficult to reject the proposition that domestic politics does affect state behavior. The nature of the government and the interests of leaders and societal groups may account for specific foreign policy choices, even if policy makers are attentive to strategic concerns and broader geopolitical considerations, for three reasons. First, systemic constraints are often indeterminate—several diverse policies can be consistent with the state's goal to survive and compete effectively with other states. Second, even if leaders' choices are a function of international distributions of power, some strategies will require that leaders be able to change foreign policy course, extract resources from society, and effectively implement selected policies. Third, states with similar power capabilities may act differently because their political values and leadership orientations vary; for example, had Hitler won World War II, the post-war international

---

98. See the chapters by Christopher Layne, Stephen Rock, and Šumit Ganguly.

system would have looked quite different from the economic and political order forged through U.S. hegemony. Thus, domestic political arguments are important because the sources of state behavior ultimately reside in how leaders view the external environment. Finally, rather than pit international against domestic level arguments, it is often more appropriate to view them as complementary. While the domestic political process can account for a given state's foreign policy orientation, international factors will often determine whether this foreign policy choice proves successful and whether the state faces sufficient opportunities to realize its agenda.[99]

In this book we argue that domestic regime type is not the only domestic political factor likely to influence war and peace decisions, and that democracy may not always be benign. Like the democratic peace theory, our critique keeps domestic politics at the forefront of the causal explanation for war and peace. But unlike the democratic peace theory, we suggest that other domestic political variables are often more important in determining foreign policy choices than the state's regime type.

The chapters that follow suggest that democracy and nondemocracy should not be treated as unified categories. In particular, proponents of the democratic peace theory fail to consider the ways in which democracies differ from one another, and how a democratic state may change over time. The theory obscures the important nuanced differences among democracies (and nondemocracies).

LEADERSHIP ORIENTATION. According to the democratic peace theory, since aggressive or defensive behavior can be inferred from domestic structures, as long as democracy persists, changes of government are irrelevant. Since all democratic leaders should be constrained by the same democratic processes and political ideologies, it matters little who rules. The theory thus underemphasizes the importance of different leaders' views on national goals and the

---

99. For example, in this book Arie M. Kacowicz suggests that weak states that lack the military capabilities to fight more powerful neighbors will refrain from going to war, even if they have aggressive intentions. Similarly, John C. Matthews III's chapter suggests that while permissive external environments allow aggressive leaders to realize their interests, nonpermissive environments can prevent decision makers from implementing aggressive foreign policy preferences. For more on how domestic political explanations can explain foreign policy orientations, while geopolitical factors ultimately account for the success or failure of these policies, see Fareed Zakaria, "Realism and Domestic Politics: A Review Essay," *International Security*, Vol. 17, No. 1 (Summer 1992), pp. 177–198.

appropriate means to achieve them; that is, the theory neglects the role that extraordinary individuals often play in war and peace decision making.[100]

In this book we claim that leader orientations are not easily inferred from the structure of the regime.[101] Leaders' opinions on the legitimacy of force vary across political regimes even though structural arrangements—democracy and nondemocracy—remain constant. Furthermore, particular foreign policy orientations are not associated exclusively with a certain type of regime—leaders in democracies may not espouse moderate views, and leaders in nondemocracies are not always hard-line. Whether or not democratic leaders embrace liberal prohibitions against the use of force is an empirical question. Hard-line, radical, and ideological leaders who come to power within democracies are more willing to use force to solve interstate disputes. By contrast, accommodationist, moderate, and risk-averse leaders who come to power in nondemocracies are less likely to lead such states down the path to war; such leaders will engage in external conflict only when important elites who brought them to power support the decision.[102] In short, whether a state is democratic or not does not by itself determine war or peace—a belligerent leader of a nondemocracy can commit to war; but he or she can also pursue peace if the public prefers war.

EXECUTIVE-LEGISLATIVE BALANCE. Leaders work within inherited domestic institutional structures. Consequently, we need to know both the leader's predisposition to use force as well as how constrained

---

100. Hermann and Kegley, "Rethinking Democracy and International Peace," p. 511.

101. See the chapters by Christopher Layne, Miriam Fendius Elman, Martin Malin, Kurt Dassel, and John C. Matthews III.

102. Hermann and Kegley, "Rethinking Democracy and International Peace"; Hagan, "Domestic Political Systems and War Proneness," p. 199. President Franklin D. Roosevelt's policies following the Munich crisis provide a good example of how leadership orientation often matters more than domestic regime type. While Roosevelt continued to believe that Stalin and Mussolini were willing to respect the norms of peaceful accommodation, Hitler's actions at Munich convinced Roosevelt that the German leader had unlimited aims. Thus, Roosevelt did not consider regime type sufficient to diagnose external threat. On the contrary, whether rival leaders preferred compromise to violence was more important than whether or not the state was a liberal democracy. For an extended discussion, see Barbara Farnham, "Roosevelt, the Munich Crisis, and the Theory of the Democratic Peace," paper presented at the annual meeting of the International Studies Association, San Diego, April 16–20, 1996.

he or she may be from acting on these preferences. For example, in decentralized democracies, leaders are especially constrained because many groups, some of whom may not agree with the leader's views, will have access to the decision making arena. Conversely, in more centralized democracies, leaders find it easier to implement their foreign policy preferences because they face fewer veto points and *ex ante* checks and balances on their decisions.[103] Thus, in more centralized democracies, groups that favor war will not win out if the executive does not favor the use of force; in decentralized democracies, groups that favor war can push the state down that road even if the executive favors more moderate action. In short, while the democratic peace theory assumes that all democracies are weak states with war-prone leaders, some democracies may have less constrained, hard-line leaders.

In this book we suggest that the extent to which leaders are constrained by the voting public and the legislature varies across democratic states, with important implications for war propensity.[104] Democracy may not have a benign impact on foreign policy when democratic structures allow skewed foreign policy making access to groups who favor the use of force. Leaders in modern democracies may be more constrained than nondemocratic leaders in their capacity to wage unpopular wars, but the constraints are a matter of degree.[105]

CIVIL-MILITARY RELATIONS. According to the institutional variant of the democratic peace theory, democracies do not fight each other because no single person can declare war. In all democracies, the military is subordinated to the civilian echelon; it tends to view its tasks as related primarily to preserving the state from external attack; and it firmly accepts the notion of civilian supremacy in war and peace decision making. Nevertheless, even within democratic states signif-

---

103. See Peterson, "How Democracies Differ"; and Thomas Risse-Kappen, "Public Opinion, Domestic Structure, and Foreign Policy in Liberal Democracies," *World Politics*, Vol. 43, No. 4 (July 1991), pp. 479–512.

104. See the chapters by Miriam Fendius Elman, Šumit Ganguly, and Lawrence Freedman.

105. Spiro, "The Insignificance of the Liberal Peace," p. 53. Constraints on the executive can vary within a given democracy as well. For example, following World War II, the U.S. executive had far greater control over foreign security policy than in previous years. After the Vietnam War, this delegation of war powers to the executive was reversed, with Congress becoming more involved in the decision making process.

icant war powers are usually delegated to small decision making groups, with important implications for war and peace outcomes. The military is likely to be more autonomous in democracies that face severe external threats. Civil-military relations in democracies that are compelled to fight and prepare for war are likely to be different from civil-military relations in democracies that face a more benign external security environment. In addition, the extent to which the military is autonomous from civilian control varies across democratic regime types. For example, because civilian institutions in the United States are divided while in Britain they are more unified, the U.S. military has far more discretion in the development of military doctrine than does the British military.[106]

In sum, we argue that the democratic peace theory, which asserts that domestic regime type matters more than other relevant domestic-level variables, must compete with a number of other plausible domestic-level theories. By focusing on the debate between the democratic peace theory and neorealism, both proponents and critics have largely ignored the importance of domestic variables other than regime type.

TOO MUCH ATTENTION ON DEMOCRATIC DYADS
Much of the current backlash against the democratic peace theory has centered on democratic dyads. Critics have not compared the relationships between pairs of states that are both democratic to those that are not; that is, they have only examined the dyadic version of the theory, and not the monadic proposition. Furthermore, the democratic peace theory makes specific predictions regarding the behavior of statesmen in both democracies and nondemocracies during crises with other states. Thus, if the theory is valid, we should find statesmen in democracies acting differently in crises from their nondemocratic counterparts. As Michael Doyle recently argued, "a fairer set of cases" designed to test the democratic peace theory would include a sample of "liberal dyads, liberal-nonliberal dyads, and non-liberal dyads, and [would] examine whether liberalism makes a difference and the liberal thesis was confirmed or disconfirmed."[107]

---

106. Deborah D. Avant, *Political Institutions and Military Change: Lessons From Peripheral Wars* (Ithaca, N.Y.: Cornell University Press, 1994). See also Lori Fisler Damrosch, "Constitutional Control Over War Powers: A Common Core of Accountability in Democratic Societies?" unpublished m.s., United States Institute of Peace, Washington, D.C.: 1995, pp. 20–21.

107. Michael W. Doyle, "Correspondence on the Democratic Peace," *International Security*, Vol. 19, No. 4 (Spring 1995), p. 181.

This book includes such cases—democratic dyads, and also mixed and nondemocratic pairs of states. In examining a democratic state's interactions with a nondemocracy, we focus on whether the regime type of the adversary made a difference in the decision making calculus. In addition, we ask whether the use of force was considered an option of last resort or a legitimate foreign policy tool. In examining the interactions of nondemocracies with each other, we focus on whether war and peace outcomes are consistent with what democratic peace proponents expect. The theory's proponents argue that pacific relations among nondemocracies is a function of the balance of power; therefore, we look to see whether nondemocratic peace can also be linked to internal constraints or domestic regime type. Since the theory's proponents presume nondemocracies are particularly aggressive internationally because of the nature of their governments, we look to see whether wars between nondemocracies can always be traced to the nature of these states' domestic regimes. The case studies that follow suggest that factors other than the features of authoritarian regimes cause war between nondemocracies; nondemocracies remain at peace for domestic reasons associated with their regime types; and the features of authoritarian regimes can help nondemocracies keep the peace.

OVER-EMPHASIS ON UNIVERSAL ARGUMENTS

Many proponents of the democratic peace proposition have sought to dismiss exceptions to the peace-proneness of democracies, and critics tend to reject the theory in its entirety. Thus, both supporters and critics of the theory have failed to delineate the conditions under which the theory is likely to have the greatest and least causal efficacy. Since social science theories are rarely either universally applicable or completely invalid, it is time to determine the boundaries of the theory's applicability and the conditions and circumstances under which democratic norms and institutions are more and less likely to explain democratic state behavior. This work is important for two reasons. First, good theories should always include clear statements of the antecedent conditions that govern their impact, as well as the evidence that would falsify them.[108] Second, conditional generalizations enable more useful policy prescriptions. As Stephen Van Evera notes, "Foreign policy disasters often happen because policymakers apply

---

108. King, Keohane, and Verba, *Designing Social Inquiry*, pp. 100–104; and Van Evera, *Guide to Methodology*, pp. 7–9.

valid theories to inappropriate circumstances."[109] To avoid mistakes, policy makers must know when democracies may be likely to use force against one another, and under what conditions and settings they will be more likely to remain at peace.

In this book we identify a number of conditions under which the democratic peace theory will apply best—and worst. For example, several authors suggest that the democratic peace theory will have less explanatory power when a state faces extreme external threat. Under these conditions, democracies will go to war even against states they perceive as democratic. Other authors suggest that the democratic peace theory may be confined to certain types of democracies. The predictions of the theory will tend to hold for decentralized democracies with war-prone leaders; they will be less robust in explaining the behavior of centralized democracies where leaders see force as a legitimate tool of foreign policy. Moreover, stable and mature democracies will also be more likely to display behavior consistent with what the democratic peace theory would lead us to expect. By contrast, new democracies with weak party systems and strong nationalist movements are not likely to conform well to the theory's predictions.

Thus, this book aims to fill the gaps in the debate over the democratic peace theory. We compare the decision making process and the foreign policy choices of democratic and nondemocratic states during international crises where there was a high risk of war. Focusing on nineteenth and twentieth century interstate crises that either escalated to war or were resolved peacefully, we explain why decision makers sometimes decided to go to war and sometimes chose to pull back from the brink. In each example of crisis diplomacy, we trace the policy process in order to determine the extent to which regime type influenced threat perceptions and foreign policy choices. Thus, using a small number of cases, many of which have raised considerable controversy in the democratic peace debate, this book focuses on leaders' deliberations in order to see whether the democratic peace theory or competing theoretical perspectives provide a better account of war and peace decision making. We test whether the democratic peace theory can be confirmed or refuted by looking at what foreign policy makers said and did when involved in interstate crises. Three central questions drive the analysis in each chapter:

---

109. Van Evera, *Guide to Methodology*, p. 8.

- Did the foreign policy decision making process unfold in a way that corresponds to the hypotheses of the democratic peace theory?
- Did domestic regime type and political ideology matter, or was the state's behavior a product of some other international or domestic factor, or both?
- If domestic politics influenced decision makers' choices, did it lead them down the road to war—and if so, is this consistent with what the democratic peace theory would lead us to expect?

In sum, we seek a better understanding of the ways in which democracy matters. Our point of departure is not to dismiss the importance of domestic politics in the foreign policy making process, or to reject the validity of the democratic peace proposition. Rather, our aim is to identify some of the international and domestic conditions under which the theory is likely to be more or less relevant. In sum, we consider the main strength of the democratic peace theory— its simplicity—also to be its central weakness. We argue that the vast complexity of war and peace decision making cannot be explained by reference to a single variable. We suggest that while domestic regime type—democracy versus nondemocracy—does matter in explaining war and peace decision making, it is not always the most important factor at play, nor is it likely to predict uniformly benign or malign international behavior.

Approach, Methods, and Cases

Each chapter tests the applicability and the explanatory power of the democratic peace theory against particular historical episodes. We look to see whether the decision making process corroborates the causal logic of the theory and its various predictions. This book relies on qualitative analysis—specifically, the case study method and process-tracing. We focus on crisis decision making that either resulted in a pacific resolution of the conflict or degenerated to war.[110]

---

110. Although each of the historical episodes presented in this book is important in its own right, our purpose is not to study particular historical outcomes, but to draw on history in order to test general theories. We view the chapter analyses as generalizable—each case study should enable us to understand other similar cases not included in this book. For more on the relationship between historical evidence and social science theory, see Olav Njølstad, "Learning From History? Case Studies and the Limits to Theory-Building," in Nils Gleditsch and Olav Njølstad, eds., *Arms Races: Technological and Political Dynamics* (London: Sage,

THE NEED FOR CASE STUDIES

Case studies can be used to develop, test, and refine theories.[111] First, case studies can be used to generate hypotheses and offer clues on cause and effect. These hypotheses can then be applied to other cases. Second, case studies can be used to corroborate or challenge existing theories. A small number of cases are investigated in detail to see if the theory's causal explanations seem valid and if events unfold in the manner predicted. Many case studies involve tracing the decision making process to see if political actors speak and act in ways that are consistent with the theory's logic. Finally, case studies can be used to repair and refine theories, by proposing a different causal process than the one hypothesized or by narrowing the scope of the existing theory's claims. Case studies can specify the antecedent conditions and particular circumstances under which the theory is likely to predict successfully—and the conditions under which it will be less likely to hold.

There are a number of reasons why case study analysis is particularly appropriate for the democratic peace theory.

CONTROVERSIAL NATURE OF THE STATISTICAL EVIDENCE. First, the quantitative, statistical studies that prove that democracies virtually never go to war with each other (the dyadic finding)—and are more peace-prone in general (the monadic finding)—remain controversial. Since both wars and democracies are historically rare, we must supplement analyses of large numbers of cases with intensive studies of individual and particularly crucial cases.[112]

EXPLAINING WHY DEMOCRACY MATTERS. Second, statistical evidence alone cannot account for *why* democracies behave differently. Statistical analyses prove correlation, but not causation. They can only supply information about the frequency of an empirical phenomenon; they do not explain why the relationship holds. In other words, aggregate data alone cannot tell us why regime type matters,

---

1990), pp. 220–246; Atul Kohli et al., "The Role of Theory in Comparative Politics: A Symposium," *World Politics*, Vol. 48, No. 1 (October 1995), pp. 1–49; and Colin Elman and Miriam Fendius Elman, "Diplomatic History and International Relations Theory: Respecting Difference and Crossing Boundaries," *International Security*, Vol. 22, No. 1 (Summer 1997).

111. See Van Evera, *Guide to Methodology*; and Alexander George, "Case Studies and Theory Development: The Method of Structured, Focused Comparison," in Paul Gordon Lauren, ed., *Diplomacy: New Approaches in History, Theory and Policy* (New York: Free Press, 1979), pp. 43–68.

112. Ray, *Democracy and International Conflict*, pp. viii, 27.

or if democracy causes peace. As Kalevi Holsti claims, "generalizations about the democratic peace are fine—we have many of them—but now is the time to explore via comparative case studies the causal chains, if they exist."[113] Indeed, even proponents of the theory argue that more case study analysis is necessary to tease out the causal mechanisms behind the democratic peace finding:

There have been by this time a number of impressive analyses of aggregate level data regarding the alleged differences in the propensity to war of democracies and undemocratic states. But a need exists to supplement the kind of evidence that can be produced by aggregate data analysis with the complementary type of evidence that can be produced by the intensive analysis of a few crucial cases.[114]

DETERMINING THE CONDITIONS UNDER WHICH THE THEORY PREDICTS BEST AND WORST. While democratic-democratic conflict is rare, studies of such cases can generate a compelling set of conditions and circumstances under which the democratic peace theory will be more—and less—applicable. Case studies are necessary because aggregate data cannot account for potential exceptions to the rule. Even studies of a few cases that fail to conform to the theory's predictions can lead to its progressive reformulation.

During the nineteenth and twentieth centuries, at least seventeen potential exceptions to the democratic peace took place.[115] Proponents of the democratic peace theory have omitted most of these cases from their quantitative studies on the grounds that at least one country involved in the conflict was not a democracy, or the conflict was too small to be coded as an international war. Yet, it is important to determine how many of these alleged exceptions to the rule really are exceptions, because even if only a handful are, the empirical finding that democracies do not go to war with each other might disappear. As James Lee Ray suggests, since wars between states are rare, the existence of even a few wars between democratic states would destroy the statistical significance in the historical rates of warfare between democratic states and all other pairs of states.[116]

---

113. Personal correspondence, February 7, 1996; see also Cohen, "Needed: A Disaggregate Approach to the Democratic-Peace Theory," p. 325.

114. Ray, *Democracy and International Conflict*, p. 42; Rousseau et al., "Assessing the Dyadic Nature of the Democratic Peace," p. 516; and Russett, "And Yet It Moves," p. 165.

115. Ray, *Democracy and International Conflict*, chap. 3. See also Russett, *Grasping the Democratic Peace*, chap. 1.

116. Ray, *Democracy and International Conflict*, pp. 27, 152–153, 159.

DO SHARED DEMOCRATIC NORMS CAUSE DEMOCRATIC PEACE?
Examining the purposes, motives, and goals of statesmen involved in
crises is crucial to determine if shared norms were an important cause
of the observed behavior or merely a rationalization for policies selected for other reasons. Indeed, leaders can invoke democratic norms as
rhetoric to justify policies. Case studies are vital for testing the democratic peace thesis because they allow us to see state behavior from
within—to assess what actors intended when they invoked liberal
norms and values.[117]

THE ARGUMENT AGAINST CASE STUDIES. While proponents of the
democratic peace theory concede that case studies can help explain
the roots of the democratic peace phenomenon, many insist that case
studies cannot be used to *test* the democratic peace proposition.
According to this view, case studies are not adequate tests because
the theory explains only trends and patterns of interstate behavior,
not individual foreign policy choices. For example, Bruce Russett
argues that by merely finding a few cases of warring democracies,
the "universal" principle of democratic peace would not be invali-
dated: "Even if there were no evidence for democratic peace considerations in four cases, that would prove nothing about their putative
absence in other instances."[118] Similarly, David Rousseau and his
coauthors suggest that "while the use of case studies is an important
step in the effort to understand fully the roots of the democratic
peace, the examination of a very limited number of cases . . . cannot
decisively disprove a probabilistic argument."[119] Thus, proponents
argue that the democratic peace theory is merely a probabilistic theory—democratic dyads have lower *propensities* to engage in war, and
democratic norms and structures reduce the *probability* of using military force. Since the dyadic democratic peace theory is not framed as
a deterministic law (that is, democracies will never wage war against
other democracies), the examination of a limited number of case
studies cannot be used to test the theory or decisively disprove it. As

---

117. For example, in chapter 6, Šumit Ganguly suggests that despite the fact that
India often referred to the nature of Pakistan's regime type, this was never the cause
of India's foreign policy toward its neighbor. India's foreign policy toward Pakistan
was driven less by the nature of the latter's regime type than by geopolitical and
cultural factors that increased or decreased India's war propensity. References to
political ideology were mere rationalizations for domestic consumption.

118. Russett, "And Yet it Moves," p. 167. See also p. 169, n. 12.

119. Rousseau et al., "Assessing the Dyadic Nature of the Democratic Peace,"
p. 516.

Bruce Russett and James Lee Ray point out: "One counter example does not refute a statement about relatively low probability."[120]

This argument is not entirely convincing for three reasons. First, democratic peace proponents have drawn on case study evidence when the results seem to fit well with the democratic peace hypothesis. Indeed, the two leading books on the democratic peace proposition devote considerable attention to detailed foreign policy cases.[121] Proponents cannot dismiss the evidence from in-depth case studies when it disagrees with the democratic peace theory, while relying on such evidence when it suits their purposes.

Second, by claiming that the democratic peace theory only explains general trends and patterns, proponents conveniently "save" the theory from potential disconfirming evidence.

Third, democratic peace theorists wish to determine how democratic norms and institutions affect the ways elites behave in negotiations, and how political actors justify their actions. The aim is not to show that decision makers act "as if" they are constrained by democratic norms and principles, but that they consciously make the calculations posited by the democratic peace model. Proponents of the theory have consistently tried to demonstrate that domestic regime type influences how decision makers think and calculate in crisis situations. Research on the democratic peace finding has sought to show how causal mechanisms work to produce the observable regularities between war and democracy.[122] Proponents have looked to see whether democratic institutions affect the bargaining and negoti-

---

120. Russett and Ray, "Why the Democratic-Peace Proposition Lives," p. 322; see also p. 319, n. 2; Rousseau et al., "Assessing the Dyadic Nature of the Democratic Peace," p. 516. According to this argument, case studies provide only weak tests of the theory. Case studies that confirm the predictions of the theory as well as cases where the theory fails are mere "straws in the wind" that weigh in the total balance of evidence but are indecisive in themselves. When historical evidence is inconsistent with probabilistic predictions, the failure simply reflects the "downside probabilities." See Van Evera, *Guide to Methodology*, pp. 40–41.

121. Russett, *Grasping the Democratic Peace*; and Ray, *Democracy and International Conflict*.

122. See, for example, Ray, *Democracy and International Conflict*, pp. 158–200; Owen, "How Liberalism Produces the Democratic Peace." In methodological terms, democratic peace theorists are scientific realists interested in identifying the underlying causal mechanisms which generate the democratic peace phenomenon. For more on the empiricist/scientific realist debate, see Alexander Wendt, "The Agent-Structure Problem in International Relations Theory," *International Organization*, Vol. 41, No. 3 (Summer 1987), pp. 350–355.

ation processes that take place as crises unfold, as well as if democratic norms affect the attitudes of leaders involved in crises. Since the democratic peace proposition is a theory of foreign policy with specific predictions about the motives that actors should reveal in crisis decision making, case studies are particularly good tests of the theory. Case studies and process-tracing are appropriate methodologies for a theory designed to predict the calculations made by decision makers in the real world.[123]

WHY CRISES?

This book focuses on instances of crisis decision making in which conflict either escalated to war or was resolved by peaceful means. This approach assumes that the behavior of states in crisis is the most useful way to test the causal claims of the democratic peace theory. To support the theory of the democratic peace, democracies have to be more than peaceful—they must also have important, opposing interests that come into conflict. Only states that have a potential for crisis and conflict are plausible candidates for testing the theory. For example, the absence of war in relations between Israel and Canada is not a vindication of the democratic peace phenomenon precisely because these democracies have no motive or opportunity to go to war in the first place. Only politically relevant pairs of states provide the context for testing the theory; states that are too far apart to have serious conflicts of interest are usually not good candidates for testing the theory.[124] In short, domestic norms and institutions should make their most visible and crucial contribution in disputes that nearly escalated to war. In such cases we can see if the disputes would have led to war but for the democratic nature of the regimes involved.[125]

THE ARGUMENT AGAINST CRISES. Advocates of the democratic peace proposition would counter that studying crises will bias our findings.

First, since democracies can assume that disputes will not escalate to war, we might find *more* crises between democratic pairs of states

---

123. Ray, *Democracy and International Conflict*, p. 154.

124. Russett, *Grasping the Democratic Peace*, pp. 9, 21; Russett, "And Yet It Moves," pp. 171–172; Layne, "Kant or Cant," p. 39; Cohen, "Pacific Unions," p. 214; Christopher Layne, "Correspondence on the Democratic Peace," *International Security*, Vol. 19, No. 4 (Spring 1995), p. 176.

125. Ray, *Democracy and International Conflict*, p. 160; Layne, "Kant or Cant," pp. 6, 13; and Morgan and Campbell, "Domestic Structure, Decisional Constraints, and War," pp. 194–195, 198.

than we would otherwise expect: "Each state might have strong incentives to [escalate the conflict] for the purpose of showing resolve ... in confidence that the other would be unlikely to reply in any substantial military manner."[126] Yet proponents of the normative version of the democratic peace theory argue that this sort of crisis bargaining is precisely what we should not expect between democracies. For example, Bruce Russett insists that democracies do not escalate their disputes into militarized disputes, are not likely to threaten to use force, and do not significantly prepare to fight each other: "Democracy/democracy pairs are ... less likely to escalate [disputes] at any level up the escalation ladder—not just at the top to war."[127] Which prediction is more valid?

Second, advocates of the theory might counter that by studying crises we ignore the numerous instances in which democracies did not come into conflict in the first place. This biases the results against the democratic peace theory, since we overlook the cases where joint democracy produces its most crucial pacifying effects.[128] To be sure, focusing on crises misses all the "dogs that did not bark"—crises that never erupted or never brought the democratic participants to the brink of war. But since non-events usually do not leave a visible paper trail from negotiations or state meetings, it would be difficult to assess whether domestic norms and institutions, or other factors, kept relations amicable. For instance, consider all the numerous reasons that can be posited to explain the long peace between the democratic great powers since 1945. In the absence of crises between these states, can we really be sure that shared democratic norms and institutions had *everything* to do with it?[129]

Finally, democratic peace theorists might argue that a book that deals primarily with crises does not offer a convincing test of the

---

126. Russett, *Grasping the Democratic Peace*, p. 42.

127. Ibid. See also Russett, "And Yet It Moves," p. 172; and Russett and Ray, "Why the Democratic-Peace Proposition Lives," p. 322.

128. Russett, "And Yet It Moves," p. 167; and Doyle, "Correspondence on the Democratic Peace," p. 182.

129. Several of the authors in this book focus on a middle category of cases in which there are serious differences between states but where conflict does not erupt into crisis. For example, Stephen Rock looks at several significant points of contention between Britain and the United States that were resolved before they approached the crisis stage. This middle category of cases can be usefully termed "dogs that growl"—a militarized dispute is avoided but the incident left a considerable paper trail for analysts to examine. I thank Stephen Rock for pointing this out to me.

theory because international crises are hard cases for domestic-level approaches. During crises, decision makers are often insulated and immune to societal pressures and are less likely to confront substantial domestic constraints. Consequently, we should not expect democratic politics to play a significant role during crises, and we should not be surprised if they do not exert a pacifying effect under these conditions.[130] In methodological terms, hard cases alone do not refute theoretical claims; that a theory fails to explain a hard case does not mean that it will be unable to explain the easier ones. The theory may be valid under certain conditions. Yet, even if we accept that domestic politics plays less of a role in crisis situations, both the normative and institutional variants of the democratic peace theory *do* make specific predictions about how actors will behave in crises. According to the institutional variant, democratic leaders may get their countries involved in militarized disputes, but are structurally constrained to pull back from the brink of large-scale war. According to the normative variant, elected leaders are supposed to have internalized liberal values and consequently will be less likely to initiate force against fellow democracies (the dyadic argument) or any type of state (the monadic argument). Furthermore, if domestic political constraints are unimportant when crises erupt, then the democratic peace theory would be relegated to explaining only those relatively uninteresting periods of "normal politics," when interstate conflict is at its lowest. Democratic peace proponents cannot argue that they can explain war and peace decision making better than neorealists, while at the same time insisting that neorealism best explains international crises.

THE THREE CATEGORIES OF CASES

In this book we focus on nineteenth and twentieth century crises in which states either went to war or backed down from the brink. Such relatively recent cases are most likely to resemble the situations in which present-day democracies and nondemocracies must make war decisions. Policy prescriptions deduced from these relatively recent historical cases are more likely to hold for contemporary situations of concern to policy makers.

All the cases in this book were selected because of their capacity to challenge received wisdoms about the sources of war and peace between democratic, democratic-nondemocratic, and nondemocratic

---

130. See Benjamin Miller, *When Opponents Cooperate: Great Power Conflict and Collaboration in World Politics* (Ann Arbor: University of Michigan Press, 1995).

pairs of states. The cases clarify what predictions can be accurately deduced from theories of the democratic peace, and what predictions are typically inferred incorrectly (see, in particular, the chapters by Arie M. Kacowicz, Martin Malin, and Kurt Dassel). Many of them were selected because of their intrinsic importance to the democratic peace debate. For example, the case of Anglo-U.S. relations was included because democratic peace proponents often cite peace between the United States and Britain since 1812 as uncontroversial proof of the democratic peace (see the chapter by Stephen R. Rock). Similarly, the case of Finland's involvement in World War II was selected because critics of the democratic peace theory often refer to this episode as an instance of democratic war (see the chapter by Miriam Fendius Elman). Finally, Indo-Pakistani relations are investigated because proponents of the democratic peace claim that we do not have to worry about a possible nuclear war between India and Pakistan; these countries are now democracies, and democracies do not fight each other (see the chapter by Šumit Ganguly).

Other cases were included because they pose strong tests. In some, the variables purported to account for the dyadic or monadic democratic peace phenomenon are abundantly present, but the predicted effect is notably absent. These outcomes are normally present but are absent in our studied cases. As a result, we can infer the circumstances and settings under which the theory will be most applicable (see the chapters by Christopher Layne, John M. Owen, Lawrence Freedman, Miriam Fendius Elman, and John C. Matthews III). In other cases, the democratic peace theory and its rival neorealist alternative make opposite predictions (see the chapters by Christopher Layne, Stephen Rock, and Šumit Ganguly); in these cases we test the relative explanatory power of the two theories by seeing whether the decision making process and foreign policy outcomes are consistent with what either theory would lead us to expect.

DEMOCRATIC PAIRS OF STATES. The dyadic version of the democratic peace theory maintains that democracies do not fight each other because of the normative and institutional features of democracy. We test this hypothesis by looking at instances where democracies defined each other as such and backed down from the brink of war. In these cases, the authors are less concerned with the outcome of the cases at hand than with the decision making process itself. The dependent variable is not whether democracies went to war or not (we know that they did not); rather, it is how democracies behaved in their interactions with one another and why they succeeded in resolving their conflicts short of war. Tracing the process of decision making is important in these cases because it helps us to judge whether state motivations are more consistent with the predictions of the democratic peace theory, or with those of its rivals. In addition, by tracing the decision making process we can assess whether democracy helped to avert war (evidence for the democratic peace theory) or whether the states' status as democracies contributed to the crisis and had to be counteracted by other factors for war to be avoided (evidence against the democratic peace theory).

We also examine cases of democratic dyads at war to determine the conditions under which wars between democracies might occur. Here, the authors are more concerned with the dependent variable of war and peace and with the independent variable of democracy. Were these states really democracies, did they see each other as such, and to what extent did they go to war with each other? Tracing the process of decision making is an important part of this analysis because it helps us determine whether hostilities between these pairs of states count as evidence against the democratic peace theory.

DEMOCRATIC-NONDEMOCRATIC PAIRS OF STATES. The monadic version of the democratic peace theory holds that the presence of one democracy in a pair of states significantly reduces the chance for war. Thus, a comprehensive test of the democratic peace thesis must include cases of "mixed dyads," where one state is democratic and the other is not.

In these cases we question whether the empirical evidence is more consistent with the monadic or dyadic version of the democratic peace theory. Thus, we ask whether the adversary's regime type influenced the decision making calculus, as the dyadic argument would lead us to expect. Did decision makers take note of the political systems of rival states? We also ask whether the democratic states involved in these crises consistently chose force only as a means of last resort, as the monadic thesis would lead us to expect. Tracing the process of decision making is important in these cases because it enables us to see whether actors perceived the regime type of the opponent as a threat, and whether this threat drove war and peace outcomes.

NONDEMOCRATIC PAIRS OF STATES. The democratic peace theory does not make predictions about when nondemocracies will use force, or why they sometimes remain at peace. Nevertheless, the received wisdom in the field is that nondemocratic states go to war because of normative and institutional features associated with their particular regime types, and that they back down from the brink of war because of strategic calculations and the balance of military power. Proponents of the democratic peace theory reinforce these conventional wisdoms in their writings. We test this scholarly consensus by including several case studies of crises between nondemocracies. We ask whether nondemocratic norms and institutions drove instances of war in these cases, as well as whether these nondemocratic features might have helped nondemocracies to preserve the peace.

In these cases, the authors trace the decision making process in order to determine what types of predictions regarding nondemocratic state behavior can be accurately deduced from theories of the democratic peace. In addition, these cases suggest possible reasons for peace among democracies. The authors look for whether the same causal mechanisms that are posited to produce peace between democracies also lead to peace between nondemocracies. In these cases, process-tracing helps us to better understand what might—and what might not—generate a separate, distinctive, and lasting peace among democratic states.

DEFINITIONS OF DEMOCRACY AND NONDEMOCRACY
Democracy is perhaps one of the most controversial and contested political terms. Few political theorists agree on the measures that should be used to operationalize democracy. Others agree that certain measures may be appropriate for particular historical eras, but that a standard set of measures is not valid for all periods. Because of these limitations, democratic peace researchers have tended to rely on subjective definitions of democracy. For example, Ido Oren argues that because the definition of democracy is "elastic over time," we need to consider the way in which actors *coded each other* during interstate crisis. Similarly, according to John Owen, "what an American political scientist codes as a democracy may not be perceived by its peer states as democratic . . . we cannot delineate an objective zone of democratic peace. Liberalism does affect states' behavior, but not in ways we can predict simply from assessing their institutions according to our own criteria."[131]

---

131. Oren, "The Subjectivity of the 'Democratic Peace'," p. 150; Owen, "How Do Liberal States Identify One Another?," pp. 2–3. Even scholars who use objective, reproducible measures of democracy recognize that perceptions matter. For example, Russett argues that we should "look for evidence that one party, correctly or not, perceives the other as not really democratic." See *Grasping the Democratic Peace*, p. 38, emphasis in the original. In ruling out a number of instances of warring democracies, Bruce Russett claims that at least one country

Such subjective analysis is likely to be especially important in considering the impact of democracy on the foreign policies of non-Western states. Indeed, many of the definitions of democracy used by democratic peace theorists correspond to modern "American" notions that exclude states that exhibit fair elections but little competition between parties. For example, Asian conceptions of democracy are inconsistent with the notion of group competition and frequent power alterations.[132] Other democracies that place group rights ahead of individual rights and do not foster clear divisions between church and state would also be excluded from definitions commonly found in the democratic peace literature.

Due to the difficulty of defining objective indicators of democracy that are transhistorical and transnational, in this book we rely on subjective indicators. We assess whether statesmen viewed each other as democratic. Cases such as these are likely to provide both the strongest challenges and the easiest cases for the democratic peace hypothesis. After all, if leaders perceive each other as democrats and yet are willing to threaten the use of force regardless of these common political ideologies, then the democratic peace theory will be far more seriously compromised than if we simply rely on the author's coding.

In a book devoted to case study analysis, an objective definition of democracy is not essential—what matters is what statesmen thought at the time, not how the analyst plans to code democracy. Nevertheless, the chapters in this volume do share a "common sense" notion of what distinguishes a democracy from a nondemocratic state. First, democracies are characterized by institutionalized competitive elections for top offices of government; the essence of democracy is public competition among different political parties. Second, political opposition groups are confident that they will not be imprisoned or tortured for espousing alternative political platforms. Third, the political opposition can be certain that a defeated incumbent will surrender political power without the use of force. Finally, incumbents can be sure that they will not be imprisoned or

---

did not consider the other democratic. See ibid., pp. 44, 57, 59, 61. Similarly, while James Lee Ray devotes considerable attention to establishing a set of indicators for judging whether a state is democratic, he too tends to focus on whether or not statesmen at the time coded each another as liberal democrats. See *Democracy and International Conflict*, pp. 107, 119–120.

132. Steve Chan, "Regime Transition in the Asia/Pacific Region: Democratization as a Double-Edged Sword," *Journal of Strategic Studies*, Vol. 18, No. 3 (September 1995), pp. 58–59.

killed when surrendering their positions after elections. In short, in democracies there is a sense of trust between incumbents and opposition. Domestic conflict is nonviolent and political opposition is not violently suppressed. As Thomas Risse-Kappen claims: "Democratic decision-making rules emphasize the peaceful resolution of conflict through compromise and consensus, penalize the threat or the use of force in domestic disputes as illegitimate, and provide for the possibility that today's minority might become tomorrow's majority."[133]

While many democratic peace researchers are likely to disagree with this definition, I find it helpful for two reasons. First, it combines liberal values with institutional procedures. Second, the definition allows for variation in a number of features commonly attributed to all democratic regimes, including the extent to which the public has access to the foreign policy making arena; the nature of the executive-legislative balance; the extent to which war powers are delegated among civilian leaders and from the civilian echelon to the military; and the degree to which the executive is accountable to the voting public and other decision making bodies. As the case studies that follow show, these factors (some of which also vary among nondemocratic regimes) can crucially affect war and peace decision making.[134]

Organization of the Study

This book is divided into four main parts. The first part focuses on two pairs of democratic states that resolved their conflicts short of war. In both cases, the authors suggest that shared democratic norms and political institutions do not provide the only—or the best—explanation for these instances of democratic peace. In Chapter 1, Christopher Layne argues that the level of hostility between France and Britain during the 1800s did not diminish, even though both

---

133. Risse-Kappen, "Democratic Peace—Warlike Democracies," p. 500. In contrast to democracies, nondemocracies are characterized by restricted or suppressed political participation; a closed process of selecting top officials; and the resort to force to solve transfers of power between incumbents and the opposition.

134. In many definitions used by democratic peace researchers, states that achieve high points on the scale have an executive who is chosen in open elections and is significantly constrained by an elected legislature. Such definitions exhibit a substantial bias in favor of U.S.-style democracies where the legislature plays an important role in the foreign policy making process and shares war powers with the executive. They are biased against democracies with strong presidents and majoritarian parliamentary regimes where the ruling party in the executive commands a majority in the legislature.

states became more democratic during this period and perceived each other as liberal. He suggests that Britain and France remained at peace not because they considered the use of force normatively unacceptable, but because neither perceived it could successfully win a war against the other. In Chapter 2, Stephen Rock also argues that geopolitical explanations go far in accounting for Anglo-U.S. peace during the 1900s. In addition, he suggests that peace has been preserved because of racial and cultural affinities extending beyond common democratic institutions.

The second part of the book examines two instances of democratic conflict. According to proponents of the democratic peace theory, democratic states rarely (if ever) engage in diplomatic crises that even remotely approach a likely step toward war.[135] We show that while many conflicts of interest between democracies may well be settled amicably, there is still the chance that democratic states will use force against each other or face off in opposing wartime alliances. In Chapter 3, John Owen suggests that even states that define each other as liberal will go to war when one seriously and unambiguously threatens the national security of the other. Focusing on the Mexican-American War, Owen argues that this conflict is a significant exception to the rule that democracies do not fight each other. Like Owen, I suggest in Chapter 4 that the democratic peace theory may cease to apply when vital security interests bring democracies into conflict. While U.S. and British behavior toward Finland during World War II is somewhat consistent with the predictions of the democratic peace theory, Finland's behavior toward the Western Allies is not. In addition, Finland's behavior suggests that the democratic peace theory may be confined to certain types of democracies. Taken together, these two chapters reinforce the need to consider potential exceptions to the dyadic democratic peace proposition.

The third part of the book is devoted to several crises involving democratic and nondemocratic states, only some of which were resolved by peaceful means. In Chapter 5, Lawrence Freedman suggests that the war between the United Kingdom and Argentina over the Falkland Islands confirms the dyadic version of the democratic peace theory but challenges the monadic model. Freedman suggests that whether a democratic state opts for war or turns back from the brink depends a great deal on the perceived legitimacy of the opponent's government: democracies will not eschew the use of force if

---

135. Russett, "And Yet it Moves," p. 167.

compromise means delivering another people to an authoritarian state. In contrast to Freedman, Šumit Ganguly suggests in Chapter 6 that neither version of the theory provides a persuasive explanation for India's foreign policies toward Pakistan. Ganguly argues that India and Pakistan have remained at peace in recent years, not because of democratization, but because of changes in the balance of military capabilities. Ganguly suggests that Pakistan's domestic regime type did not have as crucial an impact on India's decision making as the dyadic version of the democratic peace theory would lead us to expect. Furthermore, he suggests that Indo-Pakistani conflict has frequently escalated because of democratic politics.

In Chapter 7, I argue that democracies will not choose peaceful means of conflict resolution if ruling coalitions favor the use of force to solve conflicts. My analysis of Israeli decision making prior to the invasion of Lebanon in 1982 suggests that the particular features of Israel's parliamentary system, as well as the foreign policy orientations of its leadership at the time, drove the country into a war that it might have avoided. In Chapter 8, Arie Kacowicz looks at two instances where democracies and nondemocracies (Peru and Colombia and Senegal and Mauritania) resolved serious conflicts short of war. He suggests that in both cases peace was sustained because of a combination of neorealist and normative factors. In particular, he suggests that common cultural frameworks do not merely influence the behavior of jointly democratic states—they can also affect the war propensity of mixed and nondemocratic dyads.

The fourth part of the book demonstrates that nondemocratic institutions and norms are not necessarily obstacles to peace. In Chapter 9, Martin Malin focuses on the causes of peace and war between Iran and Iraq. Malin argues that because of the absence of institutional constraints on leaders, Iran and Iraq were able to transcend their differences and establish a robust peace. In addition, Malin argues that the reemergence of the Iran-Iraq conflict was determined less by autocratic forms of government than by other domestic developments. In Chapter 10, Kurt Dassel suggests that in nondemocratic states, the military's intervention in the decision making arena can often increase the likelihood for interstate peace. Focusing on Indonesia's foreign policy during the 1960s, Dassel shows that nondemocracies in which the military plays a dominant role are not necessarily more likely to pursue aggressive foreign policies. In Chapter 11, John Matthews also suggests that nondemocratic institutions can be a condition for peace, particularly when authoritarianism keeps nationalism in check. By comparing the deescalation of conflict between nondemocratic Turkey and Greece to the increasing conflict between democratizing Hungary and Czechoslovakia, Matthews underscores how democratization might undermine the prospects for inter-state peace. Focusing on the interwar period, he suggests that if Turkey and Greece had been democratic, they most probably would have gone to war.

In the conclusion, I compare and contrast the empirical findings. I provide suggestions for further research on the relationship between democracy and war, and discuss the book's implications for contemporary international relations theory and U.S. foreign policy.

Part I
Peace Between
Democracies:
Is Democracy
the Cause?

Chapter 1

Lord Palmerston and the Triumph of Realism: Anglo-French Relations, 1830-48

Christopher Layne

In this chapter I test the "democratic peace theory" by examining Anglo-French relations during the period 1830–48. During these years Britain and France were linked by a common ideology (liberalism) and, sometimes, by shared interests. Nevertheless, on at least three occasions during these years, Britain and France came near to war, and their relationship was at all times conditioned by intense geopolitical rivalry. My focus is on the basic theoretical issue of whether domestic or international level analyses offer the most powerful explanation of British and French behavior. While this case poses a hard test for realism and a favorable test for democratic peace theory, it demonstrates that realist factors have far more salience than do unit level variables in determining international political outcomes.

Unit level critiques of the democratic peace theory are important, but they are not a substitute for neorealist evaluations. Although the democratic peace theory ostensibly is a unit level ("second image") theory about the foreign policy behavior of states, its proponents assert a far more sweeping claim on its behalf.[1] For its champions, the

I wish to thank the participants at the June 1996 workshop held at the Center for Science and International Affairs to discuss the draft chapters for this volume, and especially Randall L. Schweller and Joe Hagan for reading the first draft of this chapter in its entirety. Bradley A. Thayer of CSIA also read the first draft in its entirety and I acknowledge his criticism and advice. Miriam Fendius Elman has been a superb editor and a wonderful colleague and friend. Finally, I thank the Earhart Foundation, and especially Tony Sullivan, for generously supporting my research at CSIA.

1. The classic explication of the three images, or levels of analysis, in international relations theory is Kenneth N. Waltz, *Man, the State, and War: A Theoretical Analysis* (New York: Columbia University Press, 1959).

"democratic peace" makes it possible for states to escape from the realist constraints that historically have shaped international politics. Bruce Russett, for example, asserts that in an international system comprised of a critical mass of democratic states, "it may be possible in part to supersede the 'realist' principles (anarchy, the security dilemma of states) that have dominated practice to the exclusion of 'liberal' or 'idealist' ones since at least the seventeenth century."[2] Thus, democratic peace theory contends that regime type matters more than realist factors in determining international political outcomes, so much so that changes within states can enable states to *transcend* structural constraints (anarchy and the distribution of power among states) and their consequences for international politics.[3]

The democratic peace theory, in fact, claims that all states with a similar domestic political structure will behave identically, regardless of structural constraints imposed on states by the international political system. For example, according to democratic peace theory, "perpetual peace" indeed would prevail in a world comprised solely of democratic states because, so the theory asserts, democracies do not go to war with each other and do not even threaten to use force in their relations with each other.[4] Thus, democratic peace theory seeks to move from its own realm—unit level analysis—and expand its "home court" to encompass the international systemic level of analysis as well. Hence, it is systemic—not unit—level analysis that provides the most important and telling critique of the democratic peace theory.

---

2. Bruce Russett, *Grasping the Democratic Peace: Principles for a Post-Cold War Peace* (Princeton, N.J.: Princeton University Press, 1993), p. 24.

3. The international political system's structure is defined by its ordering principle (anarchy) and the distribution of capabilities among the system's major constituent units (polarity). See Kenneth Waltz, *Theory of International Politics* (Reading, Mass.: Addison-Wesley, 1979).

4. This characterization of the democratic peace theory's claims must be qualified with the observation that the theory's proponents display a nettlesome degree of ambiguity and confusion when defining the so-called democratic peace. Some democratic peace theory proponents claim that democracies "never" go to war, or threaten to use force against each other; others say that democracies "rarely," "seldom," or "almost never" do so. Frequently, contradictory claims are made by the same individual—sometimes within a single book or article, or even in the same sentence. An example of the latter is Bruce Russett's attempt to cover all the bases when he says of democracies that "they rarely fight each other even at low levels of lethal violence, and never (or almost never) go to war against each other." Russett, *Grasping the Democratic Peace*, p. 119.

At the same time, unit-level factors can also generate traditional realist explanations of foreign policy that challenge the democratic peace theory. In the crises studied in this chapter, for example, it becomes clear that individual leaders made an important difference in determining whether Anglo-French relations were conflictive or cooperative. The crises also demonstrate that domestic political factors *do* make a difference in foreign policy—though not in the way the democratic peace theory claims. For example, in both the 1840 and 1844 crises, public opinion pushed leaders toward war rather than holding them back; this is contrary to the democratic peace theory's claims. As this chapter shows, therefore, the democratic peace theory is vulnerable to attack both from neorealist theories that focus on the importance of constraints on state behavior imposed by the international political system's structure *and* from classical realist theories that focus on the role of leaders and public opinion.

Why This Case Study? Anglo-French Relations as a Test of the Democratic Peace Theory

In this chapter I examine Anglo-French relations to shed light on the question: does the democratic peace theory explain the course of Anglo-French relations during the 1830–48 period, or were Anglo-French relations during this period shaped primarily by realist rather than unit level factors posited by the theory? To answer this question, I set out competing hypotheses derived from the democratic peace theory and realism. To determine which set of hypotheses offers the most compelling explanation of British and French behavior, I use the process-tracing method to open the "black box" of Anglo-French relations in order to ascertain the factors to which decision makers responded; how those factors influenced decisions; the actual course of events; and the possible effect of other variables on the outcome.[5] As Stephen Van Evera says, if a theory has strong explanatory power, process-tracing case studies provide a robust test because decision makers "should speak, write, and otherwise behave in a manner consistent with the theory's predictions."[6]

---

5. Alexander L. George and Timothy J. McKeown, "Case Studies and Theories of Organizational Decision Making," in Robert F. Coulam and Richard A. Smith, eds., *Advances in Information Processing in Organizations*, Vol. 2 (Greenwich, Conn.: JAI Press, 1985), p. 35.

6. Stephen Van Evera, *Guide to Methodology for Students of Political Science* (Cambridge, Mass.: MIT Defense and Arms Control Studies Program, n.d.), p. 33.

((|

This case should confirm the democratic peace theory for several reasons. First, and most obviously, Britain and France did not go to war with each other during this period. Second, during the years 1830–48, Britain and France were united by a common ideology. As the two liberal great powers in Europe, Britain and France saw themselves in common cause against the reactionary Eastern Powers that comprised the Holy Alliance: Russia, Austria, and Prussia. Third, influential members of the British "political nation" (the governing elite and that portion of public opinion attentive to foreign policy) recognized that Britain had a vested interest in bolstering the liberal July Monarchy in Paris, lest it be overthrown and replaced by a more radical and aggressive regime. Fourth, the bonds forged by liberalism carried into diplomacy. For much of this period, relations between London and Paris were described as an *entente cordiale*, and the two states collaborated closely in such important European crises as Belgium (1832) and Iberia (the 1834 Quadruple Alliance among Britain, France, Spain, and Portugal).[7] Yet, on three separate occasions—in 1831, 1840, and 1844—

---

7. Space limitations preclude extensive discussion of these instances of Anglo-French cooperation. However, it is important to note that this cooperation was driven more by realist factors than by shared ideology. On the English side, Anglo-French cooperation was the result of Lord Palmerston's desire to "manage" France, and of power balancing. On the French side, the entente was the result of Paris's desire to break out of its post-1815 diplomatic isolation. As Christopher Bartlett observes, the 1834 Quadruple Alliance (England, France, Spain, and Portugal)—the high-water mark of the entente in the 1830s—"was designed to control France and to ensure that she remained the junior partner." Bartlett, "Britain and the European Balance, 1815–1848," in Alan Sked, ed., *Europe's Balance of Power, 1815–1848* (London: Macmillan, 1979), p. 154. Palmerston believed that London could effectively restrain France by cooperating with Paris. For a general discussion of this technique of using alliances to coopt and manage a rival see P.W. Schroeder, "Alliances, 1815–1945: Weapons of Power and Tools of Management," in Klaus Knorr, ed., *Historical Dimensions of National Security* (Lawrence: University of Kansas Press, 1976), pp. 227–262. Palmerston also inclined toward the entente because, after the three Eastern powers reaffirmed their alliance at Muchengratz in 1833, England needed continental great power allies. As Palmerston said: "England alone cannot carry her points on the Continent; she must have allies as instruments to work with. We cannot have the cooperation of our old allies, the three Powers [Russia, Austria, and Prussia] because their views and opinions are now-a-days the reverse of ours." Quoted in George J. Billy, *Palmerston's Foreign Policy, 1848* (New York: Peter Lang, 1993), p. 10. France, too, needed an ally, and given the Eastern powers' suspicion of France, for Paris the entente was the sole viable option. As Roger Bullen says, for France the entente with Britain "could prevent a revival of the anti-French coalition, thus avoiding the danger of isolation." Roger Bullen, "France and Europe, 1815–48," in Sked, *Europe's Balance of Power*, p. 136.

an Anglo-French war loomed as a real possibility. Moreover, throughout the 1830–48 period, each state regarded the other as a serious geopolitical rival. This case is thus an easy case for the democratic peace theory and provides an excellent vehicle for asking whether shared domestic norms and institutions caused the absence of war between Britain and France.

Some may question the suitability of this case as a test of the democratic peace theory: it could be objected that during the period in question, Britain and France were not democracies, or they were not sufficiently developed ("mature") democracies, and hence do not provide a proper test of the theory.[8] A strong case can be made that both Britain and France, in fact, were democracies during this period. Moreover, it is incontestable that both were *liberal* states during this period, and that each was so regarded by the other.[9] In both states the domestic political structure was marked by regular, freely contested elections; executive branch actions were constrained by the legislature; the rule of law prevailed and individual rights were protected; and there was a free press and political issues were openly debated.[10]

---

8. For example, one might expect to see my use of this case criticized by Bruce Russett. He dismisses nineteenth-century examples of "near-misses" (crises where democratic states almost went to war with each other) because that "was an era of generally very imperfect democracy by modern standards." Hence, he concludes, these examples are irrelevant as potential exceptions to the democratic peace theory. Russett, *Grasping the Democratic Peace*, pp. 19–20. Russett's attempt to save the democratic peace theory by redefining the term "democracy" to explain away disconfirming cases typifies the kind of intellectual shell game tactics to which many of the theory's proponents have been forced to resort. For another example, see James Lee Ray, *Democracy and International Conflict: An Evaluation of the Democratic Peace Thesis* (Columbia: University of South Carolina Press, 1995).

9. As John Owen notes, the fact that two states are both liberal is a necessary but not sufficient condition to explain peace between them. It is also necessary that each *perceive* the other state as liberal for the democratic (or liberal) peace to hold. John Owen, "How Liberalism Produces Democratic Peace," *International Security*, Vol. 19, No. 2 (Fall 1994) pp. 96–97.

10. In describing the hallmarks of a liberal state, John Owen says that liberalism "calls for structures that protect the right of each citizen to self-government. Most important for our purposes are those giving citizens leverage over governmental decision makers. Freedom of speech is necessary because it allows citizens to evaluate alternative foreign policies. Regular, competitive elections are necessary because they provide citizens with the possibility of punishing officials who violate their rights." Owen, "How Liberalism Produces Democratic Peace," p. 99. By these standards, Britain and France clearly were liberal states during the period in question, a point Owen implicitly concedes (p. 95). Michael Doyle explicitly classifies France and Britain (from 1832 forward) as liberal states. Michael W. Doyle, "Kant, Liberal Legacies and Foreign Affairs: Part I," *Philosophy and Public Affairs*, Vol. 12, No. 3 (Summer 1983), p. 209.

As Michael Doyle and John Owen have argued, liberal ideas are the key variables leading to the "democratic peace."[11]

Borrowing from liberal ideas and the democratic peace theory, the following hypotheses can be advanced to explain the absence of war between England and France between 1830 and 1848:

- Because both states were liberal and were perceived as such by the other, neither should have regarded the other as a security threat.
- Because both states were liberal and were perceived as such by the other, neither should have regarded war with the other as a viable policy option. Public opinion in both states should have been pacific. Public opinion is important both as a domestic institutional constraint and as an indication of the mutual respect that is supposed to exist between liberal states.
- British and French decision makers should have refrained from making military threats against each other.
- In crisis situations, Britain and France should have bent over backwards to accommodate each other because ultimata, unbending hard-lines, and big stick diplomacy are the stuff of *realpolitik*, not the "democratic peace."

Neorealism yields a quite different set of hypotheses about Anglo-French relations during the 1830–48 period:

- Anglo-French relations should have been shaped by objective factors giving rise to a security dilemma between the two states—the anarchic nature of the international political system, geographical proximity, and the two states' relative power capabilities.
- To the extent that respective British and French geopolitical interests clashed, their policies toward each other should

---

11. Michael W. Doyle, "Liberalism and World Politics," *American Political Science Review*, Vol. 80, No. 4 (December 1986), pp. 1151–1169; Doyle, "Kant, Liberal Legacies"; and Owen, "How Liberalism Produces Democratic Peace." This chapter is not concerned with a detailed exploration of whether the "democratic peace" results from domestic political structures and institutions or rather from democratic (or liberal) norms and culture. Although the distinction between these two posited sources of the "Democratic Peace" is not unimportant, neither should too much be made of it. In practice, it is not so easy to distinguish between the effect of structure and institutions, on the one hand, and of norms and culture, on the other. Indeed, as Owen says, "liberal ideology and institutions work in tandem to bring about a democratic peace." Owen, "How Liberalism Produces Democratic Peace," p. 89.

have been shaped more by *realpolitik* considerations than by liberal values or the constraints posited by the democratic peace theory.

- In Anglo-French crises involving perceived vital interests, decision makers should not have been inhibited from using threats, ultimata, and big stick diplomacy.
- The absence of war between Britain and France should be attributable more to realist factors (relative military capabilities, the availability or absence of allies, the significance of the issue at stake, etc.) than to the variables associated with liberalism or the democratic peace theory.

Anglo-French Relations, 1830–48: Background

In this section, I discuss the backdrop to the 1830–48 Anglo-French relationship, including the effect of the 1815 European peace settlement; Britain's vital interests after 1815; the strategic factors that fueled the Anglo-French antagonism; Lord Palmerston's diplomatic style; and the respective domestic political structures of Britain and France.

THE SETTLEMENT OF 1815

The French Revolution plunged Europe into a quarter-century of turmoil. From 1792 until 1815, war raged almost continuously as Britain and the other European great powers sought to prevent French hegemony on the continent. The challenge posed by Revolutionary, and then by Napoleonic, France was double-edged: France used its military power to expand its geopolitical preeminence, and France also used the revolutionary ideology of nationalism and liberty to enhance its influence in Europe. Thus the French threat had both an external and internal dimension: France threatened to overturn the European balance of power, and it also threatened to undermine the domestic political and social structures of the other great powers.

During the prolonged conflict with France, Britain was the most implacable foe of French ambitions, organizing anti-French coalitions when possible but fighting on alone when necessary (as it did for much of the time between 1806 and 1812). As early as 1805, Prime Minister William Pitt (the Younger) outlined British war aims. These were to: reduce French power and force Paris to disgorge its conquests; create new territorial arrangements in post-war Europe to contain a potentially resurgent France; and establish a permanent Great Power security structure that would uphold the peace and keep France from mounting a renewed threat to Europe's stability.[12]

It fell to the British Foreign Secretary Lord Castlereagh to translate Pitt's ideas into a concrete peace settlement that would prevent French resurgence and maintain long-term stability and equilibrium in Europe.[13] In the 1814 Treaty of Chaumont, England, Russia, Austria, and Prussia pledged that upon the conclusion of the war they would enter "into defensive engagements for the protection of their respective States in Europe against every attempt which France might make to infringe the order of things resulting from such Pacification."[14] At the Congress of Vienna, Castlereagh took the lead in creating the territorial and security structure needed to contain France. France was reduced to its 1790 boundaries. To create geopolitical barriers to renewed French expansion, Prussia was awarded the Rhineland; Austrian power in Italy was augmented; and Belgium was given to Holland. Although a defeated France was admitted to the Concert of Europe established at Vienna, it is clear that France was regarded with continued suspicion by the other great powers. As F.R. Bridge and Roger Bullen observe, "the fact that it had taken the combined efforts of four powers to defeat France had given her a unique status within the new order, as the power least satisfied with the arrangements made in 1815, and the power with the greatest potential for disruption."[15]

THE STRATEGIC FOUNDATIONS OF BRITAIN'S POST-1815 DIPLOMACY

After 1815, Britain sought to bolster the security of the United Kingdom itself and to protect both the trade routes upon which Britain's worldwide commercial interests depended and the line of communications to its empire in India.[16] These general interests led to

---

12. See Henry A. Kissinger, *A World Restored: Metternich, Castlereagh and the Problems of Peace, 1812–1822* (Boston: Houghton Mifflin, Sentry Ed., n.d.), pp. 37–39; and Edward Vose Gulick, *Europe's Classical Balance of Power* (New York: W.W. Norton, 1955), pp. 143–145.

13. Muriel Chamberlain, *"Pax Britannica?" British Foreign Policy, 1789–1914* (London: Longman, 1988), p. 50.

14. Quoted in Gulick, *Europe's Classical Balance of Power*, p. 153.

15. F.R. Bridge and Roger Bullen, *The Great Powers and the European States System, 1815–1914* (London: Longman, 1980), p. 7.

16. As G.D. Clayton notes, defense of the route to India had both strategic and commercial implications. London sought control of the short route (Mediterranean-Suez-Red Sea) to India because it gave England "a decisive military advantage over other powers, and also because continued trade with India was thought vital to British prosperity." G.D. Clayton, *Britain and the Eastern Question: Missolonghi to Gallipoli* (London: University of London Press, 1971), p. 13.

a focus on very specific geographic areas. Of foremost concern to London was control of the Low Countries.[17] In the hands of France, the Low Countries could be used as a platform to interdict Britain's oceanic trade and as a springboard from which an invasion against the British Isles could be mounted. Indeed, Castlereagh believed that if Antwerp were left under French control, Britain would need to remain perpetually mobilized for war.[18] Spain and Portugal were also important to Britain because both lay astride the route to the Mediterranean, and if France gained control over Spain's overseas empire, Britain's commercial and naval interests could be threatened.[19]

Britain's other major interest was India, the "jewel" in the crown of the British Empire. Defending India was neither easy nor cheap. As the historian Malcolm Yapp has observed of India, "the difference between a jewel and a millstone was as small as that which Mr. Micawber discovered to lie between happiness and misery."[20] India's northwest frontier had to be defended from Russian advances southward from Central Asia. And because the Ottoman Empire was seen in London as a vital bulwark against the expansion of Russian naval power into the Mediterranean, British policy makers were continually preoccupied with "the Eastern Question," defined by the historian Rene Albrecht-Carrie as "the decadence of the Ottoman Empire, with the possibility of its demise and consequent partition."[21] Importantly,

---

17. As the diplomatic historians A.W. Ward and G.P. Gooch observed, "the traditional policy of England was founded on the conviction that her security required the exclusion of France from the Belgian provinces." Ward and Gooch, eds., *The Cambridge History of British Foreign Policy: Volume II, 1815–1866* (New York: Macmillan, 1923), p. 122.

18. C.J. Bartlett, *Defence and Diplomacy: Britain and the Great Powers, 1815–1914* (Manchester, U.K.: Manchester University Press, 1993), p. 9.

19. It was the need to ensure that France, which intervened militarily in Spain in the early 1820s, did not gain control over the rebellious Spanish colonies in Mexico and Latin America that prompted the tacit Anglo-U.S. cooperation that culminated in the Monroe Doctrine's proclamation. This was the basis of Foreign Secretary George Canning's famous statement that he called the New World into existence to redress the balance of power in the Old World.

20. Malcolm Yapp, *Strategies of British India* (New York: Oxford University Press, 1980), p. 590.

21. Rene Albrecht-Carrie, *Britain and France: Adaptations to a Changing Context of Power* (Garden City, N.Y.: Doubleday, 1970), p. 37. As G.D. Clayton notes, "the difficulty was that the decline of Turkey opened up too many possibilities of advantage to too many powers. It therefore became a matter of precise calculation for each power to decide whether the artificial preservation of Turkey might not be more advantageous than a total collapse—in which all powers would gain something, but none would gain enough to satisfy its 'minimal' needs." Clayton, *Britain and the Eastern Question*, pp. 9–10.

France, as well as Russia, threatened England's line of communications to India. After all, France was a major Mediterranean naval power in its own right; by 1830 it was becoming a colonial power in North Africa; and it vigorously sought to enhance its political and commercial influence in Egypt and the Near East. Indeed, during the period 1830–46, each of these areas—Belgium, Iberia, and the Near East—would become sources of Anglo-French tension.[22]

THE ANGLO-FRENCH RIVALRY

During the 1830–46 period, both Russia and France threatened Britain's vital interests. Although Russian ambitions in Central Asia and the Near East were a continual source of concern in London, it was France that was regarded as the primary threat to English interests.[23] There are three reasons for this: France's status as a dissatisfied power, France's capabilities, and geography.

First, as noted above, following the Congress of Vienna, France was a revisionist, not a status quo, power. Indeed, in this regard there is strong continuity between the foreign policies of the Bourbon Restoration, the July Monarchy, the Second Republic, and the Second Empire. As the diplomatic historian Roger Bullen notes, all French political parties condemned the 1815 settlement and wanted to revise it; more than the loss of territory, the French resented the very international order created in 1815.[24] French statesmen were highly constrained in how far they could go in challenging the 1815 settlement, but they all harbored the hope that circumstances would materialize that would present France with the opportunity to overthrow the Vienna system and reestablish France as Europe's predominant state.[25]

---

22. Anglo-French rivalry in Iberia is not discussed in this article because the fates of Portugal and, more importantly, Spain (which France regarded as part of its sphere and where it had actual political influence) did not bring England and France to the brink of war. However, especially in the 1840s, disagreements between London and Paris poisoned Anglo-French relations and contributed importantly to the entente's unraveling.

23. As the military historian Michael Partridge comments, "between 1814 and 1870 the British were convinced that the main threat to their security came from France." Michael Stephen Partridge, *Military Planning for the Defence of the United Kingdom, 1814–1870* (New York: Greenwood, 1989), p. 18. Also see Billy, *Palmerston's Foreign Policy*, p. 2.

24. Bullen, "France and Europe," pp. 124–126.

25. Diplomatic isolation was the main check on French ambitions. Simply put, the other four great powers feared France more than they feared each other. As Bridge and Bullen observe, "the French feared the continued existence of the coalition against them and their consequent isolation above all else. This balance of fear was for decades the great stabilizing factor in the Vienna states system." Bridge and Bullen, *The Great Powers*, p. 32.

Moreover, historical animosity reinforced British fears of French ambitions. As the historian Michael Partridge notes, "the French simply were not trusted in Britain."[26]

The second reason that Britain regarded France as a threat was because of the latter's material capabilities.[27] During the period in question, France was continental Europe's leading great power and England's most formidable competitor. As Paul Kennedy notes, notwithstanding "its losses during the Napoleonic War, the position of France in the half-century following 1815 was significantly better than that of either Prussia or the Habsburg Empire in many respects."[28] Unlike the other European great powers, "France had a strong economy and an efficient system of public finance."[29] Various economic indicators underscore France's relative power position. In 1830, France's GNP was slightly larger than Britain's; by 1850, Britain's GNP was a bit larger than France's.[30] In terms of per capita GNP (perhaps a better measure of the two states' relative economic power given France's larger population), England was Europe's leading power, with France a somewhat distant second.[31] In terms of per capita levels of industrialization, in 1830 England and France ranked first and second, respectively, among the European states (although by this measure, England was twice as industrialized as France).[32] In 1830, the French military establishment, just a bit smaller than the Habsburg Empire's, was the third largest in Europe (and nearly twice

---

26. Partridge, *Military Planning*, p. 18.

27. Albrecht-Carrie stresses that even after 1815, England perceived that, in terms of material capabilities, France remained the preeminent continental power and hence English efforts needed to be directed toward France's containment. Albrecht-Carrie, *Britain and France*, pp. 17–18, 39.

28. Paul Kennedy, *The Rise and Fall of the Great Powers: Economic Change and Military Conflict from 1500 to 2000* (New York: Random House, 1987), p. 166.

29. Bullen, "France and Europe," pp. 129–130.

30. Kennedy, *The Rise and Fall of the Great Powers*, p. 171. Because of Russia's large population, during the years in question it possessed the largest GNP (gross national product) of the European great powers. However, Russia lagged far behind England and France industrially and technologically.

31. Ibid.

32. Ibid., p. 169. It should also be noted that in 1830, France ranked third among the European states (just a bit behind Russia) in world manufacturing output (England, of course, was in a commanding position by this measure). By 1860 France had moved into second place in this category, though England's share of world manufactured output was more than twice as large.

as large as England's).[33] In sum, during the period 1830–46, among the European powers only France possessed the industrial, technological, financial, and administrative resources to challenge Britain. And indeed, especially from the 1840s on, France was able to draw upon these resources to mount a serious challenge to England and "run a good second" in the contest for naval supremacy.[34]

Finally, geography also contributed to shaping British perceptions of the French menace. Although insularity conferred important strategic advantages upon Britain, during the period 1830–46, defense planners never regarded the British Isles as invulnerable. Southeastern England and London were considered to be exposed to an invasion from France. During the 1840s, the increasing use of steam propulsion in warships and transport vessels heightened Britain's sense of vulnerability to a French invasion. Furthermore, French warships based at Cherbourg and Brest were well positioned to disrupt Britain's vital maritime commerce. London's concerns on this score cannot have been eased by developments in French naval strategy and technology. The French keenly appreciated the possibilities afforded by steam, both with respect to invading Britain and to sweeping British merchant ships from the seas, and they developed the doctrine of *guerre de course*. Finally, the increasingly powerful French Mediterranean fleet based at Toulon posed a direct threat to Britain's crucial Mediterranean imperial lifeline.

LORD PALMERSTON'S DIPLOMATIC STYLE

If objective factors contributed to Anglo-French tension, the presence of Lord Palmerston in the Foreign Office during much of this period certainly did not promise to ease cross-Channel friction. One historian has suggested, not unfairly, that Palmerston's diplomatic style was one based on brinkmanship—a "pronounced mixture of bluff, bluster and force."[35] Palmerston was quick to use coercive threats to

33. Ibid., p. 155.

34. C.J. Bartlett, "Statecraft, Power and Influence," in C.J. Bartlett, ed., *Britain Preeminent: Studies of British World Influence in the Nineteenth Century* (London: Macmillan, 1969), p. 183. As Bartlett notes, however, England still possessed huge advantages over France in the naval competition and "only a failure of national will or political and professional ineptitude on a massive scale could endanger her position." See also C.I. Hamilton, *Anglo-French Naval Rivalry, 1840–1870* (Oxford, U.K.: Clarendon Press, 1993).

35. Billy, *Palmerston's Foreign Policy*, pp. 8–9. Bartlett describes Palmerston's diplomacy in similar terms as an "admixture of diplomacy, bluff and coercion." Bartlett, "Britain and the European Balance," p. 154.

bolster his diplomacy. As the diplomatic historian C.J. Bartlett puts it, Palmerston "believed in making a fuss over quite small issues lest the other party should be encouraged to seek greater success and thereby precipitate a real crisis."[36] Palmerston also believed in making a big fuss over big issues.

It would perhaps be uncharitable to describe Palmerston as a francophobe. Like his Whig colleagues, he enthusiastically greeted the ascension of the July Monarchy as a triumph for liberalism, declaring that "we shall drink to the cause of Liberalism all over the world. . . . This event is decisive of the ascendancy of Liberal Principles throughout Europe."[37] Throughout his long career, Palmerston frequently proved willing to act in concert with France when London's interests overlapped with France's. Nevertheless, he was a pugnacious defender of British interests—interests he often believed were menaced by France. As he once observed:

I have for some time seen a spirit of bitter hostility toward England growing up among Frenchmen of all classes and of all parties; and sooner or later this must lead to conflict. . . . All Frenchmen want to encroach and extend their territorial possessions at the expense of other nations. . . . I do not blame the French for disliking us. Their vanity prompts them to be the first nation of the world; yet at every turn they find we outstrip them in everything. It is a misfortune to Europe that the national character of a great and powerful people, placed in the centre of Europe, and capable of doing their neighbours much harm should be as it is.[38]

Palmerston believed that the French king, Louis Philippe, hated "England from the bottom of his heart" because England was "the natural obstacle to the aggrandizement of France."[39] In criticizing the policy of his successor, Lord Aberdeen, Foreign Secretary during Sir Robert Peel's 1841–46 Tory government, Palmerston neatly captured the essence of his French policy: "We have always beaten the French

---

36. Bartlett, "Statecraft," p. 185.

37. Quoted in Kenneth Bourne, *Foreign Policy of Victorian England, 1830–1902* (Oxford: Clarendon Press, 1970), p. 29.

38. Quoted in Kenneth Bourne, *Palmerston: The Early Years, 1784–1841* (New York: Macmillan, 1982), p. 613. Palmerston was not really off the mark in this comment. After 1815 France indeed sought to carve out a sphere of influence, something denied it in the 1815 settlement. And, as Bullen comments, "in order to recover a sphere of influence for herself, France had to encroach on those of others." Bullen, "France and Europe," p. 139.

39. Quoted in Billy, *Palmerston's Foreign Policy*, p. 13.

in battle by sea and by land by the simple process of standing our ground the longest and by the same means we can always carry our points against them in diplomacy."[40]

THE DOMESTIC POLITICAL STRUCTURES OF ENGLAND AND FRANCE
British foreign secretaries enjoyed enormous power by virtue of their office. However, this does not mean that they were unfettered in the conduct of foreign policy. The most important constraint on Palmerston and Aberdeen was the principle that the Cabinet was collectively responsible for government policy.[41] In practice, however, the foreign secretary enjoyed great latitude in the conduct of diplomacy, with only the prime minister exercising close oversight.[42] Most Cabinet members normally were uninterested in foreign affairs; only during crises would the Cabinet as a whole become involved in foreign policy decision making. In theory, all Cabinet members were to be given access to official documents pertaining to foreign affairs (dispatches and memoranda, instructions to English diplomats abroad); in practice, Palmerston (like all strong foreign secretaries) was inventive in finding methods to circumvent the need to consult and inform his Cabinet colleagues.[43]

40. Quoted in ibid., p. 12.

41. Ibid., pp. 20–21; Chamberlain, *"Pax Britannica?"* pp. 11–12.

42. The degree of this oversight depended on the relationship between the prime minister and foreign secretary and the amount of confidence reposed in the latter by the former. For example, Muriel Chamberlain contends that during Palmerston's first tenure (1830–34) as foreign secretary, he was supervised very closely by the prime minister, Earl Grey. This was largely because of Palmerston's relative lack of foreign policy experience and because, as a Canningite ex-Tory in a Whig-dominated Cabinet, he was not fully trusted by some of his colleagues. (Chamberlain, *"Pax Britannica?"* pp. 70–71.) Kenneth Bourne contests Chamberlain's argument and says that Grey invested Palmerston with a high degree of autonomy. (Bourne, *Palmerston*, p. 499.) During the 1830s and 1840s, the foreign secretary had to bear his responsibilities almost single-handedly because the Foreign Office lacked a body of permanent officials with foreign policy expertise. The Foreign Office staff during this period was comprised almost solely of clerks; consequently, all substantive decisions had to be made by the foreign secretary, who did not have the luxury of being able to draw upon the knowledge and experience of professional advisers. (See Bourne, *Palmerston*, pp. 408–435, and Chamberlain, *"Pax Britannica?"* pp. 16–17.)

43. Billy, *Palmerston's Foreign Policy*, pp. 20–21; and Chamberlain, *"Pax Britannica?"* pp. 11–12. On this score, the example of Sir Edward Grey in the years prior to World War I is noteworthy. From 1906 until the very eve of war, Grey and his prime minister, H.H. Asquith, concealed from the Cabinet the terms of the military and naval understandings they had negotiated with France. See Samuel R. Williamson, *The Politics of Grand Strategy: Britain and France Prepare for War, 1904–1914* (Cambridge, Mass.: Harvard University Press, 1969).

Nevertheless, in times of serious international tension, even Palmerston was constrained by the need to gain Cabinet consent for his policies. Here, two factors were at play. First, in the 1830s, the unified Liberal Party of the latter nineteenth century had not yet emerged, and the polarization of the House of Commons associated with a two-party system had not yet taken hold.[44] The Whig-led governments of 1830–41 and 1846–51 were actually tenuous coalitions depending for their survival in office on their ability to obtain House of Commons support from radicals and nonconformists. As the historian T.A. Jenkins says, especially after 1832, the Whigs had "to embrace more fully the values and aspirations of urban and industrial Britain."[45] Second, between 1830–1841, the Cabinet included an influential group of francophile Whig ministers (the political legatees of Charles James Fox, known as "Foxites") centered around Lord Holland. Especially after the July Monarchy came to power in France, the Foxites believed that shared liberal values and institutions mandated a close Anglo-French alliance in opposition to the reactionary forces grouped together in the Holy Alliance. During the July Monarchy, the Foxites maintained close personal ties with liberal politicians in France. The Foxites were naturally distrustful of Palmerston's French policy.[46] During the Mehemet Ali Crisis (1838–41), the Foxites tried to undercut Palmerston's hard-line policy both in the Cabinet and by leaking details of the Cabinet debates to the French government. In the wake of the Mehemet Ali Crisis— which most historians regard as Palmerston's greatest diplomatic triumph—his reputation among the Foxites for bellicosity and recklessness was so great that the attempt to form a Whig-Liberal Ministry in December 1845 collapsed because Earl Grey would not join a Cabinet in which Palmerston was foreign secretary.[47]

Although the Reform Act of 1832 did not turn Britain into a mass popular democracy, public opinion—that is, the opinions of the press and the House of Commons—did affect British foreign policy. Palmerston was one of the first "modern" politicians in that he knew

44. T.A. Jenkins, *The Liberal Ascendancy, 1830–1886* (London: Macmillan, 1994), pp. 35–36, 45.

45. Ibid., p. 45.

46. On the Foxite influence in the Whig Cabinets of the 1830s, see John Clarke, *British Diplomacy and Foreign Policy, 1782–1865: The National Interest* (London: Unwin Hyman, 1989), pp. 185–186; and Roger Bullen, *Aberdeen, Guizot and the Entente Cordiale* (London: Athlone Press, 1974).

47. Chamberlain, *"Pax Britannica?"* p. 92.

how to use both public sentiment and the press to bolster his foreign policy (and, of course, his political standing).[48] By employing the rhetoric of both "liberalism" and British national interests, he mobilized popular support. With respect to the press, Palmerston (even by today's standards) was extremely dexterous in using leaks, "background briefings," and planted stories to build support for his diplomacy. Although public opinion did come to play an increasingly important role in British foreign policy, it was not the pacifying force depicted by the democratic peace theory. As the diplomatic historian Muriel Chamberlain observes:

> The intervention of public opinion in foreign affairs was by no means necessarily a benevolent force. It nearly caused war with France over the Tahiti incident in 1844. It played a major role in bringing about the Crimean War in 1854. Not for nothing did the nineteenth century believe that democracies could be more dangerous mavericks in foreign affairs than absolute monarchies.[49]

In France, the events of July 1830 "opened the way for the definitive establishment of the rules of parliamentary government along British lines."[50] In one sense, the July Monarchy was the product of the same dynamics that were shaping British politics: the rise of the commercial, professional, and industrial middle classes. It is not by accident that the July Monarchy is sometimes referred to as the Bourgeois Monarchy. However, although the July Monarchy was clearly a liberal regime, the structure of government differed in important respects from Britain's.

In both countries, the crown possessed powers with respect to foreign policy and the "royal prerogative" of appointing a prime minister.

---

48. Bourne, *Palmerston*, pp. 483–490; Jenkins, *The Liberal Ascendancy*, pp. 80–81. As Kingsley Martin observes, Palmerston "never missed an opportunity of appearing to advantage in a daily paper. Every political group employed some newspaper to represent its point of view, and even, on occasion, to make official statements on its behalf, but Palmerston was probably the first British statesman who deliberately ingratiated himself with papers of all shades of opinion. . . . It was this personal appeal to the public which differentiated Lord Palmerston from other statesmen of his period and which so often infuriated them. He knew that if he was sufficiently popular he could do what he liked." Kingsley Martin, *The Triumph of Lord Palmerston: A Study of Public Opinion in England Before the Crimean War*, rev. ed. (London: Hutchinson, 1963), pp. 55–56.

49. Chamberlain, *"Pax Britannica?"* pp. 13–14.

50. D.R. Watson, "The British Parliamentary System and the Growth of Constitutional Government in Western Europe," in Bartlett, ed., *Britain Preeminent*, p. 114.

Unlike Britain, however, where the crown gradually was being reduced to figurehead status, the French king, Louis Philippe, was very much a "hands on" monarch. This was especially true in the realm of foreign affairs, where Louis Philippe strongly advocated a cautious and pacific policy.[51] Although the French cabinet was comprised of ministers drawn from, and responsible to, the Chamber of Deputies, Louis Philippe played an active role in the formation of ministries. However, except during the 1840 crisis, when he dismissed the bellicose premier, Adolphe Thiers, he never claimed the right to ignore the will of the Chamber of Deputies. And on that occasion, Louis Philippe justified his actions by reference to his power as commander in chief to make war and peace.[52]

The role of the Chamber was crucial in the July Monarchy. The deputies had written the regime's constitution, and they believed in their primacy within the political system. Much like the British Parliament at the time, the party system was weakly developed and personalities were very important in the making and unmaking of cabinets. In contrast to Britain, however, French politics lacked underlying stability, as France was still riven by the divisions among republicans, Bonapartists, Bourbon legitimists, and Orleanists. In this political environment, "deputies regarded themselves not as legislators as much as the makers of ministries and the electors of cabinets."[53]

The volatility of French politics was enhanced by the role of public opinion. The July Monarchy was a golden age for the press in France. Noting that there was more public discussion of foreign policy in France than in any other great power between 1815 and 1848, Bullen observes that: "In French society, more than any other, foreign policy was a decisive issue; it could determine the fate of governments; it constituted an important part of opposition attacks on governments and it was part of the debate about the direction and purpose of politics since the revolution of 1789."[54] In a France externally revisionist and domestically unstable, public opinion was *not* a force for peace.

---

51. Collingham, *The July Monarchy: A Political History of France, 1830–1848* (London: Longman, 1988), p. 97.

52. Ibid., p. 102.

53. Ibid., p. 89.

54. Bullen, "France and Europe," pp. 128–129.

Anglo-French Relations, 1830–46: Cases

In this section, I analyze the Anglo-French crises of 1830–32 (Belgium), 1838–41 (the Near East), and 1844 (Tahiti and Tangier)—each of which brought London and Paris to the brink of war—to determine whether democratic peace theory or realism best explains the outcome of these events.

BELGIUM, 1830–32

Keeping the Scheldt Estuary and the port of Antwerp out of the hands of another great power "was England's most vital interest abroad."[55] At Vienna, Castlereagh had successfully pushed to have Belgium (which between 1792 and 1815 had been part of France) incorporated into the Kingdom of Holland. Britain had also helped finance the construction of a series of barrier fortresses on the Franco-Dutch (Belgian) frontier. Holland thus played a key role in England's post-1815 policy of containing France.

The revolutionary ferment that overtook Europe in the summer of 1830 set in motion events that threatened to jeopardize Britain's security interests in the Low Countries. Inspired by the July 1830 revolution in France, the Belgians staged their own popular revolt against Dutch rule. Ties of language, culture, and ideology impelled the Belgians to regard France as their patron. France regarded the events of 1830 as a possible opportunity to throw off the shackles of the 1815 Settlement and to reestablish its influence in Belgium.[56] The Eastern powers regarded the Belgian revolt as a direct challenge to the 1815 Settlement, and the possibility existed that they might assist Holland in suppressing the Belgian uprising. Such a move might trigger French counter-intervention and precipitate a general European war.

The Belgian crisis thus presented Palmerston with a formidable diplomatic challenge. He recognized that a change in Belgium's status was inevitable, but that he needed to ensure that the new arrangements for Belgium upheld Britain's strategic interests. In practice,

---

55. Bourne, *Palmerston*, p. 333.

56. France—and especially the military—had not renounced its irredentist aims in Belgium and in fall of 1829 a plan to annex Belgium was brought before King Charles X and the Council of State. And, during a private visit to Paris in 1829, Palmerston (who then was out of office) was told by the French foreign minister, General Sebastiani, that amicable relations between England and France hinged on London's willingness to acquiesce in the expansion of French power in Belgium and toward the Rhine frontier. Ward and Gooch, *History of British Foreign Policy*, p. 121.

this meant ensuring that France did not gain predominant influence in Brussels. At the same time, Palmerston needed to forestall either the Eastern powers or France from intervening in the crisis militarily (because such intervention could escalate into a general European war). Palmerston skillfully managed the Belgian crisis by playing off the Eastern powers (whose ability to intervene soon became constrained by the uprising in Poland) against the French (who, because of their diplomatic isolation, were vulnerable to Palmerston's manipulation). In the end, Palmerston achieved a peaceful settlement that preserved Britain's strategic interests by facilitating the creation of an independent but neutral Belgium.

Palmerston's diplomacy *vis-à-vis* France during the Belgian crisis is revealing; he cooperated with Paris when British and French interests coincided but he threatened war when their interests clashed. Thus, at the outset of the Belgian crisis in 1830, London and Paris acted in concert to deter possible Prussian and Austrian intervention to crush the Belgian revolt.[57] Again, in 1832, London and Paris collaborated militarily to force Holland to accept the terms imposed by the great powers. However, in 1831, the Belgian issue twice led Palmerston to threaten war against France.

The first occasion was in early 1831 when the Belgians offered the throne of their new state to the Duke of Nemours, a son of French King Louis Philippe. London understandably feared that a dynastic tie between France and the new state would transform Belgium into a French satellite. Given the implications of a French-controlled Belgium for Britain's security, it is not surprising that London resolved to risk war if necessary to compel France to decline the offer to Nemours.[58] During this affair, Palmerston bluntly told the French ambassador, Prince Talleyrand, that there would be war if Nemours became king of Belgium.[59]

---

57. The Belgian revolt had the potential to escalate into a general European war. In the summer of 1830, even in the absence of the joint Anglo-French warning, Prussia and Austria probably would not have intervened in Belgium because both were involved suppressing the uprising in Poland. However, the possibility of a general war arose again when the Dutch invaded Belgium in August 1831. The strategic situation was as follows: if all the great powers refrained from intervening, the Dutch probably would be able to suppress the Belgian revolt. However, such action by Holland probably would trigger French intervention to assist Belgium. If France did intervene, Holland would be defeated unless supported by the other great powers. And, in fact, it was likely that French intervention would prompt counter-intervention by the Germanic Confederation, led by Prussia and Austria. See Chamberlain, *"Pax Britannica?"* p. 71; Clarke, *British Diplomacy*, p. 195; and Ward and Gooch, *History of British Foreign Policy*, p. 126.

58. Ward and Gooch, *History of British Foreign Policy*, p. 136.

59. Bourne, *Palmerston*, pp. 337–338.

Ironically, the second Anglo-French approach to war over Belgium grew out of the combined diplomatic efforts of the great powers to resolve the Belgian question. In the summer of 1830, the great powers had agreed that their respective ambassadors in London should convene in a conference under the chairmanship of the British foreign secretary to negotiate a Belgian settlement. In January 1831, the London Conference adopted a protocol endorsing the creation of an independent, neutral Belgium, and subsequently the Conference drew up the territorial and financial terms that were to govern the separation of Belgium from Holland. These terms later were modified from those in the original protocol in order to make territorial adjustments in Belgium's favor (and at Holland's expense). In June 1831, King William I of Holland declared that the terms of separation were unacceptable, and in August 1831, the Dutch army invaded Belgium, which thereupon appealed to Paris for support. The London conference authorized joint intervention by the French army and the British Royal Navy to compel Dutch withdrawal.

Once 50,000 French troops were installed in Belgium, however, Paris was unable to resist the temptation to use them as leverage to gain unilateral strategic advantages. Notably, France threatened to remain in Belgium until all the barrier fortresses on the Franco-Belgian frontier were dismantled. Destruction of these fortifications would leave Belgium militarily exposed to France and thus vulnerable to French political pressure. London's reaction was swift and decisive: the French must leave Belgium unconditionally. Although some of the Foxite members of the Cabinet preferred to make concessions to France rather than risk war, Palmerston refused to submit, as he put it, to dictation "at the point of a bayonet."[60] Giving Paris a voice in determining which fortresses should be dismantled was, in his view, akin to consulting with a burglar over "which of the bars & bolts of your door & windows you might most safely dispense with."[61]

Using both official and indirect channels, Palmerston conveyed to Paris that Britain, if necessary, would go to war to compel the French to withdraw from Belgium. To his ambassador in Paris, Lord Granville, Palmerston wrote: "One thing is certain—the French must go out of Belgium, or we shall have a general war, and war in a number of days." Palmerston sent this message to Granville by regular mail,

---

60. Ibid., pp. 340–341.
61. Ibid.

anticipating correctly that it would be read by the French.[62] He also acted more directly:

Over Belgium Palmerston firmly warned Paris on 16 August 1831 that Britain would not tolerate the establishment of any separate influence in Brussels. The French, he intimated, would face "a war with all the rest of the world" in which Britain would ruin them at sea, while the eastern powers would combine to crush the Poles before joining in the conflict (presumably supported if necessary by British subsidies).[63]

Palmerston's hawkish stance on Belgium was supported by his prime minister, Earl Grey. Grey declared firmly that "the French must not remain in Belgium on any pretext whatever," and went on to observe that "public opinion in England is already very excited and any appearance of bad faith on the part of France would kindle a flame which would make war inevitable."[64]

Confronted by a resolute Britain, France backed down and war was avoided. However, this crisis's peaceful outcome does not vindicate the democratic peace theory. Notwithstanding that France was acknowledged to be a liberal state, Britain was prepared to go to war to defend a historically vital security interest. Although some Foxite ministers in the Cabinet urged that London follow a more conciliatory line toward Paris, even Earl Grey, who generally was aligned with the Foxites, strongly supported Palmerston because he recognized that Britain's security would be gravely imperiled should Belgium come under French control. To the extent that public opinion was a factor in London's decision making, it appeared to support (if not indeed demand) that Britain take a hard-line position with respect to France. Although the democratic peace theory cannot explain France's backing down from the brink of war, realism does account for the avoidance of war in 1831. Simply put, the balance of power explains why war did not occur: diplomatically isolated and facing an incipient coalition of the other four great powers, Paris elected to abandon its revisionist aspirations and withdraw from Belgium rather than risk a war it could not win.[65]

---

62. Chamberlain, "Pax Britannica?" pp. 71–72.

63. Bartlett, Defence and Diplomacy, p. 29.

64. Quoted in Ward and Gooch, History of British Foreign Policy, p. 144.

65. Albrecht-Carrie stresses that the possibility that the anti-French 1815 Quadruple Alliance would be revived was a paramount factor in Paris's decision to withdraw from Belgium. Albrecht-Carrie, Britain and France, p. 59.

The Near Eastern Crisis of 1838–41 (also known as the second
Mehemet Ali Crisis) once again brought Britain and France to the
brink of war. The underlying cause of the crisis was the Ottoman
Empire's progressive decay and the threat this posed to Britain's line
of communications to India. Even before the Napoleonic Wars, in the
latter part of the eighteenth century, the security of India and the
routes to it had come to have "an almost obsessive role" in England's
foreign policy, and the strategic importance of the Near East was held
to be as great as that of the Low Countries.[66] During the nineteenth
century, "the protection of Turkish territories was Whitehall's greatest continuing Mediterranean concern."[67] In the 1830s, Britain's Near
Eastern interests were menaced by both France and Russia.

The immediate origins of the second Mehemet Ali Crisis can be
traced directly to the outcome of the first crisis in 1832–33. Mehemet
Ali was the Pasha of Egypt. Nominally a vassal under the suzerainty
of the Ottoman Sultan in Constantinople, Mehemet Ali in fact
enjoyed considerable independence. He also was extremely ambitious and sought both recognition from the Sultan of hereditary title
to Egypt and territorial expansion. Mehemet Ali claimed that the
Sultan had promised him Syria in return for Egypt's assistance to
Constantinople during the Greek War of Independence. When the
Sultan refused to give Syria to Mehemet Ali, the Egyptian army
invaded Syria in late 1831. Soon thereafter the Sultan declared war on
Mehemet Ali. The Ottomans were soundly defeated and the
Egyptian armies marched on Constantinople.

The Ottoman Empire was saved from complete collapse only by
Russian intervention. Despite St. Petersburg's designs on the Ottoman
Empire, Czar Nicholas I apprehended that, in the short term, Russian
interests would be best served by propping up Constantinople.[68] In
July 1833, Russia used its leverage to obtain Constantinople's signature

---

66. John Marlowe, *Perfidious Albion: The Origins of the Anglo-French Rivalry in the
Levant* (London: Elek Books, 1971), p. 8.

67. Hamilton, *Anglo-French Naval Rivalry*, pp. 5–6.

68. As Bridge and Bullen observe: "He [Nicholas] saw the crisis in the Near East
as part of the revolutionary upsurge which had already disturbed Europe. To
support Turkey against her rebel subjects was consistent with his European policy of containment. Secondly, Nicholas was anxious to prevent the collapse of
Turkey; in 1829 an imperial committee had reported to the emperor that it was in
Russia's interest to support Turkey until such time as her collapse could be fully
exploited by Russia. Lastly, Nicholas wanted to prevent Mehemet Ali from taking

of the Treaty of Unkiar Skelessi. Ostensibly a mutual assistance pact, the treaty was widely believed in London to have established a virtual Russian protectorate over the Ottoman Empire. In the wake of the Treaty of Unkiar Skelessi, reducing Russian influence in Constantinople and bolstering the Ottoman Empire became overriding diplomatic objectives for London.[69] As the British diplomat Sir Stratford Canning put it in 1833, "to Great Britain the fate of this [Ottoman] empire can never be indifferent. It would affect the interests of her trade and her East Indian possessions even if it were unconnected with the maintenance of her relative power in Europe."[70]

Although London worried continually about the Russian menace to its Mediterranean and Near Eastern interests, by the late 1830s, France had emerged as an equal (and perhaps greater) threat to Britain's position in the Near East. There were three interlocking reasons for this. First, in 1830, France began its conquest of Algeria, which established it as an imperial power in North Africa and as a potential threat to England's naval control of the Mediterranean. Second, once France acquired Algeria, a powerful rationale emerged to justify expansion of French naval power in the Mediterranean— the protection of the line of communications between France and North Africa. As the historian C.I. Hamilton points out, by the mid-1830s, England and France were locked in a classic security dilemma:

Constantinople and installing himself as Sultan. He did not want an energetic and reforming ruler in control of the Ottoman Empire. Essentially Russian policy was directed towards the maintenance of the *status quo*, a weak Turkey always susceptible to Russian pressure." Bridge and Bullen, *The Great Powers*, p. 55.

69. Russia's Near Eastern diplomatic coup in 1833 was made possible by an uncharacteristic foreign policy blunder by Palmerston. He did not comprehend the gravity of Constantinople's plight, was reluctant to incur the financial consequences of intervention and a military and naval buildup, and did not wish to cooperate with Metternich in finding a multilateral solution to the crisis. Palmerston's hesitation gave Russia the opening it needed to establish its political influence in Constantinople. Ibid. Palmerston himself recognized that London had stumbled badly in 1832–33. As he wrote in 1838, "there is nothing that has happened since I have been in office which I regret so much as that tremendous blunder of the British government." Quoted in Clayton, *Britain and the Eastern Question*, p. 63.

70. Quoted in Allan Cunningham, *Eastern Questions in the Nineteenth Century: Collected Essays*, Vol. II, edited by Edward Ingram (London: Frank Cass, 1993), p. 57. This was Palmerston's view, as well. As he said, "the integrity and independence of the Ottoman Empire are necessary to the maintenance of the tranquility, the liberty, and the balance of power in the rest of Europe." Quoted in Billy, *Palmerston's Foreign Policy*, pp. 10–11.

"The danger was that each power would want to achieve maritime hegemony in the Mediterranean, the better to safeguard its own lines of maritime communication and, if necessary, to deny them to the other power."[71] Third, by the 1830s, Egypt had become a virtual French satellite. French advisers held key posts in Mehemet Ali's army, navy, and civil bureaucracy, and Paris had substantial financial, commercial, and cultural influence in Egypt, as well.[72] Indeed, the French had cultivated Mehemet Ali assiduously in the hope that their influence in Egypt could be used to shift the geopolitical center of gravity in the Near East from Constantinople (where England and Russia competed for influence) to Egypt (where French influence predominated), and obtain Mehemet Ali's military help for further French territorial expansion in North Africa.[73]

The 1838–41 Crisis was triggered when, in May 1838, Mehemet Ali announced his intention to declare independence from the Sultan. Eleven months later, the Ottoman Empire declared war on Egypt, whereupon Mehemet Ali's forces invaded Syria and quickly and decisively defeated the Ottoman Army. (The Ottoman Navy defected to Egypt.) These events created a European diplomatic crisis that Palmerston was determined to exploit for the purpose of reasserting England's interests and influence in the Near East.

Palmerston had two overarching goals during the crisis.[74] First, he wanted to defuse the threat posed to the Ottoman Empire's stability by Mehemet Ali. Mehemet Ali was a double threat to English interests. If he were able to take power in Constantinople himself, France could become the dominant power in the Near East; at the same time, continuing rivalry between Mehemet Ali and Constantinople might weaken the Ottoman Empire to the point where Russia would be tempted to intervene.[75] Second, Palmerston wanted to overturn the Treaty of Unkiar Skelessi and replace the Russian protectorate of the Ottoman Empire with collective great power responsibility for the Empire's integrity and stability. Palmerston's ultimate aim was to

---

71. Hamilton, *Anglo-French Naval Rivalry*, pp. 7–8. The classic explication of the security dilemma is Robert Jervis, "Cooperation Under the Security Dilemma," *World Politics*, Vol. 30, No. 2 (January 1978), pp. 167–214.

72. Bourne, *Foreign Policy of Victorian England*, p. 39; and Marlowe, *Perfidious Albion*, p. 226.

73. Marlowe, *Perfidious Albion*, pp. 172–173.

74. See Ward and Gooch, *History of British Foreign Policy*, p. 170.

75. Marlowe, *Perfidious Albion*, p. 215.

strengthen the Ottoman Empire so that it could withstand pressure from either Russia or France.[76]

To accomplish his goals, Palmerston needed to prevent Russia and France, each of which had Near Eastern interests antithetical to London's, from combining against Britain. This was not a difficult task, because Russia's ideological antipathy toward France ruled out cooperation between St. Petersburg and Paris.[77] At the same time, the coincidence of British and Russian interests allowed Palmerston to work in harmony with St. Petersburg to resolve the crisis. Both powers had overlapping *defensive* interests that were served by maintaining the Near Eastern status quo.[78] St. Petersburg also saw that cooperation with London afforded an opening to disrupt the (admittedly frayed) Anglo-French entente.[79]

In late 1839 and early 1840, Palmerston and the Russians reached an understanding concerning the Near East that provided for the non-renewal of the Treaty of Unkiar Skelessi and reaffirmed the principle that the Dardanelles should remain closed. London and St. Petersburg also agreed that they would collaborate with the other great powers in resolving the Mehemet Ali crisis. Palmerston and Russia were willing to concede hereditary title to Egypt to Mehemet Ali, but they insisted that he give up his conquests in Syria. If Mehemet Ali refused, the great powers would use force against him. These terms were ultimately embodied in the London Convention adopted on July 15, 1840, by England, Russia, Austria, and Prussia.

---

76. M.S. Anderson, *The Eastern Question, 1774–1923* (London: Macmillan, 1966), p. 92.

77. As Kenneth Bourne notes, "Nicholas carried his disapproval of revolution to an almost pathological hatred of the Bourgeois Monarchy and of Louis Philippe personally." Bourne, *Foreign Policy of Victorian England*, pp. 39–40.

78. Both Russia and Britain wanted the Ottoman Empire to remain intact to preserve the status quo in the Dardanelles, which prevented the Royal Navy from entering the Black Sea and the Russian Navy from entering the Aegean or Mediterranean. Russia also believed its interests would be menaced if Mehemet Ali were to come to power in Constantinople. Finally, serious financial constraints also inclined St. Petersburg to seek a diplomatic solution. See Anderson, *The Eastern Question*, pp. 90, 98; and Bartlett, "Statecraft," p. 177.

79. As Anderson points out, Nicholas and Nesselrode, his foreign minister, "realized that by negotiating with Britain alone they might be able to break the Anglo-French *entente* which, though often severely strained, had been a leading factor in European politics during the 1830s, notably in the Iberian peninsula and to some extent in Belgium. To destroy it would be a great victory for the cause of conservatism in Europe. For such a victory, Nicholas was willing to pay a considerable price." Anderson, *The Eastern Question*, p. 98.

The great powers issued an ultimatum to Mehemet Ali: if he accepted the great powers' terms immediately he could have hereditary possession of Egypt and lifetime possession of Syria; if he accepted within ten days he could have Egypt only; and if he did not accept within twenty days the offer would expire and his armies would be evicted forcibly from Syria.

Although at the crisis's outset Palmerston had hoped to enlist French cooperation, France was not included in the negotiations that led to the London Convention. This was because France had elected to support Mehemet Ali against Palmerston and the other great powers. France and Britain had begun to drift apart in the Mehemet Ali Crisis as early as summer 1839. The French prime minister, Marshal Soult, did not wish to break openly with Britain and the other powers. At the same time, Paris regarded Mehemet Ali as an important client, and France sought to mediate between Egypt and the great powers in order to secure favorable terms for Mehemet Ali (whom it viewed as a potentially useful counterweight to British influence in the Near East). In particular, France believed that Egypt's impressive military victory entitled Mehemet Ali to retain Syria; Paris opposed the use of force by the great powers to coerce Mehemet Ali; and Paris wanted the crisis settled directly by Egypt and the Ottoman Empire. Palmerston was adamant in rejecting these terms. In Palmerston's view, Mehemet Ali had to be cut down to size because he threatened the Ottoman Empire's territorial integrity, the preservation of which was crucial to Britain's interests in the Dardanelles and in the security of the routes to India.[80]

In March 1840, the Soult government was replaced by one headed by Adolphe Thiers. Thiers had little love for Britain, and he wanted to restore French preeminence in Europe.[81] Moreover, when he came to power, Thiers believed he needed to score a quick diplomatic victory in order to solidify both his own domestic political position and that of the Orleanist dynasty.[82] Thiers believed that these objectives could best be gained by a victorious war. Yet Thiers (and here he differed little from other post-1815 French leaders) understood that war posed grave external and internal risks for France. Thus, as H.A.C.

---

80. On the divergence between the Soult government and Palmerston in 1839, see Anderson, *The Eastern Question*, p. 97; and Marlowe, *Perfidious Albion*, pp. 240, 250–252.

81. Clarke, *British Diplomacy*, pp. 200–201.

82. Chamberlain, *"Pax Britannica?"* p. 74.

Collingham observes, torn between his enthusiasm for war and his fear of its consequences, Thiers turned to an aggressive foreign policy as a compromise solution.[83] The violent reaction of French public opinion against the London Convention—and Britain—reinforced Thiers's resolve to take a hard-line stance in the crisis.[84]

Notwithstanding his own bellicose posturing and French public opinion, Thiers almost certainly did not want war. However, he believed that France and Egypt would prevail in getting favorable terms by standing fast and holding out for a direct Egyptian-Ottoman settlement rather than one imposed (presumably by force, if necessary) by the other great powers. Thiers believed he could compel Palmerston to back down and acquiesce to Paris's demands. Thiers calculated that his strategy would work because Mehemet Ali was strong enough militarily to hold on to Syria; the great powers would not be able to maintain a common front; and the British Cabinet was divided, and Palmerston thus would be forced by his colleagues to adopt a more conciliatory position. In fact, Thiers's policy was based on *mis*calculation.

The great powers did not fall out—and they authorized the use of force against Mehemet Ali. Pursuant to this great power mandate, in the fall of 1840, Ottoman troops and Royal Navy forces commanded by Sir Charles Napier defeated the Egyptian forces in Syria. And, while the British Cabinet indeed was divided, Palmerston was nevertheless able to carry out his hard-line policy over the opposition of key ministers.

As a result, Thiers found himself confronting the prospect of a war he apparently did not want. Nevertheless, he was unwilling to back down. To support his policy, France mobilized the army's reserves, appropriated emergency funds for the French Navy, and proceeded with plans to strengthen Paris's fortifications.[85] These military moves

---

83. Collingham, *The July Monarchy*, p. 226.

84. Anderson describes French opinion in the wake of the London Convention as "violently anti-British." Anderson, *The Eastern Question*, pp. 101–102. Chamberlain says that the "French were furious." Chamberlain, *"Pax Britannica?"* p. 75. Marlowe says the London Convention "caused great surprise and indignation among the French public, who regarded it as an attempt by the other powers to isolate France." Marlowe, *Perfidious Albion*, p. 263. Collingham says that the whole of the French political world was "shocked and surprised" by the London Convention and that the French public reacted with "spontaneous violence" and that "everywhere there was hatred for England." Collingham, *The July Monarchy*, p. 229.

85. Collingham, *The July Monarchy*, pp. 229–230.

were mirrored by the tenor of French diplomacy. In a September 1840 meeting with the British chargé d'affaires, Thiers indicated that France regarded Mehemet Ali's demands as reasonable and just. England could join with France in compelling the Sultan to accept those terms; if not, Paris would support Egypt. Thiers concluded by posing the question: "Do you understand the gravity of what I have just said to you?"[86]

Palmerston indeed got the message, and his response was resolute: "If the French attempt to bully and intimidate us as they have done, the only way of meeting their menaces is by quietly telling them we are not afraid, and by showing them, first, that we are stronger than they are, and secondly, that they have more vulnerable points than we have."[87] Palmerston instructed the British ambassador in Paris to tell Thiers that "if France throws down the gauntlet, we shall not refuse to pick it up; and that, if she begins a war, she will to a certainty lose her ships, colonies and commerce before she sees the end of it; that her army in Algeria will cease to give anxiety and that [Mehemet] Ali will just be chucked into the Nile."[88] Palmerston did not believe that Thiers would go to war for Mehemet Ali (or that Louis Philippe would permit Thiers to do so). Nevertheless, there was the possibility that French opinion might drive Thiers into an unwanted conflict.[89] Palmerston was willing to run the risk of war, because of the interests at stake and because he believed that Paris could not prevail in a war with England.[90]

In the end, both the fear of war and Mehemet Ali's defeat prompted Louis Philippe to compel Thiers to resign, notwithstanding that the premier still commanded a majority both in his cabinet and in the Chamber.[91] As the French king observed, there was a difference between speaking of war (as did Thiers) and actually making war.[92]

---

86. Quoted in Marlowe, *Perfidious Albion*, pp. 269–270.

87. Quoted in Albrecht-Carrie, *Britain and France*, p. 73.

88. Quoted in Marlowe, *Perfidious Albion*, p. 270.

89. Bourne, *Palmerston*, p. 596.

90. See Billy, *Palmerston's Foreign Policy*, pp. 24–25; and Bourne, *Palmerston*, p. 607. As Albrecht-Carrie puts it, "Palmerston did not want war but he was willing to face the possibility of it, gambling—correctly as it turned out—on the likelihood that in the test of wills his would prove stronger than that of the French, be it Thiers' or Louis Philippe's." Albrecht-Carrie, *Britain and France*, p. 80.

91. See John M.S. Allison, *Thiers and the French Monarchy* (Boston: Houghton Mifflin, 1926), pp. 282–287; and Collingham, *The July Monarchy*, pp. 233–237.

92. Quoted in Ward and Gooch, *History of British Foreign Policy*, pp. 178–179.

The new government, with Soult again as prime minister and François Guizot as foreign minister, had a mandate to end the crisis. As Palmerston observed, "the retirement of M. Thiers and his colleagues is a sure pledge to Europe that France is not going to make war in defence of Mehemet Ali."[93]

Palmerston was able to carry out his hard-line policy despite substantial opposition from within the Cabinet. Foxites like Lord Holland and Edward Ellice believed Palmerston's policy was extremely shortsighted. They argued that the wisest course was to conciliate France—which they believed was acting from wounded pride caused by Paris's exclusion from the negotiations culminating in the London Convention—rather than antagonize Paris over Mehemet Ali.[94] As John Clarke notes, the Foxites feared that Palmerston's policy "would only humiliate Louis Philippe and precipitate a revolution in France which would give power to men who would make Thiers seem a moderate."[95] It was also argued that England, already overextended in Afghanistan, China, and North America, could ill-afford to risk a war with France. However, with the support of the prime minister, Lord Melbourne, Palmerston overrode the Foxites and carried through his policy to its conclusion, the humiliation of France.[96] As Kenneth Bourne notes, even after Thiers's fall, Palmerston did not offer France a bridge over which to retreat gracefully: "Instead he insisted on finishing off the Egyptian crisis without even the cooperation which the French then offered. Only

---

93. Quoted in Anderson, *The Eastern Question*, p. 104.

94. Palmerston did not accept the Foxite argument that French policy was being driven by wounded pride. As he wrote to the English ambassador in Paris: "As to the stale pretence of wounded *amour propre* and mortified vanity, the recent debates prove that she acted from much deeper and more rational motives than vanity or *amour propre*, and that she has laid down to herself during the last fifty years a systematic plan of aggrandizement in the Levant, to the intended detriment of England. It is the being baffled in this scheme when close upon its accomplishment that excited the fury which has lately burst forth; and the fury was the more intense and ungovernable because they who felt it would not in decency avow its real cause and were obliged to charge it upon feelings of which any man out of his teens must necessarily be ashamed." Quoted in Marlowe, *Perfidious Albion*, pp. 290–291.

95. Clarke, *British Diplomacy*, pp. 205–206.

96. In October 1840, Melbourne wrote to the Belgian King Leopold and made it clear that he backed Palmerston's policy, and that if France persisted in its military preparations, he would ask Parliament to fund countermeasures. Bourne, *Palmerston*, pp. 611–612.

when Mehemet Ali had finally submitted was France allowed to rejoin the concert."[97] And, although an Anglo-French war had been avoided for the moment, Palmerston still believed such a conflict was distinctly possible and that the "deterrence model" thus should govern England's policy toward France. As he wrote to the British ambassador in Paris at the crisis's height, "if we carry our point which I am now convinced we shall, we shall read France quietly a lesson that will be useful to her for three or four years to come. I cannot hope that anything short of a good physical thrashing will make an impression much longer than that."[98]

The democratic peace theory does not explain why Britain and France avoided war during the Mehemet Ali Crisis. On the French side, public opinion pushed Paris into a risky foreign policy. In Britain, Palmerston was able to brush aside his francophile colleagues who argued that liberal solidarity required that London should appease Paris. Contrary to the democratic peace theory's expectations, Britain's liberal elite (represented by Palmerston's foes in the Cabinet) was not able to restrain Palmerston from threatening to go to war with France.[99] And, with respect to French behavior in the crisis, one must note the irony that the liberal elements pushing France to war (Thiers, the Chamber, the press, and public opinion) had to be restrained by the most illiberal component of the French domestic political structure, the monarch.

Realism, however, does explain the crisis's outcome. Palmerston adopted a hard-line policy during this crisis because Britain's most vital strategic interests were implicated. Moreover, as C.J. Bartlett has observed, although during this crisis Palmerston showed himself an extremely skillful practitioner of *Realpolitik*, it is also true that he was playing a very strong hand.[100] In 1840, France was isolated

---

97. Bourne, *Foreign Policy of Victorian England*, p. 43.

98. Quoted in Bourne, *Palmerston*, p. 630.

99. John Owen argues that in liberal states, liberal elites act to prevent "illiberal" decision makers from pursuing belligerent policies against other liberal states. Owen, "How Liberalism Produces Peace." The Mehemet Ali crisis disconfirms Owen's argument. It should also be noted that Owen's argument is tautological. He defines liberal leaders as those who conform to the democratic peace theory's strictures. In contrast, "illiberal" decision makers in democracies are those who fail to adhere to the democratic peace theory's injunction against practicing *realpolitik* against other liberal (or democratic) states. Under Owen's approach, Palmerston would have to be considered as an example of an "illiberal" decision maker; yet, in fact, his liberal credentials are unassailable. See E.D. Steele, *Palmerston and Liberalism, 1855–1865* (Cambridge: Cambridge University Press, 1991).

100. Bartlett, *Defence and Diplomacy*, p. 42.

diplomatically in Europe. Indeed, Thiers's policy was so belligerent that, for a time in fall of 1840, Prussia, as well as England, seemed poised to go to war against France.[101] Although the immediate military balance in the eastern Mediterranean was not unfavorable to France in fall of 1840, the overall Anglo-French military balance (to say nothing of the European balance) was distinctly favorable to Britain. C.I. Hamilton has observed that in Paris it was well understood "that even if the French fleet won the first battle, it had very few reserves of men or *matériel* and could not sustain a long war."[102] This bleak view of the strategic situation indeed was held by the French ambassador in London, Guizot. As Guizot observed:

The war would be either oriental and naval, or continental and general. If naval, the disparity of forces, damages and risks is undeniable. If continental and general, France could only sustain it by giving it a revolutionary character, that is by abandoning the honest, wise and useful policy which she has followed since 1830, thus herself transforming the alliance of the four powers into a European coalition.[103]

In the end, confronting a steadfast Palmerston, Paris chose to accept diplomatic humiliation rather than fight a war it was certain to lose.

ANGLO-FRENCH RELATIONS, 1841–48: THE FALSE ENTENTE
From 1841 until 1848—that is, from the Mehemet Ali Crisis's end until the overthrow of the July Monarchy—Anglo-French relations were something of a paradox. On the one hand, at least from 1841–44, there was a revival of the *entente cordiale* that had characterized Anglo-French relations in the mid-1830s. On the other hand, each state came to regard the other as the primary threat to its security; consequently, by the mid-1840s England and France found themselves engaged in an intense naval rivalry.

The improvement that occurred in Anglo-French relations had much to do with Palmerston's departure from the Foreign Office when the Melbourne Cabinet fell and was replaced by a Tory Ministry headed by Sir Robert Peel. Peel chose as his foreign secretary Lord Aberdeen. Aberdeen's diplomatic style differed markedly

---

101. See Collingham, *The July Monarchy*, p. 229. French bellicosity in the summer and fall of 1840 provoked a strong nationalist response in Germany. It was at this time, in anticipation of war with France, that the German patriotic song "Wacht am Rhein" was composed.

102. Hamilton, *Anglo-French Naval Rivalry*, p. 12.

103. Quoted in Albrecht-Carrie, *Britain and France*, p. 77.

from Palmerston's.[104] Aberdeen possessed none of his predecessor's pugnacious nationalism.[105] Instead, he was something of an internationalist. His approach to diplomacy was patient and conciliatory. Aberdeen had an ability to understand—and respond to—the viewpoints of his interlocutors. Moreover, Aberdeen was, unusually for a Tory, a francophile. He and Peel were motivated to repair what they viewed as the damage inflicted on Anglo-French relations by Palmerston's handling of the Mehemet Ali Crisis. In this task, Aberdeen was aided by his personal friendship with the French Foreign Minister Guizot, who had previously served as French ambassador to London.

Balance of power factors also played an important role in Aberdeen's pursuit of entente with France. The new Peel Government inherited the First Opium War in China, the disastrous English defeat in the First Afghan War, and extremely tense relations with the United States. Peel and Aberdeen thought Britain should retrench. They also feared that if Britain found itself at war with either France or the United States, the other power would jump in as well. As Muriel Chamberlain observes, "the enmity of either France or the United States was an embarrassment to Britain. The simultaneous enmity of both was potentially dangerous."[106] Aberdeen also worried about the external ramifications of France's internal political instability. Aberdeen believed it was necessary to make concessions in order to keep what he regarded as a friendly government (in which Guizot was the key player) in power.[107] Aberdeen "was convinced that Guizot was the only bulwark against the triumph of revolutionary parties in France and a forward foreign policy."[108] In sum, there

---

104. The most detailed treatment of Lord Aberdeen as politician and as statesman is Muriel E. Chamberlain, *Lord Aberdeen: A Political Biography* (London: Longman, 1983).

105. See the description of Aberdeen in Chamberlain, *"Pax Britannica?"* pp. 92–93.

106. Chamberlain, *Lord Aberdeen*, p. 301.

107. Ibid., p. 84.

108. Ibid., p. 387. Of course, there are two problems with a policy such as Aberdeen's. First, it cedes to the other state a disproportionate influence over one's own policy—an influence that may be exploited to induce one to make unwise concessions in order to forestall a purportedly worse outcome. Peel eventually came to believe that Aberdeen's policy led precisely to this result and he complained "of the constant repetition of the same story 'the existing Government in France is the only security for Peace—the Powers of Europe must support it—they can only support it by concessions to the democratic and war party in the Chambers'." Quoted in Chamberlain, *Lord Aberdeen*, p. 387. The second weakness of a policy like Aberdeen's is that it is based on a personal relationship with a single counterpart rather than on a fundamental convergence of national interests; hence, if one's interlocutor should be driven from power, the entire policy is at risk of collapse.

were strategic as well as ideological and personal reasons driving the Anglo-French entente in the early 1840s.

For a time, the atmospherics of Anglo-French relations did improve. Nevertheless, beneath the surface of cordiality engineered by Aberdeen and Guizot, Anglo-French competition for political influence continued to simmer, especially in Belgium (where Guizot proposed a Franco-Belgian customs union), Greece, and Spain.[109] Then, in the summer of 1844, French designs on Morocco and a crisis over Tahiti once again brought the two nations to the brink of war.[110]

The Tahiti crisis was triggered by the unauthorized actions of a French admiral who annexed the island.[111] Although the British had exercised influence in Tahiti, the island was not under London's formal protection. Nevertheless, British public opinion was inflamed by the French annexation and this anger reached fever pitch in July 1844, when it was learned that the French admiral had arrested (and mistreated) the British consul in Tahiti, the missionary George Pritchard. To make matters worse, also in July 1844, the French threatened Morocco, and in early August they shelled Tangier, an apparent prelude to the extension of France's North African empire.[112] London opposed expansion of French influence in North Africa as a threat to its strategic interests in the Mediterranean.

For a time, Britain and France were on "the verge of war."[113] Although public opinion in both states was bellicose, neither Aberdeen nor Guizot wanted war, and a peaceful settlement was reached.[114] France agreed to refrain from annexing Morocco, to nullify Tahiti's annexation, and to pay compensation to Pritchard (which Louis Philippe paid out of his own pocket because the Chamber refused to appropriate money for this purpose). Nevertheless, Aberdeen's policy of Anglo-French entente was "in ruins" and

---

109. On the proposed Franco-Belgian customs union, see ibid., pp. 363–367. On the Spanish marriages issue, see Bullen, *Aberdeen, Guizot and the Entente Cordiale.*

110. On the 1844 crisis, see Chamberlain, *"Pax Britannica?"* pp. 89–90; Muriel E. Chamberlain, *British Foreign Policy in the Age of Palmerston* (London: Longman, 1980), pp. 54–57; Hamilton, *Anglo-French Naval Rivalry,* pp. 17–18; and Ward and Gooch, *History of British Foreign Policy,* pp. 183–185.

111. On Tahiti, see Chamberlain, *Lord Aberdeen,* pp. 363–367.

112. On the Moroccan crisis, see ibid., pp. 359–363.

113. Ward and Gooch, *History of British Foreign Policy,* p. 185.

114. On the reaction of French public opinion, see Collingham, *The July Monarchy,* pp. 321–322. In the aftermath of the summer 1844 crisis, Guizot was excoriated by his political opponents (who encompassed the French political spectrum), who regarded the outcome as a national humiliation.

friendship with France "was clearly a hopeless dream."[115] As Chamberlain says, "after the summer of 1844 no member of the British Cabinet, except Aberdeen himself, any longer had much faith in the French *entente*."[116] Instead of entente, the Anglo-French security competition intensified.

The Anglo-French security competition had actually begun even before the 1844 crisis. On both sides of the channel, the Mehemet Ali Crisis had triggered military buildups aimed at the other state. The French concluded that they might have prevailed in the 1840 showdown had they possessed a more powerful navy. They acted on this conclusion by expanding their fleet and improving it technologically (by building steam warships). Indeed, throughout the 1840s, the French Chamber lavishly appropriated funds for the navy even as the army's budget was cut back. This was, as C.I. Hamilton observes, "surely a sign of the seriousness with which the rivalry with England was taken."[117] In turn, Britain responded by enhancing its own naval power (and strengthening its coastal fortifications as a precaution against French invasion). British defense expenditures increased from nine million pounds in 1837 to over twelve million pounds in the wake of the Mehemet Ali Crisis.[118]

The 1844 crisis exacerbated the security rivalry. During the entente, the Peel government had put in abeyance England's military and naval preparations begun after the 1840 crisis. The 1844 crisis reminded Peel and the Duke of Wellington of the connection between military power and diplomacy. In the midst of that crisis, even as Aberdeen pursued conciliation with Paris, Peel urged that England embark on immediate naval and military preparations. As he told Aberdeen, "Let us be prepared for War. . . . They [the French] are much more likely to presume upon our weakness than to take offence at our strength."[119] British fears of French power deepened when, in the midst of the 1844 crisis, Prince de Joinville (one of Louis Philippe's sons) published a pamphlet arguing that steam propulsion afforded France the possibility of overcoming the Royal Navy's traditional naval superiority and successfully invading Britain. The publication

---

115. Bourne, *Foreign Policy of Victorian England*, p. 55.

116. Chamberlain, *Lord Aberdeen*, p. 367.

117. Hamilton, *Anglo-French Naval Rivalry*, p. 36.

118. Partridge, *Military Planning*, p. 15.

119. Quoted in Chamberlain, *Lord Aberdeen*, p. 361.

of de Joinville's pamphlet touched off the first of England's several nineteenth century "invasion panics."[120]

The 1844 crisis put paid to Aberdeen's policy and refocused London's attention on the Anglo-French military balance. In the midst of the 1844 crisis, Wellington wrote to Peel that "the French Government in its present State, and with its Powerful Naval Force is not capable of maintaining its Relations of Amity and Peace. That Govt. can be kept in order only, by our certain and decided Naval superiority not only to their own; but to that supported by that of the United States."[121] In response to the 1844 crisis, once again England's defense expenditures rose: from 10.5 million pounds in 1844 to 13 million pounds in 1846.[122] Alone among the Cabinet, Aberdeen opposed the naval and military rearmament occasioned by the 1844 crisis. He believed there was no real French threat and that London was acting "under the influence of mere panick."[123] Aberdeen feared that rearmament would wreck the entente that he had labored to build over the course of the three preceding years. Wellington's response was succinct: "I think it better to rely upon our own means for our defence than upon the good faith and forbearance of France."[124] On the rearmament issue, the rest of the Cabinet aligned itself firmly with Peel and Wellington, and in fall 1845 Aberdeen tendered his resignation to the Prime Minister.[125] In 1846, Palmerston returned to office as foreign secretary. From then until the July Monarchy's 1848 overthrow, Anglo-French relations continued to be marked by friction. Yet, "even before Palmerston's return, the *entente* had been a broken-backed affair."[126] The 1844 crisis had effectively ended the brief reflowering of the *entente cordiale*. In the end, liberalism could not prevail against the balance of power and the stubborn reality of conflicting great power

---

120. On London's naval and military responses to the 1844 crisis, see Hamilton, *Anglo-French Naval Rivalry*, pp. 20–29.

121. Quoted in Chamberlain, *Lord Aberdeen*, p. 301.

122. Partridge, *Military Planning*, pp. 15–16.

123. Quoted in Chamberlain, *Lord Aberdeen*, p. 371.

124. Quoted in ibid., pp. 301–302.

125. Peel refused Aberdeen's offer to resign. The Cabinet pressed ahead with rearmament while Aberdeen tried to salvage his policy of friendship with France. This cleavage remained unresolved until the Peel government fell from power in 1846, when the Tories split over the issue of repealing the Corn Laws. On the rearmament issue and the split between Aberdeen and his colleagues, see Chamberlain, *Lord Aberdeen*, pp. 371–374.

126. Hamilton, *Anglo-French Naval Rivalry*, p. 19.

interests. It was that reality that doomed the Anglo-French entente of the early 1840s, just as it had doomed a similar entente in the mid-1830s.

Conclusion

This case study disconfirms the democratic peace theory. When liberal great powers have important interests at stake, their policies toward other liberal great powers are driven by realist—that is, balance of power—considerations. When vital national interests are on the line, liberal great powers resort to coercive diplomacy against other liberal states, and are prepared, if necessary, to go to war against them. Moreover, in the cases studied, the fact that the Anglo-French crises of 1831, 1840, and 1844 did not culminate in war is explained by realism, not by the democratic peace theory. In each of these crises, the French backed down in the face of British threats because Paris realized that it would be defeated in war.[127]

No doubt some will object to these conclusions. It could be argued, for example, that I want realism to have its cake and eat it too. That is, it could be argued that realism really is indeterminate and that I therefore would use it to explain both the actual outcome of these crises (peace) or the counterfactual outcome (Anglo-French war). Such an objection would imply that realism is a theory that posits the occurrence of particular wars. But this is not true. Realism is a theory about both war *and* peace. Realists believe only that because of the anarchic, self-help nature of international politics, wars can occur and

---

127. In a June 1996 workshop held at the Center for Science and International Affairs at Harvard University to discuss the drafts of this volume's chapters, Sean Lynn-Jones noted that France's decision to back away from conflict may suggest that liberal states actually are better "realists" than nondemocratic ones. That is, liberal states are more prudent and more capable of responding appropriately to international systemic incentives than are non-liberal states. Hence, he suggested, we should expect that liberal states will be attentive to balance of power factors and will avoid war when the balance of relative capabilities is tilted against them. This argument misses the essential difference between realism and the democratic peace theory. According to the norms and culture variant of the democratic peace theory, liberal states should not need to be good "realists" in their dealings with other liberal states, because coercive diplomacy and threats to use force will not be employed by liberal states against other liberal states. In other words, according to the normative version of the theory, what makes relations between liberal states unique is precisely that balance of power concerns and *realpolitik* are absent from these relationships. For a strong statement of this position, see Russett, *Grasping the Democratic Peace*, p. 42.

sometimes do. At the same time, many realists would argue (as would I) that war, especially great power war, is rare. This is because for the great powers, war itself is a deterrent, albeit an imperfect one. Because of the uncertainties it entails, the decision to go to war is always—as German Chancellor Bethmann-Hollweg put it in 1914—"a leap into the dark." For this reason, realists would expect most great power crises to be resolved short of war. Indeed, because war is such a risky and uncertain business, realists would expect states to be extremely cautious in going to war. In other words, for realists, peace is always overdetermined. This raises the following question: what additional contribution does the democratic peace theory make to our understanding of international political outcomes? The importance of this question is underlined by the crises studied in this chapter. Indeed, what makes these crises so interesting is that balance of power factors acted as a brake to war while domestic factors pushed both France and England toward conflict. In other words, the effect of systemic and domestic factors was precisely the opposite of the expectations generated by democratic peace theory.

Although structural realism presents a devastating challenge to the democratic peace theory, this chapter also demonstrates that the theory can be attacked effectively on its own home court, the level of domestic politics. In these crises, contrary to the democratic peace theory's predictions, domestic political factors acted as an incentive to war rather than as a restraint. This underscores the theory's vulnerability. For example, as John Owen has argued, one of the democratic peace theory's central propositions is that liberal elites will restrain leaders in their state who are bent on war with another liberal state. These crises, however, suggest strongly that Owen is wrong. In 1831 and 1839–40, for example, the British Cabinet included among its members influential Whigs of pronounced francophile and liberal sentiments. Arguing that a hard-line British policy could result in the overthrow of the liberal regime in France, they tried—with a notable lack of success—to restrain Palmerston's forceful diplomacy. That is, contrary to Owen's prediction, liberal elites proved *unable* to restrain the purportedly "illiberal" (but actually impeccably liberal) Palmerston from adopting a bellicose policy.

These cases also undermine another of the democratic peace theory's key assertions, the claim that in democratic states the influence of public opinion is pacific. Contrary to the democratic peace theory's expectations, in each of these crises, rather than restraining decision makers in London and Paris, domestic public opinion powerfully pushed them toward war. For example, the angry response of English public opinion to French mistreatment of Pritchard in 1844 nearly pushed London into war over Tahiti. By the same token, in 1840, all the liberal forces in French politics and society drove Paris toward war. Indeed, these two cases illustrate precisely why nineteenth-century liberals feared the effect of mass democracy on foreign policy. They worried that irrational public impulses would override the prudent foreign policies of the political elites. Democratic peace theory also must confront the ironic impact of domestic politics on French policy during the climax of the Mehemet Ali Crisis in 1840. It was only the intervention of the monarchy—the most illiberal institution of the French government—that prevented the liberal elements of government, politics, and society from plunging France into war.

These cases also cast doubt on the democratic peace theory's claim that liberal states behave in a qualitatively different manner toward other liberal states than they do toward non-liberal states. During the 1830–48 period, Britain and France did cooperate at times. But this cooperation did not evidence the kind of "pluralistic security community" that is purported to exist among liberal states. That is, the policies that London and Paris pursued toward the other had nothing to do with the other's regime type. Cooperation occurred when it served both states' national interests. At best, however, Anglo-French cooperation produced a negative peace—merely the absence of war. But when push came to shove—that is, when crucially important national interests were on the line—Britain and France each treated the other as it would have treated any great power rival, liberal or non-liberal. In both states, regime type remained constant during periods of both cooperation and conflict. What changed—and what triggered crises during this period—was the importance of the interests at stake and the perception of threat to those interests.

Finally, these cases illuminate two further critiques of the democratic peace theory that deserve additional development. First, because the theory predicts that all democratic states will behave identically, it assumes that the role of individual leaders is irrelevant to explaining the foreign policy decisions of liberal democratic states. If anything, however, this case demonstrates that the role of individual leaders is crucial—Thiers and Louis Philippe in France and, especially, Palmerston in England. While this is not a structural realist critique of the democratic peace theory, traditional realists have always focused on the interplay between external constraints and the manner in which statesmen respond to those constraints. Indeed, few neorealists would dispute that in seeking to explain foreign policy outcomes, the state (including statecraft and statesmen) must be brought into the analysis.

Second, this case suggests that—at least in great power crises where perceived vital interests are at stake—the following things happen in liberal states: when war threatens, decision making begins to move toward the unitary rational actor model because, in a serious crisis, the decision makers who are immediately concerned with foreign policy and defense issues will assume the key roles, with others pushed to the margins of decision making. Policy outcomes will conform with realist expectations because, by virtue of their responsibilities, the key national security decision makers will be more sensitive to *realpolitik* considerations and the national interest. In the latter regard, the post-1844 marginalization of Aberdeen is intriguing. When Prime Minister Peel and the Duke of Wellington—the latter the leading figure on national security issues in Britain—concluded that France was a real threat to Britain's interests, they essentially pushed Aberdeen to the sidelines and adopted a rearmament policy over Aberdeen's objections. This suggests that, in a crisis, dovish national policy makers will tend be eclipsed by those with more realist views.

I have no doubt that the democratic peace theory's proponents will find some way to explain away the salience of the conclusions I draw from this case. This is, after all, what they do best. It could, of course, be objected that my criticism on this point is too harsh; that proponents of all theories display an imperviousness to disconfirming evidence and that the democratic peace theory's advocates are no worse than others in this regard. In my judgment, at least, this is not true. Many (although certainly not all) of the theory's proponents seem especially resistant to evidence that undermines the theory. It is not unfair to say that those proponents will *never* be convinced by any qualitative case study that disconfirms the theory, no matter how compelling the evidence. In addition, certain of the theory's leading advocates display a remarkable hostility and intolerance to those who cast doubt on the democratic peace theory's assumptions as well as its causal hypotheses and central predictions. For these individuals, the theory long ago left the realm of falsifiable scientific theory and has become a theology. For true believers, any suggestion that their faith may be flawed is perforce heresy.

If the theory's true believers want to cling to their theory notwithstanding that it has been falsified repeatedly by empirical evidence—that is by testing hypotheses against facts—that is their business.

And, if this conceit were confined behind the ivy-covered walls of academe, no harm would be done. Unfortunately, however, the democratic peace theory has more dangerous ramifications because it appeals to the messianic internationalist strain embedded in U.S. liberalism—which has impelled the United States into one futile, counterproductive crusade after another "to make the world safe for democracy." The democratic peace theory has real world consequences. Therefore, it is incumbent on international relations scholars to persist in subjecting the theory to rigorous scrutiny. While its strongest supporters may continue to cling to it, we must hope that evidence and reasoned argument may yet convince the foreign policy elite, and the American public, that the democratic peace theory is an unsound foundation upon which to base U.S. foreign policy.

Chapter 2

Anglo-U.S. Relations, 1845–1930: Did Shared Liberal Values and Democratic Institutions Keep the Peace?

Stephen R. Rock

The diplomatic history of Great Britain and the United States appears to offer striking evidence for the theory of democratic peace.[1] During the "predemocratic" era of Anglo-U.S. relations—from the Declaration of Independence in 1776 to the passing of Britain's First Reform Act in 1832—the two countries twice went to war. In the "democratic" era—from 1832 to 1997—they have not fought again.[2]

The author thanks other contributors to this volume, as well as Randall Schweller and Sean Lynn-Jones, for their comments on earlier drafts of this chapter.

---

1. This chapter tests the dyadic version of democratic peace theory, which predicts that liberal states will be pacific in their mutual relations. It has only limited relevance for the monadic variant of the theory, which predicts that liberal states will be more pacific than nonliberal ones in their relations with other states, regardless of the others' regime types. The monadic argument that democracies are more peaceful than nondemocracies cannot, of course, be tested in a case study of two democracies. However, it is possible to test the monadic claim that democracies' war and peace decisions are unaffected by the nature of other states' regimes, a claim directly contrary to the dyadic hypothesis. Evidence presented in this chapter that regime type mattered to Britain and the United States undermines the monadic version of democratic peace theory in addition to providing support for the dyadic version.

2. The United States is widely viewed by scholars as having been a liberal democracy from its founding in 1776. Most authors regard Britain as illiberal until 1832. Prior to the passing of the First Reform Act in that year, the franchise was too limited and the electoral system too unrepresentative for Britain to be considered democratic. Moreover, the cabinet, at least in theory, was responsible not to Parliament but to the Crown. See, among others, Michael W. Doyle, "Kant, Liberal Legacies and Foreign Affairs," Part I, *Philosophy & Public Affairs*, Vol. 12, No. 3 (Summer 1983), p. 209; Doyle, "Liberalism and World Politics," *American Political Science Review*, Vol. 80, No. 4 (December 1986), p. 1156; and John M. Owen, "How Liberalism Produces Democratic Peace," *International Security*, Vol. 19, No. 2 (Fall 1994), p. 111. Not everyone accepts 1832 as the dividing line between predemocratic and democratic Britain. Ephraim

Often cited in support of democratic peace theory, the long Anglo-U.S. peace thus merits serious attention.[3] But there are additional reasons why this case provides fertile ground for study. For more than a century and a half, Britain and the United States have been the most consistently liberal and democratic members of the international system. At the same time, the character of the political ideology and institutions in the two countries has not remained constant; on both sides of the Atlantic, there has occurred a broadening and deepening of democracy. Other factors have also varied over the years, including Anglo-U.S. economic connections, social and cultural links, and power relationships between these and other states. In sum, the record of Anglo-U.S. diplomacy furnishes a wealth of data on which to test democratic peace hypotheses and the predictions of competing theories.

Most scholars regard Britain and the United States as exemplars of liberal democracy. In this sense, the Anglo-U.S. peace should be a relatively easy case for democratic peace theory, one that does little to confirm its predictive power. In other respects, however, it is a hard one. Some realist theories of international politics suggest that intense rivalry and possibly war should have occurred between the two countries. For much of their history, Britain and the United States shared a (Canadian) border of several thousand miles. According to Stephen Walt, such geographic proximity is an important source of threat.[4] The hegemonic transition theories of A.F.K. Organski and Robert Gilpin would predict an Anglo-U.S. war around the turn of the century, when the United States surpassed Britain as the world's leading power.[5] And Kenneth Waltz's argument that in a world of

---

Douglass Adams, for example, writes that "the Reform Bill of 1867 changed Great Britain from a government by aristocracy to one by democracy." Ephraim Douglass Adams, *Great Britain and the American Civil War*, Vol. 2 (New York: Russell & Russell, 1924), p. 303.

3. For claims that democratic peace theory explains, or helps to explain, the Anglo-U.S. peace, see Bruce Russett, *Grasping the Democratic Peace: Principles for a Post-Cold War World* (Princeton, N.J.: Princeton University Press, 1993), pp. 5–7; Doyle, "Liberalism and World Politics," p. 1156; and Owen, "How Liberalism Produces Democratic Peace," pp. 110–119.

4. Stephen M. Walt, *The Origins of Alliances* (Ithaca, N.Y.: Cornell University Press, 1987), pp. 23–24.

5. A.F.K. Organski, *World Politics*, 2nd ed. (New York: Alfred A. Knopf, 1968); A.F.K. Organski and Jacek Kugler, *The War Ledger* (Chicago: University of Chicago Press, 1980); and Robert Gilpin, *War and Change in World Politics* (Cambridge: Cambridge University Press, 1981).

three powers the weaker two will align against the strongest predicts the formation of an Anglo-German alliance against the United States at roughly the same time.[6] Since some realist theories predict competition or even war between Britain and the United States, the fact that the two countries remained at peace suggests that powerful nonrealist factors—perhaps those identified by democratic peace theory—may have been at work.

In this chapter, I analyze five episodes in the history of Anglo-U.S. relations: the Oregon Crisis of 1845–46; the Civil War Crises of 1861–63; the Venezuelan Boundary Crisis of 1895–96; the turn-of-the-century "great rapprochement"; and naval arms control during the 1920s. These cases reflect a range of situations in which the impact of joint democracy on Anglo-U.S. diplomacy might be observed. The crises constitute "near misses" in which Britain and the United States came close to war but ultimately resolved their differences without resorting to violence. By contrast, the "great rapprochement" and naval arms control episodes represent "dogs that did not bark"; that is, "crises that never erupted or never brought the participants to the brink of war."[7] During the "great rapprochement," potentially divisive issues were settled more or less amicably as Anglo-U.S. conflict became increasingly unthinkable. Then, in the 1920s, when friendship between Britain and the United States was put to the test by naval competition, the two countries ended their rivalry before a serious rupture appeared imminent.[8]

---

6. Kenneth N. Waltz, *Theory of International Politics* (Reading, Mass.: Addison-Wesley Publishing Co., 1979), p. 202.

7. Bruce Russett, "And Yet It Moves," *International Security*, Vol. 19, No. 4 (Spring 1995), p. 167.

8. Scholars disagree about whether tests of democratic peace theory should include cases of "dogs that did not bark." Like Bruce Russett, Michael Doyle contends that they should: "One of the signs of liberalism at work will be, not the war-crises resolved, but the issues and crises that did not arise." Michael W. Doyle, "Correspondence on the Democratic Peace," *International Security*, Vol. 19, No. 4 (Spring 1995), p. 182. Christopher Layne, on the other hand, argues that researchers should focus exclusively on near misses: "nothing can be learned from mute dogs because it is difficult (if not impossible) to prove why a non-event did not happen." Christopher Layne, "Correspondence on the Democratic Peace," *International Security*, Vol. 19, No. 4 (Spring 1995), p. 176. While Layne may be right about mute dogs, this does not mean that nothing can be learned from dogs who merely growl rather than bark. As this chapter demonstrates, it is possible to learn something about the merits of democratic peace theory by examining cases in which serious issues arise but are resolved before reaching a crisis.

How does democratic peace theory explain the absence of war among liberal states? Scholars often distinguish between normative and institutional variants of the theory, but the most sophisticated formulation holds that liberal norms and democratic institutions "work in tandem: liberal ideas proscribe wars among democracies, and democratic institutions ensure that this proscription is followed."[9] There are several ways in which liberal ideas may prohibit wars among democracies. John Owen argues that liberal states perceive one another as nonthreatening. Because their interests are in harmony, war—which is costly and dangerous—is unnecessary and cannot be justified.[10] Alternatively, Michael Doyle suggests that since government in liberal states is based on popular consent, such states regard each other as legitimate and deserving of respect. For this reason, they will not wage war on one another.[11] Finally, drawing on social identity theory, it may be hypothesized that liberal states regard one another as members of an ideological "in-group" or community within which war is considered taboo.[12] Democratic institutions enforce these principles. If liberal states are not led by liberal leaders, then institutions—especially public opinion—constrain policy makers from acting contrary to liberal norms.[13]

In each of this chapter's sub-cases, I examine decision making in Britain and the United States with two objectives. First, I seek to determine whether attitudes and foreign policy conformed to the basic hypotheses of democratic peace theory listed above. Did the two countries refuse to consider war an option in their mutual relations? Did they regard one another as unthreatening, as legitimate, as members of a shared ideological community? Did pacific public opinion exercise a brake upon the bellicose policies of illiberal leaders? Second, I evaluate the importance of liberal values and democratic institutions compared to other sources of Anglo-U.S. peace.

The literature on international politics, together with histories

---

9. Owen, "How Liberalism Produces Democratic Peace," p. 119.

10. Ibid., pp. 95–96.

11. Doyle, "Kant, Liberal Legacies, and Foreign Affairs," Part I, p. 230.

12. See Margaret G. Hermann and Charles W. Kegley, Jr., "Rethinking Democracy and International Peace: Perspectives from Political Psychology," *International Studies Quarterly*, Vol. 39, No. 4 (December 1995), pp. 511–533, and Miriam Fendius Elman's introductory chapter in this volume for a discussion of this hypothesis.

13. Owen, "How Liberalism Produces Democratic Peace," pp. 99–101, 104.

of Anglo-U.S. diplomacy, suggests two principal alternatives to democratic peace theory as explanations for the absence of war between Britain and the United States. One is realism. Although, as I have noted, the Anglo-U.S. peace is contrary to the predictions of certain realist theories, it is consistent with others.[14] Realism explains the Anglo-U.S. peace as the consequence of a military balance that rendered success on the battlefield unlikely; the need for Britain and the United States to cooperate against third party threats; and the fact that vital national interests were rarely at stake in Anglo-U.S. disputes.[15] A second alternative to democratic peace theory is the cultural hypothesis, which attributes peace between Britain and the United States to the unifying influence of common history, language, and other shared attributes.[16] Throughout the chapter, I pay particular attention to the variables deemed crucial by these competing perspectives.[17]

The central argument of this essay is that democratic peace theory provides at best a partial, qualified explanation for Anglo-U.S. peace. In the early period of Anglo-U.S. relations, the theory's predictions are often not fulfilled: British and U.S. policy makers regarded each other as threatening and considered war to defend their interests;

---

14. Realism is not a monolith. Realist analyses incorporate multiple factors, which sometimes point toward different outcomes. Moreover, realist scholars may disagree about the effects of particular factors. Consider, for example, the debates within the realist school over whether a balance of power or a preponderance of power is more conducive to peace, and whether multipolar or bipolar international systems are more stable. In Anglo-U.S. relations, as in general, the realist paradigm is indeterminate. Some realist arguments predict war; others, peace.

15. At least two scholars have offered realist interpretations of the Anglo-U.S. peace. See Christopher Layne, "Kant or Cant: The Myth of the Democratic Peace," *International Security*, Vol. 19, No. 2 (Fall 1994), pp. 16–28; and William R. Thompson, "Democracy and Peace: Putting the Cart Before the Horse?" *International Organization*, Vol. 50, No. 1 (Winter 1996), pp. 159–164.

16. This theme is prominent in histories of Anglo-U.S. relations. For an argument about the importance of cultural variables in international politics, see Samuel P. Huntington, "The Clash of Civilizations?" *Foreign Affairs*, Vol. 72, No. 3 (Summer 1993), pp. 22–49.

17. In any study that employs a process-tracing approach, an assessment of the impact of various causal factors inevitably remains somewhat subjective. Nevertheless, I believe that one can, through the careful gathering and evaluation of evidence, arrive at reasonable judgments regarding the relative importance of policy makers' motives and the constraints under which they believed they were operating.

public opinion was as or more belligerent than government policy.[18] Conflict was averted in these situations mainly for reasons consistent with realism.

In later episodes, particularly beginning with the "great rapprochement," the expectations of democratic peace theory are more frequently confirmed, largely because of the increasing democratization of Britain and a growing awareness of that country's democratic character in the United States. The heightened importance of liberal values and democratic institutions in Anglo-U.S. relations at the turn of the century and after offers some confirmation of democratic peace theory.

Even more recent Anglo-U.S. relations, however, provide only limited support for the democratic peace hypothesis. The Anglo-U.S. peace was significantly overdetermined; factors besides liberal norms and democratic institutions contributed to the avoidance of war between Britain and the United States. In some situations, these factors—especially strategic imperatives and perceived cultural similarities—were more important than political ideology and institutions. This is one reason Anglo-U.S. relations before *and* after the turn of the century cannot be considered conclusive evidence for the democratic peace argument.

A second reason is that shared liberal values appear to have mattered more to Americans than to the British. To the extent that democratic peace theory explains the Anglo-U.S. peace, it does so primarily by accounting for public opinion and government policy in the United States. This raises the possibility that democratic peace theory is less a theory of international politics than a theory of U.S. foreign policy, an issue that is explored in the conclusion.

The Oregon Crisis

The Oregon Crisis had its origins in the 1790s, when British and U.S. explorers first visited the area and began staking claims. Commercial

---

18. These facts are more consistent with democratic peace theory than it might first appear; in the middle of the nineteenth century, most Americans did not regard Britain as democratic, and Britain was governed by a generally antidemocratic aristocracy. Versions of democratic peace theory that stress the importance of perceptions and of policy makers' values would not predict amicable relations between Britain and the United States during this period.

interests on both sides soon established trading posts.[19] In the War of 1812, Astoria, at the mouth of the Columbia River, was taken by the British, only to be returned to U.S. control six years later. During the three decades that ensued, the U.S. government offered on several occasions to recognize British sovereignty in the area north of the 49th parallel. In December 1843, the British foreign secretary, Lord Aberdeen, privately expressed his willingness to settle on that basis, so that by 1844 only minor issues appeared to remain.[20]

But in 1844 the United States held a presidential election.[21] The Democratic Party was badly split. A southern faction agitated for the annexation of Texas, where slavery would be legal, while a western wing demanded a free-soil Oregon as compensation. The party platform linked the issues in a single plank, which seemed to rule out any compromise: "That our title to the whole of the Territory of Oregon is clear and unquestionable; that no portion of the same ought to be ceded to England or any other power, and that the re-occupation of Oregon and the re-annexation of Texas at the earliest practicable period are great American measures, which this Convention recommends to the cordial support of the Democracy of the Union."[22] James K. Polk, the Democratic nominee, was elected president in November. In his inaugural address, Polk threw down the gauntlet, reasserting the U.S. claim to all of Oregon.

The reaction in Britain was defiant. While proclaiming his desire for a pacific settlement, Sir Robert Peel, the prime minister, told the House of Commons that Great Britain herself had rights in Oregon that were "clear and unquestionable." Aberdeen said the same to the House of Lords. Both he and Peel were supported by the opposition leader, Lord John Russell.[23] Meanwhile, the *Times* informed its readers

---

19. The Oregon Territory encompassed the present states of Oregon, Washington, Idaho, parts of Montana and Wyoming, and a large portion of British Columbia. The best source on the Oregon Crisis is Frederick Merk, *The Oregon Question: Essays in Anglo-American Diplomacy and Politics* (Cambridge, Mass.: Belknap Press, 1967). Also useful is Wilbur Devereaux Jones, *Lord Aberdeen and the Americas* (Athens, Ga.: University of Georgia Press, 1958), chap. 5.

20. Frederick Merk, "British Party Politics and the Oregon Treaty," in Merk, *The Oregon Question*, p. 257.

21. A good account is Norman A. Graebner, "Polk, Politics, and Oregon," *East Tennessee Historical Society's Publications*, Vol. 24 (1952), pp. 11–25.

22. Quoted in Thomas A. Bailey, *A Diplomatic History of the American People*, 7th ed. (New York: Appleton-Century-Crofts, 1964), p. 225.

23. April 4, 1845, Great Britain, *Parliamentary Debates*, 3rd ser., Vol. 79 (1845), cols. 120–124, 178–199.

that "the territory of Oregon will never be wrested from the British Crown, to which it belongs, but by war."[24]

In July 1845, U.S. Secretary of State James Buchanan informed the British minister in Washington, Richard Pakenham, that the United States was willing to divide the Oregon Country at the 49th parallel. Incredibly, Pakenham failed to transmit the offer to London and instead rejected it out of hand.[25] The offer was withdrawn, and Polk declared that "if we do have war it will not be our fault."[26] In his State of the Union message in December, he repeated the U.S. claim to all of Oregon and asked Congress to give Britain notice of intent to end the joint occupation of the territory in one year. At the end of that time, concluded the president, "we shall have reached a period when the national rights in Oregon must either be abandoned or firmly maintained. That they can not be abandoned without a sacrifice of both national honor and interest is too clear to admit of doubt."[27]

For reasons that are explored below, the British cabinet was not eager to fight. Nevertheless, Aberdeen was under considerable pressure to hold firm. Among the Whig opposition was the influential Lord Palmerston, whose tirades against what he regarded as the Conservative Party's weak and cowardly foreign policy had resonated with the British public and put the Tories on the defensive. Indeed, Palmerston had denounced the recent Webster-Ashburton Treaty as "one of the worst and most disgraceful treaties that England ever concluded."[28] Unless Whig support could be obtained, compromise with the United States would leave the cabinet politically vulnerable and might undermine its program of domestic reform. As one historian has noted, "to concede to the United States what previous British governments had declined to yield for over a quarter of a century was a grave political risk; to concede it after the menace of the Polk Inaugural was to expose the government to the charge of having abandoned national pride and honor. This political fear was the chief barrier in 1845-1846 to an Oregon peace."[29]

---

24. *Times* (London), March 28, 1845, quoted in Frederick Merk, "British Government Propaganda and the Oregon Treaty," in Merk, *The Oregon Question*, p. 302.

25. Merk, "British Government Propaganda," pp. 300–301.

26. Quoted in Bailey, *Diplomatic History*, p. 228.

27. Quoted in Frederick Merk, "Presidential Fevers," in Merk, *The Oregon Question*, p. 368.

28. Quoted in Merk, "British Party Politics," pp. 257–258. The Webster-Ashburton Treaty had settled a dispute between Britain and the United States over the boundary between Canada and Maine.

29. Merk, "British Government Propaganda," p. 284.

Happily, the barrier was removed, partly as a result of a propaganda campaign conducted by the British government to pave the way for compromise, and partly due to a change in political circumstances.[30] Peel's cabinet collapsed during the Corn Law crisis. Russell attempted to form a new government with Palmerston as foreign secretary, but members of his own party regarded Palmerston as too reckless, and refused to serve with him. Ultimately, Peel was asked to put together a new cabinet. With Palmerston's influence diminished, a conciliatory policy toward the United States became easier. In early February, Russell informed Aberdeen that the Whigs would not oppose a compromise over Oregon.[31]

When the Polk administration notified the British government of its intent to terminate the joint occupation of the Oregon Country, London responded by again offering to divide the territory at the 49th parallel. Although Polk expressed a desire to reject the offer, he allowed the members of his cabinet to persuade him to submit the proposed treaty to the Senate for advice. Thus the president protected himself from appearing to betray his all-Oregon supporters.[32] On June 12, the Senate advised Polk to accept the treaty as written. Polk signed the treaty on June 15, 1846, and it was ratified three days later.

IMPLICATIONS FOR DEMOCRATIC PEACE THEORY

The Oregon Crisis presents difficulties for democratic peace theory. The theory holds that in relations among liberal states, the effects of domestic politics will be benign. Yet this crisis was initiated by the United States largely because of domestic politics. In Britain, meanwhile, democratic institutions—the Whig opposition in Parliament and public opinion—constituted obstacles to the cabinet's preferred policy of compromise.

Democratic peace theory is of little value in explaining the pacific resolution of the Oregon Crisis. It is true that public opinion in the United States had shifted since Polk's inauguration and was by early 1846 generally in favor of some accommodation with Britain. According to Norman Graebner, "Polk was submerged in a plethora of argumentation for compromise from the press, personal correspondents, and from members of both parties in Congress."[33] Popular

30. See Merk, "British Government Propaganda."
31. Merk, "British Party Politics," pp. 270–276.
32. Merk, "Presidential Fevers," pp. 388–391.
33. Graebner, "Polk, Politics, and Oregon," p. 14.

opposition to war almost certainly played some role in the president's decision to settle the dispute. After all, Polk's initial bellicose stance had also been aimed at securing domestic political advantage.

Contrary to what democratic peace theory would lead one to expect, however, the change in public sentiment was unrelated to Britain's regime type and ideology. Rather, it was mainly the result of a growing recognition that the United States would gain little by insisting on the 54° 40' line. Leading journals of opinion declared that Oregon's best harbors were south of the 49th parallel and that the land north of that line was ill-suited for agriculture. Discounting the value of the disputed territory, the *North American Review* compared Oregon to Siberia.[34]

Other considerations—also unrelated to Britain's regime type and ideology—encouraged Polk to end the controversy. The crisis threatened to split the Democratic Party, as the hard-line western wing increasingly alienated the eastern and southern factions, which were more willing to negotiate with Britain.[35] In addition, the United States had in May 1846 become involved in a war with Mexico. Polk, a Southerner, regarded Texas as more important than Oregon. From a strategic standpoint, embroilment with Britain at this time was folly, particularly when London had indicated a willingness to settle on terms essentially the same as those previously proposed by Polk's administration.[36] Thus, when the British government offered to compromise, saving the president from the embarrassment of having to make the diplomatic approach himself, he accepted. As John Owen notes, some Americans, including members of Congress, invoked shared liberal values to justify peace with Britain. However, a large number of Americans did not perceive Britain as democratic. Rather, they conceived of the dispute over Oregon as a struggle between U.S. democracy and British despotism.[37] While this is consistent with

34. Ibid.
35. Norman A. Graebner, "Politics and the Oregon Compromise," *Pacific Northwest Quarterly*, Vol. 52 (January 1961), pp. 7–14; and Merk, "Presidential Fevers," p. 391.
36. H.C. Allen regards the war with Mexico as "the decisive fact leading to settlement" of the Oregon question. H.C. Allen, *Great Britain and the United States: A History of Anglo-American Relations (1783–1952)* (London: Odhams Press, 1954), p. 409.
37. John M. Owen, "Liberal Peace, Liberal War: Ideology, Institutions and Democratic Foreign Policy," pp. 171–175. This manuscript, a revision of Owen's doctoral thesis, "Testing the Democratic Peace: American Diplomatic Crises, 1794–1917" (Ph.D. dissertation, Harvard University, 1993), is scheduled for publication by Cornell University Press.

democratic peace theory, which predicts that liberals will fear and distrust states they regard as illiberal, it suggests that liberal norms and democratic institutions are not a satisfactory explanation for the pacific resolution of the Oregon Crisis. In the end, there is little evidence that Polk's decision to sign the treaty, or the Senate's decision to ratify it, was based on a desire to avoid war for liberal reasons.

The same is true of British policy in the crisis. Aberdeen wished to settle the issue peacefully because he "saw nothing in [Oregon] worth the risks of war. He conceived of its soil as a pine swamp; he knew that the great river flowing at its base . . . was for the most part unnavigable."[38] From the beginning, therefore, the foreign secretary had been eager to compromise. In proposing that the issue be submitted to arbitration, a suggestion the Polk administration rejected, Pakenham had gone so far as to tell Buchanan that "the British Government would be glad to get clear of the question on almost any terms, that they did not care if the arbitrator should award the whole territory to us (the United States)."[39]

Some British liberals believed that the United States' democratic institutions would eventually push it in a less bellicose direction. For this reason, and because they detested the notion of war with another liberal state, they argued for a softer policy on the part of London.[40] Although the attitude and preferred foreign policy of these liberals are consistent with democratic peace theory, there is scant evidence that pressure from them constrained Aberdeen and Peel. Indeed, to the extent that public opinion mattered to the British cabinet, it was regarded mainly as an obstacle to accommodation. Otherwise, no propaganda campaign in favor of compromise would have been necessary.

The public relations effort orchestrated by the Foreign Office and carried out in the press emphasized the factors that the cabinet considered crucial: the low value of Oregon and the high cost of upholding British interests there. Although the *Times* cited "identity of origin, of language, and laws—the common pursuit of similar objects, the common prevalence of similar sentiments, and the common deference to the same principles of moral action" in urging a pacific resolution of the dispute, these were not prominent themes.[41]

---

38. Quoted in Merk, "British Government Propaganda," p. 284.

39. Quoted in Allen, *Great Britain and the United States*, p. 413.

40. Owen, "Liberal Peace, Liberal War," pp. 167–168, 170–171, 175–176.

41. *Times* (London), January 3, 1846, quoted in Merk, "British Government Propaganda," p. 302.

More typical was an officially inspired article in the *Examiner*, which said of Oregon: "The only use of it to England is as a hunting ground. . . . The soil is generally mountainous, rocky, and uncultivable." The writer concluded, "The interruption of confidence for a single week costs more than the whole country is worth. A mere armament, though followed by accommodation, would cost more than a thousand times its value."[42] In sum, the British cabinet favored accommodation with the United States for realist reasons. The main barrier to this policy was opposition from the Whigs in Parliament. Once Palmerston had been neutralized and the public persuaded to accept a compromise, the path to a settlement was open.

The Civil War Crises

Less than two decades after the Oregon Crisis, the United States was consumed by civil war. Issues arising from its struggle with the Confederacy brought the Union to the brink of conflict with Great Britain on several occasions.[43]

THE TRENT AFFAIR

The most dangerous episode in Anglo-U.S. relations during the Civil War period occurred in late 1861. On November 8, the USS *San Jacinto*, under the command of Captain Charles D. Wilkes, intercepted a British steamer, the *Trent*. Aboard the *Trent* were James Mason and John Slidell, two Southern envoys on their way to England, where they hoped to persuade the British government to recognize the independence of the Confederate States. Instead, they were taken into Union custody and imprisoned.

---

42. *Examiner* (London), April 26, 1845, quoted in Merk, "British Government Propaganda," pp. 290–291.

43. Major works on Anglo-U.S. relations of the Civil War period include Howard Jones, *Union in Peril: The Crisis over British Intervention in the Civil War* (Chapel Hill: University of North Carolina Press, 1992); Adams, *Great Britain and the American Civil War*; Brian Jenkins, *Britain and the War for the Union*, 2 vols. (Montreal: McGill-Queen's University Press, 1974, 1980); Gordon H. Warren, *Fountain of Discontent: The Trent Affair and Freedom of the Seas* (Boston: Northeastern University Press, 1981); Norman B. Ferris, *The Trent Affair: A Diplomatic Crisis* (Knoxville: University of Tennessee Press, 1977); and Ferris, *Desperate Diplomacy: William H. Seward's Foreign Policy, 1861* (Knoxville: University of Tennessee Press, 1976). Works that examine Anglo-U.S. relations of the Civil War period with specific reference to democratic peace theory include Layne, "Kant or Cant," pp. 16–22; and Owen, "How Liberalism Produces Democratic Peace," pp. 110–114.

When news of these events reached London, the British government reacted vigorously. Palmerston, now prime minister, irate over the apparent violation of Britain's neutral rights, declared to his colleagues: "I don't know whether you are going to stand this, but I'll be damned if I do!"[44] At the cabinet's direction, the foreign secretary, Lord Russell, sent an ultimatum to the Union government via Lord Lyons, the British minister in Washington. The note demanded the release of the captives and a formal apology for the incident. If the demands were not met within a week, Lyons was instructed to pack his bags and return to London, severing diplomatic relations with the United States.[45]

Meanwhile, the cabinet prepared to fight. A war committee was formed. Shipments of saltpeter, arms, and ammunition to the United States were cut off. Because of Canada's extreme vulnerability, measures were taken to reinforce its defenses. More than 10,000 additional troops were sent to British North America, as well as fifteen warships. The Royal Navy drew up plans for operations against the Atlantic coast of the United States.[46]

British leaders hoped that military preparations would compel Washington to accede to their demands. The undersecretary of state for foreign affairs wrote: "Our only chance of peace is to be found in working on the fears of the Government and people of the United States."[47] Lyons had already informed London that "firmness appears to have a much more quieting effect than any amount of conciliation or concession."[48] The cabinet was far from certain, however, that diplomacy would succeed. Palmerston and his colleagues believed that the chances of avoiding war were no better than fifty-fifty.[49] The U.S. Secretary of State, William Seward, had a reputation for anglophobia, and the wild enthusiasm with which the U.S. public had greeted the seizure of Mason and Slidell had been faithfully

---

44. Jones, *Union in Peril*, p. 85.

45. Ferris, *Trent Affair*, pp. 51–53.

46. British preparations for war are detailed in Kenneth Bourne, "British Preparations for War with the North, 1861–1862," *English Historical Review*, Vol. 76, No. 301 (October 1961), pp. 600–632; Bourne, *Britain and the Balance of Power in North America, 1815–1908* (Berkeley and Los Angeles: University of California Press, 1967), chap. 7; and Warren, *Fountain of Discontent*, chap. 6.

47. Quoted in Bourne, *Britain and the Balance of Power*, p. 219.

48. Quoted in Ferris, *Desperate Diplomacy*, p. 92.

49. Bourne, *Britain and the Balance of Power*, p. 219.

reported by Lyons. To many British observers it seemed that the United States was spoiling for a fight.[50]

The cabinet was not bluffing. British policy makers were prepared to go to war, in part because they were convinced that Britain would prevail. The secretary of state for war, George Cornewall Lewis, said of the Americans: "we shall soon *iron the smile* out of their face."[51] Palmerston told Queen Victoria that Britain was in a position "to inflict a severe blow upon and to read a lesson to the United States which will not soon be forgotten."[52] Although they were confident as to the outcome of an Anglo-U.S. war, British leaders knew that victory would not be easy or inexpensive. Despite reinforcement of its defenses, Canada would be overrun and occupied by U.S. forces, and would be regained only after successful naval operations compelled the United States to retreat.[53]

British policy makers were willing to accept the humiliation of losing Canada, albeit temporarily, and the other costs associated with waging war on the United States, because they believed that Britain's reputation for defending its interests was at stake. If they did not respond decisively to this provocation, the United States would only become more aggressive. Palmerston had long believed that "with such cunning fellows as these Yankees it never answers to give way, because they always keep pushing on their encroachments as far as they are permitted to do so; and what we dignify by the names of moderation and conciliation, they naturally enough call fear."[54] Moreover, other adversaries might be emboldened to issue their own challenges. Britain's performance in the recently concluded Crimean War had already damaged its image. In the long run, the costs of inaction might be higher than the costs of action. Lord Clarendon wrote, "What a figure . . . we shall cut in the eyes of the world, if we lamely submit to this outrage when all mankind will know that we should unhesitatingly have poured our indignation and our broadsides into any weak nation . . . and what an additional proof it will be of the universal . . . belief that we have two sets of weights and measures to be used according to the power or weakness of our adversary. I have a

---

50. Ferris, *Trent Affair*, pp. 85–90; and Warren, *Fountain of Discontent*, pp. 52–66, 82.

51. Quoted in Bourne, *Britain and the Balance of Power*, p. 246.

52. Quoted in ibid., pp. 245–246.

53. Ibid., pp. 246–247.

54. Quoted in Ferris, *Desperate Diplomacy*, p. 15.

horror of war and of all wars one with the U.S. because none would be so prejudicial to our interests, but peace like other good things may be bought too dearly and it can never be worth the price of national honor."[55]

In adopting its unyielding position, the British government enjoyed the virtually complete support of the British population. Upon hearing the news of the *Trent's* seizure, the press and public exploded with anger. Seward was informed by an American in London that "there never was within memory such a burst of feeling. . . . The people are frantic with rage, and were the country polled, I fear 999 men out of a thousand would declare for immediate war."[56] A week later, the U.S. consul in London reported that there had been "no abatement to the war spirit among the people. Nearly the whole nation appears to be aroused in opposition to the North, & to be in sympathy with the South."[57] According to another observer, if the capture of the Confederate emissaries were "avowed and maintained, it means war. . . . The indignation is wild and permeates all classes."[58] Had it been disposed to take a more conciliatory stance, the cabinet might have found it impossible to do so. Charles Francis Adams, the U.S. representative to the Court of St. James, wrote that although British leaders were "believed not to be desirous of pressing matters to a violent issue," they were "powerless" to resist the war fever that had gripped the country.[59]

In the United States, public opinion was no less belligerent. Americans had long resented the right of search claimed by Britain and exercised against U.S. shipping; here at last was the chance to give Britain "a dose of its own medicine."[60] Queen Victoria's neutrality proclamation of May 1861, which granted the Confederacy belligerent status and implicitly recognized its independence, had also hardened Northern attitudes toward Britain.[61] Finally, the war against the South had been going badly for the Union. Northern forces had recently been routed at the First Battle of Bull Run. The

---

55. Bourne, *Britain and the Balance of Power*, p. 247.

56. Quoted in Jones, *Union in Peril*, pp. 83–84.

57. Quoted in Ferris, *Trent Affair*, pp. 66–67.

58. Quoted in ibid., p. 67.

59. Quoted in ibid., p. 67.

60. Adams, *Great Britain and the American Civil War*, Vol. 1, p. 219.

61. Warren, *Fountain of Discontent*, pp. 70–76.

capture of the Confederate envoys provided hope to a population desperate for some sign of success. Not surprisingly, the U.S. public erupted in a "frenzy of delight."[62] Charles Francis Adams, Jr., the son of the U.S. minister, later wrote that he could "not remember . . . any occurrence in which the American people were so completely swept off their feet, for the moment losing possession of their senses, as during the weeks which immediately followed the seizure of Mason and Slidell."[63] Although a more sober assessment of the situation subsequently produced some moderation in the press, "the universal sentiment among Americans seemed to be a determination never to relinquish the rebel emissaries."[64]

The Lincoln administration thus confronted a difficult decision. Down one path waited war; down the other humiliation abroad and public censure at home. Attorney General Edward Bates commented subsequently on the "great reluctance on the part of some of the members of the cabinet—and even the President himself" to accede to British demands for fear of "the displeasure of our own people—lest they should accuse us of timidly truckling to the power of England."[65] For two days in late December, Lincoln and his advisers discussed the issue. After considering and rejecting arbitration as a means for resolving the dispute, the cabinet chose to back down. Seward drafted a note, which was presented to Lyons on the 27th. The note did not apologize for the incident, but it promised that the prisoners would be released, asserted that Captain Wilkes had acted on his own initiative without the authority of the U.S. government, acknowledged that he had committed violations of international law, and pledged that reparations would be paid.[66] Lyons informed London that he believed Britain's demands had been "substantially complied with," a conclusion with which the British government agreed.[67]

Christopher Layne has written that "the United States bowed to London because, already fully occupied militarily trying to subdue the Confederacy, the North could not also afford a simultaneous war with England, which effectively would have brought Britain into the

---

62. Adams, *Great Britain and the American Civil War*, Vol. 1, p. 221.

63. Quoted in ibid., p. 218.

64. Ferris, *Trent Affair*, p. 112.

65. Quoted in ibid., p. 185.

66. Ibid., pp. 177–188; and Warren, *Fountain of Discontent*, pp. 181–185.

67. Quoted in Adams, *Great Britain and the American Civil War*, Vol. 1, p. 232.

War Between the States on the South's side."[68] The Lincoln administration had hoped that the British government would be constrained
from declaring war on the United States by fears that France would
seek to take advantage of Britain's embroilment with the Union. But
France had declared itself in support of London's demands.[69] Nor
was there any prospect that public opinion would exercise a moderating effect on British policy. Virtually all of Britain seemed disposed
toward war. Those sympathetic to the North, most notably the
Radical leaders Richard Cobden and John Bright, were in a small
minority. They warned their U.S. friends that unless the United States
backed down, war was certain.[70]

The United States, Bates bluntly told the cabinet in late December,
"cannot afford such a war." He argued, "in such a crisis, with such a
civil war upon our hands, we cannot hope for success in a . . . war
with England, backed by the assent and countenance of France. We
must evade it—with as little damage to our own honor and pride as
possible."[71] Seward agreed that it was foolish "to be diverted from
the cares of the Union into controversies with other powers, even if
just causes for them could be found."[72] The remainder of the cabinet,
including the president, ultimately concurred.

IMPLICATIONS FOR DEMOCRATIC PEACE THEORY. As Layne and
Owen have noted, the resolution of the *Trent* Crisis can be explained
without reference to the theory of democratic peace. The Lincoln
administration retreated in the face of British pressure for realist reasons. Engaged in a life-and-death struggle with the Confederacy, the
Union could not afford a war with Britain. Democratic institutions
did not constrain the government. If anything, the U.S. public and
Congress were more bellicose than the cabinet. There is no evidence
that liberal affinity for or trust in Britain influenced Lincoln and his
advisers' decision to back down. Indeed, in the early 1860s, few
Americans felt such an affinity. Traditional images of Britain as a
monarchic, feudal, and aristocratic state still prevailed. Nor were
these images entirely inaccurate. Although the Reform Act of 1832
had extended the franchise, only one in about twenty-four Britons

---

68. Layne, "Kant or Cant," p. 20.
69. Warren, *Fountain of Discontent,* p. 182.
70. Layne, "Kant or Cant," pp. 20–21.
71. Quoted in Ferris, *Trent Affair,* p. 182.
72. Quoted in ibid., p. 183.

possessed the right to vote, and political power remained largely in the hands of a conservative aristocracy.

British policy in the *Trent* Crisis also reflects the primacy of realist motives. Bruce Russett has argued that "to use or threaten to use force is not usually normatively acceptable behavior in disputes between democracies."[73] In this case, however, liberal Britain was not reluctant to threaten and prepare for war against the United States. Rather, the cabinet adopted a compellent strategy because of the conviction that vital British interests were at stake. There is little evidence that democratic institutions constrained the cabinet. As in the United States, public opinion was more belligerent than peace-minded.

Although most Americans in the early 1860s did not regard Britain as a democracy, Britons of all classes and political stripes recognized that the United States was democratic. However, this did not necessarily translate into sympathy for the Union. Indeed, among the aristocracy it had precisely the opposite effect. The Reform Act of 1832 had left the vast majority of Britons without the franchise. Thirty years later, the ruling classes were under pressure to accept increasing economic and political democratization. The U.S. social and political system, with its much greater equality, was a model that the British aristocracy was not eager to emulate. As Herbert Tingsten has noted, "The very word 'democracy' was hateful to the great majority of both Whigs and Tories."[74] British aristocrats "hungered for the demise of democracy in North America," hoping that dissolution of the Union would undermine the democratic movement in their own country.[75]

Because they distrusted the masses, which they viewed as ignorant and swayed by emotion rather than reason, British aristocrats also distrusted the U.S. system, which they believed was rife with corruption and the pernicious influence of party politics. In October 1861, Lyons warned that the United States was not, in contrast to Britain, "a country in which a few Statesmen decided what was for the interest of the community, and guided public opinion by their superior wisdom, talents and authority. Here the government," he said, "was in the hands of what are called in America 'politicians,' men in general of second rate station and ability, who aim at little more than at divining and pandering to the feeling of the mob of voters." Would public

---

73. Russett, *Grasping the Democratic Peace*, p. 42.

74. Herbert Tingsten, *Victoria and the Victorians*, trans. and adapted by David Grey and Eva Leckström Grey (London: George Allen & Unwin, 1972), p. 175.

75. Ferris, *Desperate Diplomacy*, p. 198.

opposition constrain the Lincoln administration from leading the country into war? Hardly. Lyons concluded, "The party in power would be more likely to be overthrown by the disasters which must immediately follow a war with Europe, than to be drawn from their posts by public opinion, in time to prevent their imprudently engaging in one."[76]

British liberals, led by Cobden and Bright, viewed the United States more favorably.[77] In 1861, however, it was not clear to what extent liberal sympathies should lie with the Union. The North was not fighting for liberal reasons. Lincoln had said in his inaugural address that his purpose was to preserve the Union, not to end slavery.[78] The Confederacy likewise argued that slavery was not the issue. As one historian has noted, "once both American antagonists had denied slavery's role in bringing on the war, the issue became clear to the British: the South wanted independence, whereas the North wanted empire."[79] For many nineteenth-century liberals, liberty meant freedom from such empire, the protection of minority "rights against the encroachments of the central government."[80] The year following the Confederate surrender, Lord Acton wrote to Robert E. Lee, "I saw in State Rights the only availing check on the absolutism of the sovereign will, and secession filled me with hope, not as the destruction but as the redemption of Democracy."[81] H.C. Allen exaggerated when he claimed that those disposed to the South "could come almost as well from the liberal as from the reactionary camps."[82] Nevertheless, he had a point: with the South's cause defined as a struggle for freedom, some in Britain saw the Confederacy, rather than the Union, as the embodiment of liberal ideals.

Liberal sympathy for the Union was also weakened by the North's protectionist economic policy, reflected first in the Morrill tariff and

---

76. Quoted in ibid., p. 199.

77. Warren, *Fountain of Discontent*, pp. 148–151.

78. In his address, Lincoln declared, "I have no purpose, directly or indirectly to interfere with the institution of slavery in the States where it exists. I believe I have no lawful right to do so, and I have no inclination to do so." Quoted in Adams, *Great Britain and the American Civil War*, Vol. 1, p. 50.

79. Jones, *Union in Peril*, p. 96.

80. Allen, *Great Britain and the United States*, p. 495.

81. Quoted in ibid., p. 495.

82. Ibid., p. 496.

then in the blockade of Southern ports.[83] Many liberals regarded
restrictions on commerce as a denial of freedom not much worse than
slavery.[84] Their moral ambivalence was captured in the opening stan-
za of "Ode to the North and South," published by *Punch* shortly
before the outbreak of the war:

> O Jonathan and Jefferson,
> Come listen to my song;
> I can't decide, my word upon,
> Which of you is most wrong.
> I do declare I am afraid
> To say which worse behaves;
> The North, imposing bonds on Trade,
> Or South, that Man enslaves.[85]

Toward the end of the *Trent* Affair, "a small but important movement" in favor of arbitration appeared. Spearheaded by Cobden and
Bright, it drew support from nonconformist churches and other liberal segments of the British population. The cabinet was concerned
that "if the antiwar movement continued to attract advocates," it
would be necessary for the government to explain publicly the legal
basis of its demand for the release of Mason and Slidell, as well as the
reasons for its refusal to arbitrate the dispute.[86] But the movement
never became this large. Because of their reservations about the
Union's liberal credentials, British liberals did not agitate as actively
as they might have against London's unyielding policy. While this
lack of vigor is consistent with democratic peace theory, which predicts that liberals will oppose war only against other states they consider liberal, it also means that British liberals exerted little or no
moderating influence on the cabinet during the crisis.

---

83. The Morrill tariff was enacted in early 1861, after Southern senators and representatives, who were generally opposed to protection, had walked out of
Congress. It was not highly protectionist; U.S. duties had been at their lowest level
since the War of 1812, and the Morrill tariff raised them by less than 10 percent.
Nevertheless, Britain, which exported large quantities of manufactured goods to
the United States and itself adhered to a policy of free trade, was distressed.

84. Ferris, *Desperate Diplomacy*, p. 182.

85. *Punch*, May 25, 1861, p. 1.

86. Warren, *Fountain of Discontent*, pp. 148–153.

BRITISH PROPOSALS FOR INTERVENTION

While the *Trent* Crisis was the most dangerous potential cause of an Anglo-U.S. war during the Civil War years, another threat to peace was the prospect that British policy makers would intervene in the conflict by recognizing the independence of the Confederacy and attempting to impose a mediated settlement. If they did so, war was virtually certain, for the Union, in an effort to preserve itself, would resist all such efforts. As Seward warned, "British recognition [of the South] would be British intervention to create within our own territory a hostile state by overthrowing this Republic itself. (When this act of intervention is distinctly performed, we from that hour, shall cease to be friends and become once more, as we have twice before been forced to be, enemies of Great Britain.)"[87]

British leaders were inclined to intervene for a variety of reasons. Strategically, a divided America would presumably be less a danger to British interests than a united one. The Russian ambassador to London reported in 1861 that "the English Government, at the bottom of its heart, desires the separation of North America into two republics, which will watch each other jealously and counterbalance one the other. Then England, on terms of peace and commerce with both, would have nothing to fear from either; for she would dominate them, restraining them by their rival ambitions."[88]

A more important impetus for intervention was the economic damage suffered by Britain as a result of Union policy. One irritant was the Morrill tariff, which had been enacted prior to the outbreak of war. Cobden and Bright, who were otherwise sympathetic to the North, deplored the tariff. The former termed it evidence of "ignorance and stupid suicidal selfishness," while the latter declared that "a more stupid and unpatriotic act was never passed." It had, he claimed, "all but destroyed" trade between two countries in certain goods.[89] The Union blockade of Southern ports, which constricted

---

87. Quoted in Ferris, *Desperate Diplomacy,* pp. 22–23.

88. Quoted in Adams, *Great Britain and the American Civil War,* Vol. 1, pp. 50–51. It could be argued that Britain's failure to support the South is inconsistent with realism, since a divided North America would have produced important strategic benefits. As I show below, however, other realist variables—cost-benefit calculations and especially the practicality of intervention—militated against such action. Thus, while the most important factors motivating British policy makers were realist considerations, not political ideology and regime type, realism was indeterminate with respect to outcome; that is, British support of either South or North could be predicted on the basis of realist principles.

89. Quoted in Ferris, *Desperate Diplomacy,* p. 181.

the supply of cotton that fed Britain's textile industry, was a more serious issue. When hostilities broke out, Britain's textile manufacturers had large surplus stocks of cotton on hand. These had been largely depleted by the middle of 1862. Prices were rising, and mills were shutting down. Fifty percent of Britain's industrial workers had been idled.[90] In Lancashire, Cheshire, and Derbyshire, where the bulk of textile manufacturing was located, conditions were especially dire. By year's end, nearly 300,000 persons were receiving poor relief. Twelve months later, 40 percent of the workers who had been employed in the mills at the beginning of the war were still out of work.[91] As some in Britain realized, the Union's closing of Southern ports was not entirely responsible for this suffering. In March 1862, the Confederate government had authorized the burning of the cotton crop in order to create a shortage and thereby put pressure on Britain.[92] Still, the cotton famine and its attendant misery were widely attributed to the Northern blockade.[93]

Perhaps the single greatest incentive for Britain to intervene in the U.S. Civil War was the humanitarian impulse. Britons were universally appalled by the carnage that was occurring on the battlefields of North America. They assumed almost without exception, moreover, that a division of the United States was inevitable, that the North could never reestablish the Union by force of arms. Thus, "the question Englishmen always put to themselves was whether they could help to end now on some such basis a war which in due course was bound to end in that fashion anyway."[94]

Within the British cabinet, there was nearly unanimous support for intervention as a matter of principle. "The whole argument," as Allen notes, "was merely as to whether the time was ripe, and the conditions determining this were in the last resort, military." The cabinet's decision would be "made on the battlefields in America."[95] Britain would intervene only if assured that there would be no war with the North. But as long as Lincoln's government remained convinced that the Union could be restored, any such action was certain to be regarded as

90. Jones, *Union in Peril*, p. 130.

91. Joseph Park, "The English Workingmen and the American Civil War," *Political Science Quarterly*, Vol. 39, No. 3 (September 1924), pp. 432–433.

92. Jones, *Union in Peril*, pp. 130–131.

93. Park, "English Workingmen," p. 432.

94. Allen, *Great Britain and the United States*, p. 479.

95. Ibid., p. 479.

a *casus belli*. The British cabinet determined therefore to wait until the North had realized "that subjugation of the South was impossible."[96] For the prime minister, this was the decisive consideration. Although disposed in August and September 1862 to favor intervention, in October Palmerston wrote to Russell, the foreign secretary, that he was "inclined to change the opinion on which I wrote to you when the Confederates seemed to be carrying all before them, and I am very much come back to our original view of the matter, that we must continue merely to be lookers-on till the war shall have taken a more decided turn."[97]

The last serious cabinet discussion on the subject of intervention was held in November 1862. Russell proposed British cooperation in a French scheme for mediation. In response, the war secretary, Lewis, circulated a lengthy memorandum, written with his nephew, William Harcourt. Lewis agreed with Russell that there existed economic and humanitarian reasons for intervening, but he raised grave legal and practical objections. Russell made no effort to answer them.[98] Palmerston offered only lukewarm support for the proposal; the remainder of the cabinet "proceeded to pick it to pieces."[99]

IMPLICATIONS FOR DEMOCRATIC PEACE THEORY. The British cabinet's decision not to intervene in the U.S. Civil War is explained largely by factors beyond the scope of democratic peace theory. As a matter of principle, most cabinet members favored intervention; they refrained from it only because of doubts regarding its feasibility.

That the cabinet's decision had nothing to do with liberal affinity for the United States is not surprising considering that Britain's ruling classes had scant sympathy for the Union on political and ideological grounds. For them, "democracy" was a dirty word. As Adams reported to Seward in August 1862, "the predominating passion here is the desire for the ultimate subdivision of America into many separate States which will neutralize each other. This is most visible among the conservative class of the Aristocracy who dread the growth of liberal opinions and who habitually regard America as the nursery of them."[100]

---

96. Jones, *Union in Peril*, p. 220.

97. Palmerston to Russell, October 22, 1862, in G.P. Gooch, ed., *The Later Correspondence of Lord John Russell, 1840–1878*, Vol. 2 (London: Longmans, Green & Co., 1925), p. 328.

98. Jones, *Union in Peril*, pp. 210–219.

99. Adams, *Great Britain and the American Civil War*, Vol. 2, p. 65.

100. Quoted in ibid., p. 285.

Attitudes were quite different among those outside of the establishment. Nonconformists, Radicals, and the working classes generally supported the North because they regarded it as a symbol of what they hoped to attain.[101] Economically, the North stood for free labor and the rights of the worker. But "freedom meant more than economic betterment; it also meant political privilege." English workers "were interested in the North because it represented democracy. They saw that democracy was on trial, and in taking sides with the North they were taking sides with themselves in their struggle for the reformation of political institutions."[102]

Led by Cobden and Bright, English liberals mounted a campaign against intervention. The movement gained strength after the Union government finally made it clear that the North was fighting against slavery. Lincoln appears to have recognized the diplomatic value of giving the war a moral purpose. He told a group of abolitionists in September 1862 that "no other step would be so potent to prevent foreign intervention."[103] In fact, the preliminary emancipation proclamation later that month had the short-term effect of encouraging intervention because it increased British fears of a bloody slave rebellion. But no servile war materialized, and after January 1863, when the Emancipation Proclamation was issued, liberal British opinion swung solidly behind the North. In March, more than 3,000 representatives of the Trades' Unions of London unanimously adopted a statement assuring Lincoln and the North "that our earnest and heartfelt sympathies are with you in the arduous struggle you are maintaining in the cause of human freedom."[104] During the spring of 1863, more than fifty public meetings were held in which "strong resolutions were passed enthusiastically endorsing the issue of the emancipation proclamation and pledging sympathy to the cause of the North."[105]

It is difficult to assess how much effect pro-Union sentiment among liberal segments of the British population had on the policy of

---

101. On the attitudes of British workers, not all of whom supported the Union, see Philip S. Foner, *British Labor and the American Civil War* (New York: Holmes & Meier, 1981).

102. Park, "English Workingmen," pp. 441–442.

103. Quoted in Jones, *Union in Peril*, p. 172.

104. John Bright, *Speeches of John Bright, M.P. on the American Question, with an introduction by Frank Moore* (Boston: Little, Brown & Co., 1865; New York: Kraus Reprint, 1970), pp. 190–193.

105. Adams, *Great Britain and the American Civil War*, Vol. 2, p. 107.

the British government. Palmerston was aware that liberal views could not be entirely ignored; he told the Russian ambassador in 1861 that there were "two Powers in this Country, the government & public opinion, & that both must concur for any great & important steps."[106] In October 1862, the prime minister informed Russell that slavery was Britain's "great difficulty" in any proposed mediation. Could the cabinet "without offence to many people here recommend to the North to sanction Slavery and to undertake to give back Runaways, and yet would not the South insist upon some such Conditions especially after Lincoln's Emancipation Decree?"[107] But public opinion does not appear at this point to have been the "main obstacle" to intervention for the prime minister or other members of the cabinet.[108] Rather, the evidence suggests that the Union's expected response and the practical difficulties raised by Lewis in his memorandum were decisive in the rejection of Russell's plan.

It is probably true that after the Emancipation Proclamation, "public opinion rendered British intervention impossible."[109] When John Roebuck, a Southern sympathizer in the Parliament, introduced a motion to recognize the Confederacy in June, opposition was so overwhelming that he withdrew it without a vote. William Gladstone, who had earlier favored intervention, spoke against the motion, arguing that "a war with the United States . . . ought to be unpopular on far higher grounds, because it would be a war with our own kinsmen for slavery."[110] Yet the arguments in favor of intervention were much weaker than before. The cotton famine had eased considerably, and Northern successes on the battlefield suggested that the war might not drag on indefinitely.

In the end, it is difficult to argue that liberal values and democratic institutions were responsible for keeping the peace between Britain and the United States during the early 1860s. Britain's failure to intervene in the Civil War was not the result of liberal sympathy for the Union within the cabinet, and, while there is some evidence that opposition by Radicals, nonconformists, and the working classes constrained the government from pursuing a more aggressive policy, this appears not to have been the decisive factor.

---

106. Quoted in Ferris, *Trent Affair,* p. 158.

107. Quoted in Jones, *Union in Peril,* p. 191.

108. For a different view, see Owen, "How Liberalism Produces Democratic Peace," p. 113.

109. Ibid., p. 114.

110. Quoted in ibid., p. 114.

Nevertheless, the sentiments and activities of liberal groups in Britain during the Civil War period do furnish support for a tenet of democratic peace theory: that liberals in one state will feel an affinity for another liberal state and will, on this basis, seek to prevent a war with it. This affinity did not significantly influence British policy simply because few effective mechanisms existed for it to do so. In the early 1860s, most workers in Britain did not possess the vote. Their political representatives, the Radicals, were badly outnumbered in Parliament and excluded from the cabinet. While Britain was liberal in many respects, it remained a country governed by an aristocracy with certain nonliberal (antidemocratic) ideals.

This situation had changed dramatically by the 1890s. The Second Reform Act, in 1867, and the Third, in 1884, radically altered the nature of British politics. The 1832 Act had extended the franchise to only about 4 percent of Britain's population. The 1867 Act doubled this percentage, and the 1884 Act gave the right to vote to a majority of Britain's adult males.[111] These reforms increased the influence of liberals on the making of British foreign policy and led more Americans to perceive Britain as democratic. As a consequence, the pacific resolution of turn-of-the-century disputes between Britain and the United States is more likely to be explained by democratic peace theory than the cases considered thus far.

The Venezuelan Boundary Crisis

The most dangerous crisis in Anglo-U.S. relations since the Civil War era erupted in December 1895. It concerned a long-standing dispute over the boundary between British Guiana and Venezuela.[112] The

---

111. Tingsten, *Victoria and the Victorians*, pp. 176, 187, 191.

112. In the following sections, I draw on my previous work, *Why Peace Breaks Out: Great Power Rapprochement in Historical Perspective* (Chapel Hill: University of North Carolina Press, 1989), chap. 2. Among the major sources on Anglo-U.S. relations of the late nineteenth and early twentieth centuries, including the Venezuelan Boundary Crisis, are Bradford Perkins, *The Great Rapprochement: England and the United States, 1895–1914* (New York: Atheneum, 1968); A.E. Campbell, *Great Britain and the United States, 1895–1903* (London: Longmans, Green & Co., 1960); Charles S. Campbell, *Anglo-American Understanding, 1898–1903* (Baltimore, Md.: Johns Hopkins University Press, 1957); Lionel M. Gelber, *The Rise of Anglo-American Friendship: A Study in World Politics, 1898–1906* (London: Oxford University Press, 1938); and Marshall Bertram, *The Birth of Anglo-American Friendship: The Prime Facet of the Venezuelan Boundary Dispute* (Lanham, Md.: University Press of America, 1992).

United States, fearful that European powers might expand their influence in the Western Hemisphere, was determined to prevent London from imposing its will. In July 1895, the U.S. Secretary of State, Richard Olney, sent a message to the British government invoking the Monroe Doctrine and requesting that the issue be submitted to arbitration.[113] Four months later, the prime minister, Lord Salisbury, issued a blunt and condescending reply in which he not only refused arbitration but rejected the Monroe Doctrine as international law.[114]

Grover Cleveland, the U.S. President, was incensed. On December 17, Cleveland told the Congress that the time had come for "the United States to take measures to determine . . . what is the true divisional line between the Republic of Venezuela and British Guiana." He asked for an appropriation that would enable him to appoint a commission for this purpose. When the commission had made its report and the report had been accepted, he concluded, it would "be the duty of the United States to resist, by every means in its power, as a willful aggression upon its rights and interests, the appropriation by Great Britain of any lands or the exercise of governmental jurisdiction over any territory which, after investigation, we have determined of right belongs to Venezuela."[115] The Congress enthusiastically complied.

The initial inclination of the British government was to stand firm. On January 11, however, over Salisbury's vehement objections, the cabinet decided to retreat. Negotiations soon began, and in February 1897, Great Britain and Venezuela concluded an agreement submitting their dispute to arbitration. Meanwhile, Britain formally declared its acceptance of the Monroe Doctrine. On February 11, 1896, Arthur Balfour, first lord of the Treasury and later prime minister, told the House of Commons that the doctrine was "a principle of policy which both they [the United States] and we cherish."[116]

IMPLICATIONS FOR DEMOCRATIC PEACE THEORY
Why did the British cabinet retreat? As Christopher Layne notes, circumstantial evidence suggests that the decision was due primarily to

---

113. Olney to Bayard, July 20, 1895, in *Congressional Record*, 54th Cong., 1st sess., Vol. 28, pp. 191–196.

114. Salisbury to Pauncefote, November 26, 1895, in ibid., pp. 196–199.

115. Ibid., p. 191.

116. Great Britain, *Parliamentary Debates*, 4th ser., Vol. 37 (1896), col. 110.

strategic considerations.[117] Since the Civil War years, British leaders had doubted their ability to win a war against the United States. Canada was bound to be overrun and occupied, and only a decisive naval victory could compel the United States to give it up. Although the U.S. Navy in early 1896 was relatively weak, possessing only three first-class battleships (with three more under construction), Britain would still need to reinforce her fleet in the Western Hemisphere. And this was simply not possible. As Arthur Marder writes, "England stood completely isolated at the beginning of 1896. Her position was scarcely endurable. France, Russia, Turkey, Germany, and the United States were openly hostile." Given Britain's vulnerability to other enemies, the cabinet was unable "to take even precautionary measures" against the United States.[118] Indeed, the admiralty refused "to contemplate the possibility of strengthening British squadrons in American waters."[119]

During the Venezuelan Crisis, Britain's strategic weakness was compounded by a dramatic deterioration in relations with Germany over South Africa. The Jameson Raid, followed by the Kruger Telegram, in which the German emperor, Wilhelm II, congratulated the Boers, brought the two countries close to war.[120] Conflict with the United States was now out of the question. J.A.S. Grenville and George Berkeley Young regard this event as crucial in explaining the shift in British policy: "In November [British leaders] believed that Britain held all the trump cards [but] the mood was no longer confident. The Cabinet was now inclined to cut Britain's losses in a world which appeared to have become suddenly hostile."[121]

---

117. Layne, "Kant or Cant," p. 25.

118. Arthur J. Marder, *The Anatomy of British Sea Power: A History of British Naval Policy in the Pre-Dreadnought Era, 1880–1905* (New York: Alfred A. Knopf, 1940), p. 257.

119. Ibid., p. 255.

120. The Jameson Raid, led by Dr. Leander Starr Jameson, was part of a plan designed by Cecil Rhodes to unify South Africa under British rule. According to the plan, British settlers in the Transvaal were to begin an uprising. Jameson and his force would then march on Johannesburg in order to defend the settlers' lives and property. However, the uprising never got off the ground, and the raiders were intercepted by the Boers and forced to surrender before ever reaching their destination.

121. J.A.S. Grenville and George Berkeley Young, *Politics, Strategy and American Diplomacy: Studies in Foreign Policy, 1873–1917* (New Haven, Conn.: Yale University Press, 1966), p. 170.

As John Owen notes, the members of the cabinet who pushed hardest for an accommodation with the United States were the liberals, led by Joseph Chamberlain.[122] But there is no concrete evidence that an affinity for U.S. democracy was decisive in determining their stance. In November, the entire cabinet, including Chamberlain, had supported Salisbury's position of not negotiating with the United States.[123] The United States had not grown more democratic by January, nor had the members of the British cabinet become more liberal. What had changed was Britain's strategic predicament. Thus, while British liberals were reluctant to go to war with the United States and the crisis was resolved in a manner predicted by democratic peace theory, shared liberal values do not appear to have significantly influenced the cabinet's policy.[124]

In Britain and especially in the United States, the outbreak of the Venezuelan Crisis at first occasioned public displays of jingoism and bellicosity. But this was rapidly replaced by a nearly universal revulsion at the prospect of conflict. In both countries, there was an "extraordinary outburst of demand . . . for some kind of permanent arbitration system that would banish for ever all possibility of Anglo-American war."[125] Letters, telegrams, and resolutions poured into Washington and London. Theodore Roosevelt was so disgusted by the demonstration of pacific sentiment that he wrote, "The clamor of the peace faction has convinced me that this country needs a war."[126]

---

122. Owen, "How Liberalism Produces Democratic Peace," p. 118. Chamberlain himself was lobbied hard by William Harcourt, the leader of the Liberal opposition and a long-time advocate of Anglo-U.S. friendship.

123. The colonial secretary apparently did so for realist reasons. According to Bertram, "Chamberlain particularly feared that if Great Britain once accepted the principle of arbitration, the wide-flung British Empire would be whittled down all over the world by neighboring states which concocted boundary disputes." Bertram, *Birth of Anglo-American Friendship*, p. 30.

124. The same was true of U.S. policy. As Owen notes, "Neither Cleveland nor Olney was part of the liberal pro-British elite." The U.S. ambassador in London, Thomas Bayard, was a liberal who believed that Britain could be trusted, but his views had little influence within the Cleveland administration. Owen, "How Liberalism Produces Democratic Peace," p. 116; Bertram, *Birth of Anglo-American Friendship*, p. 105; and Charles Callan Tansill, *The Foreign Policy of Thomas F. Bayard, 1885–1897* (New York: Fordham University Press, 1940), chap. 19.

125. Charles S. Campbell, *From Revolution to Rapprochement: The United States and Great Britain, 1783–1900* (New York: John Wiley & Sons, 1974), p. 183.

126. Roosevelt to Lodge, December 27, 1895, in Henry Cabot Lodge, ed., *Selections from the Correspondence of Theodore Roosevelt and Henry Cabot Lodge, 1884–1918*, Vol. 1 (New York: Charles Scribner's Sons, 1925), p. 205.

Public opposition to an Anglo-U.S. conflict had several bases. Particularly in the United States, there were economic reasons for avoiding war. In the aftermath of Cleveland's belligerent message, the stock market crashed. Eastern financiers were eager to prevent a conflict, as were grain producers in the Midwest, who relied heavily on the British market.[127] More potent was the idea that Britons and Americans were a single people and that a war among them would be fratricidal. Anglo-Saxonism, the belief in a common racial identity, emerged full-blown during the Venezuelan Crisis.[128] There is little evidence that public pressure had a pacifying effect on government policy in either Britain or the United States during the most acute phase of the crisis, which ended with Britain's retreat. It did, however, become an important factor in the two countries' subsequent reconciliation.

The "Great Rapprochement"

The Venezuelan Boundary Crisis was a turning point in Anglo-U.S. diplomacy. Following its resolution, relations between Britain and the United States improved dramatically. In January 1897, the two countries concluded the Olney-Pauncefote Arbitration Treaty, which was widely hailed as ending the threat of any Anglo-U.S. war. The following year, during the Spanish-American War, British public opinion sided strongly with the United States. Policy makers in London, while officially neutral, maintained a friendly attitude and helped thwart a plan by other European states to intercede on Spain's behalf. Americans, thankful for Britain's support, manifested "the most exuberant affection for England and 'Britishers' in general."[129] In an astonishing about-face, former anglophobe Richard Olney gave a speech in which he called Britain the United States' "best friend."[130]

---

127. Charles S. Campbell, *The Transformation of American Foreign Relations, 1865–1900* (New York: Harper & Row, 1976), p. 211; and Walter LaFeber, "The American Business Community and Cleveland's Venezuelan Message," *Business History Review*, Vol. 34 (Winter 1960), pp. 396–397.

128. Stuart Anderson, *Race and Rapprochement: Anglo-Saxonism and Anglo-American Relations, 1895–1904* (East Brunswick, N.J.: Associated University Presses, 1981), p. 95. Although genetically determined physical characteristics were not unimportant, notions of "race" in the late nineteenth century were grounded mainly in perceived cultural attributes.

129. Pauncefote to Salisbury, May 26, 1898, quoted in Charles S. Campbell, *Anglo-American Understanding*, p. 49.

130. Olney, "International Isolation of the United States," *Atlantic Monthly*, Vol. 81, No. 487 (May 1898), pp. 577–588. The essay was originally delivered as a speech at Harvard College on March 2, 1898.

Tensions between Britain and the United States did not vanish overnight. A dispute over the building and fortification of a canal through the Central American isthmus threatened Anglo-U.S. amity, and a controversy regarding the boundary between Alaska and the Canadian Yukon likewise carried the potential for conflict. But these issues never really approached the crisis stage and were peacefully resolved. After 1903, war between Great Britain and the United States was almost unthinkable.

ECONOMIC INCENTIVES FOR RECONCILIATION

The revolution in Anglo-U.S. diplomacy around the turn of the century was the result of several factors. One of these was a growing awareness of the devastating economic consequences of war between Britain and the United States. Each of the countries had long been the other's most important trading partner. Britain was especially dependent on U.S. cotton and foodstuffs. From 1896 to 1905, more than 75 percent of the cotton used in British textile mills was grown in the United States. From 1897 to 1901, nearly half of the wheat and wheat flour consumed in Britain was of U.S. origin.[131] Writers in British journals claimed that if trade across the Atlantic were disrupted, England would be threatened by famine within a few weeks. Textile mills would close, and unemployment would skyrocket. Concluded one, "war itself against the United States, the English base of supplies, could only result in speedy capitulation or inevitable ruin."[132]

The British government was keenly worried about the cost of food. In the debate on tariff reform, British leaders refused to consider imposing duties on U.S. agricultural goods because of the higher prices that would have resulted.[133] Clearly, a complete loss of U.S. foodstuffs in the event of war would have been far more devastating. Britain's difficulty was compounded by its less than stable relations with Russia, another major supplier of wheat. In 1897, the House of

---

131. B.R. Mitchell, *European Historical Statistics, 1750–1975,* 2nd rev. ed. (New York: Facts on File, 1981), pp. 449–452; U.S. Bureau of Foreign and Domestic Commerce, *Statistical Abstract of the United States, 1906* (Washington, D.C.: Government Printing Office, 1907), pp. 418, 426–429, 465–466; and Great Britain, *Parliamentary Papers, 1903,* Vol. 68 (Accounts and Papers, Vol. 33), "Food Supplies (Imported)," p. 9.

132. J.D. Whelpley, "American Control of England's Food Supply," *North American Review,* Vol. 174, No. 547 (June 1902), pp. 804–805.

133. See statement of Gerald Balfour, President of the Board of Trade, *Parliamentary Debates,* 4th ser., Vol. 129 (1904), cols. 661–663.

Commons passed a resolution stating that "the dependence of the United Kingdom on foreign imports for the necessities of life, and the consequences that might arise therefrom in the event of war, demands the serious attention of Her Majesty's Government."[134] The War Office noted that if war with the United States broke out, not only would supplies of U.S. grain be lost, but the flow of foodstuffs from Canada and Latin America might also be halted by U.S. military and naval action. It concluded that "such a condition of affairs might result in our being compelled to sue for peace on humiliating terms."[135]

Britain's reliance on U.S. goods was matched, more or less, by the United States' dependence on the British market. One U.S. observer noted in March 1896 that "the interruption of our commerce with Great Britain, would at once deprive a great number [of Americans] . . . of their customary occupation and means of subsistence." Before long, "the great mass of our industries would be paralyzed and brought to a state of extreme depression."[136] George Harvey, the influential editor of the *North American Review*, wrote that "a quarrel with Great Britain would be disastrous. If her ports were closed to us, we should lose our principal customer, not only for our surplus cotton, but for our surplus breadstuffs. To the farmers of our prairie States and to the planters of our Southern States, such an obstruction to the export of their staples would mean catastrophe."[137]

It is possible to regard the pacifying effects of Anglo-U.S. economic relations as evidence for democratic peace theory. Students of international politics have traditionally associated economic interdependence with "commercial liberalism," as distinct from the ideological or "republican" variety. However, to the extent that it is created and enhanced by the existence of capitalist, market economies and doctrines of free trade, interdependence is rooted in some of the same philosophical principles as liberal democracy (for example, a belief in limited government, the protection of individual rights).[138] Thus,

134. April 6, 1897, *Parliamentary Debates*, 4th ser., Vol. 48 (1897), pp. 642–676.

135. War Office, "Memorandum on the standards of defence for the naval bases of Halifax, Bermuda, Jamaica, and St. Lucia," September 17, 1903, quoted in Bourne, *Britain and the Balance of Power*, pp. 361–362.

136. Edward Atkinson, "The Cost of an Anglo-American War," *Forum*, Vol. 21, No. 1 (March 1896), p. 88.

137. George Harvey, "The United States and Great Britain: Their Past, Present, and Future Relations," *Nineteenth Century*, Vol. 55, No. 326 (April 1904), p. 533.

138. British liberals such as Cobden and Bright did not recognize a distinction between commercial and ideological liberalism. As I show above, their objections to U.S. protectionism during the Civil War period significantly weakened their liberal affinity for the United States.

Kant's prescription for a perpetual peace among republican states emphasized both economic and political ties.[139] More recently, Oneal and others have sought to reestablish the link between commercial and republican liberalism in explaining democratic peace.[140]

STRATEGIC IMPERATIVES

Although the desire to preserve valuable economic connections clearly contributed to the Anglo-U.S. rapprochement, strategic considerations were more important, especially to political leaders in Britain and the United States. Perceptions of external threat, particularly from Germany, provided strong incentives for closer Anglo-U.S. cooperation.

U.S. relations with Germany had been deteriorating since the late 1880s, largely because of trade rivalry and tariff disputes. As Germany's naval ambitions became apparent during the following decade, U.S. leaders began to fear an "'aggressive' colonial policy" aimed at Latin America.[141] By 1900, Senator Henry Cabot Lodge had become convinced that Berlin intended to establish a colonial empire in Brazil.[142] *Harper's Weekly* warned of Germany's plans to "blow the Monroe Doctrine sky-high."[143] According to the British ambassador in Washington, "suspicion of the German Emperor's designs in the Caribbean [was] shared by the Administration, the press, and the public alike."[144]

---

139. Doyle, "Kant, Liberal Legacies, and Foreign Affairs," Part I, p. 331.

140. John R. Oneal et al., "The Liberal Peace: Interdependence, Democracy, and International Conflict, 1950–85," *Journal of Peace Research*, Vol. 33, No. 1 (1996), pp. 11–28. See also Paul A. Papayoanou, "Interdependence, Institutions, and the Balance of Power: Britain, Germany, and World War I," *International Security*, Vol. 20, No. 4 (Spring 1996), pp. 42–76. The notion that interdependence leads to peace is controversial among scholars, many of whom reject the commercial-liberal thesis. For a recent attempt to resolve the dispute by identifying the conditions under which economic interdependence produces peace and those under which it produces conflict, see Dale C. Copeland, "Economic Interdependence and War: A Theory of Trade Expectations," *International Security*, Vol. 20, No. 4 (Spring 1996), pp. 5–41.

141. Memo by Charles de Kay, U.S. Consul-General in Berlin, February 1, 1896, quoted in Alfred Vagts, *Deutschland und die Vereinigten Staaten in Der Weltpolitik*, Vol 1. (New York: Macmillan Co., 1935), p. 619.

142. Anderson, *Race and Rapprochement*, p. 67.

143. *Harper's Weekly*, January 3, 1903, p. 16.

144. Herbert to Lansdowne, December 29, 1902, in G.P. Gooch and Harold Temperley, eds., *British Documents on the Origins of the War, 1898–1914*, Vol. 2, (London: His Majesty's Stationery Office, 1926–1938), p. 164.

In the face of the German threat, British neutrality, if not friendship, was vital; the United States could not hope to confront both powers simultaneously. Shortly before he became president in 1901, Theodore Roosevelt warned "that we should be exceedingly cautious about embroiling ourselves with England, from whom we have not the least little particle of danger to fear in any way or shape; while the only power which may be a menace to us in anything like the immediate future is Germany."[145] Others agreed that British support was essential if the United States were to uphold the Monroe Doctrine and resist German expansion in the Western Hemisphere. In 1905, the General Board of the Navy, after reporting on German ambitions in the West Indies, the Caribbean, and South America, concluded that "the Welfare of the United States and its immunity from entanglements with the other Powers is greatly strengthened by strong ties of friendship and by unanimity of action with Great Britain."[146]

The strategic imperative for Anglo-U.S. reconciliation was even stronger in Britain than in the United States. As the British government surveyed the geopolitical situation around the turn of the century, war with the United States appeared increasingly unpalatable. The U.S. Navy was becoming a formidable force. In early 1896, the United States possessed only three battleships, but by 1905 it had twenty-five built or under construction.[147] Meanwhile, colonial disputes with France in North Africa and Southeast Asia seemed ready to erupt into conflict. There was friction with Russia over Turkey, Persia, and Afghanistan. In 1898, Germany embarked upon a program of naval expansion so ambitious that it threatened Britain's traditional maritime supremacy. The following year, Britain found itself fighting the bloody Boer War in South Africa and facing the possibility of intervention by other European powers.[148]

---

145. Roosevelt to Lodge, March 27, 1901, in Lodge, *Selections from the Roosevelt-Lodge Correspondence*, Vol. 1, p. 485.

146. U.S. Navy, General Board, report to the Secretary of the Navy, 1906, quoted in Charles Carlisle Taylor, *The Life of Admiral Mahan* (London: John Murray, 1920), pp. 151–152.

147. Marder, *Anatomy of British Sea Power*, p. 442, n. 1.

148. The best analysis of Britain's strategic problems around the turn of the century is George Monger, *The End of Isolation: British Foreign Policy, 1900–1907* (London: Thomas Nelson & Sons, 1963). See also Aaron L. Friedberg, *The Weary Titan: Britain and the Experience of Relative Decline, 1895–1905* (Princeton, N.J.: Princeton University Press, 1988).

Although relations with France subsequently improved, Britain's strategic position remained vulnerable.[149] It was too dangerous to send a large portion of her fleet across the Atlantic to fight the United States. An admiralty memo explained: "Centuries of triumphant conflict with her European rivals have left Great Britain the double legacy of world-wide Empire and of a jealousy (of which we had a sad glimpse during the South African War) which would render it hazardous indeed to denude our home waters of the battle squadrons, which stand between our own land and foreign invasion." The admiralty concluded, "the more carefully this problem is considered, the more tremendous do the difficulties which would confront Great Britain in a war with the United States appear. It may be hoped that the policy of the British Government will ever be to use all possible means to avoid such a war."[150]

Democratic peace theorists do not deny the importance of strategic considerations in explaining the "great rapprochement." They contend, however, that British and U.S. alignment decisions were not the product of narrow geopolitical calculations, but were also strongly influenced by regime type. For John Owen, the crucial question is "why the British aligned with the United States rather than with Germany." Owen writes, "liberalism offers an answer: British liberals trusted the democratic United States more than imperial Germany."[151] Further, some democratic peace theorists have suggested that the Anglo-U.S. reconciliation was not simply balancing behavior by Britain and the United States. Rather, "the experience of near war" in the Venezuelan Boundary Crisis produced "intense reconsideration about interests and the direction of foreign policy, in which the previous antagonists' views of the democratic norms and institutions they shared played a major role in changing the way they behaved toward each other."[152] In short, these scholars argue that while strategic considerations may have loomed large in the minds of

---

149. In 1904, Britain and France concluded the famed *entente cordiale*, which settled their outstanding colonial disputes and provided the basis for Anglo-French cooperation in international diplomacy.

150. Admiralty Memo, "Defence of Canada," February 24, 1905, quoted in Bourne, *Britain and the Balance of Power*, pp. 382–385.

151. Owen, "How Liberalism Produces Democratic Peace," p. 118.

152. Russett, "And Yet It Moves," p. 166, n. 8. In previous work, I have argued similarly—though not in connection with democratic peace theory—that the Venezuelan Boundary Crisis served as a catalyst for the Anglo-U.S. rapprochement. See Rock, *Why Peace Breaks Out*, pp. 56–57.

both British and U.S. leaders, democratic peace theory is helpful in explaining turn-of-the-century alliances.

ANGLO-SAXONISM

Those who consider shared liberal values and democratic institutions key factors in the "great rapprochement" have based much of their argument on the role of Anglo-Saxonism in relations between Britain and the United States.[153] Anglo-Saxonism was "English-speaking nationalism, a belief that Englishmen and Americans, though they inhabited different lands, were a single people."[154] Many Anglo-Saxonists regarded the Anglo-Saxon "race" as superior to all others and claimed that Britain and the United States had a mission to spread enlightenment and civilization throughout the world. Expressions of Anglo-Saxonist sentiment appeared in Britain and the United States as early as the middle of the nineteenth century, but became more prevalent during the 1880s and 1890s under the influence of Social Darwinist thought and growing imperial competition.[155]

The Venezuelan Boundary Crisis prompted a veritable explosion of Anglo-Saxonism on both sides of the Atlantic. Stuart Anderson notes that the sudden threat of conflict "elicited countless expressions of kinship and good feeling from the public of both countries. Much of the public reaction against the prospect of an Anglo-American war...was rooted in the widely held belief that Englishmen and Americans were fellow Anglo-Saxons, and that a war between them would be fratricidal."[156]

In addition, important members of the policy making elite in both Britain and the United States held Anglo-Saxonist views. Within the British cabinet, Joseph Chamberlain, the colonial secretary until 1903, and Arthur Balfour, prime minister from 1902 to 1905, were leading exponents of Anglo-Saxonism.[157] Other prominent Anglo-Saxonists included Cecil Spring Rice of the Foreign Office and the future prime minister Herbert Henry Asquith. Numerous members of Parliament belonged to the Anglo-American League, which proclaimed that

---

153. Russett, *Grasping the Democratic Peace*, pp. 6–7; and Owen, "How Liberalism Produces Democratic Peace," p. 115.

154. Rock, *Why Peace Breaks Out*, p. 48. The definitive treatment of the phenomenon is Anderson, *Race and Rapprochement*.

155. Anderson, *Race and Rapprochement*, pp. 26–61.

156. Ibid., p. 95.

157. Ibid., pp. 91–94; and Rock, *Why Peace Breaks Out*, p. 51.

Britain and the United States were "closely allied by blood, inherit the same literature and laws, hold the same principles of self-government, [and] recognize the same ideas of freedom and humanity."[158]

In the United States, the list of avowed Anglo-Saxonists was equally impressive. It included John Hay, ambassador to England and later secretary of state in the McKinley and Roosevelt administrations, and Alfred Thayer Mahan, the most prominent naval strategist of the time. Even Theodore Roosevelt, who was of Dutch origin, expressed Anglo-Saxonist beliefs.[159]

On the surface, Anglo-Saxonism appears to have contributed to the "great rapprochement" in ways consistent with democratic peace theory. First, it led many Britons and Americans to feel that a war between Britain and the United States would be fratricidal and must therefore be avoided. As Balfour declared in early 1896, "The idea of war with the United States carries with it some of the unnatural horror of a civil war. . . . The time will come, the time must come, when someone, some statesman of authority . . . will lay down the doctrine that between English-speaking peoples war is impossible."[160]

Second, Anglo-Saxonism affected threat assessments. Britons perceived the United States as less menacing than Germany in part because of the affinity they felt for Americans. While they regarded German colonialism as dangerous to British interests, they enthusiastically applauded U.S. imperial efforts, seeing them as evidence that "the American Republic has now reverted to the hereditary policy of the Anglo-Saxon race."[161] Explaining the difference in Britain's attitude, Philip Kerr, later Lord Lothian, stated in 1910 that "the ideals of the United States, like her own, are essentially unaggressive and threaten their neighbours no harm." By contrast, he argued, "Germanism, in its want of liberalism . . . is dangerous."[162] U.S. perceptions were similarly affected. Alfred Thayer Mahan warned of the

---

158. Quoted in Charles S. Campbell, *Anglo-American Understanding*, p. 46.

159. Rock, *Why Peace Breaks Out*, pp. 52–54.

160. Quoted in Blanche E.C. Dugdale, *Arthur James Balfour, First Earl of Balfour, K.G., O.M., F.R.S., Etc.*, Vol. 1 (New York: G.P. Putnam's Sons, 1937), p. 164.

161. Edward Dicey, "The New American Imperialism," *Nineteenth Century*, Vol. 44, No. 259 (September 1898), p. 501.

162. Philip Kerr, "Foreign Affairs: Anglo-German Rivalry," *Round Table*, Vol. 1, No. 1 (November 1910), pp. 26–27. In 1905, the *Spectator* had written that "it would make very greatly for a better understanding between the two countries if the German government were not to show themselves so opposed to liberal ideas. . . . We admit fully that in reality the autocratic and anti-liberal system of government that prevails in Germany is no business of ours, and that we have no sort of

menace to U.S. interests posed by German ambitions, but wrote that Britain, "with her far more liberal institutions . . . has no adequate stimulus to aggression, least of all against the United States."[163]

Realists have countered each of these claims. They argue, first, that Anglo-Saxonism was a consequence rather than a cause of the Anglo-U.S. reconciliation. Britons and Americans, they contend, developed a common sense of identity to justify and render more palatable the cooperation that was necessary for strategic reasons.[164] Nor were threat assessments influenced by Anglo-Saxonism in the way that democratic peace theory predicts. Britain and the United States did not regard Germany as more dangerous because it was illiberal, and each other as less dangerous because of shared democracy. Instead, they came to see Germany as illiberal because of its menacing international behavior and the grave strategic threat it posed. Regime definition was a function of threat assessment, rather than the other way around.[165]

There is some evidence that Anglo-Saxonism was both a product and a cause of reconciliation between Britain and the United States. Richard Olney's views, for instance, appear to have shifted in response to improving Anglo-U.S. political relations. The one-time anglophobe, who delighted in "twisting the Lion's tail" and who precipitated the Venezuelan Boundary Crisis, converted to Anglo-Saxonism by September 1896, writing that "if there is anything the Americans are proud of, it is their right to describe themselves as of the English race."[166] In May 1897, Olney informed the British government that "the American people are proud of their lineage; set the highest value upon the laws, the institutions, the literature, and

---

right to object to it. Still, we cannot ignore the fact that its existence does influence men's minds here unfavourably towards the German Empire. It makes men say, in effect: 'That is not the kind of government which we can feel confidence in, or with which we should care to ally ourselves'." "A Better Understanding with Germany," *Spectator*, December 9, 1905, p. 967.

163. Alfred Thayer Mahan, *The Interest of America in International Conditions* (Boston: Little, Brown & Co., 1910), pp. 75–76.

164. Layne, "Kant or Cant," pp. 27–28.

165. See Ido Oren, "The Subjectivity of the 'Democratic' Peace: Changing U.S. Perceptions of Imperial Germany," *International Security*, Vol. 20, No. 2 (Fall 1995), pp. 147–184.

166. Olney to Chamberlain, September 28, 1896, quoted in Anderson, *Race and Rapprochement*, p. 105.

the language they have inherited; glory in all the achievements of the Anglo-Saxon race . . . and feel themselves to be . . . part of one great English-speaking family whose proud destiny it is to lead and control the world."[167] Senator Henry Cabot Lodge, another notorious anglophobe, responded to British sympathy for the United States upon the outbreak of the Spanish-American War by proclaiming joyously that "race, blood, language, identity of beliefs and aspirations, all assert themselves."[168]

These and other examples notwithstanding, Anglo-Saxonism does not appear to have been primarily epiphenomenal, the result of improved political relations between Britain and the United States. Public expressions of Anglo-Saxonist sentiment were loudest and most numerous when diplomatic relations were at their worst, during the Venezuelan Boundary Crisis. Moreover, most Anglo-Saxonists had developed their views prior to the deterioration in Anglo-German and U.S.-German relations and the recognition that Anglo-U.S. cooperation against Germany might be necessary. Joseph Chamberlain, for example, was articulating Anglo-Saxonist ideas as early as 1887, while Alfred Thayer Mahan was doing so as early as 1892.[169] Although Anglo-German and U.S.-German relations had been troubled since the middle to late 1880s, they did not worsen precipitously until after 1898, when Germany's program of naval expansion made the country a much greater threat to both Britain and the United States.[170] Between 1898 and 1901, in fact, the British government sought to conclude an alliance with Germany, indicating that Berlin was not yet regarded as an implacable foe but

167. Olney to White, May 8, 1897, quoted in ibid., p. 110.

168. Lodge to Hay, April 21, 1898, quoted in ibid., p. 118.

169. Chamberlain, speech in Toronto, December 1887, quoted in J.L. Garvin, *Life of Joseph Chamberlain*, Vol. 2, (vols. 4–6 by Julian Amery) (London: Macmillan & Co., 1932–69), p. 334. Mahan to Clarke, November 5, 1892, in Robert Seager II and Doris D. Maguire, eds., *Letters and Papers of Alfred Thayer Mahan*, Vol. 2 (Annapolis, Md.: Naval Institute Press, 1975), p. 84.

170. On German naval expansion and its effects on Anglo-German and German-U.S. relations, see E.L. Woodward, *Great Britain and the German Navy* (Oxford: Clarendon Press, 1935; reprint ed., London: Frank Cass & Co., 1964); Peter Padfield, *The Great Naval Race: The Anglo-German Naval Rivalry, 1900–1914* (New York: David McKay Co., 1974); Paul M. Kennedy, *The Rise and Fall of British Naval Mastery* (London: Allen Lane, 1976); Marder, *Anatomy of British Sea Power*; and Holger Herwig, *Politics of Frustration: The United States in German Naval Planning, 1889–1941* (Boston: Little, Brown & Co., 1976).

was still seen as a potential partner.[171]

As to the role of ideology in threat assessments: the dominant cause of germanophobia in Britain and the United States was Berlin's diplomatic and military behavior, not the nature of its political system. Much of the reason Britain perceived the United States to be less dangerous than Germany had to do with the fact that the U.S. threat was more distant, both "geographically and temporally."[172] Furthermore, as Ido Oren shows, some Americans appear to have defined the German political system as illiberal in response to the development of geopolitical tensions between the two countries around 1900.[173] Oren's argument is particularly troubling for democratic peace theory because it reverses the direction of the causal arrow between regime type and threat assessment, suggesting that liberal states see nonthreatening states as liberal and threatening ones as illiberal. Oren makes a persuasive case about U.S. views of Germany's political system.[174] Interestingly, however, U.S. perceptions of the British system (and vice versa) seem to have been more consistent and less affected by changing political and strategic relations.[175]

A more serious objection to regarding Anglo-Saxonism as evidence in support of democratic peace theory is that it was not solely an ideological phenomenon. As an expression of national identity, Anglo-Saxonism was grounded in a range of perceived cultural similarities between Britain and the United States, not simply in their shared liberal values and democratic political systems. One might argue that Anglo-Saxonism represents "an earlier form of liberalism that rooted the concepts of liberty and democratic government in shared cultural

---

171. In one sense this fact counts against democratic peace theory because it shows that British perceptions of Germany as illiberal did not lead London to regard Berlin as inherently dangerous or unsuitable as an ally. See Layne, "Correspondence on the Democratic Peace," p. 176, n. 1. However, it also suggests that British Anglo-Saxonism was not the product of strategic calculations and the perceived need for U.S. cooperation against Germany.

172. Layne, "Correspondence on the Democratic Peace," p. 176, n. 1.

173. Oren, "The Subjectivity of the 'Democratic' Peace." There is some evidence that the same is true of British perceptions of the German political system. Most references by British authors to the illiberal nature of the German system date from after 1905, by which time the Anglo-German antagonism was well established.

174. It should be noted that ultimately Oren's argument rests on an analysis of the views of two U.S. academics, only one of whom—Woodrow Wilson—altered his view of the German political system.

175. This is also the conclusion of Owen, "How Liberalism Produces Democratic Peace."

traits, not the autonomous power of political beliefs."[176] But even if this is true, in its emphasis on ethnicity and its belief in the uniqueness and superiority of the English-speaking peoples, Anglo-Saxonism was antithetical to contemporary notions of liberalism on which the logic of democratic peace theory rests. Although a *cultural* interpretation of Anglo-Saxonism and an *ideological* one overlap in the realm of political culture, they are distinct, and only the latter is consistent with democratic peace theory.[177]

It is difficult to assess the relative significance of the ideological and cultural components of Anglo-Saxonism because the two are so intertwined in the views of various individuals. John Hay, for example, stressed on one occasion that Americans were "the fortunate heirs of English liberty and English law," while on another he remarked that the people of the United States were "knitted . . . to the people of Great Britain by a thousand ties of origin, of language, and of kindred pursuits."[178] Joseph Chamberlain commented upon the "common origins, [and] common literature" shared by Britain and the United States as well as their "common laws and common standards of right and wrong."[179] And Arthur Balfour combined the cultural and political foundations of Anglo-Saxonism when he asserted that "the fact that [the United States'] laws, its language, its literature, and its religion, to say nothing of its constitution are essentially the same as those of English-speaking peoples elsewhere, ought surely to produce a fundamental harmony—a permanent sympathy."[180]

Nevertheless, it is possible to detect a basic difference between British and U.S. Anglo-Saxonism: the former placed primary emphasis on cultural connections, while the latter gave greater weight to shared liberal values and democratic political institutions. As A.E. Campbell writes, "Anglo-American sympathies . . . were based, in Britain on a sense of racial community, in America on a sense of

---

176. Sean M. Lynn-Jones, personal correspondence, June 26, 1996.

177. Russett, in *Grasping the Democratic Peace,* and to a lesser extent Owen, in "How Liberalism Produces Democratic Peace," fail to make this distinction and thus conflate the cultural and ideological bases of Anglo-Saxonism.

178. John Hay, *Addresses of John Hay* (New York: Century Company, 1906), pp. 69, 78.

179. Chamberlain to Olney, September 29, 1896, quoted in Garvin, *Life of Joseph Chamberlain,* Vol. 3, p. 168.

180. Balfour to White, December 12, 1900, quoted in Denis Judd, *Balfour and the British Empire: A Study in Imperial Evolution, 1874–1932* (London: Macmillan & Company, 1968), p. 314.

ideological community."[181] U.S. Anglo-Saxonism, then, provides considerable support for democratic peace theory. The *ideological* component was crucial; for some Americans shared democracy may even have been sufficient to produce an affinity for Britain. British Anglo-Saxonism, grounded principally in perceived cultural similarities, is another matter.[182]

Naval Arms Control During the 1920s

Anglo-U.S. relations in the years following World War I were more placid that those of the nineteenth and early twentieth centuries. No crises erupted that were comparable to the Oregon, *Trent*, or Venezuelan Boundary Crises. Nevertheless, significant tensions did arise, partly as a result of increasing economic rivalry and, more importantly, as a consequence of competition in naval armaments. Commenting on the incipient naval contest, Woodrow Wilson's trusted adviser, Colonel House, warned the U.S. president in 1919 that "the relations between the two countries are beginning to assume the same character as that of England and Germany before the war."[183]

Fortunately, the Anglo-U.S. naval arms race ended not in conflict but in compromise. At the Washington Conference in 1921–22, Great Britain and the United States agreed to equality in aircraft carriers and battleships. At the London Conference in 1930, they committed themselves to parity in submarines, cruisers, and destroyers as well.[184] For the British, acceptance of naval equality with the United States meant abandoning maritime supremacy, which Britain had

---

181. A.E. Campbell, *Great Britain and the United States, 1895–1903*, p. 204.

182. One could argue that shared democracy was necessary for British Anglo-Saxonism—after all, cultural similarities had existed between Britain and the United States since the time of U.S. independence and had not produced a sense of common identity—but it is hard to see how it could be regarded as sufficient.

183. House to Wilson, July 30, 1919, in Edward Mandell House, *The Intimate Papers of Colonel House*, Vol. 4 (Boston: Houghton Mifflin Co., 1926–28), p. 495.

184. The Washington Conference is treated in Thomas Buckley, *The United States and the Washington Conference, 1921–1922* (Knoxville: University of Tennessee Press, 1970), while the London Conference is discussed in Raymond G. O'Connor, *Perilous Equilibrium: The United States and the London Naval Conference of 1930* (Lawrence: University of Kansas Press, 1962). Additional accounts are found in Benjamin H. Williams, *The United States and Disarmament* (New York: Whittlesey House, McGraw-Hill Book Co., 1931), pp. 140–225; and Merze Tate, *The United States and Armaments* (Cambridge, Mass.: Harvard University Press, 1948), pp. 121–184.

enjoyed for more than a century and on which she had long staked the security of her people and her empire. For the United States, acceptance of naval equality with Britain meant renouncing a position of dominance that was well within its capacity to achieve.

Some of the impetus toward agreement came from factors that had little to do with democratic peace theory.[185] Memories of World War I, which had been preceded by the Anglo-German naval arms race, were still fresh; few people on either side of the Atlantic wished to repeat that experience. More important were the financial constraints on both countries. As Emily Goldman notes, "the war had left the British with insufficient resources to sustain naval competition. . . . The postwar slump was severe. Rising unemployment, stagnating trade and industry, falling prices, and mounting pressures for social reform all combined to urge fiscal retrenchment."[186] The Labour Party, under Ramsay MacDonald, was particularly interested in making sure that scarce financial resources were not diverted into excessive naval construction, but the Conservative position was not much different. Generally, politicians of all stripes saw "British taxes as being more dangerous than United States ships."[187]

Additional incentive for British leaders to compromise was provided by the simple fact that Britain would lose an unconstrained arms competition with the United States. As one Member of Parliament told the House of Commons in 1920, "if we are going to

---

185. One scholar has previously analyzed Anglo-U.S. naval arms control in terms of democratic peace theory. See Robert G. Kaufman, "A Two-Level Interaction: Structure, Stable Liberal Democracy, and U.S. Grand Strategy," *Security Studies*, Vol. 3, No. 4 (Summer 1994), pp. 690–693. My argument is similar to Kaufman's: that shared democracy contributed to Anglo-U.S. cooperation, but that international and especially domestic "structural imperatives"—e.g., lower taxes, balanced budgets—were equally or more important. For the sources of British policy in this period, see Stephen Roskill, *Naval Policy Between the Wars, Vol. I: The Period of Anglo-American Antagonism* (London: Collins, 1968); and Kennedy, *Rise and Fall of British Naval Mastery*, chap. 10. For U.S. policy, see George Theron Davis, *A Navy Second to None: The Development of Modern American Naval Policy* (New York: Harcourt, Brace, Jovanovich, 1940), chaps. 11–13; Kenneth J. Hagan, *This People's Navy: The Making of American Sea Power* (New York: Free Press, 1991), chap. 9; and Harold Sprout and Margaret Sprout, *Toward a New Order of Sea Power: American Naval Policy and the World Scene, 1918–1922*, 2nd ed. (Princeton, N.J.: Princeton University Press, 1943).

186. Emily O. Goldman, *Sunken Treaties: Naval Arms Control Between the Wars* (University Park: Pennsylvania State University Press, 1994), p. 44.

187. J.W. Hills, June 2, 1930, in *Parliamentary Debates* (Commons), 5th ser., Vol. 239 (1930), col. 1843.

enter into naval rivalry with the United States . . . one of two things is going to happen . . . we are going to be outbuilt or bankrupt."[188] Ten years later, another M.P. reminded the House that in the absence of a treaty "the United States will outbuild us at every point."[189]

The United States, which had emerged from the war in a much healthier position economically, faced fewer fiscal constraints. Pressed by naval leaders who forecast an Anglo-U.S. conflict over trade, the Harding administration initially resisted efforts to limit naval construction. It eventually succumbed, however, to popular and congressional pressure.[190] Some of this pressure was grounded, as in Britain, in concern over the financial implications of a naval armaments race. A member of the House of Representatives noted in 1919 that "the burdens of taxation resulting from this war are already falling heavily upon our people" and warned, "if we enter upon a policy of naval competition with Great Britain we can not offer to the people of this country any hope of a lessening of the burden for generations to come."[191]

Much of the pressure, however, was rooted in the belief that naval competition with Britain was unnecessary because Britain was not a potential enemy. In 1919, the *New York Times* editorialized that "the United States need not be nervous about British sea power. . . . to talk about British aggression today would be grotesque."[192] As in the pre-war period, much of the faith in British goodwill resulted from Americans' liberal affinity for England. During debate on naval appropriations, a U.S. representative from Iowa noted that "our sentiments, our hopes, our aspirations are the same. Alike in our veins courses the spirit of freedom. Alike our minds are filled with a determination to make all men equal before the law. . . . We have no occasion to be suspicious or jealous of the other, but each should rejoice as the other develops in strength and power."[193] The *Seattle Post-Intelligencer*

---

188. J.M. Kenworthy, March 17, 1920, in *Parliamentary Debates* (Commons), 5th ser., Vol. 126 (1920), col. 2346.

189. Noel Baker, June 2, 1930, in *Parliamentary Debates* (Commons), 5th ser., Vol. 239 (1930), col. 1833.

190. For the views of U.S. navy men on the prospect of war with England, see Warner R. Schilling, "Admirals and Foreign Policy" (Ph.D. dissertation, Yale University, 1954), pp. 242–249.

191. Edward Denison, February 11, 1919, in *Congressional Record*, 65th Cong., 3rd sess., Vol. 57, p. 3164.

192. *New York Times*, December 11, 1919, p. 12.

193. William Green, February 11, 1919, in *Congressional Record*, 65th Cong., 3rd sess., Vol. 57, p. 3165.

likewise argued that "we can gaze with equanimity on England's great Navy, knowing that the democratic people of the British Empire will never use that Navy wrongly. . . . The safeguard is in democracy, a democracy that has kept the two peoples at peace for over a hundred years, that brought them together at Armageddon, and will hold them stedfast friends for the future."[194] By 1921, the view of "liberal democracy as an ameliorating condition in Anglo-American relations" had taken hold even within the U.S. Navy.[195] Although linguistic and other cultural bases of common identity were sometimes cited by Americans as reasons for discounting the British threat, during the 1920s the dominant themes were clearly ideological.

Most Britons also regarded the United States as an unlikely opponent. The *Times* called building a navy against the United States "unnecessary, hateful, [and] a treachery to the future welfare of mankind."[196] H.H. Asquith, the former prime minister, told the House of Commons that he had "not the faintest apprehension of the intention or effect of what America is doing in the way of building up a Navy, or that it is directed or ever will be directed against this country." Asquith continued, between "these two great English-speaking peoples . . . fratricidal strife is, we hope and believe still, an absolute impossibility."[197] Similarly, a British naval commander told the House that "a fratricidal strike between this country and America is absolutely impossible."[198]

As in the prewar period, British expressions of common identity with the United States were grounded as much in perceived cultural similarities as in political and ideological ones. Although an Australian delegate to the Washington Conference reported that the British were willing to accept naval equality with the United States because they were convinced that "not even the wildest conception could picture the Navy of such a democracy being used aggressively against a member of the British Empire," this was not the most frequently articulated theme.[199]

194. Quoted in *Literary Digest,* January 4, 1919, p. 11.

195. Kaufman, "Two-Level Interaction," p. 713, n. 63.

196. *Times* (London), March 18, 1921, p. 11.

197. Comments on March 17, 1921, in *Parliamentary Debates* (Commons), 5th ser., Vol. 139 (1921), cols. 1788, 1795.

198. C.W. Bellairs, March 17, 1920, in *Parliamentary Debates* (Commons), 5th ser., Vol. 126 (1920), cols. 2335–2336.

199. George Foster Pearce, quoted in *Literary Digest,* March 11, 1922, p. 37.

IMPLICATIONS FOR DEMOCRATIC PEACE THEORY

Anglo-U.S. arms control during the 1920s provides some support for democratic peace theory. In the United States, strong public and congressional pressure for acceptance of naval parity with Britain helped successive administrations overcome the opposition of "big navy" advocates. Behind much of this pressure lay the belief that Britain, as a liberal democracy, posed little or no threat to U.S. interests. At the same time, however, other factors contributed significantly to the United States' rejection of a naval race. These included isolationist sentiment, which had been reinforced by the results of World War I, and reluctance to assume the fiscal burden that would have been imposed by an unconstrained arms competition. While Britain's liberal character made it easier for the U.S. government to pursue naval arms limitations, much of U.S. behavior can be explained without reference to British norms and institutions. U.S. policy makers had diverse motives for arms control, the most important of which had nothing to do with affinity for British democracy.

Democratic peace theory provides less of an explanation for British policy. As in the prewar period, Anglo-Saxonism was important, but it remained as much an expression of cultural as ideological identity. Moreover, for British policy makers, the practical constraints, primarily fiscal, on naval building were overwhelming. Anglo-Saxonism eased British minds and made the final decision to accept maritime equality less difficult. That it was the dominant factor in that decision is doubtful.

Conclusion

Were shared liberal values and democratic institutions responsible for the long Anglo-U.S. peace? The answer, for the most part, is no. Democratic peace theory does not explain the pacific resolution of the Oregon Crisis and the *Trent* Crisis. It is of limited value in explaining the decision of the British government not to intervene in the U.S. Civil War. It is of limited value in accounting for the peaceful settlement of the Venezuelan Boundary Crisis. Democratic peace theory has more explanatory power with respect to the "great rapprochement" and naval arms control during the 1920s, but in these cases liberal values and democratic institutions were not the only factors inclining Britain and the United States toward peace, and perhaps not even the dominant ones.

The theory of democratic peace is often stated in its strongest form: that shared liberal norms and democratic institutions prevent war among liberal states. Because peace between Britain and the United States was overdetermined, and because strategic calculations and cultural affinity were frequently more crucial than political ideology, the Anglo-U.S. case fails to uphold this version of democratic peace theory. It does, however, offer some support for a more modest claim: that, all other things being equal, the more liberal and democratic states are, the less likely they are to fight one another. Over time, with the deepening of democracy in Britain and the growing awareness of that country's democratic character in the United States, shared liberal values and democratic institutions became an increasingly important barrier to Anglo-U.S. war.

The impact of shared liberal ideals on attitudes and behavior was greater in the United States than in Britain. Especially during the Civil War period, British liberals felt sympathy for the democratic United States and argued for peace on this basis. But a purely ideological, liberal affinity for the United States seems to have been strongest during the 1860s, when British liberals perceived the Union as a crucial symbolic ally in their own struggle for democratization in Britain. Once the battle for democracy had been won in the Reform Acts of 1867 and 1884, the U.S. model was less salient. By the turn of the century, when Anglo-Saxonism was at its height, British affinity for the United States was based as much or more on perceived cultural similarities than on shared liberal values and democratic institutions.

In the United States, the situation was different. After the passing of the Second and Third Reform Acts, and the granting of self-government to Canada, most Americans came to regard Britain as democratic. This led U.S. liberals to trust British policy.[200] Affinity for Britain during the period of the "great rapprochement" and again in the 1920s, while grounded to some extent in perceived cultural similarities, was primarily a political phenomenon. In each of these cases, a strong sense of "ideological community" with Britain inclined U.S. liberals to press for an accommodation with the country they regarded as the source of democratic ideals.

---

200. In 1886, for example, Andrew Carnegie wrote, "Henceforth Britain is democratic." He predicted that "the British democracy is to be pacific" and "that it will not be long ere both parties in Britain pledge themselves, as both parties here have done, to offer arbitration for the settlement of international disputes before drawing the sword." Andrew Carnegie, "Democracy in England," *North American Review*, Vol. 142, No. 350 (January 1886), pp. 74, 79.

IS DEMOCRATIC PEACE THEORY A THEORY OF U.S. FOREIGN POLICY?
That shared liberal values exercised a greater impact on attitudes and behavior in the United States than in Britain suggests that democratic peace theory may be less a theory of international politics than a theory of U.S. foreign policy. Perhaps much of the absence of war among democracies, especially in this century, can be attributed to U.S. beliefs and actions. If the United States has pursued amicable relations with other liberal states, it is not surprising that they have reciprocated. After all, it is wise to cooperate with a great power, particularly one that wishes to be friendly. U.S. policy may also help to explain peace between other liberal dyads: "Countries allied with the United States are less likely to go to war, partly because they are part of the same alliance and partly because the United States will use its power and influence to keep them at peace."[201]

It is widely recognized that regime type matters more to the United States than to other countries. Since the days of Woodrow Wilson, advocates of *realpolitik* have decried the United States' tendency to base foreign policy on ideological considerations. Theorists of U.S. exceptionalism have attributed this preoccupation with liberal ideology—and its enemies—to the country's origins. As a nation of diverse immigrants, Americans lacked a unifying history, language, and culture. Consequently, they constructed a national identity on the basis of shared moral and political principles. Not surprisingly, identification with and affinity for non-Americans is grounded in similar factors.[202]

A crucial question for democratic peace theory, therefore, is whether political ideology is central to identity and community for peoples and leaders outside the United States. This chapter cannot provide an answer, but the importance of culture in British Anglo-Saxonism is one reason to think it is not. If the role of liberal ideology as the cornerstone of community is somehow unique to the United States, then ideological solidarity is unlikely to constitute a basis for

---

201. Sean M. Lynn-Jones, personal correspondence, June 26, 1996. Greece and Turkey provide the best example. Had these two democracies not been NATO allies of the United States, they might well have gone to war over Cyprus on several occasions.

202. Louis Hartz, *The Liberal Tradition in America* (New York: Harcourt, Brace & World, 1955), especially chap. 11. See also Tami R. Davis and Sean M. Lynn-Jones, "City Upon a Hill," *Foreign Policy*, No. 66 (Spring 1987), pp. 21–22.

peaceful relations among liberal states generally.[203] Indeed, democratic peace theory may be little more than an artifact of the peculiarly American worldview of those who have proposed it.

---

203. John Owen has conducted a multi-case study in which he finds considerable support for democratic peace theory. See "Liberal Peace, Liberal War." However, each of Owen's cases involves the United States, and his focus is primarily on U.S. attitudes and behavior.

Part II
Never Say Never:
Are There Exceptions
to the Rule That
Democracies Do Not
Fight Each Other?

Chapter 3

Perceptions and the Limits of Liberal Peace: The Mexican-American and Spanish-American Wars

John M. Owen

Much scholarly energy is being expended in trying to answer the question of why there is a liberal (or democratic) peace.[1] The answer could alert scholars and policy makers to any conditions under which liberal peace could fail—that is, under which liberal democracies could go to war against one another. The stakes are high: the notion that "democracies don't attack each other" is an axiom of U.S. foreign policy,[2] and policy makers need to know if there are times when the axiom does not hold.

In this chapter I use two case studies—the Mexican-American crisis of 1845–46 and the Spanish-American crisis of 1895–98—to argue that liberal peace is generally robust, but that it can break down if a crucial condition is not met: namely, that liberal states—or more precisely, liberal elites within those states—perceive other liberal states to be liberal. Typically, liberal elites perceive a foreign state to be liberal or not based on how well its domestic institutions conform to their normative vision for their own state. For these elites, a liberal

---

The author thanks Miriam Fendius Elman, Joe Hagan, and Sean Lynn-Jones, as well as the other contributors to this volume, for their comments on an earlier draft of this chapter.

---

1. Throughout this chapter I use the term "liberal state" rather than "democracy." I define a liberal state as one having institutional checks and balances on war decisions; I define democracies as states where the majority rules. Democracies may be liberal states, and vice versa; but majority rule alone does not bring a zone of peace, as the German elections of 1933 demonstrate.

2. "Excerpts from President Clinton's State of the Union Message," *New York Times,* January 26, 1994, p. A17.

state is one whose internal institutions match their vision; an illiberal state is one with an opposite, "oppressive" set of institutions. The perceptions of most of these elites generally match those of today's scholars, even though the latter may use different criteria. Thus liberal peace usually holds.

Occasionally, however, these liberal elites perceive a state to be illiberal that today's scholarly consensus would declare liberal. This chapter shows how Mexican liberals in the 1830s and 1840s, and Spanish liberals in the 1890s, came to regard the United States as illiberal, even though they had long admired their northern neighbor as a model republic. I argue that the perceptual shifts were triggered by U.S. aggressiveness: the United States, pushed by liberal elites, posed a clear and present danger to sovereign Mexican and Spanish territory, respectively.

The two cases are imperfect illustrations of a condition under which my theory of liberal peace does not apply, and thus suggest when liberal peace can collapse. The Mexican-American War is not a case of two liberal states at war, since Mexico was an unstable military dictatorship. The Spanish-American War, as explained below, is best classified as a war between a liberal and a semiliberal state. Still, domestic and interstate dynamics in the two cases show that the processes by which liberal states normally maintain pacific relations with one another can malfunction.

The cases also show that the notion that liberals are generally pacific—the "monadic" thesis—does not stand up to historical scrutiny. Liberals can be highly belligerent toward those they regard as illiberal. In fact, any discussion of liberal peace should involve its counterpart, liberal war.

Careful historical analysis must inform our understanding of liberal peace and thus our policy recommendations. In looking at any bilateral relationship today, we cannot predict violence or cooperation by simply coding the states according to ahistorical institutional criteria. Conceptions and perceptions of liberalism and democracy vary widely across time and space, and we must examine how states perceive one another to know whether they are unlikely to fight one another. The case study method is necessary to capture these conceptions and perceptions.

The next section summarizes my theory as to why liberal states rarely fight one another. I derive hypotheses from the theory, and also posit important counterhypotheses drawn from realism, ethnic identity theory, and liberal pacifism. I next present the two case studies, first giving a brief narrative account, then testing the hypotheses. The cases show that there are conditions under which my theory does not apply, and realism provides a better explanation. In other words, the cases illuminate the possible circumstances under which liberal peace can break down. Finally, I offer some conclusions for international politics today.

A Liberal Peace?

I define as liberal those states having two general sets of institutions: freedom of discussion, and regular competitive elections of those empowered to make war or those to whom they are responsible.[3] I argue that liberal states tend to remain at peace with one another because of a synergistic working of liberal ideology and institutions. The foreign policies of liberal states, especially during crises, are shaped by liberal elites—opinion leaders who are committed to having liberal institutions in their own state.[4] These elites believe it is in their nation's interest to have good relations with foreign states that have what they consider to be liberal institutions. They also believe that the national interest requires aloofness from and even hostility toward states they regard as illiberal; they may thus be likely to urge their leaders into confrontation with illiberal states. These beliefs stem from the conviction that such foreign relations serve their top priority, namely, strengthening liberalism in their own country.[5] The high value liberalism places on individual autonomy and self-determination makes liberal elites peculiarly slow to turn against those they regard as their own type. In disputes with such states they will agitate for cooperation. But they will push for confrontational policies toward states they perceive to be illiberal.[6]

3. This definition is compatible with that used by Miriam Fendius Elman in the introduction to this volume.

4. For the notion of opinion leaders, see James Rosenau, *Public Opinion and Foreign Policy: An Operational Formulation* (New York: Random House, 1961), pp. 35–39.

5. My argument is explained more fully in my *Liberal Peace, Liberal War* (Ithaca, N.Y.: Cornell University Press, 1997). Parts of the argument appear in my "How Liberalism Produces Democratic Peace," in Michael E. Brown, Sean M. Lynn-Jones, and Steven E. Miller, eds., *Debating the Democratic Peace* (Cambridge, Mass.: MIT Press, 1996), pp. 116–156.

6. Other bases for interstate identification include ethnicity, religion, and history. Below I argue that ethnic identity was not an important factor in the two cases considered in this chapter. Ideologues other than liberals (communists, monarchists, fascists) also want good relations with their own regime type, but the content of their ideologies makes them less successful than liberals at maintaining intra-regime peace.

Liberal elites, then, view foreign states with prejudice. If they live in a liberal state, their prejudices are likely to affect foreign policy. First, leaders of liberal states are likely to be liberals who hold these prejudices. Second, even if they are not, they will find themselves constrained by liberal elites, particularly during war-threatening crises. When war is possible, public attention is engaged and liberal elites agitate to persuade the electorate that their preferred policy is best. Democratically elected leaders are likely to find themselves unable to ignore the protestations of liberal elites, who will demand confrontation of illiberal states but will reject the use of force against fellow liberals.[7]

My argument is thus about liberal war as well as liberal peace. If liberals perceive a foreign state to be illiberal, they will interpret its actions as hostile. As Michael Doyle writes, "fellow liberals benefit from a presumption of amity; nonliberals suffer from a presumption of enmity."[8] These presumptions affect crisis behavior and often lead to war with states perceived to be illiberal.

How do liberals decide which states are liberal? The question is crucial; perceptions of which states are liberal are not uniform across time and space. One person's democracy is often another's despotism. In the nineteenth century, for example, many Americans regarded Great Britain as an illiberal state even though it had a free press and (after 1832) fairly competitive elections. For these Americans, Britain could not be liberal because it was a monarchy.[9]

We thus need to look at liberal peace on a subjective as well as an

---

7. Although domestic constraints are an important component of my argument, I do not elaborate on them in this chapter. See Joe D. Hagan, "Domestic Political Systems and War Proneness," *Mershon International Studies Review*, Vol. 38 (October 1994), pp. 183–207, for a call for synthesis between the literatures on liberal peace and on domestic constraints on foreign policy.

8. Michael W. Doyle, "Liberalism and World Politics," *American Political Science Review*, Vol. 80, No. 4 (December 1986), p. 1161.

9. Logically, it is not necessary that liberal states perceive one another as liberal in order for there to be liberal peace. For example, it could be that liberal states are generally more forgiving of other states (in game-theoretic terms, respond to defection with cooperation) than are illiberal states; two liberal states would thus be likely to resolve their differences pacifically even if they did not perceive one another as liberal, while a liberal state would be exploited and perhaps attacked by an illiberal state. As Bruce Bueno de Mesquita and David Lalman point out, however, liberal (dovish) states would then fear exploitation by illiberal (hawkish) states, and would thus be compelled to distinguish liberal from illiberal states. Bueno de Mesquita and Lalman, *War and Reason: Domestic and International Imperatives* (New Haven, Conn.: Yale University Press, 1992), chap. 5.

objective level. Liberals typically define a state as liberal if it has the domestic political institutions they favor in their own state. These institutions are particular to time and place. Liberals pick their institutional criteria dialectically, that is, by referring to an opposite set of "oppressive" institutions. For example, consider States A, B, and C, all of which would be considered liberal by today's scholarly consensus. A and B have universal suffrage, while C denies women the vote. Liberal elites in A who consider restrictions on voting the biggest threat to self-government in their own state will be friendly toward B and hostile toward C. Moreover, they will tend to perceive B's actions, including military spending increases, as harmless; but they are likely to be suspicious of C's actions.

One complication is that, due to their conflicting visions, liberal elites within a state often disagree over which foreign states are liberal. During the Cold War, the American Right—which favored the market over the state—tended to be friendly toward authoritarian anti-communist states. The American Left—which tended to favor more state intervention in the economy—was much friendlier toward socialist states. Both Right and Left were liberal in a general sense,[10] but disagreed as to what institutions liberalism required. Thus they perceived foreign states differently.

There are times when liberals in State A change their minds about B or C. State B, once regarded as liberal, becomes in their minds illiberal, or State C, once thought of as illiberal, is perceived as liberal. Ordinarily such changes follow either of two events: B or C changes its domestic institutions, or liberals in A change their criteria as to what constitutes a liberal state. The first type of event took place when the Spanish monarchy was overthrown in February 1873, and Americans suddenly perceived Spain as a sister republic and ceased demanding that Spain abolish slavery in Cuba. The second type took place when British conservatives, threatened by the rise of socialism in their own country in the late 1880s, decided that the American-style democracy they had long derided was an acceptable form of government after all.[11]

ALTERNATIVE EXPLANATIONS

There are a number of cogent criticisms of both the liberal peace thesis and of theories purporting to explain the peace. Here I consider

---

10. See Louis Hartz, *The Liberal Tradition in America* (New York: Harcourt Brace Jovanovich, 1955).

11. Owen, *Liberal Peace*, chap. 5.

three theories that challenge key parts of my explanation.

In general, realism asserts that power (especially military power) is the most important factor in international relations. Realists generally resist the liberal peace thesis because it would seem to undermine the primacy they accord to material power. Realists would challenge my account of how liberals come to perceive other states as liberal or not. For instance, in a provocative article, Ido Oren argues that liberal perceptions are epiphenomenal, i.e., by-products of *realpolitik* factors. The same Woodrow Wilson who took the United States to war against Germany in 1917 because it was an "autocracy" had called Germany a "progressive" state in the late nineteenth century. Wilson reclassified Germany not because of any change in the German system of government, but because of rising German threats to U.S. interests, first in the Pacific and South America, then in Europe.[12]

By this reasoning, liberal elites will code useful states as liberal, but will consider those states that threaten their interests to be illiberal. They will not define other states as liberal based on how well those states' domestic polities conform to their own liberal vision, but rather based on whether those states pose military threats to their own state.

Another alternative, the ethnic identity theory, holds that liberals identify with other states based on common ethnicity rather than form of government. For example, in this volume, Stephen Rock argues that Anglo-U.S. rapprochement in the late nineteenth century was more a product of Anglo-Saxon solidarity, especially on the British side, than of liberal affinity. What looks like liberal peace is actually *Pax Anglo-saxonica*.[13]

A third alternative actually pushes liberalism further than I. Some proponents of the liberal peace thesis have, explicitly or not, maintained that liberal states are generally more pacific than illiberal states.[14] This monadic thesis, as explained by Miriam Fendius Elman in the introduction to this volume, implies that during

---

12. Ido Oren, "The Subjectivity of the 'Democratic' Peace: Changing U.S. Perceptions of Imperial Germany," in Brown et al., *Debating the Democratic Peace*, pp. 263–300, esp. 270–271.

13. See E. H. Carr, *The Twenty Years' Crisis, 1919–1939*, rev. ed. (New York: Macmillan, 1946), 232–239.

14. See, for example, R.J. Rummel, "Libertarianism and International Violence," *Journal of Conflict Resolution*, Vol. 27, No. 1 (March 1983), pp. 27–71. Michael Howard surveys the history of this liberal pacifistic self-conception in *War and the Liberal Conscience* (New Brunswick, N.J.: Rutgers University Press, 1978).

disputes with foreign states, liberals would strive for cooperation and peace regardless of whether the other state was liberal. Since my theory encompasses liberal war as well as liberal peace, the liberal pacifism argument anticipates very different behavior by liberals and liberal states.

HYPOTHESES

My theory yields two key hypotheses:

A. 1. Liberal elites will perceive a foreign state to be liberal based on whether it has the institutions they want for their own state. *STRONG STATEMENT*

A. 2. Liberal elites will be pacific toward states they perceive to be liberal, but confrontational toward states they perceive to be illiberal.

We can determine what institutions elites want for their own state, and which states they consider liberal, by examining their writings, speeches, and voting, as well as by consulting secondary historical literature.

Realism offers a hypothesis that directly challenges A.1:

B. 1. Liberal elites will label a foreign state illiberal if it poses a material threat to their national interests.

The realist hypothesis would be supported if elites relabeled as illiberal a state once perceived as liberal when that state begins to act aggressively toward their own state. *OR DEVELOPS CAPABILITIES*

Ethnic identity challenges A.1 and B.1:

C. 1. Liberal elites will label a foreign state liberal if it is dominated by their ethnic group, and illiberal if it is dominated by a different ethnic group.

Finally, liberal pacifism challenges A.2:

D. 1. Liberal elites will be less likely to use force regardless of the regime type of the other state. *mediated by issue/justice*

In the sections that follow, I test my hypotheses, using the cases of the Mexican-American and Spanish-American Wars.

The Mexican-American Crisis of 1845–46

James K. Polk won the U.S. presidency in 1844 by calling for territorial expansion, which he and his wing of the Democratic Party (the followers of Andrew Jackson) believed was necessary to maintain American virtue and prosperity. Polk wanted to annex Texas, California, and the Oregon territory.[15] Polk's opponent in 1844, Henry Clay, was ambivalent about expansion. Clay's Whig Party feared that expansion would bring unnecessary war and jeopardize its vision of an industrial United States. Mexico had never accepted the independence of Texas, declared in 1836, and warned Washington that U.S. annexation of Texas would be seen as a hostile act. The night before Polk took office in March 1845, John Tyler, the outgoing president, offered annexation to Texas. When Polk honored the offer, Mexico broke off relations.[16]

Polk quickly ordered military and naval movements to defend Texas against possible Mexican attack. In mid-June, he sent General Zachary Taylor to move his "corps of observation" from Louisiana into Texas. Taylor moved his 4,000 men toward the Nueces River, an area claimed by both Texas and Mexico.[17]

On July 4, 1845, Texas officially accepted the U.S. annexation offer. Most of the Mexican press was livid. But the Mexican Congress balked at declaring war due to the country's difficult financial situation. Assuming that Mexican silence implied acquiescence, in November Polk sent a special envoy, John Slidell, to offer a renewal of diplomatic relations and payment of up to $25 million for California. The moderate Mexican president, José Joaquín de Herrera, wanted no war, but feared he would be charged with treason if he received Slidell. Herrera's own minister of war called for all-out war, arguing that victory would be easy. Herrera played for time, asking Slidell for better credentials and requesting advice from Mexican state governors.[18]

At this point the Spanish minister to Mexico decided the time was ripe to carry out Madrid's long-standing plans to place a Spanish monarch at the head of Mexico. Working with Lucas Alamán, a

---

15. John H. Schroeder, *Mr. Polk's War: American Opposition and Dissent, 1846–1848* (Madison: University of Wisconsin Press, 1973), pp. 3–4. Opposing this view is Justin H. Smith, *The War with Mexico*, Vol. 1 (New York: Macmillan, 1919), chap. 1.

16. David M. Pletcher, *The Diplomacy of Annexation: Texas, Oregon, and the Mexican War* (Columbia: University of Missouri Press, 1973), chap. 7.

17. Pletcher, *Diplomacy of Annexation*, pp. 255–256.

18. John Edwards Weems, *To Conquer a Peace: The War between the United States and Mexico* (New York: Doubleday, 1974), pp. 95–97; Pletcher, *Diplomacy of Annexation*, pp. 353–357.

leading Mexican intellectual and former foreign minister, the minister enlisted the conservative General Mariano Paredes y Arrillaga to overthrow Herrera and act as a transitional ruler. Paredes demanded as his price, war with the United States. The general believed Mexico would win such a war, given the strength of Mexican public opinion and political divisions within the United States. On December 18, Paredes launched a rebellion, accusing Herrera "of trying to give away national territory by negotiating the cession of Texas to the United States and with that, trying to avoid a 'glorious and necessary war.'" On January 2, 1846, Paredes marched into Mexico City and Herrera resigned.[19]

In the meantime, Polk had ordered Taylor to march to the north bank of the Rio Grande, deeper into territory claimed by Mexico. On March 28, the men camped across the river from the Mexican town of Matamoros, announcing pacific intentions to the Mexican commander there. Days later, Mexican reinforcements arrived at Matamoros and ordered the U.S. troops to march back to the Nueces within twenty-four hours. Taylor responded by asking a U.S. naval auxiliary to blockade the mouth of the Rio Grande—the sort of move normally made only in wartime.[20] In Mexico City, Paredes proclaimed a "defensive war" against the U.S. "invaders." On April 25, a reconnaissance patrol of sixty-three U.S. soldiers was ambushed by several hundred Mexicans. Sixteen Americans, including the captain in command, were killed or wounded. Taylor reported to Washington, "Hostilities may now be considered as commenced."[21]

Polk had decided to wait until Slidell returned to Washington before acting, both because he hoped that Mexican moderates would force a compromise and because he wanted to deal first with the simultaneous crisis with Britain over Oregon.[22] Upon his return to Washington, Slidell recommended war, and the president prepared a war message. Word of the Matamoros skirmish led the cabinet to vote unanimously to send the message to Congress. Polk declared that

---

19. Miguel E. Soto, "The Monarchist Conspiracy and the Mexican War," in Douglas W. Richmond, ed., *The Walter Prescott Webb Memorial Lectures, Essays on the Mexican War* (College Station: Texas A&M University Press, 1986), pp. 67–73.

20. Weems, *To Conquer a Peace*, pp. 103–112.

21. Pletcher, *Diplomacy of Annexation*, pp. 373–377; and Weems, *To Conquer a Peace*, pp. 113–114.

22. See Stephen Rock's chapter in this volume.

war already existed "by act of Mexico," and took pains to emphasize that Mexico was no longer a republic:

The government of General Paredes, having recently overthrown that of President Herrera, was a military government and depended for its continuance in power upon that allegiance of the army under his command, and by which he had been enabled to effect the late revolution. . . . The Government of General Paredes owes its existence to a military revolution, by which the subsisting constitutional authorities had been subverted. The form of government was entirely changed.[23]

In other words, Polk claimed that the U.S. Congress need not wait for its Mexican counterpart to declare war. The dictator of Mexico had already done so.

The House of Representatives easily approved the war resolution by a vote of 174–14, the only opposition coming from abolitionists, led by John Quincy Adams. Resistance in the Senate from Whigs and certain Democrats was stronger at first. A central issue was whether Mexico was still a republic; if it was, many argued, war was out of the question. On the Senate floor Thomas Hart Benton, a Missouri Democrat from the Van Buren wing of the party, read a statement by Paredes himself that only the Mexican Congress could declare war. Leading the doves was John C. Calhoun, who argued similarly that the Mexican Congress might still disavow war.[24] The argument that Mexico remained a fellow republic, constrained by its own laws from reckless war, was potentially a powerful one to Americans. Senator John J. Crittenden, a Kentucky Whig, lamented the possibility of a war on liberal grounds:

This country had regarded [the Latin American revolutions] as an imitation of our example—as a new creation of republics, united by a strong affinity, and warm sympathy. They were regarded as a portion of that great system of republics which were to stand forth in proud contrast with the Governments of the Old World. . . It was not in the amount of precious blood that had been shed that consisted the importance of [the proposed war]. No; it was the great political consequences—the bad example—the evil consequences to liberty and republicanism in every place. The hand of one republic stretched out in hostility against another!

Making the hostilities still worse for Crittenden was that Mexico was struggling even then not to fall back "into the hands of despots, and

---

23. 29th Cong., 1st sess., *Congressional Globe*, Vol. 15 (May 11, 1846), p. 783.
24. Ibid., pp. 789, 796–797.

that monarchical system from which we saw her, with pleasure, arise."[25]

Jacksonians, however, took Crittenden's last point as justifying war. The *New-York Herald* had declared the week before: "It is time for the chief magistrate of this great people . . . to begin this great movement, which will pievent a relapse of a sister republic into the arms of a monarchy, as is threatened by the English government."[26] One prowar magazine declared that "the question of extending *constitutional republican institutions* over this whole continent is one of the broadest, noblest and most important that was ever presented to any nation."[27] Expansionist senators ridiculed the idea that Mexico was a sister republic. After a sustained and vitriolic debate, antiwar votes disappeared in the face of the Matamoros incident, and the Senate passed the war resolution by a vote of 40–2.[28] Mexico was to suffer a humiliating defeat and lose half of its territory to the United States.

THE WAR AND LIBERAL PEACE

In this section I discuss whether the Mexican-American War violates the liberal peace proposition, and evaluate the various hypotheses on perceptions.

A WAR BETWEEN TWO LIBERAL STATES? The Mexican-American War does not disconfirm the dyadic version of the liberal peace thesis: while the United States was a liberal state, Mexico was not.

The first ten amendments to the U.S. Constitution guaranteed to citizens freedoms of religion, speech, the press, and assembly against federal encroachment, but did not yet apply to the states.[29] A number of laws checked the government's ability to go to war. Only Congress could declare war, and its lower house (the House of Representatives) was elected directly by the people every two years. Members of the upper house (the Senate) were chosen every six years by state legislatures, which in turn were usually popularly elected. The president

---

25. Ibid., p. 788.

26. *New-York Herald*, April 18, 1846, p. 2.

27. Letter from Parke Godwin to *Harbinger* magazine, quoted in Pletcher, *Diplomacy of Annexation*, p. 390. Emphasis in original.

28. Ibid., pp. 386–392.

29. The institution of slavery flourished, especially in the South, meaning individual rights were not recognized for all residents. The pared-down definition of liberal state used in this chapter, however, does not touch the question of slavery. Subjectively, slavery mattered a great deal to many liberals in the United States and abroad.

was selected every four years by the Electoral College, whose members were chosen either by the people or the state legislators, depending on the state. Electors were not bound by law to follow voters' or legislators' instructions, but in almost all elections they all did so. The Bill of Rights allowed highly competitive elections, and the Republican opposition was vibrant.[30] Every election, beginning in 1789, had been fairly contested; power had been peacefully handed over to the winner; and the loser had suffered no persecution.

By contrast, Mexico's political instability at the time disqualifies it from liberal status. The nation went through fourteen different presidents between 1829 and 1844.[31] In the mid-1840s these presidents gained power via the bullet rather than the ballot. In December 1844, Herrera took power from General Antonio López de Santa Anna in a coup d'état. A year later, Herrera was overthrown by Paredes.[32] Under the 1836 Constitution, only Congress was empowered to declare war; but Santa Anna had promulgated a new constitution in 1843 which gave the president war powers. It was not clear at the time—nor is it clear now—under which constitution the country was operating during the crisis with the United States in 1845–46. Paredes publicly stated that war powers resided in Congress, but he then unilaterally declared a "defensive war" against the United States. Moreover, press freedoms were often curtailed in practice.[33]

---

30. As for the voters themselves, the franchise was much more limited than today. Slaves and women, of course, could not vote. Indians living in tribal nations were not considered citizens, and, subject to separate laws and governance, could not vote either. Chilton Williamson, *American Suffrage: From Property to Democracy 1760–1860* (Princeton, N.J.: Princeton University Press, 1960), pp. 150, 156, 208–209; Robert Weil, *The Legal Status of the Indian* (New York: n.p., 1888; repr., New York: AMS, 1975), pp. 70–73.

31. Gene Brack, *Mexico Views Manifest Destiny, 1821–1846* (Albuquerque: University of New Mexico Press, 1975), p. 53.

32. George Lockhart Reeves, *The United States and Mexico 1821–1848*, Vol. 1 (New York: Charles Scribner's Sons, 1913), pp. 42–43, 262–263; Hubert Howe Bancroft, *History of Mexico*, Vol. 5 (San Francisco: A.L. Bancroft, 1885), pp. 144–146; Arthur Howard Noll, *From Empire to Republic: The Story of the Struggle for Constitutional Government in Mexico* (Chicago: A.C. McClurg, 1903), pp. 139–158; José Fernando Ramírez, *Mexico during the War with the United States*, Walter Scholes, ed., trans. Elliott B. Scherr (Columbia: University of Missouri Press, 1950), p. 12. Ramírez was a moderate liberal who kept a detailed journal on Mexican politics during this period. Scholes states that the 1843 constitution was in effect in early 1846.

33. Noll, *Empire to Republic*, pp. 139–143; Bancroft, *History of Mexico*, Vol. 5, p. 144; Brack, *Mexico Views*, p. 142.

WERE LIBERAL ELITES GENERALLY PACIFIC? In each country, large numbers of liberal elites were mistrustful and even belligerent toward the other country. As explained below, Polk and the Jacksonians were liberals in the Jeffersonian tradition (albeit more democratic than Jefferson and the early Republicans). Yet, they were hostile toward Mexico, even to the point of welcoming war.[34] In Mexico, one liberal faction, called *puros*, were strongly anti-U.S., threatening revolt if Herrera received Slidell and in the end even seeking war with the United States. Thus the evidence is inconsistent with the monadic version of the liberal peace thesis (hypothesis D.1).

HOW DID U.S. LIBERALS PERCEIVE MEXICO? Liberal elites were divided as to the liberal status of Mexico. Whigs and certain Democrats labeled Mexico a sister republic, contrasting it to the despotic monarchies of the Old World. Jacksonians called Mexico a protomonarchy, and, as such, a tool of European monarchs and a threat to the United States. The failure of the monadic argument is partly explained by the fact that Jacksonians considered Mexico illiberal.

Realism has trouble explaining the Whig-Jacksonian disagreement over the Mexican threat. On paper the Mexican army was superior to that of the United States, with roughly 32,000 men under arms in 1845; moreover, Mexico had a much stronger military tradition than the United States. But the Mexicans were poorly trained and equipped, and their country was in political chaos and fiscal crisis, making mobilization difficult. Mexico's population was only seven million; the United States's was twenty million.[35] In any event, whether or not Mexico posed an objective threat to U.S. interests, realism cannot say why the disagreement over that threat should fall along partisan lines. Ethnic identity at first blush may seem to explain the Jacksonian prejudice against Mexicans, especially since Jacksonians were more likely than Whigs to support slavery. Yet, a look at attitudes toward Mexico in the preceding decades suggests that ethnic identification was epiphenomenal, a product of the degree of British influence in Mexico. In fact, the Jeffersonian ancestors of the Jacksonians were much more pro–Latin America than were the Federalist forerunners of the Whigs.

In the 1810s and 1820s, more egalitarian U.S. elites tended to

---

34. The Jacksonians were also hostile toward England during the simultaneous Oregon Crisis.

35. Smith, *War with Mexico*, Vol. 1, pp. 105–106, 157.

perceive Central and South American states as de facto allies, while elitists scorned them. Latin American independence was seen by Jeffersonian Republicans as part of their own republican revolution and a source of sister republics to stand against the reactionary threat posed by the monarchs of Europe. A republican Western Hemisphere was to the Jeffersonian mind essential to U.S. national security. Henry Clay told Congress in 1816 that the United States should foster an "American system" and help the peoples to the south to protect themselves from European monarchists who sought to overturn republicanism everywhere:

Everyone has heard of the proceedings of the Congress of European potentates in Vienna; we heard, too, that their ideas of legitimate government were carried to an extent destructive of every principle of liberty. . . . Do we know whether we shall escape their influence? . . . This opinion I boldly declare . . . it would undoubtedly be good policy to take part with the patriots of South America. . . . I consider the release of any part of America from the dominion of the Old World as adding to the general security of the New.[36]

Thomas Jefferson, James Madison, and James Monroe agreed that the fate of republicanism in Latin America was important to U.S. security. "In the great struggle of the Epoch between liberty and despotism," Madison wrote to Jefferson, "we owe it to ourselves to sustain the former in this hemisphere at least."[37] The Monroe administration was one of the first governments in the world to recognize Mexican independence. The following year, in 1823, Monroe announced his famous foreign policy doctrine declaring the New World off-limits to any political ambitions of the European monarchies.[38]

But others, including Daniel Webster, Edward Everett, and John Quincy Adams, saw the Latin nations as irrelevant to U.S. interests. Adams responded to Clay's vision: "As to an American system, we

---

36. Arthur Preston Whitaker, *The United States and the Independence of Latin America* (Baltimore, Md.: Johns Hopkins University Press, 1951; repr., New York: Russell and Russell, Inc., 1962), p. 190.

37. Ralph Ketcham, *James Madison: A Biography* (New York: Macmillan, 1970), p. 631.

38. Monroe recognized Mexico on December 12, 1822 (Whitaker, *United States and the Independence of Latin America*, p. 390). Monroe was a lifelong antimonarchist. After his election to the presidency in 1816, Monroe explained to Andrew Jackson that he would have no Federalists in his cabinet because they had wanted to establish a monarchy in the United States. See Harry Ammon, *James Monroe: The Quest for National Identity* (New York: McGraw-Hill, 1971), pp. 370–371.

have it—we constitute the whole of it. . . . there is no community of interests or of principles between North and South America." The New Englanders tended to discount the republican potential of Hispanic, Roman Catholic societies.[39]

From the start, the rickety Mexican Republic provided support for the New Englanders' skepticism. The hero of the 1821 revolution, Agustín de Iturbide, was soon declared Emperor Agustín I.[40] By the 1830s, as dictators such as Santa Anna seemed little better than monarchs, U.S. confidence in Mexican republicanism had dwindled. Interestingly, however, by the Mexican-American crisis of the 1840s the more elitist U.S. liberals tended to regard Mexico favorably. Adams was one of these, but now so was Clay, who had left the Democrats and cofounded the Whig Party in 1834.

Ethnic identity cannot explain this curious reversal. In fact, these perceptions correlate well with the same subjects' perceptions of Great Britain, as seen in the Oregon Crisis (see Stephen Rock's chapter in this volume).[41] In the 1840s, the same Jacksonian Democrats who were anti-Mexican were anglophobic, and the same Whigs and Democrats who thought Mexico benign thought the same of England. These respective views of England derived from each faction's vision for the United States itself. For the Jacksonians, the epitome of bad government and society was Great Britain. England was monarchical, aristocratic, industrial, and slum-ridden, a land where the common man was oppressed. For the followers of Andrew Jackson, the good society was one where the small farmer and artisan flourished. They firmly believed that progress would result from territorial expansion, free trade, and equality of opportunity. They opposed centralization, industrialization, the tariff, and the Bank of the United States in favor of the Jeffersonian vision of an America of virtuous yeoman farmers.[42]

---

39. Quoted in Lester D. Langley, *America and the Americas: The United States in the Western Hemisphere* (Athens: University of Georgia Press, 1989), p. 41; and Karl M. Schmitt, *Mexico and the United States, 1821–1973: Conflict and Coexistence* (New York: John Wiley & Sons, 1974), p. 34.

40. Ibid., pp. 34–35.

41. As Pletcher writes, "Many warhawks merged the Mexican and British enemies, declaring that Britain was standing behind Mexico in her defiance." Pletcher, *Diplomacy of Annexation*, p. 390.

42. Robert V. Remini, *Henry Clay: Statesman for the Union* (New York: W.W. Norton, 1991), pp. 398–401, 458–460; and Thomas R. Hietala, *Manifest Design: Anxious Aggrandizement in Late Jacksonian America* (Ithaca, N.Y.: Cornell University Press, 1985), pp. 104–105.

The Whigs held a very different vision for the country. For them, the key to national progress was technological advancement directed by an enlightened elite. Whigs wanted a strong national government, dominated by Congress and the courts, rather than states' rights and a strong president.[43]

Democrats were more attached to "negative" liberty—that is, liberty as the absence of coercion—small, localized government, and free trade, but they were more supportive of slavery, unbridled competition, and aggressive territorial expansion. Whigs were more critical of slavery and elevated rational discussion over Darwinian competition, but favored a strong state, the tariff, and a more "positive" liberty— that is, liberty as mastery of one's bad impulses.[44] There were also more elitist Democrats who resisted various components of the Jacksonian vision. John C. Calhoun, leader of a group of Southern Democrats, helped form the Whig Party but returned to the Democrats in 1836. The wing of the party associated with Martin Van Buren, president from 1837 to 1841, was less egalitarian than the Jacksonians.[45]

The Whigs and the more elitist Democrats took a kinder view of England. They admired its ordered liberty and its industrial might. They wanted to compromise with London over the Oregon territory. The Jacksonians did not, and moreover feared that domestic instability in Mexico made that country less an autonomous republic and more a cipher for British monarchical influence. They pictured the malignant hand of England trying to hem in the United States in order to choke off American republicanism, which by its example threatened British monarchy and aristocracy. Jacksonians became taken with the thought that Mexico was most useful as a source of territory to strengthen their own republic.[46] The Whigs, meanwhile, paid little notice to alleged signs of British influence in Mexico. Van

---

43. Daniel Walker Howe, *The Political Culture of the American Whigs* (Chicago: University of Chicago Press, 1979). See also Hartz, *Liberal Tradition*, chap. 4.

44. Daniel Walker Howe, ed., *The American Whigs: An Anthology* (New York: John Wiley & Sons, 1973), p. 4. For the classic statement of the distinction between positive and negative liberty, see Isaiah Berlin, "Two Concepts of Liberty," in *Four Essays on Liberty* (New York: Oxford University Press, 1969), pp. 118–172.

45. William Brock, "The Image of England and American Nationalism," *Journal of American Studies*, Vol. 5, No. 3 (December 1971), pp. 225–245; and Robert Kelley, *The Cultural Pattern in American Politics: The First Century* (New York: Alfred A. Knopf, 1979), p. 157.

46. Schmitt, *Mexico and the United States*, pp. 42–44.

Buren had declared Britain a fellow liberal state in 1832, following the Great Reform Act;[47] as president he worked to reestablish a friendship with Mexico.[48] One branch of the Whigs, the abolitionists led by John Quincy Adams, especially admired both Britain and Mexico for having abolished slavery.[49]

Jacksonian suspicion was exacerbated by the coup of Paredes in December 1845. Polk and James Buchanan, the secretary of state, more than suspected that Paredes was carrying out a monarchical plot with the aid of the British and French. As Buchanan wrote privately to Slidell in March:

Should Great Britain and France attempt to place a Spanish or any other European Prince upon the throne of Mexico, this would be resisted by all the power of the United States. In opposition to such an attempt, party distinctions in . . . [the United States] would vanish and the people would be nearly unanimous . . . the United States could never suffer foreign powers to erect a throne for a European Prince on the ruins of a neighboring Republic, without our most determined resistance.[50]

For months, U.S. editors had been clamoring about a monarchical plot in Mexico. The *New-York Herald* announced: "Europe is adverse to liberty in Europe, and it belongs to us, the greatest republic in the whole world, to watch with zealous care, that her enmity to liberty, which reigns in her own regions, be not actively transferred to this hemisphere."[51]

Jacksonian loathing of Mexico had moreover already been stirred by the Texans' struggle for independence, especially Mexican brutality at the Battle of the Alamo. As Edward H. Moseley points out, "the new republic took the United States as its political and economic model. . . . The American press was strident in its condemnation of Mexico and its praise for the new republic."[52] The arrival of the

---

47. Van Buren was the U.S. minister to London in 1832, and was persuaded that the reforms that expanded the franchise and weakened the Crown made Britain a liberal state. Kelley, *Cultural Pattern*, p. 157.

48. Edward A. Moseley, "The United States and Mexico, 1810–1850," in T. Ray Shurbutt, ed., *United States-Latin American Relations, 1800–1850: The Formative Generations* (Tuscaloosa: University of Alabama Press, 1991), pp. 159–160.

49. Mexico abolished slavery in 1829, Britain in 1833. See Smith, *The War with Mexico*, Vol. 1, pp. 117–119.

50. Soto, "Monarchist Conspiracy," p. 78.

51. *New-York Herald*, March 25, 1846, p. 2.

52. Moseley, "United States and Mexico, " p. 147.

Republic of Texas made Mexico look less liberal by comparison.

In sum, Jacksonians saw one Mexico, and Whigs and elitist Democrats saw another. The difference was a product of their perceptions of Britain, the country that exercised the most influence in Mexico after the United States. And those perceptions of Britain derived from conflicting visions for the domestic U.S. order. I am not arguing that the Jacksonian desire to "republicanize" Mexico drove the United States to war; rather, that desire made war easier to declare when Mexico appeared on the verge of becoming a monarchy. The Jacksonian hunger for territory was the driving force behind U.S. aggressiveness.[53] But this hunger was a product of the Jacksonian domestic political program, which in turn reflected antipathy for the hierarchical nature of the British political system. In this case, ideology and interest were intertwined.[54]

HOW DID MEXICAN LIBERALS PERCEIVE THE UNITED STATES? One faction of Mexican liberals, the *moderados*, wanted to accommodate the United States and even saw their northern neighbor as a model. Another faction, the *puros*, was (like conservative Mexicans) vehemently anti-U.S. *Puros* portrayed the United States as a rapacious, racist society bent on swallowing Mexico. The story of the *puros* illustrates how the perception of significant external threats can override

---

53. There are at least two reasons to believe that war would not have happened had the United States had a less aggressive president (such as Henry Clay, whom Polk defeated in 1844). First, the Mexicans would have been reassured by a Clay victory in 1844 and may not have been as hostile during the disputes of 1845. Second, Clay may have approved of Texas annexation, but would probably not have pushed Mexico to cede California. As president, Clay would have faced enormous domestic expansionist pressure, but might have resisted it and avoided war.

54. An alternative domestic politics hypothesis is that the slavery question drove perceptions of Mexico (and Britain). In this interpretation, Jacksonians hoped and Whigs feared that land from Mexico would be slave territory. But there were Jacksonians in the North (cf. the *New-York Herald* and the *Democratic Review*) and Whigs in the South; Calhoun, slavery's most powerful advocate, opposed war with both Mexico and England; and the United States had already annexed Texas, while California was likely to be free territory. The only group the slavery hypothesis explains well is Adams's abolitionists, who admired Britain and Mexico primarily for having abolished slavery. For Adams, abolitionism overrode anglophilia: he shocked his friends by favoring war against England over the Oregon question because he wanted the United States to expand its free territory. Frederick Merk, *The Oregon Question: Essays in Anglo-American Diplomacy and Politics* (Cambridge, Mass.: Harvard University Press, 1967), pp. 227–229. But for nonabolitionists, slavery was not the primary issue at stake in the Mexican crisis.

liberal transnational solidarity.

In the first years of Mexican independence, moderate and radical liberals had admired the United States. They wanted a constitutional Mexico, with freedoms of the press and association and equality before the law for Indians. Where moderates and radicals disagreed was on how to evaluate the nation's colonial past. Radicals were staunch republicans who sought to overturn virtually every feature of the past. They wanted a strong central government actively to help the masses by seizing Church property, raising taxes, and forming a strong national army while eliminating provincial militias. They were less committed to liberal procedural correctness than to egalitarianism.[55] Moderates were less inclined to jettison the past entirely. They were less antimonarchical; they wanted to reduce the power of the Church, but slowly; they wanted a weak central government; and they wanted suffrage limited to property owners, and in general held to middle-class views of property rights.[56] Herrera, president from late 1844 until his overthrow in late 1845, was a moderate liberal.[57]

The third main faction in early republican Mexico was the conservatives, who tended toward monarchism.[58] Led by the intellectual Alamán, conservatives wanted a Mexico with a strong central government committed to property rights, Catholicism, mercantilism, and order.[59] In the 1840s, conservatives began calling for the establishment of a European prince as head of state. Alamán and his party believed that Mexico's lack of unity and progress since independence in 1821 showed that the country must become a monarchy.[60] Paredes, the general who became president by a coup in late 1845, was a conservative.[61]

In the first decade after independence from Spain, Mexican liberals tended to look on the United States as a republican exemplar. One

55. Donald Fithian Stevens, *Origins of Instability in Early Republican Mexico* (Durham, N.C.: Duke University Press, 1991), pp. 30–37.

56. Ibid., pp. 30–36.

57. Pletcher, *Diplomacy of Annexation*, p. 174.

58. Stevens, *Origins of Instability*, chap. 3.

59. Brack, *Mexico Views Manifest Destiny*, p. 30; and Stevens, *Origins of Instability*, p. 29.

60. Soto, "Monarchist Conspiracy," pp. 69–70. See also Charles A. Hale, *Mexican Liberalism in the Age of Mora, 1821–1853* (New Haven, Conn.: Yale University Press, 1968), pp. 15ff.

61. Pletcher, *Diplomacy of Annexation*, p. 172.

prominent newspaper "favored frequent elections as a way of insur-
ing stability, observing that in the United States when a government
went wrong it could be replaced by election and not by revolution."[62]
A leading liberal wrote that the U.S. Constitution had "brought glory
and prosperity in a firm and stable manner to the freest people of the
universe."[63] Charles A. Hale summarizes:

In general, the Mexican liberals of the pre-Reforma generation
approached North American society uncritically. . . . To Mexican liberals the United States was a utilitarian dream world. . . . Tadeo Ortíz,
one of the most enthusiastic of the Mexicans, referred to the United
States as "the classic land of liberty and order and the refuge of all the
social virtues."[64]

By the 1840s, however, most liberals had come to believe that
Mexico's social structure and history were too unlike those of the
United States to permit slavish imitation. From that point, some, such
as José María Gutiérrez de Estrada, became conservative under the
influence of Alamán. In the 1830s, Alamán began warning his countrymen that federalism and Enlightenment philosophy, both associated with the United States, were foreign to Mexico and should be
eradicated. In 1840, Gutiérrez admitted in an article that he had once
been "sincerely addicted to the dominant principles of our neighbors," but that it was now evident that Mexico's nature required
hereditary rather than elected government.[65] Most liberals repudiat-
ed Gutiérrez, but did conclude that the theories and experience of
continental liberalism were more relevant to their nation than
American liberalism.[66]

The event that turned so many liberals against the United States
was Texan independence in 1836. Mexico's 1836 Constitution concentrated more power in the central government than its 1824
Constitution. Some Texans, especially Anglo-Saxons, feared an unacceptable loss of state autonomy (including enforcement of the aboli-
tion of slavery), and declared Texas an independent republic. The

---

62. Brack, *Mexico Views*, pp. 17–25.

63. José María Luis Mora, quoted in Hale, *Mexican Liberalism*, p. 194. Mora's journal *Seminario politico y literario* reprinted basic U.S. documents, including the
Articles of Confederation, the Declaration of Independence, the Constitution, and
two of Washington's speeches, for Mexican readers.

64. Hale, *Mexican Liberalism*, pp. 198–199.

65. Ibid., pp. 212–213; and Pletcher, *Diplomacy of Annexation*, p. 37.

66. Hale, *Mexican Liberalism*, pp. 195–197, 206–207.

rebellious Texans eventually defeated Santa Anna at San Jacinto and forced him to agree to Texan independence. Washington recognized the Republic of Texas in 1837. But Mexicans of all political stripes rejected Santa Anna's agreement and were adamant that Texas was still a part of their country.[67]

It was becoming obvious to liberals as well as conservatives in Mexico that their Anglo-Saxon neighbors wanted not only Texas but also New Mexico and California. The leading radical Gómez Farías now wrote that if Texas were to fall into U.S. hands, the United States would eventually stretch "from sea to sea," ruining Mexico's future.[68] Any value that Mexican liberals had seen in good relations with their sister republic to the north became outweighed for many by the clear and present danger of the loss of vast tracts of sovereign Mexican territory. Mexican writers began emphasizing the more disturbing aspects of the United States, such as slavery and the persecution of Indians. Gene Brack writes that "anti-Americanism became an obsessive, transcendent issue, one by which all Mexican administrations after 1836 would be measured."[69] The United States, once a model, had become a menace. The radical liberal *puros* reclassified America as illiberal.[70]

The Mexican War is not a counterexample to the liberal peace proposition. It is, however, an example of the malfunctioning of the processes by which liberal peace is maintained. The peace depends upon liberal elites' perceiving each other's states to be liberal. The Mexican War also shows the aggressive potential of liberals— in this case, the Jacksonians—who feel threatened by an alien form of government.

The Spanish-American Crisis of 1895–98

A revolt in Cuba from 1868 to 1878—the Ten Years' War—had brought the United States and Spain to the brink of war in 1873. In February 1895, Cuban revolutionary leaders living in exile in the United States

---

67. Brack, *Mexico Views*, pp. 55–56.

68. Ibid., p. 119.

69. Ibid., pp. 54–56; see also pp. 60–61.

70. Interestingly, some liberals evidently sustained hopes of good relations with the United States even after Texas's annexation. Lorenzo de Zavala was so pro-U.S. that he settled in Texas and joined in the Anglo-Saxon revolt against Mexico, becoming vice president of the Republic of Texas. Moderates continued to favor compromise with the United States even during the war itself. Hale, *Mexican Liberalism*, pp. 202–203; Pletcher, *Diplomacy of Annexation*, p. 484.

ordered another rebellion. From Madrid, Antonio Cánovas del Castillo, the prime minister, sent a moderate general to quell the insurrection. Lack of success led Cánovas to send General Valeriano Weyler y Nicolau, a man willing to use more brutal methods, in February 1896.[71]

As the exiled Cuban junta adopted a constitution and formed a government, debate began in the United States over whether Washington ought to recognize the belligerence and even independence of Cuba. Grover Cleveland, the Democratic president, and Richard Olney, his secretary of state, were disinclined to do so, but in Congress both parties began pushing for some sort of recognition and intervention to help the Cuban rebels. U.S. pro-insurgents were variously moved by sympathy, by resentment of European colonialism, and by a desire to displace Spain as exploiter of the rich resources of Cuba. Press organs were already reporting heinous acts of Spanish oppression. In February, both houses resolved that Cleveland should recognize Cuba as a belligerent. Passage of the nonbinding resolution led Cleveland and Olney vigorously to pursue U.S. claims against the Spanish over the coming months. The U.S. administration worked with Madrid on various compromises that would allow Cuban autonomy, but to no avail.[72]

In Cuba, Weyler brutally fought the rebellion with 200,000 troops and a civilian reconcentration program. Tens of thousands of rural residents were forced into fortified towns lacking housing, food, sanitation, and medical care.[73] In June 1897, William McKinley, the new Republican U.S. president, received an official report of Weyler's atrocities and the effects of the war on U.S. investments. McKinley supervised a diplomatic note protesting "in the name of the American people and . . . common humanity," the "uncivilized and inhumane" war.[74]

---

71. John L. Offner, *An Unwanted War: The Diplomacy of the United States and Spain over Cuba, 1895–1898* (Chapel Hill: University of North Carolina Press, 1992), pp. 1–13; and Ernest R. May, *Imperial Democracy: The Emergence of America as a Great Power* (Chicago: Imprint Publications, 1991), pp. 94–100.

72. Offner, *Unwanted War*, pp. 17–36; and May, *Imperial Democracy*, pp. 84–90. It was of course up to the president to recognize Cuban belligerency.

73. By the time the Spanish-American War began in 1898, approximately 200,000 Cubans had died in Weyler's concentration camps; contemporary U.S. estimates were 400,000. Offner, *Unwanted War*, pp. 11–13; and May, *Imperial Democracy*, p. 101.

74. Offner, *Unwanted War*, pp. 44–48.

At the same time, Liberals in Spain denounced Cánovas's policies, at one point almost successfully replacing the government. On June 24, Práxedes Mateo Sagasta, the Liberal leader, issued a "Manifesto to the Nation" declaring that "all the efforts in the world [were] insufficient to maintain peace in Cuba by the bayonet alone." Four days later, Cánovas was assassinated by an anarchist.[75] Sagasta had his chance to stop the Cuban rebellion peacefully.

McKinley had threatened to recognize Cuban belligerency unless Madrid took concrete steps to end the war. Significantly, when Sagasta formed a new government on October 6, McKinley eased this pressure. The Liberals replaced Weyler in Cuba with Ramón Blanco y Erenas, who was committed to Cuban autonomy. Blanco ordered that the concentration camps be broken up and announced that as of January 1, 1898, Cuba would be self-governing under Spanish sovereignty.[76] The flood of anti-Spanish petitions to Washington slowed to a trickle. In his December annual message to Congress, McKinley portrayed the regime of the Liberals Sagasta and Blanco as radically different from that of the Conservatives Cánovas and Weyler.[77]

In Cuba, however, both rebels and reactionaries spurned the Liberal proposal. For the rebels, the autonomy offer was too little too late. For the far right, it was a betrayal: on January 12, 1898, Spanish army officers led a massive anti-autonomy riot in Havana.[78] The U.S. press made much of the riots, and congressional interest was revived. McKinley sent the U.S.S. *Maine* to pay a "courtesy call" to Havana harbor. The move was universally praised in the United States, and officially regarded by the Sagasta government as a show of solidarity with its attempt to implement autonomy.[79]

Even so, Madrid sought support from the European powers against the possibility of U.S. intervention in Cuba. Two events in early 1898 raised the likelihood of such intervention. First, a letter from the Spanish minister to Washington, Enrique Dupuy de Lôme, to a prominent Spanish Liberal in Havana ridiculed McKinley and

---

75. Ibid., 47–50; and May, *Imperial Democracy*, pp. 104–111.

76. Offner, *Unwanted War*, pp. 65–72; and May, *Imperial Democracy*, pp. 124–127.

77. May, *Imperial Democracy*, pp. 133–134; and Offner, *Unwanted War*, pp. 77–86.

78. Offner, *Unwanted War*, pp. 92–94; and May, *Imperial Democracy*, p. 135.

79. Offner, *Unwanted War*, pp. 94–100.

portrayed Blanco's program of Cuban autonomy as a ploy to fool the United States while Spain reconquered the island. Ominously, three separate resolutions appeared in Congress renewing the call for the president to recognize the Cuban rebels as belligerents.[80]

Dupuy was recalled to Spain, but on February 15 came a much worse shock: the *Maine* exploded while docked in Havana harbor, killing 266 U.S. sailors and officers. The immediate reaction in the United States to the tragedy was circumspect. Most presumed the explosion to be an accident, even if they held the Spanish indirectly responsible for not solving their Cuban problem.[81] The *Nation* argued that no American could really believe that the Spanish destroyed the *Maine*. Rather, any U.S. belligerence toward Spain was caused by the belief that it was a backward monarchy.[82]

But the general reaction to the *Maine* explosion was much darker. Clergy preached on behalf of righteous war over the selfish pacifistic interests of business, and mass meetings and newspaper editorials cried for revenge against alleged Spanish treachery. Anti-interventionist opinion began fading as the weeks passed. The *Cincinnati Enquirer* said that even if the *Maine* explosion was accidental, "we have abundant cause for interference to stop the cruel war on the island of Cuba and guarantee that island a rich place among the republics of the western world."[83] The conservative Senator Redfield Proctor of Vermont returned from a visit to Cuba, and on March 17 delivered a speech in the Senate detailing the atrocious conditions there and advocating U.S. intervention. Because he had previously opposed intervention, Proctor's speech palpably affected public opinion. As the *Literary Digest* put it, "With very few exceptions, the most conservative of newspapers now express the opinion that Senator Proctor's careful statement of conditions in Cuba . . . makes intervention the plain duty of the United States on the simple ground of humanity."[84] William Jennings Bryan, leader of the Silver Democrats, announced: "Humanity demands that we shall act. . . . The sufferings of [Cuba's] people cannot be ignored unless we, as a

---

80. May, *Imperial Democracy*, pp. 137–139; and Offner, *Unwanted War*, pp. 116–124.

81. May, *Imperial Democracy*, pp. 139–141.

82. *Nation*, March 3, 1898, p. 157. The editors stressed that this view of Spain was outdated.

83. *Public Opinion*, March 17, 1898, p. 325.

84. Offner, *Unwanted War*, pp. 98, 122–142; and May, *Imperial Democracy*, pp. 137–147.

Nation, have become so engrossed in money-making as to be indifferent to distress."[85]

Four days after Proctor's speech, a U.S. investigation of the *Maine* incident reported that the explosion came from outside the ship. A Spanish investigation held that the explosion came from within the vessel. McKinley was now working diligently to find alternatives to war, including purchasing Cuba from Spain; allowing Spain to retain nominal sovereignty but having the United States administer the island's affairs; and simply demanding a huge indemnity from Spain for the *Maine* disaster. Yet, by the end of March, congressional Republicans so feared that Democrats would use the Cuban issue against them that they began to contemplate preempting McKinley by pushing for intervention.[86]

The president and his diplomats suggested that Madrid sell the island to Washington. The cabinet rejected the proposal. At the end of March, McKinley proposed an armistice, during which time Spain would end the reconcentration program; if there were no peace agreement by October 1, the United States would act as final arbiter between Spain and Cuba. The Spanish press was in no mood to grant the United States any say over Cuba. *El Heraldo de Madríd* called for the government to stand firm against U.S. humiliation. Spaniards of all political stripes demanded defiance of U.S. demands; Sagasta refused to acknowledge McKinley's arbitration offer.[87]

The Spanish press lauded Sagasta's firmness. An armistice would be "outside intervention," said *El Correo de Madríd,* and would damage "Spain's national honor and [affect] the integrity of the nation." *El Heraldo* said, "To abandon Cuba in the midst of a rebellion offended the nation's dignity; to give it to the Yankees . . . would be even more humiliating."[88]

In early April, with bilateral diplomacy exhausted, the European powers and the pope intervened. To McKinley's disappointment, this demarche did not buy him time with Congress.[89] When the president announced he would delay submitting a message on Cuba until April 11, angry congressmen accused him of cowardice. On April 9, the Spanish cabinet acceded to the pope's request to suspend hostili-

---

85. Offner, *Unwanted War,* p. 153.

86. May, *Imperial Democracy,* pp. 139–154; and Offner, *Unwanted War,* pp. 136–147.

87. Offner, *Unwanted War,* pp. 143–156; and May, *Imperial Democracy,* pp. 138–139.

88. Offner, *Unwanted War,* pp. 156–159.

89. May, *Imperial Democracy,* pp. 154–157.

ties in Cuba. Many in the Spanish opposition, from far right to far left, denounced the decision, while moderates approved.[90]

High hopes for a peaceful settlement were dashed when McKinley received word from the Cuban junta that it would only accept the armistice if the United States recognized Cuban independence first. Meetings with Republican congressional leaders convinced the president that he could no longer delay. His own party feared it would be thrashed at the next election if it delayed war any further. On April 11, a reluctant McKinley asked Congress to approve use of the U.S. military to enforce peace in Cuba.[91]

The Spanish cabinet and press were uniformly defiant. Articles accused the United States of duplicity, and claimed that Spanish naval might far outstripped that of the United States. *El Correo Español*, an ultraconservative Carlist newspaper, called for revolution if the queen regent capitulated.[92] In the United States, conservative Republicans approved of McKinley's speech, while Democrats and liberal Republicans were disappointed that he did not ask for a war declaration. The House passed a resolution approving of the use of force that, as McKinley hoped, did not recognize the Cuban Republic. The Senate, however, in a four-day debate laced with references to a malevolent Spanish monarchy, insisted on recognition.

The press was now nearly hysterical to rid Cuba of Spanish rule. The House and Senate reconciled their resolutions in conference, defining Cuba as independent but not recognizing the Cuban Republic. Unable to fight public opinion any longer, on April 21 the president signed the resolutions. With no response from Madrid, the next day McKinley ordered a naval blockade of Cuba, and Congress passed a joint resolution retroactively declaring April 21 the start of the war. In Spain, the public rallied behind Sagasta as he took the country into one of the greatest disasters in its history.[93]

THE WAR AND LIBERAL PEACE
I now consider whether the Spanish-American War is an exception to liberal peace, and evaluate the hypotheses on perceptions.

A WAR BETWEEN TWO LIBERAL STATES? The Spanish-American War is arguably an exception to the liberal peace proposition. David A.

---

90. Offner, *Unwanted War*, pp. 172–176.

91. Ibid., pp. 177–184; and May, *Imperial Democracy*, pp. 156–157.

92. Offner, *Unwanted War*, pp. 185–186.

93. Ibid., pp. 190–193.

Lake asserts that it is; James Lee Ray and Bruce Russett both rebut that assertion.[94] Clearly the case is a difficult one for liberal peace.

The United States was a liberal state by almost any institutional definition (see the description in the Mexican case above). Spain had a number of liberal institutions and practices. It was a constitutional monarchy in which responsible ministers had to countersign all decrees of the Crown. The Cortes (national legislature) comprised a Senate elected by various entities and a Congress elected by the populace. Trial by jury and freedoms of the press and assembly were established, and universal male suffrage was restored in 1890. Power regularly shifted between the two major parties, the Liberals and Conservatives, and each party knew it would not be persecuted before taking or after leaving office.

On the other hand, Spain's corrupt electoral system keeps it from rating as highly on a liberal scale as the United States. When a government of Cánovas would fall, the monarch would ask Sagasta to form a government, and vice versa. The new premier would then schedule elections and appoint local officials, or *caciques*, who would make certain that the election results were the desired ones.[95] As José Varela Ortega writes:

In the mid-1890s, Spain's political structure was that of a two-party-system parliamentary monarchy. It was not a democracy. Elections were rigged while a network of rural bosses pulled wires on behalf of their clients. And yet, Spain was in fact a liberal country in which fundamental rights were granted by a constitution, and where the Conservative and the Liberal parties, headed by Cánovas and Sagasta respectively, had been alternating peacefully in power since 1875. Military coups seemed to be a thing of the past.[96]

During the Cuban rebellion that began in 1895, the Spanish govern-

---

94. David A. Lake, "Powerful Pacifists: Democratic States and War," *American Political Science Review*, Vol. 86, No. 1 (March 1992), pp. 24–37; James Lee Ray, *Democracy and International Conflict: An Evaluation of the Democratic Peace Proposition* (Columbia: University of South Carolina Press, 1995), chap. 3; and Bruce Russett, *Grasping the Democratic Peace* (Princeton, N.J.: Princeton University Press, 1993), p. 19.

95. H. Butler Clarke, *Modern Spain 1815–1898* (Cambridge: Cambridge University Press, 1906), pp. 402–439; Joseph McCabe, *Spain in Revolt: 1814–1931* (London: John Lane the Bodley Head, 1931), pp. 186–197; and Martin A.S. Hume, *Modern Spain 1788–1898* (New York: G.P. Putnam's Sons, 1903), p. 553.

96. José Varela Ortega, "Aftermath of Splendid Disaster: Spanish Politics before and after the Spanish American War of 1898," *Journal of Contemporary History*, Vol. 15, No. 2 (April 1980), p. 317.

ment began to shut down newspapers and forbid public gatherings to discuss policy toward the United States.[97] Most damaging to Spain's liberal status was its brutality in Cuba, which was legally part of metropolitan Spain. There, civil rights were certainly violated with abandon.

Under an institutional definition, then, Spain should be classified as semiliberal. The Spanish-American War is thus a partial exception to the liberal peace rule, and a caution to those scholars who insist that liberal peace holds across all times and places.

WERE LIBERAL ELITES GENERALLY PACIFIC? In the United States, virtually the only visible peace party by early 1898, other than the McKinley administration, comprised those business interests that feared war would disrupt commerce.[98] Liberal elites in both parties favored war with Spain to rescue the Cuban people from Spanish brutality. In Spain, the Liberal Party did not seek war until the spring of 1898, but certainly never took a pacific attitude toward the United States. The now-marginalized Republicans, meanwhile, were among the most belligerent of Spaniards. As in the Mexican case, then, the monadic thesis fails because most liberals in each state did not perceive the other state as liberal.

HOW DID U.S. LIBERALS PERCEIVE SPAIN? It is clear that during the crisis most Americans perceived Spain as a despotic monarchy. During the congressional debate in April 1898, Senator Richard Kenney of Delaware spoke for many:

Mr. President, who is it that refuses to the people of Cuba freedom? The Spanish Crown . . . . That nation that for more than four centuries has written its history in blood; that nation that conceived and brought forth the Inquisition, the doings of which put to shame the tortures of the Prince of Hell himself.[99]

Senator Frank J. Cannon of Utah also used religious language:

When the war will have ended the United States will be able, I trust, to write a story of the deed in this one sentence: "The hand of God moved this country to destroy in Cuba the divine right of kings and

---

97. *Times* (London), January–April 1898, passim.

98. Ernest May argues that most industrialists and financiers were antiwar; Walter LaFeber argues that producers of steel and other commodities likely to be boosted by the demand for armaments were prowar. May, *Imperial Democracy*, pp. 139–140; Walter LaFeber, *The New Empire: An Interpretation of American Expansion 1860–1898* (Ithaca, N.Y.: Cornell University Press, 1963), p. 385.

99. 55th Cong., 2d sess., *Congressional Record* (April 5, 1898), Vol. 31, Pt. 4, pp. 3547–3548.

established there the diviner right of the people."[100]

Senator Clarence D. Clark of Wyoming said, "We stand for freedom of peoples and for republican government, for free institutions and national honor."[101] William Randolph Hearst's *New York Journal* declared: "No considerations of loyalty to the national government can compel acquiescence in a policy which seeks to betray Cuban freedom into the clutches of Spanish monarchy."[102] Joseph Pulitzer had his *New York World* screaming for war, in part because Spain was a despotism: "War waged on behalf of freedom, of self-government, of law and order, of humanity, to end oppression, misrule, plunder and savagery, is a holy war in itself." The Cuban struggle was as righteous as that of the patriots of 1776.[103]

What accounts for these perceptions? Realism suggests that we take account of threats to U.S. interests. In fact, however, the United States faced few significant threats in the late 1890s. Spain itself was no menace: according to Spanish figures, the U.S. Navy displaced 116,445 tons, while the Spanish displaced only 56,644 tons. Although the Spanish Army in Cuba outnumbered the whole U.S. Army by 150,000 to 25,000, the Spanish had already been severely weakened by their struggles with rebels and disease in Cuba.[104] The U.S. population was approximately 76 million, while that of Spain was roughly 18.5 million.[105] The hostility Spain was displaying was defensive, a demand that the United States dissolve the Cuban junta and let Spain settle its own problems. The European powers were capable of hurting the

---

100. Ibid. (April 16, 1898), p. 3953.

101. Ibid., p. 3968.

102. *Public Opinion*, April 21, 1898, p. 483.

103. Offner, *Unwanted War*, p. 153; and John A. Heaton, *The Story of a Page* (New York: Harper & Bros., 1913), p. 162. By contrast, Pulitzer had worked vigorously for peace with Britain three years earlier, during the Venezuelan border crisis. Pulitzer tirelessly proclaimed Britain a fellow democracy. See W.A. Swanberg, *Pulitzer* (New York: Charles Scribner's Sons, 1967), p. 199.

104. David F. Trask, *The War with Spain in 1898* (New York: Macmillan, 1981), p. 63; and Graham A. Cosmas, *An Army for Empire: The United States Army in the Spanish-American War* (Columbia: University of Missouri Press, 1971), pp. 5, 76–77. Interestingly, power perceptions were not so clear at the time. In January 1898, Theodore Roosevelt, then assistant secretary to the navy, believed the two nations' Atlantic fleets to be equal; the sinking of the *Maine* convinced him that the United States's was inferior, and he knew Spain was also negotiating to buy two British-built cruisers. Offner, *Unwanted War*, pp. 128–130.

105. Colin McEvedy and Richard Jones, *Atlas of World Population History* (New York: Facts on File, 1978), pp. 100, 290.

United States, but none was threatening the United States in a way that would lead the country to balance against Spain. Realism might also suggest that the United States had a security interest in acquiring Cuba from Spain. But it would then have to explain why so many Americans wanted to grant Cuba (and the Philippines) independence following the war. In fact, leading realist writers such as George Kennan and Norman Graebner have with some annoyance treated the Spanish-American War as a violation of *Realpolitik*.[106]

One might suspect anti-Hispanic prejudice as the cause of U.S. perceptions; but in that case Americans should have been indifferent to the plight of the Cubans, a majority of whom were black as well as Spanish-speaking.

The best explanation for negative American perceptions of Spain is that Spain did not meet the a priori criteria of U.S. liberals. Its institutions were considered illiberal well before the crisis began in 1895.

Spain was little discussed in the United States in the years before 1895. Significantly, however, those who did pay attention to Spanish affairs usually emphasized that the country was a monarchy. As in the 1840s, for many Americans monarchy disqualified a nation from "liberal" status. In fact, the attachment to republicanism was evidently bipartisan. A movement of prominent U.S. leaders and academics sought to foster republicanism around the globe. In 1892, one member of the so-called Committee of Three Hundred noted, "Republicanism is a proved success, and a long stride ahead of monarchy as a matter of governmental and social evolution."[107] Andrew Carnegie, the steel magnate and Scottish émigré, was a tireless booster of republicanism; in 1887, for example, he published the 500-page *Triumphant Democracy*, with a cover illustration of a pyramid labeled "REPUBLIC" rightside up and one labeled "MONARCHY" upside down.[108]

---

106. Kennan attributes the war to imprudent economic and humanitarian impulses. Graebner calls 1898 a turning point at which the United States abandoned seeking its own national interest in favor of "ideological" policy to further U.S. "political, social, and religious beliefs." See Robert L. Beisner, *From the Old Diplomacy to the New, 1865–1900* (New York: Thomas Y. Crowell, 1975), p. 15.

107. E.P. Powell, "A World-Wide Republic," reprinted in *Literary Digest*, January 16, 1892, p. 284.

108. Andrew Carnegie, *Triumphant Democracy: Fifty Years' March of the Republic*, 1st ed. (New York: Charles Scribner's Sons, 1887). Significantly, monarchical Great Britain was now seen as a special case by many, including Carnegie; more and more Americans had begun to acknowledge Britain as a "crowned republic" since the British political reforms of the mid-1880s. See Stephen Rock's chapter in this volume; see also Owen, *Liberal Peace*, chap. 5.

Spain had been a nominal republic from 1873–75, and the United States had responded enthusiastically, even resolving the war-threatening *Virginius* crisis of November 1873 partly for the sake of republican solidarity.[109] At that time, many in the United States saw Spain as a republic fighting to stay afloat in a sea of monarchism. But in 1898, it was a monarchy struggling to survive against a just republican revolution in Cuba. Before the Cuban revolt began in 1895, Spain was perceived by Americans as a nation with a continuing liberal-republican element stymied by an outdated form of government. Commenting on an exposé of widespread corruption in Madrid in 1892, the *New York Sun* wrote: "Madrid, under a monarchy, has been more mercilessly robbed than New York was under [William Marcy "Boss"] Tweed."[110] Months later, the *New York Tribune* asserted that the Spanish crown had "constituted an obstacle to every kind of liberal doctrine, intellectual growth and national prosperity." Yet, the *Tribune* celebrated the recent election of fifty republicans to the five-hundred-member Cortes. "Under these circumstances it is not improbable that before long we may be called upon to hail the revival in Spain of that only form of government which is in keeping with the enlightened and progressive spirit of the present age—namely, a republic."[111]

An influential analysis of the Spanish system of government was published in 1889 by J.L.M. Curry, former U.S. minister to Madrid. Curry pointedly began his book:

The American idea of the derivation of political power from the people has not found lodgment, as an actuality, in Spanish politics, literature, or thought. The Constitution contains no declaration of rights, no abstract enunciation of fundamental truths and principles.

Yet, he added, "the impartial student of the science of politics can see much to encourage."[112] Among the encouragements were the fact

109. See Owen, *Liberal Peace,* chap. 5; Richard Bradford, The "Virginius" Affair (Boulder: Colorado Associated University Press, 1980); and Allan Nevins, *Hamilton Fish: The Inner History of the Grant Administration* (New York: Dodd, Mead, 1936), pp. 635–636.

110. *New York Sun,* December 10, 1892, in *Public Opinion,* December 17, 1892, p. 248.

111. *New York Tribune,* March 25, 1893, in *Public Opinion,* April 1, 1893, p. 616.

112. J.L.M. Curry, *Constitutional Government in Spain: A Sketch* (New York: Harper & Brothers, 1889), pp. 100–101.

that most governmental officials were "from the people" rather than the aristocracy, and the fact that since 1874, Spain had been a constitutional monarchy.

On the whole, then, U.S. elites regarded Spain as an illiberal state that showed signs of becoming liberal. The war in Cuba darkened U.S. perceptions of Spain. For many, no doubt, this was because U.S. property was threatened by the turmoil. U.S. business interests, however, were divided over whether to go to war. Ernest May notes that in New York, the commercial and banking classes opposed war; the story was similar in many cities of the Middle West.[113] Walter LaFeber points out, by contrast, that producers of steel and other commodities hoped production would be boosted by war.[114] Certainly those latter interests could be expected to capitalize on and exacerbate the perception that Spain was a medieval monarchy. The stronger cause behind darkening U.S. perceptions of Spain, however, is surely Spanish conduct in Cuba itself: surely a liberal state, Americans reasoned, would not treat its own people so brutally.

HOW DID SPANISH LIBERALS PERCEIVE THE UNITED STATES? Little or no affinity or respect for the U.S. system of government is in evidence among Spanish Liberals or Republicans during the 1895–1898 crisis. The Cuban affair was seen as a matter of national honor, not as a dispute with a fellow liberal state.

As with the Mexican *puros* in the 1830s and 1840s, the perceptions of Spanish liberals in the 1890s seem best explained by realism. Ethnic identity seems plausible until one considers that in the 1860s and early 1870s the same liberals, especially Republicans, greatly admired the United States.[115] Certain passages of the Constitution of 1869, heavily influenced by Republicans, appear to have been lifted directly from the U.S. Constitution. In fact, although most Republicans were adamant that Cuba was to remain in the Spanish Empire, there was even a small movement that wished to sell Cuba to the United States.[116]

By the 1890s, however, the now-fragmented Republicans were no longer pro-U.S.; Sagasta's reforms had won over the most moderate

---

113. May, *Imperial Democracy*, pp. 139–140.

114. LaFeber, *New Empire*, p. 385.

115. C.A.M. Hennessy, *The Federal Republic in Spain: Pi y Margall and the Federal Republican Movement 1868–74* (Oxford: Clarendon Press, 1962), pp. 77, 89.

116. James W. Cortada, *Two Nations over Time: Spain and the United States, 1776–1977* (Westport, Conn.: Greenwood Press, 1978), pp. 142–145.

wing, led by Emilio Castelar. Castelar had long been America's favorite Spanish statesman, and had briefly presided over the Spanish Republic in 1873. After the civil wars ended in 1874, Castelar's wing gradually scaled back its program from republicanism to universal male suffrage.[117] Once that goal was achieved in 1890, Castelar was reconciled to the monarchy and became Spain's chief apologist to the outside world. The remaining three wings of Republicanism were radicalized and marginalized.[118]

That even Spanish Republicans now were anti-American is inconsistent with the liberal ideology hypothesis (see A.2 above). While many Republicans sympathized with Cuban rebels, and all factions managed to unite in 1897 in favor of autonomy for Cuba,[119] many in the end sided against Cuban independence and thus against the United States. The most plausible explanation for their perceptions is that they saw a clear and present American danger to Spanish sovereign territory. For most, any lingering republican affinity for the United States seems to have been trumped by a very real threat to Spain's sovereignty over Cuba.[120]

As for Sagasta's Liberals, liberal ideology might explain their lack of affinity for the United States. The Liberals were constitutional monarchists, not republicans. Like their Conservative rivals, the Liberals were committed to preventing the political convulsions that had wracked Spain in the 1860s and 1870s, convulsions caused not only by Don Carlos, the ultraconservative pretender to the throne, but also by Republicans. Sagasta's stated commitment was to a "monarchy surrounded by democratic institutions and, for this reason . . . a popular monarchy."[121]

Although Republicanism was not the mass movement it once had been, it was still taken seriously as a threat by Conservatives and Liberals. Since its founding, the United States had been an inspiration to republicans in Europe and Latin America. Spanish Liberal monarchists would thus naturally be compelled to criticize the U.S. system

117. A. Ramos Oliveira, *Politics, Economics and Men of Modern Spain 1808–1946,* trans. Teener Hall (London: Victor Gollancz, 1946), p. 229.

118. Ibid., pp. 125–126.

119. May, *Imperial Democracy,* p. 105.

120. Cortada, *Two Nations over Time,* pp. 144–145; and Offner, *Unwanted War,* p. 11.

121. Oliveira, *Men of Modern Spain,* p. 125; and David Hannay, *Don Emilio Castelar* (New York: Frederick Warne, n.d.), p. 92.

of government. One Liberal leader wrote in 1895 that Americans should abandon the wish to republicanize Cuba and let Spain handle Cuban reform in its own way: "As far as we can see, republican government has nowhere been an improvement, neither in France, nor in the United States, nor in any of the South American States."[122]

Thus, although I and others today may classify Spain in 1898 as semiliberal, most Americans did not see it as liberal in the slightest. At the same time, most Spaniards had no affinity for the United States. Because the two states perceived one another to be illiberal, their contrasting liberal ideologies exacerbated the conflict and actually helped bring on the war.

Conclusion

From early on in the scholarly debate over liberal peace, the proposition that liberal states are less likely to fight one another has been seen by both sides as a potent challenge to realism. If liberal peace is true, it has been argued, then realism is false, and vice versa. A more helpful approach is to attempt to delineate the scope of the liberal peace thesis.

This chapter affirms that liberal peace is genuine by showing that liberal elites assess threats through an ideological prism. They tend to regard a foreign state as "liberal" if it has adopted institutions compatible with those they would like to see in their own polity. They are apt to regard such a state as friendly, regardless of its material power. At the same time, they regard a foreign state that has institutions that would be harmful in their own state to be "illiberal" and are suspicious of that state regardless of its power. In other words, threat assessment is a matter of ideas as well as material capabilities.[123] The existence of these biases, and their effects on policy, provide support for the liberal peace thesis.

This chapter also identifies a condition under which liberal peace

---

122. Segismundo Moret y Prendergast, writing in *España Moderna* (Madrid), quoted in *Literary Digest*, August 3, 1895, pp. 412–413.

123. According to Stephen M. Walt's variety of realism, statesmen consider not only material power in assessing threats, but also propinquity and intentions. Walt, however, explicitly separates ideology from the judgment of intentions. Stephen M. Walt, *The Origins of Alliances* (Ithaca, N.Y.: Cornell University Press, 1987), passim. In a sense, my argument is an attempt to bring ideology back into threat assessment.

may be weakened. Liberal elites may perceive as illiberal a state that we scholars categorize as liberal. The liberals of Mexico in the 1820s and Spain in the 1870s had perceived the United States as a friend because they wanted their own country to organize itself internally as it had done. But the United States, by so clearly threatening their territorial integrity, undermined their liberal biases. These perceptual shifts are important because, as U.S. actions themselves demonstrate, liberals can be quite bellicose toward states they perceive to be illiberal.

One might argue that these cases actually show that it is only *American* liberals who identify strongly with foreign liberal states. Mexican, Spanish, and other non-American liberals seem more nationalistic and "normal." This hypothesis is related to the ethnic identity explanation I considered above. The point has been made in many places that the United States is possibly unique among the world's states in being constituted more by an idea or creed than an ethno-linguistic group.[124] It is an important point, especially because in today's world the citizens of so many newly liberalizing states are tightly attached to ethnic identities. Yet, in the 1820s Mexican liberal elites craved good relations with the United States, and in the 1870s Spanish Republicans did so as well, out of admiration for U.S. institutions. Mexican and Spanish nationalism trumped liberalism only when conditions became dire.

An analogy might be instructive: you and I are alone in a field. If I am convinced that you are my friend, and you have a gun, I will not worry that you would intentionally shoot me. If you remove the safety, I will interpret the move in the best possible light; I may suppose that you are going to shoot a target to show me how accurate your aim is. But if you point the gun at me and demand my wallet, I will recategorize you as my enemy. In the late 1830s and 1840s, the United States pointed a gun at Mexico and demanded half of its territory; in the 1890s, the United States pointed a gun at Spain and demanded that it free Cuba, the brightest jewel of the remains of the Spanish Empire. Mexican and Spanish liberals had little choice but to change their minds about the United States.

We may never be able to predict precisely when a conflict of interest between two states that regard each other as liberal becomes the equivalent of a loaded gun. These cases suggest that territorial

---

124. See, for example, Samuel P. Huntington, *American Politics: The Promise of Disharmony* (Cambridge, Mass.: Belknap Press, 1981), esp. p. 4.

integrity is a bright line that liberal states should beware of crossing.[125] That territorial disputes can weaken or even wreck liberal peace is especially troubling given the increased number of sovereign states, and the concomitant increase in states that share common borders in the post–Cold War world. Some states of the former Soviet Union have erected some liberal institutions and have liberal elites similar to those studied in this chapter. But the sheer multiplication of state borders that 1991 left in its wake, and the fact that some of these borders are in dispute (most obviously between Armenia and Azerbaijan) suggest that liberalism may not be enough to keep the peace.[126] Russian power and signs of irredentism complicate matters further.

Policy makers, then, cannot assume that once liberal institutions are established in a state, that state will be nonaggressive, even toward liberal neighbors. U.S. foreign policy in the 1840s and 1890s was highly aggressive precisely because it was driven by liberal ideology. In the 1840s, Jacksonians wanted more territory to solidify liberal democracy in the United States and halt the advance of monarchism in the New World. In the 1890s, most Americans wanted to liberate Cuba from Spanish illiberalism.[127] In both cases, war was not the first resort, but neither was it the last. Liberalism does not equal pacifism. Thus, as events in Bosnia-Herzegovina at the time of this writing demonstrate, the work of bringing peace to troubled areas of the world is more than simply a matter of implementing "free and fair elections." What leaders and electors in these countries mean by liberalism or democracy, and how they perceive their neighbors, are equally consequential.

Ironically, it may be that liberals are especially prone to step over the line and fail to respect other states' sovereign territory. In the abstract, liberals tend to emphasize cosmopolitanism over state sovereignty. They naturally sympathize with Texans or Cubans fighting to be free of a mother country. When it comes to their own countries, however, liberals are as concerned with territorial integrity as

---

125. In other words, Oren's theory (see Oren, "Subjectivity of Democratic Peace") does provide a limit to liberal peace, but it only arises when B poses a clear and present danger to A.

126. For the importance of territory to war, see John A. Vasquez, *The War Puzzle* (New York: Cambridge University Press, 1993).

127. Here I ignore the question of whether the Spanish-American War—or the Mexican War, for that matter—was morally justified.

anyone. For example, during the Civil War the overriding passion of Abraham Lincoln, William Seward, and other leaders in Washington was to restore the Southern states to the Union, and they refused to allow any European mediation. This liberal double standard may incline liberals to take other liberal states' sovereignty too lightly. Western statesmen should be mindful of the importance of sovereign territory in dealing with one another and with newly liberalizing states. Liberal peace is only as strong as the perceptions of liberal people; those perceptions are written in sand, not set in stone.

Chapter 4

Finland in World War II: Alliances, Small States, and the Democratic Peace

Miriam Fendius Elman

An important benefit of the democratic peace debate is that otherwise understudied historical events have been brought to the forefront of our attention. The recent interest in Finland's role in World War II is a case in point. Proponents and critics of the democratic peace theory strongly contest how Finland's foreign policy during World War II should be interpreted. Finland was a democracy and retained its sovereignty during the war, but allied itself with an Axis power. Thus, its actions during World War II provide a rare opportunity to study whether or not a state's democratic institutions and norms determine its foreign policy decisions.

To date, both critics and proponents have focused on outcomes alone—whether or not democracies went to war—and both have been able to muster considerable evidence to support their competing claims. Indeed, the case provides ample evidence for both proponents and critics to cite. For example, proponents of the democratic peace theory note that:

- Finland insisted on remaining a cobelligerent, rather than an ally of Germany;
- German requests for Finnish participation in an offensive against Leningrad and the Murmansk Railway were refused;
- The United States refrained from declaring war on Finland;
- The British army did not engage Finnish troops, and Britain seized few Finnish ships at sea;

The author thanks Christopher Gelpi, Joe Hagan, Arie Kacowicz, and the participants at the conference held at the Center for Science and International Affairs, Harvard University, June 25–26, 1996, for their helpful comments and suggestions on an earlier draft.

- There is no record of combat casualties between Finland and any democracy during World War II. Allied forces did not shoot Finns; nor did Finnish troops engage in military action against any Western forces.

Supporters of the democratic peace theory point to Finnish interactions with the Western allies during World War II as proof that democratic norms and institutions *do* restrain democracies from direct military conflict. They argue that Finland did not go to war with the Allies, but rather pursued a separate conflict with the Soviet Union. For instance, James Lee Ray claims that "Finland was arguably democratic, but there was never any direct military conflict between Finland and Great Britain. Finland was never officially at war with the United States or France."[1] According to Ray, "this episode in which at least two democratic states (Great Britain and Finland) did find themselves officially on opposite sides of a complex multilateral war, but whose military forces never actually engaged each other in conflict, need not count as disconfirming evidence."[2] Similarly, Nils Petter Gleditsch concedes that the case provides a formal exception to the rule that democracies do not fight each other; however, because the Allies "never took up arms against Finland," he concludes that Finland's war with Great Britain and other democracies is a mere "technicality" that does not refute the democratic peace thesis.[3]

By contrast, critics maintain that the case does not provide powerful evidence in favor of the democratic peace theory. For example, critics note that:

- Britain ended all commercial interaction between the two countries by August 1941;
- Finland expelled British consuls and inspectors prior to the Continuation War, and broke off relations in July 1941;

---

1. James Lee Ray, "Wars Between Democracies: Rare, or Nonexistent?" *International Interactions*, Vol. 18, No. 3 (1993), p. 271; see also Bruce Russett, "And Yet It Moves," *International Security*, Vol. 19, No. 4 (Spring 1995), p. 168.

2. James Lee Ray, *Democracy and International Conflict: An Evaluation of the Democratic Peace Proposition* (Columbia: University of South Carolina Press, 1995), pp. 119–120.

3. Nils Petter Gleditsch, "Democracy and the Future of European Peace," *European Journal of International Relations*, Vol. 1, No. 4 (December 1995), p. 552. See also Bruce Russett, *Grasping the Democratic Peace: Principles for a Post-Cold War World* (Princeton, N.J.: Princeton University Press, 1993), p. 18.

- German and Finnish armies were intermingled and interdependent—German General von Falkenhorst had a Finnish army corps under his command, and Marshal Mannerheim's forces in Karelia included a German division;
- Finland's cobelligerency saved Germany from worrying about an extended second front, and confronted Soviet troops who would otherwise have contributed to the Allied war effort;
- Approximately 1,200 Finnish citizens were recruited for participation in the German *Waffen-SS*, the private armed forces of the Nazi party. This Finnish SS battalion was financed by funds from the Finnish defense ministry;
- Finland was the first democratic state to voluntarily join the Axis, by signing the Anti-Comintern Pact in November 1941;
- On July 30, 1941, airplanes attached to the British Navy bombed Finnish territory;
- Britain, Canada, Australia, New Zealand, and India declared war on Finland in December 1941;
- The U.S. closed the Finnish consulate, prohibited Finnish informational activities in the United States, and finally broke off diplomatic relations in June 1944.

Critics contend that conflicts between democracies undermine the theory even in the absence of large-scale violence; that is, a threshold of 1,000 battle fatalities eliminates many conflicts that nonetheless satisfy our commonsense meaning of war. For example, David Spiro points out that although "there were no attacks by Finnish troops on the armies of liberal democracies . . . the fact that [Finland] joined the opposing alliance and fought against one of the central powers in the alliance technically puts Finland at war with five liberal regimes from 1941-1944, and also France in 1944."[4] Like Spiro, Michael Doyle argues that ruling Finland out of the democratic war data set by virtue of the 1,000-battle-deaths criterion is a "useful statistical convenience" but does not resolve the issue of whether the case discredits the democratic peace proposition. As Doyle puts it, "if today the United States and Britain suddenly attacked each other, and stopped before sustaining 1000 casualties, no advocate of the liberal thesis should regard the theory as vindicated."[5]

---

4. David E. Spiro, "The Insignificance of the Liberal Peace," *International Security*, Vol. 19, No. 2 (Fall 1994), p. 61; see also pp. 73–74.

5. Michael W. Doyle, "Correspondence on the Democratic Peace," *International Security*, Vol. 19, No. 4 (Spring 1995), p. 183.

The nagging question of how to classify Finland's involvement in World War II cannot be resolved by focusing on outcomes alone—whether or not democracies went to war. Since there is a great deal of conflicting evidence, studying outcomes will not be conclusive. Instead, we should ask whether Finland was regarded as an enemy by the Allies. We should also consider what motivated decision makers in Finland, the United States, and Great Britain to take the actions that they did.

This chapter traces the decision making process during crisis to determine what motivated Finnish decision makers to behave as they did in their diplomatic interactions with Germany, the Soviet Union, and the Western democracies. This analysis is useful for several reasons. First, it can illuminate whether Finnish behavior undermines the democratic peace theory, even though armed combat did not take place. The dyadic version of the democratic peace theory says more about relations between democracies than simply whether or not they will go to war.[6] For example, it predicts that democratic states generally ally with other democracies and refuse to ally with non-democracies: "when states are forced to choose on which side of an impending conflict they will fight . . . liberals tend to wind up on the same side."[7] Thus, the fact that Finland sided with nondemocratic Germany against a democratic war-time alliance is problematic for the theory. Furthermore, Finland's actions in World War II would undermine the theory if we found that Finnish decision makers concentrated on strategic considerations rather than on domestic regime criteria; indeed, if power rather than regime type drove the decision making calculus, then the formal state of war between democratic Finland and the democratic Allies should not be excluded from the list of warring democracies.[8] Finally, a process-tracing case study of Finland's involvement in World War II can help us determine whether the finding that democracies do not fight each other breaks

6. See, for example, Bruce Russett, "Counterfactuals About War and its Absence," in Philip E. Tetlock and Aaron Belkin, eds., *Counterfactual Thought Experiments in World Politics: Logical, Methodological, and Psychological Perspectives* (Princeton, N.J.: Princeton University Press, 1996), p. 183.

7. Doyle, "Correspondence on the Democratic Peace," p. 183. See also Spiro, "The Insignificance of the Liberal Peace," pp. 84–86.

8. Michael W. Doyle, "On the Democratic Peace—Again," in Michael E. Brown, Sean M. Lynn-Jones, and Steven E. Miller, eds., *Debating the Democratic Peace* (Cambridge, Mass.: MIT Press, 1996), p. 371.

down as we extend the definitions of war and peace beyond the definitions used in the quantitative studies that first identified a democratic peace.[9] For example, that Finnish and Allied troops did not fight on the battlefield does not mean that these democracies were in a state of peace. Certainly there was a lack of the international-al collaboration we expect among liberal democracies, and the use of force was not ruled out as improbable and illegitimate.

This chapter has three sections. In the first section, I address Finnish decision making prior to the Winter War with the Soviet Union in 1939.[10] I argue that a neorealist explanation of state behav-ior does not provide a convincing account for Finnish foreign policy making. First, neorealism proves indeterminate; many possible actions would have been consistent with the prevailing distribution of power and external threats. Second, that Finland risked war with a great power is contrary to what neorealist theories would lead us to expect. I suggest that democratic politics offers a more convincing explanation: to understand the Finnish refusal to meet Soviet terms, we must consider the extent to which cabinet members' preferences diverged, as well as the effect of this impasse on foreign policy options. This case, which culminated in war between Finland and the Soviet Union, does not undermine the dyadic version of the demo-cratic peace theory, but does undermine the monadic variant. Finnish democratic institutions and the democratic process made it difficult to negotiate and compromise. Finland was therefore unable to end the crisis with the Soviet Union by peaceful means.

In the second section, I focus on Finnish foreign policy making prior to the Continuation War with the Soviet Union in 1941. Once again, neorealism falls short. While power considerations and external

---

9. Scott Gates et al., "Democracy and Peace: A More Skeptical View," *Journal of Peace Research*, Vol. 33, No. 1 (1996), pp. 7–8.

10. While democratic peace proponents and critics frequently refer to Finland in World War II, both focus solely on Finland's relations with the Allies. This is prob-lematic because historians of the case insist that Finland's decision making calcu-lus in 1940 cannot be divorced from its earlier involvement in the war. In addi-tion, by focusing solely on Finland's relations with the Allies, proponents and critics ignore additional evidence that has implications for both the dyadic and monadic versions of the democratic peace theory. Accordingly, in this chapter I separate Finland's involvement in World War II into two phases: the Winter War fought by Finland against the Soviet Union in 1939–40, and the Continuation War in which Finland fought against the Soviet Union as Germany's cobelligerent from 1941 to 1944.

threats certainly go far in explaining why Finland sided with Nazi Germany, it is unclear that choosing a course of cobelligerency with Germany was the optimal policy given external security exigencies. As with the previous case, a domestic political argument provides a closer historical fit; to understand Finnish military strategy, we must consider the executive-legislative and the executive's foreign policy preferences. While the president favored an alliance with Nazi Germany, the Finnish Parliament did not support a policy that put Finland in an illiberal, nondemocratic camp, and therefore risked a second war with the Soviet Union. Finland ultimately became a Nazi cobelligerent because in the Finnish semipresidential system, the president has almost total control over foreign affairs. Since the legislative branch does not have *ex ante* veto power over the executive's initiatives, the president faces few constraints on alliance policies or a decision to use force.[11] Thus, democratic politics matter but the democratic peace theory is not strongly vindicated. Finnish decision making prior to the Continuation War undermines the notion that democratic leaders adopt cautious foreign policies and cannot easily choose war. Advocates of the liberal thesis mistakenly assume that in all democracies, leaders cannot act autonomously. But democratically elected leaders are not always required to enlist widespread

---

11. Semipresidential systems are dual executive governments; that is, the president is elected by the people, rather than selected by Parliament, and a prime minister needs the Parliament's confidence. Semipresidential systems are not syntheses of parliamentary or presidential systems, but rather alternate between presidential and parliamentary phases. Whether the government will resemble a presidential or parliamentary democracy depends on the extent to which the president's party commands a majority in Parliament. When the president and the majority in Parliament are of the same party, semipresidential regimes will function like majoritarian parliamentary systems, where the executive also commands a majority in Parliament. When a different party has parliamentary majority, executive powers will be far less dictatorial and the kinds of executive-legislative conflict common to presidential systems will be more likely. In short, the executive (the president) in a semipresidential system has greater political leverage than does the executive in a pure presidential or a coalitional parliamentary system. However, presidential powers are strongest when the president commands a comfortable majority in the legislature. For more on presidential powers in semipresidential democracies and the implications for foreign policy, see Maurice Duverger, "A New Political System Model: Semi-Presidential Government," *European Journal of Political Research*, Vol. 8, No. 2 (June 1980), pp. 165–187; and David P. Auerswald, "Inward Bound: The New Institutionalism and the Use of Force in Comparative Perspective," paper presented at the annual meeting of the International Studies Association, San Diego, April 16–20, 1996.

support before engaging in risky foreign policies that promise large-scale violence. In some democracies, publics and legislatures do not exert a strong influence on the foreign policy making process.

In the concluding section, I argue that the Finnish case illustrates one of the boundaries of the democratic peace thesis: other things being equal, the theory is more likely to hold for decentralized democracies (those with presidential and coalitional parliamentary systems) than for more centralized democracies (those with Westminster or semipresidential systems).[12]

Finnish Decision Making Prior to the Winter War, 1939–40

As Max Jakobson correctly points out, "the Winter War was part of the great European crisis of the 1930's, or rather one of its products, and cannot be understood except in the context of the international situation of the time."[13] During this period, the Soviet Union faced a threatening security environment—it was isolated from the Western democracies and could not rely on peace with Germany. Indeed, Soviet demands for guarantees that Finland would not side with Germany in a war against the Soviet Union must be considered in light of German military successes. Initial negotiations began in April 1938 between Finnish Foreign Minister Rudolf Holsti and Boris Yartsev, Second Secretary of the Soviet delegation at Helsinki. The Soviet Union offered military and economic assistance to help Finland resist a German invasion. According to the Soviets, Finland could not defend its neutrality alone, and would surely fall into German hands without Soviet support. Thus, Yartsev's principal task was to ensure that the Soviet Red Army would be able to advance as

---

12. However, the type of democracy does not determine war propensity; leaders' preferences are also an important variable. For instance, a centralized democracy will not be aggressive abroad if the executive views force only as a means of last resort.

13. Max Jakobson, *The Diplomacy of the Winter War: An Account of the Russo-Finnish War, 1939-1940* (Cambridge, Mass.: Harvard University Press, 1961), p. 7. See also Albin T. Anderson, "The Origins of the Winter War: A Study of Russo-Finnish Diplomacy," *World Politics*, Vol. 7, No. 2 (January 1954), p. 170; Yohanen Cohen, *Small Nations in Times of Crisis and Confrontation* (Albany: State University of New York Press, 1989), pp. 241–242; and Anthony F. Upton, *Finland in Crisis, 1940-1941: A Study in Small-Power Politics* (London: Faber and Faber, 1964), pp. 24–25.

far as possible to engage the enemy.[14] He explained that the Soviet Union had no intention of sending the Red Army to Finland or occupying Finnish territory; rather, Finland would receive arms and its sea coasts would be defended. A defense treaty would merely enable the Red Army to advance into Finland if war loomed large.

Finland rejected Yartsev's proposals. The Finnish reply, drafted by Prime Minister A.K. Cajander, stated that the acceptance of the Soviet proposals would violate Finnish sovereignty and its declared neutrality.[15] The Soviet Union then conceded that if Finland could not sign a military treaty, it should provide a written commitment to prevent a German attack by calling on the Soviet Union for military aid. Moscow also consented to the fortification of the Aaland Islands, but requested that Finland permit the Soviets to construct sea and air defenses on the islands of Suursaari or Hogland. In return, the Soviet Union would guarantee Finnish territorial integrity; provide aid on favorable terms; and conclude a trade treaty advantageous to Finnish industrial and agricultural sectors.[16]

Once again, the Finnish government rejected Yartsev's proposals on the grounds that they would compromise Finnish sovereignty and neutrality, and it offered no counterproposals as a substitute for the Soviet request to fortify Suursaari or Hogland.[17] In March 1939, the Soviets contacted Foreign Minster Eljas Erkko, who had taken over Holsti's position, with a proposal to lease Hogland and several other small islands in the Gulf of Finland for a period of thirty years. These islands would serve as naval posts along the approaches to Leningrad. In return, Finland was offered a portion of Soviet Karelia and economic collaboration.[18] Once again, Finland rejected the proposals: "Eljas Erkko declared that [Finland] could not consider leasing to a foreign power the islands referred to because they were

---

14. Jakobson, *The Diplomacy of the Winter War*, pp. 11, 49; Vaino Tanner, *The Winter War: Finland Against Russia 1939-1940* (Stanford, Calif.: Stanford University Press, 1957), p. 4; Marshal Mannerheim, *The Memoirs of Marshal Mannerheim*, trans. Count Eric Lewenhaupt (London: Cassel, 1953), p. 293; and C. Leonard Lundin, *Finland in the Second World War* (Bloomington: Indiana University Press, 1957), pp. 42–43.

15. Jakobson, *The Diplomacy of the Winter War*, p. 45.

16. Lundin, *Finland in the Second World War*, p. 43; and Richard W. Condon, *The Winter War: Russia Against Finland* (New York: Ballentine Books, 1972), pp. 12–13.

17. Tanner, *The Winter War*, p. 10.

18. Mannerheim, *Memoirs*, pp. 299–300.

inseparable parts of an area whose independence the Soviet Union had recognized and [Finland] would violate its neutrality by even undertaking to discuss the question."[19] Instead, Finnish decision makers argued in favor of a joint Finnish-Swedish defense of the Aaland Islands. But far from pacifying the Soviet Union, the prospect of a Finnish-Swedish alliance appeared even more threatening—this prospect of collaboration harked back to earlier centuries when just such an alliance threatened Soviet borders. Fearing that Swedish participation in defense of the Aaland Islands might bring it into conflict with the Soviet Union, Sweden quickly withdrew its support for the defense scheme.

In August 1939, the Soviet Union secured German support in the Nonaggression Treaty, an agreement that gave the Soviet Union a free hand in the Baltics. Since the agreement had been forged at the expense of the Baltic states, Stalin's demands on Finland were bound to increase. Thus in March 1939, when the Soviet Union felt threatened by Germany and ignored by the West, it might have been possible for Finland to secure concessions; however, the opportunity to bargain with Moscow was lost in August. In September and October 1939, the Soviet Union concluded alliance treaties with Estonia, Latvia, and Lithuania, each of which granted the Soviet Union a number of air bases it had lost in World War I. Shortly thereafter, the Finns received an invitation from Foreign Minister Vyacheslav Molotov to discuss "concrete political questions," and Juho Kusti Paasikivi, the Finnish minister in Stockholm, was chosen to represent Finland in this next round of negotiations.[20] Paasikivi was instructed to tell the Soviets that Finland would not compromise its independence, and that any agreement made in Moscow would have to be ratified by the Finnish Parliament.[21]

The Soviet leaders were determined to push the frontier on the Karelian Isthmus back from its close proximity to Leningrad, and to establish a naval base on the Finnish coast at the mouth of the Gulf of Finland.[22] In Josef Stalin's words:

---

19. Tanner, *The Winter War*, p. 14.

20. The importance that the Soviets attached to these negotiations with Finland was exhibited by the fact that Stalin participated in each of the discussions.

21. Jakobson, *The Diplomacy of the Winter War*, p. 109.

22. Lundin, *Finland in the Second World War*, p. 51. The naval base would be established opposite the newly acquired bases in Estonia. Thus, any hostile naval force coming through the Gulf of Finland would be faced with Soviet crossfire.

It is no one's fault that the geographical relationships are such as they are. We must be able to block entrance to the Gulf of Finland. If the channel to Leningrad did not run along [the Finnish] coast, we should have no need at all to take up the question . . . We cannot move Leningrad, and therefore the boundary must be moved.[23]

Once again Molotov asked whether Finland would agree to a mutual assistance treaty similar to that which the other Baltic states had recently concluded with the Soviet Union. When Paasikivi argued that such a treaty would compromise Finnish neutrality, Molotov suggested instead that the existing Finnish-Soviet Nonagression Pact be amended to include a provision that Finland would not join an alliance directly hostile to the Soviet Union. Molotov also insisted that Finland lease Hanko for a period of thirty years, as well as cede the islands in the Gulf of Finland, that had been mentioned in earlier talks. In addition, Molotov stated that the Soviet-Finnish border, which at the time was only twenty miles from the outskirts of Leningrad, should be moved farther north, and fortifications on the Karelian Isthmus should be demolished. As compensation, the Soviets offered to cede a district of Soviet Karelia "twice as large . . . as the combined area of the territories to be given up by Finland." Molotov was also willing to let Finland fortify the Aaland Islands, provided that no other country contributed to the project.[24]

The Finnish cabinet agreed to a revision of the Karelian Isthmus frontier and was also willing to cede the southern half of the island of Hogland. But it was not willing to give up Hanko or the area on the Karelian Isthmus. By November, the negotiations had reached a stalemate and Foreign Minister Erkko authorized Paasikivi to break off the talks if the Soviet Union would not agree to Finland's concessions. Molotov replied that "we civilians seem to be able to do nothing more in the matter; now it is the turn of the military circles to speak their mind."[25] On November 26, 1939, shots were fired in the border town of Mainila, and Moscow revoked its non-aggression pact with Finland. Soviet troops crossed the Finnish frontier shortly thereafter.

---

23. Quoted in ibid., pp. 52–53.

24. Tanner, *The Winter War*, p. 25; and David Vital, *The Survival of Small States: Studies in Small Power/Great Power Conflict* (London: Oxford University Press, 1971), p. 101, n. 4.

25. Quoted in Tanner, *The Winter War*, pp. 66–67.

The Finnish army was initially able to take advantage of terrain, but the Soviet Union's overwhelming superiority in manpower and arms inevitably worked in the Soviets' favor. Soviet campaigns in December 1939 failed to break the main line of Finnish defenses on the Karelian Isthmus, and the Soviet Eighth Army's advance north of Lake Ladoga and a converging attack on Suomusalmi were stopped with great losses to the Soviets.[26] When the Soviets began a new offensive in February 1940, Finnish casualties mounted. By March, Soviet forces had established themselves on the western shore of Viipuri and had gained a foothold in the Karelian Isthmus. In the Gulf of Finland, Soviet forces advanced against the mainland from the islands of Suursaari and Lavansaari.

Soviet fears of an Allied expedition compelled the Soviet Union to abandon the hope of total victory. Stalin wanted to remain outside the European war, and a French-British military expedition would have involved the Soviet Union in the war as Germany's ally. Stalin also wanted his forces free for the new campaigning season and the greater priority of the European conflict. But while it was important to end the war before an Allied military presence appeared in the Baltic, it was also necessary to convince the world (especially Germany) that the Soviet Union had won the war; Stalin would not settle for the terms that had been offered in earlier Soviet-Finnish talks.[27] Finland was forced to make peace on terms far worse than it had initially rejected. Stalin got the air base he wanted, and much more territory than he had originally demanded. Nearly the entire population of the ceded territory elected to move across the new frontier, creating over 500,000 refugees. In addition, Finnish losses in the war were close to 25,000 dead and nearly 44,000 wounded—a high proportion for a nation of less than

---

26. The Finns, however, paid heavily for these victories. For example, after a twelve-day battle near Lake Ladoga, in which the Soviet 75th and 139th Divisions were defeated, the Finnish units engaged in the fight lost 30 percent of their officers, and 25 percent of their rank and file. See Lundin, *Finland in the Second World War*, p. 59.

27. See Upton, *Finland in Crisis*, pp. 27–28; Annette Baker Fox, *The Power of Small States: Diplomacy In World War II* (Chicago: University of Chicago Press, 1959), pp. 58–59; H. Peter Krosby, *Finland, Germany, and the Soviet Union, 1940-1941: The Petsamo Dispute* (Madison: University of Wisconsin Press, 1968), pp. 10, 68; and Martti Häikiö, "The Race for Northern Europe," in Henrik S. Nissen, ed., *Scandinavia During the Second World War* (Minneapolis: University of Minnesota Press, 1979), p. 84.

four million.[28] In Marshal Mannerheim's words,

Finland's strategic situation had been dealt a crushing blow. All advantages which had given [Finland] a chance of closing the gates to an invader were lost. The new frontier left the country open to attack and the Hanko base was like a pistol aimed at the heart of the country . . . The Peace Treaty deprived [Finland] of security and freedom of action in foreign affairs.[29]

THE NEOREALIST ARGUMENT

Finnish foreign policy prior to the Winter War is inconsistent with neorealism in four ways. First, given the distribution of power between Finland and the Soviet Union, we would have expected Finland to acquiesce to Soviet territorial demands rather than risk national survival. According to the neorealist hegemonic stability theory, peace is preserved largely because secondary states see the futility of fighting a preponderant state.[30] Similarly, balance-of-power theory would also predict that Finland acquiesce to Soviet demands; this theory argues that weak states are compelled to bandwagon with threatening and geographically proximate great powers.[31]

Second, according to neorealism, states should avoid wars when they are likely to lose, or win at an unacceptable cost. Neorealism would predict that Finland should have given in to Soviet demands: "[its] stubbornness had little relation to the resources at [its] disposal."[32] Indeed, Finland took great risks in refusing to settle its differences with the Soviet Union. In October 1938, a Defense Council report claimed that "the armed forces must at present be described as totally unfitted for war." By November 1939, Finland's domestic arms industry had not been adequately expanded and arms supplies from abroad had not been secured. Rifle and machine gun ammunition

---

28. Fox, *The Power of Small States*, p. 57; Lundin, *Finland in the Second World War*, pp. 78–79; and Mannerheim, *Memoirs*, p. 388. A similar proportion of the United States' 1940 population of 130 million would have been 2.6 million dead or wounded in only 105 days. See Eloise Engle and Lauri Paananen, *The Winter War: The Russo-Finnish Conflict, 1939-1940* (New York: Charles Scribner's Sons, 1973), p. 143.

29. Mannerheim, *Memoirs*, p. 388.

30. A.F.K. Organski, *World Politics* (New York: Knopf, 1968), p. 294.

31. Stephen M. Walt, *The Origins of Alliances* (Ithaca, N.Y.: Cornell University Press, 1984), p. 31, see also pp. 24, 29–30; Michael Handel, *Weak States in the International System* (London: Frank Cass, 1981), pp. 183–187.

32. L.A. Puntila, *The Political History of Finland, 1809-1966* (London: Heinemann, 1975), p. 162.

would last for only two months by the government's estimate. Shells for heavy artillery, field howitzers, and field guns would last for only a few weeks. The Finnish forces had few anti-tank weapons, only a few batteries of anti-aircraft guns and heavy artillery, and only sixty tanks from World War I. Moreover, frontier defenses in Karelia amounted to little more than a thin string of machine gun nests, unsatisfactory tank traps, and trenches dug hastily by students and school boys.[33] Facing this scantily equipped Finnish force of approximately 127,000 men, the initial Soviet forces sent to the Finnish theater included close to 500,000 soldiers equipped with hundreds of artillery pieces, tanks, and aircraft. All Soviet divisions included an anti-tank section, and an armored battalion with fifty tanks; the Finnish divisions possessed no corresponding formations. Finally, the Soviet forces also had a virtually unlimited supply of ammunition.[34]

Third, Finnish leaders had strong reasons to assume that Western support would not be forthcoming. As early as June 1939, the British government stated that it "fully appreciated that the military occupation of one of the Soviet Union's North-West neighbors . . . might be regarded by the Soviet Union as a threat to its security."[35] Later, both France and Britain considered plans to aid Finland by a joint expedition, but they were more concerned with how such an expedition would affect their conflict with Germany.[36] It was also doubtful that the Allies would force their way through Norway and Sweden, which had denied transit to Allied troops. Nor could the Finns count on support from the United States. Given isolationist sentiment in Congress, President Franklin D. Roosevelt had to move cautiously during the Winter War despite his preference for a more interventionist foreign policy.[37] In short, Finland had strong reason to suspect that a policy of balancing against the Soviets by allying with other great powers

---

33. Cohen, *Small Nations in Times of Crisis*, p. 264; Lundin, *Finland in the Second World War*, pp. 57–58; and Condon, *The Winter War*, pp. 30, 32.

34. Mannerheim, *Memoirs*, p. 324; Lundin, *Finland in the Second World War*, pp. 57–58; and Vital, *The Survival of Small States*, p. 102.

35. June 12th directive to Ambassador Leeds, quoted in Jakobson, *The Diplomacy of the Winter War*, p. 84.

36. Aimo Pajunen, "Finland's Security Policy," *Cooperation and Conflict*, Vol. 3 (1968), p. 76. Specifically, the possibility of denying Germany iron ore was one of the most important motives for considering a Scandinavian front. See Cohen, *Small Nations in Times of Crisis*, p. 285–287.

37. On British-French vacillations regarding an expeditionary force to Scandinavia and Roosevelt's inability to commit more to a Finnish defense, see

would not work to its advantage: "the Western allies were strategically remote from Finland. Thin, insupportable affirmations of loyalty
coming from great-power friends at a distance or from closer small
states could not save a small state in Finland's predicament."[38]

Finally, Finnish intransigence appears even more detached from
external circumstances if we consider that the Soviet Union's
demands were fairly circumscribed. The Soviet Union did not
demand that Finland give up its independence altogether, and it was
willing to make concessions. Moreover, the Soviet Union continually
made it clear that its demands were motivated by its own security
dilemma. Soviet intentions were not overly hostile; the Soviet government was not interested in annexing Finland, but merely wanted
assurances that Leningrad would not come under attack through
Finnish territory. Finland had everything to fear from Soviet capabilities, but less to fear from Soviet intentions. Thus, both balance-of-
power theory and balance-of-threat theory would predict Finnish
compliance with Soviet demands.[39]

In short, by tenaciously refusing to negotiate a settlement, Finland
risked the costs of war with a great power. By refusing to assent to a
limited number of concessions which would have contributed to
Soviet security, the Finns were subsequently forced to cede much
larger areas after the Soviets took by force what they could not secure
by diplomatic means.[40]

Cohen, *Small Nations in Times of Crisis*, chap. 20; Lundin, *Finland in the Second
World War*, pp. 68–76; and R. Michael Berry, *American Foreign Policy and the Finnish
Exception: Ideological Preferences and Wartime Realities* (Helsinki: Suomen
Historiallinen Seura, 1987), pp. 69–74.

38. Fox, *The Power of Small States*, p. 53.

39. For more on balance-of-threat theory, and its relationship to balance-of-power
theory, see Walt, *The Origins of Alliances*.

40. Numerous historians suggest that Finland should have made minor territorial adjustments in order to avoid the costs of war with the Soviet Union. For
instance, according to Jakobson, the balance of power compelled the Finns to
acquiesce to Soviet attempts to improve the security of Leningrad. Jakobson considers the Finnish government's refusal to yield as "foolhardy." Similarly, Fox
notes that Finland should not have resisted Soviet pressure. Anderson argues that
during the Finnish-Soviet negotiations, Finland failed to act with "the kind of
prudence which small powers perforce must exercise when living under the
shadow of a big neighbor." Lundin also notes that in view of the increasing belligerence of the German Reich, the Soviet proposals of 1938 were not "unreason-
able" and that Finland should have conceded to them rather than risk war.
Finally, in his memoirs, Mannerheim suggests that the Finnish government

DEMOCRATIC POLITICS AND FINNISH DECISION MAKING

How can we account for Finnish intransigence prior to the Winter War? One possible explanation is that Finnish decision makers misperceived Soviet intentions and were motivated by psychological biases. As Yohanen Cohen points out, "Both sides adhered to their declared position; each ignored the other's point of view. . . . Both sides misread each other's intentions and signals." Similarly, according to Annette Baker Fox, "part of Finland's suffering during World War II arose because each actor in the situation imperfectly or incorrectly perceived what the other actors wanted or would do."[41]

According to this explanation, Soviet attempts to protect the security of Leningrad were seen through the prism of past experiences, including Soviet attempts to "Russify" the Finns prior to World War I, and the Soviet attempt to extend the Bolshevik Revolution into Finland in 1918. Thus, however legitimate the Soviet Union's security concerns in 1939, Finland interpreted the current situation in the context of prior Russo-Finnish relations: "Finnish ideas about Russia were built on impressions gained during the last period when there had been contact, the period 1918 to 1920. It had been a period when the USSR was trying to export revolution to its neighbors. . . . There was almost total ignorance in Finland of the changes wrought by Stalin in the 1930s."[42] Indeed, the Soviet government's insistence that Hitler was ready to attack the Soviet Union and that his plans included the use of Finland as a northern base was considered a mere pretext for Finland's absorption into the Soviet Union.[43] Soviet concessions were interpreted as mere steps toward the ultimate takeover of the Finnish state, rather than attempts to meet the Finns halfway. In

---

would have strengthened its position by offering concessions at a time when the Soviets felt threatened by Germany and abandoned by the West. According to Mannerheim, the Finnish government failed because it did not "adapt" itself to external circumstances. See Jakobson, *The Diplomacy of the Winter War*, pp. 3–4; Fox, *The Power of Small States*, p. 44; Lundin, *Finland in the Second World War*, p. 44; and Mannerheim, *Memoirs*, p. 302.

41. Cohen, *Small Nations in Times of Crisis*, pp. 250, 255; and Fox, *The Power of Small States*, p. 77.

42. Upton, *Finland in Crisis*, p. 43. For more on the tendency to interpret incoming information based on preexisting images, see Robert Jervis, *Perception and Misperception in International Politics* (Princeton, N.J.: Princeton University Press, 1976), chap. 4.

43. Häikiö, "The Race for Northern Europe," p. 63.

Jakobson's words: "Admittedly the initial Soviet approach was far from menacing in tone; it was an offer of protection, not a threat of domination. But to the Finnish mind, the two were virtually synonymous: to accept Soviet protection meant submitting to Soviet domination."[44] In sum, the "tragic failure" of Finnish foreign policy was an inability to "appreciate the apprehensions and desire for security of an isolated great power."[45]

Equally important was that Finland's security had always been preserved by virtue of German-Russian rivalry. As Jakobson points out, "it had been regarded as axiomatic that Germany was always bound to resist a Russian attempt to advance in the Baltic area and thus provide Finnish neutrality with a natural cover."[46] The signing of the German-Soviet Nonaggression Treaty did little to dispel the ingrained belief in German support against Soviet encroachment. Finally, Finnish decision makers did not believe that the Soviet Union would go to war over minor territorial demands: "the possibility of a Soviet attack on Finland hardly existed in the minds of the Finnish political leaders . . . the idea that the Russians might go to war to enforce their claims seemed too fantastic to be taken seriously."[47] Significantly, Foreign Minister Erkko was convinced that Stalin was merely using Hanko and other territorial demands as bargaining chips: "If Finland sticks to her guns over Hanko, the Russians will climb down. . . . In any case, the Soviet Union will not allow a conflict to develop."[48] Finnish decision makers discounted the Soviet Union's dissatisfaction with the status quo and underestimated the extent to which the Soviets considered the benefits to be gained from war—an adequate defense—to be worth the perceived minimal costs of war with Finland. In short, having dismissed the possibility of Soviet aggression, Finland found it unnecessary to weigh its chances in a Finnish-Soviet conflict:

---

44. Jakobson, *The Diplomacy of the Winter War*, p. 10. See also p. 12.

45. D.G. Kirby, *Finland in the Twentieth Century* (Minneapolis: University of Minnesota Press, 1979), p. 107, emphasis in the original; see also pp. 118–119; and Puntila, *The Political History of Finland*, p. 162.

46. Jakobson, *The Diplomacy of the Winter War*, p. 99; see also p. 110; and Lundin, *Finland in the Second World War*, pp. 30–32.

47. Jakobson, *The Diplomacy of the Winter War*, p. 100; see also pp. 150–151.

48. Quoted in Jakobson, *The Diplomacy of the Winter War*, p. 131; see also Tanner, *The Winter War*, pp. 57–58; Anderson, "Origins of the Winter War," pp. 180, 182, 186; and Lundin, *Finland in the Second World War*, pp. 56–57.

Erkko was convinced that the Russians would retract their pressure and dangerous demands when faced with an unequivocal, proud, and consistent stance. The inverse was also valid: any Finnish concession would provoke further pressure. He considered every new alternative presented by Stalin during the talks as confirmation of his assumptions, and dismissed the possibility of war as so much hollow threat and bluff.[49]

While these misperceptions go far in explaining Finnish military strategy prior to the Winter War, several problems remain. First, Finnish decision makers held different foreign policy views—not all were suffering from cognitive errors and biases. Thus, as I suggest below, in order to understand Finnish decision making we need to know who suffered from cognitive errors, and why these particular actors had greater weight in the decision making process. Second, arguments that stress the cognitive and motivational errors of individual decision makers ignore how particular foreign policies would affect domestic political goals and priorities. As I argue below, rather than view Finnish foreign policy as an error in judgment, we can see it as a strategy to maintain domestic political consensus.

FINNISH FOREIGN POLICY: AN INSTITUTIONAL ARGUMENT. Finnish foreign policy decision making prior to the Winter War must be seen in light of the elections of 1937, which threw the conservatives into opposition and secured a coalitional cabinet composed of Social Democrats, Agrarians, and Liberals. The conservative cabinet that had retained power throughout the 1930s was replaced by a coalition in which, for the first time since the Finnish Civil War of 1918, the Social Democrats cooperated with two non-Socialist parties. Known as the "Red-Mud" alliance, this center-left coalition government faced bitter opposition from the right-wing parties that found themselves excluded from their traditional political influence in the government. Given Finland's semipresidential system, these changes need not have affected foreign policy outcomes. In most semipresidential systems, the president is given special constitutional authority over foreign policy and defense. Thus, in times of international crisis, the

---

49. Cohen, *Small Nations in Times of Crisis*, p. 255; see also P.K. Killinen, "Direction of the War in Finland During World War II," *Revue Internationale d'Histoire Militaire*, No. 47 (1980), p. 26. According to Jervis, Finnish decision makers relied on multiple reinforcing arguments. Those who believed that concessions to Russia would only lead to greater demands also thought that the Soviets would back down if Finland remained firm. See Jervis, *Perception and Misperception*, pp. 134–135.

executive's political influence is bound to increase. In addition, the president has substantial political leverage because he or she is meant to stand above party strife as a "supra partisan representative" of the national interest.[50] However, President Kyösti Kallio had little interest in foreign affairs. Thus, "by default, foreign policy was left in the hands of the Cabinet, or more precisely, of its two liberal members, Prime Minister Cajander and Foreign Minster Holsti."[51]

Cajander and Holsti refused to endorse a pro-German position. Assuming that Germany would draw Finland into a German-Soviet conflict, they considered a close association with Germany as a threat to Finnish security. For Cajander and Holsti, "the immediate task of Finland's foreign policy . . . was to disassociate herself from Germany and convince the world of the genuineness of her neutrality, and this in turn required a show of reconciliation with the Soviet Union."[52] However, they faced a conservative opposition in Parliament that would veto a conciliatory policy towards the Soviets, and the left of center parties that made up the new Cajander government would similarly refuse to support a policy that put Finland in alliance with Germany.[53] Indeed, since there was no majority party in Parliament, the Finnish cabinet was unable to carry out any policy that it could not persuade the major parties to accept. While the Finnish right urged the government not to neglect relations with Germany, the Finnish left refused to support a policy that advocated collusion with the German Reich.

Thus, it was inconceivable that Parliament, which would have had to ratify an agreement along the lines suggested by Yartsev in 1938, would have accepted military cooperation with the Soviet Union in any form. In order to agree with most of Stalin's demands, the cabinet would have had to obtain a parliamentary vote to amend the Constitution, which would require a five-sixths majority. Cabinet

---

50. Thomas A. Baylis, "Presidents versus Prime Ministers: Shaping Executive Authority in Eastern Europe," *World Politics*, Vol. 48, No. 3 (April 1996), p. 308. See also pp. 313–314.

51. Jakobson, *The Diplomacy of the Winter War*, p. 20.

52. Ibid., pp. 21–22.

53. Conservatives claimed that Finland could not "afford to offend Germany" now that it was the dominant power on the European continent. While right-wing groups insisted that the Finnish public would not endorse Holsti's anti-German policy, these groups did not have a majority to advance their preferred foreign policy agenda in Parliament. Lundin, *Finland in the Second World War*, p. 34.

members were convinced that such deliberations would create a public struggle likely to last for months.[54] In short, any suggestion of military cooperation with the Soviet Union would have outraged conservative parties in the Finnish Parliament. Similarly, it was no longer possible to pursue a pro-German policy given the foreign policy views of the new coalitional cabinet. In the end, the only policy to which all groups could agree was military cooperation and unity among the Scandinavian countries.

As a former tsarist officer, Marshal Mannerheim appreciated the strategic thinking behind the Soviet proposals and urged President Kallio, Prime Minister Cajander, and Foreign Minister Erkko to bargain with Moscow. Mannerheim pointed out that the islands in the Gulf of Finland had little military value to Finland and could not be defended in time of war. Giving them up would be a small concession to ensure Soviet good will. In Mannerheim's words:

> I was of the definite opinion that we were bound to meet the Russians in some way if this was likely to lead to improved relations with our mighty neighbor . . . the islands were of no use to [us] and . . . we had no means of defending them. . . . On the other hand, the islands were of real importance to the Russians, as they commanded the entrance to their naval base at the bay of Luga, and by leasing them we should draw advantage from one of the few trumps we had.[55]

Moreover, Mannerheim insisted that Finnish military resources were not sufficient to warrant a rigid and inflexible foreign policy position and urged Paasikivi that "you must absolutely come to an agreement."[56] Nevertheless, civilian political leaders did not support Mannerheim's assessment. Basing their decision on the perceived domestic political repercussions, they argued that the new coalitional government would not "survive the public outcry that

---

54. The Soviet proposal of early March 1939 would have required parliamentary approval; according to Finland's Constitution, Finnish territory was "indivisible," so the government did not have the authority to negotiate over Finnish frontiers. See Tanner, *The Winter War*, pp. 14, 30. Similarly, during the negotiations of October 1939, Paasikivi told Stalin and Molotov that Finland could only grant Soviet territorial claims by constitutional amendment, which required support of five-sixths of Parliament. Apparently Stalin had little understanding of Finnish domestic constraints. He told Paasikivi not to worry, declaring that he would get "99% of the votes." See Jakobson, *The Diplomacy of the Winter War*, p. 119.

55. Mannerheim, *Memoirs*, p. 300.

56. Quoted in Jakobson, *The Diplomacy of the Winter War*, p. 150.

would follow the suggestion of territorial sacrifices."[57]

Like Mannerheim, both Paasikivi and Finance Minister Väinö Tanner, who accompanied Paasikivi to Moscow in October 1939, believed that the territorial concessions were not worth the risk of war with the Soviet Union. According to Tanner, the rejection of the Soviet claims could mean war and the consequences of war might be "the destruction of Finland, perhaps even the establishment of the Bolshevik system and the annexation of the country."[58] Similarly, Paasikivi thought Finland should not risk war over a few islands that "most Finns had never heard of." Both Tanner and Paasikivi thought that Soviet territorial demands were intended to be used in defense of Leningrad, not as pressure against Finland. Giving up these minor territorial claims would not increase Finland's dependence on the Soviet Union; once Stalin satisfied his strategic needs, he would leave Finland alone.[59]

But the Tanner-Paasikivi viewpoint was a minority position in the cabinet. The majority assumed that once the Red Fleet was anchored off the coast of Finland, there would be little to stop the Soviet Union from "forcing [Finland] into servitude." The cabinet's rigid guidelines tied the delegation's hands, precisely at a time when Stalin was more willing to compromise. Paasikivi and Tanner were left with little diplomatic leeway: "the negotiators that were sent to Moscow enjoyed almost no freedom of maneuver. They were shackled by strict orders as to what they might and what they might not talk about; and the sense of urgency which the delegates received in the course of the discussions failed to make much impression in Helsinki."[60] As Tanner notes:

If the Soviet Union should make proposals affecting Finland's territorial inviolability or sovereignty, the negotiators were to declare that none of them was authorized to make promises that would violate the national constitution, but that according to the parliamentary system prevailing in Finland it fell to the government and the Diet to approve or reject such undertakings as the Soviet Union proposed.[61]

57. Mannerheim, *Memoirs*, p. 300; see also Anderson, "Origins of the Winter War," p. 176.

58. Quoted in Jakobson, *The Diplomacy of the Winter War*, p. 126.

59. Lundin, *Finland in the Second World War*, p. 56.

60. Ibid., pp. 54–55.

61. Tanner, *The Winter War*, p. 23.

In short, due to President Kallio's lack of experience in foreign affairs, foreign policy making reverted to a coalitional cabinet that diluted Finnish security policy to command the support of various parties. The cabinet had to secure support from both the left and the right-wing opposition in order to retain legislative confidence. Consequently, Finnish foreign security policy was tailored toward maintaining consensus. Since any decisive action—either acquiescence to Soviet demands or obtaining German support—would be vetoed by either the left or the right, the coalitional government sought a middle-of-the-road alternative. Indeed, the attempt to seek Swedish support can be considered a carefully balanced position that would command the support of both the Agrarians and Social Democrats within the government as well as the right-wing opposition. The Swedish initiative was the only policy upon which everyone could agree.

Thus, there were two domestic political problems. First, there were great divergences among the parties' foreign policy preferences. Second, the president, who should have exerted a personal influence over foreign policy, abdicated responsibility. As a result, parliamentary control over foreign policy became stronger at the same time that divisiveness within parliament was increasing. As Joe Hagan notes:

Deep leadership cleavages can prevent foreign policy makers from committing their nation's resources to a particular course of action. Even if not all members of a regime's coalition actually participate in the making of policies, decision makers must still be concerned that their decisions do not alienate crucial members of the ruling coalition.[62]

Finland's foreign policy prior to the Winter War shows why states sometimes choose foreign policies that stand little chance of international success: leaders judge foreign policy options based on how these various choices will affect their domestic political standing. Thus, foreign policies may often appear anomalous from a neorealist perspective. Indeed, while for Finland a more conciliatory policy would have been rational in light of the balance of power, such a policy could not be sustained given the dynamics of Finnish domestic politics at the time. Finland was too ideologically polarized to pursue

---

62. Joe D. Hagan, "Regimes, Political Oppositions, and the Comparative Analysis of Foreign Policy," in Charles F. Hermann, Charles W. Kegley, Jr., and James N. Rosenau, eds., *New Directions in the Study of Foreign Policy* (Boston: Allen and Unwin, 1987), p. 344.

a policy of accommodation with the Soviet Union.

CRITIQUE OR CONFIRMATION OF THE DEMOCRATIC PEACE THEORY?
Proponents of the democratic peace hypothesis would argue that
Finnish foreign policy prior to the Winter War is either irrelevant to
the democratic peace theory or supportive of its claims. On the one
hand, since Finland went to war with a nondemocracy in 1939, democratic peace theorists could claim that it does not disconfirm the
dyadic version of the democratic peace theory, which only purports to
explain why democracies are conciliatory and peaceful with each
other. On the other hand, proponents of the dyadic democratic peace
argument could also argue that the case confirms the theory. A central
claim of the dyadic explanation is that democratic states cannot trust
nondemocratic counterparts and will find it unwise to negotiate with
them. Leaders in nondemocracies are socialized into an environment
where the use of force is considered legitimate. Consequently, it
would not be surprising to find that democratic states adopt hard-line
and aggressive policies toward nondemocratic states: "The expectation that . . . non-democratic opponents will often resort to force
and/or will refuse to negotiate in good faith leads democratic decision makers to adopt more coercive foreign policies."[63]

This argument fails for three reasons. First, while Finnish decision
makers did invoke the Soviet Union's regime type, Finland did not
define the Soviet Union as threatening merely because it was a nondemocracy. Rather, the Soviet Union was considered a threat because
it was a great power with the material capability to conquer Finnish
territory. The balance of power trumped norms, ideology, and
domestic institutions as the criterion for determining whether the
Soviet Union was a threat. A state as powerful as the Soviet Union
would appear threatening to Finland, regardless of whether it was
democratic or not.

Second, despite the fact that coercion and violence were considered
legitimate means of domestic conflict resolution, the Soviets were not
adverse to compromise and negotiation with the Finns. The Soviet
Union was willing to negotiate and was prepared to provide substan-

---

63. David L. Rousseau et al., "Assessing the Dyadic Nature of the Democratic
Peace, 1918-1988," *American Political Science Review*, Vol. 90, No. 3 (September
1996), pp. 512–533. See also Russett, *Grasping the Democratic Peace*, pp. 32–33; and
Michael Doyle, "Kant, Liberal Legacies, and Foreign Affairs," in Brown, Lynn-
Jones, and Miller, eds., *Debating the Democratic Peace*, pp. 30–43.

tial concessions. Indeed, the fact that the Soviets frequently initiated negotiations undermines the notion that nondemocracies externalize domestic norms when dealing with international actors. The domestic systems of nondemocracies may make leaders more tolerant of the use of force against domestic opponents, but contrary to the claims of some democratic peace proponents, aggressiveness or peacefulness abroad cannot be readily inferred from the degree of violence in a state's domestic arena.[64] Domestic norms are not a fool-proof means of anticipating the way a state will act internationally.

Finally, the dyadic argument asserts that authoritarian leaders may exploit democracies by attacking first because they expect that democracies are more likely to capitulate. Nondemocracies view democratic institutions as a source of weakness, and this encourages them to "threaten or bully a democracy to make concessions."[65] Yet, while Finland did eventually become a target of Soviet aggression, the Soviet Union did not exploit Finnish domestic institutional weaknesses. Rather, democratic politics made it difficult for Finland to effectively conduct foreign policy and meet the Soviets halfway.

Finnish foreign policy during the Winter War undermines the monadic variant as well. Proponents of the monadic hypothesis argue that democracies are generally more likely to settle disputes short of war. More often than other states, democracies choose mediation, negotiation, or other forms of diplomacy, and they refrain from escalating disputes to the point of war. They are less likely to resort to large-scale violence to resolve disputes if the prospects for peaceful resolution remain high. Since democratic norms and institutions are consistent with a strategy of reciprocity, democracies need not fear exploitation. States will not initiate wars on democracies because they expect that democratic leaders will prefer bargaining, mediation, and compromise over forceful coercion to resolve disputes.[66]

Contrary to these claims, this case shows that a democracy may

---

64. For the argument that domestic norms are good predictors of a state's predisposition to resolve international disputes nonviolently, see especially John R. Oneal et al., "The Liberal Peace: Interdependence, Democracy and International Conflict, 1950-85," *Journal of Peace Research*, Vol. 33, No. 1 (1996), pp. 11–28.

65. Russett, *Grasping the Democratic Peace*, p. 39.

66. Charles W. Kegley, Jr., and Margaret G. Hermann, "Ballots, a Barrier Against the Use of Bullets and Bombs: Democratization, Military Intervention, and the Democratic Peace," paper presented at the annual meeting of the International Studies Association, San Diego, April 16–20, 1996.

choose policies that increase the likelihood of war, even when alternatives for peaceful accommodation are available. Thus, that a state is a
liberal democracy does not indicate that it is "dovish." Simply because
a country chooses its leaders through the ballot does not mean that
they will be willing or able to negotiate disputes or accept mediation.
Moreover, the case suggests that democratic politics may often make it
more difficult to reach a negotiated settlement and deter attack: democratic politics can make matters worse! In the Winter War case, democratic institutional imperatives—which required the avoidance of controversy—increased the likelihood of war by preventing Finland from
formulating a decisive policy to deter or reassure the Soviet Union.
Division within the Finnish government prevented reconciliation with
the Soviets, even though military capabilities were clearly skewed in
the Soviets' favor and the prospects for a peaceful resolution to the
conflict were high. The Finnish democratic framework—foreign policy
making within a divided cabinet—meant that anti-Soviet actors could
veto any attempt to resolve the conflict through negotiation.[67]

The monadic democratic peace theory fails because it assumes that
international negotiation is domestically cost-free.[68] On the contrary,
interstate negotiation and compromise are often difficult because deci-

---

67. According to James Fearon, democratically elected leaders can commit to war
because backing down from an initially hard-line position entails a significant loss
of voter support. By contrast, nondemocratic leaders do not face these domestic
audience costs, and thus cannot convince opponents that their threats are credible.
Fearon suggests that because democracies can more easily commit to war, opponents are pressured into settling disputes by peaceful means. See James D. Fearon,
"Domestic Political Audiences and the Escalation of International Disputes,"
American Political Science Review, Vol. 88, No. 3 (September 1994), pp. 577–592. This
case is somewhat inconsistent with Fearon's argument. First, that Stalin attended
the meetings with the Finnish negotiators and agreed to numerous territorial concessions suggests that nondemocracies can also send "costly" signals of their
intentions and thus create credible foreign policy commitments. As historians of
the Winter War are quick to note, Finnish leaders could have assumed that Stalin
would face a heavy international, and to some extent domestic, price for conced-
ing the issues at stake. Thus, the Finnish negotiators had every reason to view the
Soviets' willingness to fight as credible. Second, while Finland's negotiating
position was clearly linked to anticipated voter reactions, its commitment to a
hard-line stance did not decrease the likelihood of war. Contrary to Fearon's
conclusions, being locked into a position due to unfavorable domestic political
consequences does not necessarily increase the chances for a negotiated settlement. In the event, the Soviet Union did not shy away from the contest.

68. Proponents of the democratic peace theory have largely ignored a substantial
body of literature emphasizing the problems that democratic states face in

sion makers need to avoid contradictory policies that will jeopardize a fragile ruling coalition. Indeed, democratic institutions can make it difficult to resolve disputes peacefully because power-sharing minimizes the possibility of developing a coherent foreign policy platform. Due to imbalances in the distribution of power, Finland had strong incentives to settle its dispute with the Soviet Union without the escalation to war. The Soviet Union's concessions also should have given the Finns a reason to compromise. Yet Finnish leaders could not easily negotiate with the Soviet Union because of divisions in the ruling coalition.[69]

Finnish Decision Making Prior to the Continuation War

Although the Finnish government insisted on its neutrality during World War II, ample evidence confirms German-Finnish military collusion and consent for a German base of operations in northern Finland well before Hitler's attack on the Soviet Union.[70] Indeed, according to C. Leonard Lundin, "it is simply not believable that [Mannerheim] and his colleagues can have remained unaware that the Germans were preparing to strike at Murmansk through Finland." Similarly, according to Anthony F. Upton, "The Finnish command could be certain that an offensive war was being contemplated, and that if it was executed, Germany was expecting Finland to take part in it."[71] Thus, while decision makers later claimed that Finland sought to remain neutral in the approaching German-Soviet confrontation, "the picture of a Finnish

---

conducting interstate negotiations. On how domestic political constraints make it difficult for democracies to negotiate at the international level see, for example, Robert Putnam, "Diplomacy and Domestic Politics: The Logic of Two-Level Games," *International Organization*, Vol. 42, No. 3 (Summer 1988), pp. 427–461.

69. Democratic peace proponents assert that democracies are slow and reluctant to fight because elected leaders must first mobilize support from the voting public. It is this difficult and lengthy process of securing domestic support that provides the opportunity to reach a negotiated settlement. See Russett, *Grasping the Democratic Peace*, pp. 38–39. However, when war is imminent, negotiated outcomes must be delivered quickly. In this case, the Soviet Union could not wait for a negotiated settlement with Finland. Given its acute security dilemma, time was of the essence. Thus, Finland's democratic decision making process failed to provide an opportunity for reaching a speedy agreement with the Soviet Union.

70. See Lundin, *Finland in the Second World War*, pp. 95–104; Krosby, *Finland, Germany, and the Soviet Union*, pp. 157–158, 172–176; Ohto Manninen, "Operation Barbarossa and the Nordic Countries," in Nissen, ed., *Scandinavia During the Second World War*, pp. 144–145.

71. Lundin, *Finland in the Second World War*, p. 97; and Upton, *Finland in Crisis*, p. 218.

government and military high command firmly declining to make promises to Germany and hoping against hope that the country might be spared another war," is not confirmed by the available evidence.[72] Finnish leaders not only expected to be involved in the war, but they made Finnish collusion with Germany inevitable, merely leaving the Soviet Union with the responsibility for initiating hostilities.

On June 22, 1941, the Germans crossed the demarcation line, and Hitler declared that German and Finnish troops stood side by side for the defense of Finnish soil. With German troops poised for attack, the Soviet Union opened hostilities through extensive air attacks of Finnish territory. Initially, the Finnish counterattack was successful. Yet, as the war began to turn against Germany, Finland put out peace feelers.[73] Moscow's terms for peace were harsh. Finland was required to lease to the Soviet Union an area on the Porkalla peninsula, only a few miles from Helsinki; free communication by rail, road, and water between Finland and the Soviet Union was to be guaranteed; air fields near the southern coast of Finland were to be placed at Soviet disposal; the Finnish merchant marine had to be relinquished to the Allies; and Finland had to cede the Petsamo area to the Soviet Union.[74] On September 2, 1944, roughly two-thirds of Parliament voted to accept the government's decision to sign an armistice with the Soviet Union.

THE NEOREALIST ARGUMENT

Faced with the threat of both the Soviet Union and Nazi Germany, Finland had a number of options from which to choose, each of which can be considered consistent with neorealism. First, Finland

---

72. Lundin, *Finland in the Second World War*, p. 101.

73. Britain and the United States also insisted that Finland sue for peace. The United States opposed Finland's military strategy because it aided Germany and thus contributed to bringing the war closer to the United States. Once the United States entered the war, its policy toward Finland reflected a long-term desire to balance a strong postwar Soviet Union by retaining the independence of its border states and an immediate need to prevent Finland from contributing to the German war effort. That Finland was a democracy had little to do with these calculations. See Berry, *American Foreign Policy and the Finnish Exception*, pp. 138–144, 186–191, 288–297.

74. In addition to these territorial losses, 55,000 Finnish citizens lost their lives in the Continuation War. The German high command viewed Finland's capitulation to the Soviet Union as an act of treason and a breach of Finland's earlier commitment. In the brief Lapland War that followed, Finland lost more lives and property to the German army, which was intent on remaining in northern Lapland to protect the nickel mines at Petsamo.

might have bandwagoned; small states often join a superior power rather than balance against it in order to remove the possibility of future attack.[75] Second, Finland could have balanced. Balancing against superior force ensures national survival in the long run. As a result, even small states will prefer to balance rather than bandwagon.[76] Finally, Finland could have remained neutral. As a small state with insufficient resources, a neorealist argument would predict that Finland stay outside of great power conflicts rather than risk its survival by entering these controversies.[77] By choosing sides, Finland risked alienating one great power and becoming dependent on the other. Indeed, we would expect that Finland renounce expansionist policies that could only be realized at the expense of the Soviet Union. As Lundin suggests, "Prudence would seem to dictate . . . that the political leaders of the small country . . . avoid every appearance of constituting a threat to the security of the [more powerful] neighbor, particularly at times of international tension."[78] Similarly, Fox argues that Finland's mistake was siding with Germany against the Soviet Union rather than playing the two great powers against each other. While it did gain support from Germany to counter Soviet pressure, Finland should have made a comparable effort to use Soviet power to curb the German threat to Finnish security.[79]

In short, a neorealist argument cannot determine whether Finland should have balanced against Nazi Germany or the Communist Soviet Union; both posed threats to Finnish security. Indeed, German aggression could not be ignored—the Germans had just occupied Denmark and Norway, a fact that seemed to have very little effect on Finnish opinion at the time. Consequently, siding with the Soviet Union against Germany, allying with Germany against the Soviet Union, or maintaining strict neutrality would all have been consistent with international constraints. External exigencies thus did not sweep Finland along like a piece of driftwood—Finnish decision mak-

---

75. Walt, *The Origins of Alliances*; see also Fox, *The Power of Small States*, p. 187.

76. Eric J. Labs, "Do Weak States Bandwagon?" *Security Studies*, Vol. 1, No. 3 (Spring 1992), pp. 383–416.

77. Because of their placement in the international system, small states are more able to "hide" from great power conflicts. See Fox, *The Power of Small States*, pp. 1–9, 180–188; and Paul W. Schroeder, "Historical Reality vs. Neo-realist Theory," *International Security*, Vol. 19, No.1 (Summer 1994), pp. 117–119.

78. Lundin, *Finland in the Second World War*, p. 12.

79 . Fox, *The Power of Small States*, p. 64; see also Upton, *Finland in Crisis*, p. 198.

ers made conscious decisions, even if they did not have many options to choose from. As Jakobson notes:

The Finns had no more than marginal control over the external circumstances of their country during the Second World War. Their freedom of choice more often than not was freedom to choose between the bad and the worse. But ultimately it was their own decisions, not decisions imposed by others, that determined their fate.[80]

Finland's choice of cobelligerency with Germany, a choice it made without much reluctance, and without a search for alternative foreign policy options, can only be explained by looking at who advocated such a foreign policy agenda, and at how these actors came to dominate the decision making process. David Spiro puts it well:

Faced with a choice of surrendering to the USSR in June 1944 or allying with Germany . . . President Ryti decided to bind with Germany . . . two months later Ryti was replaced in elections by Mannerheim, who began peace negotiations with the USSR. Thus, in a democratic state, a leader who pursued an alliance with fascists and who declared war on democracies was not re-elected, and his successor chose a different policy . . . The fact that Mannerheim pursued peace with the USSR should prove it was possible for Presidents Kallio and Ryti to have made different choices before 1944.[81]

DEMOCRATIC POLITICS AND FINNISH DECISION MAKING

As with the Winter War, cognitive and motivational biases provide a partial explanation for Finnish foreign policy in 1940–41. Once again, the Finns perceived Soviet actions as aggressive rather than defensive: "Because neither Soviet nor Finnish leaders fully appreciated the defensive security considerations of the other party, both Soviet and Finnish interpretations of past Russo-Finnish relations. . . contributed to making the security dilemma. . . a self-fulfilling prophesy."[82]

Finnish decision makers viewed Soviet behavior as a reaction to

---

80. Max Jakobson, *Finland: Myth and Reality* (Helsinki: Otava Publishing Co., 1987), p. 46. By contrast, Finland continually claimed that it was compelled to side with Germany because of the threat of Soviet aggression. In the official Finnish view, Finland was waging a separate "Continuation" war, which had begun when the Soviets attacked Helsinki in November 1939. Jakobson, *Diplomacy of the Winter War*, p. 257; Berry, *American Foreign Policy and the Finnish Exception*, pp. 100–101; and Henrik S. Nissen, "Adjusting to German Domination," in Nissen, ed., *Scandinavia During the Second World War*, p. 105.

81. Spiro, "The Insignificance of the Liberal Peace," pp. 61–62.

82. Berry, *American Foreign Policy and the Finnish Exception*, pp. 96–97.

Finnish policy, rather than as a response to the German threat. For example, President Risto Ryti considered the reinforcement of the Soviet garrison on the Karelian Isthmus as a "clear indication of plans for land operations against Finland" rather than as a defensive measure against anticipated German aggression. The Soviet construction of roads, airports, and railways in Eastern Karelia was also deemed a "military deployment for a crushing blow against Finland."[83] The Finns also failed to consider the Soviet annexation of the Baltic Republics in June 1940 as a function of its security dilemma; rather, this was merely another indication that Finland would soon be absorbed into the Soviet empire. As R. Michael Berry notes, "the Soviet annexation of the Baltic states was a logical continuation of an effort to strengthen Soviet security at a time when Germany was becoming stronger but was still committed elsewhere. It does not necessarily follow that the Soviet Union had intended all along to . . . occupy Finland."[84] Later, when the Soviets insisted that Finland grant the nickel concession at Petsamo to the Soviet Union, Finnish decision makers once again viewed Soviet demands as an indication of sinister Soviet designs on Finland. They failed to realize that the extension of Germany's military power into northern Norway was bound to trigger a Soviet countermeasure.[85] Conversely, the more Finnish decision makers sided with Germany, and the more powerful Germany became, the stronger the confirmation of the Soviet Union's belief that it would have to preempt. Upton puts it well: "the Finnish leaders were psychologically blind and deaf . . . [Ryti] was convinced that Soviet Russia would never give up its attempt to conquer Finland . . . Finland's only salvation was that Germany should smash the Soviet Union."[86]

In sum, psychological explanations go far in accounting for Finnish foreign policy prior to the Continuation War. Nevertheless, such explanations ignore the fact that Finland's pro-German policy ran counter to the preferences of a majority in Parliament. To understand why Finnish decision makers ultimately chose this foreign policy

---

83. Lundin, *Finland in the Second World War*, p. 85.

84. Berry, *American Foreign Policy and the Finnish Exception*, p. 94.

85. For more on the Finnish-Soviet negotiations over the Petsamo area, see Krosby, *Finland, Germany, and the Soviet Union*. According to Krosby, "the real motive behind the Soviet Union's demand on Finland was to prevent any great power, including Germany, from getting a foothold in the Petsamo area" (p. 88).

86. Upton, *Finland in Crisis*, pp. 238–239.

option over other viable alternatives, we need to know who advocated this particular policy and how domestic institutions made it easier for these actors to win the foreign policy debate. In the following section, I argue that Finland's form of democratic government played an important role in the decision to side with Nazi Germany in 1940 and risk the costs of a second war with the Soviet Union; Finland ultimately chose this course of action over other options because particular democratic institutions made it easier for the executive to win the foreign policy debate.

FINNISH FOREIGN POLICY: AN INSTITUTIONAL ARGUMENT. Various Finnish political parties gave either passive or active support to different foreign policy options due to their "divergent views about how Finnish society should be organized and governed."[87] The conservatives supported a pro-German policy; the Progressives advocated a pro-British policy; the Swedish People's Party supported a policy of joint Finnish-Swedish defense of Scandinavia; and the radical left favored cooperation with the Soviet Union. The Social Democrats and the Swedish-speaking Finns were willing to fight to regain the areas lost in the Winter War, but they were reluctant to annex Eastern Karelia and build a "greater" Finnish society. By contrast, right-wing groups, including the military, wanted to annex Eastern Karelia for strategic, economic, and cultural reasons.[88] Ultimately, the foreign policy views of these right-wing groups won out, largely because they were dominant in the inner circle of the cabinet. This right-wing bias in the composition of the Finnish government was reinforced after the election of President Risto Ryti in 1940. The new cabinet formed with J.W. Rangell as Prime Minister concurred with Ryti's pro-German policy. As Henrik S. Nissen notes, "The Finnish government . . . was, to be sure, a national government, but it did not reflect proportionately the balance of strength in the Finnish parliament. The Right was clearly overrepresented, especially after a representative of the [pro-fascist] IKL [People's Patriotic Movement] was admitted to the government during the winter 1940-1941."[89]

Events leading up to the Continuation War emphasize the extent of the executive's foreign policy discretion. Most significant was

87. Berry, *American Foreign Policy and the Finnish Exception*, p. 152; see also Henrik S. Nissen, "The Nordic Societies," in Nissen, ed., *Scandinavia During the Second World War*, p. 43.

88. Berry, *American Foreign Policy and the Finnish Exception*, p. 53.

89. Nissen, "Adjusting to German Domination," p. 102.

Finland's decision to allow the transit of German troops and supplies through Finnish territory, a concession that would have far-reaching implications for Finland's status as a cobelligerent. When Germany approached Mannerheim regarding an agreement to permit the transit of German supplies and troops across Finnish territory to the German post in northern Norway, Mannerheim replied that only the civil authorities could negotiate such an agreement. The only civilians that needed to be consulted were the prime minister and acting President Ryti, who both advocated a pro-German policy, and both gave an affirmative answer. The Finnish Parliament was not aware of the negotiations, and most members of the cabinet did not learn of the agreement until the first German transports began.

On June 13, as a partial mobilization of Finnish troops was taking place, Finnish Foreign Minister Rolf Witting finally informed Parliament's Committee on Foreign Affairs that "war is at the door." The committee chairman protested that Finland had sided with Germany without Parliament's approval, and the leader of the Agrarian Party claimed that "a foreign power has occupied Finland." Witting presented the Finnish military preparations as defensive measures against Soviet aggression—the committee was therefore unable to judge the government's policy of risking the costs of war by collaborating with the Germans for an offensive attack.[90]

Indeed, because of the structure of Finland's democratic system, the Parliament could exercise little direct influence over the executive in the area of foreign security policy—members of the foreign affairs committee did not have to be consulted in advance and thus were in no position to suggest alternative courses of action. The foreign affairs committee was informed of developments long after decisions had been reached and policies implemented. Thus, if Parliament had been more involved in the policy making process, a pro-German policy might not have emerged: the Finnish Parliament would have opposed the pro-German drift in Finnish foreign policy. After all, the Social Democratic party, which insisted that Finland retain strict neutrality, was the largest single party and represented over 40 percent of the electorate.[91] Although a sizable portion of the electorate favored a pro-German course, it was no overwhelming majority. If the Finnish government had wanted to reverse the drift

---

90. Lundin, *Finland in the Second World War*, p. 106.
91. Upton, *Finland in Crisis*, pp. 248.

toward a German military alliance, it would not have lacked domestic support.

According to Lundin, the fact that Finnish military strategy could be decided by a "handful of military leaders" demonstrates that "Finland's democracy was not functioning on this occasion."[92] On the contrary, Finnish democracy was operating. In the Finnish semipresidential system, only the president has the constitutional power to call the commander in chief to account in the making of military policy. But neither Kallio nor Ryti chose to exercise this constitutional power. Thus, the military did not take power away from civilian authorities prior to the Continuation War; rather, civilian authorities abdicated responsibility to a "tiny group of soldiers" and allowed them to take decisions with important consequences for Finnish national security. As president, Ryti was able to give the military a free hand.[93] In fact, Finnish Minister of the Interior Baron Ernst von Born understood that military control of the decision making process was only possible if the president approved this expanded role: "Soldiers are now important policy makers, [and] they are strongly oriented towards Germany. But this direction is followed with the understanding of the president."[94] That Ryti, Rangell, and Mannerheim alone decided to let the Germans into the country is consistent with foreign policy making in a semipresidential system, where the president has wide-ranging foreign policy powers; the military can determine foreign policy outcomes if the head of state concurs with its views; and the president and prime minister often share common foreign policy preferences.[95]

The Finnish government insisted that Finland would only fight if

---

92. Lundin, *Finland in the Second World War*, p. 90.

93. Upton, *Finland in Crisis*, pp. 80, 148.

94. Quoted in ibid., p. 245.

95. Prior to the Winter War, Mannerheim had begged a skeptical government to concede to the Soviet Union's demands. Following the war, Mannerheim's autonomy increased considerably, largely because Presidents Kallio and Ryti agreed to transfer the responsibility for the details of military strategy to military authorities. For example, the government left the implementation of the military transport agreement with Germany entirely in Mannerheim's hands. Ryti made no attempt to supervise the transports, and government officials never knew how many German soldiers were in the country at any time. Later, Mannerheim put the Finnish battalion at Petsamo and the Fifth Army Corps under German command. Ryti, Walden, and Witting were left to merely "search for a suitable diplomatic formula in which to clothe this decision." (Ibid., pp. 262–263.)

first attacked by the Soviet Union. In effect, Finnish leaders were asking that Germany arrange matters so that Finland not appear to be taking the initiative in a war against the Soviet Union.[96] The executive approved of the German plan to attack the Soviet Union—its only concern was that Finland "not appear the aggressor state, but that . . . she should be 'drawn in' to the conflict after it had started. There was no attempt to set any other relevant political condition for Finland's participation."[97] This policy was crucially linked to anticipated domestic reactions in Parliament. Ryti insisted that the German forces start operations before the main Finnish army began a general mobilization: "In this way it would be much easier to carry the [Parliament] and the general public along with the government's policy."[98] The strength of the Social Democrats in Parliament compelled the executive not to take an initiative in the attack; thus the Finnish army could not be used to begin hostilities, nor could Finnish territory be used to launch the initial attacks.[99]

The executive had predicted the reactions of the Socialists in Parliament well. On June 17, the party told other members of Parliament that it would not support an offensive war and believed that Finland should remain neutral if war broke out between Germany and the Soviet Union. As Upton argues, "the opposition to an offensive war was sufficiently strong and well organized to make it understandable why Ryti was so anxious that Finland should not appear to take the initiative against the USSR. If serious internal discontent was to be avoided, the USSR must somehow be made to seem the aggressor."[100] Thus, by inviting a Soviet attack, the Finnish executive created the circumstances under which the Finnish Parliament would have no recourse but to vote in favor of war. With Finnish

---

96. Ibid., p. 263; see also p. 220.

97. Ibid., p. 264.

98. Ibid., p. 274.

99. Here, democratic peace supporters might claim that the case provides strong support for the theory because public opposition prevented Finland from initiating force—even against the nondemocratic Soviet Union. However, this conclusion would be misleading. Rather than prevent the initiation of force, anticipated parliamentary reactions merely compelled the Finnish executive to find alternative means for waging war. That the executive was able to bypass domestic opposition and fight a war it wanted from the start is inconsistent with what the democratic peace theory would lead us to expect.

100. Upton, *Finland in Crisis*, pp. 277–278.

preparations for an offensive under way, the Soviets could not continue to treat Finland as a nonbelligerent and a defensive counterattack became imperative. Once Soviet air strikes began, the Finnish executive had an appropriate *casus belli*.[101] Given the Soviet initiation of hostilities, the Finnish Parliament had to accept Finnish-German collusion and vote for war with the Soviet Union.

In short, Ryti's ability to set the foreign policy agenda, thereby limiting the options for Parliament, made it difficult for legislators to change course. By "moving first" and committing Finland to a particular foreign policy course, Ryti effectively removed alternative options, and a costly war became more likely. Thus, policy making within this particular democratic setting *generated* dangerous international security environments: Finland created its own security dilemma.

Once the tide began to turn against Germany and Finland, it was difficult to negotiate a separate peace with the Soviet Union largely because Germany insisted that any agreement made behind its back would be considered a betrayal. Germany demanded that Finland sign a formal pact not to make a separate peace, and it was in a powerful position to punish the Finns for any such move. However, a treaty that pledged Finland not to conclude a separate peace would have been unconstitutional without the consent of Parliament, and the Finnish government could not bring the matter to the Finnish Parliament because of the dissension it was likely to cause. Consequently, Finland avoided giving the Germans a definitive answer, despite the German interruption of food and other supplies and its capacity to inflict other reprisals.

With the Soviet successful offensive on the Karelian Isthmus in June 1944 and the German demand that Finland publicly forgo a separate peace, the Finnish government was stuck between a rock and a hard place: "Faced with the appalling alternatives of binding the nation to a Germany surely doomed to defeat or committing it to an unconditional surrender to dreaded Russia, the government of

---

101. Upton, Krosby, and Manninen argue that even if the Soviets had not attacked on June 25, the Finnish government would have found another incident to use as a *casus belli*. Since Finland had no desire to remain neutral and was not seeking to avoid a conflict with the Soviet Union, the Finnish-German offensive would have proceeded as planned. See Upton, *Finland in Crisis*, pp. 292–293; Krosby, *Finland, Germany, and the Soviet Union*, pp. 182–183; and Manninen, "Operation Barbarossa and the Nordic Countries," pp. 151–152.

Finland seemed paralyzed."[102] Once again, a lack of parliamentary consensus prevented any decisive action. The Agrarians, the IKL, and members of the Concentration Party insisted that the government obtain German aid, while the Social Democrats, members of the Swedish People's Party, and the Progressives demanded that the government sue for peace.

Ultimately, Finland obtained German aid without committing the country to a German alliance. Instead of Parliament committing itself to Germany, it was decided that only President Ryti would sign the declaration. As a result, *only he would be bound by the agreement*.[103] The commitment to Germany was in the form of a statement signed solely by President Ryti. There was no countersignature of any minister and there was no specific claim that the president was speaking with the support of the cabinet or Parliament. As such, this mere presidential letter of intent could be discarded at a later date and would not be binding on a new government. The promise given by Ryti would apply during the time he remained in office, and would bind the cabinet since it had advised Ryti to sign the agreement. But the election of a new president would allow for a reorientation of Finland's foreign policy position.[104] Ryti explains the decision to deceive the German High Command:

The discussion of the agreement in Parliament would generate bitter differences of opinion . . . It would probably lead to a cabinet crisis . . . Under such circumstances a formula [had to] be found that would make it possible for Finland, at the right moment, to free itself without being crushed. Such a formula was viable, and I took upon myself the entire responsibility, thus reserving for Parliament full moral freedom and freedom of action, when it should be necessary to bring about a change . . . I announced to the members of the cabinet that I was ready to resign from the post of President of the Republic as soon as such a moment had come.[105]

---

102. Lundin, *Finland in the Second World War*, p. 214; see also Aage Trommer, "Scandinavia and the Turn of the Tide," in Nissen, ed., *Scandinavia During the Second World War*, p. 261; and Berit Nøkleby, "Adjusting to Allied Victory," in ibid., pp. 283–285.

103. According to Lundin, the Finnish commitment to Germany was "one of the few successful frauds ever practiced on Hitler, and certainly one of the slickest tricks of the Second World War." Lundin, *Finland in the Second World War*, p. 215.

104. The text is printed in Lundin, *Finland in the Second World War*, p. 216.

105. Quoted in ibid., p. 218. Interestingly, not all the cabinet members viewed the agreement as a deliberate attempt to deceive the Germans. The five representatives

Thus, the executive exploited Finland's domestic political features to secure aid.

Germany fully acknowledged the presidential letter, and in return sent arms, troops, and other supplies to stiffen the Finnish resistance. This material proved most helpful—the Soviet attempts to cross the Bay of Viipuri were repelled, and the line defending the approach into southern Finland remained unbroken. By the end of June, a German division joined the Finns in fighting against the Russian offensive, and a brigade of self-propelled artillery was received. Anti-tank weapons, abundant ammunition, and grain deliveries stabilized the situation and created a basis for a more equitable settlement between Finland and the Soviet Union.[106]

The German government was deceived largely because it expected the Finnish government to behave like itself. Accustomed to an authoritarian way of thinking, Joachim von Ribbentrop did not appreciate the "backdoors" of the Finnish democratic system. Lundin puts it well:

[The Germans] seem actually to have believed that in a country in which the Constitution expressly reserved to Parliament a power of consent in 'all decisions with respect to peace and war' they could, by the blackmail of a war emergency, override the Constitution and the Parliament and, by the use of illegal presidential signature, bind the nation to take orders from Berlin indefinitely. They seem to have thought that the Finns, like the Germans, would continue fighting a hopeless fight . . . merely because the executive power told them to do so.[107]

In sum, although Finland was pressured by both Germany and the Soviet Union, it did have choices. Finland was able to change foreign policy course largely by relying on the character of its own democratic political institutions.

CRITIQUE OR CONFIRMATION OF THE DEMOCRATIC PEACE THEORY?
My analysis suggests that Finnish democracy influenced its military

---

of the socialist party voted against sending the agreement. These representatives and the socialist members of Parliament even discussed leaving the cabinet and going into open opposition. But after Tanner convinced the party committee that no great value should be placed on the "scrap of paper," the Social Democrats agreed to remain in the government. Ibid., p. 219.

106. Mannerheim, *Memoirs*, p. 483; Nøkleby, "Adjusting to Allied Victory," pp. 284–285; and Killinen, "Direction of the War in Finland," p. 35.

107. Lundin, *Finland in the Second World War*, p. 220.

strategy during World War II, but not in the ways assumed by the democratic peace theory. Most problematic for the monadic version of the theory is that Finland chose a course of action that risked high costs, poor outcomes, and a severely violent war with a great power. Advocates of the monadic hypothesis assert that democracies are less likely to pursue risky foreign policies and will hesitate to fight costly wars.[108] Yet, Finnish democratic institutions did not prevent war, but rather made it more likely—the features of Finnish democracy got the Finns involved in a costly war that they could have avoided.

The case also challenges the institutional variant of the democratic peace theory. According to this argument, democratic institutions allow for public control over foreign policy and ensure that citizens have leverage over war decisions. This case shows that democratic systems that do not separate the powers of the executive and legislative branches, and provide few *ex ante* checks on the executive's foreign policy making authority, do not prevent war-prone leaders from leading the state into war. For example, semipresidential democracies, which allow the president to direct foreign security policy and set the agenda of military strategy, make it difficult for the legislature to consider alternative foreign policy options. Indeed, the absence of the kinds of checks on presidential foreign policy making found in most West European coalitional parliamentary systems and in the U.S. presidential system made it *easier* for the executive to direct Finland's foreign policy course in the direction of either war or peace.[109]

By privileging a president who favored a pro-German policy and undermining the bargaining power of more moderate forces represented in Parliament, semipresidential democracy decreased the chances of a Soviet-Finnish peace in the aftermath of the Winter War. This argument is significantly different from Spiro's explanation for

---

108. See especially R.J. Rummel, "Democracies ARE Less Warlike Than Other Regimes," *European Journal of International Relations*, Vol. 1, No. 4 (December 1995), pp. 457–479; and Randolph M. Siverson, "Democracies and War Participation: In Defense of the Institutional Constraints Argument," *European Journal of International Relations*, Vol. 1, No. 4 (December 1995), pp. 481–489.

109. Finnish leaders were certainly more constrained than leaders in nondemocracies. But they were less constrained than leaders in other types of democracies, and they found it easier to direct Finland's foreign policy course than have leaders in other democratic regime types. Although this finding is not a direct refutation of the democratic peace theory, it does suggest that the theory—particularly its institutional variant—may apply to some democracies more than others.

the Continuation War. Spiro argues that "democratic checks and balances" did not prevent President Ryti from siding with Nazi Germany and declaring war on the democracies. In his view, the Continuation War supports neorealism and proves that a "conflict of interest may be so deep" that "nations fight despite the fact that they are . . . liberal democracies." By contrast, I argue that neorealism is less persuasive. Democratic rules and structures *did* influence Finnish military strategy. Indeed, the features of semipresidential democracy made it easier for the president to direct military strategy and delegate decision making to the military—hard-liners had it easy because Finland's domestic institutions were biased in their favor.[110]

In sum, while leaders in democracies may be more constrained than leaders in nondemocracies to commit their nations to war, these constraints vary and are a matter of degree. In a semipresidential system, the executive has more autonomy than in other democratic systems and is nearly solely responsible for national security policy. In these democracies, a war-prone president can more easily mobilize (or circumvent) public opinion for a war he or she wishes to initiate. The executive will find it easier to implement its preferred foreign policy agenda because it faces fewer veto points, and there are no other institutions to directly block the executive's decision for war. Simply put, "what matters in a crisis is the organization of foreign policy authority—the centralization of the executive and its autonomy from the legislature—not merely whether the state is democratic or not."[111]

Finally, Finland's alignment policies challenge the causal logic of institutional democratic peace approaches. The institutional variant asserts that if an incumbent government pursues unpopular policies, it can be replaced at the next election. Regular elections give leaders an incentive to forgo risky policies *in advance* in order to avoid losing office in the future; the source of peaceful policy is the voting public.

---

110. However, the case does not support the notion that civilian control of the military decreases foreign aggression. President Ryti delegated the formulation of military strategy; unrestrained military leaders did not "capture" the state.

111. Susan Peterson, "How Democracies Differ: Public Opinion, State Structure, and the Lessons of the Fashoda Crisis," *Security Studies*, Vol. 5, No. 1 (Autumn 1995), p. 5. Berry suggests that Finland's "authoritarian form of political democracy" explains its ability to survive the crises of the 1940s. See Berry, *American Foreign Policy and the Finnish Exception*, p. 440. By contrast, I have suggested that executive autonomy and near total control of foreign policy agenda-setting helps to explain why Finland got involved in the Continuation War in the first place.

Yet, in this case it was not the public that was most instrumental in changing Finland's foreign policy course and getting the country out of a costly war; it was the Ryti government which manipulated both the public and democratic accountability. By forwarding a mere presidential letter to Germany and resigning shortly thereafter, Ryti was able to guarantee German military aid without surrendering to the Soviet Union. Thus, the *absence* of the kind of checks on presidential foreign policy initiatives that are common to West European coalitional parliamentary systems and the U.S. presidential system—which guarantee that a commitment by the executive cannot be easily overturned if a majority of legislators have established vested interests in the old policy—facilitated the adoption of a different foreign policy agenda once a new president (Mannerheim) was elected.[112]

Conclusion

Finland's involvement in World War II is partially consistent with the democratic peace theory. First, British and U.S. foreign policy toward Finland is consistent with what a strict reading of the theory would lead us to expect. That these democratic great powers avoided attacking Finnish troops and either reluctantly broke off diplomatic relations (the United States) or declared war on Finland (Britain) is evidence in favor of the democratic peace thesis. Moreover, decision makers in both the United States and Britain referred to Finnish democracy in justifying their policies. That Finland's regime type played an important role in the decision making calculus of the Western allies is strong evidence for the dyadic democratic peace proposition.[113]

Nevertheless, while the United States and Britain did not shoot Finns, the case undermines the claim that joint democracy averts not

---

112. In his discussion of the Finnish case, Spiro ignores this domestic institutional manipulation. According to Spiro, President Ryti was not reelected because he was "a leader who pursued an alliance with fascists and who declared war on democracies." Thus, according to Spiro, "democratic checks and balances led to Mannerheim's election" and contributed to the subsequent changes in Finland's pro-German foreign policy course. See Spiro, "The Insignificance of the Liberal Peace," pp. 61–62. By contrast, I have suggested that the executive (rather than the voting public) was responsible for getting Finland out of the war.

113. For more on U.S. and British responses to Finnish policies, and how the perception of shared democratic institutions and norms stalled the deterioration of Allied-Finnish relations, see Berry, *American Foreign Policy and the Finnish Exception*, pp. 175–186, 194–195, 412–417.

only war, but also makes the threat of force nonexistent.[114] In this case, the Western Allies and Finland were not able to settle their disagreements by mediation, negotiation, or peaceful diplomacy; the United States eventually broke off diplomatic relations with Finland, and Britain declared war. Relations between these democracies during World War II certainly do not fit into the category of "stable peace."

While U.S. and British policies toward Finland are somewhat consistent with the theory, Finnish foreign policy toward the Western allies is less supportive. On the one hand, the case confirms the central premise of democratic peace theory—that domestic regime type influences international conflict. Consistent with the democratic peace theory, the case suggests that the attributes of a state's domestic political system do affect its foreign policy choices. Consequently, neorealists are wrong to claim that democracy and other internal characteristics are irrelevant to whether states will or will not fight each other. The nettlesome question of why Finland chose its disastrous foreign policy during World War II can be resolved by focusing on the competing foreign policy preferences of various domestic groups, and how certain domestic institutions influenced which group would ultimately win the foreign policy debate. Finland's form of democratic government played an important role both in its willingness to resist Soviet demands in 1939 and in its decision to side with Nazi Germany in 1940.

On the other hand, the case undermines the central hypothesis of the monadic variant—that democratic institutions generate moderation in foreign policy making and prevent the emergence of belligerent policies that provoke war. Indeed, prior to the Winter War, Finnish democratic institutions made war more likely. The features of semipresidential democracy got Finland involved in a war that it should have avoided. Prior to the Continuation War, the Finnish domestic political system made it more difficult for moderate groups to influence the foreign policy making process. Here too, the features of semipresidential democracy generated foreign policy strategies that risked the costs of war with the Soviet Union.

Even more problematic for the dyadic version of the democratic peace theory is that joint democracy did not prevent Finland's elected

---

114. For the argument that joint democracy eliminates threats to use force, see Russett, *Grasping the Democratic Peace*, p. 42; and Russett, "Counterfactuals About War and its Absence," p. 180.

leaders from joining an alliance against the Western democracies and collaborating with their enemy. There is no question that Finnish policies prior to the Continuation War threatened the national interests of the democratic Allied forces. Finland's alliance with Germany and its military activities in Soviet territory undermined U.S. and British efforts to keep the Soviet Union in the war in order to defeat Germany. The important point is that regime type was largely irrelevant to Finland's alliance choices—it was certainly not an important criterion for determining which states should be treated as threatening. While a substantial proportion of the Finnish Parliament did not favor an alliance policy that put Finland in an illiberal nondemocratic camp and risked a second war with the Soviet Union, the Finnish president preferred to side with Nazi Germany. Ryti viewed Nazi Germany as the lesser threat (despite its illiberal regime) because of power and strategic considerations. As Berry states, "the efforts of the Roosevelt administration to support Britain and the Soviet Union combined with the popular image of Finland to determine United States policy toward Finland. Concurrently, Finland viewed its national interests through the prism of a German counterbalance to the Soviet Union."[115]

Ryti's calculations are not surprising; for small states facing severe external pressures, strategic calculations are often more important than considerations of regime type affinity.[116] The president's views prevailed because in the Finnish semipresidential system the president has great leeway in foreign policy making, can delegate war powers to the military, and need not heed the *ex ante* views of parliament when planning military strategy. In short, whether democracies ally against or fight other democracies depends as much on the *type* of democratic regime as on how particular elected leaders view the security environment and the legitimacy of using force. Finland's declaration of war against the Western democracies and its alliance with Nazi Germany shows that even democratic pairs of states cannot count on enjoying pacific relations indefinitely.

The upshot is not that we should discard the democratic peace theory. Instead, the next round of theory testing should identify its

---

115. Berry, *American Foreign Policy and the Finnish Exception*, p. 93.

116. For more on the claim that the democratic peace theory will be less useful for explaining the foreign policy choices of small democracies, see Randall Schweller, "Domestic Structure and Preventive War: Are Democracies More Pacific?" *World Politics*, Vol. 44 (January 1992), pp. 235–269.

boundaries of applicability. In this essay, I have suggested two contingencies under which the theory may be less applicable. First, small democratic states that face severe external threats are more likely to exhibit foreign policies that diverge from the expectations of the theory; that is, foreign policy decision makers will be compelled to base foreign policies on strategic considerations and the balance of power. By contrast, great power democracies will be more likely to display foreign policies that conform to the theory's predictions. Foreign policy decision makers will have more options because great powers rarely face threats to national survival; consequently, considerations of the opponent's regime type may play just as important a role in the decision making calculus as do neorealist variables. Second, the nature of the executive-legislative balance of power varies among democracies, and the democratic peace theory is likely to work better in some variations and worse in others. Centralized democratic institutions will facilitate aggressive behavior when leaders prefer war. By privileging the executive over the legislative branch, such structures can lead the state down the road to war, perhaps even against fellow democracies. By contrast, decentralized democracies will be better able to constrain a leader bent on war. Since the executive must share foreign policy making powers with other groups, separating the foreign policy powers of the executive and the legislative branches will constrain war-prone leaders. In sum, since executive autonomy varies across democratic regime types, democratic institutions may be just as likely to drive states to war as they are to restrain them from it. Democracy matters, but not in any determinate way.

Part III
Democracies in the
World at Large:
Are They Generally
More Pacific and
Prudent?

Chapter 5

How Did the Democratic Process Affect Britain's Decision to Reoccupy the Falkland Islands?

Lawrence Freedman

In this chapter, I consider the influence of democracy on the origins and conduct of the 1982 Falklands War between Britain and Argentina.[1] At the start of April 1982, Britain was a democracy and Argentina was not.[2] The hostilities between the two, which concluded with the surrender of the Argentine garrison on June 14, 1982, and led to a return of the Falkland Islands to British sovereignty, was a war.[3]

Two types of democratic peace theory have been identified by Miriam Fendius Elman. According to the dyadic position, democracies

The author wishes to thank Chris Baxter for his help researching this paper, and Miriam Fendius Elman, Arie Kacowicz, and Chris Gelpi for their comments.

1. I refer to the "Falklands War" and to the territory in dispute as the "Falkland Islands" partly because one consequence of the war was to confirm this identity. Naturally, an Argentine analysis would refer to the "Malvinas." Some analysts, seeking to avoid pronouncing on the merits of the case, refer to the "Falklands/Malvinas," giving equal weight to the British and Argentine names. This seems unnecessarily clumsy.

2. Debates about the quality of British democracy concerning such matters as the culture of official secrecy and the nature of military rule in Argentina, for example, concerning its complex roots, are not germane to this analysis.

3. One of the interesting features of the Falklands War for the democratic peace theory is that the accepted casualty level of about 950 puts it just below the 1,000 battle casualties that Small and Singer use to separate wars from other forms of organized violence. Russett uses this definition for coding purposes, but nonetheless recognizes that it would be odd not to include the Falklands War. Bruce Russett, "The Fact of Democratic Peace," in Michael E. Brown, Sean M. Lynn-Jones, and Steven E. Miller, *Debating the Democratic Peace* (Cambridge, Mass.: MIT Press, 1996), p. 70. This chapter is reprinted from Russett's book, *Grasping the Democratic Peace* (Princeton, N.J.: Princeton University Press, 1993). R.J. Rummell

236 | PATHS TO PEACE

do not fight wars against each other, but are neither less conflict-prone nor less belligerent than nondemocracies when they are fighting nondemocracies because of their competing ideologies. According to the monadic position, democracies are inherently pacific.[4] Since only one of these states involved in this war was democratic, this chapter cannot confirm the most important claim of the dyadic position. Clearly, the readiness of Britain to fight for the Falklands challenges the view that democratic states are deeply reluctant to go to war, especially when confronting a nondemocratic state. It shows that democratic states can accept belligerency, but throws little light on their inherent belligerency because Britain did not seek a war with Argentina. The first moves in 1982 were made by Argentina; the issue for Britain was whether or not to respond. However, Britain's willingness to fight does support the view that once democratic states are roused they can be formidable opponents.[5]

Despite these modest conclusions, and the equally modest role played by this war in the scholarly debate,[6] there are four reasons why the Falklands War does deserve close attention. First, there are few recent cases in which two countries have allowed a dispute to be settled so decisively on the battlefield; in which there was no direct participation of other states; and in which the contrast in regime type was so stark. Second, because the case is comparatively recent, the characteristics of the democratic state might be considered to have a more general application to contemporary policy debates, to which

---

also deals with this issue in "Democracies ARE Less Warlike Than Other Regimes," *European Journal of International Relations*, Vol. 1, No. 4 (December 1995), p. 469, as does Miriam Fendius Elman in the introduction to this volume. My own view is that the possibility of excluding the Falklands War on these grounds is indicative of the problems with quantitative definitions. It will be interesting to see how the Western involvement in Bosnia comes to be coded in future analyses.

4. See Miriam Fendius Elman's introduction to this volume.

5. See, for example, David Lake, "Powerful Pacifists: Democratic States and War," *American Political Science Review*, Vol. 86, No. 1 (March 1992), pp. 24–37; Randall L. Schweller, "Domestic Structure and Preventive War: Are Democracies More Pacific?" *World Politics*, Vol. 44, No. 2 (January 1992), pp. 235–239; and R.J. Rummell, "Democracies ARE Less Warlike Than Other Regimes," pp. 457–479.

6. It appears to be insufficiently anomalous. Another reason may be that it occurred too late to appear in the most important data set for those given to this form of analysis: Melvin Small and J. David Singer, *Resort to Arms* (Beverly Hills, Calif.: Sage, 1982).

much of the democratic peace thesis is clearly directed. Third, the Falklands War occurred at a time when there were strong grounds for assuming that public opinion in a democratic state would tend to be pacific. In the early 1980s, there were regular demonstrations on the streets of Western capitals against nuclear weapons; moreover, this was also a time when the best recent evidence was that Western states were not only disinclined to fight wars, but also incompetent in military operations.

Fourth, and particularly important, the Falklands War was about democracy. Britain went to war in support of the democratic principle of self-determination. An additional normative influence was a belief that international law had been violated, and that compliance with Argentine demands would therefore mean rewarding aggression. Questions of national prestige and honor were also, of course, extremely significant. Nonetheless, it is impossible to make sense of the events of April–June 1982 without understanding the importance of the principles believed to be at stake. As one analyst later observed, the Falklands War was

an unusual opportunity to see how a Parliamentary democracy . . . thinks through in public debate the rights and wrongs of going to war to defend national interests or to remedy breaches of international law.[7]

The next section outlines the specific hypotheses of the democratic peace theory that can be tested in the Falklands case, and discusses the democratic value of self-determination. I then trace the events of the crisis and war, focusing particularly on how Britain justified its actions, and the role of public opinion. I seek to answer the question: how did democracy shape Britain's response to the Argentine seizure of the islands? Finally, the conclusion suggests the case's implications for the democratic peace theory.

---

7. Robert Andrew Burns, *Diplomacy, War, and Parliamentary Democracy: Further Lessons from the Falklands, or Advice from Academe* (Lanham, Md.: University Press of America, 1985), p. 6. He adds: "Of course, the vital British interest at stake was not the first-order concern for the national security of the homeland. The crisis affected only the periphery of the national identity and raised more controversial considerations of principle (self-defense against an illegal use of force, self-determination, and territorial sovereignty) and national honor (a British willingness to defend a small group of people for whom they were responsible and to show that aggression "does not pay"). It is not surprising, however, that the war evoked strong passions and the kind of patriotic posturing which makes rational analysis of the sensible response so difficult"(p. 6).

The Behavior of Democracies

The Falklands case offers evidence on three hypotheses about the behavior of democracies: that public opinion in a democracy is a force for peace; that democracies regard nondemocracies as warlike; and that democratic values are a source of a democracy's peaceful behavior (according to the monadic version) or its unwillingness to make war on democracies (according to the dyadic version). It also encourages a careful consideration of the meaning of democratic values in conflicts such as this. It suggests that those features of democratic ideology most germane to the conflict will tend to be emphasized as governments seek to justify the use of force at home and abroad. While all relevant values were stressed to both domestic and world audiences when justifying the use of force by Britain, the need to uphold the rule of international law was highlighted more at home, and the principle of self-determination was underscored abroad. In addition, values such as these may not be allowed so prominent a role when democratic governments hope for more peaceful relations with nondemocratic governments. Up to this point Britain had shown few qualms about developing close relationships with countries such as Chile and Argentina, despite their poor human rights records, and it moved even closer to Chile during the conflict. Thus, though this case study supports the importance of normative factors in explaining international behavior, it demonstrates that the character of these norms may be complex and conditional.[8]

In the democratic peace literature there is often an assumption that public opinion in a democracy is a force for peace, restraining elites who might otherwise be more belligerent. Democratic peace theorists tend to assume that while sometimes the external challenge is so great that the public can be mobilized, significantly strengthening a government in the conduct of war, in general the public will be far more impressed by opportunities for negotiated, compromise settlements and alarmed by the prospect of heavy casualties should battle be joined in earnest. Nondemocratic states, by contrast, are supposed to be more vulnerable to the capriciousness of whimsical supreme leaders and the rapacity of power-hungry oligarchies.

The Falklands case study shows that public reaction is conditional

---

8. Thomas Risse-Kappen, "Democratic Peace—Warlike Democracies? A Social Constructivist Interpretation of the Liberal Argument," *European Journal of International Relations*, Vol. 1, No. 4 (December 1995), pp. 491–517.

on the issues at stake. Public opinion, or at least sections of it, can be moved to contemplate war for reasons that do not touch on the fundamentals of national security but do touch on questions of prestige and principle. Democracy has to be understood not only as a set of mechanisms—a "regime type"—but a set of values. In this context, democracy has two important qualities: it provides conditions through which misgivings about belligerency, or for that matter passivity, can be made known, and also defines a shared normative framework that helps both the public and policy makers alike differentiate between right and wrong in the conduct of international affairs. It can thus provide legitimacy to war-like acts performed in its name.

HOW DEMOCRACIES PERCEIVE NONDEMOCRACIES

The dyadic version of the democratic peace thesis argues that the conduct of democratic politics creates expectations that disputes in society will be resolved through consultation, mediation, and the rule of law rather than through crude power plays, and that this expectation will spill over into the resolution of disputes with other democracies. Opposing expectations are created when dealing with nondemocratic states. Regimes that take an aggressive stance when dealing with their own people are likely to be even more aggressive in their external relations.

The Falklands case study provides support for this view of the difference between the two types of regime, but it takes it even further. British opinion at all levels saw Argentine behavior as displaying the characteristically aggressive pathology of authoritarian regimes; this behavior was contrasted with Britain's own democratic nature. In addition, from the beginning of the crisis, popular consent was recognized by the British government as critical. It was conscious of the need to frame war aims in terms that would maximize support. It is significant that these war aims were increasingly framed in terms of democratic norms: the material interests involved were negligible and were increasingly played down.

That Britain was a democracy and Argentina was not affected not only the origins of the conflict but also its conduct; however, it is doubtful that any a priori propositions could have helped predict how the characters of the two states would affect their decision making. In war, judgments must be tested in battle as well as against public opinion. Strategy requires great sensitivity to external factors, including allies and international organizations as well as the enemy, and this affects the role that can be played by domestic institutions, limiting the options available while potentially magnifying the impact of individual decisions. Both Britain and Argentina could claim a popular mandate. Both found public opinion pushing them as much in hawkish as in dovish directions, allowing them to negotiate while setting limits on the areas of compromise.

THE IMPORTANCE OF SELF-DETERMINATION

It is important to specify the values believed to be at stake in any conflict before their influence can be properly assessed. The norm of self-determination arises out of democratic theory, but it is by no means dependent upon it. It also has an uneasy relationship with liberalism.[9] Equally, the precise ideologies adopted by illiberal or nondemocratic regimes can vary considerably, and can involve an embrace of the norm of self-determination, especially when the government has a nationalist ideology and claims for itself a unique insight into the will of the people.[10]

The norm grew in importance during the nineteenth century as individual European nations demanded freedom from colonial restraints, and in particular those imposed by the Austro-Hungarian and Ottoman empires. As the twentieth century progressed, this developed into a challenge against all colonial regimes. Struggles were waged against the British, French, Dutch, Belgian, Portuguese,

---

9. While the literature treats liberalism and democracy as though they are synonymous, they are not. Liberalism puts the greatest stress on individual liberties, and so may be a moderating force through encouraging checks and balances on the executive. Democracy, in its stress on the will of the majority, may be more prone to waves of popular feeling. The political practices associated with both liberalism and democracy have changed dramatically over the past two centuries, as a result of industrialization, mass suffrage, and modern communications. So too have the nature of the challenges they face. In the U.S. literature, emphasis is understandably placed on republicanism, which was often contrasted at the time with monarchical government. Ido Oren makes the important point that prior to World War I, Imperial Germany was admired by early political scientists such as Woodrow Wilson for its constitutionalism, and that notions of what it means to be a democracy were redefined as a result of the war. Oren,"The Subjectivity of the 'Democratic' Peace," *International Security*, Vol. 20, No. 2 (Fall 1995), pp. 147–184.

10. Jeane Kirkpatrick, U.S. Ambassador to the United Nations at the time of the Falklands War, and an advocate of a neutral U.S. policy that did not alienate Argentina, had earlier written a notorious article that stressed the variations in nondemocratic regimes. See Jeane Kirkpatrick, "Dictatorship and Double Standards," *Commentary* (November 1979).

and Soviet empires after World War II. During the course of these struggles, democratic states found themselves accused of disregarding their own democratic principles by denying popular demands for independence. In some cases this profoundly affected the character of their regimes. For example, in 1958, during the "generals' revolt" in Algeria, French democracy almost broke down. By contrast, the strain of Portugal's colonial rule prompted a democratic revolution in Portugal in 1974.

A legacy of the processes of decolonization, in their peaceful as well as their violent manifestations, was to elevate the principle of self-determination as a democratic norm. The British and other former imperial powers came to accept that past conquests no longer carried the right to rule over people who had explicitly rejected that rule. The democratic principles that these powers accepted for themselves could not be ignored when it came to subject peoples.

In its simplest form, self-determination involves no more than a restatement of the foundation of any democratic system: governments should be accountable to those they claim to represent. In the West, periodic free elections remain the best means devised to secure accountability. Self-determination, however, is generally considered to be a right of groups, rather than of individuals. This notion gained currency in the nineteenth century as various nationalist movements argued that distinctive communities of people had a right to govern themselves on the basis of their shared language, culture, and traditions. States should be constructed to give expression to the aspirations of coherent national groupings, whether by dismantling empires to liberate oppressed nationalities, or by transcending established borders in an effort to unify national groups.

Self-determination has not always led to democratic forms of government. As a nationalist slogan, it requires only that a government be drawn from the host population and that it not be an alien imposition. Many governments have claimed that the wishes of the people can be discerned without Western-style elections, and in particular without sanctioning a political opposition. More radical governments often claim that they grasp the needs of the people better than the people themselves, and that excessive democracy would result in a long-term political vision being compromised continuously for reasons of short-term expediency.

Various groups' demands for self-determination can contradict each other. This can lead to bitter conflicts, as has been seen since the end of the Cold War. Such conflicts can have important implications for the democratic peace thesis, for they point to circumstances in which two sets of democratic wills can seem fated to clash. This is particularly evident when one or more groups feels denied the opportunity for self-determination within state institutions dominated by another group, even though the state is formally democratic.

The Falklands case illustrates a different type of problem with self-determination, one that arises when decolonization would lead not to self-rule but to a transfer of sovereignty to another state, normally one occupying adjacent territory. In such situations, self-determination—the inspiration for decolonization—also helps to define its limits. For example, in each of Britain's significant residual territories—Gibraltar, the Bahamas, the Falklands—local sentiment remains firmly with retaining the British connection. Even with Northern Ireland, an integral part of the United Kingdom, the British government has asserted that it has no "selfish" strategic or economic needs to hold on to sovereignty. If a majority voted for union with Southern Ireland instead of Britain, that would be acceptable, at least in theory. In Hong Kong, the principle of self-determination was only overcome because Britain had a lease with a fixed expiration date and not a freehold. Here, as with the Falklands and Gibraltar, the issue has been whether the people most affected should be allowed to veto a transfer of sovereignty.

In all of these cases, self-determination is hardly a pretext for holding on to a highly desirable property; continuing colonial administration has carried the risk of a potentially expensive and hazardous conflict with aggrieved local powers. The circumstances in the Falklands War were unusual, but the essential issues are raised any time a political settlement appears to involve handing over the destiny of one political community to one that is larger and whose interests are inimical.

Britain and Argentina

Neither the British nor the Argentine governments enjoyed great popularity in the opening months of 1982; only in Britain did the government have to consider the prospect of defeat at the polls. The Conservative government led by Margaret Thatcher had been in power since May 1979 and was only starting to recover electoral support after taking the country through a deep recession. The government was accused of policies that had willfully aggravated economic hardships. In Argentina, the junta was led by General Leopoldo

Galtieri, who had been in office since December 1981, when he had taken over from the previous junta led by General Roberto Viola. All these juntas lacked popular support due to both the harsh measures through which the military had sustained itself in power since 1976 and the perilous state of the economy.

Regime type was one of two important differences between the two countries. The other was their attitudes toward a set of barely populated islands in the South Atlantic that they both claimed—the Falklands. The islands were governed by Britain, and the local population (1,800) considered itself British. Local government on the islands was not itself a model of democracy, with a colonial governor and a strong influence from the main employer, the Falkland Islands Company, but the islanders considered the government to be sufficiently democratic to provide a stark contrast to Argentina.[11] As David Gompert notes:

Socially, culturally, and politically . . . the Falkland Islanders considered themselves British. They enjoyed what they considered their democratic political institutions and disdained Argentina's political tradition and its military government.[12]

General Galtieri had put the Falklands dispute at the top of his agenda. From its distinctive geopolitical perspective, the junta saw the islands as occupying a critical location, particularly relevant in terms of Argentina's ongoing dispute with Chile and also wider international negotiations on the future of Antarctica. It was also a straightforward issue of national pride. When asked during the war to explain why his country had acted as it did, Galtieri dismissed material explanations—"Not gold, not oil, not the strategic position." It was all about, he insisted, "the sentiment of the Argentine nation since 1833."[13] Thus 1982, the year before the 150th anniversary of the British seizure of the islands, was seen as a critical year of decision. After a decade and a half of fruitless negotiations, Galtieri had

---

11. See G.M. Dillon, *The Falklands, Politics and War* (London: Macmillan, 1989), chap. 3. The Falkland Islands Company owned over 40 percent of the land, and provided essential shipping, banking, distribution, and marketing services. It was owned by the Coalite Group.

12. David Gompert, "American Diplomacy and the Haig Mission," in D.B. Bendahmane, and J.W. McDonald, eds., *Perspectives on Negotiation: Four Case Studies and Interpretations* (Washington, D.C.: Center for the Study of Foreign Affairs, 1986), p. 62.

13. Interview with Iriana Fallaci, *Times* (London), June 12, 1982.

already decided on military action if necessary, though he had not expected to take such a drastic step as early as April.[14]

Britain, by contrast, did not want to make any decisions on the future of the Falklands. It had no obvious strategic or economic interest in holding on to the islands. The overall contraction of the British Empire had left the Falkland Islands with no role left to play in any grand imperial design. Surveys suggested exploitable resources, including possibly oil, but their extent was uncertain and they could not be exploited in any event so long as the dispute with Argentina rumbled on.[15] The local economy was largely geared to sheep and controlled by the Falklands Islands Company. The needs of the islanders had not loomed large in British policy making, whether in terms of defining their nationality rights, planning their economic development, or even guaranteeing their security. Indeed, in the summer of 1981 the government had sent a clear signal that it did not intend to spend much on the defense of the islands when it announced its decision to scrap HMS *Endurance,* an ice patrol ship connected to the British Antarctica Survey, which had also been used to demonstrate a commitment to defend the Falklands.

The main influence that the islanders had on their own future was that they had managed to impose a veto on any attempt to hand the islands over to Argentina. Successive British governments had judged that there was little to be gained politically by relinquishing the islands and a certain amount to lose because the Falkland Islands lobby could mobilize vocal support in the House of Commons and the media, with bipartisan support whenever there was ever any suggestion of a deal with Buenos Aires. At best, the government hoped that closer links with the mainland, including air and sea communications, would gradually persuade the islanders that their long-term future lay with Argentina; active negotiations with deadlines threatened this gradualist approach. The Argentine junta, however, was in a hurry. The crisis of 1982 arose from the clash of these timetables. The two sides had met in February 1982 in New York. London hoped that modest progress on procedural matters would satisfy Buenos Aires; Buenos Aires was convinced that Britain was procrastinating.

---

14. Unless otherwise stated, the analysis in this chapter follows Lawrence Freedman and Virginia Gamba-Stonehouse, *Signals of War: The Falklands Conflict of 1982* (London: Faber and Faber, 1990).

15. Lord Shackleton, *Economic Survey of the Falkland Islands* (London: Her Majesty's Stationery Office [HMSO], 1976).

The Crisis and War

The trigger to the conflict over the Falklands was a complicated and in many ways farcical episode involving Argentine scrap metal merchants who landed, without seeking permission from Britain, at an old whaling station on the island of South Georgia, a dependency of the Falklands. The British assumed that the Argentine navy was using the scrap metal merchants as a means to establish an illegal presence on South Georgia, and it therefore demanded that they leave and sent HMS *Endurance*, then on its last patrol, to encourage it to do so. The junta feared that those within the British government who were opposed to any deal with Argentina were using the crisis to revive Britain's local military presence, and thereby reverse established policy. This perception, which was reinforced by inaccurate reports in the London press suggesting that an attack submarine might also be dispatched to the South Atlantic, led the junta to suppose that unless it used force quickly it would soon lose a military option. On March 26, the junta determined to occupy the Falkland Islands forthwith; this was achieved on April 2. South Georgia was taken the next day.

The Argentine junta's analysis of British policy making was sophisticated but wrong. It had correctly assessed the British government's marginal interest in the islands themselves and the readiness of the Foreign and Commonwealth Office to rely on diplomacy to manage lingering colonial problems, as it had successfully done in 1980 over Rhodesia. It also correctly judged that the United States would be unhappy at the prospect of two allies going to war with each other and would feel obliged to offer mediation, and that Britain would always find it difficult to ignore U.S. views (as had been shown during the 1956 Suez Crisis). There were good grounds also for supposing that the British armed forces would advise their political masters that a military expedition to retake the islands would be hazardous and possibly impractical.

This latter matter was, however, in part one of timing. The first military appreciation given to the British government argued that a task force could be sent with some prospect of success, although at a risk of high casualty. Military operations were only possible because the 1981 defense review, which had set in motion major cuts in Britain's naval forces, had yet to be fully implemented, and because many ships were in port for Easter and there was still time for the task force to get to the South Atlantic before the onset of winter conditions. A few months later, Britain's military options would have been much less impressive.

However, the junta's major miscalculation was its failure to recognize how the British public would react to the occupation of the Falklands, which was seen as an aggressive act. The junta had hoped that a relatively bloodless occupation would not earn the ignominy normally associated with armed aggression. It also presumed that it could not aggress against territory that was rightfully its own. However, images of the small detachment of Royal Marines lying face down with their hands clasped to the back of their heads were sufficient to send tremors of outrage through the British media and Parliament.

British Prime Minister Margaret Thatcher was faced with the alternatives of either negotiating a face-saving solution in a hopelessly weak position, or sending a task force to bolster the country's bargaining position and provide a military option should negotiations fail. When the House of Commons met in emergency session on April 3, Thatcher announced that the second course would be followed. The naval task force would include Britain's only two aircraft carriers and the bulk of the available fleet. This was not the response that the junta had expected, and it never adjusted to its consequences.

Motives for War

Both countries were surprised that they found themselves at war in April 1982, and that Britain had managed such a substantial military response. For Argentina the dispute was over the ownership of some islands in the South Atlantic; for Britain it was over the fate of the island's 1,800 inhabitants.

When U.S. President Ronald Reagan wondered aloud why two of his country's allies could be getting so passionate about "that little ice-cold bunch of rocks," few in Britain would have disagreed with the assessment. The islands were a burden; they did not support wider British interests. Nor were they just one small issue in a much broader dispute with Argentina. Absent the Falklands controversy, relations would have been cordial and unproblematic. Perhaps inconsistently with the dyadic version of the democratic peace theory, Britain had been trying to improve relations and prevent the Falklands from acting as a source of tension despite Argentina's authoritarianism. It had even sold Argentina important weapons systems, including destroyers and defensive missiles.[16] The problem

16. At the same time the nature of Chile's regime, which was attracting even more international opprobrium for its repressive and authoritarian quality than that of Argentina, enjoyed good relations with Britain.

was that the people who lived on those rocks considered themselves to be British and did not wish to accept the choice of either becoming part of another country or leaving their homes. In the absence of the islanders' determination to retain the link with Britain, the Falkland Islands would have been transferred to Argentina many years ago.

While the islanders' fate remained the core issue, the means by which it was put on the agenda were also critical in shaping the British attitude. Argentina's sudden seizure of the islands was an affront to British pride, as well as to democratic norms. "Aggression must not be rewarded" became as much a slogan of the British campaign as did the notion of "self-determination." Most members of the cabinet accepted that if a response had not been found to this "national humiliation," and if the episode was seen throughout the political spectrum as a deep blow to national prestige imposed by a reactionary militaristic regime, then not only the foreign secretary, who described the event in this way and effectively cast himself into the role of scapegoat,[17] but the whole government might have to resign. This would bring to a premature end the whole Thatcherite experiment, although not necessarily Conservative rule. While many members of the cabinet accepted neither the policies nor the style of the prime minister, the sense that they were fighting for their political lives must have added to the relief among ministers that a show of military strength turned out to be feasible.[18] This does not mean that the task force was sent solely for domestic political purposes.

The British government did not want a war, nor was it looking for something dramatic and popular to distract the people from their economic woes. In the days leading up to the Argentine occupation, the British government accepted that it had no adequate form of defense against a determined Argentine attack, and consequently sought a diplomatic solution. After taking a tough stance over the South Georgia incident, and then discovering that they could not back it up, they attempted to avoid further provocation and encouraged the United States to restrain Argentina.[19] Contrary to the claims of democratic peace proponents who insist that regime type determines the distinction of friends from foes, Britain did not need to look

---

17. Lord Carrington, *Reflect on Things Past* (London: Collins, 1988), pp. 368–371.

18. Nonetheless, the Secretary of State for Defence, John Nott, who had sought to cut back the Royal Navy the previous June, remained uncomfortable throughout the military operation.

19. *Falkland Islands Review: Report of a Committee of Privy Counsellors*, Chairman, The Rt. Hon. Lord Franks, Cmnd. 8787 (London: HMSO, 1983).

at the authoritarian regime in Buenos Aires to be leery of any future Argentine promises—its behavior was eloquent enough. As one scholar has observed, "British policymakers suddenly discovered that their adversarial partner had changed the rules of the game and was, therefore, no longer to be trusted."[20] Britain had hoped it had the measure of Argentina; now it realized that it did not and so had little choice but to assume the worst.

Once Thatcher decided to send the task force, the issue that was both "more immediate and more manageable" was "how to deal with public opinion at home in the intervening period," before the task force reached its destination. Her concern was not the initial support for the task force, but its durability. Sustaining support required that Thatcher maintain unity among those who, like herself, suspected that war was all but inevitable; those who doubted that such a drastic step would be either necessary or desirable; and those who thought it would be both necessary and desirable but doubted that the government would dare to fight. She stated:

> I knew, as most MPs could not, the full extent of the practical military problems. I foresaw that we could encounter setbacks that would cause even some of the hawkish disposition to question whether the game was worth the candle. And how long could a coalition of opinion survive that was composed of warriors, negotiators and even virtual pacifists?[21]

The role of democratic values and international legal norms was critical. Agreement was soon reached on a precise, political objective that was essentially a return to the status *quo ante bellum*: "that the islands would be freed from occupation and returned to British administration at the earliest possible moment." Opinion became mobilized behind this objective during an extraordinary meeting of the House of Commons of April 3, 1982, which some commentators have described as being as critical as the previous evening's meeting of the war cabinet in shaping British policy. While the cabinet made the decision to send the task force, Parliament set the tone for the subsequent diplomatic and military campaign.

Some important themes were voiced from the start of the debate: this was sovereign British territory; the Argentine attempt to decide a dispute through force broke a basic principle of international law;

---

20. Dillon, *The Falklands, Politics and War*, p. 93.

21. Margaret Thatcher, *The Downing Street Years* (London: HarperCollins, 1993), p. 184.

the islanders wished to remain British and had a right to self-determination; and the Argentine regime was essentially fascist. As the prime minister summed it up: "We cannot allow the democratic rights of the islanders to be denied by the territorial ambitions of Argentina."[22]

The most important aspect of the debate was the strength of the Labour Party's support for a tough line against Argentina. The leader of the opposition, Michael Foot, had made his name in the 1930s as a campaigner against appeasement and more recently as a campaigner for disarmament. He stood for high principles in international affairs. His speech demanded action on this basis:

The rights and circumstances of the people in the Falkland Islands must be uppermost in our minds. There is no question in the Falkland Islands of any colonial dependence or anything of the sort. It is a question of people who wish to be associated with this country and who have built their whole lives on the basis of association with this country. We have a moral duty, a political duty and every other kind of duty to ensure that is sustained.[23]

With the Labour leadership's support, and support from the center parties as well, there was no serious organized opposition in Parliament to the later conduct of the war. The Labour front bench confined itself to arguing for a more imaginative diplomacy, though some of its backbenchers did take a more dissident line.

As might be anticipated from the dyadic democratic peace argument, Argentina's authoritarian regime was considered a permissive condition for a military response to the crisis. One of the most senior Conservative backbenchers, Sir Bernard Braine, captured the importance of this feature of the opponent in his contribution:

We are dealing here not with a democratic country that has some claim to the Falkland Islands—with which the matter could be thrashed out in a civilized way—but with a Fascist, corrupt and cruel regime.[24]

Yet in British political tradition and culture, a military response to foreign policy problems is a more acceptable—and feasible—option

---

22. The important debates are reproduced in House of Commons, *The Falklands Campaign: A Digest of Debates in the House of Commons, 2 April to June 1982* (London: HMSO, 1982), p. 5.

23. Ibid., pp. 8–9.

24. Ibid., p. 16.

than it might in other liberal democracies. In Britain, war is not seen in a wholly negative light, as something that must be avoided at all costs. For the British political class, World War II remains the country's "finest hour," and the appeasement of Hitler during the preceding years a warning of the dangers of putting a yearning for peace above all other values. The prime minister put this view in a nutshell in a Commons statement on April 14:

We have a long and proud history of recognizing the right of others to determine their own destiny. Indeed, in that respect, we have an experience unrivalled by any other nation in the world. But that right must be upheld universally, and not least where it is challenged by those who are hardly conspicuous for their own devotion to democracy and liberty.[25]

Francis Pym, secretary of state for Foreign and Commonwealth Affairs, later claimed that the development of cross-party support through the workings of Parliament was "a very good example of the way in which our democratic procedures in Parliament are a source of strength to our nation."[26]

The values the British believed themselves to be upholding were esteemed as international values—especially the reluctance to reward aggression and the disinclination to deny the islanders political rights. Britain had to make its case to the United Nations and gain support from allies that had no direct interest in the conflict; in one extremely important case, the United States, had reasons for sympathizing with Argentina. This created important problems of legitimacy, which have become even more pressing for Western military actions since the end of the Cold War.

The government could point to the extent to which international opinion supported Britain, as reflected in trade sanctions against Argentina, and the passage of Resolution 502 in the United Nations Security Council, passed on April 3 (ten votes in favor, one against, and four abstaining). The resolution did not name Argentina as an aggressor, but did associate it with a breach of the peace and demanded a withdrawal of its forces from the islands. No similar demands were placed on British forces, although a call was made to both countries to "seek a diplomatic solution to their differences." The resolution reinforced the legal basis for the task force—the right

---

25. Ibid., p. 77.
26. Ibid., p. 101.

to self-defense under Article 51 of the UN Charter. The role played by Resolution 502 and Article 51 in the construction of the official British position indicates a sensitivity to problems of both international and domestic legitimacy. Whether Britain would have taken a markedly different stance if UN support had not been forthcoming is difficult to say, but its availability was considered at the time to be a major advantage.[27]

Preparations for War

It is easy enough to satirize the sentiments expressed in the parliamentary debates and the posturing that accompanied them. In one critique, Anthony Barnett picked up on the habitual desire of British politicians to acquire the mantle of Winston Churchill, and the extent to which this allowed the rights and wrongs of the conflict to be simplified and the significance of the British stance to be exaggerated beyond all proportion. Barnett listed the "essential symbols" that were to be found in the fate of the Falkland islanders:

an island people, the cruel seas, a British defeat, Anglo-Saxon democracy challenged by a dictator, and finally the quintessentially Churchillian posture—we were down but we were not out. The parliamentarians of right, left and centre looked through the mists of time to the Falklands and imagined themselves to be the Grand Old Man. They were, after all, his political children and they too would put the 'Great' back into Britain.[28]

For many observers, the jingoism that surrounded the campaign and the treatment of combat as a spectator sport were distasteful, as was Britain's poor management of the underlying dispute and the March 1982 crisis, and its readiness to make deals with an unattractive junta when arms sales were at stake.[29]

The decision to send the task force undoubtedly carried high risks. The British military had recent experience in supporting the civil power in Northern Ireland, and in this could draw on its former

---

27. Sir Anthony Parsons, "The Falklands Crisis in the United Nations, 31 March-14 June 1982," *International Affairs*, Vol. 15, No. 2 (Spring 1983).

28. Anthony Barnett, *Iron Britannia: Why Parliament Waged its Falklands War* (London: Allison & Busby, 1982), p. 48. A similar point is made by Dillon in *The Falklands, Politics and War*, p. 136.

29. On the excesses of some of the press, see Robert Harris, *Gotcha: The Media, The Government and the Falklands Crisis* (London: Faber and Faber, 1983).

expertise in imperial policing and counterinsurgency warfare (as had been exhibited in Malaya). But it had been many years since Britain had mounted a conventional military campaign. The dominant memory remained the Suez fiasco of 1956, when economic pressure from the United States had obliged Britain to abandon an attempt, in collusion with France and Israel, to topple Nasser's government in Egypt.[30] In 1967, when Britain decided to abandon its military presence "East of Suez," there was a presumption that the time had passed when it would regularly go to war in areas distant from the European continent.

As for the faraway Falkland Islands, 8,000 miles away from Britain and close to the Argentine coast, internal studies had shown that there was little that could be done to defend them. The small Royal Marine garrison there supposedly provided some deterrent, but had actually been sent originally to combat any private enterprise by Argentine nationalists.[31] In June 1981, when the Conservative government confirmed the European focus of defense policy, it announced an intention to end the patrols of HMS *Endurance*.

The initial steps approved on April 2, 1982, as the Argentine seizure of the islands was confirmed, did not necessarily mean that Britain was going to war. They could be justified as strengthening Britain's bargaining position in any negotiations while creating an option for future military action. The more fateful decisions to use armed force came later. Nonetheless, the British considered that the Argentine moves had already created, in effect, a state of war. British units on the Falklands and its dependency of South Georgia had put up a fight before acknowledging the futility of resistance against overwhelming odds, and had inflicted some casualties on the Argentine forces. The decision to send the task force was not a decision to resume the fight,

---

30. A case could have been made for using force to put down the white minority regime in Rhodesia (now Zimbabwe) after a unilateral declaration of independence was made in 1965, or to take action in Cyprus in 1975, after a coup inspired by the Greek military junta. In both cases the government decided against military action.

31. In September 1966, in "Operation Condor," an armed group of twenty young Argentines hijacked an Argentine Airlines DC-4 and forced it to land on the race course at the Falklands capital of Port Stanley. British military strength at the time was down to an officer and five men, a reduction from the platoon (thirty-two men) sent after a similar incident in 1964. After this incident, numbers were raised again to platoon strength. During the 1982 invasion, there was double this strength because one platoon was relieving another.

although it made a future fight possible.[32] Whether battle was to be joined again in the future was to depend on diplomacy, but there was to be no waiting for diplomacy. For the moment, the threat to the Argentine position posed by the task force was the only way to ensure that diplomacy would be over anything other than the terms of the transfer of British sovereignty. Margaret Thatcher observes in her memoirs that the task force was sent with some anxiety about what would await it, both because Argentina would have time to prepare defenses and the "bitter winds and violent storms of the southern winter approached." For many, she also notes, the anxiety was eased because they saw the task force as "a purely diplomatic armada that would get the Argentineans back to the negotiating table."[33]

At the same time, the use of force was not conditional on anything other than the military situation, and given the pressures of time, the task force commanders were always reluctant to delay operations for diplomatic reasons. There was never any intention to develop a close linkage between the unfolding of the military operation to retake the islands and the ebb and flow of diplomatic activity. Any military action could always be rationalized as additional pressure on Argentina to make concessions. On April 7, Britain announced a maritime exclusion zone around the islands, to take effect on April 12, when the first submarines would arrive. This was later turned into a total exclusion zone at the end of April, when surface ships and aircraft moved into position to prevent Argentina from reinforcing its Falklands garrison. South Georgia was recaptured with some difficulty, but with no casualties, on April 25.

Britain's knowledge of the Argentine forces was scanty when the task force was sent, and strategy was developed *en route.* Intelligence on certain crucial matters was poor. Certainly those charged with planning an eventual amphibious landing were hardly confident of the outcome. Many senior officers were aware of all the measures that a prudent enemy might take. The military was concerned that

---

32. On the impact of taking military measures for diplomatic reasons, and on the later pressures for war, see Colin Seymour-Ure, British "War Cabinets" in Limited Wars: Korea, Suez and the Falklands (Freiburg-Im-Breisgau: European Consortium for Political Research Workshops, March 1983), p. 22. Max Hastings and Simon Jenkins note that "once the great machine had been set in motion, only the most astonishing change of heart in Buenos Aires could have halted it." The Battle for the Falklands (London: Michael Joseph, 1983), p. 97.

33. Thatcher, The Downing Street Years, pp. 181–184.

Argentine forces would be able to use their time in occupation of the islands productively to improve their defenses; that an opposed landing on the islands would be extraordinarily difficult if local air and sea superiority had not been gained; and that waiting for a propitious moment for a landing, or delaying one while diplomacy took its course, could leave the fleet and the thousands of troops they were carrying exposed to the growing hazards of a South Atlantic winter.

The conflict was not a typical Third World contest, as it was fought with conventional forces on both sides rather than as a guerrilla campaign.[34] This made it more of a "level playing field" for Britain, as its strengths in training and professionalism could make themselves felt,[35] and Britain also had some advantages in military equipment (although here the gap between the two sides was not great and in some instances favored Argentine forces). Because of logistical constraints, neither Britain nor Argentina could bring the full weight of its military resources to bear on the combat, so that battle was a test of the morale and raw fighting abilities of the troops on the ground.[36] None of this could, however, be known with confidence in April.

From the start, Britain's strategy was based on getting as many men and as much matériel to the South Atlantic as possible over the attenuated supply lines; seeking psychological advantage over the enemy by taking victories wherever they could be found;[37] and, most importantly, establishing superiority over the Argentine Navy and Air Force. To establish superiority, Britain needed opportunities to take on and destroy Argentine forces; this helps explain why the first serious engagements of the war were as fierce as they were.

At the start of May, once the bulk of the task force was in place, British aircraft began to strike Argentine positions, including the run-

---

34. Argentina's status as a member of the Third World, though trumpeted as a feature of Argentine diplomacy during the conflict, was in fact rather tenuous. It reflected economic decline since the early decades of the century, rather than the self-image of the political elite.

35. Norma Kinzer Stewart, *South Atlantic Conflict of 1982: A Case Study in Military Cohesion*, Research Report 1469 (Washington D.C.: U.S. Army, Research Institute for the Behavioral and Social Sciences, April 1988).

36. This case supports David Lake's proposition that democracies tend "to win the wars that they do fight," partly due to their internal structures. Argentine armed forces suffered both from their politicization at the higher levels, and their general gearing toward local repression. Nonetheless, the recapture of the Malvinas was a genuinely popular cause in Argentina. David A. Lake, "Powerful Pacifists: Democratic States and War."

37. One example is the retaking of South Georgia on April 25 and the move against Goose Green once the bridgehead on the island had been secured.

way at the islands' capital, Port Stanley. This was intended to draw out Argentine air and naval forces. With the air force, this strategy largely failed. However, the Argentine cruiser, the *General Belgrano*, was sunk by a nuclear submarine, with the loss of 360 lives. This discouraged the Argentine fleet from leaving port thereafter, though Argentina did sink a British destroyer, HMS *Sheffield*, on May 4, using an air-launched *Exocet* missile.[38]

For the commanders, however, a far greater concern at the start of May lay in the failure to impose attrition on the Argentine Air Force. By mid-May, when the government approved the decision to land at Port San Carlos, the logic of the situation left them with very little choice. The UN negotiations had failed and the task force was as ready as it was ever going to be. However, at the war cabinet meeting on the morning of May 19, at which the chiefs of staff pressed for approval for the landing, ministers were also warned of the possibility that a ship carrying hundreds of troops could be lost. In short, the military situation influenced political calculations as a dawning realization that battle was likely, rather than as a sudden, sharp, definite demand for military action. When the time for decisive action came, it was recognized that victory could well come at a high price.[39]

On May 21, a few days after the UN negotiating effort concluded without a result, British troops landed at Port San Carlos. The landing was successful, but was followed by days of air assaults against the British ships attempting to get supplies ashore. Many Argentine aircraft were shot down and three British warships were sunk, as was

---

38. Success in the naval battle cost Britain dearly internationally, as many were shocked at the considerable loss of life when the *Belgrano* went down. Allies kept their distance, and before the fighting was over, Britain found itself vetoing a Security Council resolution calling for an immediate cease-fire. The sinking of the ship did not become a *cause célèbre* in Britain until after the war, as evidence accumulated that the cruiser was sailing away from the British task force at the time it was sunk, rather than toward it, as had been claimed at the time. House of Commons, Third Report of the Foreign Affairs Committee, Session 1984–85, *Events of the Weekend of 1st and 2nd May 1982* (London: HMSO, 1985). The sinking is explained, without resort to conspiracy theories, in Freedman and Gamba-Stonehouse, *Signals of War*, chap. 16.

39. Though the first substantial British casualties had come with the twenty lives lost on the *Sheffield*, the bulk came once British forces had landed at Port San Carlos and were trying to move men and equipment onto the bridgehead, and then in the moves against Argentine positions on the islands. As the battle later moved toward Port Stanley, there was also concern that the civilian population could be at risk, although its small and scattered nature was a limiting factor. One woman was killed and two others were wounded by British shell fire. Many islanders left for the duration of the conflict.

one merchant ship, the *Atlantic Conveyor*, carrying a number of helicopters and other vital equipment. The first major land engagement after the landing came on May 28, when 600 British troops defeated a larger Argentine garrison at Goose Green, after heavy fighting during which the commanding officer, Colonel "H" Jones, was killed. The land forces moved towards the main Argentine garrison based in and around Port Stanley. The greatest single disaster was on June 8, when the troopship *Sir Galahad* was caught by Argentine aircraft at Port Fitzroy. Gradually, using combinations of artillery bombardments and infantry attacks to dislodge spasmodic but sometimes fierce resistance, the British took the high ground around Port Stanley. On June 14, the Argentine garrison surrendered.

Public Opinion and the Anticipation of War

According to the democratic peace thesis, the prospect of casualties is believed to represent an important limitation on a democratic government's freedom of maneuver. The Falklands War was a situation in which casualties could become heavy, representing possibly a substantial proportion of the total task force of 28,000 men and women and an even larger proportion of the civilian population whose right to self-determination was being defended. Yet, the impact of casualties on public opinion was qualified by a number of factors. First, as noted earlier, the British tend to see a readiness to go to war as a necessary component of a responsible foreign policy. Second, the British armed forces do not rely on conscription but are composed of volunteer professionals, who are presumably willing agents of foreign policy. Third, the first shots had already been fired by Argentina and so the country was not divided on the need to restore the Falkland Islands to British administration; the purposes for which force might be used was not contested. Fourth, casualties were not seen as an inevitable consequence of the dispatch of the task force.

From the start of the conflict, polls suggested that over 80 percent of the population cared that the islands should be regained, although a good number of these did not care very much, while a sizeable majority consistently supported the sending of the task force and the overall crisis management.[40] This majority grew steadily during the conflict, with the only wobble coming after the sinkings of the

---

40. All the material on polls is taken from Lawrence Freedman, *Britain & the Falklands War* (London: Basil Blackwell, 1988), chap. 8. The bulk of the polls was conducted by the British polling organization MORI. After an initial poll of 1,018

Belgrano and HMS *Sheffield*. Many more opponents of government policy criticized it for being too soft than for being too tough.

While respondents were not asked directly about support for the principle of self-determination, a critical factor in popular support was clearly that the Falkland Islands were British territory whose inhabitants identified themselves as British. If there was to be a negotiated solution, most respondents preferred that the islands be handed over to UN administration. Though consistently high numbers supported the proposition that the islanders should have the final say over the transfer of sovereignty, the limits to self-determination were recognized in one important respect. In a poll in late May that asked whether the long-term policy on the Falkland Islands should be determined by the wishes of the islanders alone, or by the interests of Britain as a whole taking the islanders' views into account, 72 percent supported the latter. As discussed below, this language was closer to that used by Argentina in the negotiations, while Britain stressed the importance of the islanders' wishes. Interests were not necessarily best judged by the islanders themselves. As far as the public was concerned, "not rewarding aggression," a slogan with echoes of the struggle against Nazism, was a more popular theme than self-determination.

On April 14, one British poll found that 20 percent of the population expected that Argentina would give up the Falklands without a fight; 16 percent expected a diplomatic outcome such as Britain leasing back the islands from Argentina; and 6 percent accepted that Britain might have to back down completely. Half expected a fight, and equal numbers (25 percent) thought that a naval battle would be sufficient, or that troops would eventually have to land. Thus, around one quarter correctly predicted the course of the conflict. Nonetheless, from the start a clear majority (56 percent) was prepared to see the islands regained by force, with a significant minority (24 percent) prepared to see the Argentine mainland attacked.

In another mid-April poll, only 2 percent said that their views—allowing Argentina to keep the islands—were governed by a fear of

---

adults on April 14, 1982, for *The Economist*, between 450 and 550 of the respondents were re-interviewed every few weeks until the end of the conflict. Other MORI polls were conducted on April 26, 1982, and April 30, 1982, with 600 and 1,178 adults respectively. The MORI poll evidence is discussed in Robert Worcester and Simon Jenkins, "Britain Rallies Round the Prime Minister," *Public Opinion* (June/July 1982). Other polls were conducted by Gallup and National Opinion Polls.

bloodshed. Except on the eve of hostilities, when opinion was equally divided, there was never a majority tolerating the loss of Falkland Islanders' lives, although the majority narrowed from 55 percent (with 36 percent against) at the start of the conflict, to 48 to 45 percent a month later. At the start of the conflict, a majority would not tolerate the loss of servicemen's lives (49 percent, compared to 44 percent who would tolerate such a loss), but on the eve of actual hostilities, there was a substantial majority tolerating a loss of life (58 to 37 percent), declining slightly as the first lives were lost (53 to 43 percent), and then picking up well into the campaign (62 to 34 percent). After the fighting was over, by which time some 250 British and 750 Argentine servicemen had lost their lives, some 76 percent felt that the retention of the islands had been worth the loss of lives, with only 22 percent against. In sum, the notion that democratically elected leaders can only fight "cheap" wars because the voting public will not condone wars with high costs is not borne out in the Falklands case.

Democracy and the Negotiation of Peace

Consistent with the monadic version of the democratic peace theory, the British government accepted that it must show both domestic and international opinion that force was a last resort, and that Britain was serious in its efforts to find a negotiated solution. Throughout the conflict, the prime minister frequently had to be persuaded that an uncompromising stance would create major presentational problems, especially in getting U.S. and European opinion "on side." In the end, Thatcher was vindicated in her basic belief that there was no obvious point of compromise between the British and Argentine positions. The more dovish members of her government were also vindicated in that Britain's appearance of a readiness to compromise, and the clumsiness of Argentine diplomacy, gave London an aura of reasonableness that made it easier to justify the later use of force.

For much of April, as the task force proceeded to the South Atlantic, there was intensive diplomatic activity as the U.S. Secretary of State, Alexander Haig, shuttled between London and Buenos Aires in search of a compromise solution.[41] It was only on April 30, when this effort had clearly failed, that Haig formally announced a U.S. tilt in favor of Britain. Even then diplomatic activity continued, first in the form of a

---

41. Haig describes his shuttle, not always accurately, in Alexander Haig, *Caveat* (London: Weidenfeld & Nicholson, 1984).

largely amateur initiative led by the president of Peru, Belaunde Terry, and then a more professional effort handled in New York by another Peruvian, UN Secretary General Javier Perez de Cuellar. The norma-tive foundations for the British position were gradually refined during these three efforts. At its core lay not the principle of sovereignty, as might have been expected, but rather that of self-determination.

norms

The arguments over the sovereignty of the Falkland Islands origi-nate in the inconclusive colonial expeditions mounted by Britain, Spain, and France.[42] In 1816, after the end of Spanish rule in that area, the then unoccupied islands were claimed by the government of Buenos Aires for the United Provinces, the forerunner of Argentina. They were occupied in 1820, and sovereignty was officially imple-mented in 1829. Britain had previously settled West Falkland (while Spain settled East Falkland), and it declared that it had never relin-quished its claim. It now protested the claim by Buenos Aires and in 1833 expelled the Argentine garrison. Thereafter Britain occupied the islands, and its claim to the title rested upon this.[43]

Argentina has always been unhappy with this state of affairs and never relinquished its claim, although for long periods it did little about it. In the mid-1960s, Argentina made some headway by phras-ing the issue as an example of colonialism. On December 16, 1965, UN General Assembly Resolution 2065 considered the Falklands an instance of colonialism and urged the British and Argentine govern-ments to find a "peaceful solution to the problem, bearing in mind . . . the interests of the population of the Falkland Islands (Malvinas)." The resolution was passed by 45 votes to zero, with 14 abstaining, including Britain. This resolution maintained the principle of self-determination, but the phrase "bearing in mind . . . the interests" was to haunt future negotiations. Discussions between the two countries began the next year.[44]

---

42. The Argentine term "Malvinas" comes from the French *Iles Malouines*, the name given to the islands by French sailors from St. Malo in Brittany in the eigh-teenth century.

43. The literature on the origins of the dispute is substantial. See, for example, Ralph Perl, ed., *The Falkland Islands Dispute in International Law and Politics: A Documentary Sourcebook* (London: Oceana Publications, 1983); and Lowell S. Gustafson, *The Sovereignty Dispute over the Falkland (Malvinas) Islands* (New York: Oxford University Press, 1988).

44. Peter Beck, "Cooperative Confrontation in the Falkland Islands Dispute: The Anglo-Argentine Search for a Way Forward 1968-81," *Journal of Interamerican Studies and World Affairs*, Vol. 24, No. 1 (February 1982).

There were many views of the islanders' best "interests." It could be claimed that in the long run they would be best served through a close association with the mainland. This was largely the view of the British Foreign Office in the 1960s. It indicated in March 1967 that it would contemplate a transfer of sovereignty. The islanders, however, were not prepared to be transferred. They claimed that they were the best judges of their interests, and established the Falkland Islands Emergency Committee to press their case in London, which it did to great effect. In 1968, Britain acknowledged a readiness to recognize Argentine sovereignty, but now the "wishes" rather than the interests of the islanders were to be critical, and these wishes were made abundantly clear whenever a government minister took the long journey to the islands to explain the current thinking in Westminster.

Britain had suggested to Argentina that its best bet was to win over the islanders through practical demonstrations of the benefits of closer ties. In September 1971, air and sea links were established. Argentina found that these links merely rendered the status quo more viable, rather than rendering the islanders more amenable. There was no evidence of a shift in popular attitudes. Argentina therefore shifted the operative language back from wishes to interests, and worked to counter the influence of the islanders.

Part of Argentina's strategy in April 1982 was to encourage U.S. pressure on Britain. The United States initially played its role almost according to this Argentine script. The Reagan administration could see no obvious reason for the British to want to retain the islands, and with two allies about to come to blows over such an inconsequential piece of land, felt that its duty was to find a compromise. This approach initially tended to trivialize the dispute. Only during the course of Secretary of State Haig's shuttle diplomacy did Washington come to recognize that small territories with small populations can raise large issues of principle. The test of any principle is to be found in marginal cases, and the political rights of 1,800 people came into that category. There was also a second principle at stake, since one side had sought to obtain a better agreement than it might have otherwise obtained through the use of armed force. This contradicted a basic principle of international law, and Argentine actions could be seen as a dangerous precedent in this regard. To the British, the belief that aggression should not be rewarded reinforced their reluctance to give ground on the principle of self-determination.

Thatcher never saw diplomacy as a search for a bargain from which both parties could emerge with honor satisfied, with mutual "face-saving" the prime objective. An appeal from Haig to consider the political needs of General Galtieri received a stony response, with references to the hazards of appeasement. She refused to accept a symmetry between herself and Galtieri, as if they were two politicians trying to cling to power in desperate circumstances. Thatcher told Haig "that it was essentially an issue of dictatorship versus democracy."[45] For his part, Galtieri was unmoved by Haig's accounts of Thatcher's political problems. He had obtained a level of political popularity to which few military juntas ever aspire; reclaiming the Malvinas was a truly national cause, and he was reluctant to let the islands be taken from him again, whatever economic pressures or military threats he faced.

A peaceful settlement of the dispute needed three key elements: a formula for getting the Argentine forces off the islands without allowing British forces to return; an interim administration while negotiations on the long-term future of the islands got under way; and a prospectus for the substantive negotiations. The first two elements were difficult enough, but the crux of the dispute was the third. Britain found it easy to agree to the processes of negotiation but not to any specified outcome. Argentina saw negotiations without an agreed outcome as providing more opportunities for British procrastination. In the end, diplomacy foundered because no formula that was acceptable to Britain could simultaneously guarantee the transfer of sovereignty Buenos Aires demanded.

Argentina was ready to accommodate the interests of the islanders by creating special inducements for them to stay in a special Argentine economic zone or else sufficient incentives for them to emigrate. It was prepared to offer Britain access to the suspected oil reserves and other natural resources it believed (erroneously) were Britain's prime motivation in sustaining a presence in the South Atlantic. If the international community refused to acknowledge anything other than the islanders' wishes, then Argentina would insist on the rights of its own citizens to live, work, and own property on the islands. With sufficient immigration, the majority view on the islands would soon change.

The Argentine position as stated in its proposal of April 19 was that a definitive agreement be reached by December 31, 1982, that would include "due consideration of the rights of the inhabitants and the

---

45. Thatcher, *The Downing Street Years*, p. 198.

principles of territorial integrity in this dispute."[46] Before that, under the interim administration, the islanders would continue to enjoy rights "relating to freedom of opinion, religion, expression, teaching, movement, property, employment, family, customs and cultural links with the countries of origin." However, there would also be an active promotion of the movement of people from the mainland who would be able to acquire property. Islanders who did not want to stay would be offered compensation.[47]

The final Haig proposal of April 24 contained clauses not dissimilar to these,[48] but also included a provision for a virtual referendum:

The manner of taking into account the wishes and interests of the islanders, insofar as islands with a settled population are concerned, based on the results of a sounding of the opinion of the inhabitants, with respect to such issues relating to the negotiations, conducted in such manner as the [Special Interim] Authority may determine.

The junta objected to any attempt to discern the "wishes" of the islanders, as well as the lack of a guaranteed transfer of sovereignty.[49] Yet, as Thatcher noted, the Haig plan potentially put Argentina in a strong position. It would have a strong presence in the Special Interim Authority. In addition:

the wording relating to the Argentine residence and property...would effectively have allowed them to swamp the existing population with Argentineans.

In addition, Haig's proposal apparently ruled out the possibility of a return to the situation enjoyed by the islanders before the invasion:

---

46. An earlier version had used the word "interests." The language of "rights" was seen in Buenos Aires as a significant concession. Argentina rejected an attempt by Haig to insert the word "fundamental" before "rights."

47. The quotations are taken from an unofficial translation in Desmond Rice and Arthur Gavshon, *The Sinking of the Belgrano* (London: Secker & Warburg, 1984).

48. It included the promotion and facilitation "on a non-discriminatory basis" of the movement of people and the acquisition of residency and property rights (6.1) and allowing existing inhabitants the same "rights and guarantees" as before (6.2). It also referred to "due regard for the rights of the inhabitants and for the principle of territorial integrity" when describing the basis for an eventual settlement, which would be geared to removing the islands from the UN's list of "Non-Self-Governing Territories," rather than necessarily organizing a transfer to Argentina, although such a step was not precluded (7.0).

49. See text of response from Argentine Foreign Minister, Nicanor Costa Mendez in Rice and Gavshon, *The Sinking of the Belgrano*, pp. 192–194.

"We would have gone against our commitment to the principle that the islanders' wishes were paramount and would have abandoned all possibility of their staying with us."[50]

Foreign Secretary Francis Pym, who felt that the text was the best that could be expected in a negotiated settlement, proposed acceptance, but the rest of the war cabinet was not convinced. Rather than take the risk of alienating the United States by rejecting the draft, the war cabinet decided to reserve its position until the Argentine position was known; this was done in the correct expectation that the junta would not see the opportunity the Haig plan provided, and that it would reject the plan. The core British position was stated to the Commons by Pym on April 27:

Our basic position is that Britain is ready to co-operate in any solution which the people of the Falkland Islands could accept and any framework of negotiation which does not pre-determine and does not prejudice the eventual outcome.[51]

After the failure of his own initiative, Haig saw the readiness of Peru to get involved as a way to maintain momentum, but this mediation also amounted to little.[52] It was only during the final negotiating round, conducted under the auspices of the UN, that Britain developed its own proposals.[53] Britain stressed that the islanders' "interests" were paramount. In seeking to make this sound more positive, Pym held out at least the theoretical possibility that the islanders might change their minds:

---

50. Thatcher, *The Downing Street Years*, p. 207.

51. House of Commons, *The Falklands Campaign*, p. 180.

52. The "Peruvian Initiative,"as this stage in the diplomacy became known, was overshadowed by the start of serious hostilities, and in particular by the sinking of the *General Belgrano*. The Peruvian plan consisted of a number of headline points, purposefully kept simple, which were to be presented by Peruvian President Belaúnde Terry to Galtieri, and by Haig to Pym, on May 2. It never got very far, despite later claims by Belaúnde to the contrary, because it offered no real advance on previous plans. For our purposes, the relevant clause stated that "the two governments would recognize the need to take the viewpoints and interests of the islanders into account in the final solution." In the Belaúnde-Galtieri conversations, this became "viewpoints concerning interests" *(puntos de vista sobre los intereses)*. Costa Mendez appears to have considered favorably the word "aspirations" (taken from Article 73 of the UN Charter) as less supportive of the islanders than "wishes." This language was no more acceptable to London.

53. Government of the United Kingdom, *Falkland Islands: Negotiations for a Peaceful Settlement* (London: May 21, 1982).

The islanders will wish to consider, after a period of respite and recuperation, how their prosperity and the economic development of the islands can best be furthered, how their security can best be protected and how their links with the outside world can best be organized.[54]

That principles of self-determination per se, rather than liberal ideology and the nature of the Argentine regime, were crucial became clear when Thatcher, after the conclusion of the UN effort, explained to the Commons:

If the islanders wished to go to Argentina, I believe that this country would uphold the wishes of the islanders. After their experience, I doubt very much whether that would be the wishes of the islanders. Indeed, I believe that they would recoil from it.[55]

The outcome of the war not only helped revive the fortunes of Thatcher's government but also the reputation of the British armed forces, and altered the widespread presumption of the time that in a contest between Western states and the Third World, the former would probably lose. It also triggered the transformation of Argentina into a democracy.

Conclusion

The Falklands case offers evidence on three hypotheses about the behavior of democracies: that public opinion in a democracy is a force for peace; that democracies regard nondemocracies as warlike; and that democratic values are a source of a democracy's peaceful behavior (according to the monadic version) or its unwillingness to make war on democracies (according to the dyadic version). It also encourages a careful consideration of the meaning of democratic values in conflicts such as this. It suggests that those features of democratic ideology most germane to the conflict will tend to be emphasized as governments seek to justify the use of force at home and abroad. These same features may not be so prominent when governments hope for more peaceful relations. Though this case study supports the importance of normative factors in explaining international behavior, it warns against a facile presumption of what these norms might entail.[56]

54. House of Commons, *The Falklands Campaign*, p. 241.
55. Ibid., p. 278.
56. Thomas Risse-Kappen, "Democratic Peace—Warlike Democracies?"

David Welch notes that the Falklands War "is difficult to explain from a Realist perspective":

Were it not for the intensity of the Argentine sense of injustice, invading the islands could have served no economic, strategic or political purpose; were it not for the firmness of the British commitment to the self-determination of the islanders, the islands would long since have been handed over to Argentina anyway.[57]

Other governments, whether democratic or not, would have responded to events differently because their political and military cultures were different. It would therefore be unwise to generalize too much from this case study, or draw too many implications for the democratic peace thesis. Nonetheless, the Falklands War does provide another example of a democratic state taking on a nondemocratic state and winning. It confirms the proposition that if two countries are in dispute, and that one is democratic and the other nondemocratic, this fact alone may increase the probability that the two will come to blows. There are good reasons for this: both types of regimes define each other by negative reference to the other. Democracies scorn unaccountable governments that suppress and ignore popular opinion; nondemocracies often believe themselves to be more decisive and less corrupt in pursuit of the interests of the nation.

While Argentine decision making is not explored here, this chapter provides no support for the assumptions that nondemocracies are incapable of acting in accordance with normative principles and with popular support. Equally, democratic foreign policy does not need to reflect a chronic fear of casualties and a desperate search for compromise. The Falklands case indicates the importance of norms and values in gaining support for the use of armed force, and of a culture that accepts armed force as an instrument of diplomacy, even if it hopes that threats will suffice so that actual use can be avoided. In domestic debate, questions of national pride and sovereignty remain important, but at the international level, justifications for force can be strengthened by reference to the need to uphold international law and the principle of self-determination. This has an important consequence for the conduct of war. Once the objectives are set by reference to such values as self-determination and denying rewards to aggressors, then simple cost-benefit analyses become difficult. All

---

57. David Welch, *Justice and the Genesis of War* (Cambridge: Cambridge University Press, 1993), pp. 184–185.

communities accept some limits to self-determination but tend to draw the line at foreign domination. The interests of the islanders—and of Britain—might have pointed to an expenses-paid move to a new and probably more comfortable home, but if they did not wish to move nor be governed by a military junta with a poor record on human rights, how can a value be put on their liberation? Would the principle have been any different if instead of 1,800 inhabitants there had been 180 or 1,800,000?

Chapter 6

War and Conflict between India and Pakistan: Revisiting the Pacifying Power of Democracy

Šumit Ganguly

At the end of the Cold War, South Asia remains one of the most conflict-ridden regions of the world. In addition to the various insurgencies and civil wars that have wracked the subcontinent, the two major powers in South Asia, India and Pakistan, have fought three wars: in 1947–48, 1965, and 1971. More recently, in 1987 and 1990, India and Pakistan have teetered on the brink of war, and border skirmishes are common. The central dispute in the region, the Indo-Pakistani conflict over the state of Jammu and Kashmir, continues to animate national elites and mass populations in both states. Since 1989, India has been suppressing an insurgency in Kashmir—an insurgency that, despite formal denials from Islamabad, Pakistan has been aiding since at least early 1990. While Pakistan's involvement in the uprising has renewed Indo-Pakistani tensions, it is unlikely that either side will deliberately precipitate a fourth war in the region; nevertheless, another war could ensue from a spiral of hostility and mutual misperception, such as occurred in 1987 and 1990.[1]

The author thanks Traci Nagle and Jack Snyder for comments on a draft of this chapter. Any errors of fact or interpretation are necessarily mine.

---

1. In 1987 and in 1990, processes of brinkmanship and misperception almost led to full-scale conflict. On the 1987 crisis, see Kanti P. Bajpai, Pervaiz Iqbal Cheema, P.R. Chari, Stephen P. Cohen, and Šumit Ganguly, *Brasstacks and Beyond: Perception and the Management of Crisis in South Asia* (New Delhi: Manohar, 1995). On the 1990 crisis, see Devin Hagerty, "Nuclear Deterrence in South Asia: The 1990 Indo-Pakistani Crisis," *International Security*, Vol. 20, No. 3 (Winter 1995/96), pp. 80–114.

Contrary to popular belief, the Indo-Pakistani relationship has not been bereft of cooperation.[2] Yet the enduring conflict-ridden state of Indo-Pakistani relations raises questions for the proposition that democratic states do not fight other democracies.[3] Is this hypothesis supported in the South Asian context? Given the long history of conflict between the two states since their creation, realist explanations focusing on the balance of power and external threat should account well for Indo-Pakistani relations. Consequently, the Indo-Pakistani case is a "hard test" for the democratic peace hypothesis—support for this hypothesis within the South Asian context would greatly increase our confidence in the dyadic version of the democratic peace argument.

This chapter, which aims to determine whether the democratic peace accounts for war and peace outcomes in South Asia, is divided into six sections. The first provides the definition of democracy, and discusses the nature of democracy in the South Asian context. The next three sections focus on the three Indo-Pakistani conflicts, and analyze their implications for the democratic peace proposition. The fifth section discusses the crises of 1987 and 1990 and attempts to explain why they did not culminate in full-scale war. The sixth and final section evaluates the likelihood of future conflict between India and Pakistan, and examines whether a democratic peace exists in South Asia.

What Is Democracy?

Conceptions and definitions of democracy vary widely.[4] Democratic institutions alone do not make a democracy; new democracies (and

---

2. For background on the wars and conflicts as well as the moments of cooperation between India and Pakistan, see Šumit Ganguly, "Conflict and Crisis in South and Southwest Asia," in Michael E. Brown, ed., *The International Dimensions of Internal Conflict* (Cambridge, Mass.: MIT Press, 1996); Šumit Ganguly, *The Origins of War in South Asia: The Indo-Pakistani Conflicts Since 1971* (Boulder, Colo.: Westview, 1994); and Šumit Ganguly, "Discord and Collaboration in Indo-Pakistani Relations," in Kanti Bajpai and H.P. Shukul, eds., *International Politics and International Society: Essays for A.P. Rana* (New Delhi: Sage, 1995). No clear-cut generalizations obtain about the international, regional, and domestic contexts that proved conducive to Indo-Pakistani cooperation.

3. For a survey and assessment of the literature on this subject, see James Lee Ray, *Democracy and International Conflict: An Evaluation of the Democratic Peace Thesis* (Columbia: University of South Carolina Press, 1995).

4. See, for example, Robert A. Dahl, *Democracy and Its Critics* (New Haven, Conn.: Yale University Press, 1989).

countries where periods of democracy are punctuated by periods of authoritarian rule) are not fully democratic.

For the purposes of this chapter, a state is a democracy if it holds free and fair elections; provides (and attempts to implement) constitutional guarantees for the protection of religious, linguistic, and ethnic minorities; adheres to the due process of law for all citizens; and has an independent judiciary and a free press. In South Asia, where every state is polyethnic, constitutional protections for minorities take on special significance. Even well-established democracies in the region—India and Sri Lanka, for example—have fallen short on this score. In India, the 1996 electoral successes of a jingoistic Hindu party, the Bharatiya Janata Party (BJP), pose a significant threat to India's secular policies and concomitantly to the status of Muslims, India's largest religious minority.

The relationship between democracy and the process of democratization also needs to be addressed.[5] At least two states in South Asia, Pakistan and Bangladesh, have experienced intermittent periods of military and authoritarian rule. Neither of these states can be considered consolidated democracies; at best, they are states on the path to democratization. Pakistan saw the end of an eleven-year period of military rule in 1989. Since then, Pakistan has successfully held free and fair national elections, but the country fails to meet many of the other criteria that would qualify it as a consolidated democracy. Civil liberties are severely constrained. The press, while largely free, is not bound by appropriate norms of probity and fairness. Minority rights are largely honored in the breach.

Since India can be considered a democracy, fluctuations in Pakistan's regime type allow us to test both the monadic and dyadic versions of the democratic peace theory. Indeed, although India underwent a brief period of authoritarian rule between 1976–77, it has been a democracy for most of the years since its founding in 1947.

The Legacy of Partition in 1947

In 1947, on August 14 and 15 respectively, India and Pakistan emerged as self-governing dominions from the detritus of the British Indian empire. The transfer of power from Britain to these two emergent states was quite sanguinary. After nearly two hundred years of imperial conquest and consolidation, Britain left the continent in

---

5. For an early treatment of the transition from authoritarian to democratic rule, see Dankwart Rustow, "Transitions to Democracy: Toward a Dynamic Model," *Comparative Politics*, Vol. 2 (April 1970).

haste and made inadequate efforts to maintain order during the transfer of power.[6] The first war between India and Pakistan, in 1947–48, stemmed directly from the ill-managed process of colonial withdrawal from the subcontinent.

Under British rule, two classes of states had existed on the subcontinent. One group of states was under the direct tutelage of the British Crown. A second group, the so-called princely states, were notionally independent as long as they accepted the "paramountcy" of the British Crown. The monarchs of the princely states had control over all matters save defense, foreign affairs, and communications. As the time of the transfer of power approached in 1947, Lord Louis Mountbatten, the last viceroy, declared that paramountcy would lapse and that the monarchs would have to accede to either India or Pakistan, basing their decisions on the demographic composition and geographic location of their states. Independence was not an option.

The state of Jammu and Kashmir posed a peculiar problem. Its monarch, Maharaja Hari Singh, was a Hindu, but his population was predominantly Muslim. In addition, Kashmir abutted both incipient states—India and Pakistan. Despite Lord Mountbatten's injunction, the maharaja vacillated on the question of accession, hoping to gain independence.

In October 1947, a tribal rebellion broke out in Poonch, in the western reaches of Kashmir. The rebels, who found support from the newly created government of Pakistan, made quick work of the maharaja's forces. Toward the end of October, the rebel forces approached Srinagar, the capital of Kashmir. In a panic, the maharaja appealed to the Indian government in New Delhi for military assistance. Prime Minister Jawaharlal Nehru agreed to provide military assistance only after two conditions were met. First, the maharaja had to join India and sign the Instrument of Accession. Second, Sheikh Mohammed Abdullah, the leader of the popular Jammu and Kashmir National Conference, had to grant his imprimatur to the Instrument of Accession. Only after both conditions were met did Nehru send Indian troops to Kashmir.[7]

---

6. For a useful account, see Leonard Mosley, *The Last Days of the British Raj* (London: Weidenfield and Nicholson, 1961).

7. The origins of the tribal rebellion, Pakistan's support for the rebels, and Kashmir's accession to India are all subjects of some contention. For a discussion of the origins of the rebellion, see H.V. Hodson, *The Great Divide* (Oxford: Oxford University Press, 1969). The most explicit account of Pakistan's complicity in aiding and abetting the tribal rebellion is Akbar Khan, *Raiders in Kashmir* (Karachi: Pak Publishers, 1970). For a critique of Kashmir's accession to India, see Alistair

Nehru's insistence on ascertaining Sheikh Abdullah's views about accession is important. Under the terms of the Indian Independence Act, it was clearly the maharaja's legal prerogative to accede to India. But Nehru, a staunch democrat, was also acutely concerned about the legitimacy of Kashmir's accession.[8] Nehru deemed that Abdullah's views were critical in conferring a degree of legitimacy to the Instrument of Accession due to his stature in the politics of Kashmir.[9]

THE ONSET OF WAR

After the Instrument of Accession was signed on October 27, 1947, an Indian infantry brigade was airlifted into Srinagar, and it quickly stopped the tribal advance. In early November, the Indians counter-attacked and broke through the tribal defenses. But after this early success, the Indian Army suffered an important setback in December. On January 1, 1948, at the instance of Lord Mountbatten, Prime Minister Nehru of India referred the dispute to the United Nations Security Council. As Indian and Pakistani representatives debated the merits of their respective positions in the Security Council, the war in Kashmir proceeded apace.

In the spring of 1948, India mounted another offensive to regain some lost ground. Soon thereafter, Pakistani Army units entered the fray. Later in the year, as the Indian Army maintained its offensive, the Pakistani Army brought in a parachute brigade, two field artillery regiments, and a medium artillery battery west of Jammu. These troop deployments enabled Pakistan to threaten the tenuous Indian lines of communication, which ran from Amritsar in Punjab to Pathankot, Jammu, and to Poonch in Kashmir. For the remainder of 1948, the war followed a desultory course, with neither side making any further territorial gains.[10]

Lamb, *The Birth of a Tragedy: Kashmir, 1947* (Hertingfordbury, U.K.: Roxford Books, 1994). For a defense of Kashmir's accession to India, see Prem Shankar Jha, *Kashmir, 1947: Rival Versions of History* (Delhi: Oxford University Press, 1996).

8. Richard Sisson and Leo E. Rose, *War and Secession: Pakistan, India, and the Creation of Bangladesh* (Berkeley: University of California Press, 1990).

9. In 1952, Sheikh Mohammed Abdullah, the prime minister of Jammu and Kashmir, and Jawaharlal Nehru concluded the Delhi Agreement, which reaffirmed Kashmir's accession to and special status in the Indian Union. Specifically, the Delhi Agreement codified that India's role in Kashmir would be confined to defense, foreign affairs, and communications.

10. Much of this discussion has been drawn from Šumit Ganguly, "Wars Without End: The Indo-Pakistani Conflict," *Annals of the American Academy of Political and Social Science*, No. 541 (September 1995), pp. 167–178.

On January 1, 1949, the United Nations declared a cease-fire, which brought the hostilities to a close. When the hostilities ended, Pakistan controlled about one-third of the state (which they called "Azad Kashmir"—literally, "Free Kashmir") and India two-thirds. A UN observer group (the United Nations Military Observer Group in India and Pakistan) took up positions along both sides of the cease-fire line.

A FAILURE OF THE DEMOCRATIC PEACE THEORY?

At a superficial level the 1947–48 war would seem to challenge the basic premise of the dyadic version of the democratic peace theory; notionally, both India and Pakistan were democratic states when the war started. But a closer examination of the evidence suggests otherwise. Certainly, some democratic structures were in place when India and Pakistan obtained their independence from Great Britain. For example, both India and Pakistan had inherited the British colonial legislative, judicial, and administrative institutions. These institutions had been created during the early part of the twentieth century under the pressure of nationalist movements in British India. The last of these legislative directives, the Government of India Act of 1935, had created a strong executive and a weak legislature. Under the aegis of this act, two elections, in 1937 and 1946, had been held in the states of British India. However, many of the other attributes normally associated with a democratic state were lacking. For example, owing to the imperatives of colonial control, laws governing press freedoms and peaceful assembly were still severely restrictive.

This limited conception of democracy that the British colonial authorities had grudgingly conceded was the common heritage of the two nationalist movements. Beyond this shared legacy, sharp organizational and ideological differences characterized the Indian and Pakistani nationalist movements.[11] The Indian nationalist movement had started out with a reformist agenda and with an anglicized, upper-middle-class political base. Under the influence of Mohandas Gandhi in the 1920s and 1930s, this movement transformed itself into a largely secular, democratic, and mass-based political party that sought to represent the interests of all Indians. The Pakistani nationalist movement, in marked contrast, had both a limited geographical and organizational base. It was primarily confined to the United

11. Paul Brass, *Language, Religion and Politics in North India* (Cambridge: Cambridge University Press, 1968).

Provinces in northern India and revolved around the personality of Mohammed Ali Jinnah, the leader of the Muslim League. The organizational structure of the League remained elitist and it failed to create a mass political base. In the aftermath of independence, these ideological and organization differences had profound consequences for nation-building and helped shape the political institutions that emerged in the two states.[12]

In 1947–48, executive power was highly concentrated in both states. However, despite his towering stature, Indian Prime Minister Jawaharlal Nehru faced important informal and formal constraints on the exercise of executive authority. The Indian National Congress, the party that had brought India independence, was a highly institutionalized organization. The norms of consultation and consensus-building were of considerable importance.[13] The governor-general of Pakistan, Mohammed Ali Jinnah, who was the principal architect of Pakistani nationalism, faced far fewer constraints on his actions. Jinnah's stature in the Pakistani nationalist movement was *primus inter pares*.[14] Furthermore, the organizational structure of the Muslim League was markedly different from that of the Indian National Congress. Unlike the Congress Party, the League lacked internal democracy, and best represented the corporate interests of the Muslim landed gentry of northern India. Indeed, many in the upper echelons of the League were actually contemptuous of democracy. The following quotation is illustrative of their sentiments about the rough-and-tumble character of democratic politics:

They [illiterate peasants] elect crooks and scalawags who promise the moon. The scalawags make a mess of everything, and then I have to clean up the mess. Democracy requires education, tradition, and breeding, and pride in your ability to do something well.[15]

---

12. A military coup brought democracy to an end in Pakistan in 1958. Apart from a brief period of authoritarian rule in 1976–77, democracy has thrived in India. See Leo E. Rose, "Pakistan: Experiments with Democracy," and "India: Democratic Becoming and Combined Development," in Larry Diamond, Juan J. Linz, and Seymour Martin Lipset, eds., *Democracy in Developing Countries: Asia* (Boulder, Colo.: Lynne Rienner, 1989).

13. On this point, see Rajni Kothari, *Politics in India* (Boston: Little, Brown, 1972).

14. Khalid Bin Sayeed, *Pakistan: The Formative Phase, 1857–1948* (Karachi: Oxford University Press, 1968). Also see Ayesha Jalal, *The Sole Spokesman* (Cambridge: Cambridge University Press, 1985).

15. Minister of Interior Iskander Mirza, as quoted in Khalid Bin Sayeed, *The Political System of Pakistan* (Boston: Houghton Mifflin, 1967), p. 76.

In contrast to the Pakistani political elite, the Indian political leadership, which had already internalized many of the norms of democratic conduct, evinced a willingness to resolve the dispute over Kashmir through peaceful, multilateral means. Accordingly, it was India that referred the case to the UN Security Council.

In short, the outcome of the 1947–48 crisis appears consistent with the predictions of the monadic version of the democratic peace theory. First, in contrast to the Pakistani political leadership, the Indian political elite had internalized many of the norms of democratic conduct and were amenable to settling the dispute over Kashmir through peaceful, multilateral means. Pakistan showed no such willingness. Accordingly, it was India that referred the case to the UN Security Council. Second, democratic India saw war as an option of last resort. Finally, Pakistan's lack of democratic constraints on decision making made it easier for decision makers to resort to war. It is at least plausible to argue that had democratic structures and norms been in place, Pakistani leaders might have been more willing to explore strategies other than war. Nevertheless, while the outcome of this crisis is consistent with the predictions that the dyadic argument makes for democratic-nondemocratic interactions, this does not mean that Pakistan's regime type drove India's decision making process. The onset of war had little to do with the particular regime types of the two states. The real roots of the war can be traced to the process of colonial disengagement and the quest for territorial aggrandizement.

The Second War over Kashmir in 1965

The second Kashmir war, which took place in August and September 1965, also started without a formal declaration of war. In this instance, international, regional, and domestic politics combined to propel the two adversaries into a second war.[16]

THE INTERNATIONAL DIMENSION

Internationally, the UN mediation process that was started after the 1947–48 war had proved unfruitful. Initially, Prime Minister Nehru had expressed a willingness to settle the Kashmir dispute on the basis

---

16. For a detailed discussion of the forces that contributed to the 1965 war, see Šumit Ganguly, "Deterrence Failure Revisited: The Indo-Pakistani War of 1965," *Journal of Strategic Studies*, Vol. 13, No. 4 (December 1990), pp. 77–93.

of a plebiscite, as had been suggested in the UN Security Council Resolution of April 21, 1948.[17] But India soon moved away from this position for two compelling reasons. First, Pakistan proved unwilling to abide by the first component of the resolution, which called for Pakistan to withdraw its troops and the Azad Kashmir rebel forces. Second, after 1954 and the emergence of a U.S.-Pakistani military alliance, Indian domestic politics significantly reduced Nehru's room for maneuver.[18] Eventually, the unwillingness of the two parties to implement the UN resolutions led the United Nations to lose interest in the Kashmir dispute.

THE REGIONAL DIMENSION

At a regional level, a second conflict had important repercussions for the Indo-Pakistani conflict. In October 1962, after the failure of border negotiations, the People's Republic of China (PRC) attacked India. The Indian forces, which were thinly deployed along India's Himalayan borders, proved a weak match for the ferocious Chinese People's Liberation Army (PLA). Within two weeks, the PLA forces had routed the Indian troops and had seized some 14,000 square miles of territory claimed by India. Compounding India's humiliating defeat, the PLA forces declared a unilateral cease-fire.[19]

After this military debacle, India sought to rebuild its forces, and it appealed to both the United States and the United Kingdom for military assistance. Both states came to India's assistance, but with important conditions. Among other matters, they urged India to start negotiations with Pakistan to settle the Kashmir dispute.[20] Grudgingly, Prime Minister Nehru agreed to hold bilateral discussions with Pakistan, and six rounds of talks were held between December 1962 and May 1963. The talks quickly became deadlocked, however, and failed to produce an agreement.[21]

---

17. Ishtiaq Ahmed, *State, Nation and Ethnicity in Contemporary South Asia* (London: Pinter, 1996), p. 143.

18. On this point, see Escott Reid, *Envoy to Nehru* (New York: Oxford University Press, 1981). Reid was the Canadian high commissioner to India during the 1950s.

19. Steven Hoffmann, *India and the China Crisis* (Berkeley: University of California Press, 1990).

20. Dennis Kux, *Estranged Democracies* (Washington, D.C.: National Defense University Press, 1994).

21. Denis Wright, *India-Pakistan Relations, 1962–1969* (New Delhi: Sterling, 1989).

Meanwhile, India's defense modernization plans proceeded apace. Plans were drawn up for the creation of a forty-five-squadron air force with modern, supersonic aircraft; the raising of the service ceiling of the Indian Army to one million; the creation of ten new mountain divisions equipped for high-altitude warfare; and the modernization and expansion of the Indian Navy.[22] While the military expansion was driven by the newly perceived Chinese military threat and India's resulting vulnerability, it created a security dilemma for Pakistan.[23] Some Pakistani analysts believed that India's increased military strength could threaten Pakistan's very survival, and the Pakistani elite also realized that its ability to wrest Kashmir from India through force would soon erode.

THE DOMESTIC DIMENSION

Finally, domestic politics within India and Pakistan played an important role in precipitating the second Indo-Pakistani conflict.

In 1963, in an attempt to further integrate Kashmir into the Indian Union, the Indian central government introduced legislation in Parliament to begin eroding Kashmir's special status (that is, its local control over all areas save, defense, communications, and foreign affairs). Understandably, Pakistan feared that its legal claim on Kashmir was being undermined, and protested vehemently in bilateral and multilateral fora. India nevertheless went ahead with its plans.

India's efforts to integrate Kashmir suffered a brief setback in December 1963, after a holy relic—reputedly a hair of the Prophet Mohammed, was stolen from from the Hazratbal mosque in Srinagar. Anti-Indian riots and demonstrations swept through the Kashmir Valley until the relic was recovered. The Pakistani leadership of President Mohammed Ayub Khan construed this display of anti-Indian sentiment as Kashmiri interest in integration with Pakistan.

In early 1965, President Ayub Khan, who had assumed power in a military coup in 1958, was faced with the beginnings of a challenge

---

22. Raju G.C. Thomas, *The Defence of India* (Delhi: Macmillan, 1968).

23. The concept of a "security dilemma" is discussed in John Herz, "Idealist Internationalism and the Security Dilemma," *World Politics*, No. 2 (January 1950). The "security dilemma" stems from the anarchic features of the international system. The international arena is deemed to be anarchic in that it lacks a supreme authority to enforce order. As a consequence of this anarchic structure, each state is ultimately responsible for its own security. In this milieu, the acquisition of military power by one state for defensive purposes may be construed as being threatening by an adversary.

to his stature in the Pakistani polity. His attempt to partially democ-ratize his regime through the creation of the "Basic Democracies" system, an elaborate mechanism of indirect representation, had revealed the limits of his public support. Even though he had hand-somely defeated his only presidential opponent, Fatima Jinnah, in West Pakistan, his margin of victory in East Pakistan was consider-ably smaller.[24] Furthermore, a charismatic young politician from the province of Sindh, Zulfiquar Ali Bhutto, was assuming greater prominence in Pakistani politics.

Faced with the decline of international interest in Kashmir, India's steady integration of Kashmir, and incipient challenges to his posi-tion within Pakistan, Ayub Khan needed a dramatic event to bolster his regime's sagging fortunes. A war with India over the issue of Kashmir was seen as a way to help revive the Kashmir issue at an international level and also to generate popular support for his regime.[25] Accordingly, Ayub Khan tested India's battle-readiness with a series of incursions along a poorly delineated border in the marshes of the Rann of Kutch in the western Indian state of Gujarat between January and April 1965. The Indian response was less than vigorous. The Indian military, under the command of General J.N. Chaudhuri, realized that the terrain favored the aggressor. Moreover, the new Indian prime minister, Lal Bahadur Shastri, agreed with Chaudhuri's assessment that the Rann of Kutch had little economic, political, or military significance. After a series of border skirmishes between Indian and Pakistani troops, at the instance of the British prime minister, Harold Macmillan, India agreed to refer the dispute to the International Court of Justice.

The Pakistani leadership construed this Indian willingness to settle the dispute through international arbitration as a sign of Indian pusillanimity. This fundamentally flawed inference was reinforced by the Pakistani leadership's reliance on colonial notion that Muslim

---

24. For a description and analysis of the Basic Democracies system, see Lawrence Ziring, *The Ayub Khan Era* (Syracuse, N.Y.: Syracuse University Press, 1971).

25. For a discussion of the propensity of authoritarian regimes to resort to "diversionary wars," see Jack S. Levy and Lily I. Vakili, "Diversionary Action by Authoritarian Regimes: Argentina in the Falklands/Malvinas Case," in Manus I. Midlarsky, ed., *The Internationalization of Communal Strife* (London: Routledge, 1992), pp. 118–146. For a thorough discussion of the relationship between weak institutional structures and internal and external conflict see Michael E. Brown, "Introduction," in Michael E. Brown, ed., *The International Dimensions of Internal Conflict*, pp. 1–31.

soldiers were better fighters than Hindu soldiers.[26] Finally, Foreign Minister Zulfiquar Ali Bhutto, in particular, believed that Indian Prime Minister Shastri, who lacked Nehru's charismatic hold over India's masses, would prove inadequate to the task of governing his fractious, polyethnic, and socioeconomically divided country.[27]

THE ONSET OF WAR

Having convinced themselves of India's lack of military and political resolve, the Pakistani military and civilian elites conceived of a bold plan to seize Kashmir. This strategy, formulated by Major General Akhtar Husain Malik, Foreign Minister Bhutto, and Foreign Secretary Aziz Ahmed, was known as "Operation Gibraltar." Their strategy involved infiltrating regular Pakistani troops disguised as local tribesmen across the Cease Fire Line (CFL) into the Kashmir Valley throughout the summer of 1965. These troops were expected to mingle with the Kashmiris and help foment a rebellion; taking advantage of the turmoil within the valley, the Pakistani Army would then attack and seize a substantial body of territory in a short, sharp incursion. Finally, the Pakistani political leadership would appeal to the international community as India attempted to counterattack and dislodge the Pakistani forces.

This strategy went awry from the outset. Far from welcoming the Pakistanis as potential liberators, the Kashmiris reported them to the local authorities. Once the Indian Army was apprised of this infiltration, it quickly moved to seal the porous border. Despite the loss of strategic surprise, Pakistan went ahead with its plan. Unable to stop the infiltration, the Indian forces attacked across the CFL, launching a strike into Azad Kashmir on August 15, 1965. Over the course of the next two weeks the fighting intensified. The Pakistani forces successfully counterattacked on September 1, dealing the Indian forces heavy losses. On September 5, the Pakistani forces captured the village of Jaurian, fourteen miles inside Indian territory. From this strategic location they could easily proceed to the town of Akhnur, from which they would be able to seal off Jammu and Kashmir from the rest of India.

To relieve pressure on Akhnur, the Indian forces resorted to a contingency plan: horizontal escalation. They attacked in the neighboring state of Punjab near the Pakistani city of Lahore. The Indian

26. The concept of "martial races" is discussed in Stephen P. Cohen, *The Indian Army* (Berkeley: University of California Press, 1971).

27. Dilip Mukherjee, *Zulfiquar Ali Bhutto* (Delhi: Vikas, 1972).

threat to Lahore led to a further escalation of the conflict, including a pitched tank battle in the Sialkot sector of Punjab. By mid-September the war was reaching a stalemate, and the UN Security Council unanimously passed a resolution on September 20 calling for a cessation of hostilities. The government of India accepted the cease-fire resolution on September 21, and the government of Pakistan did the same on September 22.

The United States, one of the few countries that had significant influence in both New Delhi and Islamabad, showed scant interest in brokering a post-bellum agreement. U.S. abstention permitted the Soviet Union to step into the breach, and Prime Minister Alexei Kosygin invited the warring parties to the Central Asian city of Tashkent to negotiate an end to the dispute. The Tashkent Agreement of 1966 between Mohammed Ayub Khan and Lal Bahadur Shastri succeeded only in restoring the *status quo ante*. In the interests of securing peace, India made substantial concessions, including returning the strategic Haji Pir pass to Pakistan over the objections of the Indian military.

CRITIQUE OR CONFIRMATION OF THE DEMOCRATIC PEACE THEORY?

At the time of the 1965 war, only India could be properly called a democracy. It had a written constitution that guaranteed a range of procedural and substantive rights, including the freedom of expression, assembly, movement, and religion, as well as due process. It also provided for the protection of private property.[28] The Indian judiciary was independent, and the country had a lively and contentious press. Significantly, the nation had held three national elections on the basis of universal adult franchise. In the first general election, held in 1952, 60 percent of the eligible electorate voted.[29] All three of India's elections to date are widely considered to have been both free and fair. Vigorous parliamentary debates took place regularly, on a range of subjects. Finally, after Nehru's death in 1964, political succession had adhered to constitutional procedures.

However, there was some abridgement of democratic procedures. In the aftermath of the 1962 border war with China, a constitutionally sanctioned "state of external emergency" had been declared. Under the terms of the emergency, the government had invoked the

---

28. Granville Austin, *The Indian Constitution: The Cornerstone of a Nation* (New York: Oxford University Press, 1966).

29. Francine R. Frankel, *India's Political Economy, 1947–1977: The Gradual Revolution* (Princeton, N.J.: Princeton University Press, 1978), p. 93.

Defence of India Rules (DIR), which harked back to the days of British colonialism. The DIR enabled the government to limit the rights of habeas corpus. Yet these measures were clearly seen as temporary measures designed to cope with an exigent situation, and not as a failure of democracy.

The Pakistani polity in 1965, on the other hand, was far from democratic. Pakistan's first constitution, which had been promulgated in 1956, had been suspended following Ayub Khan's military coup in October 1958. Between 1958 and 1962, Pakistan remained under martial law. During this period, Ayub Khan held the positions of president and chief martial law administrator. The civilian bureaucracy offered no resistance, and, in fact, worked closely with the military authorities.

In June 1962, Ayub Khan instituted a new constitution that granted extensive powers to the executive and created a weak and ineffectual legislature, and also created the Basic Democracies system. Among other matters, the constitution permitted the president to declare a state of emergency if the country faced either internal disturbances or an external threat. Both the judicial and legislative branches were subordinated to the executive. For example, neither the courts nor the unicameral assembly had the authority to question the president's decision to proclaim a state of emergency. Furthermore, once a state of emergency was declared, the president could assume virtually dictatorial powers.[30] Such a state of emergency came into force when Pakistan went to war with India in September 1965.

Some analysts of the democratic peace contend that democratizing states, which are characterized by weak institutional structures and manipulative elites, may be more war-prone than states in which democratic procedures and norms are well entrenched.[31] Did the limited opening up of the Pakistani political order under the Basic Democracies system contribute to war? Not really. Ayub Khan's Basic Democracies system did not genuinely broaden political participation. Press freedoms were still sharply curbed. The civilian bureaucracy was complicit, the judiciary was pliant, and the national legislature was weak. The narrow political elite could act with

---

30. Hasan-Askari Rizvi, *The Military and Politics in Pakistan* (New Delhi: Konark, 1988), pp. 112–114.

31. Edward D. Mansfield and Jack Snyder, "Democratization and the Danger of War," *International Security*, Vol. 20, No. 1 (Summer 1995), pp. 5–38.

impunity in matters relating to national security.[32] Once Foreign Minister Bhutto had successfully convinced Ayub to make war, few institutional or popular checks could constrain the undertaking of military action. Had such institutional or normative constraints existed, they might have prevented Bhutto or Ayub Khan from whipping up popular passions around the rancorous memories of the partition of the subcontinent and the unresolved status of Kashmir.

The evidence from this case shows limited support for the dyadic version of the democratic peace, which asserts that because of domestic weaknesses, democracies will often become the targets of attack by nondemocracies. India's willingness to negotiate an end to the Rann of Kutch dispute clearly emboldened the Ayub Khan regime and thereby contributed to Pakistan's decision to go to war. The examination of this case also provides some support for the monadic version of the democratic peace. India, as the democratic state, did not escalate the Kutch conflict and evinced a willingness to settle the dispute through negotiation.

Yet this case may suffer from overdetermination. While Pakistan's nondemocratic features undoubtedly contributed to its war-proneness, an equally compelling balance-of-power explanation can be constructed. Ayub and his advisers feared that the international community was losing interest in the Kashmir dispute. Moreover, India's rearmament program in the wake of the Sino-Indian border war would soon have given India conventional superiority, which would have foreclosed the possibility of Pakistan's wresting Kashmir away through force. In sum, while Pakistan's belligerence is consistent with the predictions of the dyadic version of the democratic peace theory, competing realist arguments can equally account for the war decision.

When Democracies Turn Belligerent: The 1971 War

The origins of the 1971 war were markedly different from those of the two previous Indo-Pakistani conflicts.[33] It arose from profound internal political developments within Pakistan, not territorial disputes and international power struggles.

---

32. One important measure of the significance attached to national security issues was the Pakistani defense budget. In 1964–65, the budget amounted to 46.07 percent of Pakistan's total expenditures. The following year it rose to 53.67 percent. Rizvi, *The Military and Politics in Pakistan,* p. 125.

33. The two best accounts of the 1971 war are Robert Jackson, *South Asian Crisis* (New York: Praeger, 1975); and Sisson and Rose, *War and Secession.*

The failure to resolve the Kashmir problem proved costly for President Ayub Khan. Many in the armed forces blamed him for their lackluster performance against India.[34] Furthermore, the failure to resolve the Kashmir dispute through war generated popular disaffection with the regime. This disenchantment was also rooted in the regime's failure to promote social justice and economic equity. Pakistan had grown at an extraordinarily rapid rate during Ayub Khan's rule, but the benefits of this growth had been highly concentrated.[35]

Ayub's troubles worsened when Zulfiquar Ali Bhutto, the principal architect of the 1965 war plans against India, resigned from the foreign ministry in 1966 and created his own political party, the Pakistan People's Party (PPP), in November 1967.

In early 1968, Ayub Khan's health started to fail. Against the backdrop of an ailing dictator and rising popular discontent, Bhutto started a public campaign against the regime and held rallies throughout West Pakistan. On March 25, 1969, in poor health and faced with a rising tide of disaffection against his regime, Ayub Khan resigned. The chief of staff of the Pakistani Army, General Yahya Khan, assumed office.

DEVELOPMENTS IN EAST PAKISTAN

Discontent against the western wing of the country had long existed in East Pakistan.[36] Among other matters, the predominantly Bengali-speaking population in East Pakistan had long resented the imposition of Urdu as the national language. Furthermore, the bulk of the government's industrial investment went to West Pakistan; East Pakistan's economy remained dependent on the production of primary commodities, especially jute, rice, and tea.

East Pakistani resentment grew after the 1965 war. East Pakistan had been left largely undefended during the war. The Ayub Khan

---

34. Rizvi, *The Military and Politics in Pakistan*, p. 148.

35. In a public speech in Karachi in 1968, Mahbub ul Haq, the military regime's chief economist, disclosed that some twenty-two industrial families controlled the bulk of the productive resources in Pakistan. See Shahid Javed Burki, *Pakistan: A Nation in the Making* (Boulder, Colo.: Westview, 1986), p. 60.

36. See J. Lee Auspitz, Stephen A. Marglin, and Gustav F. Papanek, "History of Economic and Political Domination of East Pakistan," in *The Bangla Desh Papers* (Lahore: Vanguard, n.d.). Also see Raonaq Jahan, *Pakistan: Failure in National Integration* (New York: Columbia University Press, 1972).

regime had argued that "the defense of the East lay in the West"; in other words, if India militarily threatened East Pakistan, the Pakistani forces would mount attacks against Kashmir and Punjab, thereby drawing the Indians away from the east. Although India had conducted only limited military operations in East Pakistan, the Bengali population there realized that their security depended to a large extent on India's sufferance.

These grievances against the West Pakistani regime contributed to an incipient East Pakistani demand for regional autonomy. This demand coalesced around the Awami League, a regional political party led by a charismatic Bengali politician, Sheikh Mujibur Rehman. Faced with rising pressures for democratization, General Yahya Khan decided to hold nationwide elections in December 1970; the Awami League won 160 out of a possible 162 seats in East Pakistan, and Zulfiquar Ali Bhutto's PPP won 81 out of a possible 138 seats in West Pakistan. Having won a sweeping mandate in East Pakistan, the Awami League made it clear that it wished to implement its election manifesto, which included a "Six-Point Program" for the autonomy of East Pakistan.[37] The military regime saw these demands as verging on secession and fought the Awami League's demands to form a government in Islamabad. Negotiations between the military regime, Bhutto, and Sheikh Mujibur Rehman quickly became deadlocked.[38] By early March 1971, the Awami League tired of the temporizing tactics of the West Pakistanis and started to publicly air secessionist sentiments.

Faced with growing public disturbances in East Pakistan, the Pakistani military started "Operation Searchlight" on March 25, 1971.[39] This military operation involved a systematic massacre of students, university professors, journalists, lawyers, and other members of the Bengali intelligentsia, primarily in the East Pakistani city of Dacca (now Dhaka). Sheikh Mujibur Rehman and a number of other Awami League leaders were promptly arrested and whisked away to prison in West Pakistan.

---

37. For a discussion of the Six-Point Program, see Herbert Feldman, *The End and the Beginning* (Karachi: Oxford University Press, 1975).

38. For details of these negotiations, see Sisson and Rose, *War and Secession*.

39. For a detailed description of "Operation Searchlight," see Anthony Mascarhenas, *The Rape of Bangla Desh* (Delhi: Vikas, 1971).

THE ROAD TO WAR

The military pogrom against the Bengalis sent a dramatic exodus of refugees into the neighboring Indian state of West Bengal. The influx of refugees reached its peak in May 1971; the total number of refugees reached nearly ten million.[40] Faced with this extraordinarily large influx of refugees, the government of Prime Minister Indira Gandhi initially sought two forms of external assistance and intervention. It appealed to the major powers and international aid organizations to relieve the financial costs of the refugee burden. The international community was quite responsive to the refugee burden. However, the major powers, and the United States in particular, showed scant interest in India's other request: placing pressure on Pakistan to move toward a political solution to its civil crisis.[41]

Faced with the unresponsiveness of the global community, by midsummer of 1971 the government in New Delhi decided that it was easier to resort to war than to absorb another several million people into the politically volatile state of West Bengal. Accordingly, Indira Gandhi and her closest political advisers fashioned a politico-military strategy that would both assure a return of the refugees to East Pakistan and also lead to the creation of a new state on the subcontinent, thus greatly weakening Pakistan.[42] To this end, in August 1971, Indira Gandhi signed a treaty of "peace, friendship, and cooperation" with the Soviet Union; Article Nine made it incumbent on each party to come to the other's assistance in the event of a threat to national security.[43] The treaty virtually guaranteed the support of a veto-wielding power in the Security Council to block any possible censure of India's actions in East Pakistan.

---

40. Ganguly, *The Origins of War in South Asia*, p. 97.

41. The paucity of U.S. interest in exerting pressure on Pakistan to reach a political settlement deserves comment. The United States had used the military regime of General Yahya Khan as a conduit for Henry Kissinger's secret talks with the People's Republic of China. Furthermore, President Richard Nixon had a personal animus against Prime Minister Indira Gandhi. For a discussion and critique of the U.S. role in this crisis, see Roger Morris, *Uncertain Greatness: Henry Kissinger and American Foreign Policy* (New York: Harper and Row, 1977). For an alternative formulation, see Sisson and Rose, *War and Secession*.

42. A good discussion of the politics of this decision can be found in Pran Chopra, *India's Second Liberation* (Delhi: Vikas, 1973).

43. Within India, Indira Gandhi was widely criticized for signing this treaty with the Soviet Union. Her critics contended that she had compromised nonalignment. For an analysis of the treaty, see Robert Horn, *Soviet-Indian Relations: Issues and Influence* (New York: Praeger, 1982).

In October 1971, Indira Gandhi toured a number of Western capitals to apprise them of the refugee burden and India's security concerns, as well as to exhaust all possible diplomatic initiatives before making war on Pakistan. Simultaneously, she gave a free hand to the Indian military to make preparations for a major land offensive in East Pakistan. Along with the Indian military, India's principal counterintelligence and espionage organization, the Research and Analysis Wing, started to recruit, organize, and train Bangladeshi insurgents. These insurgents, known as the Mukti Bahini (literally, "freedom force") started to harry the West Pakistani forces in East Pakistan. Pakistan repeatedly protested India's support for the Mukti Bahini. Unable to deter the Indian support, the Pakistani Air Force attacked India's northern airfields on December 3, 1971. The Indian Air Force retaliated the next day, penetrating deep into Pakistani territory. During the course of the next two weeks (the entire duration of the war), the Indian Air Force maintained complete air superiority. On December 17, 1971, Lieutenant-General Jagjit Singh Aurora, the senior Indian commander in the eastern sector, obtained an unconditional surrender from his Pakistani counterpart, Major General A.A.K. Niazi. The third Indo-Pakistani conflict had come to a close.

INDIA: SHREWD INITIATOR OR HAPLESS VICTIM?
Which state initiated the 1971 war? The question is far from trivial, and has important implications for an assessment of the democratic peace theory. In a strict sense, Pakistan can be held responsible for *starting* the war: it was the Pakistani air attack on India's northern airfields on December 3, 1971, that formally began the war. Furthermore, it was Pakistan's repression of its population that led to the exodus of refugees into India in late March 1971. Nevertheless, India's persistent support for the Mukti Bahini was vitally important in provoking the conflict. Thus, it would seem that contrary to the claims of the monadic democratic peace argument—which asserts that democracies will pursue war only as a last resort, and only after all alternative methods of conflict resolution are exhausted—India, after a certain stage of the crisis, was looking for a war. Below I discuss further the implications of the case for the monadic peace argument.

In 1971, with some limitations, democratic institutions had taken firm root in India. The country had twice witnessed the peaceful transfer of power at its highest levels. The Indian military was under firm civilian control. Elections were openly contested. The political spectrum included parties of a range of political persuasions. The Indian press, both English-language and vernacular, was free and feisty. With marked exceptions, civil liberties were largely respected. One exception was in the state of West Bengal, where civil liberties had come under siege after a violent Maoist urban guerilla movement, the Naxalites, had unleashed a campaign of mayhem and terror. In an attempt to suppress the Naxalites, the state authorities had resorted to many extra-judicial measures. Nevertheless, on balance, India could be characterized as a democratic state.

Why did India choose to become involved in Pakistan's internal conflict? Two interrelated factors prompted India to intervene, but only one of these had anything to do with the adversary's domestic regime type; on the contrary, the first factor was strategic. K. Subrahmanyam, a prominent Indian bureaucrat and strategist, made the initial case for military intervention. In a closed-door session, he contended that unless India intervened in East Pakistan, several million predominantly Muslim refugees would have to be absorbed into India, which could give rise to communal tensions in eastern India. Furthermore, Subrahmanyam contended that China was unlikely to intervene, given its low stakes in the issue.[44] Finally, although Subrahmanyam did not explicitly spell it out, most Indian decision makers saw a military intervention in East Pakistan as an opportunity to fundamentally weaken their principal adversary.

Yet, the decision to intervene cannot be explained solely in strategic terms. India's democratic status, at least in part, influenced its decision to intervene. As Prime Minister Indira Gandhi stated in parliament:

Something new has happened in East Bengal—a democratic election in which an entire people had spoken with almost one voice. We had welcomed this, not because we had wanted to interfere in another country's affairs *but because the values for which the victorious Awami League stood were our values . . . for which we have always stood and for which we have always spoken out.*[45]

What were these shared values to which Indira Gandhi alluded? She was drawing attention to the Awami League's democratic, secular, and socialist agenda. Although it was not always able to realize

---

44. K. Subrahmanyam, *Bangla Desh and India's Security* (Dehra Dun: Palit and Dutt, 1972).

45. Indira Gandhi, *India and Bangla Desh* (New Delhi: Orient Longman, 1972), pp. 9–10. Emphasis added.

them in practice, India too espoused these principles. Presumably, a democratic neighbor would be easier to deal with and would create fewer conflicts of interest than the religiously based military regime based in Islamabad.

A prominent Anglo-Indian member of the Lok Sabha (the lower house of the Indian Parliament), Dr. Frank Anthony, echoed Gandhi's sentiments in discussing the Pakistani repression of the Awami League:

It is a challenge to our whole polity—challenge not only to the form, but to the content of our political way of life, *to our secular motive* to which we are passionately committed and indeed, to the whole concept of the integration of the people of a secular society.[46]

No doubt the defense of secular principles played an important role in India's decision to become involved in the civil war in East Pakistan. However, while political ideology—support for democracy and democratization—can account for India's decision to use force, it only provides a piece of the puzzle: India also had important strategic reasons to go to war. Furthermore, contrary to the democratic peace theory's assertion that opposing political ideologies of democracy and nondemocracy drive war outcomes, in this case the norms that mattered were only partly related to the *political* organization of the polity.

PAKISTAN: DEMOCRATIZATION AND WAR-PRONENESS?

Pakistan's political orientation in 1971 was far more complex than India's. Martial law had been eased in January 1970. A directive issued in March 1970 (the Legal Framework Order) had further lifted curbs on political activity.[47] Indeed, the December 1970 elections were widely considered to be the only free and fair election that Pakistan had held since its independence in 1947.

But these political and institutional changes within Pakistan did not make it a democracy.[48] Pakistan lacked both democratic structures

---

46. Frank Anthony, as quoted in *Lok Sabha Debates, May 25, 1971* (New Delhi: Government of India, 1971), p. 239. Emphasis added.

47. G.W. Choudhury, *The Last Days of United Pakistan* (Bloomington: Indiana University Press, 1974), p. 94.

48. The definition of a democracy can vitally influence the extent to which the democratic peace theory is vindicated or refuted. For more on how definitions of democracy have changed over time, see John M. Owen, "How Liberalism Produces Democratic Peace," *International Security*, Vol. 19, No. 2 (Fall 1994), pp. 87–125.

and democratic norms. In 1970–71, the military was in charge of the Pakistani polity, despite emerging challenges. If the military had not sought to thwart the outcomes of the democratic election, Pakistan might have started down the path toward democracy. The norm of fair, honest, and open contestation, so vital to a democratic polity, simply did not exist in Pakistan. In effect, Yahya Khan's decision to start opening up the political system unleashed forces that neither he nor unscrupulous politicians such as Zulfiquar Ali Bhutto were prepared to countenance. The initial demands of the Awami League were not secessionist, but focused on regional autonomy. Only after the explicit unwillingness of Bhutto to share power with the League in Islamabad did the demands take on a secessionist hue. The military crackdown in Dacca, of course, created an unbridgeable rift between the two parties.

Pakistan's fitful efforts to move toward a democratic polity and the onset of the 1971 war do seem to confirm, at least partially, Edward Mansfield and Jack Snyder's hypothesis about the war-proneness of democratizing states. They argue that groups that are threatened by social change and democratization often take an inflexible view of their interests. This was precisely the case with the Pakistani military and civilian oligarchies. Yahya Khan's opening of the political system enabled the Awami League to put forward and press for its "Six-Point Program" for regional autonomy. If Sheikh Mujibur Rehman had been able to implement all the components of that program, the corporate interests of the Pakistani military would have been threatened.[49] More to the point, the military was opposed to democratization and genuine power-sharing within Pakistan. The Awami League, given its ideological abhorrence of the Pakistani military and its numerical majority in parliament, would have insisted on a transformation of the political order within Pakistan. Consequently, it was no surprise that the military, as well as Bhutto, thwarted the demands of the Awami League and ultimately plunged the country into a brutal civil war to protect their entrenched privileges. The Indian intervention in East Pakistan was a consequence of the refugee burden that the military crackdown and the subsequent civil war in East Pakistan had spawned.[50]

---

49. Mansfield and Snyder argue that groups that are threatened by social change and democratization often take an inflexible view of their interests. This was precisely the case with the Pakistani military and civilian oligarchs. See Mansfield and Snyder, "Democratization and the Danger of War," p. 27.

50. Richard Sisson and Leo E. Rose, *War and Secession*, p. 149.

NOT QUITE THE DEMOCRATIC PEACE

India's decision to resort to war had little to do with Pakistan's non-democratic status. However, proponents of the monadic version of the democratic peace argument may find some support from this case.[51] According to that theory, democracies do not promptly resort to war against authoritarian adversaries even when limited opportunities present themselves. Initially, Indian decision makers had hoped that the Pakistani leadership would see reason and negotiate with Sheikh Mujibur Rehman and the Awami League. They did not seek militarily to exploit Pakistan's domestic turmoil. They confined their efforts to expressions of concern about Pakistan's domestic developments.

The Indian position changed quite dramatically after the military crackdown in East Pakistan and the flight of millions of refugees into India. Faced with the extraordinary refugee onus, Indian decision makers concluded that a political solution to the East Pakistan crisis was all but impossible. Within two months of the military crackdown in March 1971, sensing a unique opportunity to deliver a *coup de main* against its principal adversary, India chose war. In the ultimate analysis, then, the decision to go to war stemmed from strategic imperatives; India could ill afford to absorb the refugees into the politically sensitive state of West Bengal without significant and adverse social, political, and economic consequences.

The "Long Peace" in South Asia: 1972–97

In 1972, President Zulfiquar Ali Bhutto and Prime Minister Indira Gandhi met at the hill resort of Simla in northern India to discuss a settlement to the 1971 war.[52] In Simla, the two sides agreed to abjure the use of force to settle outstanding disputes.[53] Despite crises in 1987 and 1990, full-scale war has not broken out between India and Pakistan since 1972. What explains this "long peace" in South Asia? Several factors are at work, and they must be carefully disaggregated.

---

51. For a discussion of the monadic version of the democratic peace argument, see Ray, *Democracy and International Conflict*, pp. 16–21. Also see Miriam Fendius Elman's introduction to this volume.

52. Bhutto assumed the presidency on December 20, 1971, three days after Pakistan's military defeat.

53. For an analysis of the Simla Agreement, see Thomas P. Thornton and Imtiaz Bokhari, *The 1972 Simla Agreement: An Asymmetrical Negotiation* (Washington, D.C.: Foreign Policy Institute, Johns Hopkins School of Advanced International Studies, 1988).

PAKISTAN: BREAKDOWN, DICTATORSHIP, AND TRANSITION

On April 12, 1973, Prime Minister Bhutto gave the country a new constitution, which, unlike its 1962 predecessor, emphasized the powers of the prime minister over those of the president. It also created a bicameral legislature and declared Islam to be the state religion of Pakistan. However, Bhutto disregarded the constitutional provisions that guaranteed nondiscriminatory treatment of opposition regional governments. In February 1974, he dismissed the opposition government of the province of Baluchistan on the grounds that it had encouraged its people to challenge central authority; this act led the government of the Northwest Frontier Province to resign in protest. In May of the same year, Bhutto passed an amendment to the constitution that gave the executive the authority to declare illegal any political party that acted in a manner detrimental to the sovereignty or integrity of Pakistan. This power was to be exercised with the approval of the Supreme Court. It was successfully used to ban the National Awami Party.[54] Despite the extraordinary powers that he came to wield under the constitution and the strength of the PPP, Bhutto resorted to various forms of electoral malfeasance in the elections of March 1977.[55] Widespread disturbances broke out in the wake of this compromised election.

With rising disorder in Pakistan, General Mohammed Zia-ul-Haq, the chief of army staff, organized and implemented a successful coup against President Bhutto's regime on July 5, 1977. He promptly declared martial law, took over as the Chief Martial Law Administrator, suspended the 1973 Constitution, and dissolved the federal and provincial cabinets.[56] In 1979, General Zia-ul-Haq sent the deposed president to the gallows on the grounds that he had orchestrated the murder of a political opponent. With minor modifications, the military regime of Zia remained in place until his death in a mysterious plane crash on August 17, 1988.[57]

Following Zia's death, Benazir Bhutto, the daughter of Zulfiquar Ali Bhutto, became prime minister in an open election. Nevertheless, the military remains one of the principal institutions within the Pakistani state apparatus, alongside the office of the president and

54. Burki, *Pakistan: A Nation in the Making*, pp. 71–73.

55. Marvin Weinbaum, "The March 1977 Elections in Pakistan: Where Everyone Lost," *Asian Survey*, Vol. 17, No. 7 (July 1977), pp. 559–618.

56. Rizvi, *The Military and Politics in Pakistan*, p. 225.

57. Martial law was formally lifted on December 30, 1985.

the permanent civilian bureaucracy. Under the Eighth Amendment to the 1973 Constitution, which was passed by a supine National Assembly in 1985, during the period of military rule, the president of Pakistan possesses sweeping powers, which include that of dismissing the prime minister. On March 31, 1997, Prime Minister Nawaz Sharif, in a bold and unprecedented step, introduced legislation to abolish significant sections of the Eighth Amendment to the Pakistani Constitution. Specifically, under the terms of the new legislation, the Thirteenth Amendment, which passed on April 1, the president's power to dismiss elected governments was severely curtailed. The prime minister also won back the right to appoint the three military service chiefs. Sharif was able to pass this legislation because he commanded an overwhelming majority in both houses of parliament. Even the opposition did not stand in his way because they too stood to gain from this new law.[58]

INDIA: FITFUL DEEPENING OF DEMOCRACY

After she inflicted a humiliating defeat on India's longstanding and principal adversary, Indira Gandhi won an overwhelming electoral victory in 1972. Despite this extraordinary mandate, she presided over the deinstitutionalization of Indian politics during the 1970s and early 1980s. She increasingly resorted to populist appeals and plebiscitary electoral tactics. While these measures exacted an important toll on institution-building, her populist slogans and policies succeeded in mobilizing large sections of the Indian populace.[59]

India underwent a brief period of authoritarian rule between 1976 and 1977, under Indira Gandhi. This episode was precipitated when a defeated political opponent successfully moved a lower court judgment against Gandhi for a series of minor electioneering offenses. With opposition parties publicly clamoring for her immediate resignation, Gandhi obtained a stay order from a higher court, declared a state of internal emergency, and then used her parliamentary majority to retroactively alter the law under which she had been prosecuted. During this span of authoritarian rule, civil liberties were suspended, the judiciary silenced, the press muzzled, and political

---

58. Mohammed Waseem, "Pakistan's Lingering Crisis of Dyarchy," *Asian Survey*, Vol. 32, No. 7 (July 1992), pp. 617–634; Ahmed Rashid, "Clipped Wings," *Far Eastern Economic Review*, April 10, 1997, p. 18.

59. Lloyd I. Rudolph and Suzanne Hoeber Rudolph, *In Pursuit of Lakshmi: The Political Economy of the Indian State* (Chicago: University of Chicago Press, 1987).

activity sharply curtailed. When Gandhi finally called an election in 1977 to legitimize her rule, the Indian electorate promptly threw her out of office. The new coalition government of Prime Minister Morarji Desai moved to restore press freedoms and civil liberties.

Since 1977, despite India's widespread political instability, the democratic process has expanded and deepened.[60] Political participation, particularly by India's poor, lower castes and minorities, has dramatically increased. One of the most striking indicators of the increased inclusiveness of Indian democracy is the composition of the eleventh Lok Sabha. For example, the percentage of legislators from the so-called backward castes rose from 13 percent in 1971 to 23.3 percent in 1996. The number of legislators from rural, agrarian backgrounds increased from 33.2 percent in 1971 to 51.8 percent in 1996.[61] As an institution, Parliament has become far more representative of the country.

Political mobilization and participation have come at a price. India's political institutions have eroded to varying degrees. Parliamentary norms are routinely flouted, most political parties lack ideological coherence; elections are increasingly plebiscitary exercises; and the probity of key institutions, such as the civil service, has markedly declined. In the wake of the 1996 general election, which brought a minority coalition government to power, hopes for some reform of India's compromised institutions were raised. However, the decline of other countervailing institutions during the 1980s produced an extremely powerful executive that is largely free from legislative scrutiny. The decline of bureaucratic norms and routines, which started as early as the 1970s, has also enabled the office of the prime minister to exercise overweening power. These forms of institutional decline have eroded the usual constraints on democratic control over foreign and security policy issues.

THE "BRASSTACKS" CRISIS OF 1987

Relations between India and Pakistan deteriorated after the Soviet invasion of Afghanistan. Although India was distressed by the Soviet

---

60. In the eleventh general election in 1996, some 590 million people were eligible to vote; candidates from 500 recognized parties participated; and the overall turnout was around 64 percent. See "India's Epic Election," *New York Times*, April 30, 1996, p. A20; and "India Spurns the Congress Party," *New York Times*, May 11, 1996, p. A18.

61. Harinder Baweja, "Changing Face of Parliament," *India Today*, July 15, 1996, pp. 25–36.

entry into Afghanistan, it was unwilling to criticize publicly the Soviet decision, for fear of jeopardizing the carefully constructed Indo-Soviet arms transfer and security relationship.[62] Pakistan, which was by now seen as a vital conduit of weaponry to the Afghan resistance, initially rebuffed U.S. President Jimmy Carter's offer of $400 million in economic and military assistance. In 1981, the Reagan administration, which dubbed Pakistan a "front-line state," provided a five-year package of military and economic assistance worth $3.2 billion. This package included F-16 fighter aircraft and military hardware. India reacted to this U.S. military assistance with considerable vigor, obtaining the latest-generation Soviet MiG-29 aircraft to offset the Pakistani acquisition. As an incipient arms race developed on the subcontinent, the political relationship between New Delhi and Islamabad plummeted. Matters worsened when Pakistan was implicated in supplying weaponry to the Sikh insurgency in Punjab. Although that insurgency had indigenous roots, Pakistani involvement raised the level of violence.[63]

Even though Pakistan faced a live border with Afghanistan, it sought to exploit India's troubles in Punjab. India's exasperation with Pakistan's continued assistance to the Sikh insurgents coincided with profound organizational changes that were taking place in the Indian Army. General Krishnaswami Sundarji, the Indian Army's flamboyant chief of staff, wanted to induct two new infantry formations and a mechanized brigade into the army. He was also interested in testing Plan AREN, an indigenously developed and produced communications grid, and a C[3]I (command, control, communications, and intelligence) system. This military exercise, code-named "Brasstacks," was the largest of its kind in India's independent history.[64]

The scale and long duration of this military exercise, held in the Rajasthan desert, was clearly designed in part to convey a message to the Pakistani military leadership that India could exert military pressure on Pakistan at will, despite the problems in Punjab. To the shock of India's decision makers, as the exercise drew to a close in December 1987, Pakistan, which was also holding its winter military exercises "Saf-e-Shikan" and "Flying Horse," moved its forces to the

62. Horn, *Soviet-Indian Relations*.

63. See Raju G.C. Thomas, *Democracy, Security, and Development in India* (New York: St. Martin's, 1996).

64. Bajpai et al., *Brasstacks and Beyond*, p. 29.

strategic Shakargarh bulge in Punjab. More distressingly, in early January 1988, Pakistan's Army Reserve South forces crossed the Lodhran bridge on the Sutlej River. From this position they were within striking distance of a number of key towns in Indian Punjab, including the city of Amritsar.

The possible intent of these troop movements caused considerable alarm in New Delhi and generated a flurry of diplomatic activity. The minister of state for external affairs, Natwar Singh, met with the Pakistani ambassador, Humayun Khan, to convey India's concerns about the Pakistani troop movements. Simultaneously, the Indian minister for external affairs, Narayan Dutt Tiwari, met with the Soviet ambassador Vassily Rykov, while the Indian minister of state for defense, Arun Singh, conducted a parallel meeting with the U.S. ambassador, John Gunther Dean. On the other side of the border, the Pakistani minister for foreign affairs, Zain Noorani, contacted the Indian ambassador to Islamabad, S.K. Singh, to convey Pakistan's interest in lowering the rising level of tension along the Indo-Pakistani border in Punjab.

The crisis began to defuse shortly after January 25, 1988, when India agreed to hold talks with Pakistan. On January 26, Pakistani spokesmen announced that Foreign Secretary Abdul Sattar would meet with his Indian counterpart, Alfred Gonsalves, to defuse the border tensions. By February 4, both sides had agreed to a phased withdrawal of their own troops from the border regions.

Analysts of South Asian regional security studies debate whether there was a nuclear dimension to this crisis. Although this debate is far from settled, one fact is certain. Abdul Qadir Khan, widely known as the "father" of Pakistan's quest to obtain a nuclear weapon, gave an interview to a prominent Indian journalist, Kuldip Nayar, on January 28. In this interview he asserted that Pakistan had enriched uranium to weapons-grade quality. This interview was published in the London *Observer* on March 1, 1988. Khan could not have granted this interview without the prior knowledge and permission of the Pakistani military. Yet, if his interview was intended as a nuclear signal, it was poorly timed. The "Brasstacks" crisis had all but blown over. Quite possibly, it was a signal to India that in the future it would have to take account of the possibility that Pakistan had nuclear weapons before engaging in coercive behavior.[65]

---

65. Much of this discussion is drawn from Šumit Ganguly, "Arms Control in South Asia: History and Prospects," *Defense Analysis*, Vol. 12, No. 1 (1996), pp. 65–75.

THE 1990 CRISIS

In early 1990, a second crisis punctuated Indo-Pakistani relations. Some scholars have argued that this crisis definitely had a nuclear component.[66] In December 1989, the insurgency in Kashmir had peaked.[67] Indian decision makers had sufficient evidence that Pakistan was systematically organizing, training, and arming various Kashmiri insurgent groups, but they were unable to stop the infiltration of insurgents across the porous Line of Control. Some analysts argue that key Indian decision makers decided to draw up plans for striking deep into Azad Kashmir to destroy training camps. Pakistani intelligence picked up signs of increased Indian troop movements in Kashmir. Because Pakistan's conventional capabilities were markedly inferior to India's, decision makers reportedly placed key squadrons of the Pakistani Air Force on alert and armed them with nuclear weapons.[68]

U.S. intelligence agencies apparently picked up evidence of the Indian and Pakistani moves. Fearing that escalating tensions could culminate in full-scale war, President George Bush dispatched his deputy national security adviser, Robert Gates, and Richard Haass, the senior staff member of the National Security Council with responsibility for the Near East and South Asia, to Islamabad and New Delhi. The principal aim of the U.S. mission to the South Asian capitals was to counsel restraint. In Islamabad, Gates informed the government that the Pentagon had simulated every imaginable scenario, and that in every one of them Pakistan was defeated. Consequently, if Pakistan wished to avoid war, it should cease support to the Kashmiri insurgents. In New Delhi, Gates counseled Indian leaders not to carry out strikes into Azad Kashmir. He contended that such strikes would inevitably provoke full-scale war with Pakistan. The impact of the Gates-Haass mission is difficult to assess. In any event,

---

66. Hagerty, "Nuclear Deterrence in South Asia."

67. As with the insurgency in the Punjab, the origins of the Kashmiri insurgency are indigenous; however, it has been greatly exacerbated by Pakistani involvement. For a discussion of the origins of the insurgency, see Šumit Ganguly, "Explaining the Kashmir Insurgency: Political Mobilization and Institutional Decay," *International Security*, Vol. 21, No. 2 (Fall 1996), pp. 76–107.

68. It is impossible to state with any certainty whether Pakistan armed its aircraft with nuclear weapons. The most alarmist account is Seymour Hersh, "On the Nuclear Edge," *New Yorker*, March 29, 1993, pp. 56–73. For a more balanced account, see Mitchell Reiss, *Bridled Ambition: Why Countries Constrain Their Nuclear Capabilities* (Washington, D.C.: Woodrow Wilson Center Press, 1995).

296 PATHS TO PEACE

war was averted. The insurgency in Kashmir continues, however, and Pakistani support to the insurgents has not stopped.

A DEMOCRATIC PEACE IN SOUTH ASIA?

Several features of this "long peace" in South Asia require comment. First, despite changes in regime type in both India and Pakistan, peace, meaning the absence of full-scale war, has been uninterrupted since 1971. For example, during India's period of authoritarian rule in 1976–77, its behavior toward democratic Pakistan was not especially belligerent. Nor did its behavior change substantially when the tables were turned in 1978. Thus, the evidence does not readily support either the monadic or dyadic versions of the democratic peace theory.

Second, despite India's uninterrupted democratic record since 1977, it is ironic that it steadily moved toward the Soviet Union (until around 1990) and against the United States during much of this period. Ideology had little to do with this foreign policy shift. Few in the Indian foreign policy elite had much affinity for the Soviet Union. India's willingness to align with the Soviet Union stemmed from straightforward balance-of-power considerations: the Soviet interest in containing China coincided with Indian misgivings about growing Sino-U.S. strategic cooperation.

Third, India and Pakistan were both democratic states after 1989, but their relations since then have been marked by continuing acrimony, border clashes, and at least one major crisis. This situation challenges Michael Doyle's expectation that substantial democratization within a dyad should lead to reduced levels of conflict.[69]

In effect, the "long peace" in South Asia is deceptive. India and Pakistan came perilously close to war on two occasions. And since 1989, India has been harshly suppressing a rebellion in the Kashmir Valley.[70] Close to 20,000 individuals have been killed in this conflict since its outset. The possibility of war, though small, continues to stalk the region. "Peace," therefore, is a contestable description for the current situation in the region.

But what explains the lack of a full-scale war since 1971? The period

---

69. Michael W. Doyle, "Michael Doyle on the Democratic Peace—Again," in Michael E. Brown, Sean M. Lynn-Jones, and Steven E. Miller, eds., *Debating the Democratic Peace* (Cambridge, Mass.: MIT Press, 1996), pp. 364–373.

70. The harsh methods that India has adopted to quell the Kashmir insurgency are certainly corrosive to democratic values. Nevertheless, Indian democracy remains robust.

between 1972 and 1987 does not require a great deal of explanation; India possessed overwhelming conventional superiority over Pakistan. After witnessing India's assistance in the breakup of Pakistan in 1971, no Pakistani leader could seriously contemplate another war with India. Furthermore, after 1979 it became even harder for Pakistan to start a war with India due to the Soviet presence along the Afghan-Pakistani border. This Soviet presence imposed constraints on a military adventure against India. Even after Pakistan acquired substantial quantities of weaponry from the United States, the military balance still favored India.

Apart from its intervention in East Pakistan in 1971, India has been a status quo power in the region. After the Simla Agreement was concluded with Pakistan, most Indian leaders believed that the Kashmir problem had been resolved. Apart from a handful of unrequited members of India's jingoistic Bharatiya Janata Party, few leaders seriously contemplated seizing the remainder of Kashmir from Pakistan. Consequently, India had little interest in starting a war with Pakistan during this period.

What factors, then, explain the "near miss" of 1987? At the time, Pakistan was a military dictatorship and India a democratic state. Yet India initiated the exercise that set off the escalatory spiral. Why did India behave in this bellicose fashion? First, as argued earlier, there was Pakistani provocation, in that Pakistan was aiding the Sikh insurgents. Second, and more importantly, despite the existence of democratic institutions in India, the realms of defense and foreign policy making remained an elite preserve. Public and even ministerial expertise in these areas is still woefully limited. Consequently, senior bureaucrats and military planners have considerable leeway in making decisions, and public scrutiny and analysis of decision making is idiosyncratic and often poorly informed. Third, decision making, particularly in areas pertaining to foreign and defense policy, had become highly centralized under Rajiv Gandhi. The prime minister's secretariat, which had grown in power under Indira Gandhi's rule, had become the locus of much decision making. Consequently, General Sundarji, an ambitious and articulate military officer, could easily sway a neophyte prime minister and a coterie of bureaucrats. Only after "Brasstacks" provoked a vigorous Pakistani reaction and the Indian government held a press conference did the Indian press start to question the wisdom of the military exercise.[71]

---

71. Bajpai et al., *Brasstacks and Beyond*, pp. 167–168.

The 1990 crisis poses more of a conundrum. Pakistan had made a fitful transition to democracy in 1989 after the death of General Zia-ul-Haq in 1988. In India, in the 1989 ninth general election, the ruling Congress (I) Party was defeated. A coalition government led by Vishwanath Pratap Singh had recently assumed power in New Delhi when the insurgency abruptly erupted in Kashmir. Notionally, both states had democratic governments.

Yet democratic institutions had not been consolidated within Pakistan. Both structurally and normatively, Pakistan was far from being a full-fledged democracy. The prime minister served at the sufferance of the military and the president.[72] The Inter-Services Intelligence (ISI) organization, the principal military entity responsible for funneling weaponry to the Afghan insurgents, had become a virtual "state within a state." The principal opposition party, the Islamic Jamhoori Ittehad, which was led by Punjabi industrialist Mian Nawaz Sharif, was largely a creation of the Pakistani Army and the ISI.

Furthermore, societal forces vitiated democratic norms in Pakistan. For example, newfound press freedom generated considerable reckless reporting on India.[73] When the Kashmiri insurgency erupted, Benazir Bhutto quickly adopted a belligerent posture toward India in an attempt to outflank her opponents and critics. For example, in a National Assembly session she called for a *jihad* (holy war) against India.[74]

Did the presence of democratic institutions in both states enable them to avoid escalation and war? The evidence points to the contrary. The Pakistani civilian leadership was particularly truculent once the insurgency started in Kashmir. Evidence exists that the ISI quickly became involved in supporting the insurgents.[75] In India, an

72. Waseem, "Pakistan's Lingering Crisis of Dyarchy," p. 630.

73. See *FBIS Media Guide: Pakistan* (Washington, D.C.: Foreign Broadcast Information Service, 1996).

74. Madhu Jain, "Pakistan: Raising the Stakes," *India Today*, February 28, 1996, pp. 19–23. Also see Shekhar Gupta, "'Jehad' for Kashmiris," *India Today*, May 31, 1990, pp. 14–15. It may well be asked why it was not popular to adopt a more conciliatory posture toward India now that Pakistan had made a transition to democratic rule. The answer is simple. During more than a decade of military and authoritarian rule, the Pakistani public had been fed a steady diet of vicious anti-Indian propaganda, creating a large reservoir of distrust of and hatred toward India. A weak prime minister could ill-afford to resist the temptation to stir this cauldron of anti-Indian sentiment.

75. Anthony Davis, "The Conflict in Kashmir," *Jane's Intelligence Review*, Vol. 7, No. 1 (1995), pp. 41–46.

untested coalition government, surprised by the abrupt outbreak of widespread disaffection in Kashmir, responded in a ham-handed fashion. Thus, the presence of democratic governments in both states had little to do with the avoidance of war; on the contrary, democratic political processes in both states pushed toward increasing conflict. In all likelihood war was avoided because of the existence of nuclear weapons on both sides.[76] India and Pakistan pulled away from the brink because they feared nuclear escalation.

A Future Unlike the Past?

The foregoing analysis of war and conflict in South Asia does not entirely support either the dyadic or monadic version of the democratic peace theory. However, advocates of the democratic peace proposition could contend that the hypothesis has not been adequately tested in the region. Today, despite limitations, India is a successfully consolidated democracy. Even jingoistic political leaders in India will now face important constraints on their behavior. Many political institutions that atrophied during the 1980s are showing renewed health and vigor.[77]

Pakistan has only just embarked on the long road toward democratic consolidation, despite two peaceful transfers of power in the 1990s. Although the road is strewn with many obstacles that will not be easy to remove, it is unlikely that Pakistan will initiate a war with India in the foreseeable future. The acquisition of crude nuclear capabilities by India and Pakistan appears to have brought some degree of stability to the region, and despite widespread international (and especially U.S.) pressure, neither country is about to renounce its nuclear weapons program.[78] Furthermore, no Indian government will permit India's substantial conventional superiority over Pakistan to erode. India's pace of economic growth, which has picked up considerably since economic reforms were initiated in 1991, is sufficient to sustain the necessary defense outlays.

---

76. See Hagerty, "Nuclear Deterrence in South Asia." The Gates-Haass mission may have reinforced the caution induced by the existence of nuclear weapons on both sides.

77. Peter Waldman, "India's Supreme Court Makes Rule of Law a Way of Governing," *Wall Street Journal*, May 6, 1996, p. A8.

78. Stephen P. Cohen, "1990: South Asia's Useful Nuclear Crisis," paper presented at the annual meeting of the American Association for the Advancement of Science, Chicago, Illinois, February 6–7, 1992.

Since these factors can deter war even in the absence of strong democratic constraints and norms, a more compelling test of the democratic peace proposition will have to be deferred to a time when both India and Pakistan are robust, mature democracies and face a compelling security crisis.

Chapter 7

Israel's Invasion of Lebanon, 1982: Regime Change and War Decisions

Miriam Fendius Elman

In the social sciences, definitions can make or break a theory. For example, the way researchers define democracy and war determines how many international conflicts can be coded as democratic wars and as disconfirming evidence for the democratic peace theory; that is, analyses based on select definitions of democracy and war can make the democratic peace theory appear more robust than it really is.[1] Consider Israel's invasion of Lebanon in 1982. Proponents of the democratic peace theory tend to give this case short shrift: James Lee Ray does not include it in his list of alleged wars between democracies; Bruce Russett points out parenthetically that Lebanon was not democratic at the time.[2] Nevertheless, critics of the democratic peace theory count the case as an instance of warring democracies. For example, David Spiro claims that the case should not be excluded even though Lebanon's government was "in shambles," and the armies of Syria and

The author thanks Joe Hagan, Arie Kacowicz, and the participants at the conference held at the Center for Science and International Affairs, Harvard University, June 25–26, 1996, for their helpful comments and suggestions.

1. David E. Spiro, "The Insignificance of the Liberal Peace," *International Security*, Vol. 19, No. 2 (Fall 1994), pp. 51, 54–55.

2. James Lee Ray, *Democracy and International Conflict: An Evaluation of the Democratic Peace Proposition* (Columbia: University of South Carolina Press, 1995), pp. 86–87; and Bruce Russett, *Grasping the Democratic Peace: Principles for a Post-Cold War World* (Princeton, N.J.: Princeton University Press, 1993), p. 18. Proponents might also exclude the case on the grounds that Lebanon was a failed state, much less a democracy, and because Israel's prime target was not Lebanon but Syria and the Palestine Liberation Organization (PLO).

the Palestine Liberation Organization (PLO) were already operating on its territory.[3] Similarly, Charles W. Kegley, Jr. and Margaret G. Hermann code Lebanon as partially free in 1982. Thus, Israel's intervention in Lebanon is inconsistent with the predictions of the democratic peace theory.[4]

Whether or not Lebanon is defined as a democracy, Israel's invasion in 1982 does challenge the monadic variant of the democratic peace argument. According to the monadic hypothesis, the more democratic a state, the less likely it is to initiate the use of force regardless of the adversary's regime type: "Democracies are less likely than nondemocracies to initiate crises against all other states."[5] As Kegley and Hermann put it: "Democracies have associated with their behavior the perception that they will abide by the neoliberal tenet that bargaining works—or, at least, is worth a try . . . Countries which choose their leaders through the ballot and hold them accountable signal to the external world a willingness to negotiate disputes and accept mediation."[6]

Contrary to this monadic argument, Israel's behavior in 1982 suggests that democracies may in fact initiate crises and will not necessarily choose peaceful means of conflict resolution, even when alternative nonviolent strategies are available. They are especially likely to initiate conflicts if ruling coalitions favor the use of force to solve international conflicts. In this chapter, I argue that a number of domestic factors account for why Israel initiated a costly war that it could have avoided: the foreign policy orientation of Israel's leadership in 1981–82; changes in the composition of the coalition government that increased the bargaining leverage of certain political actors; and Israel's rules that regulate civil-military relations. According to

---

3. Spiro, "The Insignificance of the Liberal Peace," p. 60.

4. Charles W. Kegley, Jr. and Margaret G. Hermann, "Military Intervention and the Democratic Peace," *International Interactions*, Vol. 21, No. 1 (July 1995), p. 10. The authors note that "the fact that free states intervene against partly free states suggests that any union of democratic countries may contain a danger zone. Members of the democratic community may sometimes resort to, or believe themselves forced to resort to, the use of military intervention to resolve conflicts among themselves." See ibid.

5. David L. Rousseau et al., "Assessing the Dyadic Nature of the Democratic Peace, 1918–1988," *American Political Science Review*, Vol. 90, No. 3 (September 1996), pp. 512–513.

6. Charles W. Kegley, Jr. and Margaret G. Hermann, "Ballots, a Barrier Against the Use of Bullets and Bombs: Democratization, Military Intervention, and the Democratic Peace," paper presented at the annual meeting of the International Studies Association, San Diego, April 16–20, 1996, pp. 5, 25.

the prevailing versions of the democratic peace theory, democratic norms and institutions play a greater role in foreign policy making than do the people involved in making foreign policy decisions.[7] By contrast, I suggest that changes in leadership can dramatically affect the war-proneness of a democratic state. Since new leaders may hold different foreign policy beliefs than their predecessors, intra-regime changes can crucially influence whether a democratic state will choose to solve external conflicts by force. In addition, by treating democracy as a unified category, the democratic peace theory obscures the different ways in which military power is delegated between civilian leaders and the military. While democracy ensures some civilian control over the military, this control is a matter of degree that varies significantly among democratic regime types.[8]

Neither the democratic peace theory nor neorealism provides a good explanation of why Israel went to war in 1982. Israel's war decision was inconsistent with what the monadic version of the democratic peace theory would lead us to expect. Furthermore, intra-regime changes led to changes in Israel's foreign policy toward Lebanon, even though regime type—democracy—remained stable. Neorealism also fails to account for Israel's war decision because Israel was facing fewer external threats than in the past. In addition, a full-scale invasion was inconsistent with Israel's traditional military doctrine. In short, the democratic peace theory does not fail to explain Israel's invasion of Lebanon because external threats or the distribution of power matter more; rather, the democratic peace theory gets it wrong because it fails to adequately capture the *domestic* mechanisms that lead to war and peace. By focusing solely on types of government—democracy versus nondemocracy—the theory conceals the many other domestic political factors that affect decisions about war and peace.

Israel's War in Lebanon

Well before the invasion of Lebanon in June 1982, Israel had been concerned about political developments in its divided northern

---

7. For more on this point, see Margaret G. Hermann and Charles W. Kegley, Jr., "Rethinking Democracy and International Peace: Perspectives From Political Psychology," *International Studies Quarterly*, Vol. 39, No. 4 (December 1995), pp. 511–533.

8. See Deborah D. Avant, *Political Institutions and Military Change: Lessons From Peripheral Wars* (Ithaca, N.Y.: Cornell University Press, 1994).

neighbor. From as early as the 1950s, successive Israeli governments supported the Christian Maronite faction in Lebanon, which was perceived as more likely to initiate peace negotiations with Israel if it established majority control.[9] By the late 1970s, when it became clear that the Christian Maronites would not establish majority control, they increasingly sought Israeli intervention both to rid Lebanon of Syrian influence and to eliminate their domestic political rivals. Yet, contrary to the Maronite leader Bashir Jumayyil's belief that "[Israeli Prime Minister] Menachem Begin's government would be more likely to take a forceful position on the Lebanese question," when Begin came to power in 1977, the Israeli government continued with its cautious policy.[10] For example, the Litani Operation of March 1978 was far smaller than the Maronite leader had expected from the new right-wing Israeli government. Throughout this IDF (Israeli Defense Forces) operation in southern Lebanon, no attempt was made to engage Syrian army units; instead, Israel aimed to punish the PLO for recent terrorist attacks and to create a security zone that could subsequently be patrolled by UN peacekeepers.[11]

In the summer of 1981, renewed PLO attacks on Israel's northern border convinced Prime Minister Begin that Israel had to mount a large-scale operation to drive the PLO out of southern Lebanon. Begin brought a plan for such a major military initiative (code named ORANIM or Big Pines) to the cabinet for approval in December 1981. The plan, which called for a major assault toward the Beirut-Damascus highway and the outskirts of Beirut in a joint operation by the IDF and Bashir Jumayyil's Phalangists, was not approved by the cabinet.[12] Then, on June 3, 1982, after an Israeli ambassador was attacked in London, Israeli air strikes were authorized even though

---

9. For good overviews of Israel's policy toward Lebanon, see Ze'ev Schiff and Ehud Ya'ari, *Israel's Lebanon War* (New York: Simon and Schuster, 1984); Avner Yaniv, *Dilemmas of Security: Politics, Strategy, and the Israeli Experience in Lebanon* (New York: Oxford University Press, 1987), chap. 2; and Itamar Rabinovich, *The War for Lebanon, 1970–1983* (Ithaca, N.Y.: Cornell University Press, 1984).

10. Schiff and Ya'ari, *Israel's Lebanon War*, p. 24.

11. On the Litani operation, see Yair Evron, *War and Intervention in Lebanon: The Israeli-Syrian Deterrence Dialogue* (Baltimore, Md.: Johns Hopkins University Press, 1987), pp. 71–82.

12. The explicit goals of ORANIM included the creation of a twenty-five-mile (forty-kilometer) PLO-free zone north of Israel's border; the withdrawal of all Syrian forces from Lebanon; the destruction of PLO headquarters in Beirut and the expulsion of all PLO forces from Lebanon; and a peace treaty with a unified

the prime minister, chief of staff, and the heads of military intelligence knew that the PLO had recently issued a directive to respond to any further air bombardments by shelling Israeli settlements. As Katyusha rockets once more fell on the Galilean settlements, the cabinet was convened for an emergency session to vote on a full-scale operation designed to silence the PLO artillery once and for all. This June 5 cabinet meeting approved Operation Peace for Galilee by a vote of 14 to 2. The following day, the IDF's regular forces and reserve personnel were ordered to cross into Lebanon.[13]

CAN NEOREALISM ACCOUNT FOR THE WAR DECISION?

Critics of the democratic peace theory might argue that neorealism can better account for Israel's war decision. According to this argument, the Israeli invasion was a reaction to the increased PLO threat and new external conditions that provided opportunities for war. A neorealist account thus dismisses the role of domestic politics in the war decision, assuming that *any* Israeli government would have acted in the same manner given Israel's external situation. Like the democratic peace theory, neorealism ignores the details of a country's government at any given moment.[14]

Lebanon, under the domination of the Christian Maronites. An implicit goal was to change the military and strategic status quo in the Middle East. The Begin government hoped to increase Israeli control over the West Bank and Gaza strip by initiating a process that would lead to the establishment of a Palestinian state in Jordan. With an Israeli military victory, the terrorists gone from Lebanon, and the PLO in ruins, Defense Minister Ariel Sharon believed that moderate Palestinian leaders in the West Bank would be willing to negotiate for an "autonomy" plan. On the motivations behind the war, see Shai Feldman and Heda Rechnitz-Kijner, *Deception, Consensus and War: Israel in Lebanon* (Tel Aviv: Jaffee Center for Strategic Studies, October 1984), pp. 3, 10–25; Shlomo Aronson, "Israel's Leaders, Domestic Order and Foreign Policy, June 1981–June 1983," *Jerusalem Journal of International Relations*, Vol. 6, No. 4 (1982–1983), pp. 21–22; Dan Horowitz, "Israel's War in Lebanon: New Patterns of Strategic Thinking and Civilian-Military Relations," *Journal of Strategic Studies*, Vol. 6, No. 3 (September 1983), p. 91; Rabinovich, *The War for Lebanon*, p. 122; and A. Mack, "Israel's Lebanon War," *Australian Outlook*, Vol. 37, No. 1 (April 1983), pp. 5–6.

13. As I suggest below, the cabinet did not approve ORANIM on June 5, 1982. Nevertheless, during the course of the war, Israel incrementally implemented this large-scale military initiative. Operation Peace for Galilee eventually became indistinguishable from the plans for ORANIM that the cabinet had rejected earlier.

14. On the neorealist explanation for Israel's military strategy, see Yaniv, *Dilemmas of Security*; and Avner Yaniv and Robert J. Lieber, "Personal Whim or Strategic Imperative? The Israeli Invasion of Lebanon," *International Security*, Vol. 8, No. 2 (Fall 1983), pp. 117–142.

According to some proponents of the democratic peace argument, severe external threats may override the pacifying effects of democracy. For example, Randall Schweller suggests that the foreign policies of small democratic countries will often fail to conform to the predictions of the democratic peace argument. Citing Israel as a deviant case, Schweller argues that the foreign policies of small democracies will not be "constrained by those elements that have ruled out preventive war for other democracies—liberal moral values, party politics, pacifistic public opinion, and liberal complaisance."[15]

If extreme external threats override the otherwise pacifistic tendencies of democracy, then Israel's invasion of Lebanon would merely be an outlier case that would not pose a serious challenge to the democratic peace theory. However, as I argue below, Israel's foreign policy choice is not explained by its external security environment. As a result, Israel's war decision presents a substantial challenge to the democratic peace argument.

In order to see Israel's invasion of Lebanon in 1982 as a rational response to external constraints, we must conclude that the PLO would not be able to return to southern Lebanon following the war; the Syrians would be quickly defeated; the Christian Maronites would succeed in creating a new ruling coalition after the war; and the war would not jeopardize the Israeli-Egyptian peace treaty. In 1982, there was little reason to have confidence in any of these conclusions.

First, unless Israeli troops were to remain in postwar Lebanon— an impossibly expensive commitment—there would be little to stop the PLO or Syria from returning.[16] Second, the need to move cautiously due to lack of cabinet approval for ORANIM was bound to benefit Syria; it would allow Syria the time to reinforce its positions and attack the slow-moving IDF: "Israel's ability to defeat the Syrians quickly and forcefully was . . . undermined by the requirements of deception on the Israeli domestic plane."[17] Moreover, an attack on the Syrians that was not preceded by a Syrian provocation

15. Randall L. Schweller, "Domestic Structure and Preventive War: Are Democracies More Pacific?" World Politics, Vol. 44, No. 2 (January 1992), p. 267.

16. Feldman and Rechnitz-Kijner, Deception, p. 7.

17. Ibid., p. 69. Feldman and Rechnitz-Kijner argue that the cabinet's rejection of ORANIM meant that the "architects of Israel's intervention" had to misrepresent the true objectives of the war both prior to the war decision on June 5 and during the war's initial stages. As a result, there could be no quick and decisive thrust into Lebanon. Since the cabinet had not approved a large-scale operation, the IDF

would be more likely to spill over to the Golan Heights, provide an incentive for Soviet intervention, or impel other Arab states to join the battle against Israel.[18] In addition, Israel could not expect an easy victory despite its local qualitative and quantitative superiority. In the event, the Syrian air force and air defense systems were quickly defeated, but its ground troop formations did not collapse.[19]

Third, the fact that Lebanon was divided among a number of powerful forces meant that the Christian Maronites could not succeed in solidifying their rule in a new government. Moreover, the Israeli leadership had little reason to assume that, even if the Christian Maronites were able to suppress their rivals, they would adopt a pro-Israeli position.[20] Fourth, a full-scale invasion might cause a negative reaction in Egypt and jeopardize the newly achieved peace. As Efraim Inbar notes, "The Peace Treaty . . . [was] an additional political constraint on Israel's freedom of action. One consequence of the Treaty [should have been] a greater Israeli consideration for Egyptian sensitivities to Israeli-initiated regional moves."[21] Peace with Egypt made Israel *more* rather than less secure, and hence removed an incentive to initiate war in the early 1980s: "The Peace Treaty with Egypt . . . offered Israel the possibility of at least partial tranquillity obtained through political means, without the recurrent need to resort to military power."[22]

---

could only advance incrementally and gradually toward Beirut and the Beirut-Damascus highway. Inevitably, this meant that Israel was bound to lose. See Feldman and Rechnitz-Kijner, *Deception*, especially pp. 37, 41, 66, 70; see also Schiff and Ya'ari, *Israel's Lebanon War*, pp. 109–110, 203.

18. Feldman and Rechnitz-Kijner, *Deception*, pp. 7–8; and Evron, *War and Intervention*, pp. 189, 201.

19. Furthermore, given the fact that Syria had long played a stabilizing role in Lebanon, it is odd that Israel would view Syria as a threat in 1982. Prior to the Lebanon war, Syria avoided taking any actions that might provoke the IDF to attack. In Amos Perlmutter's words, "Syria was acting as a status-quo Arab power, not as a belligerent and recalcitrant Arab neighbor." Amos Perlmutter, "Begin's Rhetoric and Sharon's Tactics," *Foreign Affairs*, Vol. 16, No. 1 (Fall 1982), p. 78; see also Evron, *War and Intervention*, especially pp. 191, 200, 206.

20. Schiff and Ya'ari, *Israel's Lebanon War*, pp. 242–245; Feldman and Rechnitz-Kijner, *Deception*, p. 7; Rabinovich, *The War for Lebanon*, p. 168; and Evron, *War and Intervention*, pp. 102, 166–167.

21. Efraim Inbar, "Israeli Strategic Thinking After 1973," *Journal of Strategic Studies*, Vol. 6, No. 1 (March 1983), p. 49.

22. Horowitz, "Israel's War in Lebanon," p. 91.

Fifth, Israel's response in June 1982 appears to be an instance of overkill. The Israeli forces participating in the war were four times greater than the Syrian forces based in Lebanon before the war and six times greater than the PLO forces.[23] Indeed, external threats from Lebanon in the early 1980s did not require a large-scale military initiative. As Shai Feldman and Heda Rechnitz-Kijner state, "Israel's tanks did not simply roll into Lebanon on June 6 in an angry response to PLO shelling. Nor was the invasion merely an effort to silence the sources of PLO fire." Similarly, Yair Evron concludes that "it seems that Israel was not over concerned about the danger of [PLO] escalation . . . the threat of instability was in fact sought by Israel."[24]

Sixth, a neorealist argument does not explain why the invasion took place in 1982, and not earlier. If changes in the external situation in Lebanon after 1977 account for the government's decision, then why didn't a full-scale invasion occur in 1978, 1979, 1980, or 1981? Syria had mended its fences with the PLO by the late 1970s, and the PLO had already taken on the trappings of a conventional armed force long before June 1982. Why did it take five years for Israel to react to this new strategic situation?

Finally, a large scale invasion was not the optimal military solution, even though Israel has traditionally advocated an offensive strategy. Neorealists could argue that Israel's resource constraints dictate its military doctrine—an offensive doctrine and strategy linked to Israel's lack of strategic depth, limited manpower capabilities, and difficulties of resupply.[25] These constraints compel Israel to fight on enemy territory; initiate war rather than wait to absorb the first strike; and decisively defeat the enemy rather

---

23. Ibid., p. 100, n. 24. The size of the Syrian deployment in Lebanon suggests that it was not intended for an attack on Israel. In fact, the imbalance of Syrian and Israeli forces in Lebanon and Syria's deteriorating relations with Iraq and Egypt made Syria reluctant to confront Israel in Lebanon. See Evron, *War and Intervention*, pp. 130, 201.

24. Feldman and Rechnitz-Kijner, *Deception*, p. 21; and Evron, *War and Intervention*, p. 111. PLO activity against Israel in the year preceding the war supports Evron's claim. Direct threats to the northern settlements had been removed by U.S. mediation, and the number of Katyusha attacks had become negligible. See Horowitz, "Israel's War in Lebanon," p. 91; and Dan Horowitz and Moshe Lissak, "Democracy and National Security in a Protracted Conflict," *Jerusalem Quarterly*, Vol. 51 (Summer 1989), p. 8.

25. See Major General Israel Tal, "The Offensive and the Defensive in Israel's Campaigns," *Jerusalem Quarterly*, Vol. 51 (Summer 1989), pp. 41–47; and Horowitz and Lissak, "Democracy and National Security in a Protracted Conflict," p. 20. In general, offensive doctrines are more useful for small states, such as Israel, that have few resources to absorb a first strike and cannot sustain drawn-out wars of attrition.

than merely limit the damage to its own armed forces.[26]

At first glance, Israel's intervention in Lebanon appears consistent with its offensive military doctrine: the military initiative took the battle to the enemy's territory and delivered the first strike. Indeed, Begin justified the invasion in preventive terms—a first strike was required to eliminate the threat of a PLO presence in southern Lebanon and deter the Arabs from planning a future war against Israel. An Israeli first strike would prevent the PLO from starting a war in the future, weaken the PLO's patron (Syria), and establish a friendly regime under Bashir Jumayyil.[27] As Avner Yaniv and Robert Lieber note, "any lengthy delay of a major Israeli move posed serious risks. Specifically, by leaving the initiative to the PLO, Israel faced the near certainty of yet another war of attrition on the July 1981 scale—or larger—but initiated by the Palestinians at a time of their own choosing."[28]

Nonetheless, ORANIM was inconsistent with Israel's traditional military doctrine in three ways. First, to rid the whole of Lebanon of PLO units, the IDF would have had to engage in lengthy low-level warfare in urban environments populated by thousands of civilians. Certainly this kind of warfare was not consistent with Israel's traditional strategy of quick, decisive advances.[29] Second, in order to realize the far-reaching goals of the plan, Israel would have had to retain a police force in Lebanon to ensure that the PLO did not return to the south, as well as to bolster the Christian Maronite contingent. Such a police force would have been costly, and would have been inconsistent with Israel's traditional policy of avoiding long, drawn-out wars of attrition. Third, prior to the war, there was no reason to assume

---

26. Randall Schweller puts the point well: "the strategic military doctrine of the Israeli Defense Forces (IDF) stresses speed, maintaining the initiative, and the iron law of fighting on—or quickly transferring the fighting to—the opponent's territory. To meet these requirements, the IDF will not hesitate to launch a preventive attack if the security of the state is endangered; it is an offensive doctrine motivated by self-defense." See "Domestic Structure and Preventive War," p. 266; see also Horowitz, "Israel's War in Lebanon," p. 89.

27. See Aronson, "Israel's Leaders," p. 20. Sharon also defined Operation Peace for Galilee as a preventive war—the invasion prevented the planned PLO destruction campaign for northern Israel. See *Ma'ariv* (Israel), July 7, 1982.

28. Yaniv and Lieber, "Personal Whim or Strategic Imperative?" p. 132.

29. Evron, *War and Intervention*, pp. 138–139. The IDF is organized around armored divisions with few first-line infantry units, and is better suited to fighting in large open spaces than in built-up urban areas.

that Israel would achieve a visible, decisive victory—a key prerequisite to Israel's offensive doctrine. The likelihood that the Soviet Union
would intervene when the Syrian forces were attacked was bound to
undermine Israel's willingness to seek a rapid operative success on
the battlefield.[30] Nor was it advisable for Israel to reveal its high-tech
weaponry in an initiative that did not threaten Israel's survival: "The
air-force's stunning victory over the surface-to-air missiles came at
the cost of disclosing the possession of technology that would have
been better saved for the contingency of a genuine war of survival."[31]
In short, it is not at all clear that a large-scale military initiative in
Lebanon was the best solution:

In the invasion of Lebanon, the IDF and [Defense Minister Ariel]
Sharon adhered to a purely offensive doctrine despite geographic,
demographic, and political circumstances that made a quick and
decisive victory impossible. If such a victory was unlikely, then a
defensive approach offered a better chance to reduce casualties and
increase stamina. Sharon's plan was implausible.[32]

To sum up, the neorealist argument is inconclusive. Since Israel's
security environment would have equally supported a decision not
to go to war, neorealism does not explain why Israel chose
war. Moreover, a large-scale military operation would undermine
Israel's security and hinder effective deterrence. While a small-scale
invasion along the lines of the Litani Operation would have been
consistent with external exigencies, Israel's invasion of Lebanon in
1982 does not satisfy our expectations of how Israel should have acted,
given its external constraints. As Michael Handel puts it: "the war in
Lebanon was a strategic blunder—an unnecessary self-inflicted disaster . . . Under Begin, Israel's national security policy became even further removed from an objective evaluation of its situation."[33]

---

30. Despite Israel's qualitative and quantitative advantage, PLO strongholds in
southern Lebanon could not be defeated in just a few days. It took the IDF well
over a week to reach the Phalange, a distance of only ninety kilometers. In particular, the IDF encountered difficulties in the refugee camps near Tyre and in
Sidon, where PLO forces fought fiercely. On how the PLO resistance thwarted the
Israeli timetable, see Schiff and Ya'ari, *Israel's Lebanon War*, chap. 8.

31. Ibid., p. 307; see also Michael Handel, "The Evolution of Israeli Strategy: The
Psychology of Insecurity and the Quest for Absolute Security," in Williamson
Murray, Macgregor Know, and Alvin Bernstein, eds., *The Making of Strategy:
Rulers, States, and War* (New York: Cambridge University Press, 1995), p. 551.

32. Handel, "The Evolution of Israeli Strategy," p. 575.

33. Ibid., pp. 570, 574.

Similarly, according to Zeev Maoz:

What was supposed to be a "quick and efficient" military operation gradually turned into a military and political disaster lasting nearly three years. When Israel pulled out of southern Lebanon in June 1985, it was no better off than when it had started the invasion, especially when the economic costs of the war and the concomitant social turmoil in Israel are considered.[34]

DOMESTIC POLITICS AND ISRAEL'S WAR DECISION

If neorealism fails to explain Israel's decision to invade Lebanon in 1982, can a domestic political explanation do better? Israel's war decision might be explained if we can trace the war decision to the military's involvement in the decision making process.[35] ORANIM was an IDF initiative that was well suited to the military's own needs; an emphasis on diplomacy and negotiation would have relegated the army to a secondary role in national security policy making. According to Yoram Peri, "The Prime Minister . . . blindly followed the recommendations of the powerful Chief of Staff, his top military adviser." Similarly, Athanassios Platias argues that "Israel's offensive strategy [in the Lebanon war] can be explained in terms of the parochial interests of the military and its power in the decision-making system."[36]

This explanation misses the mark. Israel was not transformed into a garrison state, and the military did not drag civilian leaders into an unwanted war. The general staff was not running the government; the government was not a mere rubber stamp for the military's proposals; nor did the civilian echelon abdicate responsibility for mili-

---

34. Zeev Maoz, "Power, Capabilities, and Paradoxical Conflict Outcomes," World Politics, Vol. 41, No. 2 (January 1989), p. 257.

35. For studies that trace aggressive military strategies to the military's preferences, see, for example, Scott D. Sagan, "More Will Be Worse," in Scott D. Sagan and Kenneth N. Waltz, The Spread of Nuclear Weapons: A Debate (New York: W.W. Norton, 1995); Barry Posen, The Sources of Military Doctrine: France, Britain, and Germany Between the World Wars (Ithaca, N.Y.: Cornell University Press, 1984); and Jack Snyder, The Ideology of the Offensive: Military Decision Making and the Disasters of 1914 (Ithaca, N.Y.: Cornell University Press, 1984). For a critique, see Elizabeth Kier, "Culture and Military Doctrine," International Security, Vol. 19, No. 4 (Spring 1995), pp. 65–93.

36. Athanassios G. Platias, "High Politics in Small Countries: An Inquiry into the Security Policies of Greece, Israel and Sweden," Ph.D. dissertation, Cornell University, 1986, p. 436; and Yoram Peri, Between Battles and Ballots: Israeli Military Politics, 2nd ed. (New York: Cambridge University Press), p. 268.

tary strategy and doctrine. In fact, the IDF's operations followed the orders of the defense minister. It was Ariel Sharon who advocated a major thrust toward Beirut's outskirts and the Beirut-Damascus highway. He (and the cabinet) gradually permitted the IDF to exceed the limited twenty-five mile deep invasion of Lebanon. Moreover, the IDF did not exploit numerous military advantages on the field; this is also inconsistent with the argument that the military was to blame. As the chief of the northern command later claimed:

This war was characterized . . . by the intervention of the political echelon in all the stages of the battle . . . the IDF did not exploit its success against the Syrians, which was quite tempting, and did not take control of territories, which are now occupied by the enemy, [but] were then empty of enemy forces. This was the result of the special character of the war, one in which the considerations were not only military.[37]

Moreover, ORANIM was formulated under the directives of the civilian defense minister, though Chief of Staff Rafael Eitan certainly agreed with most aspects of it. While Eitan was certainly more sympathetic to the Likud's ideology than his predecessor had been, the "main changes in Israeli strategic thinking [from 1980] are connected however to Ariel Sharon's ascendance in security affairs."[38] Nor did the military as a whole endorse an offensive strategy in Lebanon. In short, the problem was not that the military echelon undertook actions that civilian leaders had not authorized. On the contrary, the IDF followed the instructions of the defense minister to the letter: "Even if Sharon did not have the full Cabinet behind him, his words were law in the army."[39] As Yehuda Ben Meir notes, "[The Lebanon War] is a typical example of the military echelon under explicit instructions from the minister of defense creating a fait accompli in the field and thereby maneuvering the civilian echelon into an impossible position."[40]

If the military cannot be held responsible, how can we explain the decision to go to war? I argue that democratic Israel chose war in 1982 because of the distribution of domestic power. In the sections

---

37. Quoted in Feldman and Rechnitz-Kijner, *Deception*, p. 33.

38. Inbar, "Israeli Strategic Thinking," p. 37.

39. Schiff and Ya'ari, *Israel's Lebanon War*, p. 214.

40. Yehuda Ben Meir, *Civil-Military Relations in Israel* (New York: Columbia University Press, 1995), p. 154.

that follow, I examine the foreign policy preferences of the main political parties, the Labor Alignment and the Likud; shifts in the distribution of domestic political power in 1981, which led to a more
centralized government; and civil-military relations. Together, these
factors created an environment that led to the implementation of a
military operation whose goals were very similar to ORANIM.

In the 1977 elections, the Likud wrested power from Labor, which
had long dominated Israel's government.[41] Labor- and Likud-led
governments had very different foreign policy orientations. Since
each party attached different degrees of legitimacy to the use of force,
military strategy was bound to change as one leadership replaced the
other. I link changes in Israel's military strategy to these fundamental domestic political realignments. Specifically, the Likud's leadership was consolidated in 1981, when the ruling coalition became both
less heterogeneous and more right-wing; this provided a more hospitable environment for war-prone actors to act on their preferences.
Sharp breaks in Israel's foreign policy toward Lebanon were bound
to occur not because the external environment had changed or the
military preferred the use of force, but because the second Begin government was both willing and able to alter previous policies.

THE LEGITIMACY OF FORCE. The different views of left and right
regarding the legitimacy of using force to solve international conflicts
can be traced to the first years of the new state. Labor's belief was
that "without military strength Israel would not survive, but that it
could not survive on military strength alone. It was not enough to
have a policy of war; it needed to have a policy of peace."[42] To be
sure, Labor-led governments were more than willing to use force to
preserve the status quo and punish attempts to violate Israel's territorial integrity. But since the Labor party believed that the Arab-

---

41. In 1977, Labor lost office after a rule of twenty-nine years after independence
and fifteen years prior to statehood. The Likud party (45 seats) was able to form
a government with Moshe Dayan's party (1 seat), the religious Mafdal party (12
seats), the religious Aguda party (4 seats), and the Democratic Movement for
Change (15 seats). The new ruling coalition thus had the support of 77 Knesset
members out of 120 votes. For a good overview of how increasing tension
between the Ashkenazi and the Sephardic communities in Israel contributed to
the 1977 electoral realignment, see Efraim Torgovnik, "Likud 1977–81: The
Consolidation of Power," in Robert O. Freedman, ed., *Israel in the Begin Era* (New
York: Praeger, 1982).

42. Peter Y. Medding, *The Founding of Israeli Democracy, 1948–1967* (New York:
Oxford University Press, 1990), p. 46.

Israeli conflict could not be solved by military means, it consistently rejected going to war for goals beyond national survival. The Labor leadership developed a strategy of deterrence that, without excluding the possible use of force, placed emphasis on realizing political objectives by accumulating power rather than by its actual application. War was legitimate only if it was defensive and only if the Arab states provided the country with "no choice."[43]

By contrast, according to Herut—and later the Likud—leaders, the only way to achieve a stable peace was to use force to drive out the Arab invaders. During the battle for independence, the forerunners of the Likud perceived military force as a legitimate means for resolving international conflicts. In fact, during the 1940s, during the British mandate, both Begin and Yitzhak Shamir objected to the Hagana's policy of self-restraint, and demanded a large-scale offensive against the British.[44] As Peter Y. Medding points out, the Israeli right "continued to advocate the use of force and militarily imposed solutions in Israel's relations with its neighbors, in pursuit of Israel's undisputed historical rights to the territories on both sides of the Jordan."[45] Thus, the Likud ascendancy in 1977 was not a trivial domestic political development.

Consistent with the legitimacy it assigned to the use of force, the Likud looked for opportunities to use the IDF to change Israel's strategic situation once it gained control of the government in 1977.[46] It believed that Israel's military power could dictate at least a partial resolution to the Israeli-Palestinian conflict. Prior to the Lebanon war, both Sharon and Begin indicated that military action could arrange the domestic political order in Lebanon to Israel's advantage. Begin identified "wars of choice" as legitimate; Sharon assumed that force should be used to attain national objectives, and not simply for self-defense; and Chief of Staff Eitan argued that the IDF war machine should be put to good use by going to war against the PLO. In other

---

43. Efraim Inbar, *War and Peace in Israeli Politics: Labor Party Positions on National Security* (Boulder, Colo.: Lynne Rienner, 1991), pp. 123–124.

44. Medding, *The Founding of Israeli Democracy*, p. 64.

45. Ibid.

46. Horowitz, "Israel's War in Lebanon," p. 93. See also Inbar, "Israeli Strategic Thinking." Inbar argues that under the Labor-dominated government, Israel's military doctrine reflected a defensive posture. From 1973–77, Israel attempted to create defensible borders in order to absorb a first strike. This new doctrine was partly a reflection of the new borders established in 1967, but it was also a function of Labor's rejection of an offensive doctrine.

words, there was a consensus that Israel's military superiority should be used for purposes other than ensuring the country's independence and its survival. Under Begin's Likud-dominated government, there was less willingness to rely on diplomacy to solve security problems and an increased tendency to authorize preemptive strikes.[47]

In contrast, in April 1982, when Begin and Sharon briefed the Labor opposition in the Knesset regarding ORANIM, Party Secretary (and former IDF chief of staff) Chaim Bar-Lev argued that the goals of expelling the Syrians from Lebanon and creating a pro-Israel government "did not justify such a war." Later, the Labor opposition supported the Likud government's decision to invade Lebanon only because it was couched as a defensive action: "Unquestionably, most Laborites . . . preferred an enlarged version of the March 1978 Litani Operation, which was characterized by modest political goals, a limited territorial scope, and avoidance of contact with the Syrians."[48] Only the creation of a twenty-five-mile free zone justified the deployment of the IDF in the name of self-defense. Thus, changes in the strategic philosophies of Israel's rulers led to increasing legitimization of the use of force for purposes other than national survival. This suggests that we must examine the attitudes of important decision makers in assessing whether a country is likely to make war.

PARLIAMENTARY DEMOCRACY AND THE USE OF FORCE. While the defeat of the Labor Alignment in the May 1977 elections brought the hawkish Likud party to power, the Likud's capacity to implement its foreign policy preferences were limited in the first Begin government because it shared power in a coalition government with more moderate groups. Since the Likud did not command a clear majority of votes, a vote of no confidence from its coalition partners could bring down the government. The Likud could not afford to alienate these parties.

The Democratic Movement for Change (DMC) was a particularly powerful member of the ruling coalition. It had been the pivotal party in the post-election coalition negotiations, dictating whether Labor or the Likud would serve as the dominant member of the new ruling coalition. This gave the DMC a great deal of leverage

---

47. See *Ma'ariv*, August 20, 1982; *Yediot Acharonot* (Israel), May 14, 1982; *Ha'aretz* (Israel), November 24, 1982; and Feldman and Rechnitz-Kijner, *Deception*, p. 18.

48. Inbar, *War and Peace in Israeli Politics*, pp. 126–127.

over both ministerial postings and policy outcomes. Since the defection of the DMC or any other significant member of the coalition would cause the government to collapse, the Likud members of the government had to avoid any policy which would antagonize them.

In practice, this meant that more moderate ministers in the cabinet such as Defense Minister Ezer Weizman, Deputy Prime Minister Yigal Yadin, and Foreign Minister Moshe Dayan were able to vote against the hawkish moves proposed by the Likud.[49] For example, Sharon's campaign to expand Jewish settlement in the occupied territories was stymied by the combined opposition of Likud moderate Weizman and DMC leader Yadin. Yadin's opposition also helped to postpone the transfer of two hawkish Likud ministers (Sharon and Yitzhak Moda'i) to head the ministries of defense and foreign affairs. In David Pollock's words:

As long as [the DMC] was in Begin's government, it did have some influence on policy, at least in foreign affairs . . . speeding up the treaty with Egypt and slowing down the growth of settlements on the West Bank . . . the prospect of a divisive cabinet or Knesset confrontation, and the occasional procedural delays even after . . . decision[s] were announced, did "complicate" settlement policy to some extent . . . Clearly, the party was able to exert some "moderating" influence on Begin's government.[50]

In short, during Begin's first term in office, "people alien to the Herut movement—Moshe Dayan, Ezer Weizman, and others—went against the grain of the Herut movement's policies and diluted its message."[51] Coalitional politics stymied the extremism of the Herut faction of the Likud bloc. Begin and other Herut supporters bowed to the views of their coalition partners in order to maintain the Knesset's confidence; the constraints of a parliamentary democratic system ensured that the hard-line Herut was unable to implement its preferred military strategies.[52]

---

49. Avi Shlaim and Avner Yaniv, "Domestic Politics and Foreign Policy in Israel," *International Affairs* (Spring 1980), pp. 246, 255–256.

50. David Pollock, "Likud in Power: Divided We Stand," in Freedman, ed., *Israel in the Begin Era*, pp. 31–32; see also p. 50.

51. Rabinovich, *The War for Lebanon*, p. 127; and Perlmutter, "Begin's Rhetoric and Sharon's Tactics," pp. 67, 71.

52. While in this case the diversity of political parties helped to moderate foreign policy, fragmentation can also generate adverse outcomes such as logrolling and deadlock. For more on the foreign policy implications of divisions within the

By contrast, the coalition government that emerged following the 1981 elections gave Herut a far more dominant position and minimized the ideological differences among the coalition members.[53] Parties that had previously been essential for the maintenance of legislative confidence were no longer needed to make up the new government. Thus, the ruling coalition had far less need to emphasize consensus and compromise. Indeed, the government was much more homogeneous with the resignation of partners from the old regime— i.e., the DMC members, headed by Deputy Prime Minister Yigal Yadin, and Dayan. Even within Herut itself, there was a weakening of the dovish sector, headed by Ezer Weizman. It was then that the security conception changed.[54]

In sum, contrary to popular belief, it makes little sense to attribute Israel's decision to use force solely to the idiosyncratic views or the decision making style of Defense Minister Ariel Sharon. To be sure, Sharon did exploit his position as Defense Minister. But Sharon did not evade the supervisory controls of the country's parliamentary system. On the contrary, it was the nature of Israel's parliamentary system that provided Sharon with new-found room to maneuver in the early 1980s. The increased cohesiveness of the Likud ruling coalition after the 1981 election made war a possible solution to Israel's security problems. Israel's foreign policy toward Lebanon changed in lock-step with changes in the composition of the governing coalition. As Israeli democracy took on more of the features of a majoritarian-type system, foreign security policy shifted to reflect the views of the Herut majority. In the second Begin government, Herut was freed from the fetters that previously constrained its control over foreign

---

government, see Joe D. Hagan, "Domestic Political Systems and War Proneness," *Mershon International Studies Review*, Vol. 38, No. 2 (October 1994), pp. 192–198.

53. In 1981, the ruling coalition consisted of Likud (48 seats), Mafdal (6 seats), Tami (3 seats), and Aguda (4 seats). The Techiya (Rebirth) party (3 seats) also supported the government but did not participate in the coalition.

54. Aronson, "Israel's Leaders," p. 17. The Likud did not have to contend with the moderate DMC, but it did have to retain the confidence of the more right-wing Techiya party, which had gained three seats in the elections. The Likud coalition had a mere 61 Knesset seats out of 120. With this one-vote majority, the government had a strong incentive not to antagonize Techiya's representatives by being too moderate. Furthermore, the need to retain the confidence of Sharon's supporters in the Knesset also influenced foreign policy outcomes. After the 1981 elections, Begin was obliged to turn the post of defense minister over to Sharon in exchange for his followers' support. See Aronson, "Israel's Leaders," pp. 171–178; see also Perlmutter, "Begin's Rhetoric and Sharon's Tactics," p. 73.

policy. Indeed, the Likud victory in the 1981 elections meant that Begin could form what amounted to a war cabinet, since hawkish Herut ministers took the place of the moderates of the first Begin cabinet. Thus, foreign policy did not change simply because the Likud had different ideas regarding the use of force and national security; rather, the Likud, which had long advocated the use of force to generate changes in the status quo, was finally in a position where its views were bound to count.

CIVIL-MILITARY RELATIONS AND THE USE OF FORCE. While Israel's military has often played an important role in determining both military strategy and domestic political developments, by and large the military echelon upholds the "principle of the subordination of the armed forces to political authority."[55] As Ben Meir puts it:

Time and again throughout Israel's short history, the military has complied . . . with the operational directives of its civilian superiors—even when these directives were diametrically opposed to the recommendations, desires, and judgment of the military leadership.[56]

Nevertheless, Israel's civil-military relations are characterized by a great deal of overlap among the responsibilities of the defense minister, prime minister, and chief of staff. In the Transition Law of 1949, the defense minister was authorized to act for the cabinet. The army was subordinate to the defense minister, and the cabinet's dealings with the armed forces would be through his post.[57] Thus, the defense minister is both a representative of the government and the "supreme chief" of the army. He or she effectively becomes the primary link between the government and the army.[58] Since the defense minister is the representative of the government to the army and can authorize military operations, he or she can cut off the rest of the political echelon from military developments. Yet, as head of the cabinet (i.e., "first among equals"), the prime minister is also granted authority regarding the use of force. The defense minister cannot authorize

55. See, for example, Moshe Lissak, "Paradoxes of Israeli Civil-Military Relations: An Introduction," *Journal of Strategic Studies*, Vol. 6, No. 3 (September 1983), p. 2; and Shimon Shetreet, "The Gray Area of War Powers: The Case of Israel," *Jerusalem Quarterly*, Vol. 45 (Winter 1988), p. 29. For more on how the military has influenced war and peace decision making, especially before the Six Day War, see Peri, *Between Bombs and Bullets*, pp. 245–251.

56. Ben Meir, *Civil-Military Relations in Israel*, p. 128.

57. Ibid., pp. 31, 35.

58. Ibid., p. 41.

actions without the prime minister's approval since this would contravene the wishes of the cabinet, to which all ministers are subordinate.[59] As Ben Meir states, "if they stand together, they are almost unbeatable; apart, each walks on thin ice . . . Without the support of the prime minister, the defense minister could find it very difficult to retain the confidence of the cabinet."[60] Finally, the chief of staff (*Ramatkal*), who is responsible for the operational dimensions of the IDF and is subordinate to the defense minister, is also granted an important role in the decision making process. In the 1976 "Basic Law: The Army," the chief of staff is designated as the commander of the army, albeit subordinate to the authority of the cabinet.[61] Since the defense minister appoints the chief of staff subject to cabinet approval, a government that commands the support of a majority in the Knesset can select an officer whose views correspond with its own interpretation of national security.

When these three posts have been filled by representatives of rival political parties (or rival factions of the same party), each has checked the actions of the others. When the posts have been held by actors from the same party, checks to executive action were effectively removed. For example, when David Ben Gurion was both prime minister and defense minister and also had a loyal chief of staff, he was able to authorize and implement far-reaching military actions without prior cabinet approval. Ben Gurion's defense policy, which led to

---

59. Shetreet, "The Gray Area of War Powers," pp. 33–34; and Ben Meir, *Civil-Military Relations in Israel*, pp. 61, 74. According to the 1976 "Basic Law: The Army," the authority of the cabinet to control the army is vested in the minister of defense, thus defining his role as a "superior chief of staff." Yet, the "Basic Law" can also be interpreted as granting the minister this role only to the extent that the cabinet and the prime minister give it to him. See Daniel Shimshoni, *Israeli Democracy: The Middle of the Journey* (New York: Free Press, 1982), p. 196. This distinction proved important in decision making prior to (and during) the Lebanon invasion. Sharon was able to direct the military initiative as he saw fit because he had Begin's support. But once he lost this support, his ability to act as a "superior chief of staff" was removed.

60. Ben Meir, *Civil-Military Relations in Israel*, pp. 102–103.

61. Shetreet, "The Gray Area of War Powers," p. 32; and Ben Meir, *Civil-Military Relations in Israel*, pp. 42–43. During the "waiting period" before the Six Day War, Chief of Staff Yitzhak Rabin had almost full ministerial responsibility thrust upon him. And following the surprise of the Yom Kippur War, the Agranat Committee suggested that the chief of staff, rather than the defense minister, should be held responsible for the mishap. See Shetreet, "The Gray Area of War Powers," p. 35; and Ben Meir, *Civil-Military Relations in Israel*, p. 39.

the Israeli agreements with France and Britain, is a case in point. Israeli commitments were given without cabinet knowledge. In addition, the decision to undertake the Sinai campaign of 1956 was made by Ben Gurion alone; only after the decision had been made did he inform his cabinet colleagues.[62] Later, Deputy Minister of Defense Shimon Peres was able to go above the head of then Chief of Staff Chaim Laskov and give direct orders to the military because he had the support and backing of Prime Minister Ben Gurion. By contrast, when Moshe Sharett served as prime minister, his capacity to control and direct foreign policy was limited because Defense Minister Pinchas Lavon was loyal to a different Laborite faction, one that had opposing foreign policy preferences.

Similarly, chiefs of staff and other high-ranking military officers have often checked the actions of defense ministers. For example, shortly after the Yom Kippur War, when Defense Minister Dayan ordered an operation that General Israel Tal thought had partisan political aims, Tal insisted on cabinet approval. Since Dayan was largely acting outside the cabinet's authorization, this ultimatum effectively constrained his capacity to initiate any military action.[63] Similarly, when Dayan instructed the commanding officer of the southern command to attack an Egyptian division during the Yom Kippur War, he refused to execute the order until it was also conveyed by the chief of staff. On this occasion, Chief of Staff David Elazar stated: "Whatever the minister tells you is very interesting. However, orders you receive only from me."[64]

Significantly, none of these checks were operative prior to the Lebanon War in 1982. Since Sharon had the support of the prime minister and the chief of staff, and since no other government ministers were high-ranking military officers, he was able to deploy IDF forces without adequate control by the other cabinet members; that is, other cabinet members had no means to ensure against error or fraud.[65]

---

62. Aronson, "Israel's Leaders," p. 6; and Ben Meir, *Civil-Military Relations in Israel*, p. 60. Ben Gurion did discuss the matter with Chief of Staff Dayan and Director General of the Defense Ministry Shimon Peres. Both Dayan and Peres were from the same party as Ben Gurion, and hence loyal to his views; they served less to check Ben Gurion's decision than to confirm it.

63. Peri, *Between Battles and Ballots*, pp. 254–259.

64. Ben Meir, *Civil-Military Relations in Israel*, p. 66.

65. Chief of Staff Rafael Eitan was a firm supporter of continued Israeli control over greater Israel. In 1978, he declared that Israel should never give up the West

Ze'ev Schiff and Ehud Ya'ari put it well:

The three men with rich military experience in the first [Begin] government—Dayan, Weizman, and Yadin—consistently restrained the Cabinet from plunging into any imprudent ventures . . . Other Cabinets had always comprised ministers espousing a variety of views on defense questions, thereby providing a sense of equilibrium in the decision making process. But in Begin's new government, for the first time in the state's history, the group of leading figures who monopolized defense and foreign affairs was monolithic in its hawkish views and its readiness to employ Israel's military power for objectives that went well beyond the country's security needs.[66]

Due to the nature of civil-military relations in Israel and the support of Begin and Eitan, Sharon was able to direct and control the foreign policy making process.[67] Indeed, the cabinet was presented with faits accompli that escalated actions in Lebanon and incrementally led to the implementation of ORANIM. Since Sharon was both a minister in the government and the government's representative in the IDF, he could order military actions, decide on operational matters, and create conditions in the field that compelled the cabinet to authorize an increased Israeli presence in Lebanon. Sharon could move first, while the rest of the cabinet could only respond to actions that he had already taken. In short, Sharon was the primary link between the government and the army, since military strategy was delegated to the defense minister, as in many parliamentary systems. His position

---

Bank, thus identifying the IDF with Herut, one of Israel's domestic political parties. Later, he insisted that the war in Lebanon was a battle for greater Israel. Of particular importance is the fact that he avoided attending cabinet meetings during the first week of the Lebanon invasion, so that he would not be available for comment on Sharon's operational suggestions. See ibid., p. 62.

66. Schiff and Ya'ari, *Israel's Lebanon War*, pp. 38–39.

67. Perlmutter, "Begin's Rhetoric and Sharon's Tactics," pp. 72–73. Scholars disagree as to whether Begin was an accomplice or a victim of Sharon's manipulation of the cabinet. Evidence suggests that Begin was fully aware that Operation Peace for Galilee would extend beyond the twenty-five-mile limit. Begin had advocated a large-scale initiative before Sharon assumed the position of minister of defense, and he had also declared that the IDF would go "as far as Arafat's bunker" to eliminate the PLO threat. Moreover, Begin had previously claimed that if he gave Sharon the position of defense minister, Sharon would surround the Knesset with tanks and stage a coup d'état. Surely one of the reasons Begin appointed a minister he knew would act with or without cabinet approval was that he had already decided to go to war. On Begin's role in the decision making process, see Yaniv, *Dilemmas of Security*, pp. 92–93.

meant that he "dragged the Israeli Cabinet behind him, step by step, into moves that he claimed were dictated by the situation on the ground but were in fact elements of his original grand design."[68] As Arye Naor puts it: "The cabinet . . . was not the one that determined the strategic goals [of the war] . . . Its authority as the supreme commander of the army 'dribbled' and drained into the defense minister's office."[69]

For example, prior to the invasion of Lebanon, the Cabinet's rejection of ORANIM did not mean that ORANIM was shelved. On the contrary, Begin and Sharon implemented it in incrementals. Presenting a modest war plan and gaining approval for a limited initiative was satisfactory; military developments in the field would ensure an expanded Israeli initiative in any case.[70] Indeed, by getting the cabinet to authorize a limited Israeli initiative, the IDF could create conditions in the field that would leave the cabinet with little choice but to authorize greater and greater involvement. Thus, in January and April 1982, after the cabinet had rejected ORANIM, Begin and Sharon proposed that Israel respond to terrorist activity by bombing PLO air bases. Ostensibly, they were trying to create a *casus belli*: "the plan [was] aimed at *inducing* the PLO to react by artillery shelling of Israel's north which, in turn, would provide ample ground for Israel to invade Lebanon . . . the air force raid was intended to catalyze a sequence of events allowing [for] an Israeli

---

68. Shiff and Ya'ari, *Israel's Lebanon War*, p. 302 ; see also Ben Meir, *Civil-Military Relations in Israel*, p. 154; and Arye Naor, "The Israeli Cabinet in the Lebanon War (June 5–9, 1982)," *Jerusalem Quarterly*, Vol. 39 (1986), p. 4.

69. Naor, "The Israeli Cabinet in the Lebanon War," p. 4.

70. That Sharon had decided from the start to implement ORANIM is clear from his statements following the initiation of the war. On interviews given from June 14–18, Sharon claimed that the IDF should hit PLO targets beyond the twenty-five-mile range; that an Israeli presence north of the twenty-five-mile limit was always part of the Peace for Galilee initiative; and that the cabinet had never agreed to the immunity of the PLO beyond this limit. See *Ha'aretz*, June 14, 1982; *Yediot Achronot*, June 18, 1982; and *Ma'ariv*, June 18, 1982. Prime Minister Begin later justified going beyond the twenty-five-mile limit by insisting that the IDF had to advance its force when the Syrians attacked (see *Ha'aretz*, January 25, 1983); this argument is groundless, since an attack on the Syrian forces in Lebanon was part of ORANIM. Indeed, at the start of the war Sharon attempted to goad the Syrians into striking IDF units as a pretext for initiating an Israeli offensive. Sharon reportedly told IDF officers: "It is not clear what the Cabinet will say about the attack on the Syrians. We must therefore continue to advance without creating the impression that a major war is taking place." Quoted in Feldman and Rechnitz-Kijner, *Deception*, p. 31.

invasion."[71] Similarly, when the invasion plan was presented to the cabinet on June 5, Begin and Sharon were careful that the wording of the official cabinet communiqué not limit their options. Vague wording would later allow for a deeper penetration into Lebanon.[72]

Not only did the cabinet ministers assume they were voting in favor of a limited military offensive in Lebanon, but they also assumed that Israeli forces would not confront Syrian armed forces in Lebanon.[73] Indeed, the cabinet war decision states that the "IDF must refrain from attacking the Syrian army." Similarly, in the June 6 Order of the Day, Eitan noted that "this is not a war against Syria." However, Sharon was well aware that Syrian forces were positioned south of the twenty-five-mile line, and that it was therefore unlikely that the PLO forces could be removed without a confrontation.[74] Sharon proposed to the Cabinet that the IDF compel the Syrians to withdraw from positions south of the twenty-five-mile zone by presenting a threat to their rear. He argued that an Israeli presence at the northwestern flank of Syria's forces would compel them to straighten their lines so as not to leave these forces exposed, thus removing their troops from the Beqa'a region. But Sharon, with his military background in fighting Syrian forces, would have known that this reasoning was flawed: in past wars, the Syrians had rarely withdrawn their forces from one area in order to strengthen other positions. Thus, by arguing that an IDF move north of Jazzin was

---

71. Ibid., pp. 26–27 (emphasis added).

72. In the communiqué, the government instructed the IDF to take all the Galilee settlements out of fire-range of terrorists who are "concentrated, they, their headquarters and their bases, in Lebanon." The main headquarters of the PLO was in Beirut, however, well beyond the twenty-five-mile limit. See ibid., p. 11; see also Naor, "The Israeli Cabinet," p. 6; and Evron, *War and Intervention*, p. 127.

73. After the invasion, Minister of Communications Mordechai Zipori, Deputy Prime Minister Simcha Erlich, and Minister of Interior Yosef Burg each stated that they had approved only a twenty-five-mile operation. In Feldman and Rechnitz-Kijner's words, "the weight of evidence is that at the decisive Cabinet meeting on June 5, the operational plan presented was limited to the twenty-five-mile depth." See *Deception*, p. 29; and Schiff and Ya'ari, *Israel's Lebanon War*, pp. 103–106.

74. Ben Meir, *Civil-Military Relations in Israel*, p. 153. Although he told the cabinet otherwise, Sharon later admitted that he knew the Syrians would intervene and that Israel's war aims would include conflict with Syrian ground forces in Lebanon. On June 25, he stated that Israel's war aims included the expulsion of the Syrians from Lebanon. See *Ma'ariv*, June 18, 1982, and June 27, 1982; and *Ha'aretz*, June 30, 1982.

merely a flanking operation to rid the twenty-five-mile zone of Syrian troops, Sharon maneuvered the cabinet into accepting an expanded role for the IDF *north* of the twenty-five-mile zone: "Sharon probably hoped that such a movement would lead the Syrians to attack the IDF units advancing in very close proximity to their own forces stationed in Jazzin, thus providing him with a pretext for opening an offensive against the Syrian forces."[75] Indeed, the Syrian military engagement of the IDF was an inevitable outcome of the advance of this Israeli formation in the central sector in the direction of the Beirut-Damascus highway. While Sharon could not authorize the use of force against the Syrian army on the Beirut-Damascus highway without Cabinet approval, he could order the IDF to "creep northward, hill by hill."

In voting for Operation Peace for Galilee on June 5, the Cabinet was also assured that Beirut was beyond the scope of the invasion. According to Deputy Prime Minister Simcha Ehrlich, Sharon reportedly told the Cabinet that

Beirut is outside the picture. There are foreign embassies there. We must keep away from that place. The aim of Operation Peace for Galilee is to push the [PLO's] artillery and rockets away from our settlements, and not to conquer Beirut. We are today talking about a 25-mile range. This is what the Cabinet is approving.[76]

Yet, since institutional rules gave Sharon control of the IDF, he could authorize its entrance into Beirut, thus compelling the cabinet to deal with these new conditions. In this way, the cabinet was unwittingly compelled to adopt ORANIM even though it had previously rejected it. As Feldman and Rechnitz-Kijner note:

The need to make such tactical choices was thrust upon the Cabinet by a strategic reality which most of its members did not help create. Only after the IDF had already penetrated Beirut's southern and southeastern suburbs was the Cabinet called upon to face this new reality . . . The Cabinet did not decide that Beirut should be the central focus of Israel's effort until the reality of the IDF's presence in Beirut's outskirts had already dictated such a role. The problem of *how* to deal with the PLO in Beirut was thus thrust upon a Cabinet that had never decided *whether* an effort to expel the PLO

---

75. Feldman and Rechnitz-Kijner, *Deception*, p. 31; see also Naor, "The Israeli Cabinet," pp. 5, 9; Horowitz, "Israel's War in Lebanon," p. 86; and Schiff and Ya'ari, *Israel's Lebanon War*, pp. 112–113, 156.

76. Quoted in Feldman and Rechnitz-Kijner, *Deception*, p. 78, n. 48.

from Beirut was worthwhile.[77]

Finally, once hostilities had been initiated, the cabinet had little ability to limit the operational dimension of Peace for Galilee; any move to curtail the scope of the military initiative was bound to harm the troops already on the field. Sharon was able to expand the scope of the war by insisting that further operational measures were essential to protect the lives of Israeli soldiers.[78] As Education Minister Zvulun Hammer put it: "Sharon would draw maps for us with all sorts of unacceptable situations, such that if we were to refuse to approve one move or another which he had proposed, we would have been responsible for numerous casualties among our forces. This did not leave us much choice."[79] In the Knesset, opposition to the war was also muted for weeks due to the perceived need to "rally around the flag" and support the troops in the field. Thus, after the twenty-five-mile limit was crossed, the Labor opposition sided with the Likud to defeat a vote of no confidence by 94-3. The party leaders reasoned that as long as the fighting continued and the safety of the IDF was at stake, criticism must be saved for later.[80]

In sum, the nature of civil-military relations—that both civil and military authority over the IDF was concentrated in one person—forced the rest of the cabinet to move second, so that Begin and Sharon fought the full-scale war they had wanted from the beginning. Yet, the cabinet was hardly blameless.[81] On June 5, Sharon did receive support from most cabinet members for Operation Peace for Galilee; on June 27, the cabinet did not rule out a military move into Beirut; and on October 30, the cabinet demanded that the conditions for an Israeli pullout from Lebanon include the evacuation of all PLO forces from Lebanon, including Beirut. The cabinet went along with

---

77. Feldman and Rechnitz-Kijner, *Deception*, pp. 15–16; and Schiff and Ya'ari, *Israel's Lebanon War*, chap. 10.

78. Feldman and Rechnitz-Kijner, *Deception*, pp. 31–32; and Schiff and Ya'ari, *Israel's Lebanon War*, pp. 165–166.

79. Translated from quotes in *Ha'aretz*, December 20, 1985.

80. Feldman and Rechnitz-Kijner, *Deception*, p. 44; and Inbar, *War and Peace in Israeli Politics*, p. 127.

81. Feldman and Rechnitz-Kijner put the blame for the Lebanon War squarely on Sharon's shoulders, but concede that Sharon did not face strong opposition in the cabinet. Here, posing the counterfactual is helpful. Had Operation Peace for Galilee occurred during the first Begin government, it would have been much harder to "deceive" the cabinet, due to its greater ideological diversity.

most of Sharon's proposals largely because it was an ideologically cohesive coalition that was far more right of center than the previous ruling coalition had been. As Valerie Yorke states:

With Menachem Begin's accession to power in May 1977, Israel's confrontation with Palestinian nationalism was inevitable . . . the traditional Labor-dominated coalition, which had always favoured partition of Palestine, was now replaced by a right-wing coalition committed to the retention of all of Eretz Israel.[82]

Thus, while Sharon manipulated the delegation of war powers to his advantage, it is also important that even the ministers who opposed the war agreed with the Likud's basic policy objectives. Indeed, Feldman and Rechnitz-Kijner concede that "the IDF's advance towards Beirut was not halted by a shortage of Cabinet approvals . . . there is no evidence that the Cabinet rejected any operation which Sharon proposed during the first week of the war." Similarly, according to Charles Freilich, "To a certain degree . . . the war in Lebanon was sanctioned, as Sharon himself has repeatedly claimed, by far greater cabinet approval than any other war in Israel's history." The cabinet allowed itself to be lied to: "they were . . . willing to hide behind a cloak of ostensible ignorance in the hope that Sharon could 'pull it off'."[83]

Israel's Intervention in Lebanon: Critique or Confirmation of the Democratic Peace?

This case study provides disconfirming evidence for many of the tenets of the democratic peace theory, and identifies its shortcomings. The democratic peace theory is wrong to suppose that democratic values that are applied within a country will also be applied in its foreign affairs. The theory also misleads by treating all democracies as like units, and by assuming that democracy restrains war-prone leaders. As this chapter suggests, some democracies may not include enough guarantees to keep one person with many posts from becoming a "rogue elephant."

---

82. Valerie Yorke, *Domestic Politics and Regional Security, Jordan, Syria and Israel: The End of an Era?* (Brookfield, Vt.: Gower, 1988), p. 185.

83. Feldman and Rechnitz-Kijner, *Deception,* pp. 33–34; and Charles David Freilich, "Realism and Messianism: National Security Decision Making in Israel," Ph.D. dissertation, Columbia University, 1992, p. 421.

First, contrary to the dyadic version of the democratic peace theory, Israel consistently acted to undermine Lebanon's democratic system. One goal of the war was to create a government dominated by the Christian Maronites that would be capable of signing a peace treaty with Israel. Instead of supporting democracy in Lebanon, Israel consistently acted to undermine Lebanon's democratic system by increasing the political power of one group (i.e., the Christian Maronites) over others. Israel did not want a representative liberal state in Lebanon, where elections would ensure that the Maronite leadership would be balanced by other parties. Nor did Israel want a participatory democratic Lebanon, where majority rule would minimize the influence of the pro-Israel Maronite minority. The timing of the 1982 invasion was linked to the upcoming Lebanese presidential elections. Sharon and Begin wanted to make sure that the opponents of Bashir Jumayyil, the Maronite candidate, were eliminated prior to the elections. The architects of ORANIM did not shrink from using the IDF to determine the Lebanese elections—the army was to be in Beirut to make certain that Lebanese democracy worked as Israel wanted and that Jumayyil was installed as president.

Contrary to the democratic peace thesis, which implies that democracies prefer democratic neighbors, democratic Israel did not prefer a democratic Lebanon. Since democracy would allow anti-Israeli political groups into the decision making arena, a democratic Lebanon was not likely to be a trustworthy and friendly neighbor. The idea that anti-Israeli parties would share power with their Christian Maronite allies was anathema to the Israeli government, which would have preferred an authoritarian Lebanon under the strong control of the Jumayyil family. As Ben Meir puts it, "Sharon intended to become kingmaker in Lebanon, backed up as needed by Israeli bayonets."[84] In sum, contrary to what the normative model of the democratic peace theory would lead us to expect, Israel did not work to strengthen Lebanon's democratic institutions. What Israel preferred was a strong government, and its aim in the war was to redraw the Lebanese domestic political map in favor of the Christian Maronites. The Israeli government was not concerned with Lebanon's domestic regime type, but with which Lebanese made up the ruling coalition.[85]

---

84. Ben Meir, *Civil-Military Relations in Israel*, p. 150.

85. For more on how democracies have used coercive diplomacy to undermine the democratic process in other states, see Kegley and Hermann, "Military Intervention

Second, the structural-institutional explanation for the democratic peace overstates the capacity of the public to restrain an executive bent on war. As this case study shows, when parliamentary democracies consider whether to go to war, it is the executive that constrains itself through party competition; therefore, a party that can form a government with the sustained confidence of a majority in the legislature has few *ex ante* constraints on its capacity to initiate war. While a failure to achieve the goals of the war can mean a vote of no confidence and a reversal of fortune in the next elections, public opinion and elections do not stop leaders from choosing war in the first place. By contrast, in coalitional cabinets, where parties with diverse ideological positions must cooperate to sustain the government, the extremism of any one party is more likely to be moderated. Because parties holding competing foreign policy preferences must reach consensus in order to sustain the government, under these conditions there are substantial *ex ante* constraints on the decision to go to war; an extremist party will be restricted significantly by its coalition bonds. In short, the institutional model for the democratic peace, which assumes that democratic states are less war-prone due to institutional constraints on the executive, is flawed; it overlooks the fact that parliamentary systems have few institutional safeguards to restrain a homogeneous executive that has majority support in the legislature.[86]

For example, Israel's decision making supports the notion that, while they cannot prevent war initiation, democratic publics can stop military actions that have become costly and ineffective: "In Israel ... parliament can prevent the government from continuing to wage war by casting a vote of no-confidence, thereby forcing the govern-

---

and the Democratic Peace," pp. 1–21; Stephen Van Evera, "American Intervention in the Third World: Less Would Be Better," *Security Studies*, Vol. 1, No. 1 (Fall 1991), pp. 4–8; David P. Forsythe, "Democracy, War, and Covert Action," *Journal of Peace Research*, Vol. 29, No. 4 (1992), pp. 385–395; and Patrick James and Glenn E. Mitchell II, "Targets of Covert Pressure: The Hidden Victims of the Democratic Peace," *International Interactions*, Vol. 21, No. 1 (July 1995), pp. 85–107.

86. In the Israeli system, executive powers are impressive. The cabinet declares war without the consent of the Knesset and can conduct military operations without consulting the Knesset's foreign and defense relations committees: "The political system in Israel is a highly centralized one, lacking effective checks and balances ... As long as the government enjoys a majority in the Knesset, the parliament has a very limited control and influence on the government." See Avraham Brichta and Yair Zalmanovitch, "The Proposals for Presidential Government in Israel: A Case Study in the Possibility of Institutional Transference," *Comparative Politics*, Vol. 19, No. 1 (October 1986), p. 61.

ment to resign."[87] Increased protest in the Knesset and at public rallies did force the government to seek an end to a war that was viewed as avoidable and unsuccessful. This lends some support to the monadic democratic peace argument that democracies will give up wars when the human and material costs of maintaining them become too high.[88] Nevertheless, public dissent did not lead to immediate changes in executive policies. In fact, as public protest mounted, the government became even more adamant in achieving its goals in Lebanon. Sensing that failure would result in an electoral defeat, increased domestic protest provided the Begin government with an incentive to begin a new offensive. Thus, contrary to the claims of the monadic variant, the fear of political punishment may not necessarily make democratically elected leaders more sensitive to the human costs of war. Yaniv puts it well:

mounting public pressure acted as an added inducement for the government to come up with clear results to prove that the casualties and other costs of the war were justified . . . Instead of feeling . . . obliged to yield to public pressures, [the Cabinet became] more belligerent and more prone to entrench themselves further in their positions.[89]

Third, the case suggests that supporters of the monadic version of the democratic peace thesis are wrong to assume that democracies will generally seek peaceful means for conflict resolution, rather than war. According to the monadic variant, democracies value negotiation and compromise, and eschew violence as a result of the externalization of domestic norms of conflict resolution. On the contrary, the avoidance of political repression at home does not always indicate the degree to which the government will resolve international disputes nonviolently. Israel's invasion of Lebanon in 1982 is a case in point. Since 1975, the PLO had increasingly shown signs of being prepared to modify its ambitions. Yasser Arafat and other PLO pragmatists were willing to give up their campaign of terror, provided that Israel also ended its attempt to eradicate the Palestinian nationalist movement, and was willing to make peace in exchange for Palestinian independence. Indeed, Arafat was well aware that PLO terrorist activities merely served to weaken Israeli doves while strengthening the

---

87. Feldman and Rechnitz-Kijner, *Deception*, p. 73.

88. Randolph M. Siverson, "Democracies and War Participation: In Defense of the Institutional Constraints Argument," *European Journal of International Relations*, Vol. 1, No. 4 (December 1995), pp. 481–489, especially pp. 486–487.

89. Yaniv, *Dilemmas of Security*, pp. 159–160.

position of hard-liners. Negotiation, then, was a possibility in the early 1980s; that the Israeli government chose war instead is a serious indictment of the monadic democratic peace argument. Clearly the Begin government preferred to use force to resolve the Israeli-Palestinian dispute. Contrary to what the monadic hypothesis would lead us to expect, war was a choice of *first* resort. In Andrew Mack's words: "in the case of the Lebanon war there *clearly* was an alternative—dialogue, directly or indirectly, with the PLO with the aim of creating a settlement . . . a potentially non-violent alternative to war existed and was ignored."[90] In short, the monadic variant of the democratic peace theory incorrectly assumes that what holds true for citizens also holds true for the state. The monadic theory infers that democracies will behave in a tolerant and conciliatory manner because voting citizens advocate these norms. But while the public may put a heavy premium on peaceful methods of conflict resolution, the government may still behave in a very intolerant manner.[91]

Fourth, the case underscores the danger of disregarding the preferences of particular parties in a democratic state. According to democratic peace proponents, regime type is a good indicator of whether a state will be prone to using force: "the highly visible character of regime type does influence the odds or the risk that one is facing a state adverse to the use of force."[92] Yet, Israel's foreign policy toward Lebanon changed not because of shifts in domestic structure—Israel remained a democracy throughout—but because the Likud-led coalition that gained power in 1977 valued the use of force. As Joe Hagan points out:

Leader orientations . . . can . . . vary across time even though structural arrangements remain constant. . . This insight requires that domestic political constraints be conceived in terms of the ruling group (or coalition) that controls the state at any point in time . . . A leadership's core shared beliefs form an important motivational basis for the overall direction of a state in the march to war.[93]

---

90. Mack, "Israel's Lebanon War," p. 8.

91. James and Mitchell, "Targets of Covert Pressure," pp. 86–87.

92. Bruce Bueno de Mesquita and David Lalman, *War and Reason: Domestic and International Imperatives* (New Haven, Conn.: Yale University Press, 1992), p. 156; Thomas Risse-Kappen, "Democratic Peace—Warlike Democracies? A Social Constructivist Interpretation of the Liberal Argument," *European Journal of International Relations*, Vol. 1, No. 4 (December 1995), p. 492.

93. Hagan, "Domestic Political Systems and War Proneness," pp. 187, 198; see also Hermann and Kegley, "Rethinking Democracy and International Peace."

Thus, the important consideration is not whether a country is democratic or not, but whether its ruling coalition is committed to peaceful methods of conflict resolution. There is no reason to expect that all domestic groups in a democratic state will eschew the use of force, expansion, and aggressive foreign policy. Indeed, even in democracies there are always likely to be elites who view force as the best means of ensuring national security. Thus, by focusing solely on domestic regime type, the democratic peace theory obscures the extent to which hard-line leadership orientations are often a prerequisite to war. Leaders in nondemocracies may espouse moderate leadership orientations; leaders in democracies can hold militant and radical orientations.[94]

Finally, this chapter suggests that the democratic peace theory overemphasizes domestic regime type to the exclusion of other domestic political variables that crucially affect war and peace decisions. Specifically, Israel's intervention into Lebanon suggests that civil-military relations can affect war initiation, even in democratic states. The Israeli cabinet *did* constrain those who supported ORANIM by compelling them to reject operations that other cabinet members were likely to veto. But given the delegation of war powers in Israel, this did not present much of a check on Sharon's actions. In Israel, domestic institutional rules regarding war powers delegate control over the armed forces by a large, unwieldy body (the cabinet) to a single, unified body (the minister of defense). Inevitably, this serves to increase the autonomy of the defense minister. As Dan Horowitz notes, the defense minister enjoys a "special status" as the connecting link between military and political levels, and on more than one occasion defense ministers have tended to see themselves as representative of the army before the government rather than the reverse.[95] Thus, the cabinet did not prevent Sharon from implementing operations consistent with ORANIM—it merely compelled him to implement it in an incremental, gradual, and ad hoc fashion: "The . . . leaders responsible for the operation had . . . to design a plan which would eventually lead to the same military and political objectives envisaged for the 'Big Plan', but which would do it in a somewhat more gradual way."[96] In short, the structural-institutional explanation for the

---

94. For more on how leadership orientations affect how states deal with international conflicts, see Hagan, "Domestic Political Systems and War Proneness."

95. Horowitz, "Israel's War in Lebanon," p. 94.

96. Evron, *War and Intervention*, p. 131.

democratic peace asserts that democracies are less war-prone because the power to wage war is not concentrated in the hands of one person. Yet, many democracies *do* delegate war powers, increasing the chances that military strategy will reflect the views of a small group of civilian and military figures. As Naor writes:

It would be an unsatisfactory conclusion to attribute what happened entirely to the personality of the Defense Minister Ariel Sharon and to the manipulative talents he displayed. Beyond the personal dimension lies the institutional factor too: the events were made possible because the government lacked the appropriate tool to successfully carry out the job of supreme commander of the army.[97]

Conclusion

In this chapter I have suggested that, contrary to the expectations of the monadic variant of the democratic peace theory, democracies do not necessarily pursue more pacific foreign policies. By classifying states as either democratic or nondemocratic, the democratic peace theory obscures other domestic political institutions and dynamics that lead to more (or less) belligerence. Variation in leadership orientation, intra-regime changes, and the nature of civil-military relations are more important predictors of a state's external behavior than its regime type.

First, my analysis suggests that the ways in which war powers are delegated significantly influence war and peace outcomes. While democracies do not place war and peace decision making in the hands of one person, foreign policy is often delegated to smaller, expert decision making groups, especially in times of crisis. Because civilian control over the military is subject to institutional rules that vary across democratic regime types, the war propensities of democratic states are unlikely to be uniform.

Second, the case illustrates that whether democratically elected leaders will prefer compromise to violence is an empirical question; it cannot be assumed a priori.[98] As Barbara Farnham states: "what is important is not solely the perception that a state is a liberal democracy, but rather that its leaders espouse the norms of political

---

97. Naor, "The Israeli Cabinet," p. 15.
98. Hermann and Kegley, "Rethinking Democracy and International Peace."

accommodation which makes it possible to work with them."[99] The ruling coalition that came to power in Israel following the 1981 elections perceived the use of force as legitimate, and it initiated crises to advance its conception of national security. Far from viewing compromise and bargaining as a means of first resort, the Israeli leadership was wary of negotiation and preferred to use force.[100]

Finally, the chapter illustrates that intra-regime changes affect the extent to which war-prone leaders can implement their preferences. Changes in the degree of regime fragmentation go far in explaining shifts in war propensities. Before 1981, Herut was unable to pursue its foreign policy agenda in a fragmented ruling coalition that included moderates. Herut's ability to control the agenda increased substantially following the 1981 elections, when moderate factions could no longer make or break the government. In both periods, coalition dynamics affected Israel's policies toward Lebanon. Prior to 1981, smaller moderate parties diluted Herut's preferred policies. Later, the pivotal smaller parties were more extremist than the Likud mainstream and helped to push the state down the road to war.[101] In short, when democratic peace proponents argue that regime change

---

99. Barbara Farnham, "Roosevelt, the Munich Crisis, and the Theory of the Democratic Peace," paper presented at the annual meeting of the International Studies Association, San Diego, April 16–20, 1996, abstract.

100. The implications for the contemporary Middle East peace process are telling. Israel's neighbors take little comfort in the fact of Israeli democracy. Indeed, what is critical for the Arab states is not whether Israel is democratic, but whether Israel's ruling coalition is likely to reject the use of force and value negotiation. In the Middle East, at least, threat perceptions are less a function of domestic regime type than of who holds power. Arab perceptions of the Israeli threat have tended to vary with whether Likud-led or Labor-led coalitions have been in power.

101. Recent electoral reforms in Israel should decrease the ability of smaller parties to hold the government hostage. To be sure, the direct election of the prime minister allows voters to split their ticket, thus ensuring the multiplicity of parties in the Knesset, many of which represent only narrow interests. Yet, this fragmentation does not mean that these smaller parties can make extortionist demands on the government. Under the old parliamentary system, pivotal but small parties could make excessive demands on the prime minister because they could jeopardize the government's existence. Currently, however, since the prime minister is voted into office by a separate ballot, there are institutional incentives for smaller parties to conform to the prime minister's views, lest he or she look elsewhere for coalitional partners. Because of the prime minister's permanence, parties have much to gain from participating in the ruling coalition and a great deal to lose from exclusion. For more on how Israel's electoral reforms increase the independence of the prime minister while minimizing the leverage of minor

is important, they base their case on states that changed their foreign policies after liberal revolutions brought new democratic regimes to power. This chapter shows that foreign policy should not be considered a constant even within mature democracies, and that changes *within* regimes matter as much as changes *of* regimes. In sum, the democratic peace hypothesis is correct in insisting that much of international politics cannot be explained without reference to domestic level factors. But the case of Israel's foreign policy toward Lebanon suggests that while domestic politics matters, this is not a concession that gives the game away. Scholars and policy makers must look far beyond a simple coding of "democratic" or "nondemocratic" to predict a state's foreign policy.

---

ity parties, see Bernard Susser, "'Parliadental' Politics: A Proposed Constitution for Israel," *Parliamentary Affairs*, Vol. 42, No. 1 (January 1989), pp. 112–122. For alternative views, see Amos Perlmutter, "The Splinter Factor," *New York Times*, May 31, 1996; and Shai Feldman, "Netanyahu's Victory Opens a New Mideast Era," *International Herald Tribune*, June 1–2, 1996.

Chapter 8

Peru vs. Colombia and Senegal vs. Mauritania: Mixed Dyads and "Negative Peace"

Arie M. Kacowicz

In this chapter I examine two serious militarized crises in the Third World that did not escalate into full-fledged wars: the Leticia dispute between nondemocratic Peru and democratic Colombia, and the Senegal Valley River dispute between nondemocratic Mauritania and democratic Senegal. These two crises took place in two regions of the world that have enjoyed long periods of international peace: South America and West Africa. Although the countries involved in these two conflicts reached the verge of war, broke diplomatic relations, and were involved in armed skirmishes and sporadic battles, they ultimately did not escalate them from a militarized crisis to a full-scale war. I argue that a fragile "negative peace" was maintained within these mixed dyads due to several domestic and international factors, including the lack of material means to wage international wars; sudden leadership changes; the pacifying role of regional hegemons (Brazil and France) and of international institutions (the League of Nations and the Organization of African Unity); and a normative regional consensus in favor of peaceful settlement of disputes and respect of the existing international borders (the principle of *uti possidetis*).

To what extent is the democratic peace theory relevant to these cases? Since Colombia in 1932–33 and Senegal in 1989–90 were both democracies, these crises make it possible to examine the behavior of

The author thanks Miriam Avins, Miriam Fendius Elman, Elizabeth Finkelstein, Orly Kacowicz, Randall L. Schweller, and the other participants of the CSIA Harvard Workshop on "Paths to Peace" for their comments and suggestions; Mirav Yaacovson for research assistance, and the Israeli Foundations Trustee and the Leonard Davis Institute for their financial support.

democracies toward their nondemocratic counterparts.[1] The empirical evidence is not inconsistent with the predictions of the dyadic version of the democratic peace theory, which claims that democracies are no less warlike than other regimes except with fellow democracies, but emphasizes its limitations; specifically, the cases illustrate that the peaceful resolution of serious international crises can be explained without reference to the domestic political regimes of the countries involved. Indeed, the regime types of the states involved in these two crises had little or nothing to do with how the crises were resolved.

To understand the outcome of these crises, it is important to differentiate between negative peace (the mere absence of war) and stable peace. Negative peace is defined as the absence of systematic, large-scale collective violence among or between political communities. International negative peace is the absence of war among or between independent states. An unstable or fragile peace is usually maintained by threats, deterrence, or a lack of will or capabilities to engage in violent conflict. By contrast, stable peace implies a "state of peace" in which there are no expectations of violence, since war has been ruled out as a legitimate or likely recourse.[2] In this chapter I focus on the condition of negative, fragile, or precarious peace, which does not require that both states be democratic; hence, it is unrelated and irrelevant to the dyadic version of the democratic peace argument. At the same time, it examines the monadic claims of the democratic peace theory regarding the inherent peaceful behavior of democracies. Although

---

1. According to Michael Doyle's categorization, both countries are democracies. Colombia was a liberal democracy between 1910 and 1946, with a democratic record equaled only by Uruguay in Latin America. Senegal since 1981 can be also coded as a democracy, or at least as a "quasi-democracy." See Michael W. Doyle, "Liberalism and World Politics," *American Political Science Review*, Vol. 80, No. 4 (December 1986), p. 1164; Alexander W. Wilde, "Conversations among Gentlemen: Oligarchical Democracy in Colombia," in Juan J. Linz and Alfred Stepan, eds., *The Breakdown of Democratic Regimes: Latin America* (Baltimore, Md.: Johns Hopkins University Press, 1978), pp. 28–81; and Christian Coulon, "Senegal: The Development and Fragility of Semidemocracy," in Larry Diamond, Juan J. Linz, and Seymour Martin Lipset, eds., *Democracy in Developing Countries: Africa* (Boulder, Colo.: Lynne Rienner, 1988), pp. 141–178.

2. See Michael W. Doyle, "Michael Doyle on the Democratic Peace—Again," in Michael E. Brown, Sean M. Lynn-Jones, and Steven E. Miller, eds., *Debating the Democratic Peace* (Cambridge, Mass.: MIT Press, 1996), p. 365; Arie M. Kacowicz, "Explaining Zones of Peace: Democracies as Satisfied Powers?" *Journal of Peace Research*, Vol. 32, No. 3 (August 1995), p. 268; and Kenneth Boulding, *Stable Peace* (Austin: University of Texas Press, 1978).

democracy is not a necessary condition for the peaceful resolution of serious militarized disputes involving nondemocratic or mixed dyads, it is very relevant for understanding the evolution and deepening of peaceful relations from mere negative peace toward a stable, lasting peace, as in the Southern Cone of Latin America since the mid-1980s.

In the following pages I describe the Leticia and the Senegal Valley disputes, as well as the regional negative peace in South America and West Africa.[3] These two militarized crises are assessed within the context of a general absence of international wars in these two regions. For each crisis, I first present a brief historical overview, and then I assess how the domestic political regimes of the countries involved affected their handling of the crises. Next, to account for why these two crises did not escalate into full-fledged wars, I offer four alternative explanations to the democratic peace argument: the role of a regional normative consensus against war; the pacifying effects of regional and extra-regional hegemons, aided by regional and international institutions; the geographical irrelevance and material impotence to fight international wars, associated with the fact that those states were usually weak in both domestic and international terms; and sudden leadership changes, as in the case of Peru. Some of these explanations transcend the explanatory range of the democratic peace theory by stressing the role of regional hegemons, geopolitical considerations, and a lack of material power. Two other explanations—normative consensus and leadership changes—highlight domestic political variables that lie outside the scope of the democratic peace thesis. Thus, nondemocracies or mixed dyads can have a common normative foundation for peace, and variables specific to domestic politics—such as leadership changes—can keep mixed dyads at peace. Finally, I examine the implications and relevance of these empirical cases for the democratic peace theory.

The Leticia Crisis, 1932–33

South America has had fewer wars than many other areas of the developing world. Despite the frequency and intensity of several ter-

---

3. For a review of South America and West Africa as zones of "negative peace," see Arie M. Kacowicz, *Zones of Peace in the Third World: South America and West Africa in a Comparative Perspective* (Albany: State University of New York Press, forthcoming); and Kalevi J. Holsti, *War, The State, and the State of War* (Cambridge: Cambridge University Press, 1996).

ritorial conflicts, South American states have fought only two wars in the past one hundred years: the Chaco War of 1932–35 between Bolivia and Paraguay, and the brief Ecuadorean-Peruvian war of 1941, which was followed by a sequel of iterated armed skirmishes in 1981 and 1995. The region is no stranger to violence; it has been beset by internal conflict, military coups, and virulent civil wars. Furthermore, military force has been a consistent means of communication in the foreign policies of several countries, including threats and other minor uses of military force, short of full-fledged wars. Nevertheless, war has been the exception rather than the rule in South America since 1883; during the twentieth century, the region has been characterized by mutually peaceful relations and nonviolent modes of conflict resolution, even though the majority of the political regimes were not democratic before the end of the 1970s and the beginning of the 1980s.[4]

While boundary problems have been a fertile source of international conflicts in South America since the beginning of the nineteenth century, the Leticia dispute between Peru and Colombia—which evolved into a serious crisis in 1932–33 that led the two countries to an armed confrontation and to the verge of war—was an unusual episode in the international relations of the region, comparable to a similar militarized confrontation that took place between Argentina and Chile over the Beagle Channel in December 1978.[5] What were the causes of this conflict and why did it evolve into a serious militarized crisis? Why and how was the crisis managed or mismanaged?

THE DISPUTE

The Leticia dispute arose over a Peruvian attempt to repudiate a valid international treaty, and to regain by violence territory ceded to

---

4. See Wolf Grabendorff, "Interstate Conflict Behavior and Regional Potential for Conflict in Latin America," *Journal of Interamerican Studies and World Affairs*, Vol. 24, No. 2 (August 1982), pp. 267–294.

5. On the Beagle crisis, see Miguel A. Scenna, *Argentina-Chile: Una Frontera Caliente* (Buenos Aires: Editorial Belgrano, 1981); Roberto Russell and Laura Zuvanic, "Argentina: Deepening Alignment with the West," *Journal of Interamerican Studies and World Affairs*, Vol. 33, No. 3 (Fall 1991), pp. 119–120; and James L. Garrett, "The Beagle Channel: Confrontation and Negotiation in the Southern Cone," *Journal of Interamerican Studies and World Affairs*, Vol. 27, No. 3 (Fall 1985), pp. 81–110.

Colombia in 1922.[6] From 1911 to 1932, Peru and Colombia feuded over possession of the strategic Amazon port city of Leticia. Peru's economic interests, particularly its search for raw materials after its defeat in the Pacific War of 1879–83 against Chile, led it to claim this area in the Upper Amazon basin.

In 1922, Peru and Colombia concluded the Salomon-Lozano Treaty, by which an area of about 4,000 square miles was ceded to Colombia, including the left bank of the Putumayo River and a corridor to Leticia, in exchange for other border areas with Ecuador that were in Colombian possession. The Leticia area included fewer than 500 white inhabitants, 300 of them in Leticia, and about 1,500 Indians. At its northeast corner on the Putumayo stood the town of Tarapacá, and at its southeast corner on the Amazon, 2,500 miles from the Atlantic Ocean, the town of Leticia. The agreement, which was very unpopular in Peru, was reached by the authoritarian government of Augusto Leguía without consulting the Peruvian inhabitants of the Loreto area.

A military revolt led by Colonel Luis M. Sánchez Cerro deposed President Leguía on August 25, 1930. Following a chaotic year in Peruvian politics, elections were held on October 11, 1931. Sánchez Cerro was elected president. The new Peruvian regime was supported by the army and by several groups of conservatives, notably the Civilista Party. The Salomon-Lozano Treaty of 1922 was one of Leguía's achievements that the Civilistas wished to nullify; in this effort they found allies among the rough and ready frontiersmen of Loreto, who held that the Amazon should be a wholly Peruvian stream from its source to the Brazilian border.[7]

On the night of August 31, 1932, an armed band of some three hundred Peruvian civilians entered Leticia, seized the public

---

6. For a general overview of the Leticia dispute, see Gordon Ireland, *Boundaries, Possessions, and Conflicts in South America* (Cambridge, Mass.: Harvard University Press, 1938), pp. 196–206; Manley O. Hudson, *The Verdict of the League: Colombia and Peru at Leticia* (Boston: World Peace Foundation, 1933); Jayme de Barros, *Ocho Años de Política Exterior del Brasil* (Rio de Janeiro: DNP, 1938), pp. 29–34; Augusto Bourouncle, *Reconstrucción Política de Fronteras: Perú-Colombia* (Arequipa, Peru: Edición Leer, 1934); and Alfonso López, *La Política Internacional* (Bogotá: Imprenta Nacional, 1936), pp. 19–24. For the antecedents of the crisis previous to 1932, see Thomas J. Dodd, "Peru," in Harold E. Davis and Larman C. Wilson, eds., *Latin American Foreign Policies: An Analysis* (Baltimore, Md.: Johns Hopkins University Press, 1975), p. 364.

7. Bryce Wood, *The United States and Latin American Wars, 1932–1942* (New York: Columbia University Press, 1966), pp. 174–175.

buildings and town offices, expelled the Colombian officials, and raised the Peruvian flag. Later, they extended their occupation to the entire area. Although the Peruvian government disavowed the action at the beginning of the crisis, local Peruvian authorities in Loreto furnished military support, and on November 26, 1932, Peruvian regular troops were said to have occupied Leticia. The Peruvian government did not interfere with the support by local authorities, arguing that the patriotic aspirations of the local population should be respected, and that the 1922 treaty should be revised.

Colombia decided to take measures to restore "normal conditions" in the Leticia area, "under the aegis of Colombian laws and Colombian authorities." Colombia prepared a naval expedition of six vessels and 1,500 men under the leadership of General Alfredo Vázquez Cobo; it was to sail around the Atlantic coast and all the way up the Amazon River as a police expedition to restore the law in its usurped territory. Yet, what was regarded by Colombia as a "police expedition," sent to operate in Colombian territory, was perceived by Peruvians as a "punitive expedition" designed to commit aggression against Peruvian troops and civilians.[8]

During the months of January and February 1933, the Colombian naval expedition slowly approached the Leticia area, while diplomatic efforts to avoid war were undertaken by Brazil, the Pan-American Union, the United States, Argentina, Chile, and the League of Nations. As early as September 1932, the Peruvian government sought to submit the dispute to the Washington Conciliation Commission, as provided by the Gondra Treaty of 1923 and the Washington Convention of 1929. Colombia rejected the arbitration plea, arguing that the events at Leticia were "strictly and exclusively of an internal nature." The Colombian expedition reached Manaos on January 9, and remained there until January 23, when it sailed for the upper Amazon. On January 24, Colombia sought the intervention of the parties to the Kellogg-Briand Anti-War Pact, and of the League of Nations, to remind Peru of its international obligations. The following day, U.S. Secretary of State Henry L. Stimson condemned the Peruvian occupation of Leticia and decided to intervene through the League of Nations to avert war. By the beginning of February, Brazil abandoned its mediation

---

8. This account is based on Hudson, *The Verdict of the League*, pp. 5–6; and Ireland, *Boundaries*, pp. 198–200. Contrary to the monadic claim, democratic Colombia was not conciliatory as it prepared itself for an armed confrontation with Peru.

efforts as the disputing parties increased their war preparations.[9]

On February 14, Peru and Colombia clashed on Brazilian territory, near the Leticia area, as Peruvian planes unsuccessfully attacked the Colombian flotilla. The following day the countries broke off diplomatic relations. Instead of continuing southeast toward Leticia, the Colombian expedition decided to attack the town of Tarapacá, in the northeast corner of the area. The successful recapture of Tarapacá was a moral rather than a military victory for Colombia, since it involved almost no casualties for both sides. On February 17, Colombia appealed to the Council of the League under Article 15, which stated that the Council should endeavor to effect a peaceful settlement of any international dispute. On February 18, a street mob in Lima attacked and burnt the Colombian legation. On February 25, a League mediation committee proposed that a League commission administrate the territory of Leticia for a transitional period.

Following the battle of Tarapacá, the crisis further escalated as the two countries finalized their preparations for a general war, including levying war taxes and mobilizing personnel. On February 28, the League of Nations ordered a halt to the conflict. On March 1, the League adopted a peace plan to administer the territory, and on March 18, the League Council demanded that Peru surrender "Colombian territory." On March 26, the Colombian expedition reported that it had captured the Peruvian Fort Guepi on the south bank of the Putumayo. This new engagement was seen as the beginning of a Colombian offensive. Since Peru maintained its flat refusal to evacuate Leticia, and Colombia became convinced that a peaceful settlement had proved futile, war seemed now to be inevitable. A temporary military impasse developed in April, while Peru sent its own naval expedition, including warships and submarines, through the Panama Canal. A general war—one that might expand to include also Brazil and Ecuador—now seemed imminent.[10]

---

9. See Hudson, *The Verdict of the League*, p. 8; and *New York Times*, January 2, 1933, p. 17; January 3, 1933, p. 9; January 8, 1933, p. 21; January 10, 1933, p. 10; January 13, 1933, p. 4; January 15, 1933, p. 17; January 18, 1933, p. 8; January 25, 1933, p. 1; January 27, 1933, p. 11; January 31, 1933, p. 7; February 7, 1933, p. 8; February 8, 1933, p. 16; and February 11, 1933, p. 8.

10. See Hudson, *The Verdict of the League*, pp. 10–13; and *New York Times*, February 16, 1933, p. 14; February 18, 1933, p. 10; February 19, 1933, p. 1; February 20, 1933, p. 6; February 23, 1933, p. 8; February 25, 1933, p. 5; February 26, 1933, p. 15; February 28, 1933, p. 3; March 7, 1933, p. 11; March 16, 1933, p. 12; March 20, 1933, p. 7; April 16, 1933, p. 22; and April 23, 1933, p. 30.

On April 30, 1933, Peruvian president General Sánchez Cerro was assassinated. His death unexpectedly opened the way to resolve the Leticia crisis by peaceful means; he was known to be the moving spirit both of the illegal occupation of Leticia and of Peru's refusal to accept the decision of the League of Nations to restore Leticia to Colombia. The new president, General Oscar Benavides, happened to be a personal friend of a prominent Colombian diplomat and Liberal presidential candidate, Alfonso López. In a matter of days, the crisis de-escalated as López flew to Bogotá and conferred with Colombian President Enrique Olaya Herrera, and then flew to Lima to directly negotiate with President Benavides from May 15 to May 20.

On May 10, the League advisory committee had proposed the Peruvian evacuation of Leticia, and a temporary occupation of the territory in the name of Colombia for one year, followed by direct negotiations for a permanent settlement of the territorial question. Colombia accepted these proposals on May 12, and Peru agreed to them on May 24, after the López-Benavides meetings. A preliminary agreement ending the military crisis was reached on May 25, 1933. Exactly one year later, on May 24, 1934, the two countries signed the Protocol of Friendship and Cooperation in Rio de Janeiro, ending their conflict. Leticia was transferred back to Colombia from the temporary League administration on June 19, 1934. The war over Leticia never took place.[11]

DEMOCRATIC COLOMBIA'S CRISIS MANAGEMENT

Unlike Peru and most of the South American republics, Colombia in 1932–33 was a democracy. Though it shared with the rest of Latin America the usual impediments to democracy—a high rate of illiteracy, widespread poverty, a powerful Catholic church, a dominant landowning class, poor national integration, and an ingrained heritage of political violence and civil wars—between 1910 and 1949 Colombia managed to create and develop a political system of notable stability, openness, and competitiveness between the Conservative and Liberal parties. In the 1930s, Colombia was a matured "oligarchical (limited) democracy," in which elections were held regularly every four years. A Liberal government had been in

---

11. See *New York Times*; May 1, 1933, p. 1; May 12, 1933, p. 11; May 18, 1933, p. 13; May 22, 1933, p. 6; and May 26, 1933, p. 3; Ireland, *Boundaries*, pp. 201–202; and especially the exchange of letters between Dr. Alfonso López and President General Oscar R. Benavides in López, *La Política Internacional*, pp. 19–25.

power since 1930, after fighting among Conservatives had opened the way to a relatively easy victory for Enrique Olaya Herrera, an enlightened moderate who had been serving as ambassador to the United States.[12]

Did democracy help Colombia to manage its conflict with Peru peacefully, did it merely exacerbate the crisis, or was it irrelevant for its handling? The forceful Peruvian occupation of Leticia posed a serious problem for the popularity and legitimacy of the Liberal government. For example, as President Olaya argued about the Peruvian appeal for an arbitration commission in September 1932:

No government in Colombia could last an hour that would agree to participating in such a commission at this time. . . . We cannot allow any commission to discuss our right to recover territory which has been taken from us illegally by force. As I see the matter now, it seems that either I must fall or Sánchez Cerro must fall.[13]

Moreover, the Colombian president had at stake a matter of personal prestige that may have affected his attitude. Olaya had been the foreign minister during the crisis of 1911, when Peru had successfully pushed its border demands in a previous episode. However, the Colombian government was fearful that the war would increase the role of the military. As the Colombian Liberal leader, Alfonso López, candidly recognized, "Colombia does not want war. . . . The Liberal party especially had fought the military clique in Colombia and had broken down the military caste."[14] Its fine achievements could easily be jeopardized by the prospects of a long war with Peru. Hence, while President Olaya did not wish to cross the threshold of war, he was compelled to take an activist policy toward Peru.

During the early months of 1933, Colombia elaborated a strategy that combined military and diplomatic options: it would send a naval expedition up the Amazon River to recover Leticia in a "police action," and it would seek the mediation efforts of Brazil, the United States, and the League of Nations. The procrastination of the military

---

12. On the Colombian democracy, see Wilde, "Conversations among Gentlemen," pp. 29–31; and Jonathan Hartlyn, "Colombia: The Politics of Violence and Accommodation," in Larry Diamond, Juan J. Linz, and Seymour Martin Lipset, eds., *Democracy in Developing Countries: Latin America* (Boulder, Colo.: Lynne Rienner, 1989), pp. 291, 300, and 321.

13. Olaya quoted in Wood, *The United States and Latin American Wars*, pp. 177–178.

14. Quoted in ibid., p. 195.

344 | PATHS TO PEACE

expedition in January and February 1933 was an attempt to gain time for the Brazilian mediation.

However, President Olaya also faced a restless military, a vociferous Conservative opposition, and the pressure of public opinion. Hence, when speeches by the opposition or critical editorials seriously weakened his domestic standing, or when he felt Colombia's dignity could bear inaction no longer, he would redress the balance by having the naval expedition of Vázquez Cobo traverse a few more miles of the Amazon.[15]

The slow pace of crisis management could not last forever: an armed encounter between the two countries was only a matter of days away. The battle of Tarapacá, on February 15, 1933, increased the popular enthusiasm with the prospects of a rapid military victory. Yet, the Liberal party increasingly feared the enhanced presence of General Vázquez Cobo and the preponderant role the military might play in domestic politics in case of war. This fear might explain Colombia's intense appeal to the League of Nations to act diplomatically and help it avoid the war, and the continuing caution and procrastination in the planning of the military moves in March and April 1933.

It is evident that public opinion in Bogotá pushed the country toward war. After Peru rejected the Council's Resolution of March 18, President Olaya apparently concluded that he must act, both to ensure the safety of the expedition and to show Colombian public opinion that he was continuing an active policy. On March 27, Fort Guepi was captured, assuring an open supply to Colombian troops. Providentially, the Guepi engagement proved to be the final encounter in the Leticia conflict; the unexpected assassination of Sánchez Cerro opened the way for Olaya and Alfonso López to peacefully manage the resolution of the crisis with the new Peruvian leadership.

In sum, the picture that emerges from Colombia's management of the crisis in 1932–33 is of a cautious, even reluctant escalation in the direction of an armed confrontation. The Colombian leadership did not want a general war, but decided to regain the occupied territory by diplomacy if possible, and by force if necessary. Public opinion, precisely because the population could vote freely, and the existence of a free press pushed in the direction of war. Thus, contrary to the claims of the monadic version of the democratic peace argument, democratic politics and the influence of public opinion encouraged

---

15. Ibid., p. 206.

the civilian leaders to adopt more aggressive policies. Conversely, the civilians' fear of the military, and the traditional Colombian predilection for legalism pushed in the directicn of peace.

NONDEMOCRATIC PERU'S CRISIS MANAGEMENT

In August 1930, a military revolt led by Colonel Luis M. Sánchez Cerro brought down the Leguía dictatorship; and not until the next summer did the country settle down enough to hold a presidential election. On October 11, 1931, the elections took place; the candidates were Sánchez Cerro and Victor Raúl Haya de la Torre, leader of APRA (American Revolutionary Popular Alliance, or Aprista Party). Sánchez Cerro was returned to power after a close race and serious allegations of electoral fraud.

In February 1932, Sánchez Cerro transformed his regime into a repressive autocracy. Confronting revolutionary plots and army unrest, he closed all opposition newspapers, arrested a former minister of war, repressed a naval mutiny in July 1932, and crushed a revolutionary movement in Trujillo with more than 1,000 casualties. In response, APRA escalated the cycle of violence, including making assassination attempts against Sánchez Cerro.[16]

It is against this troublesome domestic political scene that the Peruvian government became involved in the Leticia crisis on September 1, 1932. At first, Sánchez Cerro officially disclaimed any responsibility for the seizure of the town, and even blamed the Communists and the Aprista Party. Peru, which was initially much stronger than Colombia at Leticia, did not make serious preparations for war, and even showed surprise at the determination of Bogotá as manifested by the dispatch of a naval expedition to retake Leticia.

Yet, by the beginning of 1933, under the pressure of Aprista propaganda calling for strong action and his increasing unpopularity at home, Sánchez Cerro gradually hardened his attitude toward Colombia until war became imminent. He adduced that the Leticia affair had aroused nationalistic demands that he could not resist if his government were to remain in power; the legitimacy of his autocratic rule increasingly depended upon his degree of activism and professed patriotism in the Leticia area.

---

16. On Peruvian domestic politics, see Robert Marett, *Peru* (London: Ernest Benn, 1969), pp. 157–162; and James D. Rudolph, *Peru: The Evolution of Crisis* (Westport, Conn.: Praeger, 1992), pp. 39–40.

Peru's mismanagement of the crisis illustrates an initially unintended linkage between domestic and international conflict: the political survival of Sánchez Cerro became inextricably associated with the continuing occupation of the Leticia area. As in Colombia, public opinion pushed for activism and war, without any democratic opposition striving for peace. It remains unclear whether Sánchez Cerro really wanted a war with Colombia; he also delayed his military moves (for instance, the Peruvian naval expedition was sent only after March of 1933). Thus, it seems that Sánchez Cerro wanted to profit politically from the crisis and the popular mobilization, but without necessarily crossing the threshold of a general war. In any case, the assassination of Sánchez Cerro on April 30, 1933, and the new policy of his successor, General Oscar Benavides, opened the way for peace. Benavides could see no point in fighting an expensive war over Leticia, and he also realized the weakness of Peru's legal position in South America, and *vis-à-vis* the international community as a whole.

The Senegal River Valley Dispute, 1989–92

Of the several African regions, West Africa stands out as the only zone of negative peace in that continent since the beginning of the decolonization process after World War II. With the exception of the brief and inconsequential war between Mali and Burkina Faso in December 1985, there have been no international wars among the sixteen members of the Economic Community of West African States (ECOWAS) that constitute West Africa. This situation of negative peace is quite remarkable, considering the multiethnic and multinational character of the member-states, and the persistence of numerous territorial disputes. As in South America, the lack of international wars starkly contrasts with widespread domestic violence, military coups, and virulent civil wars, such as the Nigerian-Biafran conflagration of 1967–70 and the Liberian civil war of 1990–96. There were almost no democratic regimes in this region until the beginning of the 1990s, with the exceptions of Gambia (until 1994), and Senegal (since the late 1970s).

One can argue that this negative regional peace is the result of a rational policy adopted by the West African states to respect their international borders in order to avoid the implementation of separatist, irredentist, and self-determination claims by ethnic groups. Although the boundaries of West Africa were determined arbitrarily by colonial administrators, they have been thoroughly respected by the new independent West African states. In West Africa, as in South America, the principle of retaining the colonial borders at the time of independence (i.e., *uti possidetis*) has been adopted partly as a response to the institutional, economic, social, and political weaknesses of the new countries; and most of the West African states realized that they had a reciprocal interest in respecting their international borders.[17] Moreover, at the regional and international levels, this commitment to inherited borders has been furthered by the norms of behavior developed by the Organization of African Unity (OAU), and by the international community that upholds the "juridical" sovereignty of all African states. Yet, despite the widespread recognition of the legitimacy of the international borders in West Africa, these boundaries have been very permeable since precolonial times. The permeability of these borders has been manifested through transnational transactions involving people (labor and refugee migrations, guerrilla fighters), and commodities (smuggling and "non-official" trade).

The Senegal River Valley dispute arose from border tensions between Senegal and Mauritania. During the crisis, Mauritania and Senegal severed diplomatic relations, militarized their common borders, and prepared for a war that never took place. There were even sporadic armed clashes between the two countries in 1989–90. The dispute also led to the worst intercommunity violence that ever took place—between Moors and Black Africans within Senegal and Mauritania—and to a massive population transfer of Mauritanians and Senegalese who resided in each other's country. It has been estimated that about 2,200 people in Mauritania and about 60 in Senegal died as a result of ethnic riots. After two years of negotiations and the active mediation of the Organization of African Unity, the two countries agreed to reopen diplomatic relations by April 1992. The crisis destroyed the sense of neighborliness that had characterized the relations of these two states, which are close to each other geographically, historically, and ethnically. Before the crisis took place, Mauritania and Senegal had experienced peaceful relations, were making

---

17. See Jeffrey Herbst, "The Creation and Maintenance of National Boundaries in Africa," *International Organization*, Vol. 43, No. 4 (Autumn 1989), pp. 673–692; Jeffrey Herbst, "War and the State in Africa," *International Security*, Vol. 14, No. 4 (Spring 1990), pp. 117–119; and Robert H. Jackson and Carl G. Rosberg, "Why Africa's Weak States Persist: The Empirical and the Juridical in Statehood," *World Politics*, Vol. 35, No. 1 (October 1982), pp. 1–24.

progress in joint economic development efforts, and their markets were intertwined through trade and labor migration.[18] Though the issues of the crisis were deep-rooted, the passions unleashed within the respective populations caught both governments off guard, making the dispute one of the most virulent interstate crises in the region.[19]

THE DISPUTE

Mauritania and Senegal both gained independence from France in 1960. As an outcome of its Sahelian location, Mauritania has been inhabited by two racial groups that have never been able to tolerate each other: a majority of white Moslem Berber-Arabs (about 80 percent), and a minority of Sudanese Black Africans, ethnically linked to Senegal and other West African states. Unlike Senegal, Mauritania is a state without a defined nation behind it. By contrast, Senegal has been freed of serious ethnic and religious tensions, with an ethnic equilibrium centered around the Black African Wolof group (about 41 percent), and the predominance of Islam as a national religion (about 90 percent).[20]

The Senegal-Mauritania border tensions were rooted in a long history of land disputes among individuals and communities living along both banks of the Senegal River. Desertification pushed nomadic Arab herders south, in the direction of sedentary Black

---

18. Thus, the crisis also challenges the validity of arguments that link economic interdependence to peace. See Ron Parker, "The Senegal-Mauritania Conflict of 1989: A Fragile Equilibrium," *Journal of Modern African Studies*, Vol. 29, No. 1 (January 1991), p. 155. I thank Randall L. Schweller for pointing this out to me.

19. For an overview of the dispute, see Mark Doyle, "Blood Brothers," *Africa Report*, Vol. 34, No. 4 (July–August 1989), pp. 13–16; Parker, "The Senegal-Mauritania Conflict of 1989," pp. 155–171; François Soudan, "Interview: Maaouya Ould Taya: 'Le Sénégal Nous Veut Du Mal,'" *Jeune Afrique*, No. 1513 (January 1, 1990), pp. 34–37; Gilbert K. Bluwey, "Mauritania," in Timothy M. Shaw and Julius Emeka Okolo, eds., *The Political Economy of Foreign Policy in Ecowas* (London: Macmillan, 1994), pp. 86–102; Anthony G. Pazzanita, "Mauritania's Foreign Policy: The Search for Protection," *Journal of Modern African Studies*, Vol. 33, No. 2 (April 1992), pp. 281–304; Geeta Chowdry and Mark Beeman, "Senegal," in Shaw and Okolo, *The Political Economy of Foreign Policy in Ecowas*, p. 165; and Sheldon Gellar, *Senegal: An African Nation Between Islam and the West* (Boulder, Colo.: Westview, 1982), pp. 72–73.

20. See Bluwey, "Mauritania," p. 86; and Christian Coulon, "Senegal: The Development and Fragility of Semidemocracy," in Diamond, Linz, and Lipset, *Democracy in Developing Countries: Africa*, pp. 163–164.

African farmers who inhabited both banks of the river, which divides the two states.[21]

A potential source of conflict between the two countries was the dissatisfaction of large segments of Mauritania's Black African minority concentrated along the Senegal River with the Arabization programs imposed by the Moorish majority since independence. The French-educated Toucoulor (Black African) elite led the fight against Arabization, which it saw as reducing the Black African minority to second-class status. There has always been tension between the people in the river area and Moors who dominate Mauritanian politics. These tensions were exacerbated by the construction of a dam and the improvement of irrigation in the valley after 1985.[22]

Before the crisis, between 200,000 and 300,000 Mauritanians (or Naars, as they are called by the Senegalese) lived and worked in Senegal, about one third of them in Dakar. They controlled 80 percent of the petty commerce sector as corner shopkeepers. Similarly, communities of Senegalese fishermen had lived along the rich Atlantic coast of Mauritania for generations, and other Senegalese worked as plumbers, masons, carpenters, and electricians, constituting an integral part of the Mauritanian economy. This massive presence of Senegalese and Mauritanians caused racial tensions, which were aggravated by serious economic crises in both countries, leading to social unrest in the 1980s. Senegalese living in Mauritania and Mauritanians living in Senegal were deprived of political rights, and had to confront the animadversion and even racism of their "host" populations. Relations between Black Africans and Moors within both countries became increasingly volatile, following coup attempts by the Toucoulor opposition to the Mauritanian government, supported by Senegalese groups, and the concomitant repression of the black ethnic groups in Mauritania. Ultimately, the explosion of violence in both countries seems to have been about land: mutual claims, latent ethnic mistrust, and economic deprivation made a politically dangerous combination.[23]

21. A.I. Asiwaju, "West Africa," in UN Regional Centre for Peace and Disarmament in Africa, *Workshop on the Role of Border Problems in African Peace and Security* (New York: United Nations, 1993), p. 83; and Parker, "The Senegal-Mauritania Conflict of 1989," p. 155.

22. See Gellar, *Senegal*, p. 73; and Mark Doyle, "One Foot in Black Africa," *West Africa*, July 24–30, 1989, pp. 1200–1201.

23. See *African Research Bulletin*, Vol. 26, No. 5 (May 15, 1989), p. 9241.

At the end of the 1988 rainy season, Black African cultivators preparing fields on the northern bank of the Senegal River were chased away by Beydanes (white Moors) from Nouakchott, Mauritania's capital. As a reprisal, in January 1989, Senegal banned fresh fish, mineral water, and other food imports, and Mauritania responded with embargoes on vegetable oil, animal feed, and fresh vegetables. The threatening situation was eased in late January by President Houphouet-Boigny of Ivory Coast, who brought the two countries' heads of state together for a meeting.[24]

Relations between Senegal and Mauritania were dealt a lasting blow by a serious crisis involving the two countries on April 9, 1989. The crisis began at Diamara village in Ndounde-Khore, a small island near the southern shore of the Senegal River. A watchman had the responsibility of warning the crop farmers if he saw Mauritanian herders and their flocks coming into their fields. Alerted by him in the early afternoon of Sunday, April 9, 1989, the farmers went to chase away the flocks. Four uniformed Mauritanians (border guards) opened fire; they killed two farmers, wounded three, and took thirteen prisoners to Mauritania.

Upon learning about the incident, Senegalese youths retaliated and sacked Mauritanian-owned shops in Bakel on April 11. On April 19 and 20, there were more confrontations between Black Africans and Beydanes in border villages; afterwards, violence escalated rapidly. In a bid to contain the anger of his people, Senegalese President Abdou Diouf requested a meeting with his Mauritanian counterpart, who instead sent his interior minister to Dakar. On his arrival at Dakar airport, the minister, Djibril Ould Abdulahi, told a television news crew that the shooting on April 9 "should not be accorded an importance which surpasses reality." The Senegalese were infuriated at the implication that Senegalese lives were unimportant.

As a result of the minister's visit to Dakar, the two governments formed a joint commission to study the causes of the conflict in the river valley. However, the commission failed to resolve the problem, and the head of the Mauritanian delegation refused to sign the meeting's minutes, which specified that the incident had taken place "on Senegalese soil." On April 22, when the commission convened, thousands of Mauritanian-owned shops in Dakar were looted; when they learned of the thefts, on April 24, Mauritanians began to attack and

24. Parker, "The Senegal-Mauritania Conflict of 1989," p. 155.

to kill Senegalese living in Nouakchott and in Nouadhibou, Mauritania's two largest cities. A systematic pogrom against black Mauritanians and Senegalese living in Mauritania was organized by the Ba'athist movement, an extreme Moslem group. As a result, 3,000 black Mauritanians and 2,000 Senegalese were murdered. On April 27, the Senegalese government published a protest "against the lack of protective measures in Mauritania." Senegal also declared a state of emergency and instituted a curfew in Dakar.

A semblance of order was restored when the two governments agreed, following a Moroccan diplomatic initiative, to an airlift of their respective people out of the main towns of both countries. The operation was carried out from April 28 to May 7 with the assistance of France, Spain, Morocco, and Algeria. Some 200,000 Mauritanians and 70,000 Senegalese were returned to their countries of origin. The mutual exodus had catastrophic economic consequences for the economies of both countries, and ruined Mauritania's rural development plans, which depended upon good relations with Senegal.[25] Unfortunately, the repatriation of Mauritanians and Senegalese did not resolve the crisis. The conflict further escalated, exacerbated by racial tensions within Mauritania, and by economic and social problems within Senegal.

Mauritania and Senegal incessantly blamed each other for the crisis, and on August 21, 1989, they severed diplomatic relations, curtailed all trade, militarized their common border, and turned to a limited use of force. Commentators suggested that a war that neither side wanted nor could sustain for long was imminent. At the same time, Mauritania confronted armed opposition from guerrillas operating out of Senegal and Mali against the thinly spread Mauritanian army.[26] In November 1989, the deployment of Mauritanian troops along the Senegalese border was substantially increased. Senegal and Mauritania exchanged heavy artillery for the first time in January 1990, near Senegalese border villages. Throughout the rest of 1990, Mauritania also resisted the guerilla attacks of the African Forces of Liberation in Mauritania (FLAM), the armed Black African opposition to the Nouakchott regime.[27]

---

25. In specific terms, the Gorgol valley irrigation scheme and the Boghe and Djama dam projects were based on the free flow of water from the Senegal River. See Bluwey, "Mauritania," pp. 97–98.

26. Pazzanita, "Mauritania's Foreign Policy," p. 298.

27. See ibid., p. 298; and Parker, "The Senegal-Mauritania Conflict of 1989," p. 167.

The conflict escalated yet further in political terms, when both countries broadened the issues at stake in the early months of 1990. Mauritania used the crisis with Senegal as a pretext to repress and expel Black Africans, who were considered potential political opponents of the Arab-dominated regime. Senegal claimed its sovereignty over the entire Senegal River basin, on the basis of a 1933 treaty that established the "real" border as the north bank at its highest point. Ultimately, the de-escalation of the conflict after September 1990 and the resolution of the dispute were facilitated by the recognition of the existing borders, and a commitment not to interfere in each other's domestic affairs. After two years of negotiations and mediation by the OAU, the two countries agreed to reopen diplomatic relations in April 1992.[28]

DEMOCRATIC SENEGAL'S CRISIS MANAGEMENT

Unlike Mauritania and most of its West African neighbors (with the exception of tiny Gambia), Senegal has been a relative democracy since 1981. As the majority of African regimes worked to consolidate single-party rule in the mid-1970s, Senegal moved in the opposite direction, gradually re-creating a multiparty system and reestablishing the institutional framework of a democracy, including widespread freedom of expression and open political opposition. As a result, Senegal has managed to project a positive international image since the days of President Leopold Senghor (1960–81), despite its relative lack of military and economic power. In many respects the Senegalese political system could be considered at least as a "semi" or "quasi" democracy, in which a dominant party has been able to gradually liberalize the political system while maintaining a hegemonic position through an extensive network of patronage ties.[29] For the purpose of this study, Senegal—as Colombia before it—was democratic enough that we should expect the monadic version of the democratic peace theory to be applicable.

The 1988 Senegalese elections were a moment of high drama in Senegal's political evolution. Four presidential candidates and six party lists for National Assembly seats participated in a contest

---

28. See Chowdry and Beeman, "Senegal," p. 165.

29. See Ousmane Kane and Leonardo Villalón, "Islam and Democracy in Senegal: The Crisis of Legitimacy and the Emergence of a Muslim Opposition Movement," paper presented at the annual meeting of the International Studies Association, Chicago, February 22–25, 1995; and Coulon, "Senegal," pp. 141–178.

marked by increasingly heated debate; and although incumbent President Diouf received 72 percent of the vote, the opposition parties charged him with fraud. What distinguished these elections from previous ones was the willingness and capability of the opposition to challenge the official results in the streets during a time of economic hardship and urban discontent. To address increasing popular unrest, student strikes, and lack of personal security in the streets, Diouf orchestrated after the elections a "roundtable" with the major political parties, and forged a rocky alliance with two opposition parties—the Socialist Democratic Party (PDS) and the Independence and Labor Party (PIT). To add to the political fragility of Senegal's government, the economic and social climate was also very volatile, following the austerity measures adopted with the assistance of the International Monetary Fund.[30]

During April and May 1989, the government of President Diouf combined both activism and prudence in its approach to the dispute with Mauritania, with the result that the PDS criticized it for appearing timid. Its initial response to the crisis was measured, and designed to preserve Senegal's reputation as a moderate country that can serve as an international mediator. President Diouf condemned the human rights violations in what he called "the inhuman and degrading treatment" of Senegalese in Mauritania and said, "I understand the pain and anger that the Senegalese people feel," but he appealed for an end to vengeance. "An attitude of vendetta would put at risk the lives of our fellow countrymen left in Mauritania," he said in a broadcast on April 30. Diouf blamed Mauritania for the border incident, and said he would welcome an international committee to investigate it.[31] This moderation was also apparent in May 1989 at the summit of French-speaking countries held in Dakar; Senegal asked the other participants in the conference not to make an issue of its differences with Mauritania.

The opposition, some of whose leaders came from the Senegal River Valley region, heavily criticized President Diouf for failing to protect the rights of indigenous blacks in the border areas with Mauritania and in Mauritania itself. Thus, while Diouf pronounced

---

30. See Crawford Young and Babacar Kante, "Governance, Democracy, and the 1988 Senegalese Elections," in Goran Hyden and Michael Bratton, eds., *Governance and Politics in Africa* (Boulder, Colo.: Lynne Rienner, 1992), p. 57; and Kane and Villalón, "Islam and Democracy in Senegal," p. 6.

31. Quoted in *African Research Bulletin*, Vol. 26, No. 5 (May 15, 1989), p. 9242.

himself opposed to war, he had to take into account public opinion, which accused him of weakness over the Mauritanian issue. Considering the economic situation, some in the government could see war as a way of escaping from domestic problems and bolstering the regime's decreasing domestic popularity. [32]

The opposition took advantage of the volatile social and economic situation to mobilize the public in massive demonstrations and protests, forcing the regime to take a harder line. This harder line was manifested in the breakdown of diplomatic relations on August 21, 1989, and the redeployment of Senegalese troops from Gambia to the Senegalese-Mauritanian border. Moreover, citizens from the Senegal River Valley were forming powerful lobbies. It was after the religious leader Thierno Mountaga had made his position against Mauritania public that President Diouf proposed that the Senegalese frontier be extended some miles to include both banks of the river. To make things even worse for the government, the same year the Senegambia Confederation was dissolved, relations with Guinea Bissau over a territorial dispute worsened, and the MFDC (Mouvement des Forces Démocratiques de Casamance), a terrorist group, threatened the secession of the Casamance province. In sum, the democratic character and the relative openness of the Senegalese society, linked to its chaotic economic, social, and political situation, pushed the country in the direction of war.

By the end of 1989, Senegalese Foreign Minister Ibrahim Fall stressed that his country would never initiate an armed conflict with Mauritania, but warned that Senegal would defend its territorial integrity at all costs, using force if necessary. He said that the border incidents took place because some of the 48,000 Mauritanians deported to Senegal by Mauritania in 1988–89 on racial grounds— they were all Black Africans—crossed back over the Senegal River to recover their lost property. He added that to date, the Senegalese army had not been implicated in any border incidents, but said that gunshots had been heard on the Mauritanian side.[33] By the beginning of 1990, the Senegalese and Mauritanian armed forces exchanged sporadic artillery salvos along the border.

---

32. The fact that democratically elected leaders often escalate international conflicts as a way to divert attention from pressing domestic problems or to bolster support for the regime is logically inconsistent with the monadic version of the democratic peace theory. I thank Miriam Fendius Elman for her suggestions on this point.

33. *West Africa*, November 13–19, 1989, p. 1910.

In sum, the picture of the Senegalese management of the crisis is a complex one, and similar to Colombia's behavior during the Leticia crisis. At the beginning of the crisis (April–May 1989), President Diouf adopted a conciliatory tone and insisted upon the formation of a binational commission to investigate the events that led to the crisis with Mauritania. Later on, as he had to confront a very difficult social, economic, and political situation at home, an activist public opinion, and a militant political opposition, Diouf gradually hardened his position; for instance, he made revisionist claims regarding the border demarcation with Mauritania. These revisionist demands clearly contradicted the accepted principle of *uti possidetis* and even the agreements that had founded the Organization for the Development of the Senegal River in 1972. Ultimately, and despite the heightened tension in 1990, the democratic government of President Diouf managed to avoid a full-fledged war with Mauritania.

NONDEMOCRATIC MAURITANIA'S CRISIS MANAGEMENT

Unlike Senegal, Mauritania was not democratic in 1989–90. Mauritania had been under military rule since 1978, when military officers ousted President Ould Daddah. In 1984, Colonel Maaouya Ould Sid'Ahmed Taya seized power in a bloodless coup; his authoritarian regime has been accused of ethnic cleansing, slavery, repression and detention of opposition leaders, continued human rights violations, and widespread discrimination against black Moors and Black Africans. The white Beydanes (Moors) dominate the country politically and economically. They maintain a political alliance with their former black slaves or *haratines* and other "black Maures." Since 1987, the regime had faced increasingly active opposition from many of its own citizens, in addition to an unaccustomed degree of international scrutiny regarding its violations of human rights.[34]

Mauritania's handling of the crisis reflected its unstable and unintegrated nature. The issue of race permeated most of the political problems in the country. From July 1978 to April 1992, Mauritania passed through a succession of three military regimes. The Ould Taya government withstood a coup attempt in October 1987. This attempted coup was the most dramatic action to date of militant Toucoulor opposition to the Moorish government, and it was

---

34. See Pazzanita, "Mauritania's Foreign Policy," p. 294; and *Freedom in the World: The Annual Survey of Political Rights and Civil Liberties, 1994–1995* (New York: Freedom House, 1995), pp. 395–396.

supported by a clandestine group based in Dakar called FLAM, which has sought to exploit historical tensions between the Moorish cultural majority and Black ethnic groups. The lack of national integration was also amply demonstrated in the territorial dispute that erupted between Mauritania and Senegal in April 1989. A clandestine Moslem group known as the Ba'athist movement had emerged in the country in the early 1970s. Its philosophy was ultra-Arabic, anti-Black and anti-Christian. In the April 1989 conflict, it organized a pogrom against non-Arab and particularly black Mauritanians. Thus, the Ba'athists took advantage of the international crisis with Senegal to increase their control of the domestic political scene.[35]

Before April 1989, Mauritania's relations with Senegal were already strained. Land reform in Mauritania at the expense of Toucoulor farmers only exacerbated the tensions between the two countries. Once the crisis detonated in April 1989, it is clear that the escalation of the conflict in Mauritania resulted from the regime's racism and animadversion toward the black minority. The mounting Black African opposition to the regime provided a strong incentive for the government to incorporate the border problem with Senegal into the larger racial and domestic context, which led it to act forcefully; among other actions, Mauritania expelled thousands of its own Black African citizen across the border, according to its "Arabization program."[36]

Mauritania turned to Iraq for military assistance as it prepared for a possible war with Senegal in the fall of 1989 and the beginning of 1990. Yet, the regime wanted to ensure its political survival, rather than fight an international war that it could not win. Mauritania felt that the international crisis had been orchestrated by Senegal, due to its own domestic political problems. According to this view, the deterioration of the domestic situation in Mauritania simply provided Senegal with a convenient pretext for taking actions that had little to do with the fact that Mauritania was an authoritarian state that violated human rights. In the words of Mauritanian President Maaouya Ould Taya:

It was Senegal that organized the events. It was Senegal that on August 21 broke diplomatic relations between the two countries. It is Senegal that keeps under practically forced labor thousands of Mauritanians, and organizes armed groups that cross the river. . . .

---

35. See Bluwey, "Mauritania," p. 93.

36. See Parker, "The Senegal-Mauritania Conflict of 1989," p. 161; and *Africa Confidential*, September 22, 1989, pp. 3–4.

The FLAM is a Senegalese invention, organized and armed by the Senegalese authorities. . . . The territorial demands by Senegal stand in contradiction to the convention of the OMVS (Organization for the Development of the Senegal River) signed in 1972. . . . As a matter of fact, Senegal has sustained bad intentions against Mauritania since 1981, when its domestic political situation started to deteriorate. The incident at Sonko was resolved by the visit of the Senegalese interior minister to Nouakchott. After that, Senegal suddenly ignited the candle. This coincided with a political crisis in Senegal. . . . We in Mauritania have received so far about 240,000 expelled citizens [from Senegal]. . . . The issue is not a domestic problem [within Mauritania], but an international one. . . . The territorial problem was created by a certain ethnic group from Senegal, which has decided to appropriate Mauritanian territory.[37]

While Senegal accused Mauritania of serious violations of human rights and mistreatment of Black Africans, Mauritania charged the Senegalese government with raising illegal revisionist claims about their common border, and also blamed the Senegalese press for creating a "climate of tension" that constituted "a danger to stability and peace in the region."[38] Interestingly, each country attributed the escalation of the crisis to the other's domestic political troubles. Senegal saw the crisis as a Mauritanian manipulation to crush its Black African opposition. Mauritania saw the crisis as a golden opportunity for Senegal's democratic regime to rally its tarnished popularity. Whether both Senegalese and Mauritanians were right or wrong in their assertions, neither the nondemocratic nor the democratic government was eager to start a full-fledged war; the differences in their regime type do not seem to have affected their predisposition toward war or peace. Indeed, as in the Leticia case, the eventual resolution of the crisis can be explained without any reference to the differences in Senegal and Mauritania's political regimes.

Alternative Explanations to the Democratic Peace Argument

In accounting for the peaceful resolution of the crises between Peru and Colombia and between Senegal and Mauritania, the domestic regime types of the countries involved played a minimal role. This section assesses four plausible and not mutually exclusive explana-

---

37. Quoted in Soudan, "Interview," pp. 34–37 (my translation from French).
38. *West Africa*, November 13–19, 1989, p. 1910.

tions for why war was averted. Two are based at the international level of analysis, and two at the domestic level. First, a regional normative consensus affected the predisposition of the states involved against war. Second, regional and extra-regional hegemons, assisted by regional and international institutions, assisted in the mediation and resolution of the crises by peaceful means. Third, the material impotence, evidenced by the lack of economic, military, and even political means of weak powers and weak states, impeded fighting full-fledged wars. Finally, sudden leadership changes led to significant shifts in the formulation of foreign policy and the peaceful resolution of the crises.

THE ROLE OF A REGIONAL NORMATIVE CONSENSUS AGAINST WAR
In both the Leticia and the Senegal River Valley disputes, a regional normative consensus facilitated the crises' peaceful management and resolution. One can argue that these two crises stemmed from the practical difficulties of implementing the accepted norms of peaceful settlement and *uti possidetis*, and were aggravated by domestic problems and a limited use of force. The effectiveness of the regional normative consensus suggests that nondemocratic regimes do not necessarily apply their internal norms of political behavior to their foreign relations. In other words, both Mauritania and Peru were able to invoke norms of conflict resolution, compromise and bargaining, and mediation at the international level, though they ignored similar norms at home.

THE SOUTH AMERICAN NORMATIVE CONSENSUS AND THE LETICIA CRISIS. In the past one hundred years, the South American countries have gradually established a unique Latin "diplomatic culture" that has helped their governments to resolve their international conflicts short of war. Based upon a common historical and cultural framework, the South American nations have built a strong regional normative consensus, which includes a normative and legal reluctance to engage in war against fellow South American nations. The major norms and principles of South America's diplomatic system include: *uti possidetis* (recognition of the former colonial borders); peaceful international coexistence (the principle of *convivencia*); non-intervention and mutual respect of national sovereignties; and the peaceful settlement of international disputes, including the use of arbitration, mediation, and similar juridical and diplomatic techniques.[39]

---

39. See Holsti, *War*; John R. Redick, "The Tlatelolco Regime and Nonproliferation in Latin America," *International Organization*, Vol. 35, No. 1 (Winter 1981), p. 111;

During the Leticia crisis, both Peru and Colombia invoked various multipartite instruments relating to the peaceful settlement of disputes. Peru appealed to the Treaty to Avoid Conflicts (the Gondra Treaty) of 1923 for arbitration and to the Inter-American Conciliation Convention of Washington of 1929, for the legal revision of the 1922 treaty by which it had transferred Leticia to Colombia. Colombia appealed to the Covenant of the League of Nations (1919), and to the Kellogg-Briand Anti-War Pact of 1928 to condemn the illegal Peruvian occupation of Leticia. Peru's legal position against the principle of the observance of treaties was based upon three arguments: first, the principle of *rebus sic stantibus* (the occupation of Leticia led to a change in conditions); second, the fact that the 1922 treaty was finalized by Leguía, a tyrannical dictator without democratic approval; and third, that the principle of self-determination of the inhabitants of the Leticia area should be respected. In addition, Peru directly appealed to the South American normative consensus against war in the expectation that this would prevent Colombia from escalating the crisis into a full-fledged war. A Peruvian editorial summarized this normative position:

The attitude of Colombia would have been quite different if, instead of making its declaration on the intangible sanctity of treaties, and instead of peremptorily recommending to Peru the acceptance of Brazilian mediation without changes, . . . it should understand that the peace of America stands above all other considerations, and that the keeping of the peace should never be sacrificed to the text of a diplomatic agreement which, while negotiated to promote harmony among peoples, was converted into an instrument of hatred and a cause of war.[40]

After the assassination of Sánchez Cerro, the new Peruvian president was seriously concerned about the possible reactions of other

---

Peter H. Smith, "Political Legitimacy in Spanish America," in John J. Johnson and Peter J. Bakewell, eds., *Readings in Latin American History*, Vol. II (Durham, N.C.: Duke University Press, 1985), p. 155; Ronald H. Ebel, Raymond Taras, and James D. Cochrane, *Political Culture and Foreign Policy in Latin America: Case Studies from the Circum-Caribbean* (Albany: State University of New York Press, 1991); and Luis Quintanilla, "Latin America," in Philip W. Buck and Martin B. Travis, eds., *Control of Foreign Relations in Modern Nations* (New York: W.W. Norton, 1957), pp. 175–181.

40. Editorial of *El Comercio* (Lima), March 3, 1933, quoted and translated in Wood, *The United States and Latin American Wars*, p. 216.

South American countries in case of war. Similarly, the Colombian government, following its traditional recourse to legalism and diplomatic procedures, underlined the need to avoid the war to maintain South America's normative consensus. In an exchange of telegrams with President Benavides, Alfonso López, the Colombian negotiator, underlined that:

The peaceful resolution [of the crisis] will set a precedent for the Latin American peoples, underlining the norm that among them there should not be territorial conflicts that would lead to armed interventions. . . . We have to respect the diplomatic tradition and the international conventions.[41]

Thus, although the normative consensus that existed between Peru and Colombia could not keep the dispute from becoming a serious military crisis, it helped to prevent the Leticia crisis from exceeding the bounds of a fragile, negative peace.

THE WEST AFRICAN NORMATIVE CONSENSUS AND THE SENEGAL RIVER VALLEY DISPUTE. As in South America, the West African states have developed a normative consensus to respect the norms of territorial integrity and *uti possidetis*. The norms of behavior sanctioned by the Organization of African Unity in 1964 in favor of the "freezing" of the international borders were designed to keep the international peace in the region, and to delegitimize international war as a mechanism to resolve international disputes. The policies of the vast majority of African states have reflected their respect for their existing borders; the major exceptions are Somalia, Morocco, Ghana, and Togo in 1957–66, and to a lesser extent, Senegal's claims in 1989–90. The basic norms among the African states include: non-intervention in the domestic affairs of other African states; non-recourse to force in inter-African relations, so that interstate wars were not considered as legitimate policy alternatives; a preference for African solutions to African problems; and respect for the territorial status quo, as established by the colonial powers.[42]

The adoption of the principle of *uti possidetis* helps keep territorial disputes from proliferating and escalating into armed conflagra-

41. Letter from Alfonso López to President Benavides, May 10, 1933, in López, *La Política Internacional*, pp. 22–24 (my translation from Spanish).

42. See Claude E. Welch, *Dream of Unity: Pan-Africanism and Political Integration in West Africa* (Ithaca, N.Y.: Cornell University Press, 1966), pp. 14–23; and Jon Kraus, "The Political Economy of African Foreign Policies: Marginality and Dependency, Realism and Choice," in Shaw and Okolo, *The Political Economy of Foreign Policy in Ecowas*, pp. 269–270.

tions. Yet, it does not address the possible conflicts arising from different interpretations of documents defining the border demarcations (as in the cases of Mauritania-Senegal and Burkina Faso–Mali), as well as disputes related to irredentist claims based on historical demands dating from before the colonial period (as in the cases of Morocco and Somalia).

In the case of the Senegal River Valley dispute, the African norm of respect for the territorial status quo was challenged by Senegal's revisionism about its border with Mauritania, despite the claim by Senegalese officials that they were simply applying the OAU principle of the inviolability of colonially inherited boundaries. Senegal invoked a colonial treaty signed in 1933 as the legal basis for its claim; this retrospective implementation, more than fifty years later, could not receive the support of the OAU or of ECOWAS because of its dangerous implications for other boundaries of the continent. It was obvious that Mauritania was not likely to negotiate peacefully the loss of large tracts of fertile land.[43] Hence, Senegal had to confront and resolve the inherent contradiction between its revisionist challenge to the norm of *uti possidetis* and its conservative and moderate foreign policy in the region in general, including its professed predilection for the peaceful settlement of international disputes. Ultimately, as in the Leticia case, the normative consensus facilitated the de-escalation and conciliation between these two francophone states.

HEGEMONS AND INTERNATIONAL INSTITUTIONS

The normative consensus in favor of keeping the negative peace in both South America and West Africa has been facilitated by the action of a regional or extra-regional hegemon, assisted by the work of regional and international institutions. The regional hegemon and the international institutions can fulfill the roles of mediators, peacemakers, and peacekeepers. In the Leticia crisis these roles were filled by Brazil, the United States, the League of Nations, and to a lesser extent Argentina and Chile. In the Senegal-Mauritania dispute, France, the Organization of African Unity, and ECOWAS had pacifying effects upon the resolution of the crisis.[44]

---

43. Parker, "The Senegal-Mauritania Conflict of 1989," p. 169.
44. On the role of regional hegemons and hegemons in general, see Robert Gilpin, *War and Change in World Politics* (Cambridge: Cambridge University Press,

HEGEMONS AND INTERNATIONAL INSTITUTIONS IN THE LETICIA CRI-SIS. Several international actors played a significant role in defusing the Leticia dispute in the early months of 1933. Brazil, the prospective South American hegemon, was particularly prominent in the peaceful resolution of the crisis. Both Colombia and Peru had agreed to the Brazilian mediation since the beginning of the crisis, with the support of the United States. On December 30, 1932, Brazilian Foreign Minister Afranio de Mello Franco, had proposed to Colombia a plan for Peru to deliver Leticia to Brazil, and for Brazil to restore it to Colombia, with the understanding that Colombia and Peru would settle their territorial dispute in talks in Rio de Janeiro, with Brazil acting as a mediator. Although the plan was not accepted by the parties, it was adopted by the League of Nations in March 1933 as a basis for its own interim administration of Leticia. The parties to the dispute accepted the League Plan by the end of May 1933, initiated negotiations under Brazilian auspices, and signed a final peace agreement in Rio de Janeiro the following year.[45]

The United States, Argentina, Chile, the Pan American Union, and the League of Nations also played important roles in deterring the parties from escalating their crisis into a full-fledged war. On January 24, 1933, U.S. Secretary of State Henry L. Stimson consulted the Kellogg-Briand Anti-War Pact signatories about Colombia's plea that Peru was an aggressor, and decided to condemn Peru's occupation of Leticia in strong terms. Similarly, on March 18, 1933, the League Council demanded the complete evacuation by the Peruvian forces of the whole territory of Leticia.[46]

1981); Raymond Aron, *Peace and War: A Theory of International Relations* (New York: Doubleday, 1966), pp. 152–153; and David J. Myers, "Threat Perception and Strategic Response of the Regional Hegemons: A Conceptual Overview," in David J. Myers, ed., *Regional Hegemons: Threat Perception and Strategic Response* (Boulder, Colo.: Westview, 1991), pp. 1–29.

45. On the role of Brazil in South America, see Robert A. Humphreys, *The Evolution of Modern Latin America* (Oxford: Clarendon Press, 1946), pp. 142–143; Philip Kelly, "Geopolitical Tension Areas in South America: The Question of Brazilian Territorial Expansion," in Robert Biles, ed., *Inter-American Relations: The Latin American Perspective* (Boulder, Colo.: Lynne Rienner, 1989), pp. 190–209; and David J. Myers, "Brazil: The Quest for South American Leadership," in Myers, *Regional Hegemons: Threat Perception and Strategic Response*, pp. 225–268. On Brazil's role in the Leticia dispute, see Barros, *Ocho Años de Política Exterior del Brasil*.

46. On the role of the League of Nations, see Stan Windass, "The League and

HEGEMONS AND INTERNATIONAL INSTITUTIONS IN THE SENEGAL RIVER VALLEY DISPUTE. France has maintained its overarching presence over its former colonies in West Africa, sometimes preventing the outbreak of serious civil or interstate wars throughout most of the region. At the end of the 1980s, France still sustained a clear post-colonial commitment to its former dependencies, based upon cultural, economic, strategic, and prestige considerations. During the Senegal River dispute, France maintained good relations with both Senegal and Mauritania, and joined forces with Nigeria, Mali, Algeria, Saudi Arabia, ECOWAS, and the OAU to resolve the crisis by peaceful means.[47] In addition to France, ECOWAS, which since the early 1980s has been an important political forum for the consensual behavior of its member states,[48] worked with the OAU to normalize the relations between the two countries with relative ease.

As the conflict escalated by the end of 1989, each side tried to involve its external allies. Senegal turned to ECOWAS and to the Organization of African Unity; Mauritania turned to the Arab League and to the recently created Maghreb Arab Union. Much to their credit, these regional and international organizations refused to be partisan, and worked together to contain the crisis without apportioning blame and responsibility. Thus, the peaceful outcome was ultimately the common effort of all these international institutions, in addition to France, Nigeria, Mali, Togo, Morocco, Algeria, and Saudi Arabia.[49]

Territorial Disputes," in Evan Luard, ed., The International Regulation of Frontier Disputes (London: Thames and Hudson, 1970), pp. 77–81. On the U.S. role, see Wood, *The United States and Latin American Wars.*

47. On the French role in West Africa, see I. William Zartman, "Africa and the West: The French Connection," in Bruce E. Arlinghaus, ed., *African Security Issues* (Boulder, Colo: Westview, 1984), p. 40; R. Omotayo Olaniyan, "Nigeria and West Africa: Problems and Prospects in Future Relations," *Nigerian Journal of International Affairs,* Vol. 12, No. 1–2 (1986), p. 148; and Bola A. Akkinterinwa, "The Role of France in Nigeria's Relations with its Neighbors," *Jerusalem Journal of International Relations,* Vol. 12, No. 1 (1990), pp. 112–147.

48. See Baffour Agyeman-Duah and Olatunde J.B. Ojo, "Interstate Conflicts in West Africa: The Reference Group Theory Perspective," *Comparative Political Studies,* Vol. 24, No. 3 (1991), pp. 299–318.

49. Bluwey, "Mauritania," pp. 98, 100.

MATERIAL IMPOTENCE TO FIGHT FULL-FLEDGED WARS

The absence of war and the ultimate peaceful resolution of the two crises could be attributed to a factor that is unrelated to the regional normative consensus and the presence of hegemons and international institutions: the plain material impotence of all the states involved to fight international wars across their borders. A scarcity of interstate transportation linkages, poor technology, underdeveloped economies, and the want of the material basis to sustain long and modern wars have clearly deterred many states, especially in the Third World, from engaging in full-fledged international wars. In other words, a negative peace is sustained not because of any lack of will, but because of a lack of money and infrastructure. The cases of Leticia and the Senegal River Valley provide powerful support for this argument.

Many developing countries are weak states; they have low levels of political institutionalization, legitimacy, and stability, and high levels of domestic conflict. Such weak states, which are usually also weak powers in international relations, seem to concentrate their political efforts upon the domestic arena. Rather than fight across their borders to augment their domestic base of support, weak nondemocratic states are usually not eager to become involved in international wars. Thus, paradoxically, it is precisely their institutional weakness and sense of insecurity at home that explain the cautious and even conservative foreign policies of weak states, and their predisposition to maintain the regional order.[50]

This argument is illustrated by the behavior of authoritarian regimes ruled by the military. As Stanislav Andreski eloquently argues, military dictatorships are not predisposed to fight international wars. He suggests that there might be an intrinsic "incompatibility between the internal and external uses of the armed forces, which makes them less apt for one if they are being employed for the other."[51] That is, weak states tend to be immersed in domestic conflicts and even civil wars, though they are reluctant to be involved in international wars.

---

50. See Mohammed Ayoob, "The Third World in the System of States: Acute Schizophrenia or Growing Pains?" *International Studies Quarterly*, Vol. 33, No. 1 (March 1989), p. 71; Brian L. Job, "The Insecurity Dilemma: National, Regime and State Securities in the Third World," in Brian L. Job, ed., *The Insecurity Dilemma: National Security of Third World States* (Boulder, Colo.: Lynne Rienner, 1991), pp. 12–13; and Jackson and Rosberg, "Why Africa's Weak States Persist."

51. Stanislav Andreski, *Wars, Revolutions, and Dictatorships* (London: Frank Cass, 1992), p. 104.

MATERIAL IMPOTENCE, GEOGRAPHICAL ISOLATION, AND THE FUTIL-ITY OF A WAR OVER LETICIA. The lack of economic resources by both Peru and Colombia affected their disposition to engage in a full-fledged war. In addition, the remote location of Leticia deterred a war of conquest and expansion. Moreover, despite the divergence in their political regimes, in 1932–33 both were weak states that focused their political efforts upon problems of domestic stability and legitimacy. Hence, although both regimes wanted to profit domestically from the crisis over Leticia, they were able to assess the danger of a full-fledged armed confrontation.

For both countries, Leticia was remote. Trans-Andean communications were extraordinarily difficult, and the only way either Peru or Colombia could bring heavy military equipment to the Leticia area was to bring it up over the top of South America, to the Amazon River, through Brazil. Leticia was 1,700 miles from Pará, Brazil, at the mouth of the Amazon. From Pará to Barranquilla, the nearest port in Colombia, the distance was about 2,200 miles. From Callao, the closest port in Peru on the Pacific Ocean, the voyage through the Panama Canal to Pará and then to Leticia was about 5,500 miles.[52]

Both countries encountered serious financial problems in preparing for war, but neither could expect any financial return from the control over Leticia that could compensate for the exorbitant costs of a prolonged conflict, such as the Chaco war being fought at about the same time.

For Peru, one reason to accept the peace plan in May 1933 was the lamentable unreadiness of the Peruvian navy compared with the capacity of Colombia, which was demonstrated when two transports with 1,650 troops bound for Leticia arrived in Trinidad on May 22.[53]

It is clear that Colombia was also aware of the "ruinous consequences of an armed conflict, especially given the economic situation of both nations." For example, in May 1933, Alfonso López wrote to his former diplomatic colleague, Peruvian President Benavides, asking him to cooperate and to improve Colombia's political and economic links with Peru, rather than fight a futile war. In response, President Benavides wrote:

Under the present economic conditions, the armed conflict cannot be sustained over long time without bringing misery and mourning to

---

52. Wood, *The United States and Latin American Wars*, p. 180.
53. Ibid., p. 244.

two fraternal peoples. . . . There is a need to end the war preparations in both sides of the border. . . . As you say, the Bolivarian nations need to cooperate to defend their common economic interests.[54]

Thus, economic and financial conditions, and serious difficulties in mobilizing the national economies for a long war acted to defuse the crisis and to find a peaceful resolution of the dispute over Leticia.

MATERIAL IMPOTENCE AND THE FUTILITY OF A WAR OVER THE SENE-GAL RIVER VALLEY. The most important sources of threats to the West African states have been domestic, rather than international. Since they are immersed in dealing with their domestic problems, the issue of interstate wars has been quite irrelevant. Furthermore, they have been quite unable to fight among themselves. Thus, the negative regional peace is not only the consequence of French or Nigerian hegemony, or a result of a normative consensus against war institutionalized through the work of ECOWAS; it is also a result of their material impotence to fight international wars. The typical military forces of these states are very weak, and are organized for neither border defense nor aggressive attacks. This military weakness is a direct result of the underdeveloped state of their economies, which has acted as a deterrent to fight extended external wars. Thus, territorial expansionism has been very rare in Africa in general, and in West Africa in particular, leading to a widespread respect for the territorial status quo.[55]

In the Senegal-Mauritania dispute, a major reason why the crisis never escalated into a full-fledged war was the economic hardships experienced by both countries at that time. The massive repatriation of Senegalese and Mauritanians destroyed vital sectors of both countries' economies. In addition, Mauritanian plans for agricultural development were seriously affected by the worsening of relations with Senegal. It seems that neither country was economically or

---

54. Letter from López to Benavides, May 2, 1933; letter from Benavides to López, May 8, 1933; quoted in López, *La Política Internacional*, pp. 19–22 (my translation from Spanish). The Bolivarian nations are Peru, Colombia, Venezuela, Ecuador, and Bolivia.

55. Robert O. Matthews, "Interstate Conflicts in Africa: A Review," *International Organization*, Vol. 24, No. 3 (Spring 1970), pp. 356–357; Henry Bienen, "African Militaries as Foreign Policy Actors," *International Security*, Vol. 5, No. 2 (Fall 1980), pp. 168–186; and Robert H. Jackson, "The Security Dilemma in Africa," in Job, *The Insecurity Dilemma*, pp. 88–90.

militarily prepared for a full-fledged war, despite the alleged military assistance of Iraq to Mauritania and the prestige Senegal enjoyed within French West Africa. As President Diouf of Senegal summarized these material constraints in July 1989, "You have to be mad in today's world to look for a war, especially when you are not only an under-developed country, but also a Sahelian one."[56]

Paradoxically, while the Senegal-Mauritania conflict revealed the domestic weaknesses of both states, the militarization of the dispute helped to strengthen and validate the legitimacy of both regimes. That is, the perception of a common threat, linked to the expulsion of incompatible (foreign) elements within the nation, aggravated the crisis but helped the threatened political regimes. Yet, the negative effects of the crisis and its ultimate peaceful resolution suggest that poor African economies cannot bear the costs of a "European" pattern of state-building, by which "states make wars" and "wars make states."[57]

LEADERSHIP CHANGES

A second domestic-level explanation can account for why Peru and Colombia backed down from the brink of war: domestic changes within political regimes can bring to power new and more moderate political leadership.

An abrupt leadership change took place during the Leticia dispute after Sánchez Cerro was assassinated on April 30, 1933. The new president, General Oscar Benavides, was a close personal friend of Alfonso López, a prominent leader of the Liberal Party in Colombia; this soon became vitally important to the peace negotiations. Only two days after the death of Sánchez Cerro, direct negotiations over Leticia commenced between the two countries.

The leadership change in Peru was crucial in resolving the dispute, though Peru did not change its regime type—it remained an authoritarian state. The resolution of the crisis shows that regime change is important insofar as it brings new leaders to power who might be more moderate. This case highlights that the relatively unchanging nature of a state's regime type—democratic versus nondemocratic—is not the only domestic variable that might account for peace and war.

---

56. Quoted in *Africa Research Bulletin*, Vol. 26, No. 9 (September 15, 1989), p. 9370.

57. See Charles Tilly, "War Making and State Making as Organized Crime," in Peter B. Evans, Dietrich Rueschemeyer, and Theda Skocpol, eds., *Bringing the State Back In* (Cambridge: Cambridge University Press, 1985), pp. 169–191; and Parker, "The Senegal-Mauritania Conflict of 1989," p. 171.

Implications and Relevance for the Democratic Peace Theory

The Leticia and Senegal River Valley crises tend to disconfirm the monadic version of the democratic peace theory. Although these two crises did not escalate into wars, the evidence does not show that the behavior of Colombia and Senegal was inherently more peaceful (or more belligerent) than that of Peru and Mauritania. The cases neither confirm nor disconfirm the dyadic claim that democracies do not fight each other. The theory does not rule out the possibility that mixed dyads might maintain a fragile negative peace, although it suggests that peace might be more difficult to achieve in a mixed dyad than in a democratic one. Thus, the democratic peace theory does not account well for instances of negative peace in the Third World between nondemocratic or mixed dyads; however, it might be very relevant to assessing the "upgrading" of the quality of peace, once the process of democratization makes a mixed dyad into a democratic dyad.

Peace and war in the two cases analyzed in this chapter were apparently unrelated to the fact that the political regimes of the countries involved were very different. Senegal, one of the most democratic African regimes, was the revisionist party, not Mauritania. Colombia decided to risk a war that was ultimately avoided because of the assassination of the Peruvian president. Hence, these cases require explanations that focus on variables other than regime type.

Two empirical findings from the cases seem to contradict, or at least transcend, the tenets of the democratic peace theory: the detrimental role of public opinion, and the very positive role played by regional normative consensus. Public opinion and domestic interest groups tend to play a detrimental or negative role in terms of crisis management. This happens especially within democratic regimes, such as Colombia and Senegal. Thus, democratic regimes are often more vulnerable to undesired escalation than their nondemocratic counterparts: due to institutional constraints and the influence of opposition parties that can often manipulate public opinion, the escalation of international disputes can become a requirement for retaining domestic political power.

Conversely, regional normative frameworks play a very positive role regarding peaceful management of international crises. These normative frameworks do not merely influence the behavior of democracies—they can also affect the war and peace propensities of nondemocratic or mixed dyads. Thus, nondemocracies, as well as mixed groups of states, can establish and maintain peaceful relations among themselves, including possible zones of stable peace.

Nonetheless, regional democratization seems to be crucial in defining the quality of that peace, and democratic dyads may enjoy a more stable peace. For example, democratization played a crucial role in the movement from negative peace to stable peace in the evolving relations between Peru and Colombia, once both countries became democratic. Thus, democratic peace theory—in its dyadic form—may help explain how stable peace and pluralistic security communities evolve, while it may be less helpful in explaining the emergence of a peace that is characterized simply by the absence of war. In short, whether democracy reduces international conflict depends not only on the way we define democracy and war, but also on the way we think about peace.

Part IV
Nondemocratic War
and Peace: Is
Authoritarianism the
Culprit?

Chapter 9

Is Autocracy an Obstacle to Peace? Iran and Iraq, 1975–80

Martin Malin

Democratic states have rarely if ever gone to war with one another. The most important and widely accepted explanations for this observation identify specific internal norms and institutions that are thought to prevent decision makers from using force when two democracies have a dispute. This chapter examines what happens when democratic norms and institutions are absent. What are the implications of democratic peace theory for relations among non-democratic states, and what lessons can the behavior of autocratic states yield for those who wish to understand the causes of peace among democracies? An investigation of the causes of peace and war between Iran and Iraq in the 1970s and 1980s suggests some answers to these questions.

A study of relations between autocratic states can offer valuable insights into the separate peace among democracies. First, it provides a basis for comparison. If characteristics peculiar to democracies account for their separate peace, then the foundations of peace between autocracies should be built from different stuff than that which undergirds peace among democracies. Democratic peace theorists do not claim that peace is impossible outside the democratic "zone"; however, many do claim that whereas democracies are capable of constituting and maintaining peaceful relations founded upon shared norms of behavior, autocratic states can enjoy peace only when it is backed up by coercive threats or calculations of strategic advantage. No study has yet

The author thanks F. Gregory Gause, Michal Hershkowitz, Randall Schweller, and Miriam Fendius Elman and the other authors in this volume for helpful comments on the first draft of this chapter.

tested the claim that shared *democratic* norms are a necessary condition for establishing a principled peace.

Second, several of the causal arguments developed to explain why democracies do not go to war with one another imply a corollary relationship between autocratic political norms and structures and greater war propensity.[1] No case studies of war or crises between nondemocracies have examined whether these causal mechanisms are indeed at work. Thus, an examination of the behavior of autocratic states can help to refine the various hypotheses advanced by democratic peace theorists, and to integrate them with the more general literature on the domestic origins of war and peace.

A detailed study of relations between Iraq and Iran in the 1970s and 1980s is ideal for a number of reasons. First, Iran and Iraq are both highly repressive regimes. If the nature of peace is related to the internal attributes of states, then Iranian-Iraqi relations should contrast sharply with relations among democracies. Likewise, if any states are likely to exhibit unconstrained aggressive behavior attributed to nondemocracies by some democratic peace proponents, Iran and Iraq should do so. Second, the relationship between Iran and Iraq underwent dramatic change in the period under study. A deeply rooted and violent conflict between the two states was first peacefully settled in 1975, and then reemerged in 1980 when Iraq initiated war after the Iranian revolution. This variation makes it possible to uncover both the causes of peace in the 1970s and the reasons for war in 1980, while holding constant contextual factors such as culture and geography. Finally, the Iranian-Iraqi relationship is a valuable case study for investigating the sources of international cooperation and conflict because of the Persian Gulf's importance in the international political economy, and the long history of great power involvement there.

The investigation yields some surprising results. In the 1970s, I find that despite the violently antidemocratic norms of conflict resolution in both countries, and because of the absence of governmental and societal constraints on foreign policy, Iran and Iraq were able to transcend their long-standing differences in the 1975 Algiers Accord. Contrary to the predictions of democratic peace hypotheses, the agreement did not merely reflect the absence of conflict due to stalemate,

---

1. Often these corollaries are made explicit. See, for example, Bruce Russett, *Grasping the Democratic Peace* (Princeton, N.J.: Princeton University Press, 1993), pp. 35, 40; Zeev Maoz and Bruce Russett, "Normative and Structural Causes of Democratic Peace, 1946–1986," *American Political Science Review*, Vol. 87, No. 3 (September 1993), p. 626; and David Lake, "Powerful Pacifists: Democratic States and War," *American Political Science Review*, Vol. 86, No. 1 (March 1992), pp. 24–35.

coercion, or coincidental interests. Instead, like the "democratic peace," it was founded upon shared norms and principles such as reciprocity and respect for sovereignty. Thus, the absence of internal democratic norms and structures in warring states does not preclude either negotiated conflict resolution or the establishment of norm-governed peace.

In 1980, Iran and Iraq behaved at first glance much as would be predicted by democratic peace theorists: internal conflict associated with the Iranian revolution spilled over the borders and Iraq took forceful action in response to the new threat. However, despite the combined effects of overwhelming opportunities for Iraq to enhance its relative position, and domestic conditions in each state that either permitted aggression or pushed decision makers in a bellicose direction, the war was quite slow to erupt; it was not until nearly two years after the Shah of Iran was overthrown that the Iraqi government finally took forceful action. The lag indicates that the earlier peace was indeed quite robust, and that the predisposition of autocratic states to aggressively exploit international opportunities for aggrandizement may not be as pronounced as suggested by at least some of the proponents of the democratic peace theory.

Finally, there are practical lessons to be drawn from the case of Iranian-Iraqi relations. Although there are many good reasons to encourage democratic reform around the world, the promotion of international peace and stability may not be one of them. Autocratic states can create and enjoy stable peace, based on shared principles. Likewise, conflict among autocratic states should not be treated as if it is intractable by the United States and its democratic allies simply because of the domestic political characteristics of the adversaries.

In the following sections, I review the chief hypotheses that purport to explain peace among democracies, calling particular attention to the corollary causal claims about relations among nondemocracies. I then examine Iranian-Iraqi relations in the 1970s and 1980s, comparing the causes of peace and war suggested by the historical record to the predictions of democratic peace hypotheses. I conclude with a summary of my findings and their implications for the democratic peace proposition.

Democracy and Autocracy: Causal Paths to Peace and War

Two sets of arguments have been proposed to explain the existence of exclusive "zones of peace" among democracies. Both also suggest why autocracies may be more warlike. The first set of arguments highlights the effects of governmental and societal structures on foreign policy choices. The second set of arguments focuses on how domestic political norms affect a state's international relations. For most democratic peace theorists, it is the cumulative effect of a number of probabilistic causes that underpins the claim that democracy is sufficient to produce peace. The same logic leads them to propose that autocratic rule not only readily permits aggressive foreign policy, but may also predispose the state to such behavior. In short, for democratic peace advocates, autocracy is both a necessary cause of international conflict and a condition that increases the probability of war.

STRUCTURAL CAUSES OF WAR AND PEACE

One set of arguments for why democracies do not fight one another focuses upon the domestic structural features of democratic rule.[2] The governmental "checks and balances" common in democracies limit the autonomy of the executive and slow down the decision making process when the use of force is being considered, thus reducing the chances of war.[3] The deliberate nature of decision making in democracies also reduces the likelihood of miscalculated escalation. Conversely, the relative absence of checks and balances in the decision making process frees autocratic leaders to act on impulse. The lack of institutionalized processes for self-evaluation in strategic decision making increases the probability of miscalculation. It also increases the haste with which leaders can respond to perceived threats with force. When a dispute develops between autocracies, centralized decision making processes may obscure each state's intentions toward the other and exacerbate the security dilemma. According to Zeev Maoz and Bruce Russett: "Conflicts between nondemocratic systems are . . . more likely to escalate because both leaderships operate under relatively few structural constraints. The failure of initial efforts to find a peaceful solution may result in a rapid flare-up of the conflict into a violent level."[4]

---

2. See for example, Russett, *Grasping the Democratic Peace*, chap. 2; James Lee Ray, *Democracy and International Conflict: An Evaluation of the Democratic Peace Proposition* (Columbia: University of South Carolina Press, 1995), pp. 30–37; Maoz and Russett, "Normative and Structural Causes of Democratic Peace," pp. 625–626; Sally H. Campbell and T. Clifton Morgan, "Domestic Structure, Decisional Constraints and War: So Why Kant Democracies Fight?" *Journal of Conflict Resolution*, Vol. 35, No. 2 (June 1991), pp. 189–193.

3. Russett, *Grasping the Democratic Peace*, p. 40.

4. See Maoz and Russett, "Normative and Structural Causes of Democratic Peace," p. 626.

A related argument claims that in democracies, societal pressures exerted through institutionalized channels constrain costly, aggressive foreign policies. Competitive elections enable citizens to hold leaders accountable for burdensome wars and exercise a "citizen's veto" over costly policies.[5] The protection of free expression encourages public debate, keeping the electorate informed and increasing the sensitivity of decision makers to the domestic political costs of their choices. This sensitivity makes leaders more cautious. Public scrutiny also inhibits leaders from using force when the strategic rationale for war cannot be reconciled with the values of a liberal democratic society.[6] By contrast, the absence of institutionalized channels for public expression gives leaders in nondemocratic states more leeway to use force. The absence of competitive elections unshackles autocratic leaders from the restraints imposed by cost-averse publics. Restrictions on freedom of expression and the government's control of information inhibit public education about the likely costs of war, and raise the costs to those contemplating opposition to the regime or its policies.[7] Thus, the absence of popular constraints enables autocratic leaders to assume greater risks and higher costs in their decision calculus. As Russett has argued, "leaders of nondemocracies are not constrained as leaders of democracies are, so they can more easily, rapidly, and secretly initiate large-scale violence."[8]

David Lake proposes that the lack of societal constraints on leaders has an even more pernicious and direct effect on the foreign policies of autocratic states. According to Lake, autocracies are not only free to act aggressively, they are predisposed to do so: autocratic states "will possess an imperialist bias and tend to be more expansionist and, in turn, more war-prone."[9] Because autocratic states are less hindered by societal opposition than are democracies, they are able to engage in intensive and predatory domestic resource extraction, or "rent-seeking." The unbridled pursuit of societal resources, according to Lake, is the source of the autocratic proclivity for expansionism; expansion of

5. Michael Doyle, "Liberalism and World Politics," *American Political Science Review*, Vol. 80, No. 4 (December 1986), p. 1160; and Morgan and Campbell, "Domestic Structure, Decisional Constraints and War," pp. 190–191.

6. Randall Schweller, for example, has found that democratic states do not engage in preventive war. See "Domestic Structure and Preventive War: Are Democracies More Pacific?" *World Politics*, Vol. 44, No. 2 (January 1992), pp. 235–269.

7. Lake, "Powerful Pacifists," p. 26.

8. Russett, *Grasping the Democratic Peace*, p. 40.

9. Lake, "Powerful Pacifists," p. 24.

the territory and population under the state's control increases the state's extraction opportunities. Moreover, the process of external expansion—the provocation of crises, and war itself—provides leaders with the perfect pretext for scapegoating foreigners and extorting ever more resources from their citizens.[10]

NORMS AS A CAUSE OF WAR AND PEACE

A second set of arguments highlights the role of domestic political norms. Domestic political norms, especially those governing conflict resolution, spill over into international relations, with important implications for the causes of war and peace. Within a democratic political culture, political competition is bounded by the rejection of violence and coercion. All sides to a conflict understand that "winning does not require the elimination of the opponent, and losing does not prohibit the loser from trying again."[11] This internal consensus on the norm of peaceful competition is transmitted to international relations when a democracy finds itself in a dispute with another democracy.[12] Because each side shares common norms for conflict resolution, force is neither contemplated as a quick means to victory, nor even considered as a strategy of last resort. Moreover, according to William Dixon, not only are democracies less quick to fight, but also their shared norms of conflict resolution make them "better equipped" for negotiating peaceful settlements when disputes arise.[13]

---

10. Ibid., pp. 24–30. One could supplement Lake's causal claims with the argument that the governing coalitions in authoritarian regimes are likely to be composed of precisely those groups best positioned to benefit from aggressive foreign policies. Military, bureaucratic, and industrial interest groups with narrowly focused interests in expansion are commonly at the center of authoritarian political coalitions. See Jack Snyder, *Myths of Empire* (Ithaca, N.Y.: Cornell University Press, 1991).

11. Maoz and Russett, "Normative and Structural Causes of Democratic Peace," p. 625. William Dixon also discusses the idea of bounded competition and its implications for international conflict resolution at length. See William Dixon, "Democracy and the Peaceful Settlement of International Conflict," *American Political Science Review*, Vol. 88, No. 1 (March 1994), pp. 14–32.

12. According to Maoz and Russett, "political culture and political norms constitute images that a state transmits to its external environment." See "Normative and Structural Causes of Democratic Peace," p. 625. See also Michael Doyle, "Kant, Liberal Legacies, and Foreign Affairs," in Michael E. Brown, Sean M. Lynn-Jones, and Steven E. Miller, eds., *Debating the Democratic Peace* (Cambridge, Mass.: MIT Press, 1996), p. 26; and John Owen, "How Liberalism Produces Democratic Peace," *International Security*, Vol. 19, No. 2 (Fall 1994), pp. 96–98.

13. See Dixon, "Democracy and the Peaceful Settlement of International Conflict," pp. 14–32.

Just as shared democratic norms are thought to produce peace, the lack of nonviolent norms of conflict resolution in nondemocratic polities is presumed to increase the likelihood of war. First, competition for power or resources among groups within states may turn violent when the prevailing political culture provides no strong norms for the peaceful resolution of conflict. This violence may become externalized if elites make scapegoats of foreign nationals to unify their mass support. Alternatively, state leaders may provoke international crises as a means of diverting the attention of the public from the suffering associated with civil strife.[14] Second, the violent internal political practices of autocratic states cause others to be doubly suspicious when such states become involved in international disputes. Since the use of force cannot be ruled out, the pernicious effects of international anarchy are exacerbated. As Russett has argued, "in nondemocracies, decisionmakers use, and may expect their opponents to use, violence and the threat of violence to resolve conflict as part of their domestic political processes. . . . Therefore, nondemocracies may use violence and the threat of violence in conflicts with other states, and other states may expect them to use violence and the threat of violence in such conflicts."[15]

The presence or absence of democratic norms not only influences how conflicts are resolved, it also gives shape to the nature of the ensuing peace. Michael Doyle, drawing on the ideas of Immanuel Kant, draws the distinction between the foundations of peace among liberal democracies, and those which exist outside of the "pacific union."[16] According to Doyle, the principles and norms shared by liberal democracies tame the effects of international anarchy and produce the stable, liberal peace. The "political bond of liberal rights and interests have proven a remarkably firm foundation for mutual nonaggression."[17] Peace between autocracies, by contrast, is primarily founded upon either coercion or the mere absence of conflicting interests. In the first instance, the propensity for autocratic states to

---

14. On the use of foreign policy as a diversion, see Jack Levy, "The Diversionary Theory of War: A Critique," in Manus Midlarsky, ed., *Handbook of War Studies* (Boston: Unwin and Hyman, 1989), pp. 259–288.

15. Russett, *Grasping the Democratic Peace*, p. 35.

16. See Doyle, "Kant, Liberal Legacies, and Foreign Affairs," pp. 3–27. See also Kenneth Boulding, *Stable Peace* (Austin: University of Texas Press, 1979); and Arie Kacowicz's distinction between "negative" and "stable" peace in his chapter in this volume.

17. Doyle, "Kant, Liberal Legacies, and Foreign Affairs," p. 27.

threaten and use force results in a peace grounded in either deterrence and stalemate, or in the imposition of a settlement by a more powerful external actor. The coercive use of military power undergirds such a peace. In the second instance, autocratic peace may merely reflect the absence of conflicting interests, rather than institutionalized agreements based on shared norms and principles.

In sum, the hypotheses draw a sharp contrast between the behavior of democratic and autocratic states, and the nature of the peace they will enjoy. Democratic states tend to be constrained by their internal structures from taking forceful action, especially against fellow democracies; autocratic states are free to act without regard to the wishes of their citizens and are expected to aggress against others given the power and the opportunity.[18] Democracies apply internal norms of conflict resolution to their international relations, at least when they encounter other democracies; autocracies, lacking such norms, tend to externalize their internal conflicts. Democracies enjoy a principled, "warm" peace; autocracies find peace by coincidence or create it with coercion.

Autocracy and Peace: The 1975 Algiers Accord

In March 1975, at the conclusion of an Organization of Petroleum Exporting Countries (OPEC) summit meeting in Algiers, then Iraqi Vice President Saddam Hussein and the Shah of Iran issued a joint communiqué announcing the settlement of disputes that had plagued relations between the two countries. The statement, which came as a surprise to most observers of politics in the region, promised "a new era in the relations between Iran and Iraq in the higher interest of the future of the region."[19] The agreement, known thereafter as the Algiers Accord, addressed border demarcation disputes, both in Iraq's central region and along the Shatt al-Arab waterway, and associated security problems.[20]

---

18. Russett, *Grasping the Democratic Peace*, p. 32.

19. "Algiers Declaration of March 6th, Joint Communiqué between Iran and Iraq," in Tareq Ismael, *Iraq and Iran: Roots of Conflict* (Syracuse, N.Y.: Syracuse University Press, 1982), p. 62.

20. Discussions of the 1975 Algiers Accord can be found in Majid Khadduri, *The Gulf War* (New York: Oxford University Press, 1988), pp. 57–63; Christine Moss Helms, *Iraq: Eastern Flank of the Arab World* (Washington, D.C.: Brookings Institution, 1984), pp. 144–151; and R.K. Ramazani, "Iran's Search for Regional Cooperation," *Middle East Journal*, Vol. 30, No. 2 (Spring 1976), pp. 177–179.

The Algiers Accord, a peaceful settlement between highly autocratic states, represents an interesting puzzle for the democratic peace hypotheses outlined above. Those hypotheses suggest that the internal structures of nondemocratic states permit or predispose leaders to engage in international conflict, while internal norms of political interaction handicap their international conflict resolution skills. However, if this is true, then the case of the 1975 Algiers Accord should include evidence of at least some of the following conditions. First, the issues that the accord settled should not have been very difficult ones to resolve, and their political and economic stakes should have been low. Second, if the stakes were significant, then the agreement should have been founded upon vague, weakly institutionalized commitments that would allow each side to quickly reverse itself and resume violent conflict. Finally, if real conflicts of interest did exist, there should have been significant signs of external coercion undergirding the agreement; that is, either a third party should have compelled the parties to settle, or a settlement should have been imposed by the stronger party on the weaker one. In short, the democratic peace hypotheses outlined above would explain Iranian-Iraqi peace between 1975 and 1980 as either insignificant, fictional, or forced.

In this section, I review the nature and intensity of the conflict between Iran and Iraq prior to their 1975 accord, and examine the peace accord and its significance for Iranian-Iraqi relations. I then consider the international and domestic causes of the 1975 accord. I find, contrary to what the democratic peace hypotheses would predict, that Iran and Iraq were able to overcome significant and deeply rooted conflicts through peaceful negotiation and to establish warm, peaceful relations. This outcome was not compelled by changes in the international system. To the contrary, it was facilitated by domestic political and economic conditions in Iran and Iraq.

THE CONFLICT PRIOR TO 1975: DEEP ROOTS AND HIGH STAKES
The differences between Iran and Iraq in the late 1960s and early 1970s ran deep and were often deadly.[21] At stake were billions of dollars in

---

21. For accounts of the conflictual relations between the two states in the 1960s and 1970s, see Majid Khadduri, *Socialist Iraq: A Study in Iraqi Politics Since 1968* (Washington, D.C.: Middle East Institute, 1978), pp. 148–153; Marion Farouk-Sluglett and Peter Sluglett, *Iraq Since 1958* (London: KPI, 1987), pp. 164–170; and Edmund Ghareeb, "The Roots of the Conflict," in Christopher Joyner, ed., *The Persian Gulf War* (Westport, Conn.: Greenwood, 1990), pp. 23–29.

oil revenues, and each state's strategic position in relation to the other and the rest of the Gulf region. More serious still, the conflict posed a threat to the survival of both regimes, though the danger was worse for Iraq. Prior to the Algiers agreement, neutral observers believed the conflict to be intractable: the two states engaged in frequent border disputes and skirmishes, and each interfered in the internal affairs of the other through clandestinely organized and in some cases armed opposition groups. The salience of the outstanding issues between the two countries and the intensity of the conflict highlight the significance of the shift toward a peaceful settlement.

BORDER DISPUTES. Two regions in particular were a source of tension in the years immediately prior to the Algiers Accord: the border region in central Iraq to the northeast of Baghdad, and the southern border, along the Shatt al-Arab waterway. The central border region was endowed with oil reserves that spanned the border, and was home to a high concentration of Iraqis of Persian origin. The Shatt al-Arab, a waterway formed by the confluence of the Tigris and Euphrates rivers, flows for approximately one hundred miles into the Persian Gulf. Along the lower half of the waterway, the two countries share a border. As Iraq's only outlet onto the Gulf, the Shatt al-Arab is a vital artery for Iraqi commerce and oil production. Iran has also used the waterway extensively, building a major oil facility on its shores at Abadan and a port at Khorramshahr.

Border conflicts in this region have centuries-long historical roots.[22] The Ottoman and Persian empires came to an agreement in 1847 at Erzurum; the Persian border was drawn at the eastern bank of the Shatt al-Arab, excepting those regions where Persia had ports of commerce, where the border was to be the median point of the waterway. The agreement was short-lived, as were numerous subsequent arrangements. After World War I, Britain turned over the Basra port on the waterway to what became modern Iraq, but Iran refused to recognize Iraqi control, persisted in using its own pilots to navigate the waterway, and disputed the border established in earlier agreements. Though a partial settlement was reached in 1937 with the help of the League of Nations, tensions continued to fester.

The Shah of Iran took up the issue immediately after the fall of the

---

22. Historical accounts of the border disputes in the region are provided by Kaiyan Homi Kaikobad, *The Shatt-al-Arab Boundary Question* (New York: Oxford University Press, 1988); and Ismael, *Iraq and Iran*, pp. 1–23.

Iraqi monarchy in 1958. In 1969, the issue came to a head following disputes over Iran's refusal to pay tolls to the Iraqi authorities, to lower the Iranian flag while navigating the waterway, to comply with Iraqi regulations in the Basra port, and to keep Iranian naval personnel out of Iraqi ports. Iran unilaterally abrogated the 1937 treaty, placed naval and air forces on full alert, and sent an armed escort with a vessel down the waterway. Iraq responded by expelling tens of thousands of Iranian pilgrims visiting Shi'ite holy sights. With both sides of the river heavily fortified, a standoff ensued. Following a failed coup attempt in which Iran was implicated, Iraq broke off diplomatic relations in May 1970. Tension escalated further when the Shah increased the pressure on the Iraqi regime by engaging in military maneuvers in Iraq's central border region, and openly assisting Kurdish rebels in northern Iraq.

In 1970, and again from 1972 to 1974, a series of border clashes took place along a 125-mile stretch of Iraq's central border region with Iran, northeast of Baghdad. Each side alleged that the other had violated the border, and each side incurred casualties in the military skirmishes. The most serious fighting occurred in early 1974, in which a total of more than fifty Iranian and Iraqi soldiers were killed. The United Nations mediated a cease-fire, and in May 1974, the secretary general announced that the two sides had agreed to a simultaneous withdrawal from the disputed region. However, the cease-fire broke down later in the summer.[23] It was not until the March 1975 accord that the border both in the central region and on the Shatt al-Arab was finally stabilized.

SUBVERSION. The border conflagrations between Iraq and Iran occurred against the backdrop of efforts by each side to weaken or subvert the domestic political position of the opposing regime. When tensions over the Shatt al-Arab rose in 1969, Iraq began broadcasting to Arabic-speaking residents of the oil-rich region of Khuzistan in Iran. Reviving Iraq's earlier claims to that area, the broadcasts encouraged the residents of the region to revolt against the Shah's rule.[24] Iraq also at times encouraged the anti-Shah political activities of Shi'ite religious leaders. The Ayatollah Ruhollah Khomeini, then residing in the Shi'ite holy site of Najaf in Iraq, was among those

---

23. Khadduri, *Socialist Iraq*, pp. 150–151; and Helms, *Iraq*, pp. 147–148.

24. R.K. Ramazani, *Iran's Foreign Policy, 1941–1973* (Charlottesville: University Press of Virginia, 1975), p. 418.

solicited by the Iraqi regime to participate in Iraqi efforts to weaken the Shah at home. Khomeini kept his distance from the Iraqi government, but his anti-Shah positions were well known, and he occasionally issued appeals from Najaf to the Iranian people to demonstrate against the Iranian regime's secular, Western-oriented policies.[25]

Iran's interference in Iraqi affairs was far more extensive. A January 1970 coup attempt by retired Iraqi military officers who had coordinated their planning with and received weapons from Iran was exposed, and the perpetrators placed under arrest. During their trial, Iraqi prosecutors made public evidence of taped conversations between the coup plotters and Iranian officials.[26] The plotters received death sentences. It was immediately after the failed coup that border skirmishes began in the central border region, and many expected that full-scale war was imminent.

More serious still was Iranian support for Kurdish rebels in northern Iraq. Iraqi Kurds were engaged in a protracted war with the Iraqi government over their demands for greater autonomy. Fighting against the Ba'ath government had first broken out in 1969, when it became clear to Kurdish leader Mullah Mustafa Barzani that the government would not fulfill its original promises to grant Kurdish autonomy. The Shah, initially fearing that Kurdish nationalist violence in Iraq could spread to the Iranian Kurdish community, offered only limited support. Beginning in 1972, however, with the active encouragement of the United States, Iran's support of the Kurdish revolt became much more substantial. As a result, the Kurds succeeded in tying down four-fifths of the fully mobilized Iraqi military in a costly civil war, inflicting heavy casualties. The Kurds not only fought with U.S. and Israeli arms supplied by Iran, but in December 1974 and January 1975, the Shah deployed Iranian forces to "liberated" Kurdish areas in Iraq near the border, offering artillery and anti-aircraft support to the insurgents.[27] Three months later in Algiers, Iran and Iraq announced their intention to settle their differences peacefully.

---

25. See James Bill, *The Eagle and the Lion* (New Haven, Conn.: Yale University Press, 1988), p. 185; and Dilip Hiro, *The Longest War* (London: Grafton Books, 1989), p. 26.

26. Khadduri, *Socialist Iraq*, pp. 53–56; Helms, *Iraq*, p. 145.

27. On Iranian support for the Kurds in the early and mid-1970s, see Edmund Ghareeb, *The Kurdish Question in Iraq* (Syracuse, N.Y.: Syracuse University Press, 1981), chaps. 7–8; Khadduri, *The Gulf War*, pp. 52–56; Hiro, *The Longest War*, p. 16; and Helms, *Iraq*, p. 148.

THE ALGIERS ACCORD AS A FOUNDATION FOR PEACE

Both the border conflicts and the issue of subversion were resolved by the 1975 accord. In Algiers, Iran and Iraq decided upon a "definitive demarcation of their land frontiers," and pledged to "restore security and mutual trust along their common boundaries."[28] A formal treaty was negotiated in June, in which the borders were defined in detail. The border along the Shatt al-Arab was placed at the median point of the waterway for the length of the border, and each side enjoyed complete freedom of navigation within the waterway. Iran conceded certain disputed territories to Iraq in the central border region, and a joint commission was established to survey the region and demarcate the boundary. In addition, the two states put "a definitive end to all acts of infiltration of a subversive character."[29] Iranian support for the Kurdish revolt came to an abrupt halt, and Iraq quickly defeated the rebels and imposed its control on the region. Iraqi propaganda in support of Arab opponents of the Shah in the Khuzistan region also ceased.

The horrors of the subsequent eight-year-long Iran-Iraq war, which began in 1980, have cast a long shadow over the 1975 settlement, and have caused some scholars to question the significance of the accord.[30] For example, Daniel Pipes has argued that the Algiers agreement constituted an Iraqi capitulation to Iran—that Baghdad chafed at its concession on the Shatt al-Arab, and exploited the first opportunity to recover its lost position on the waterway. From this perspective, the peace agreement was founded upon Iranian coercion, as might be predicted by democratic peace theorists. However, were such an interpretation correct, one would expect to find evidence of a "cold peace" between Iran and Iraq between 1975 and 1979. The evidence indicates otherwise.

Between 1975 and the departure of the Shah from Iran amidst the revolutionary turmoil of early 1979, relations between Iran and Iraq were completely normalized. Trade relations expanded. The numbers of Iranian Shi'ite pilgrims visiting holy sites in Iraq mushroomed

---

28. "Algiers Declaration of March 6th, 1975," in Ismael, *Iraq and Iran*, p. 61.

29. Ibid.

30. See, for example, Shahram Chubin and Charles Tripp, *Iran and Iraq at War* (Boulder, Colo.: Westview, 1988), p. 23; and Daniel Pipes, *The Long Shadow: Culture and Politics in the Middle East* (New Brunswick, N.J.: Transaction Publishers, 1989), p. 84.

(these visits had been restricted prior to 1975). In 1977, an Iraqi foreign ministry delegation visited Iran and met with the Shah and other Iranian officials to discuss issues ranging from consular affairs to trade to oil policy to tourism.[31] The Shah was accorded full respect in the Iraqi press. Iran and Iraq formed a united front within OPEC, pushing the organization to take a hawkish stand in its pricing policies.[32] There were even discussions of forming a joint security organization. Saddam Hussein commented publicly in 1976 that the "Iranian-Iraqi rapprochement has permitted discussions for establishing a Gulf security agreement."[33] Cooperation over internal security matters was extensive. When rioting against the Iraqi government by Shi'ite opposition groups erupted in 1977, the Shah dispatched the Empress Farah Diba to the Iraqi holy sites to address the crowds and help the government restore order. Likewise, Iraq made no effort to exploit the Shah's domestic difficulties when his country descended into revolutionary chaos. In fact, at the Shah's request, Khomeini was expelled from Iraq for his anti-Shah rhetoric in 1978. Finally, even after the Shah had fallen, Iraq cautiously welcomed the new regime in Tehran, expressed hope that the friendly relations that had grown in recent years would continue, and inquired in particular about the revolutionary regime's intentions regarding the 1975 agreement.[34] It was only when Tehran did not reciprocate that the disputes between the two states began to reemerge.

The evidence of friendly relations between 1975 and 1979 clearly indicates that the Algiers accord was a stable, peaceful settlement in which respect for agreed-upon norms and principles played a central role. The agreement reflected neither an Iraqi bandwagoning strategy, nor a continuation of the hard-nosed balance-of-power politics that had characterized Iranian-Iraqi relations prior to 1975. Instead, the new cooperative arrangement allowed the two states, under the regimes that negotiated it, to transcend centuries-old differences and

---

31. Helms, *Iraq*, pp. 150–151.

32. F. Gregory Gause, "Gulf Regional Politics: Revolution, War, and Rivalry," in Howard Wriggins, ed., *Dynamics of Regional Politics* (New York: Columbia University Press, 1992), p. 47; and Ramazani, "Iran's Search for Regional Cooperation," pp. 177–178.

33. Quoted in Edmund Ghareeb, "Iraq: Emergent Gulf Power," in Hosein Amirsadeghi, ed., *The Security of the Persian Gulf* (London: Croom Helm, 1981), p. 213.

34. Khadduri, *The Gulf War*, pp. 68–69; and Edmund Ghareeb, "The Roots of the Crisis," pp. 29–31.

put an end to untold losses of blood and treasure.[35] Each side made commitments that were not cast aside when opportunities to gain unilateral advantage presented themselves. According to historian Majid Khadduri, until the Iran-Iraq war, the Algiers Accord represented "the most significant milestone in Iraqi-Iranian relations since the turn of the century."[36]

MOTIVATIONS FOR THE 1975 ACCORD
The Algiers Accord rested upon important domestic political and normative foundations. The peace did not emerge from changed international conditions that removed earlier conflicts of interest. Nor was the peace imposed. International conditions did not compel either side to come to a settlement. Instead, the desire by both the Iranian and Iraqi governments to concentrate on internal political problems; the absence of domestic constraints on the negotiators; and the prospect of increasing externally derived rents from oil sales combined to motivate decision makers to come to a peaceful settlement. In addition, the expectation of reciprocity and the institutional forum provided by OPEC facilitated the achievement of the settlement.

INTERNATIONAL INCENTIVES. International and regional circumstances provided mixed incentives to Iranian and Iraqi decision makers regarding each state's policies toward the other in the mid-1970s. Changes in the international environment did not dissolve earlier disputes, though they did provide some new motivation for reaching an accommodation.

The most important international condition that moved the two sides toward a peaceful settlement was the post-1973 oil boom.[37] Leaders in both states understood that the opportunity costs of continued conflict were potentially enormous. War would drain resources from economic development projects at precisely the time

---

35. Paul Schroeder has defined "transcendence" in international relations as a strategy of "attempting to surmount international anarchy and go beyond the normal limits of conflictual politics: to solve the problem, end the threat, and prevent its recurrence through some institutional arrangement involving international consensus or formal agreement on norms, rules, and procedures for these purposes." The Algiers Accord clearly reflects such a strategy. See Paul W. Schroeder, "Historical Reality vs. Neo-realist Theory," *International Security*, Vol. 19, No. 1 (Summer 1994), p. 117.

36. Khadduri, *Socialist Iraq*, p. 153.

37. For an analysis of the effects of the oil boom on regional politics, see Gause, "Gulf Regional Politics," pp. 41–44.

when sufficient capital was available. Discord within OPEC hindered the extent to which each could take advantage of the benefits of the oil boom. Furthermore, oil revenues increased the independence of each state from its respective superpower patron, freeing each from the pressures of satisfying Cold War concerns in Washington and Moscow, and relaxing the polarization of the region. Nonetheless, given the history of conflict between the two states, leaders on both sides could not easily neglect the strategic concern for maintaining their relative position, especially in a period of such rapid economic and military expansion. Moreover, newfound autonomy from the superpowers meant that the constraints each patron imposed on the actions of its regional ally were weakened. Thus, the oil boom's pacifying effects on foreign policy were tempered by an exacerbation of the security dilemma in the region, which might have elevated suspicions on both sides.[38]

If international factors were primarily responsible for the Iran-Iraq accord, then the case would not seriously contradict the logic of democratic peace theory. However, the mixed incentives emanating from the international system are not sufficient to account for the shift in Iranian and Iraqi policies. In fact, contrary to the predictions of democratic peace theory, the domestic political and economic goals of each country carried greater weight in bringing about the accommodation.

DOMESTIC POLITICS, AUTOCRACY, AND PEACE. Domestic political concerns played a crucial role in moving both Iran and Iraq toward a settlement in 1975. At least three causal mechanisms were at play. First, especially for Iraq, but also for Iran, the settlement was motivated by a desire to dedicate greater resources to the consolidation of the regime and the suppression of its internal opponents.[39] The Algiers Accord allowed both states to pursue their internal goals. These cases, therefore, do not appear to support the claim that among regimes that lack peaceful norms of conflict resolution, internal and external aggression will be positively related. Instead of externalizing the violence within their borders by making scapegoats of one another and by adopting aggressive, diversionary foreign policies,

---

38. Ibid., p. 44.

39. On the logic of seeking a pacific international environment to permit the achievement of domestic goals, see Stanislav Andreski, "On the Peaceful Disposition of Military Dictatorships," *Journal of Strategic Studies*, Vol. 3, No. 3 (December 1980), pp. 3–10.

Iran and Iraq negotiated a peaceful relationship that permitted each greater success in quelling opponents at home.

In Iraq, the government's desire to prevail in its war against the Kurds was a central motivation for reaching an accord with Iran.[40] The agreement with Iran cut off the Kurds' principal source of external support, and allowed the government to intensify its war against the insurgents while alleviating concern over an expansion of hostilities on the Iranian front.[41] The government began its offensive within six hours of the announcement of the Algiers Accord, and Kurdish resistance was stamped out just over two weeks later.[42] Iran had similar domestic motives for putting an end to the conflict with Iraq. In the early to mid-1970s, state violence against dissenters became increasingly commonplace. The settlement with Baghdad enabled a diversion of resources away from the conflict with Iraq, which could be put to good use against domestic opponents.[43] The Shah hoped that the accord, which ended Iraqi support and inspiration for opponents to his regime, would make easier the job of silencing domestic critics. It is likely that the Shah's decree establishing a single-party system just prior to his departure for Algiers—further consolidating the position of the monarchy—was part of a coordinated plan.[44] Thus, for both the Shah and the Iraqi regime, the Algiers Accord was a means to ease the demands of the regional system in order to focus on trouble at home.

---

40. Helms, *Iraq*, p. 150; Ghareeb, *The Kurdish Question in Iraq*, pp. 171–172; and Hiro, *The Longest War*, p. 17.

41. The Iraqi government's accommodation of Iran is a case of what Steven R. David has called "omnibalancing," in which state leaders seek to eliminate their most pressing internal opponents by allying with the latter's primary external patron. See Steven R. David, "Explaining Third World Alignment," *World Politics*, Vol. 43, No. 2 (January 1991), pp. 233–256.

42. On the post-Algiers Iraqi political and military suppression of the Kurds, and the collapse of the Kurdish resistance, see Ghareeb, *The Kurdish Question in Iraq*, pp. 171–174; and Farouk-Sluglett and Sluglett, *Iraq Since 1958*, pp. 187–190.

43. The Shah's support of Iraqi Kurds not only consumed resources that might be better spent at home, but also created the possibility of new domestic problems. Success of the Kurdish forces in Iraq, it was feared, could have a contagious effect on the large Kurdish population in Iran. See Bill, *The Eagle and the Lion*, p. 207; Hiro, *The Longest War*, p. 16; and Ramazani, "Iran's Search for Regional Cooperation," pp. 177–178.

44. On the Shah's efforts to consolidate his rule in the early and mid-1970s, including the establishment of a single-party system, see Ervand Abrahamian, *Iran Between Two Revolutions* (Princeton, N.J.: Princeton University Press, 1982), pp. 439–446; and Bill, *The Eagle and the Lion*, pp. 186–192.

A second attribute of domestic politics in Iran and Iraq that contributed to the conclusion of the Algiers Accord was the absence of
societal demands and governmental structures in either state that
could constrain the foreign policy choices of state leaders. Whereas
democratic peace adherents claim (with some justification, as demonstrated below) that the absence of such constraints makes it easier for
autocratic leaders to use force, in the cases of Iran and Iraq, the freedom of the executive also made it easier to negotiate a peaceful settlement. Neither government had to fear the domestic political
consequences of an unpopular peaceful settlement.

In fact, the agreement was not popular, but societal opposition and
dissent within decision making circles imposed no serious restraint
on the Shah or on the Iraqi Ba'athist Revolutionary Command
Council (RCC) when the issue of rapprochement was placed on the
table. In Iraq, Ba'athist true believers despised the Shah. In both
countries, Shi'ite activists hated the existing secular regimes, and correctly perceived the agreement as directed against them. However,
there is no evidence that either the Iranian or Iraqi government was
concerned with public opinion about the accord. Nor is there evidence that elite political or bureaucratic opponents imposed constraints. In the case of Iran, there is little evidence that the Shah
discussed the Algiers Accord with any members of his cabinet prior
to the negotiations.[45] Vice President Saddam Hussein, who negotiated the agreement from the Iraqi side, operated under somewhat
greater expectations of accountability; there may have been dissent
within the military and the ruling RCC over the shift in policy, yet
none sufficient to prevent a border concession on the Shatt al-Arab
that Iraqi leaders had avoided for two centuries.[46] The Shah and
Saddam Hussein negotiated the accord personally, with only
Algerian President Houari Boumedienne present as a mediator.

Third, rent-seeking played a decisive role in both states' decisions
to settle their differences. However, the desires to maximize rent
extraction resulted in a different causal process, and had precisely the
opposite causal effect, than that proposed by Lake.[47] Extraction

---

45. According to Khadduri, prior to the trip to Algiers, "the Shah made no public
announcement about his departure, nor did he inform his ministers. They were
informed from the plane only after he had left the country." *The Gulf War*, p. 57.

46. Hiro, *The Longest War*, p. 17, notes that the agreement was divisive in Iraqi
political and military circles.

47. Lake, "Powerful Pacifists," p. 24.

efforts were indeed expansive and targeted externally, but they did not require a belligerent revision of state boundaries; on the contrary, rent-seeking through oil sales was facilitated by a more peaceful regional environment and a legitimation of the status quo.[48]

Both Iran and Iraq reaped enormous rents from the explosion in oil prices in the early 1970s.[49] The windfall had profound domestic consequences. The new financial resources allowed each regime to purchase an enhanced capacity for coercion and thereby bolster itself against domestic opposition. Oil rents were also distributed to various societal groups in hopes of buying quiescence, if not loyalty. Both Iraq and Iran initiated enormous economic development and welfare projects in the mid-1970s, and each regime understood that the maintenance and growth of oil rents were the key to domestic consolidation.[50] Thus, Iranian and Iraqi rent-seeking, motivated by domestic political goals, pushed each state to settle with the other.

In sum, domestic conditions in Iran and Iraq had a crucial effect on the decision to seek an accommodation. The absence of nonviolent norms of conflict resolution *within* Iran and Iraq gave rise to efforts to

---

48. The political-economic organization of both Iran and Iraq has been so dominated by the states' pursuit and distribution of oil rents that they have been deemed "rentier states" among scholars of comparative political economy. On the characteristics of rentier states see, for example, Giacomo Luciani, "Allocation vs. Production States: A Theoretical Framework," and Hazem Beblawi, "The Rentier State in the Arab World," in Giacomo Luciani, ed., *The Arab State* (Berkeley: University of California Press, 1990), pp. 65–98; and Hootan Shambayati, "The Rentier State, Interest Groups, and the Paradox of Autonomy: State and Business in Iran and Turkey," *Comparative Politics*, Vol. 26, No. 3 (April 1994), pp. 307–331.

49. In Iran, oil revenues increased from $1.1 billion in 1970, to $18.4 billion in 1975. Meanwhile, the share of oil revenues to total state revenues increased from 45 percent in 1970 to 76 percent in 1975. In Iraq, the picture is similar, though on a smaller scale. In 1970, Iraqi oil revenues totaled $500 million; by 1975 they had increased fifteen-fold to $7.5 billion. See Ian Skeet, *OPEC: Twenty-Five Years of Prices and Politics* (New York: Cambridge University Press, 1988), p. 240; and Shambayati, "The Rentier State, Interest Groups, and the Paradox of Autonomy," p. 318.

50. Iraqi economic development plans in this period are discussed by Phoebe Marr, *The Modern History of Iraq* (Boulder, Colo.: Westview, 1985), pp. 240–244 and chap. 9; Farouk-Sluglett and Sluglett, *Iraq Since 1958*, pp. 227–254; and Joe Stork, "State Power and Economic Structure: Class Determination and State Formation in Contemporary Iraq," in Tim Niblock, ed., *Iraq: The Contemporary State* (London: Croom Helm, 1982), pp. 32–44. Iranian economic development under the Shah in the 1970s is described in Nikkie Keddie, *Roots of Revolution* (New Haven, Conn.: Yale University Press, 1981), pp. 160–182; and Jahangir Amuzegar, "The Iranian Economy Before and After the Revolution," *Middle East Journal*, Vol. 46, No. 3 (Summer 1992), pp. 413–425.

create such norms *between* the two states. The absence of societal and governmental constraints on foreign policy made the accord possible, despite strong internal opposition to it. Meanwhile, the desire to convert oil rents into domestic political and economic gains caused each state to strike conciliatory postures in response to mixed international political incentives.

IMPLICATIONS FOR THE DEMOCRATIC PEACE PROPOSITION

The causes and substance of the peace between Iran and Iraq from 1975 to 1980 are inconsistent with the predictions of the democratic peace hypotheses outlined earlier. Iran and Iraq were able to transcend their deep divisions and long history of conflict through the process of peaceful negotiation. Despite long-standing and deeply rooted disputes, the two autocratic states came to a warm accommodation in which self-restraint and respect for agreed-upon peaceful norms of conduct played a central role. In fact, this case suggests that many of the same norms and principles that constitute the democratic peace may also underlie peaceful relations among nondemocracies.

Moreover, elements of the Iranian and Iraqi autocratic political structures actually facilitated the peaceful outcome. The relationship between these autocracies' domestic and international practices differed significantly from the one described by democratic peace theorists. Violent domestic conflict was not externalized, but rather served as an impetus to peaceful international settlement. Unconstrained leaders exercised their freedom of action to make peace rather than war. Ambitious rent-seeking goals translated into cooperative, concerted strategies rather than unilateral, aggressive policies. This case suggests, therefore, that at least some of the hypotheses on the international behavior of autocratic states deduced by democratic peace theorists should be reconsidered.

Autocracy and War: The 1980 Persian Gulf War

Though the 1975 accord underpinned a significant warming trend in Iranian-Iraqi relations, the period of peace was a brief one. In September 1980, a year and a half after the revolutionary uproar in Iran began, Iraqi President Saddam Hussein announced that Baghdad considered the 1975 Algiers Accord "null and void."[51] Within a few days of the announcement, Hussein ordered a full-scale Iraqi offensive across the Iranian border, launching what would

---

51. President Hussein's statement is quoted in Khadduri, *The Gulf War*, p. 85.

become the most costly war in the history of the modern Middle East. What accounts for the deterioration of Iranian-Iraqi relations in 1979–80? Did aspects of each state's autocratic form of government cause Iran and Iraq to resort more quickly to the use of force once tensions began to emerge?

At first glance, the answers to these questions appear to be consistent with what democratic peace theorists would expect: internal politics in both Iran and Iraq appear to be closely associated with the failure of the Algiers Accord and the outbreak of war. In Iran, the new revolutionary regime exported its Islamic ideology and externalized its domestic turmoil as a means of consolidating its power. Saddam Hussein's decision to respond with force was unconstrained by domestic considerations.

However, the association drawn by democratic peace adherents between autocratic government and war, though present, does not establish cause and effect. To examine the democratic peace hypotheses with greater rigor, I consider what alternative explanations could account for the outcome of war; how war should have developed if domestic factors were a precipitating cause; and whether the outcome would have been different had it not been for the proposed domestic causes.[52]

My investigation of the causes of the Iran-Iraq war suggests that, unlike in the mid-1970s, pressures and opportunities emanating from the regional and international system had a compelling effect on the Iraqi decision for war. Although domestic conditions in both Iran and Iraq undoubtedly pushed each state in a more belligerent direction, neither revolutionary Iran nor the Ba'ath regime of Saddam Hussein behaved in quite the manner suggested by the democratic peace hypotheses.

THE IRANIAN REVOLUTION AND THE WEAKENING OF THE ALGIERS
ACCORD

A broad coalition of groups worked to overthrow the Shah's regime in 1978. The Shah's policies had alienated and embittered the country's merchants, workers, students, leftist political groups, and, of

---

52. On the use of counterfactual reasoning in social science explanation, see James Fearon, "Counterfactuals and Hypothesis Testing in Political Science," *World Politics*, Vol. 43, No. 2 (January 1991), pp. 169–195; and Philip Tetlock and Aaron Belkin, "Counterfactual Thought Experiments in World Politics: Logical, Methodological, and Psychological Perspectives," in Aaron Belkin and Philip Tetlock, eds., *Counterfactual Thought Experiments in World Politics* (Princeton, N.J.: Princeton University Press, 1996).

course, its Muslim clerics. The regime had made weak efforts to liberalize in 1977, but these merely served to unleash the forces that had
been driven together by the Shah's repressive policies. By late 1978,
the Shah had lost control, and in January 1979, he left the country,
never to return. Ayatollah Khomeini arrived in Iran soon thereafter to
take the reins of the revolutionary movement and establish a new
Islamic republic in Iran.[53]

Though the uncertainty produced by the turmoil in Iran could not
have been a source of comfort for the government in Baghdad, the triumph of the revolutionary movement was initially welcomed by
Iraq.[54] Until November 1979, nine months after Khomeini's return to
Iran, relations remained reasonably cordial. Invitations to normalize
relations were extended by Baghdad; Iraq welcomed its neighbor's
withdrawal from the pro-Western Central Treaty Organization,
encouraged Iran to join the nonaligned movement, and lauded its
statements denouncing Israel and the United States. Iraqi efforts at
maintaining good will in the relationship continued after Saddam
Hussein succeeded Ahmad Hassan al-Bakr as Iraqi president in July
1979. However, relations quickly soured after November 1979, when
Mehdi Bazargan resigned as head of the provisional government in
Iran in response to the student takeover of the U.S. embassy in
Tehran, an act encouraged by Ayatollah Khomeini.

As the struggle for power within Iran intensified, so too did tensions with Iraq.[55] Iranian support for Iraqi Shi'ite opposition groups
became more strident and overt. In April 1980, following the first
anniversary of the proclamation of the Islamic Republic, Shi'ite assas-
sins, allegedly acting with Iranian support, made an attempt on the
life of then Vice Prime Minister Tariq Aziz.[56] The Iraqi government
retaliated by expelling thousands of Shi'ites to Iran and by ordering

---

53. On the causes of the Iranian Revolution, see Keddie, *Roots of Revolution;* Said
Arjomand, *The Turban for the Crown: The Islamic Revolution in Iran* (New York:
Oxford University Press, 1988); and Shaul Bakhash, *Reign of the Ayatollahs: Iran
and the Islamic Revolution* (New York: Basic Books, 1986).

54. Khadduri, *The Gulf War,* pp. 80–81; and R.K. Ramazani, *Revolutionary Iran:
Challenge and Response in the Middle East* (Baltimore: Johns Hopkins University
Press, 1988), pp. 58–59.

55. Accounts of the deterioration of Iranian-Iraqi relations in 1979–80 can be
found in Jasim M. Abdulghani, *Iran and Iraq: The Years of Crisis* (London: Croom
Helm, 1984), pp. 178–193; Ramazani, *Revolutionary Iran,* pp. 59–69; Hiro, *The
Longest War,* pp. 27–39; Helms, *Iraq,* pp. 151–162; and Gause, "Gulf Regional
Politics," pp. 50–55.

56. Helms, *Iraq,* p. 156; and Farouk-Sluglett and Sluglett, *Iraq Since 1958,* p. 200.

the execution of a number of Shi'ite leaders who had expressed sympathies with the Islamic revolution. Among those killed was the most prominent Shi'ite leader in Iraq, who was also a personal friend of Khomeini, Ayatollah Muhammad Baqir Sadr. When Khomeini learned of the Iraqi action, he began openly calling for the Iraqi people to rise up and overthrow their government. Border skirmishes increased in frequency and intensity. At the same time, leaders of the Iraqi Kurds returned from Tehran prepared to resume their struggle against the Iraqi government. Finally, in September 1980, Saddam Hussein declared Iraq's abrogation of the 1975 Algiers Accord and launched the Iraqi invasion of Iran.

Saddam Hussein had anticipated a short, low-cost war in which Iraq would reestablish complete control of the Shatt al-Arab, enhance Iraqi access to the Gulf, and seize parts of the oil-rich region of Khuzistan in Iran.[57] The Iraqi air force hit military and economic targets along the border, while five armored divisions crossed into Iran, seizing disputed territory in the central border region and along the Shatt al-Arab.[58] On September 28, six days after launching the offensive, Saddam Hussein indicated that Iraq was willing to consider a cease-fire. However, Iraq had badly miscalculated Iranian cohesion and defense capability. The Iranian government refused to consider a cease-fire and fighting continued. By 1982, the early Iraqi gains had been reversed; Iran then decided to carry the war into Iraq. The fighting ended in a stalemate eight years after it began.

THE CAUSES OF THE IRAN-IRAQ WAR

What caused Iran and Iraq to become more bellicose toward one another? Why did each side fail to find a peaceful way to resolve the problems in their relations after the revolution? How well do the predictions of the democratic peace hypotheses stand against the empirical record, and to what extent are the specified causal mechanisms operating? Clearly, internal conditions contributed to the deterioration of the Iranian-Iraqi relationship following the revolution in Iran: the lack of democratic institutions to limit the authority of state leaders and to channel popular pressures appears to have contributed to the radicalization of both states' foreign policies; and the opposing ideological foundations of the two regimes made it difficult for state

---

57. On Iraqi war objectives, see Helms, *Iraq*, pp. 163–166; and Phoebe Marr, "The Iran-Iraq War: The View from Iraq," in Joyner, *The Persian Gulf War*, pp. 59–64.

58. On the initial military developments, see Hiro, *The Longest War*, pp. 40–49.

leaders to find common ground for the peaceful resolution of their disputes. However, as I argue below, these explanatory factors are outweighed by a set of international conditions that better account for the delayed timing and limited nature of the Iraqi war decision. In autumn 1979, Iraq confronted a set of highly compelling international threats, and after attempting numerous diplomatic strategies in response, it finally turned to the use of force.

AUTOCRACY AS A CAUSE OF THE IRAN-IRAQ WAR. One characteristic of the deterioration of Iranian-Iraqi relations that would be familiar to democratic peace theorists is that internal conflict between state authorities and popular opposition groups in each country was linked to increasingly hostile foreign policies. Iran's revolutionary leaders faced two types of threats from below. First, segments of the highly mobilized urban masses, whose support was crucial for carrying off the revolution, soon threatened to join liberal and leftist opponents of the clerics, especially as economic conditions in Iran deteriorated.[59] The aggressive foreign policy rhetoric, which mixed Iranian nationalism with a universalistic imperative to "export" the Islamic revolution, served to both marginalize critics on the left and keep the popular classes mobilized by directing their energies outward.[60] Second, ethnic opposition to the revolutionary regime from both Kurdish and Arab minorities, fanned especially in the latter case by Iraq, created the danger that the revolution would dissolve into an ethnic conflict. This threat, however, also provided a ready excuse for religious ideologues to hijack Iranian foreign policy by making Iraq the scapegoat for the internal strife while simultaneously gaining the upper hand at home.

Iraq's Ba'ath government was also vulnerable to popular opposition, particularly from Shi'ite sympathizers with the revolutionary movement in Iran. In 1980, after the Iraqi government became convinced that Iran's revolution posed a threat to internal order, internal repression went hand in hand with external belligerence. After years

---

59. Between 1978 and 1980, Iran's GNP declined by nearly 20 percent, owing largely to the drop in oil exports. Government subsidies were cut nearly in half over the same period. See Setareh Karimi, "Economic Policies and Structural Changes since the Revolution," in Nikkie Keddie and Eric Hoogland, eds., *The Iranian Revolution and the Islamic Republic* (Syracuse, N.Y.: Syracuse University Press, 1986), pp. 32–54.

60. Thom Workman, *The Social Origins of the Iran-Iraq War* (Boulder: Lynne Rienner, 1994), pp. 90–97; Chubin and Tripp, *Iran and Iraq at War*, p. 37; and Hoogland, "Iran 1980–85: Political and Economic Trends," in Keddie and Hoogland, *The Iranian Revolution and the Islamic Republic*, p. 24.

of attempting to buy popular complacency by investing a share of the government's oil wealth in the Shi'ite community while simultaneously repressing troublemakers, the Iraqi regime found itself confronting a potentially dangerous surge of opposition whose source of inspiration and material support was the Iranian revolution.[61] Iran became an obvious scapegoat to justify not only the further repression of the Shi'ite activists as a fifth column, but also to rally greater support to the government.

Also consistent with the democratic peace hypotheses is the fact that the absence of institutionalized restraints in the foreign policy decision making processes of both countries appears to have played an important role in the rapid deterioration in relations in the fall of 1979. In Iran, poorly institutionalized and somewhat decentralized control over foreign policy made the issue an important proving ground in the internal struggle for power, resulting in increasingly bellicose rhetoric and policies. The first leader of the provisional government after the revolution, Mehdi Bazargan, favored a pragmatic nationalist approach to foreign policy that required a moderate stance toward both Iraq and the United States.[62] However, even before Bazargan's resignation, as struggles between liberal, leftist, and clerical factions intensified, the clerics used hostility toward Iraq—expressed in terms of outrage at the oppression of Iraqi Shi'ites and the corruption of the secular Ba'ath regime—as an important tool for the consolidation of their power.[63] According to R.K. Ramazani, "armed pro-Khomeini factions roamed the country and, in defiance of the Bazargan government, assaulted the security forces of the provisional government, which sought to protect foreign interests, including Iraqi interests, in Iran."[64] Thus, the internal struggle for power in Iran included competition for control of foreign policy, and hostility toward Iraq became an important tool of the clerics.

In Iraq, it is likely that the highly centralized decision making

---

61. Farouk-Sluglett and Sluglett, *Iraq Since 1958,* pp. 190–200.

62. Even Iraqi officials have acknowledged in retrospect that Prime Minister Bazargan was "cooperative and tried to strengthen relations between the two countries [Iran and Iraq]." See Ramazani, *Revolutionary Iran,* pp. 58–59; Shireen Hunter, *Iran and the World: Continuity in a Revolutionary Decade* (Bloomington: Indiana University Press, 1990), pp. 56–57.

63. Thom Workman finds that there "was a direct link between the aggression against Iraq and the rhetorical world that sustained Iran's revolutionary zeal and consolidated clerical power." See Workman, *The Social Origins of the Iran-Iraq War,* p. 96.

64. Ramazani, *Revolutionary Iran,* p. 59.

structure for foreign policy allowed Saddam Hussein to guide Iraqi policy as he wished with little or no resistance. Saddam Hussein's ascension to the presidency in July 1979 was not trouble-free; however, through a combination of skill and brutality, his elimination of political rivals within the inner circle of the Ba'ath party was thorough.[65] Upon assuming office, Saddam had a number of his rivals on the Revolutionary Command Council put to death. Thereafter, it is quite plausible that dissension over policy choices, even at the highest level, was highly curtailed. This degree of centralization arguably had two effects on the decision to go to war against Iran. First, the decision was likely to have been uncontested. Second, and related, the merits of the decision and the various contingencies associated with it may not have been fully debated by the Iraqi president and his advisers; the origins of Iraqi miscalculations of the strength and cohesiveness of Iranian defenses may lie in the highly centralized Iraqi decision making process.

Finally, democratic peace theorists might contend that the opposing ideological bases of the two regimes made it very difficult for leaders on each side to overcome images of the other as hostile.[66] The Islamic republic's revolutionary mission was to export its vision of an independent Islamic government. Export of the revolution was justified in Iran as a form of self-defense, but its rhetoric undermined the very basis of secular rule in Iraq. The Islamic ideology espoused by the Iranian clerics who were rapidly establishing control over the revolutionary movement contrasted sharply with the secular, Arab nationalist ideology of the Iraqi Ba'ath. Iraqi leaders were alarmed that Iraqi citizens were organizing in support of such principles with Iranian encouragement and finances. Meanwhile, to Khomeini, the secular, socialist Ba'ath regime in Iraq represented not merely a threat to Iran but also an ideological repudiation of Islamic principles.

Though each of these arguments is compelling, each would predict an Iraqi war decision characterized by haste, opportunism, and unlimited goals. However, although Baghdad did eventually initiate the war, it did not act rashly to exploit opportunities to attack a weakened Iran. To the contrary, it made numerous attempts at diplomacy in hopes of maintaining cordial relations. On February 13, 1979, two

---

65. On Saddam Hussein's path to the presidency, see Khadduri, *The Gulf War*, chap. 7; and Helms, *Iraq*, pp. 94–96.

66. The ideology of the Islamic revolution and its effect on Iranian foreign policy is described by Ramazani, *Revolutionary Iran*, pp. 19–31; Hunter, *Iran and the World*, pp. 36–45; and Abdulghani, *Iran and Iraq*, pp. 181–193.

days after the Iranian revolutionaries had established a provisional government under Ayatollah Khomeini, the Iraqi government sent a memorandum reaffirming the Ba'ath government's commitment to pursue friendly relations with Iran, based on the principles of respect for sovereignty and noninterference in domestic affairs as specified in the 1975 Algiers Accord. The memorandum applauded the revolutionary leaders' denunciation of Zionism and the United States, and expressed Iraq's hope "to deepen its friendly relations [with Iran], promote mutual interests, and maintain stability and peace in the region, based on freedom and justice."[67] Later, in April 1979, President Bakr sent congratulations to Ayatollah Khomeini on the occasion of the latter's proclamation of the Islamic Republic. On another occasion, at the meeting of nonaligned states in Havana in 1979, the Iraqi president attempted to initiate high-level talks with Bazargan and his foreign minister on normalization. It was only well after these initiatives failed that the decision to go to war was made.

This evidence of caution and attempted diplomacy in Baghdad is particularly noteworthy given Iraq's enormous opportunities for aggrandizement in the aftermath of the revolution across the border. One crude indicator of the reversal in the two states' relative capabilities is illustrated by oil production trends. Between 1978 and 1980, Iraq more than doubled its own oil income, surpassing Iranian production for the first time in history. Iranian production fell over the same period by 35 percent.[68] Iran's military capabilities were also weakened by the revolution; suspected by the revolutionaries for its former loyalty to the Shah, the military was decimated. Desertions from Iran's 171,000-strong army depleted the force by 60 percent. An additional 12,000, mostly officers, were purged.[69] Finally, the deterioration of the military left the oil fields across the Shatt al-Arab in Khuzistan relatively unprotected. The target was a lucrative one; seizure of Khuzistan oil fields in Iran would have augmented Iraqi income, increased Baghdad's influence in OPEC, and solved the problem of Gulf access.

Additional regional and international incentives should have increased Iraq's temptation to gain relative superiority in the Gulf. The 1978 decision of Egypt, Iraq's traditional rival, to make peace

---

67. Khadduri summarizes the memorandum. See *The Gulf War*, pp. 80–81.

68. Skeet, *OPEC*, p. 240.

69. On the disintegration of the Iranian military after the revolution, see Chubin and Tripp, *Iran and Iraq at War*, p. 33; and Sepehr Zabih, *Iran Since the Revolution* (Baltimore, Md.: Johns Hopkins University Press, 1982), pp. 15–19.

with Israel caused a series of regional realignments, and opened the way for an Iraqi bid for leadership in inter-Arab politics.[70] Turmoil in Iran, coupled with Egypt's isolation (which was engineered by Iraq at the Arab summit in Baghdad in 1979), made Iraq well poised to emerge as a new regional broker in inter-Arab politics. The value of this role was not limited to prestige; as the Cold War was reheated following the Soviet invasion of Afghanistan, Iraq's independence and regional influence promised to win Baghdad new arms and allies in Western Europe and the United States.

The democratic peace propositions cannot explain Iraqi hesitation in the face of opportunity. Most of the above incentives for war were evident by mid-1979, when Saddam Hussein assumed power in Iraq, yet the decision to invade was delayed until September 1980. The democratic peace hypotheses would predict a more rapid exploitation of such overwhelming opportunities. Instead, Iraq attempted to salvage the principles of Iranian-Iraqi relations that had been enshrined in the Algiers Accord.

EXTERNAL THREATS AND THE IRAQI WAR DECISION. A more powerful explanation for why Iraq chose to attack Iran in September 1980 is that the decision was a response to the overwhelming threat posed by Iran.[71] Insecurity, rather than opportunity, motivated Iraq's choice of strategies. According to Iraq experts Efraim Karsh and Inari Rautsi, "war was not his [Saddam Hussein's] first choice but an act of last resort, taken only after trying all other means for deflecting Iran's pressure."[72] As Stephen Walt has found in a recent work, the Iraqi response was a typical one for any state—regardless of regime type— faced with a revolutionary threat. According to Walt: "Like the wars of the French Revolution and the Russo-Polish war, the Iran-Iraq war was a direct consequence of the revolution itself. Both Iran and Iraq saw the other as a potential threat, and each exaggerated its ability to reduce the danger through the use of force."[73]

Iran's deliberate and increasingly bold attempts to topple the Ba'ath government and replace it with an Islamic one in its own image forced Saddam Hussein to attempt to contain the threat militarily. Iraq's relatively modest territorial aims (control of both banks of the Shatt

---

70. Gause, "Gulf Regional Politics," p. 51; Stephen Walt, *The Origins of Alliances* (Ithaca, N.Y.: Cornell University Press, 1987), p. 137.

71. See, for example, Efraim Karsh and Inari Rautsi, *Saddam Hussein* (New York: Free Press, 1991), pp. 147–148.

72. Ibid., p. 148.

73. Stephen Walt, *Revolution and War* (Ithaca, N.Y.: Cornell University Press, 1996), p. 243.

al-Arab and parts of the Khuzastani oil fields) and its early exploration of opportunities for a settlement (declaring a readiness for a
cease-fire as urged by the United Nations only six days after its initial attack) are further evidence that its motives were not overly
ambitious.[74] Iraqi statements emphasized the limited, defensive
nature of its war aims.[75]

The breakdown of reciprocity in the previously cooperative relationship was crucial to Iraq's assessment of the Iranian threat. Iraqi
diplomatic overtures in the months following the revolution were met
mostly by silence. Just as in the 1970s, when the norm of reciprocity
was a central element of the peaceful settlement, so in the 1980s, the
absence of any signal that Iraqi cooperation would be reciprocated by
Iran devastated the relationship. The decision by Iran to carry the war
into Iraq in 1982, at a time when reciprocation of Iraqi willingness to
work toward a settlement would have ended the war, also helps
explain the conflict's duration. An Iranian offer of cooperation would
have attenuated many of the domestic forces pushing Iraq toward the
brink of war.

In addition, the cycle of threats and counterthreats was reinforced
by a failure on the part of international institutions, primarily the
United Nations in this case, to provide proper mediation. According
to Cameron Hume, "despite much huffing and puffing by council
members . . . both governments had grounds to conclude that the
Security Council was unlikely ever to take decisive action."[76] One
might speculate that had there been mediation efforts within an effective institutional context, cooperation might have been advanced
despite the tensions created by the revolution.

In sum, the Iranian Revolution posed an overwhelming threat to
the Iraqi regime, one sufficient to compel a forceful response.[77] The
threat was highlighted by the breakdown of reciprocity in Iranian-
Iraqi relations and compounded by the failure of international insti-

---

74. Karsh and Rautsi, *Saddam Hussein*, p. 148; and Helms, *Iraq*, pp. 166–175. For
an alternative point of view, see Shireen Hunter, who argues that "Iraq's ambitions, as the emerging regional power and as custodian of the Arab nationalist
mantle, and Iran's weakness created an irresistible temptation and triggered the
war." *Iran and the World*, p. 105.

75. See, for example, the discussion in Abdulghani, *Iran and Iraq*, pp. 204–205.

76. Cameron Hume, *The United Nations, Iran, and Iraq* (Bloomington: Indiana
University Press, 1994), p. 34.

77. The threat from Iran may qualify for what Schweller has deemed "extreme
systemic constraints." He argues that such conditions are sufficient to cause even
democratic states to launch preventive war. See "Domestic Structure and
Preventive War," pp. 264–267.

tutions to mediate the emerging conflict. Although Iran's temporary weakness made the use of force an attractive option, Iraq initiated war only after exhausting all other alternatives.[78] Further, Saddam Hussein did not adopt highly ambitious goals. The autocratic nature of the Iranian and Iraqi regimes may have contributed to the deterioration of the relationship, but international compulsion is a stronger explanation for why the war erupted in 1980.

IMPLICATIONS FOR THE DEMOCRATIC PEACE PROPOSITION

The claim advanced by democratic peace theorists that autocracy is a necessary condition for war rests not only upon statistical evidence (which cannot be contested by a case study of two autocracies at war), but also upon an illumination of causal mechanisms that link domestic politics with aggression or war. The evidence from the Iran-Iraq war suggests that external forces moved Iraq toward war; the autocratic nature of the regimes was of secondary importance. Moreover, the role played by domestic politics in causing the war is not explained well by the democratic peace propositions. According to the criteria for coding regime type provided by democratic peace proponents, there was no change in the internal politics of Iran and Iraq in the late 1970s that might account for the change in relations. Neither state became more autocratic. In fact, in Iran significant new channels for popular expression and new standards of accountability emerged during the revolution. Nevertheless, despite the massive revolutionary change that occurred in Iran, and despite the fact that it was this domestic transformation that contributed to the deterioration in the Iranian-Iraqi relationship, democratic peace proponents would not code the Iranian revolution as a regime change. The insights of democratic peace proponents could be made more useful if they were integrated with the larger literature on domestic causes of conflict and cooperation, where dichotomous distinctions such as democracy versus autocracy are broken down further.

Autocracy, Peace, and War

I have reviewed a number of arguments drawn from the literature on the democratic peace, and examined cases in which the proposed causes of peace are absent and the causes of war very much present.

---

78. For accounts that emphasize both the threats and opportunities underlying the Iraqi war decision, see Gause, "Gulf Regional Politics," p. 56; Ramazani, *Revolutionary Iran*, pp. 68–69; and Walt, *Revolution and War*, pp. 238–243.

What I have found in the cases of the 1975 Algiers Accord between Iran and Iraq and the Iran-Iraq war in 1980 has at least two implications for the democratic peace hypotheses.

First, democratic peace theorists have claimed that the causes and nature of peace among democracies are unique. Whereas democratic states can enjoy peace that is domestically rooted in shared norms and principles, autocratic states lack the requisite norms and structures to settle their disputes peacefully. Peace prevails among autocracies only when interests do not conflict, when power balances opposing power, or when peace is imposed by a state with preponderant power. The 1975 Algiers Accord, however, demonstrates that the causes and nature of democratic and autocratic peace are not always different. Iran and Iraq transcended deep differences and achieved a peaceful settlement that was both domestically motivated and founded on agreed-upon norms of conduct. This outcome was permitted by the absence of governmental and societal constraints on foreign policy choices in each country. The accord was also produced by the desire on the part of both Iranian and Iraqi leaders to create order in their external relations so that they could devote more attention to the repression of internal opposition. The case demonstrates that democratic peace theorists have incorrectly deduced that nondemocratic regime characteristics tend to generate belligerence. On the contrary, nondemocratic regime features can at times promote a principled peace. More comparative research on the domestic sources of international peace would be useful, as would research comparing the nature of peace among various regime types.

Second, although evidence from the Iran-Iraq case cannot directly challenge the claim made by democratic peace theorists that autocracy is a necessary condition for conflict, it does raise questions about the existing explanations of that claim. The causal paths from peace to war were only partly predicted by the democratic peace hypotheses. Iran did externalize its internal unrest as democratic peace theorists might expect; however, it did so in the context of its revolution. Its aggressive behavior was determined less by its autocratic form of government than by its revolutionary nature. More importantly, when the Iran-Iraq conflict reemerged after the Iranian revolution, Iraq was quite slow to react and undertook numerous initiatives to avoid war. Prolonged and intense antagonism that threatened Iraq from within and without was finally met with violence only after all attempts to uphold the peaceful relations established at Algiers were rebuffed. When violence was used, its aims were initially quite modest. Iraqi behavior at the outset of the war is thus inconsistent with the predictions of democratic peace theorists, who would have expected Iraq to rapidly exploit opportunities to revise the status quo as soon as international conditions permitted. In addition, the propositions generated in the democratic peace literature, which dichotomize regime type (democracy versus autocracy), *cannot* account for the change in Iran and Iraq's relationship. The regime in each state remained constant according to democratic peace theory, despite the fact that Iran experienced a revolution. This suggests that dichotomous regime typologies are far too blunt to account for peace and war. More work must be done to increase our understanding of how particular internal attributes, especially in nondemocratic states, cause aggression. Meanwhile, in the policy realm, autocratic states should not necessarily be treated by the United States and its democratic allies as obstacles in the path to a peaceful international order.

Chapter 10

Domestic Instability, the Military, and Foreign Policy: Indonesia, 1956–71

Kurt Dassel

The argument and evidence I present in this chapter are not so much a critique of the democratic peace theory as a supplement to its central claim, and a useful counterpoint to its potential implications. The central claim of the dyadic version of democratic peace theory is that democratic dyads are far less likely to fight than are dyads with at least one nondemocracy. An implication that many proponents infer from the theory is that authoritarian regimes are more aggressive than democracies because they lack certain democratic characteristics. I will argue that the central claim is somewhat misleading, and that a type of authoritarian regime is at least as pacific as democracies. Under certain conditions, those authoritarian regimes with unstable political institutions (e.g., countries experiencing revolutions, frequent regime transitions, and state formation) will pursue aggressive foreign policies, but under different conditions they will pursue pacific peace-promoting foreign policies.[1]

Institutional instability tends to have two consequences. First, it threatens the core organizational interests of the military, for example its existence as an organization, its internal unity, its monopoly of

The author is indebted to David Baldwin, Rachel Bronson, Michael Brown, Miriam Fendius Elman, Joe Hagan, John Matthews, Helen Milner, Eric Reinhardt, and Jack Snyder for their comments. I would also like to thank the United States Institute of Peace for its generous financial assistance.

1. For an extensive exposition of this argument, and case studies of Indonesia (1956–71), Argentina (1969–82), Germany (1888–1914), Japan (1926–41), and Pakistan in its 1965 war with India, see Kurt Dassel, "Domestic Instability, the Military, and War," Ph.D. dissertation, Columbia University, 1996.

force, and its political prerogatives.[2] Thus, institutional instability increases the degree to which the military is motivated by parochial concerns; this can make the military more willing to take extreme actions to protect and advance its interests, including the use of force across or within state borders.[3] Second, institutional instability tends to deprive civilians of institutional devices to control the military, so the military will be more able to use force in the manner it wishes.

Whether the military is likely to advocate external aggression depends upon the consequences of using force in the domestic arena. If the military can use force domestically without splitting apart, then it will prefer to repress domestic opponents. It will also avoid foreign conflicts in order to concentrate its coercive capabilities on domestic targets. If, however, using force domestically will divide the military against itself and precipitate a civil war, it will use force abroad. The military will provoke an external threat that will increase its importance, thus allowing it to protect its organizational interests. Usually, the military can use force domestically and maintain its unity; hence, it usually uses force domestically and pursues a pacific foreign policy in order to maximize its chances of successfully repressing domestic opponents. In other words, a sizeable subset of nondemocracies—those experiencing institutional instability—will usually pursue pacific foreign policies toward all other regime types, and will do this because, when institutions are unstable, the military controls the use of force abroad.

This chapter is divided into five sections. First I discuss what democratic peace theory does and does not say about the international behavior of authoritarian regimes, and the relevance of my argument to the democratic peace theory. Next, I present the general logic of my argument. The third section briefly reviews neorealist and domestic-level explanations of Indonesia's foreign policy from 1956–71. This period poses a difficult challenge for any explanatory theory because Indonesia shifted rapidly and dramatically from a relatively pacific foreign policy (1956–61), to an aggressive foreign policy (1961–65), and then back to a pacific foreign policy, even

---

2. These are generally accepted as important interests of the military. See Samuel E. Finer, *The Man on Horseback* (Baltimore, Md.: Penguin, 1975), pp. 41–49; Eric Nordlinger, *Soldiers in Politics: Military Coups and Governments* (Englewood Cliffs, N.J.: Prentice-Hall, 1977), p. 65.

3. Of course the military is not only motivated by threats to its organizational interests; other factors will also affect officers' decisions about using force abroad.

cooperating with its former enemies (1966–71). In the fourth section, I argue that Indonesia pursued a fairly pacific foreign policy in the earlier and later periods because the military could protect its organizational interests by using force domestically, and hence preferred to avoid international conflict. Conversely, in the middle period (1961–65), the military could not use force domestically without risking intramilitary civil war, and hence it used force abroad to provoke a foreign threat and so enable itself to protect its organizational interests. The final section discusses implications of my argument for democratic peace theory.

Democratic Peace Theory and the Behavior of Authoritarian Regimes

The democratic peace theory argues that democracies will almost never fight each other. The most prominent explanations for this behavior are that democracies have political institutions that subject foreign policy makers to checks and balances; that they possess nonviolent norms of domestic conflict resolution that are carried over to international relations; or both.[4] These arguments imply that the presence of at least one authoritarian regime is a necessary condition for war, but beyond this implication, democratic peace theory is silent about the foreign policies of nondemocracies. As a body of intellectual thought, the dyadic version of democratic peace theory does not explain patterns of war and peace outside of democratic pairs of states.

Nevertheless, it is very tempting to draw on the theory to explain the occurrence of war. One inference scholars often draw is that the lack of institutional constraints on decision makers or the lack of nonviolent norms of conflict resolution makes the nondemocracies more aggressive. This inference, however, is a logical leap that cannot be derived from democratic peace theory. The only valid inference that follows from democratic peace theory is that the absence of constraining institutions or the absence of norms of nonviolence makes war possible. Only in their absence will war occur, but given this permissive condition, other factors ultimately determine war and peace outcomes among nondemocratic regimes and mixed dyads. In the final account, constraining institutions and norms of domestic conflict resolution have a varied effect on the relative war-proneness of

---

4. See Miriam Fendius Elman's introduction to this volume.

authoritarian regimes; as I demonstrate in this chapter, regimes with very few institutional checks on foreign policy decision makers, and where domestic conflicts are resolved through massive violence, may pursue very pacific foreign policies.

This argument cautions against explaining the international behavior of authoritarian regimes by drawing on theories purporting to account for the democratic peace. Factors that affect the war-proneness of authoritarian regimes may be quite different from the factors that encourage peace between democracies, so that a particular type of authoritarian regime is very pacific. Finally, my argument warns against the presumption that authoritarian states are predisposed to external aggression. Since only certain authoritarian states will use force abroad, treating *all* nondemocracies as potential aggressors has dangerous policy implications—it could lead democracies to provoke conflict and war with nondemocracies.

The Military, Its Organizational Interests, and War and Peace

I focus on the subset of authoritarian regimes with unstable domestic political institutions. By political institutions, I mean explicit rules and implicit norms that govern how various political actors interact.[5] Political institutions regulate who is eligible to hold high office, who participates in choosing these leaders, how societal groups interact with the state, and how branches within the state interact with each other.[6] Unstable institutions are either changing or are susceptible to change.[7] In other words, my argument essentially applies to countries experiencing revolutions, failed revolutions, regime transitions, and failed transitions.

---

5. Jack Knight, *Institutions and Social Conflict* (New York: Cambridge University Press, 1992), pp. 2–3.

6. The literature on regimes and the state identifies these institutions. See Juan J. Linz, "Totalitarian and Authoritarian Regimes," in F. Greenstein and Nelson Polsby, eds., *Handbook of Political Science* (Reading, Mass.: Addison-Wesley, 1975), pp. 179–185, 187–196, 264–285; Giovanni Sartori, *Parties and Party Systems* (Cambridge: Cambridge University Press, 1976), pp. 119–129; Phillipe Schmitter, "Still the Century of Corporatism," in James Molloy, ed., *Authoritarianism and Corporatism in Latin America* (Pittsburgh, Penn.: University of Pittsburgh Press, 1977), pp. 93–97, 102–105; Michael Mann, "The Autonomous Power of the State," *Archives Européennes de Sociologie*, Vol. 1 (1984), pp. 187–192; and Theda Skocpol, "Bringing the State Back In," in Peter Evans, Dietrich Rueschemeyer, and Theda Skocpol, eds., *Bringing the State Back In* (Cambridge: Cambridge University Press, 1985), pp. 11–20.

7. A structure can be unstable without actually changing. For example, a house

Institutional instability produces two important consequences for the military. First, instability promotes grave threats to core interests of the military, and tempting opportunities for it to advance its interests. Second, instability deprives civilians of the institutional devices to control the military. When political institutions are unstable, the military will be more willing and able to use force to protect its organizational interests.

Faced with threats to its core interests, the military could use force domestically, such as launching a coup or repressing domestic opponents. Alternatively, it could use force abroad. It could provoke an external threat, and use its increased importance as the only organization capable of protecting the country from this threat, to protect its own parochial interests. If the armed forces can use force domestically and maintain its unity, it will prefer to pursue repression at home, and avoid conflict abroad. Using force at home allows the military to directly attack groups that threaten its interests, while using force abroad only temporarily buffers the military from such threats. In order to concentrate its coercive capabilities internally, the military will prefer to avoid foreign conflicts; consequently, it will pursue a pacific foreign policy that avoids war. However, if the military cannot use force internally without dividing the military and risking civil war, then it will reject this option. Under these conditions, the military will use force abroad to protect its interests.

UNSTABLE INSTITUTIONS, THREATS, AND OPPORTUNITIES
To understand the constraints and opportunities that the military faces when political institutions are unstable, consider the situation when the rules are stable. Stable political institutions constrain and channel behavior. They prescribe acceptable means by which political actors can resolve their disputes. They enable actors to resolve their disputes through votes, logrolling, and compromise, rather than through bribery, corruption, and violence. When political institutions are unstable—when rules and norms are changing or susceptible to change—actors are not similarly constrained. It is unclear how disputes will ultimately be resolved, whether other actors will accept unfavorable votes, and whether they will honor their commitments.

---

of cards may remain standing for some time, but will fall down at the slightest breeze; it is hardly stable. Considering institutions that are susceptible to change as being unstable makes measuring instability more difficult, but is conceptually proper. In any case, Indonesia's institutions were changing throughout the 1956–71 period, so demonstrating instability is not difficult.

If an actor continues to obey some set of institutions—if it pursues its ends only through some set of rules and norms—it may put itself at a serious disadvantage in its competition with other actors.

Since disagreements cannot be resolved through institutions, extra-institutional means will be used, including coercion (the use of force). Cognizant that coercive means may well be used to resolve political disputes, civilian groups will seek coercive capabilities. As the country's premier coercive organization, the military becomes the focus of unwanted attention; civilians seek to control it; to control some fraction of it; to form a non-military coercive organization to counter it; or some combination of the above. Civilians may try to limit the military's prerogatives; they may try to gain authority to command the military, to decide promotions, and to control its budget in order to bend it to their own purposes. Civilians may try to weaken military unity; they may try to gain the loyalty of particular officers, units, or branches within the military.[8] Civilians may try to break the military's monopoly of force; they may try to acquire their own coercive capabilities (such as palace guards, militias, guerrilla armies) with which to counter the military. Finally, civilians may try to destroy the organization itself, and replace it with one loyal to them.[9] Once force becomes a usable means for achieving domestic political ends, civilians tend to attack the core interests of the military in an effort either to control or counter it.

Of course, the military is an actor in its own right, and military officers might seek to determine which set of political institutions will be imposed upon the country (for example, it might prefer a military dictatorship to a multiparty democracy). The military, no longer constrained by institutions, acting in an environment in which force is usable, and faced with an opportunity to shape institutions to its benefit, may be sorely tempted to use force.[10]

In addition, the military recognizes that civilians fear and covet it, and civilians recognize the military's temptations. Even if the military did not want to advance its interests, it might try to do so as a

8. Alfred Stepan, *The Military in Politics* (Princeton, N.J.: Princeton University Press, 1971), pp. 165–171; and Nordlinger, *Soldiers in Politics*, pp. 71–75. Such tactics are common, and not only against the military: see Joel Migdal, *Strong Societies and Weak States* (Princeton, N.J.: Princeton University Press), pp. 214–226.

9. This frequently happens after a successful revolution (as in Cuba, Russia, and China).

10. Samuel P. Huntington, *Political Order in Changing Societies* (New Haven, Conn.: Yale University Press, 1968), p. 194.

defensive measure in anticipation of civilian attacks. Even if civilians did not want to attack the military's interests, they might do so to prevent the military from advancing them. Civilians and the military find themselves in something of a security dilemma: because the fears and temptations are common knowledge, self-restraint becomes doubly difficult.

In this environment, the military will be inclined to take whatever steps are necessary to protect and advance its interests. Inaction would be very costly; the military must do something to employ those means it has at its disposal to protect its organizational viability. These means generally include the use of force.

Unstable institutions not only create the need for the military to protect its parochial interests, they also make it possible for the military to do so. The absence of strong, stable political institutions deprives civilians of the mechanisms by which they control the military. Stable institutions identify which civilians have authority over the military, the extent of that authority, and the procedures by which the civilians and the military can resolve their disagreements. But when institutions are unstable, when they are changing or are likely to change, the locus and extent of civilian authority and the conflict-resolving procedures are unclear. When institutions are unstable, there are no commonly accepted rules governing civilian control of the military. This does not mean the military is omnipotent, or that it controls the state, but it does mean that civilians will have great difficulty controlling the military. They will also have great difficulty controlling the tools with which wars are fought. A purportedly authoritative civilian command to pursue war (or peace) may be ignored. Without stable political institutions, civilians lose their control of the military; it is the military that decides whether the country pursues peace or war.

INTERNAL REPRESSION OR EXTERNAL AGGRESSION?
How will the military counter the threats to its organizational interests and seize the opportunities to advance its interests? It will likely use coercion.[11] This is not to say that coercion is the only means the military will employ, but given that such vital interests are at stake, there is no reason to suppose that coercive means will be excluded.

---

11. In Huntington's words, "each group employs means which reflect its peculiar nature and capabilities. The wealthy bribe; students riot; workers strike; mobs demonstrate; and the military coup." Huntington, *Political Order in Changing Societies*, p. 196.

The military has powerful incentives to use force abroad, since it is the organization most capable of protecting the country from external threats. If it can provoke such a threat, civilians will become dependent upon it, allowing it to protect and even advance its parochial interests. As S.E. Finer notes, "war-time is exceptional, and . . . in such circumstances, the military's claim to create the conditions for its own success is more plausible and likely to be acceded to [by civilian authorities] with much less reluctance."[12] Alternatively, the military could use force at home—it could repress or eliminate groups that threaten its organizational viability. The important point is that deciding to use force in one arena precludes the use of force in the other arena. If the military chooses to use force at home, it will strive to make peace abroad, and vice versa.

A strongly united military that can wield force domestically without splitting apart will generally prefer domestic repression to external aggression. It might rule the country itself or, more often, choose acceptable civilians to govern on its behalf. A united military will prefer domestic repression for several reasons. First, whereas external aggression only temporarily buffers the military from threats to its interests, domestic repression directly targets groups threatening the military's interests, and may allow it to restabilize institutions on a favorable basis. Second, a united, well-organized, and determined military is usually all but unstoppable when it employs its coercive capabilities against domestic opponents. Because it can protect its interests through repression at home, external aggression becomes unnecessary, and since aggression is inherently risky, the military will prefer to avoid an unnecessary risk.[13]

Thus, the military is usually a force for peace in countries with unstable political institutions. Interestingly, the reasons the military acts in this way are counter to what the democratic peace theory would lead us to expect. Specifically, the military prefers to pursue peace abroad because of the absence of norms of nonviolent conflict resolution. Furthermore, the military is able to pursue peace abroad because of the absence of institutions through which civilians constrain the military. Whereas democratic peace theorists would tend to

---

12. Finer, *The Man on Horseback*, p. 43.

13. An obvious exception to this logic occurs when the military faces an armed internal opponent. In this case, the military may be very stoppable. Nevertheless, external aggression would be unlikely to help the military in its battle with domestic opponents. The military will still prefer to pursue peace abroad and concentrate its capabilities against domestic opponents.

argue that the absence of these factors should encourage war, I argue that their absence can promote peace.

However, if the military cannot use force domestically and maintain its unity, it is likely to provoke other states so that it can protect the country from these outside threats. If some officers want to use force internally to deal with threats and opportunities but others are adamantly opposed to this solution, so that using force internally might cause violent confrontations within the military, the military will use force abroad to provoke an external threat.[14] Once called upon to protect the country from the threat it provoked, it will be able to buffer itself from civilian encroachments and protect its prerogatives, unity, monopoly of force, and existence.

Indonesian Foreign Policy

In the 1960s, Indonesian foreign policy shifted from pacifism to aggression and back to pacifism in quick succession. Since it gained independence in 1947, Indonesia had been using peaceful means to persuade the Netherlands to vacate West Irian, the last Dutch colony in the Indonesian archipelago. In 1961, Indonesia began to send regular army units into West Irian to foment rebellion, and began to organize a large-scale invasion. Rapid capitulation by the Dutch prevented further violence, but Indonesia immediately turned its aggression to the quixotic goal of preventing the formation of an independent Malaysia from the British colonies in the region. Again, the tactic was low-intensity guerrilla warfare by regular Indonesian troops, with plans for larger-scale operations in the works. After four years of skirmishing, and at least one near instance of major escalation by the British, Indonesia suddenly ended its "Crush Malaysia" campaign in 1966, and sought peaceful relations with its former enemies. Indeed, within a year of ending the campaign, Indonesia and Malaysia were engaged in joint military counterinsurgency operations along their common border in North Borneo.[15] In a brief seven-year span, Indonesia shifted from a pacific policy toward the Dutch,

---

14. Thus, the internal use of force can create the very problems it is intended to solve; using force internally risks destroying military unity and hence breaking its monopoly of force. Moreover, a divided military will have difficulty protecting its prerogatives and will be more vulnerable to any groups that wish to eliminate it. Just as inaction threatens the military's interests, so too can internal repression.

15. Michael Leifer, *Indonesia's Foreign Policy* (Boston: George Allen & Unwin, 1983), p. 122.

to aggressive policies, first against the Dutch and then against the British and Malaysians, and then back to a peaceful, indeed cooperative, policy toward its former enemies. Indonesia's rapid shifts in foreign policy are difficult for any theory to explain.

ALTERNATIVE EXPLANATIONS OF INDONESIAN AGGRESSION

In this section I outline several competing explanations of Indonesia's aggression.

NEOREALISM. A neorealist approach can do a fairly good job of explaining Indonesia's shift to aggression against the Dutch in West Irian. The Indonesian state had always claimed to represent the people of the former Dutch East Indies. Since this territory included West Irian, the continued Dutch occupation was perceived to be illegitimate (despite general support for the Dutch presence within West Irian). Since independence, Indonesia had sought to gain sovereignty over West Irian through bilateral negotiations with the Dutch, appeals in the United Nations, and economic sanctions. By the early 1960s, force was the only means yet to be tried. Hoping to avoid war, Indonesia signaled its willingness to use force with its low-intensity guerrilla attacks and preparations for large-scale operations. The Dutch were not willing to fight a major war over West Irian, and pulled out after a successful mediation effort by then U.S. Attorney General Robert Kennedy.

A neorealist explanation has more trouble explaining the violent confrontation with Malaysia. George Kahin notes that, because Indonesia is a regional power, many Indonesian leaders, "even the moderates among them believe that Djakarta has as much right as Kuala Lumpur to control Sarawak and Sabah [two territories to be incorporated into Malaysia]."[16] One could argue that Indonesia used force in the hope of preventing these territories from being included in the new state, but interestingly no scholar suggests this was the primary cause of aggression, and most scholars do not even discuss these neorealist considerations.[17] This is because Sarawak and Sabah were not strongly coveted territories, unlike West Irian. Indonesians did not

---

16. George McT. Kahin, "Malaysia and Indonesia," *Pacific Affairs*, Vol. 37 (Fall 1964), p. 261.

17. Scholars who note the partial utility of neorealist factors include Donald Hindley, "Indonesia's Confrontation with Malaysia," *Asian Survey*, Vol. 4 (June 1964), pp. 906–908; and Kahin, "Malaysia and Indonesia," pp. 262–264. Scholars who do not even discuss them include Bernard Gordon, "The Potential for Indonesian Expansionism," *Pacific Affairs*, Vol. 36 (Winter 1963–64), pp. 378–380;

feel that they belonged solely to Indonesia. While it is conceivable that the leadership might try to extract some kind of payment from the British in return for Indonesia's acceptance of their incorporation into Malaysia, it is implausible that they would risk war with the British over the issue. Moreover, even if Indonesia was willing to use force, why not wait until after the British left? That is, why not agree to the formation of Malaysia until the superior British forces withdrew, and then use force against a much weaker opponent? Finally, this argument cannot explain why confrontation ended in 1966. Indonesians continued to believe they had as much right to govern Sarawak and Sabah as Malaysia, and the distribution of power between the two states was roughly the same.[18] Neorealist variables did not change, and yet the aggressiveness of foreign policy did.

Neorealism's inability to explain the confrontation with Malaysia casts some doubt on the validity of its explanation for Indonesia's aggression against West Irian. The facts that Indonesia immediately used force abroad after the Dutch capitulated, that the nature of the violence was the same (low-intensity guerrilla warfare), and that all the domestic actors who supported violence against West Irian also supported confrontation with Malaysia suggest that the two campaigns are linked. Whatever caused one probably caused the other.

DOMESTIC-LEVEL EXPLANATIONS. Since neorealist explanations fall short, most scholars subscribe to some domestic-level explanation of Indonesia's aggression. The most common domestic-level explanation is that the President of Indonesia, Ahmed Sukarno, and his most powerful pillar of civilian support, the Indonesian Communist Party (PKI), preferred external aggression in 1961, and that their support

---

J.A.C. Mackie, *Konfrontasi* (Kuala Lumpur: Oxford University Press, 1974), pp. 326–333; and Ulf Sundhaussen, *The Road to Power* (Kuala Lumpur: Oxford University Press, 1982), pp. 168–170.

18. The British had some 10,000 troops in Borneo and some 50,000 in Southeast Asia, while Indonesia had some 15,000–30,000 in Borneo and some 330,000 total (Mackie, *Konfrontasi*, p. 215). Not all of Indonesia's troops were well equipped and well trained. At one point, Britain had 80 warships defending Malaysia, including 4 aircraft carriers (Arnold Brackman, *Southeast Asia's Second Front: The Power Struggle in the Malay Archipelago* [New York: Praeger, 1966], pp. 241–242). In 1965, Indonesia had 26 submarines, 1 cruiser, 12 destroyers, and "scores of other warships" (ibid., p. 99). Indonesia's air force included over 100 MiGs of various types (27 MiG-16s, 50 MiG-17s, 13 MiG-19s, and 17 MiG-21s; ibid., p. 99). These large numbers are probably misleading; many were apparently short of parts. It seems the British were confident they could cripple both Indonesia's air force and navy. See Mackie, *Konfrontasi*, pp. 261–262.

was for an aggressive foreign policy.[19] In other words, it was more Sukarno and the PKI, and less the military, that caused Indonesia to pursue an aggressive foreign policy. This argument is plausible, but partial at best. Sukarno certainly preferred an aggressive foreign policy, and the PKI certainly preferred a radical foreign policy (though probably not an aggressive one).[20] But their preferences were largely irrelevant because they lacked the power to implement their wishes. For the first year of the "Crush Malaysia" campaign, operations proceeded roughly in accord with the military's wishes. Aggression was relatively modest, enough to provoke a credible external threat, but not enough to push Britain into an outright attack on Indonesian territory. In September 1964, however, Sukarno and his closest advisers escalated the conflict against the wishes of the army. Regular troops under the command of Air Marshal Omar Dhani landed on the Malaysian Peninsula itself. This greatly concerned the army, since it risked provoking a British counterattack. Consequently, the army immediately reorganized the chain of command, gained control over operations, moderated the aggression, and sent secret emissaries to the British to communicate its opposition to escalation.[21] As soon as confrontation strayed from what the army perceived as acceptable boundaries, it asserted its control over the means of coercion, and returned to low-intensity tactics.[22] Despite Sukarno's expressed desire for a more confrontational policy, the army would not budge. As I suggested earlier, when political institutions are unstable, it will be the military that controls the means of coercion. It will be the military, and the military alone, that decides whether and how to use

---

19. Hindley, "Indonesia's Confrontation," pp. 909–913; Franklin Weinstein, *Indonesian Foreign Policy and the Dilemma of Dependence* (Ithaca, N.Y.: Cornell University Press, 1976), pp. 303–310; and Sundhaussen, *The Road to Power*, pp. 168–170.

20. Rex Mortimer, *Indonesian Communism Under Sukarno* (Ithaca, N.Y.: Cornell University Press, 1974), p. 204.

21. Harold Crouch, *The Army and Politics in Indonesia* (Ithaca, N.Y.: Cornell University Press, 1978), pp. 69–75.

22. The army's decision to moderate its aggressive foreign policy is somewhat problematic for my argument, which would predict that the military would continue to use force abroad. However, within a year of moderating external aggression, the military suffered the expected consequence—it divided in the coup attempt of September 1965. While the army's reluctance to aggress abroad is somewhat puzzling, the fact that the military did divide against itself shortly thereafter tends to support the underlying logic of the argument. See Dassel, "Domestic Instability," pp. 119–126.

force abroad. Thus while Sukarno preferred an aggressive foreign policy, and the PKI preferred a radical policy, their advocacy was not the primary cause of the "Crush Malaysia" campaign.[23]

The Military's Role in Determining Indonesia's Foreign Policy

My alternative domestic-level explanation of Indonesia's foreign policy emphasizes the role of the military, not civilians. I certainly do not argue that it was the sole determinant of this aspect of foreign policy. President Sukarno, the PKI, and the international distribution of power, for instance, all affected the relative aggressiveness of Indonesian foreign policy. Nevertheless, compared to the influence of the military, these other factors were of marginal importance.

Indonesia's unstable political institutions not only created threats to the military's organizational interests, but also freed it from civilian control and allowed it to largely determine how it would use its coercive capabilities. From 1956–61, rebellious military units who had broken off from the official military were fighting a guerrilla war on several of the Outer Islands.[24] The high command did not have to worry that using force domestically would cause intramilitary divisions, because these divisions had already occurred. To leave the rebels alone would have allowed them to grow and organize themselves further. Hence, prior to 1961, the military preferred to use force internally to protect its interests, and to avoid international conflicts. Between 1961 and 1965, the military was unable to use force internally. The rebellion was defeated in 1961, and so the charismatic President Sukarno no longer supported the military's use of force internally. Because many Indonesian soldiers were intensely loyal to Sukarno, defiance of Sukarno's wish would have provoked an intramilitary split and risked civil war. Since the military was unable to use force domestically, it preferred to use force abroad to protect its interests. Finally, a coup was attempted in September 1965, and the military was able to blame it on the communists, and to implicate Sukarno with them. This tended to discredit Sukarno, and enabled the military to use force internally without dividing against itself. After 1965, the military used force internally to protect and advance its interests, and ended the Crush Malaysia campaign. Within a year,

---

23. For a more lengthy rebuttal to these arguments, see ibid., pp. 79–83, 126–131.

24. Indonesia is an archipelago whose main island is Java. The "Outer Islands" are the islands other than Java.

Indonesia's armed forces were actually engaged in joint military operations with its recent enemy, the Malaysian army, to fight insurgents on their common border.

INSTITUTIONAL INSTABILITY IN INDONESIA

Indonesia's political institutions were clearly unstable during the 1956–71 period. Upon achieving independence after World War II, Indonesia adopted a parliamentary democracy. In the years after independence, however, these institutional arrangements proved unsatisfactory, and by mid-1956, few influential groups supported parliamentary democracy.[25]

Over the next three to four years, parliamentary democracy was disassembled and replaced by "Guided Democracy."[26] In this system, President Sukarno, the army, and later the PKI were locked in a tense struggle for control, a struggle in which civil war was always a possibility. Only Sukarno's influence as a coordinator of contending groups prevented internal violence and maintained the institutional structure.[27] An extremely charismatic and dominating personality, Sukarno's word was law.[28] Nevertheless, he did not control a large, well-organized group of his own, and hence feared becoming too dependent upon the army to mobilize support for his government and to implement its policies. Consequently, he cultivated and protected the PKI to provide himself with a measure of independence from the army. Because Sukarno publicly supported the PKI's political role, the army could not overtly attack it, violently or otherwise. The army depended upon Sukarno to limit the PKI's influence, and the PKI depended upon Sukarno for its very survival; by playing the two organizations against each other, he could maintain his role as Indonesia's leader within the institutional structure of Guided Democracy.

Guided Democracy ended in September 1965. On September 30,

---

25. See Herbert Feith, *The Decline of Constitutional Democracy in Indonesia* (Ithaca, N.Y.: Cornell University Press, 1962), pp. 507–520.

26. On Guided Democracy, see Herbert Feith, "Dynamics of Guided Democracy," in Ruth McVey, ed., *Indonesia* (New Haven, Conn.: Southeast Asia Studies, Yale University with Hraf Press, 1967), pp. 325–342; and Crouch, *The Army and Politics in Indonesia*, pp. 43–68.

27. Herbert Feith, "President Soekarno, the Army and the Communists: The Triangle Changes Shape," *Asian Survey*, Vol. 4 (August 1964), pp. 977–979.

28. J.D. Legge, *Sukarno* (New York: Praeger, 1972), p. 311; Crouch, *The Army and Politics in Indonesia*, pp. 43–44, 176–177; and Sundhaussen, *The Road to Power*, pp. 172–173.

while giving a speech, Sukarno himself collapsed on stage and was taken to a hospital. Shortly after this, pro-Sukarno elements of the air force, army, and presidential guard attempted a coup against the central army leadership.[29] Six top-ranking generals, including the commander of the army, General Achmad Yani, were killed. The plotters' motives remain unclear, though they probably feared that the central military command would seize the opportunity to depose Sukarno and destroy the communists. General Suharto, who survived the coup, rallied the army and blamed the coup attempt on the PKI. This charge was accepted by most Indonesians, and hence the failed coup provided the army with the opportunity it needed to dismantle Guided Democracy.

In the months following the coup attempt, the army massacred hundreds of thousands of PKI members,[30] and eased President Sukarno from power by March 1967. The military and its civilian allies essentially governed the country while formulating a new political system. By the elections of July 1971, a stable bureaucratic-authoritarian regime, known as the New Order, was firmly in place. In fifteen years, Indonesia had changed from a parliamentary democracy, to a "Guided Democracy," to the "New Order."

THE MILITARY AND DOMESTIC REBELLION: 1956–61

As the institutions of Indonesia's parliamentary democracy broke down, several regions in the Outer Islands declared their independence from Indonesia and formed the Revolutionary Government of the Republic of Indonesia (PRRI). Military units in these localities frequently joined the secessionists. Until they surrendered in 1961 (most between February and October), the army claimed that some 100,000 rebels were at large.[31] Moreover, disparate rebel units on different islands were trying to organize themselves into a more coordinated force. In this period, using force domestically would not cause intramilitary splits because these splits had already emerged. Indeed,

---

29. Mortimer, *Indonesian Communism*, pp. 387–399; Crouch, *The Army and Politics in Indonesia*, pp. 97–134; and Sundhaussen, *The Road to Power*, pp. 194–207.

30. Crouch, *The Army and Politics in Indonesia*, pp. 135–220; Justus van der Kroef, *Indonesia after Sukarno* (Vancouver: University of British Columbia Press, 1971), pp. 1–44; Mortimer, *Indonesian Communism*, pp. 387–394; Legge, *Sukarno*, pp. 385–409; and Sundhaussen, *The Road to Power*, pp. 207–254.

31. Feith, "Dynamics of Guided Democracy," p. 346. Sundhaussen doubts official reports, estimating rebel troops at under 20,000 (Sundhaussen, *The Road to Power*, pp. 119, fn. 199).

had the military not used force against the rebel units, further defections may well have occurred. The military enabled the civilian government to rule by protecting them from internal rebels.

My argument predicts that Indonesia would pursue a relatively pacific foreign policy from 1956–61 because it wished to concentrate its coercive capabilities on internal foes; it could already protect its interests by using force domestically; and using force abroad would introduce unneeded risks. Indeed, Indonesia's foreign policy was relatively pacific; it did not use force abroad. By itself, the absence of violence abroad is not strong evidence that domestic factors *caused* the lack of violence. Peace is usually a "non-decision" in that leaders do not consciously decide to stay at peace. In the Indonesian case, however, peace was consciously chosen. The Netherlands had refused to leave all of its East Indies colonial territories. Although use of force was considered in the 1956–60 period, Indonesia pursued its claim through bilateral negotiations with the Dutch, through the United Nations, and by use of economic sanctions. Of course, a neorealist approach can also explain why Indonesia rejected aggression, and such considerations probably did affect Indonesia's behavior. Rather than reject a neorealist explanation, the following subsections simply aim to show that the military's efforts to protect its organizational interests also encouraged a pacific foreign policy.

INSTABILITY AND THREATENED INTERESTS. The regional rebels' efforts to secede—that is, to fundamentally change the political institutions governing relations between the center and the Outer Islands—gravely threatened the army's monopoly of force. In addition to the units that rebelled, many remained loyal to the central command, but strongly sympathized with the rebels. For example, the commander of South Sumatra took de facto control of the area and refused to let the government use his territory as a base against the rebels; this was a significant move, since most of the rebels were located in West and North Sumatra.[32] The West Java division, where Jakarta and central command headquarters are located, essentially refused to contribute troops for suppressing the rebellion.[33] Indeed, in 1956, several units from this division had participated in coup attempts against the central command.[34] The rebel defections broke the army's monopoly of force; had the center failed to deal quickly

---

32. Sundhaussen, *The Road to Power*, pp. 103, 107.

33. Ibid., pp. 108–110.

34. Ruth McVey, "The Post-Revolutionary Transformation of the Indonesian Army," *Indonesia*, No. 11 (April 1971), pp. 161–170.

and effectively with the rebels, the defections may well have spread and precipitated a more serious civil war.

A second threat to the army's interests came from the PKI, which was moving closer to Sukarno and using him as a shield from the military. Its desire to radically reshape Indonesia's political institutions in a way that was antithetical to the predominately Muslim officer corps necessarily brought the PKI into conflict with the military. The PKI saw the army as its chief enemy and sought to limit its powers, break its near monopoly of force, and weaken its unity. As early as 1957, the PKI began to directly cultivate supporters from within the officer corps.[35] A greater concern for the army was that about 30 percent of the enlisted men voted for the PKI in 1955.[36] Thus, the potential defection of a few officers in conjunction with ample support from the ranks constituted a serious threat to army unity. The PKI also sought to create its own paramilitary force. In December 1957, the communist's veterans' organization (PERBEPSI) included 300,000 members, men with military training from their service in the armed forces.[37] According to Donald Hindley, "the greatest value of Perbepsi for the PKI was that it constituted a paramilitary organization that would be available in the event of a major political crisis."[38] The PKI's efforts to shape institutions threatened the army's autonomy, its monopoly of force, its unity, and ultimately its very existence.

USING AND MANIPULATING THE DOMESTIC THREAT. Although the army could not use force against the PKI, it could advance its interests by using force domestically against the rebels. As Daniel Lev put it, a "major consequence of the rebellion . . . was that it emphasized the importance of the army and gave it a stronger position in the national government, in addition to justifying the continuation of martial law."[39] Martial law was declared in those regions of the country with active rebel forces, and it not only gave the army dictatorial powers in much of Indonesia, it also enabled the army to acquire and operate the newly nationalized Dutch firms. In addition, army officers assumed many seats in the cabinet, legislature, Consultative

---

35. Crouch, *The Army and Politics in Indonesia*, pp. 82–83; and Mortimer, *Indonesian Communism*, p. 426.

36. McVey, "Post-Revolutionary Transformation," p. 138.

37. Donald Hindley, *The Communist Party of Indonesia* (Berkeley: University of California Press, 1964), p. 217.

38. Hindley, *The Communist Party of Indonesia*, p. 217.

39. Daniel Lev, "The Political Role of the Army in Indonesia," *Pacific Affairs*, Vol. 36 (Winter 1963–64), p. 354.

Assembly, and various governorships.[40] Thus, the army was able to acquire considerable power from its de jure administrative positions, its economic patronage, and its source of funds that was independent of the government's budget.

In fact, the domestic threat was probably not great enough to justify such power, but the army exaggerated the size of rebel forces in its official statements. The figures that the commander of the army, General Abdul Nasution, cited to domestic audiences ranged from "100,000 men" to "130,000 rebels" to "200,000 direct actors of the rebellion."[41] Ulf Sundhaussen suspects that General Nasution's lower estimate of 20,000, given at an overseas speech in Bangkok, is more accurate.[42] Thus, the army consciously manipulated the danger posed by the armed rebels in order to advance its organizational interests.

OPPOSITION TO INTERNATIONAL AGGRESSION. So long as a credible domestic threat existed and could be manipulated effectively, the army had little interest in provoking international threats. In fact, Indonesia's foreign policy aimed to cultivate good relations with its neighbors in order to help the struggle against the rebels. As Herbert Feith notes, "between 1958 and 1961 a principal purpose of Indonesian diplomacy was to counter the overseas activities of the PRRI rebels. Efforts were made to persuade neighboring Southeast Asian governments to expel PRRI agents from their countries and to prevent them from shipping supplies to rebel held areas of Indonesia."[43] Confrontation with its neighbors could only strengthen the position of the armed rebels.

While civilians began to consider using force against the Dutch in West Irian, the army stressed the domestic threat. In 1959, the cabinet announced its short-term goals as first providing food and clothing for the people, second restoring internal security, and third recovering West Irian. For General Nasution, internal security was the highest priority.[44] Early in 1961, Nasution argued for a delay in military action against West Irian until internal security had been achieved. Even as late as August 1961, Nasution argued in a closed army

40. Crouch, *The Army and Politics in Indonesia*, pp. 34, 39–40, 46–48.

41. Abdul Nasution, *To Safeguard the Banner of the Revolution* (Jakarta: Delegasi, 1964), pp. 21, 52–53.

42. Sundhaussen, *The Road to Power*, p. 119, n. 199.

43. Feith, "Dynamics of Guided Democracy," p. 351.

44. Sundhaussen, *The Road to Power*, pp. 154–155.

lecture that West Irian should be subordinated to internal security needs. But the argument held less and less weight as the rebels surrendered. As Nasution explained, "After the restoration of [internal] security, 75% of our military forces are being concentrated for the military confrontation which, in a short time . . . would be ready any time to destroy the Dutch Armed Forces in West Irian. We have needed time to build up a powerful military confrontation. Prior to our return to the 1945 Constitution (in 1959), the West Irian was settled through political channel(s) and the recent rebellions had forced us to concentrate our forces to crush some 100,000 rebels . . . who, three years ago controlled one-sixth of the Indonesian territory."[45] Not until internal threats were effectively eliminated would the army support or allow the use of force against West Irian.

As hypothesized, Indonesia pursued a relatively pacific foreign policy. While this policy was overdetermined—the Dutch were a formidable military opponent, and other less costly options had not yet been exhausted—peace was consciously chosen. Leaders discussed the idea of using force to acquire West Irian, but rejected it until 1961. Their debates left a paper trail which suggests that, while other factors may have played a role, the military was a strong supporter of peace, and it supported peace because this best served its organizational interests.

AGGRESSION ABROAD, THE WEST IRIAN CONFLICT AND
KONFRONTASI: 1961–65

Once the rebels surrendered, the military no longer had an acceptable target of domestic coercion. Since political institutions remained unstable, Sukarno and the PKI sought to acquire coercive capabilities in case the system broke down, thus threatening the military's interests. But, without the danger of armed rebel groups, President Sukarno became opposed to the military's use of force domestically, either against his new ally, the PKI, or of course himself. Were the high command to disobey the president, it would have provoked Sukarno's supporters within the military to come to his aid. As Daniel Lev argues:

Soekarno was popular and the army was not. Since 1957. . . the army had become increasingly unpopular because of its heavy handedness in dealing with civilians and because of the corruption of some

---

45. From a speech given in April 1962, cited in Nasution, *To Safeguard the Banner*, p. 62.

of its officers . . . Second, Soekarno as paramount leader relieved the general staff of the onerous burden of responsibility which it would have to bear if it tried to run the government alone . . . for [there were] many trying issues that might cause political disruption within the army. Third, the officer corps was divided in its attitudes towards Soekarno, many Javanese officers in particular being personally quite loyal to him.[46]

The use of force internally would have divided the military.

Therefore, the military pursued an aggressive foreign policy to maintain its unity and protect its other interests. The conflict over West Irian escalated in 1961, and entailed a brief naval battle, the infiltration of over 500 troops, and plans for larger operations should Robert Kennedy's mediation efforts fail.[47] Beginning in 1963, similar tactics were used against the British in Malaysia, and some 625 battle deaths occurred.[48]

INSTABILITY AND THREATS TO THE MILITARY'S INTERESTS. While the army would have been content sharing power with Sukarno in the early 1960s, he treated it more as a rival. The army was "the one group in Indonesian society he never managed to understand or control. Sukarno could therefore be expected to try to undermine both Nasution's position in the army and the unity of the officer corps."[49] One of his strategies for controlling the army (or at least lessening his dependence on it) was to promote the PKI as an integral component of Guided Democracy, largely at the expense of the army.[50] Particularly damaging was the lifting of martial law in the formerly rebellious territories in 1963. The army expected to play an important role in Indonesian politics.[51] As General Yani summed up the army's long-standing position in 1965, "the armed forces are recognized as having played a principal role during the Revolution and as such are awarded a share in the determination of national policies, equal to

---

46. Lev, "Political Role," pp. 358–359.

47. Mackie, *Konfrontasi*, pp. 99–101; Justus van der Kroef, "The West New Guinea Settlement," *Orbis*, Vol. 7 (Spring 1963), pp. 126–128, 145; and William Henderson, *West New Guinea: The Dispute and its Settlement* (South Orange, N.J.: Seton Hall University Press, 1973), pp. 78–79.

48. Mackie, *Konfrontasi*, pp. 237, n. 26.

49. Sundhaussen, *The Road to Power*, p. 137.

50. Feith, "President Soekarno, the Army and the Communists," pp. 974–975, 977–978.

51. Sundhaussen, *The Road to Power*, pp. 125–127.

political parties and other bodies."[52] Sukarno's efforts to reduce his dependence on the military jeopardized this role.

Furthermore, the PKI continued trying to weaken military unity and to break its monopoly on the use of force until it was destroyed in 1966. First, the PKI demanded the creation of an armed "Fifth Force" outside the control of the military. A single veterans' organization largely under army control had been formed in 1959 and PERBEPSI, the PKI's veterans' organization, had been forced to join as well. Ever since, the communists had been calling for the arming of the people. During the West Irian and Malaysia campaigns, Sukarno supported the idea, and once arranged to have 100,000 small arms delivered from China for the Fifth Force. During 1965, some 1,200 people were trained at Halim Air Base and used as a reserve force in the September 30, 1965, coup attempt. A second PKI strategy was to try to insert civilian "advisory teams" into the armed forces in the hope of gaining influence, or at least information, on military decisions. A third strategy was to recruit army officers sympathetic to the PKI and perhaps form communist cells within the military. PKI leaders claimed they had "regular contact with 250 officers in Central Java, 200 in East Java, 80–100 in West Java, 40–50 in Jakarta, 30–40 in North Sumatra, 30 in West Sumatra, and 30 in Bali."[53] Finally, the PKI endeavored to pit the navy, air force, and police against the army.[54] The PKI's most notable success was in gaining the sympathy and active support of many high-ranking air force commanders, including both chiefs of staff between 1960 and 1966.[55] Air force officers went so far as to train Fifth Force civilians, and many participated in the September 30 coup. Ultimately, the PKI's growing influence threatened the existence of the military organization itself. If the PKI were to acquire a Fifth Force, and to succeed Sukarno, it would replace the military with a force of its own creation. The army and the PKI simply could not tolerate each other over the long run. Instability and the possibility that force would become the means to resolve disputes were threatening the most vital of the military's organizational interests.

---

52. "The Indonesian Army's Doctrine of War," cited in Sundhaussen, *The Road to Power,* p. 172.

53. Crouch, *The Army and Politics in Indonesia,* p. 83.

54. On all these tactics, see Crouch, *The Army and Politics in Indonesia,* pp. 82–94; Mortimer, *Indonesian Communism,* pp. 117, 198, and 371; Sundhaussen, *The Road to Power,* pp. 183–194.

55. Crouch, *The Army and Politics in Indonesia,* p. 84.

OFFICERS' ATTITUDES TOWARD THE PKI. Although domestic opponents actively threatened the military's interests, violence against them was risky. Sukarno was shielding the PKI from the military and using it as a counterweight to the military. His opposition to internal violence tended to divide the military into two camps: those who favored domestic repression, and those who did not. Inaction in the face of institutional instability would threaten the military's interests, but so too would domestic repression. Consequently, external aggression became a more attractive policy.

While most army officers were staunchly anti-communist, there was no consensus about how to deal with the PKI. Rather than confront the president directly, the commander of the army, General Yani, preferred to accept Sukarno's policies and demands, but interpret them as he desired. Many non-Javanese and Outer Island officers, who centered around the former commander of the army, General Nasution, favored a more aggressive and openly critical approach.[56] Over time, as the PKI membership grew, its popular support increased, and Sukarno more openly and frequently sided with it. The Yani group grew more disposed towards an aggressive response. For example, Yani revived the career of Kemal Idris, a strong anti-Sukarnoist. "Kemal . . . was almost equally hostile to Sukarno as to the PKI, [and] had assembled his troops in front of the presidential palace on 17 October [1956]," and would again lead troops in an implicit coup threat against Sukarno in 1966.[57] While the army publicly denied any intention of launching a coup, "opinion was building up within the army that something had to be done, even if it meant an open break with Sukarno . . . and rumors about the possibility of a military coup were heard more frequently."[58] The army always contained an element prepared to directly confront Sukarno's support for the PKI, and this contingent grew in size and determination over time.

Another contingent of officers were very loyal to Sukarno and saw efforts to defy him as treasonous. They were not communists them-

56. Ibid., pp. 78–82. For example, the regional commanders in South Sumatra, South Kalimantan, and South Sulawesi banned the PKI in 1960, and it took some time and considerable pressure from Sukarno to get the bans lifted. Sundhaussen, *The Road to Power*, pp. 178–180.

57. Sundhaussen, *The Road to Power*, p. 172.

58. Crouch, *The Army and Politics in Indonesia*, p. 94. See also Sundhaussen, *The Road to Power*, pp. 199–200.

selves, but followed Sukarno's lead and accepted the PKI as an integral part of Indonesia's political system. They opposed attacks on the PKI not due to communist sympathies, but because doing so defied Sukarno's wishes. A particularly important Sukarnoist was the Sudanese commander in West Java, Ibrahim Adjie. Because Jakarta and other presidential residences were in West Java, "with Adjie in control of West Java a physical threat by the Army against his [Sukarno's] person or position had become close to impossible."[59] These pro-Sukarno sentiments were even more widespread among officers and enlisted men (and indeed among the entire Javanese population) in Central and East Java. They favored protecting the military's interests, but linked these interests closely with loyalty to Sukarno. Any armed move against Sukarno would have provoked a violent response from these units.

THE MOTIVES FOR EXTERNAL AGGRESSION. Institutional instability threatened the military, yet it could not use force against either Sukarno or the PKI. Since the costs of both inaction and domestic repression were high, the military began to consider international aggression.

A foreign conflict, especially with an imperialist Western power such as the Netherlands or Great Britain, would help the military justify its extensive role in Indonesian politics. Because the military was the only organization that could prosecute the campaign, foreign conflict would help the military retain its monopoly on the use of force. It would also be less politic for Sukarno or the PKI to be seen meddling in the military's internal affairs during an international crisis, so it would be more difficult for them to divide the loyalties of the officer corps. Most importantly, since a conflict would help the military protect its organizational interests without using force domestically, the prorepression-antirepression split within the military would not be exacerbated. The disadvantage was that external aggression risked provoking war with powerful foreign states. Yet, both inaction and domestic repression created the risk of war as well—a civil war between fellow officers. All options risked war of some variety, but external aggression was the better choice for the military.[60]

This sort of calculus seems to have motivated the West Irian campaign. As soon as the internal rebellions ended and could no

---

59. Sundhaussen, *The Road to Power*, pp. 150–151.

60. I would also argue that a war against a powerful foreign state would be preferable to a civil war against one's fellow officers.

longer provide a justification for the army's considerable political role, it executed an abrupt about-face on the tactics for regaining West Irian. "For much of 1961 [before many rebels had surrendered] its leaders seemed to stake their hopes on a diplomatic victory gained as a result of United States and other Western pressure on Holland. In the second quarter of 1962 the emphasis changed, with a highly influential group of officers arguing, 'Now that our preparations are as far advanced as this, let us fight with all we have and win decisively.'"[61] As long as the domestic threat existed, the army opposed the use of force against the Dutch; after the last of the rebels had surrendered in October 1961, the army began to advocate a massive invasion of West Irian. In the end, the dispute was settled before the army had completed preparations for a large-scale invasion, and so the army was unable to increase its prestige and influence as much as it might have.[62]

Nevertheless, the army did gain from the external threat. The military was concerned that the rebels' surrender would lead to budget reductions and eagerness to counter the growth of the PKI's mass organizations; the West Irian campaign "provided a rationale for major new purchases of arms (for the army as well as the other services) and for extending the influence of the army among students, youth organizations, and the civilian population in general."[63] Furthermore, the military used the external Dutch threat to continue martial law.[64] Martial law was not lifted until May 1, 1963, the day Indonesia took control of West Irian from the Dutch. Finally, the need to mobilize against the Dutch enabled the army to maintain and increase the number of officers in the cabinet, parliamentary bodies, governorships, and informal but more powerful decision making bodies.[65] Having achieved what it could from the rebel threat, the

---

61. Feith, "Dynamics of Guided Democracy," p. 354. See also Mortimer, *Indonesian Communism*, pp. 192–193; and Mackie, *Konfrontasi*, p. 101.

62. Because the army was unable to launch a full invasion, Feith ("Dynamics of Guided Democracy," p. 354) and Mortimer (*Indonesian Communism*, p. 193) argue that the army did not benefit as much from the Irian campaign as did Sukarno and the PKI. In other words, had the army been able to use more force before the Dutch capitulated, it would have benefitted more politically.

63. Feith, "Dynamics of Guided Democracy," p. 353; and Leifer, *Indonesia's Foreign Policy*, p. 61.

64. Crouch, *The Army and Politics in Indonesia*, p. 54; Weinstein, *Indonesian Foreign Policy*, p. 313.

65. Crouch, *The Army and Politics in Indonesia*, pp. 47–48. The informal decision making bodies included Koti (short for the Supreme Command for the Liberation

military escalated the violence against the Dutch to justify the extensive administrative powers it enjoyed through martial law and to claim as much credit for the confrontation as possible.

Once the Netherlands capitulated and left West Irian for Indonesia to govern, it looked for several months as though the Sukarno government might focus on pressing internal economic problems. But a focus on internal problems would have been dangerous for national unity. Sukarno, the army, and the PKI each had different ideas about the policies Indonesia should pursue and about who should lead the country. The differences among these groups, particularly the PKI and the army, were irreconcilable, and they knew it. Yet no group, the army, Sukarno, or the PKI, was confident it would win a domestic confrontation. Consequently, economic reforms were abandoned, and the confrontation against Malaysia began in 1963.

The army was grimly determined to use the confrontation to protect its organizational interests.[66] Crouch reports that the commander of the army, General Yani, supported confrontation primarily because it would aid the army's domestic political position and ability to obtain armaments. Yani also apparently hoped that the army might gain control of British firms, as it had with Dutch firms in 1957.[67] In addition, the army used the confrontation to achieve a partial restoration of martial law throughout much of Indonesia in September 1964, and managed to increase the number of army officers occupying governorships.[68]

TRIUMPH AT HOME AND PEACE ABROAD: 1966–71

From 1961–65, the military pursued an aggressive foreign policy because it could not use force internally to protect its interests, but with the attempted coup against army high command on September 30, 1965, the loyalty to Sukarno of the Javanese people, including Javanese officers, began to weaken. The army managed to blame the attempt on the PKI and to implicate Sukarno as well. Over the next ten months,

---

of West Irian) and Peperti (Supreme War Authority), which were formed as alternative decision making councils to the cabinet.

66. Crouch, *The Army and Politics in Indonesia*, p. 69; Mackie, *Konfrontasi*, pp. 327–329; Weinstein, *Indonesian Foreign Policy*, pp. 320–321; and Sundhaussen, *The Road to Power*, pp. 173–174.

67. Crouch, *The Army and Politics in Indonesia*, pp. 59–60, from an interview with General Nasution.

68. Ibid., pp. 76–77.

Sukarno's authority ebbed, and with it the loyalty of the Javanese officers. The army gradually became more confident in its ability to use force domestically without provoking intramilitary divisions.

INSTITUTIONAL INSTABILITY, THREATS, AND OPPORTUNITIES. Shortly after the coup attempt, peaceful relations between the army and the PKI were probably not possible; one of them had to go.[69] The military saw the PKI as an immediate though not terribly dangerous threat to its own existence, and it dealt with this threat quickly and brutally, massacring hundreds of thousands of communists in late 1965 to early 1966.

Peaceful though inharmonious relations between Sukarno and the military probably were possible; he was not necessarily a threat to the military's existence, but he was a threat to its unity.[70] Sukarno recognized that the military high command was intent on subordinating him to its influence without formally removing him from the presidency.[71] In order to retain more than figurehead status, Sukarno needed to cultivate support to replace the PKI. Some of his most ardent and useful supporters were in the military.

Following the destruction of the PKI, many army officers, particularly those in Central and East Java, wanted to rule with Sukarno, much as they had in the late 1950s and early 1960s. Efforts to undercut Sukarno's power would not be supported by these men.[72] Indeed, it was fears of his losing influence that encouraged the 1965 coup attempt in the first place. Support for Sukarno was even stronger in the predominantly Javanese air, navy, and police forces. Not only did these groups identify with Sukarno as a Javanese, but they were also fearful of losing power relative to the army.[73] It was unclear whether the military high command actually commanded the loyalty of all its troops. Thus, as late as September 1966, Sukarno was a powerful threat to the military's unity, its monopoly of force, and its political prerogatives.

After Sukarno was eased from power in March 1967, the military no longer faced serious threats to its organizational interests; instead, it had an opportunity to advance its interests beyond where they had been before the coup. Indonesia's political institutions remained unstable, and while the military was certain to play the primary role

---

69. Sundhaussen, *The Road to Power*, p. 214.

70. Crouch, *The Army and Politics in Indonesia*, pp. 158–159.

71. Ibid., p. 160.

72. Ibid., pp. 158–159; and Sundhaussen, *The Road to Power*, pp. 227, 243–244.

73. Crouch, *The Army and Politics in Indonesia*, p. 159; and Sundhaussen, *The Road to Power*, pp. 227, 243–244.

in Indonesia's polity, the extent of its institutionally sanctioned power had yet to be determined. Without Sukarno, the military needed to legitimate its government (or else rule by force indefinitely); indeed, the commander of the army, General Suharto, had felt it necessary to use the Provisional People's Consultative Assembly (MPRS) to formally remove Sukarno, and confer the presidency on himself. As Nawaz Mody notes, "technically, at least, he [Suharto] committed himself to a political system where the President was answerable to the MPRS and subject to re-election."[74] As Harold Crouch argues, "political stabilization in the long run, it seemed, would require the setting up of a new political framework within which civilian groups could be accommodated."[75] In the years after Sukarno's ouster and before the July 1971 elections, the military was to shape institutions and control the political parties in order stabilize institutions as much as possible with as little accommodation as possible.[76] Initially motivated by the fear of threats to its organizational interests, later motivated by the opportunity to advance its organizational interests, the military was willing to use force so long as Indonesia's political institutions remained unstable.

USING FORCE DOMESTICALLY. Just after the coup attempt, it was unclear whether the military could use force within Indonesia. The high command's control of the air force, navy, and most army units in Central and East Java was tenuous at best. The fear that motivated the coup attempt—that the high command would oust Sukarno—was widespread, and was hardly lessened by the destruction of the PKI and the high command's effort to implicate Sukarno in the coup attempt. As long as Sukarno retained his tremendous prestige and authority, the military high command could not confidently use force domestically.

After the coup attempt, even Sukarno's staunchest civilian and military supporters favored brutal repression of the PKI. Indeed, it is a measure of Sukarno's decreasing authority that his clearly expressed desire that the PKI be left unharmed was flagrantly disregarded. The military was on safe grounds when it eradicated the communists. Still, no one expressed anti-Sukarno sentiments for several months after the coup attempt. Thus, excepting the communists, civilian unity against domestic violence continued for some time.

---

74. Nawaz Mody, *Indonesia under Suharto* (New Delhi: Sterling Publishers, 1987), p. 210.

75. Crouch, *The Army and Politics in Indonesia*, p. 245.

76. Ibid., pp. 245–272.

However, after the coup attempt, the army was able to acquire administrative power throughout Indonesia.[77] In this environment, anti-Sukarno groups were able to operate more freely than they had under Guided Democracy. The first organized groups to publicly oppose Sukarno were several student groups: KAPPI, KAMI, and KASI (high school, college, and graduate students respectively). These groups were also the effective representatives of many members and supporters of the banned Masjumi party and Indonesian Socialist Party (PSI).[78] They initially voiced support for Sukarno, but his appointment of an anti-army, left-leaning cabinet on February 21, 1966, and his banning of KAMI shortly thereafter, pushed them into direct opposition.[79] As J.D. Legge states, "their new wave of demonstrations reflected the presence of an extraordinarily sophisticated organization, with an effective communications system to coordinate action."[80] Further evidence of division within civilian ranks came on March 10, when all parties, except the Indonesian National party (PNI) and Partindo party, would only condemn the means of the students, not their ends.[81]

Encouraged by the massive demonstrations against Sukarno's cabinet, the army took a bolder though less bloody step; it made a show of force outside the presidential palace during a cabinet meeting.[82] While the troops probably had no intention of moving against Sukarno himself (though they may well have arrested some of his ministers), he nevertheless "escaped" by helicopter to another residence in Bogor. General Suharto then sent three generals to Bogor,

---

77. After the coup attempt, Sukarno formally conceded responsibility for restoring security and order to Suharto. Suharto interpreted his responsibilities broadly, ignoring Sukarno's appointed commander of the army and effectively commanding the army himself (with widespread backing from the army).

78. The Masjumi was the top vote getter in the Outer Islands in the 1955 elections, and was banned in 1960 for its involvement with regionalist rebellions. The PSI was more a party for intellectuals; its influence exceeded its polling numbers.

79. Crouch, *The Army and Politics in Indonesia*, pp. 181–187; and Sundhaussen, *The Road to Power*, pp. 230–234.

80. Legge, *Sukarno*, p. 401.

81. Crouch, *The Army and Politics in Indonesia*, p. 187, including n. 16.

82. It is doubtful that Suharto knew the exact plans of the officers who organized this show of force. Crouch believes Suharto had told them to foster chaos in the capital so he could play the role of the moderate to whom Sukarno would have to turn. Crouch, *The Army and Politics in Indonesia*, pp. 185–190.

where they extracted a signed letter from Sukarno handing executive powers over to Suharto.[83] With these powers, Suharto unequivocally broke civilian unity: he banned the PKI, purged the bureaucracy, and reformed the cabinet. Significantly, he was able to bring prestigious civilians, such as the sultan of Jogjakarta, and the left-nationalist Adam Malik into the cabinet. With this increase of support, the military dared to use more force; Suharto compelled the PNI, Sukarno's strongest supporter, to hold a party conference in April where, again due to army pressure, the left-wing faction was removed from positions of leadership and replaced by a more "realistic," though still Sukarnoist, right-wing faction. Finally, in late June, the assembly (MPRS) gave its approval to the March 11 letter and forbade Sukarno to issue presidential decrees and regulations.[84]

By July 1966, Sukarno's authority was severely limited. As J.D. Legge wrote, "Sukarno found that his words on [the destruction of the PKI] and other matters were now simply ignored. He could maintain the appearance of leadership but its reality had slipped from him. He could no longer impose his personality on others."[85] The most vocal civilian groups, the students, explicitly supported the military's threats of force, such as the show outside the presidential palace. Most other civilian political actors—many of the parties, the MPRS, the sultan of Jogjakarta, and Malik—implicitly supported the military's use of threats by sanctioning the results—Suharto's assumption of the presidency—and by participating in Suharto's government. Sukarno's strongest civilian supporters, the PKI and PNI, were bullied into silence and grudging acceptance. Between late February and early July 1966, the military regained the ability to use force internally without dividing against itself.

ENDING AGGRESSION ABROAD. As Sukarno's authority declined, and as the military grew increasingly confident in its ability to use force internally, it gradually ended its aggressive foreign policy. Until late February–early March 1966, it seemed possible that Sukarno would preserve his authority and prevent a military coup against himself. Consequently, the military used force domestically to the extent that it could: it eradicated the PKI. It also intensified its rhetoric against Malaysia, but the military did not use force against

83. Exactly what happened at this meeting is not known. Ibid., pp. 190–191.

84. Ibid., pp. 192–203; and Sundhaussen, *The Road to Power,* pp. 236–239.

85. Legge, *Sukarno,* p. 400.

Malaysia.[86] Thus, until Sukarno's authority broke down, the military could not entirely abandon the option of foreign aggression.

As the military became increasingly sure of its ability to further its interests by using force domestically if necessary, it sought officially to end confrontation with Malaysia. As Franklin Weinstein writes, "in 1964, the army could use confrontation to avoid a post–West Irian campaign demobilization and the restoration to civilian control of key administrative positions held by army officers. By March 1966, however, the army no longer needed a foreign crisis to justify its retention of administrative posts."[87] In the tense days after the show of force outside Sukarno's palace on March 11, 1966, the military continued its belligerent rhetoric, sounding "almost desperate lest anyone get the wrong idea."[88] But shortly after General Suharto brought prominent civilians into his cabinet on March 27, he said that Indonesia was open to peace talks. On April 7, "a tabloid believed to represent the view of certain army elements made the first public criticism of confrontation, terming the 'physical confrontation or war' something 'inspired by the Indonesian Communist Party for the interests of China' [and] suggested 'peaceful confrontation' as an alternative to war."[89] After the manipulation of the PNI's leadership in early April, the government moved more explicitly to a policy of "peaceful confrontation." In early June, Foreign Minister Adam Malik negotiated an agreement to end confrontation with Malaysia. Finally, after the MPRS endorsed Sukarno's letter to Suharto in June 1966, the agreement to end confrontation was ratified and signed on August 11, 1966. Each step in the dissolution of Sukarno's authority was matched by increasingly bolder uses of force in domestic politics—first against the broadly condemned PKI, then the veiled threat toward Sukarno himself, then the actual use of force against Sukarno's strongest supporter, the PNI. Each successful use of force in domestic politics was matched by increasingly open and serious efforts by Indonesia to end confrontation against Malaysia.

The military leadership did not stop at a simple cease-fire with Malaysia, at an ambiguous relationship between confrontation and cooperation. Shortly after the agreement ending confrontation was signed, the militaries of the two countries were engaged in joint

---

86. Franklin Weinstein, *Indonesia Abandons Confrontation* (Ithaca, N.Y.: Southeast Asia Program, Cornell University, 1969), pp. 23–24.

87. Ibid., p. 41.

88. Ibid., p. 31, n. 95.

89. Ibid., p. 37.

counterinsurgency operations along their common border in North Borneo. This cooperation was officially confirmed by an exchange of letters in March 1967.[90] Indonesia also fostered a broader regional organization, the Association of South-East Asian Nations (ASEAN), which was established in August 1967. For all its members, one purpose of ASEAN was "the institutional encapsulation of the most powerful state in the region (Indonesia) . . . envisaged both as a means to satisfy its natural ambition and also to contain its more objectionable hegemonic disposition."[91] This purpose was not something to which Indonesia grudgingly acceded; indeed, it was an incentive to join. As Evelyn Colbert writes, "for Indonesia, ASEAN provided an opportunity to dispel old antagonisms and create new and more congenial relationships."[92] Thus, not only did Indonesia end confrontation, but it also cooperated militarily with its former enemy, and joined and encouraged an organization that constrained its opportunities for expansion in order to allay its neighbors' fears.

Conclusion

The shifts in Indonesia's foreign policy from relative pacifism to aggression against the Dutch and then the British, and then back to pacifism and even cooperation, provide a hard test for any general explanation of foreign policy. The shifts cannot be adequately explained by a neorealist account; perhaps anarchy and the distribution of power can explain why Indonesia eventually resorted to force to drive the Dutch out of West Irian, but they cannot explain why Indonesia used force to prevent the formation of Malaysia, or why Indonesia eventually abandoned this aggressive foreign policy. Anarchy and the distribution of power were constants, and yet Indonesia initiated and then ended a policy of aggression against the British and Malaysian forces.

Domestic-level explanations that place Sukarno and the PKI alongside the military as causes of aggression provide a richer account of Indonesia's foreign policy shifts. However, they fail to identify the

---

90. Leifer, *Indonesia's Foreign Policy*, p. 122.

91. Leifer, *Indonesia's Foreign Policy*, pp. 120–121. For a similar assessment, see Amitav Acharya, "Regionalism and Regime Security in the Third World," in Brian Job, ed., *The Insecurity Dilemma* (Boulder, Colo.: Lynne Rienner, 1992), p. 150.

92. Evelyn Colbert, "Southeast Asian Regional Politics," in W. Howard Wriggins, ed., *Dynamics of Regional Politics* (New York: Columbia University Press, 1992), p. 233.

military as the necessary driving force behind the use of force abroad. Sukarno and the PKI were unceasing in their belligerent rhetoric, but had the military not preferred an aggressive foreign policy, Indonesia would not have taken the ultimate step of using violence abroad.

I argue that Indonesia's foreign policy choices were primarily products of the military's efforts to protect its organizational interests. More generally, in countries with unstable political institutions, the military is both willing and able to use force as it wishes to protect and advance its interests. If the military can use force domestically without dividing against itself, it will do so, and will pursue a pacific foreign policy abroad. If, however, using force domestically will divide the military against itself, it will use force abroad to provoke an external conflict and threat.

This argument does not challenge the empirical finding that democratic dyads are peaceful, nor does it disconfirm the explanations for this phenomenon.[93] It is a useful counterweight to some of the claims and implications of the dyadic version of the democratic peace theory. First, the central claim of the democratic peace theory is misleading. If we compare democratic dyads to all other dyads, it might be true that the democracies are less likely to fight each other. But if we compare subsets of these other dyads to the democratic dyads, I suspect this claim will not stand. Nondemocratic dyads that include a state whose military can use force domestically will be unlikely to fight. That is, the democracy versus nondemocracy dichotomy is misleading, since there are many types of nondemocracies, some of which are inclined toward aggressive behavior, and some toward pacific behavior. The prevalence of peace in South America tends to support this claim. Since World War II, many of these countries have had repressive militaries, and there have been no wars among them. Most prominently, between 1930 and 1970, the relative power of the two strongest states on the continent, Brazil and Argentina, reversed, and yet they did not come close to war. In both countries, the military used domestic coercion to protect its interests. While this evidence is hardly conclusive, it does suggest that zones of peace might exist among nondemocracies.[94]

---

93. The evidence in this chapter is compatible with the dyadic version of democratic peace theory, since the only near wars discussed in this chapter were between an authoritarian regime and democracies. Moreover, since the theory does not assert that democracy is a necessary condition for peace, or that authoritarian regimes never pursue peace and cooperation abroad, finding that Indonesia has done so is not an indictment of the theory.

94. See Arie M. Kacowicz's chapter in this volume.

Second, we must be careful to distinguish between propositions that can be logically deduced from the democratic peace theory, and propositions that cannot. It is easy to leap from explanations of the democratic zone of peace to unwarranted and erroneous explanations for the causes of nondemocratic war and peace. If the democratic peace theory is correct, then the presence of an authoritarian regime is a permissive condition for war, but not necessarily a contributing cause of war. Even if democracies do not fight each other, we cannot infer that the sources of aggression lie in authoritarian regimes. More specifically, we cannot infer that the absence of any institutional checks on foreign policy decision makers or the absence of any norms of nonviolent domestic conflict resolution will dispose a state toward aggression. In Indonesia during the 1956–61 and 1966–71 periods, the relative absence of institutional checks on the military and the military's ability to use force domestically to protect and advance its interests were the very factors that encouraged it to pursue peace abroad. Conversely, from 1961 to 1965, it was the military's inability to use force domestically that encouraged it to pursue aggression abroad. Thus, the democratic peace theory cannot account for the behavior of authoritarian regimes—the factors that determine the foreign policy of nondemocratic regimes cannot be identified from the theory's propositions about democratic behavior.

Third, democratic peace theory does not provide leaders of democracies with useful guidance for dealing with authoritarian regimes. Even if it is true that democracies rarely fight each other, this does not mean that authoritarian states are the source of aggression. Nor are all authoritarian states equally inclined to use force abroad. As Bruce Russett notes, the danger is that political leaders may conclude that "democracies must be eternally vigilant and may even need to engage in defensively motivated war or preemptive action anticipating an immediate attack."[95] If they do, then it will be the democracies that provoke avoidable conflicts. Peaceful and cooperative relations are possible with a significant number of authoritarian countries—a group that includes, though is probably not restricted to, countries in which the military uses domestic coercion.

---

95. Bruce Russett, "Why Democratic Peace?" in Michael E. Brown, Sean M. Lynn-Jones, and Steven E. Miller, eds., *Debating the Democratic Peace* (Cambridge, Mass.: MIT Press, 1996), p. 93.

Chapter 11

Turkish and Hungarian Foreign Policy During the Interwar Period: Domestic Institutions and the Democratic Peace

John C. Matthews III

The relationship between Greece and Turkey has been relatively hostile since at least 1821. During the nineteenth century, the hostility was largely an outgrowth of Greece's successful bid for independence from the Ottoman Empire; in the post–World War II period, the enmity has continued, making these two NATO partners strange "allies" at best. The militarized dispute in 1996 over the small contested islands in the Aegean only reiterates the broader historical disputes. Yet during the interwar period, relations between these two states were quite peaceful due largely to Turkish efforts. Indeed, by the early 1930s, Turkey and Greece formed the cornerstones of a Balkan alliance designed to preserve the status quo in the face of many possible competing irredentist claims. In this chapter, I examine Turkey's peaceful foreign policy between World Wars I and II, including its relations with Greece. I argue that the Turkish case challenges explanations for the democratic peace phenomenon that focus on democratic institutions as the locus of pacific behavior. The chapter then compares the Turkish case with that of Hungary during the same period.

Since many theories of the democratic peace argue only that democracy is a sufficient rather than necessary cause of peace, the logical inferences that can be made about nondemocratic states' behavior are limited. Nevertheless, some democratic peace theorists

I would like to thank the other contributors to this volume and all of the participants in the preparatory workgroup for this book for their insightful comments and critiques of my chapter. I would also like to acknowledge the support of the Center for Science and International Affairs and the Institute for the Study of World Politics for supporting this research.

maintain that nondemocratic states are likely to be more aggressive for domestic reasons. For example, some institutional democratic peace arguments suggest that nondemocratic states may be more aggressive because they do not have to contend with a cost-conscious, constraining public.[1] Nondemocratic states may be peaceful, but generally it is thought that external exigencies rather than domestic factors account for this behavior. In contrast, I argue that domestic constraints and opportunities led nondemocratic Turkey to pursue a moderate foreign policy toward nondemocratic Greece. Turkey's foreign policy is especially puzzling because it had multiple opportunities during the interwar period to pursue a more expansionist security policy with relatively low cost and with few risks. Nevertheless, Turkey chose not to aggress. I argue that this was due to domestic factors; furthermore, if Turkey had been more democratic, it would have been aggressive and expansionist because of the likely influence of certain elites and masses who were instead excluded from politics.[2]

I trace Turkey's pacific security policy during the interwar period to the creation of a strong political party—the Republican People's Party—which enabled the leadership to exclude from the decision making process those politicians who advocated more aggressive foreign policy options. The Republican People's Party served to screen out actors who, for ideological reasons such as Pan-Turkist nationalism and Pan-Islam, wished to be more expansionist. Had Turkey not been an exclusionary regime, that is, had it been more democratic, these actors would likely have been able to mobilize significant support for Turkey to expand beyond its Anatolian frontiers.

The critical variable discussed in this chapter, strong political parties, tends to be present in stable democratic states as well as in

---

1. Bruce Russett argues that "leaders of nondemocracies are not constrained as leaders of democracies are, so they can more easily, rapidly, and secretly initiate large-scale violence." Bruce Russett, "Why Democratic Peace," in Michael E. Brown, Sean M. Lynn-Jones, and Steven E. Miller, eds., *Debating the Democratic Peace* (Cambridge, Mass.: MIT Press, 1996), p. 103.

2. This counterfactual claim challenges arguments that suggest that democracy, understood as political openness and participation, has pacifying effects. For a similar argument about how openness and participation can lead to international conflict in poorly institutionalized settings, see Edward D. Mansfield and Jack Snyder, "Democratization and the Danger of War," *International Security*, Vol. 20, No. 1 (Summer 1995), pp. 5–38. For more on the use of counterfactuals in international relations, see James Fearon, "Counterfactuals and Hypothesis Testing in Political Science," *World Politics*, Vol. 43, No. 2 (January 1991), pp. 169–195.

many nondemocratic states. Thus, the "democratic" peace may not be caused by the institutions of democracy, but by other domestic institutions. If so, the empirical finding of a separate democratic peace may need to be expanded to include nondemocratic states with strong parties or certain other institutions.

This chapter begins with a discussion of how the existence of a strong moderate political party can lead a state to maintain a status quo foreign policy. It then examines the interwar history of Turkey, focusing on its domestic political developments, especially institutional developments, and Turkey's foreign policy choices with regard to Greece and other key states. The next section briefly examines Hungary during the interwar period, looking at the same set of variables and demonstrating how Hungary's more open institutions led to a very belligerent foreign policy, most notably toward Czechoslovakia. Finally, the conclusion discusses the consequences of these cases for theories of democratic peace.

Political Institutions and Foreign Policy

Democratic peace proponents correctly point to the importance of domestic institutions in explanations of foreign policy outcomes. However, in focusing on a state's regime type, they often fail to examine the most important institutional variable—in the cases of Turkey and Hungary,—the role of political parties.[3]

Political parties have been, and continue to be, the principal organizations that control political recruitment and channel political participation in most democracies and authoritarian regimes.[4] Parties are strong when they have a monopoly or oligopoly on the political resources that are necessary to attain power. Sometimes this comes

---

3. The institutionalist literature is extensive. For recent representative examples, see Walter W. Powell and Paul J. DiMaggio, eds., *The New Institutionalism in Organizational Analysis* (Chicago: University of Chicago Press, 1991); James G. March and Johan P. Olsen, *Rediscovering Institutions: The Organizational Basis of Politics* (New York: Free Press, 1989); Jack Knight, *Institutions and Social Conflict* (New York: Cambridge University Press, 1992); and Kenneth Shepsle, "Studying Institutions: Some Lessons from the Rational Choice Approach," *Journal of Theoretical Politics,* Vol. 1, No. 2 (Spring 1989), pp. 131–147.

4. See, for example, Joseph LaPalombra and Myron Weiner, eds., *Political Parties and Political Development* (Princeton, N.J.: Princeton University Press, 1966); and Seymour M. Lipset and Stein Rokkan, eds., *Party Systems and Voter Alignments: Cross-National Perspectives* (New York: Free Press, 1967).

from constitutional provisions that give parties the formal ability to form lists for offices. Sometimes parties control resources such as money, political training, access to the media, and the ability to mobilize support nationally. If one or a few parties securely control these resources, they are strong. If control over the resources is broadly diffused, parties are weak. When political parties are relatively strong, and the leadership of the state and party is moderate, radical actors, including those who advocate a more aggressive foreign policy, tend to be screened out. In these cases, nationalism and religion help to legitimize the party and state leaderships' rule and do not become sources for direct political competition.

When parties are weak, however, nationalism becomes a convenient and powerful tool that politicians can use in competing for political power. Rather than having to satisfy the leaders of parties, politicians appeal directly to more broadly based support groups; they have an incentive to employ ideological tools. Under these conditions, it is more likely that a state will be pushed toward a more aggressive foreign policy that corresponds with the expansionist inclinations of nationalist appeals, regardless of its regime type or the preference of its political leaders.[5]

Thus, the democratic peace theory may point to the wrong independent variables to explain the lack of war among established democracies. That is, it is not the features of democratic government, such as popular participation and electoral restraints, that determine whether a state will tend to be pacific or aggressive. As many critics have noted, and as this case will illustrate, mass publics are often more willing to support aggressive foreign policies than is the executive

---

5. Both leadership orientation and party strength are important. If leaders are moderate but have weak parties, they will be unable to restrain ideological competition and will likely be pushed toward more aggressive policies. A radical leader with a strong party may pursue an aggressive foreign policy; in many such cases, however, it is prior institutional weakness and ideological competition that bring radicals to power who then construct strong parties. It is rare that ideological competition occurs when parties are already strong, and it is thus through institutional weakness that radicals tend to come to power in the first place. For example, the Nazis rose to power in Germany through ideological competition in an environment of rapidly crumbling institutions, including weak parties in a fragmented political system. Only after it controlled the Reichstag did the Nazi party become a strong party according to the definition used in this chapter.

6. John Mearsheimer, "Back to the Future: Instability in Europe After the Cold War," *International Security*, Vol. 15, No. 1 (Summer 1990), p. 185.

branch of the state.[6] Rather, it is the institutions that provide the rules for competition and participation that are responsible for foreign policy choices. If established democracies are more peaceful, it is because these states generally have strong institutions, including parties that screen out the more radical actors from political life. Most explanations for the democratic peace have ignored these institutional features, features that are shared with some nondemocratic states.

Turkey in the Interwar Period

In this section, I argue that Turkey's pursuit of a status quo foreign policy was a consequence of the strength of the Republican People's Party (RPP) and Mustafa Kemal's leadership. This section first reviews the period of 1918–23, showing developments that easily could have led Turkey toward an irredentist foreign policy later in the interwar period, and tracing the development of the institutionalist precursors of Kemal's RPP that prevented such a policy. It then shows how the RPP under Kemal's leadership was able to exclude politicians who advocated an aggressive foreign policy, and prevented political competition based on increasing nationalist appeals for the recovery of territory or the expansion of borders.

TURKEY AFTER WORLD WAR I

Turkey emerged as a state only at the conclusion of World War I. Prior to that it had formed the center of the extensive Ottoman Empire, which had existed for centuries and extended well beyond the current Anatolian boundaries of Turkey. With the Ottoman defeat in World War I, this empire disintegrated.[7] Aside from a few notable victories, such as Mustafa Kemal's at Gallipoli, Turkey's experience in World War I was dismal, suffering successive defeats on almost all fronts. With the end of the war, the three leaders of the Empire during the war, Enver, Talat and Djemal Pashas, fled the country. An interim government led by Ahmed Izzet Pasha was appointed by Sultan Mehmed Vahideddin to negotiate the peace with the Allies, and an armistice was signed that delimited Turkey's borders to essentially what exists now as Turkey, the Anatolian peninsula.

---

7. For a good account of the period of 1876–1908, including the role of Mustafa Kemal in the nascent CUP movement, see Erik Jan Zurcher, *The Unionist Factor: The Role of the Committee of Union and Progress in the Turkish National Movement, 1905–1926* (Leiden: E.J. Brill, 1984), pp. 9–44.

The terms of this armistice and the peace that was expected to come out of it stripped the Ottoman Empire of almost all of its non-Turkish territory.[8] No longer would it exercise control over Arab lands that were granted independence under the protectorates of the great powers. Turkey also lost any remaining territory on the European continent. In addition, many Turks were left out of the new state, including some Ottoman Turks who had once lived inside the Ottoman Empire, and the ethnic Turks in places like Central Asia, who had been considered by many before and during the war to be integral components of the Turkish nation.

Despite these large losses, many analysts believe that had the Allies consistently followed the armistice terms, and had they formed the basis for the peace treaty, the Turks would have acquiesced.[9] However, the Turks believed, with good justification, that the Allies were instead continually looking for ways to erode what remained of Turkey, and were likely to interpret any ambiguities in the armistice to the detriment of the Turks.[10] In response to both the Western violations and the Ottoman government's weakness, a new movement began to grow among the remaining high-ranking Ottoman officers; its goal was an ambiguous notion of a "stronger" Turkey.[11]

When Greek troops landed in Turkey in May 1919 with the blessing of the Allies, the movement quickly picked up steam, with self-defense organizations forming throughout Turkey. Meanwhile, the Ottoman government in Istanbul took no measures to resist the Greek landing. The nationalist forces in the interior, which now included some regular Turkish forces under Mustafa Kemal's command, combined with

---

8. For a brief account of the terms of the settlement, and particularly of the Treaty of Sevres, an even harsher settlement than was anticipated based on the armistice agreements that reduced the Empire to Anatolian Turkey, see George Lenczowski, *The Middle East in World Affairs*, 4th ed. (Ithaca, N.Y.: Cornell University Press, 1980), pp. 98–102.

9. Bernard Lewis, *The Emergence of Modern Turkey*, 2nd ed. (New York: Oxford University Press, 1968), p. 241.

10. The British, for example, pushed forward to occupy Mosul after the armistice had been concluded and forces were supposed to stay in place. Edward Reginald Vere-Hodge, *Turkish Foreign Policy, 1918–1948* (Ambilly-Annemasse, France: Imprimerie Franco-Suisse, 1950), p. 17; Lord Kinross, *Ataturk: A Biography of Mustafa Kemal, Father of Modern Turkey* (New York: William Morrow and Company, 1965), pp. 155–158.

11. Zurcher, *The Unionist Factor*, pp. 96–105.

the self-defense organizations to create a new government that was headquartered in Ankara. Kemal's government competed with the interim Ottoman government, still located in Istanbul, for control of the county.[12] It continued to gain support throughout its war with Greece, but was not formally recognized as the legitimate government of Turkey until it occupied Istanbul in 1922.

After a prolonged Greek advance,[13] Kemal was able to concentrate his forces, taking command of them himself in July 1921 at the Sakarya River in a pivotal battle that lasted three weeks and forced the Greeks into retreat.[14] Only twelve months after the battle at Sakarya, the Greek forces were pushed out of Anatolia, and the Turkish nationalist forces approached the Dardanelles in September 1922 and moved to take back Istanbul, which was under British control.[15]

At first it appeared that Britain would make a stand and engage the Turks. However, the British were left standing alone by the other great powers who had by now accepted the Kemalist-led government as the legitimate ruler of Turkey.[16] The British evacuated in October 1922, and the nationalist forces formally took control of all of Anatolia and negotiated a new peace treaty that recognized the full Anatolian boundaries as defined by the armistice agreement, and also afforded Turkey significantly more financial and political independence than did the peace treaties concluded with the other losing

12. In anticipation of their military needs, nationalist commanders in the interior of the country had been hindering demobilization and storing weapons, so that in 1921 the nationalist forces numbered some 100,000, some of whom were well armed. A.L. Macfie, *Ataturk* (New York: Longman, 1994), pp. 50–55.

13. Greece advanced rapidly largely because Kemal's army first had to face the French and Italians, sometimes in combat. These states had troops occupying parts of the former Ottoman Empire after World War I. Turkey finally secured an agreement with both the French and Italians for their evacuation from Anatolia, and the French knowingly left behind some heavy weapons that were quite useful to the Turks against Greece. See Lenczowski, *The Middle East in World Affairs,* pp. 104–105.

14. Kinross, *Ataturk,* pp. 319–322, gives a good account of this battle.

15. Lenczowski, *The Middle East in World Affairs,* p. 105.

16. Richard Robinson, *The First Turkish Republic: A Case Study in National Development* (Cambridge, Mass.: Harvard University Press, 1963), pp. 74–75. At first, local French and Italian commanders lent token forces of about 100 men to the British cause, but orders from their governments led to a quick evacuation, leaving the British alone. Stephen F. Evans, *The Slow Rapprochement: Britain and Turkey in the Age of Kemal Ataturk, 1919–1938* (Walkington, U.K.: Eothen Press, 1982), pp. 52–57.

states. Certain difficult issues such as the status of Mosul, a town claimed by Turkey, were left to later settlement.[17]

Thus, by 1923 Turkey's relations with Greece and Great Britain were extremely hostile. Turkey had just concluded a bitter war with Greece, which was regarded as an enemy and inferior. There remained "Turks" inside of Greece, and parts of Thrace were coveted by many in Turkey. Turkey had almost gone to war with Great Britain over control of the Straits and of Istanbul. Nevertheless, the nationalists had succeeded in reestablishing the boundaries of Turkey, and in setting Turkey on firm footing internationally.

DOMESTIC POLITICS IN INTERWAR TURKEY

Below I examine the institutional developments and ideological cleavages in interwar Turkey.

POLITICAL CONTESTS AND IDEOLOGICAL COMPETITION. During the war with Greece, Turkish politics in many respects resembled those in a democratic state. First, there was real competition for seats in the National Assembly, and no single person, group, or party dominated the elections for these positions.[18] Participants in the Assembly included former members of the prewar Committee of Union and Progress (CUP); local politicians and elites who were not necessarily part of the political leadership prior to World War I; the military, through its political control of some self-defense organizations; and religious figures from the interior of the country. These groups competed for power, mobilized popular support, and participated in reasonably free and fair elections that drew the participation of a significant portion of the Turkish population.[19] Though the nationalist Assembly was not formally broken down into parties or factions (it was ostensibly unified in order to best prosecute the war), there were divisions

---

17. These also included the ultimate status of the Straits of Bosporus, the Dardanelles, and the Narrows, which remained for the time being internationalized and nonmilitarized. These had always been considered the critical strategic area of Turkey since they gave the only access to the Black Sea and gave Istanbul its access to the Mediterranean Sea. Leczowski, *The Middle East in World Affairs*, pp. 106–107.

18. Ergun Ozbudun, "Turkey," in Myron Weiner and Ergun Ozbudun, eds., *Competitive Elections in Developing Countries* (Durham, N.C.: Duke University Press, 1987), p. 336; Zurcher, *The Unionist Factor*, pp. 125–129; Dankwart Rustow, "The Development of Parties in Turkey," in La Palombra and Weiner, eds., *Political Parties and Political Development*, p. 120; and Feroz Ahmad, *The Making of Modern Turkey* (New York: Routledge, 1993), p. 53.

19. Rustow, "The Development of Parties in Turkey," p. 120.

that were important to political outcomes. These divisions were to some degree muted during the Greco-Turkish war, but did flare up at times. They were most noticeable at the end of this war, promising to expand into intense political conflicts after the war.[20]

Furthermore, this period was marked by real divisions of power; Kemal, as president, was not able to pursue all of the policies he wanted. A provisional constitution guaranteed substantial power to the legislature populated by members who espoused a more aggressive international policy.[21] Even though Kemal was regarded as a war hero, was considered the leader of the nationalist movement, and exercised executive authority, he was heavily constrained in his actions.[22] The legislature often balked at his demands. For instance, at one point in 1920 it appeared that the Ottoman government in Istanbul was going to accept nationalists into its body. Elections were held and the nationalists did very well, sending a majority to the new parliament. Kemal told the nationalist representatives to elect him as leader of the government, but they did not do so.[23] Even after power shifted back to Kemal's government in Ankara when the British closed the Ottoman Parliament, he was elected as the executive of the provisional Assembly by a vote of 110-109.[24]

Moreover, because of the constitutional limits on his power, and therefore the need to gain approval from the legislature for most governmental actions, Kemal spent most of his time during the war with Greece trying to bargain with and persuade the Assembly that it should go along with his plans, rather than leading the Turkish military forces himself. That is why he did not take actual command of the Turkish forces until Sakarya, a battle that took place only a few miles away from the nationalist capital of Ankara.[25] Institutionally, then, across a variety of measures, Turkey had become an emerging democracy during its war to expel Greece from Anatolia.

---

20. Ibid., p. 120; and Macfie, *Ataturk*, pp. 103, 129–130.

21. Frederick W. Frey, *The Turkish Political Elite* (Cambridge, Mass.: MIT Press, 1965), p. 8.

22. Erik Jan Zurcher, *Political Opposition in the Early Turkish Republic: The Progressive Republican Party, 1924–1925* (Leiden: E. J. Brill, 1991), p. 17.

23. The conflict was made moot once the British intervened to close this last Ottoman Parliament because of nationalist successes. For a good account of the episode, see Macfie, *Ataturk*, pp. 92–95.

24. Ibid., pp. 101–102.

25. Kinross, *Ataturk*, pp. 271, 307.

While there was political contestation, there were no strong political parties. Diverse groups opposed Kemal's leadership, but neither he nor the opposition had powerful organizations behind them.[26] That is, no group could reliably command a secure constituency; had control over large-scale financial resources; or was truly national in its scope.[27] Therefore, political parties were not the mechanisms of either political recruitment or the channeling of political participation. Instead, relatively loose agglomerations of similarly minded people were grouped into competing factions. What actually drove political competition and accounted for political success was the extensive use of competing ideologies.

In fact, the factions were largely defined by their use of different ideological, or normative, appeals. There were three main ideologies: Pan-Turkism, Pan-Islam, and constrained Turkish nationalism. The first was expounded mostly by former members of the CUP, which had strongly promoted a very expansive view of Turkish nationalism that included Turkic peoples who had never lived inside the Ottoman Empire, particularly those in Central Asia and Southern Russia.[28] Pan-Turkism was one of the strands of nationalism that emerged from the development of Turkish cultural studies, the goal of which was the establishment of a distinct Turkish identity. Nationalist studies were begun in the nineteenth century, as it was becoming evident that the empire was facing severe internal problems related to the development of national identity among non-Turks.[29] Nationalist studies strived to identify certain linguistic and cultural markers that would define a specifically Turkish nation.

---

26. Macfie, *Ataturk*, pp. 129–130.

27. The remnant of the CUP was closest to having some strong party structure, but even it was quite fragmented, being split between defense-of-rights groups, CUP organizational successors, and followers of Kemal. In addition, the CUP was made illegal, and while this did not halt its operations in practice, it did make it more difficult to keep the CUP intact as a national party. See Zurcher, *The Unionist Factor*, pp. 72–92.

28. Ibid., pp. 125–130. There was fairly extensive support in some of the more radical CUP circles for the return of Enver Pasha, the main CUP proponent for a Pan-Turkist policy during World War I. Enver's return was blocked by Kemal, and Enver went on to attempt to organize Pan-Turkist movements outside of Turkey.

29. Historically, ethnicity had not been important in gaining access to political power. Any Greek, Slav, Albanian, Kurd, or Arab could become part of the Ottoman elite, so long as he spoke Turkish and practiced Sunni Islam. Lewis, *The Emergence of Modern Turkey*, pp. 7–8, 344–345.

These markers were often found in Turks living outside of Turkey. In fact, many students of Turkish nationalism romanticized the degree to which Turks who lived outside the Ottoman Empire might reflect "true" Turkism better than the Anatolian Turks.[30] This Pan-Turkic movement was partly driven by immigrants from Southern Russia; but the Ottoman Turks themselves were generally favorably inclined toward this perspective.[31]

Writings of prominent Ottoman Turks prior to World War I indicate that Turkish nationalism was often thought to be inextricably linked to Pan-Turkism.[32] The ideology became politically relevant through the CUP prior to World War I, when certain nationalists were brought into positions of authority within the party and began to affect its policy. It reached its pinnacle during World War I when Enver Pasha, perhaps the best known of the triumvirate that led the Empire during the war, mobilized large-scale support for the Pan-Turkic cause, and designed military actions to try to realize such a vision of an expanded Turkish political unit.[33] In the immediate aftermath of the war, it was difficult to separate Turkish nationalism from Pan-Turkism. Those Turks who were mobilized by nationalism frequently associated it explicitly with the expansionist notion of Pan-Turkism that was espoused by many who had been CUP elites.[34] While the CUP was banned in 1918 when Turkey capitulated because of its "culpability" for World War I, it continued to influence politics in Turkey.

Religious ideology was also an important competitive tool. Islam was a core feature of what constituted the Ottoman identity, and was a

---

30. David Kushner, *The Rise of Turkish Nationalism, 1876–1908* (Totowa, N.J.: Frank Cass, 1977), pp. 42–43.

31. Lewis, *The Emergence of Modern Turkey*, p. 348.

32. Masami Arai, *Turkish Nationalism in the Young Turk Era* (Leiden: E.J. Brill, 1993), chaps. 4–5. See also Jacob M. Landau, *Pan-Turkism in Turkey: A Study of Irredentism* (London: C. Hurst, 1981) for an excellent study on the development of Turkish nationalism and its connections with irredentism.

33. Lewis, *The Emergence of Modern Turkey*, p. 351; and Landau, *Pan-Turkism in Turkey*, p. 54. Landau makes a more general argument that Turkey's entrance into World War I was largely inspired by the possibility of taking in the Turks of the Russian Empire and building a new Turkish Empire. Upon entry into the war, the Ottoman government issued a statement that "participation in the World War represents the vindication of our national ideal. The ideal of our nation and our people leads us towards the destruction of our Muscovite enemy, in order to obtain thereby a national frontier to our Empire, which should include and unite all branches of our race." Quoted in Landau, *Pan-Turkism in Turkey*, p. 52.

34. Lewis, *The Emergence of Modern Turkey*, p. 358.

critical link between the Turks and Arabs.[35] Furthermore, *Ulema*—official religious authorities—were important to the Empire in their function as legal authorities who oversaw the interpretation and enforcement of the *Shari'a*—the Islamic legal code—for Muslim subjects of the Empire. Most important during this period was that Islam was a core identity feature of almost all Turks. Religious leaders could thus rely on support based on their appeals to shared Muslim identity.[36]

Religious ideology tended to produce Pan-Islamic politics.[37] There was nothing unique about Turkey as an Islamic state, or Turks as Muslims; therefore, for many who identified themselves primarily through religion, creating a political unit to correspond to Islam meant expansion well beyond Anatolian frontiers. At the least, Turkey should have actively sought to reacquire most of its lost imperial territory, especially to the south where many of the most important holy places were, and which were predominantly populated by Muslims.[38]

The third competing ideology was that of a constrained Turkish nationalism. This fairly new vision of Turkish nationalism was championed by Kemal, beginning sometime around July 1919.[39] It recognized the important connections between Anatolian Turks and other Turkic people, but maintained that there were also important differences that made the realization of a larger Turkish nation-state impossible. It drew upon Turkish nationalist studies, but tried to

---

35. Islam was powerful enough to keep most Arabs loyal to the Empire during World War I. While many popular Western histories focus on the Arab Revolt and the Arab participation on the side of the Allies against the Ottoman Empire, most Arabs were not participants. Kemal noted that Arab soldiers continued to fight bravely for the imperial forces under his command at Gallipoli, where Kemal's strategy was to take high casualties while wearing down the British forces. He knowingly sent thousands of soldiers to their deaths, and they knew their probable fate. He maintains that Arabs went as willingly as any other soldiers, and that they believed that dying in this way would make them martyrs and assure their entrance into heaven. See Macfie, *Ataturk,* pp. 40–42. See also Mehmet Yasar Geyikdagi, *Political Parties in Turkey: The Role of Islam* (New York: Praeger, 1984), pp. 30–31.

36. Lewis, *The Emergence of Modern Turkey,* p. 329.

37. Ibid., p. 13.

38. Even the Ottoman leadership during World War I had used Pan-Islam in attempts to cleave Muslim parts of the British Empire from the Western Allies. See Jacob M. Landau, *Pan-Turkism: From Irredentism to Cooperation* (Indianapolis: Indiana University Press, 1995), pp. 49–50.

39. Robinson, *The First Turkish Republic,* p. 69.

place limits on the degree to which Ottoman Turks shared an identity with other people of Turkic background.[40]

The political consequence of this ideology was an attempt to create a state corresponding to the Anatolian borders. The movement was sustained largely by Kemal's own reputation.[41] As the only Turkish commander to have won a major victory in World War I, Kemal had a reputation that went a long way toward establishing this constrained nationalism as a legitimate political force that could mobilize support. While Kemal saw the establishment of an Anatolian Turkish state as an end goal, those who advocated Pan-Turkism or Pan-Islam saw it as a way station on the path to a larger and more inclusive political unit. The danger was that, despite Kemal's personal power, both of the expansionist ideologies were stronger and more popular than Kemal's more limited version of Turkish nationalism.[42]

THE CREATION OF A STRONG PARTY. What prevented this ideological competition from dominating Turkish interwar politics and propelling Turkey to an aggressive security policy was the construction of a dominant political institution, the Republican People's Party (RPP), led by Mustafa Kemal.[43] Kemal's general strategy in building institutions was to merge or take over existing institutions. The RPP was constructed out of two important institutional legacies, the CUP and the self-defense organizations.[44] Kemal himself had been a CUP

---

40. In many ways, even this limited nationalism was quite problematic. Most of Anatolia had poor lines of communication, and many villages had unique cultural heritages that made speaking about a Turkish nation more difficult. See Robinson, *The First Turkish Republic*, pp. 37–42.

41. Lewis, *The Emergence of Modern Turkey*, p. 358.

42. For instance, the three ideological pillars of the late Ottoman governments had been Pan-Turkism, Pan-Islam, and Ottomanism. People simply had not been mobilized around Kemal's more limited notion of Turkish nationalism. See Landau, *Pan-Turkism*, chap. 2.

43. For the role of Kemal and the RPP in making Turkey a status quo state, see Dankwart A. Rustow, "Ataturk as an Institution Builder," in Ali Kazancigil and Ergun Ozbudun, eds., *Ataturk: Founder of a Modern State* (London: C. Hurst, 1981).

44. Ahmad, *The Making of Modern Turkey*, p. 48. To a degree, the distinction between the CUP and self-defense organizations is difficult to make since the latter drew heavily on the CUP at its inception. See Arif T. Payaslioglu, "Political Leadership and Political Parties: Turkey," in Robert E. Ward and Dankwart A. Rustow, eds., *Political Modernization in Japan and Turkey* (Princeton, N.J.: Princeton University Press, 1964), p. 417. The self-defense organizations, however, tended to be more locally focused and penetrated somewhat more deeply into society than the CUP had.

member, and was tied into the CUP network.[45] More importantly, the remnants of the illegal CUP leadership became willing to follow Kemal's leadership.[46]

Particularly at the local level, the nascent RPP simply took over the financial, organizational, and personnel assets of the old CUP. While some of the local members of the CUP had moved into the self-defense groups, the national leadership had retained control over the formal organization by setting up direct successors to the CUP, such as the Renovation Party and Karakol.[47] Thus, by adopting this CUP legacy, Kemal was able to appropriate some key political resources.

In addition, Kemal incorporated many of the local self-defense organizations.[48] At the outset, these groups saw Kemal as an outsider and were reluctant to cede the command to him. When Kemal first came to Anatolia in 1919 as the inspector of Ottoman forces in charge of demobilizing troops, he set out to take control of the young nationalist movement. Resistance to him was strong, however, and his attempts to lead the first national congresses in Erzerum and Sivas were strongly contested.[49] Nevertheless, in the end Kemal gained control over most of these groups and established himself as the main leader of the self-defense movement, merging many of the regional groups into larger organizations such as the Erzerum and Trabzon self-defense groups.[50]

The CUP gave Kemal a cadre of well-trained party bureaucrats in most major towns, as well as financial and organizational resources; ties with the self-defense groups expanded and deepened his control over Turkish society, allowing him to mobilize at the local level better than he could have otherwise done. Thus, the RPP allowed Kemal to "recruit and organize persons loyal to [Kemal] Ataturk and his

---

45. Zurcher, *Political Opposition in the Early Turkish Republic*, p. 11.

46. Zurcher, *The Unionist Factor*, p. 135. By the time of the 1923 elections for the Assembly, the CUP chose not to put up independent candidates, and instead supported those of Kemal.

47. Zurcher, *The Unionist Factor*, pp. 72–82, 88–92.

48. Geyikdagi, *Political Parties in Turkey*, p. 55.

49. Macfie, *Ataturk*, pp. 68–69; and Kinross, *Ataturk*, pp. 207–208.

50. Macfie, *Ataturk*, p. 71. Even as late as the summer of 1923, the Trabzon branch of the Association for the Defense of Rights resisted Kemal's trying to turn it into an RPP branch. By August, however, the RPP had officially taken over all assets of the self-defense groups. Zurcher, *Political Opposition in the Early Turkish Republic*, pp. 27–30.

policies," and securely mobilize and channel popular support.[51] It managed popular support more by depoliticization than by large-scale mobilization.[52]

By 1923, the nationalist movement had accomplished its basic goals of securing the sovereignty of Turkey from Greek and Western control, and moved to assume power over the whole state. At this point divisions emerged. As the Assembly began to break into factions, Kemal moved to transform his heretofore loose organizational tool into a dominant party. In 1921, Kemal had formed the Defense of Rights Group in the Assembly, and others had formed the "Second Group."[53] As victory over Greece and the Allies approached, the divisions that had created this split became more important, leading Kemal to strengthen his support and turn the Defense of Rights Group into a real party, the RPP. By the time of the elections in summer of 1923, he had succeeded in doing this.[54] His electoral victory and party strength allowed him to force out of office those who directly hindered his plans. RPP dominance had become a fact.[55]

The RPP's dominance effectively ended Turkish democratization. For the remainder of the interwar period, Turkish politics were determined by Kemal and the RPP.[56] To have a political career, or any political voice at all, one had to be a member of the RPP and approved by its leadership.[57] Kemal himself selected which RPP members would be put on the ballot for elections to the Assembly; in most cases this amounted to deciding who would be elected.[58] Thus,

---

51. Payaslioglu, "Political Leadership and Political Parties: Turkey," p. 418.

52. Ergun Ozbudun, "The Nature of the Kemalist Political Regime," in Kazancigil and Ozbudun, eds., *Ataturk: Founder of a Modern State*, pp. 92–93.

53. Zurcher, *The Unionist Factor*, p. 129.

54. Kinross, *Ataturk*, pp. 415–416; Macfie, *Ataturk*, pp. 130–131.

55. Ahmad, *The Making of Modern Turkey*, p. 53. In fact, in the 1923 elections, only 3 of the 118 members of the informal "second group" that had been Kemal's main opposition were reelected. See Frey, *The Turkish Political Elite*, pp. 312–313.

56. Ahmad, *The Making of Modern Turkey*, p. 54.

57. For a description of the process by which one became an RPP member, see Walter Weiker, *The Modernization of Turkey: From Ataturk to the Present Day* (New York: Holmes and Meier Publishers, 1981), p. 120.

58. Not until electoral reforms in 1942 was the RPP given formal legal control over nominations. That year, it became a requirement that the RPP give its consent before a candidate was eligible for office. However, this new law was nothing more than a codification of an institution that had been at work in Turkey since at least 1927. See Frey, *The Turkish Political Elite*, p. 13.

after the war with Greece, Turkey became an authoritarian system. It did not exhibit free political contestation, and never approached the degree of democratic choice displayed in the Provisional Assembly during the war with Greece.

Furthermore, the RPP and Kemal pursued a range of reforms that required a fair degree of coercion, and, Kemal believed, an authoritarian state.[59] The most contested reforms aimed to secularize Turkey. These reforms occurred despite the fact that Anatolian *Ulema* had been instrumental in providing a foundation of support for Kemal's nationalist movement during the war with Greece. Almost immediately after the war was concluded, however, Kemal and the RPP began introducing measures designed to remove religious figures from positions of political or legal authority, and eventually to remove religion from political life altogether.[60]

First, Kemal pushed a declaration through the Assembly that stated that Turkey was to be a republic. The Ottoman Empire had a long tradition of a dual political authority from both secular and religious sources. For Kemal, the declaration of a republic was seen as the first step in the transformation of Turkey into a Westernized state. The move to become a republic was important because Turkey's political and religious authority had traditionally been held by one person, the Sultan, who was also the Caliph. By removing the Sultan from the head of government, and abolishing the sultanate, Kemal was dismantling positions through which Islam could hold sway in government.

Next Kemal implemented a series of more controversial reforms.[61] The RPP abolished the office of the caliphate over the strenuous objections of Muslims both within and outside Turkey.[62] Kemal forced out most religious leaders from public office, and then excluded them from politics for the remainder of the interwar period. The RPP-led Assembly passed legal reforms based mostly on German and Swiss law that removed the *Ulema* from their historic role as legal authorities based on their application of the *Shari'a*. As of 1927, Islam was no longer the official religion of Turkey. New rights for women

---

59. Robinson, *The First Turkish Republic*, pp. 32–33.

60. On this point, see Geyikdagi, *Political Parties in Turkey*, pp. 40–42.

61. An extensive list of these secularizing reforms can be found in ibid., pp. 3–4.

62. Ahmad, *The Making of Modern Turkey*, p. 54. In quick order after this, Kemal also abolished the religious schools and the religious court system. Lewis, *The Emergence of Modern Turkey*, pp. 264–265.

were introduced that sought to entirely transform their place in Turkish society.

In sum, Kemal and the RPP forced Turkey to accept a new subordinate and nonpolitical role for religion, a radical change for a state and society that had long thought of itself as an Islamic state. Most of these reforms were strongly opposed, though the opposition was so effectively kept off of public stages that little of it surfaced. With no *Ulema* in the Assembly and tight control over the media, the RPP could ensure that opponents of the reforms had few opportunities to mobilize organized and widespread public support.[63]

In general, Kemal was able to ignore the significant opposition because Kemal and the RPP were in secure control of the state's coercive apparatus. As Bernard Lewis writes, "by 1927 all opposition to the regime . . . had been silenced, and when elections were held in August and September 1927 for a third Assembly of the Turkish Republic, only one party, the Republican People's Party of Mustafa Kemal, was there to take part in them."[64] With the RPP, Kemal could prohibit any opposition from congealing. He could exclude religious figures from politics, and demobilize their supporters. In severe crises he could count on the military to support his reforms to the point of using force, as in the Kurdish-Dervish Revolt of 1925. Thus, in addition to constructing institutions that limited open competition for political office, Turkey was also nondemocratic in the interwar period in that it coercively excluded a major segment of opinion from politics, and forced reforms through a society that resisted them. It is impossible to imagine Kemal's reforms being as rapid or deep had he not had strong institutional mechanisms at his disposal, and had Turkey not been an authoritarian state.[65]

INTERWAR TURKISH FOREIGN POLICY

Along with the exclusion of the religious elite from politics, the RPP also excluded actors advocating an aggressive international policy. Advocates of any expansionist security policy were forced out of the Assembly, and then not allowed on the RPP lists. These included the

---

63. There were periodic expressions of overt hostility to the reforms such as the Dervish-led uprising among the Kurds in 1925, which was violently suppressed by the Turkish military. See Lewis, *The Emergence of Modern Turkey*, p. 266.

64. Ibid., p. 276.

65. Robinson, *The First Turkish Republic*, pp. 32–33; and Payaslioglu, "Political Leadership and Political Parties," pp. 418–419.

few Ottomanists remaining who favored some resumption of the Empire. More important, it excluded those proposing a policy premised on Pan-Islam or Pan-Turkism, both of which were prominent in the Assembly during the war with Greece.[66]

As the patron of an Anatolian-based Turkish nationalism who wished to improve relations with Europe, Kemal was committed to the status quo. Therefore, he made it clear that anybody who advocated a belligerent international posture was not welcome in the RPP, and certainly not in the Assembly. As early as 1921, Kemal publicly stated that "neither Islamic union nor Turanism may constitute a doctrine, or a logical policy for us. Henceforth the government policy of the new Turkey is to consist in living independently, relying on Turkey's own sovereignty within her national frontiers."[67] Once the RPP achieved political dominance and could remove aggressively inclined politicians from power, it was able to use its control over political resources as selective incentives. That is, in return for allowing somebody into the RPP and supporting their bid for political office, the RPP could demand adherence to the party's domestic and foreign policy program. Thus, the breakdown of democratic institutions and the construction of the RPP muted support for an expansionist security policy.

During the entire interwar period, Turkish policy aimed to preserve the status quo. Mustafa Kemal and his close followers were most responsible for the articulation and pursuit of a limited strategy that would stop at the armistice boundaries; this is in fact what happened. Turkey could have continued to prosecute the war against Greece and, as it will be shown below, there were good reasons to expect Turkey to do so. Yet once it reached its previously declared objectives of reestablishing Turkish control over that territory that was "rightfully" Turkey's by prior agreement, Turkey halted its activities and concluded peace treaties with its former enemies.[68] For the remainder of the interwar period, Turkey was a staunch defender of the territorial status quo in the Balkans.[69]

---

66. Landau, *Pan-Turkism in Turkey*, p. 73.

67. Quoted in ibid., p. 72.

68. The Turks were quite conciliatory in many respects. For example, Kemal did not pursue war reparations against the Greeks, feeling that it was preferable to begin building better relations. Charles Sherrill, *A Year's Embassy to Mustafa Kemal* (New York: Charles Scribner's Sons, 1934), p. 227.

69. Lenczowski, *The Middle East in World Affairs*, p. 122.

During the 1920s, Turkey made great efforts to improve its relations with the two states that had been its principal antagonists immediately after World War I, Greece and Great Britain. The relationship with Greece was soured by a number of important factors. First, Greece was seen as instrumental in the nineteenth-century breakdown of the Ottoman Empire. Egypt had gained a large measure of independence prior to Greece, but Egypt was far from the Empire's core, and whatever the reality of the political relationship, Egypt was still formally part of the Ottoman Empire.[70] In the Greek case, a newly independent state was established next to the heart of the Ottoman Empire.

That Greece took advantage of Turkey's internationally isolated and internally weak situation to take territory was a sign of the state of Greco-Turkish relations in 1920, and obviously hurt the relationship further. Additionally, when Turkey halted its own advance, a large population of ethnic Turks remained within the boundaries of Greece; this provided many in Turkey with a powerful incentive for war. Thus, the Greco-Turkish relationship was one of almost unmitigated animosity.

Yet Kemal gradually constructed a new relationship with Greece throughout the 1920s. First, the two states agreed to a population transfer of unprecedented size. Rather than taking the territory that the remaining ethnic Turks in Greece lived on, Kemal chose to exchange the Turks for Greeks living in Anatolia.[71] Provisions were made for the Greek Orthodox population in Istanbul to remain there given the centrality of the city, formerly Constantinople, to the Orthodox Church. In addition, Turks in western Thrace were also allowed to remain in place. This was a potentially explosive decision since Turkey wanted the territory despite the agreement, and the Muslim population there was discriminated against.[72] These factors could have easily become focal points for a revisionist policy by Turkey. Second, at the end of the 1920s and beginning of the 1930s, Turkey began courting Greece to enter into an alliance. Greek President Eleutherios Venizilos visited Turkey in October 1930 to sign a treaty of friendship, and press reaction was quite favorable.[73]

---

70. See Arthur Goldschmidt, *A Concise History of the Middle East*, 3rd ed. (Boulder, Colo.: Westview, 1988), pp. 157–160, 173–178.

71. Kinross, *Ataturk*, p. 406.

72. Vere-Hodge, *Turkish Foreign Policy*, pp. 54–55.

73. Ibid., p. 57.

A more comprehensive Balkan Pact was signed in February 1934. This astonishing arrangement made Greece and Turkey partners in a pact that was geared toward the preservation of peace in the region, and guaranteed the territorial status quo in the Balkans, a goal that Turkey had been explicitly pursuing since 1930.[74] The alliance included provisions that if a state was attacked by an outside power, the others would come to its assistance militarily. While the treaty amounted to little once Germany began its revisionist efforts, the treaties of 1930 and 1934 are the best indication that Turkish foreign policy was aimed at peace, accommodation, and the status quo.

Turkey adopted a similar line with respect to Great Britain, despite the hostility that remained from the conflict over the Straits and Istanbul in 1922 and despite Turkey's perception, based on considerable evidence, that Britain had been the strongest great power backer of the Greeks, and of the final Ottoman government.[75] In particular, Turkey wanted Britain to support Turkey's taking over full control of the Straits. By the early 1930s, Turkey persuaded the British that it was reliable enough to run this strategic point, and that it could be trusted to responsibly arm the area for defense. By 1936, Turkey obtained enough international support to take over the Straits, in large part due to British backing.[76] The British-Turkish relationship had come full circle from 1922, when Britain nearly went to war to prevent a Turkish presence in the Straits.[77]

A second issue involving Britain was the status of Mosul. Because it had been contained in the original National Pact, the nationalist Assembly's provisional constitution that defined Turkey's borders based on the armistice agreements, the city and region were important to Turkey. Furthermore, Mosul had a large Turkish population, and was strategically and economically important. The British, however, maintained that Mosul should be granted to Iraq.

The matter was sent to arbitration at the League of Nations. The League decided that Turkey's claim was probably more valid, but that since Iraq was a protectorate of Britain, the region would be better served and developed if it went to Iraq.[78] Many members of the

---

74. Ibid., pp. 80–81, 96–97.

75. In addition to the episodes already mentioned, the British even had individual Ottoman commanders removed from their posts or their responsibilities and had their power downgraded. They attempted to force Kemal out of the army in this way as well. Kinross, *Ataturk*, p. 168.

76. Vere-Hodge, *Turkish Foreign Policy*, pp. 122–124.

77. Ibid., pp. 119–120.

78. Ibid., pp. 59–63.

Assembly called for armed action to take Mosul by force if necessary. Kemal, however, backed down after a bit of saber-rattling. He quieted the Assembly and made it accept the fact that Mosul was lost to Britain and Iraq. Calls to war quickly subsided and Turkey accepted the British victory.[79]

These events are excellent illustrations of Turkey's foreign policy during the interwar period. It is clear that Kemal and the RPP wanted to improve relations and resolve even the most heated issues through negotiation rather than armed conflict. Creative solutions were sometimes found, as with the populations exchange with Greece. Other resolutions involved giving in, as in the case of Mosul. Finally, Turkey took active steps to preserve the status quo, as in its alliance with Greece.

Yet there were both international and domestic reasons to expect that Turkey would be far more aggressive. At the international level, one might have expected Turkey to be expansionist because of its substantial military success. As George Lenczowski notes, "victory over their enemies gave Kemal and his followers tremendous confidence in their own strength and ability and raised the morale throughout the entire nation. It would have been easy to adopt a dangerous and ambitious course of aggrandizement."[80] During the war with Greece, Turkey had demonstrated that it could decisively defeat its neighbor's forces. By the time Turkey began its counteroffensive, Kemal had constructed an able force with a high-quality command. Turkey had also received some weaponry from an agreement with the Soviet Union, and from supplies intentionally left by the French after their negotiated withdrawal from parts of Turkey.[81] Moreover, by the end of the conflict, even the British were backing away from supporting Greece, and France and Italy had already done so since they considered Greek success to be inimical to their own interests in the region.[82] Thus, Turkey seemed to have a real military advantage:

79. Ibid, pp. 63–64.

80. Leczowski, *The Middle East in World Affairs,* p. 122.

81. An agreement with the Soviet Union was reached by August 1920, but was not signed until seven months later due to Soviet concerns over Pan-Turkic activity aimed at the Caucasus. Roderic Davidson, "Turkish Diplomacy from Mudros to Lausanne," in Gordon Craig and Felix Gilbert, eds., *The Diplomats, 1919–1939* (New York: Atheneum, 1963), pp. 184–185.

82. By January 1921, Turkey was beginning to talk with Italy and France over withdrawal in return for some sort of economic concessions. In October 1921, France signed the Treaty of Ankara with Turkey; it evacuated French forces, left equipment and recognized the nationalists in return for minor concessions over part of the Baghdad Railway. In effect, this was a bilateral revision of the terms of Sevres. Davidson, "Turkish Diplomacy from Mudros to Lausanne," p. 193.

Greek troops were in full retreat, and Turkey could have pressed on to greater territorial gains, particularly in Thrace, where the Turks had claimed an interest and where large pockets of ethnic Turks resided. The likelihood of great power intervention to aid Greece appeared low. Despite these advantages and the opportunity for large gains at low costs, Turkey still halted its advance.

The Turks also had a local military superiority over the great powers with forces in the region. The French and Italians agreed to withdraw their forces from Turkey, instead concentrating their attention on the peripheral areas of the former Ottoman Empire such as the Levant and North Africa.[83] Britain demonstrated its continuing interest in Anatolia, or at least the northwest corner of it, with its stand against Kemal's army. But in backing down, the British revealed a deep reluctance to enmesh themselves in another costly and probably protracted war with the Turks. As previously noted, part of this was due to the disinterest of the other major Western states; but there was also domestic pressure for Britain to back down. Contemporary British newspapers reveal popular opinion against beginning a new war with Turkey so soon after the end of World War I, and also a fair amount of sympathy for the nationalist forces in Turkey.[84] If Britain did not defend the part of Turkey that had been most important to it historically, there was little reason for Turkey to worry that the British would engage in a large-scale war with Turkey over the smaller issue of Mosul. The fact that Britain was unlikely to intervene made the Turkish Assembly's call for war all the more attractive, and made a Turkish victory appear possible.[85] In short, then, there were no actors that could have been expected to stop Turkish expansion. Greece seemed unable, and the great powers unwilling.

Domestic politics provided additional reasons to expect a more aggressive and revisionist foreign policy, since many of the politicians in the Provisional Assembly, which formed the nationalist

---

83. Vere-Hodge, *Turkish Foreign Policy*, pp. 34–35.

84. Evans, *The Slow Rapprochement*, p. 59.

85. In fact, during the negotiations for the Treaty of Lausanne there was serious opposition to the concessions that Ismet, the Turkish nationalist negotiator, gave to the West. Ismet, for instance, agreed to international control over the Straits, with the possibility of reconsideration at a later date. For this he was widely attacked, and only Kemal's intervention saved his position and allowed the treaty to be ratified. Many in the Assembly were quite willing to go back on the offensive to take what they believed they deserved. Davidson, "Turkish Diplomacy from Mudros to Lausanne," pp. 202–207.

legislature during the war with Greece, were committed to an ideology that advocated a larger political area for Turkey than just Anatolia. Those who wanted a Muslim state generally wanted boundaries to expand toward the south, to bring in Arab Muslims. Those whose focus was on Turkish nationalism often looked toward the north and east for expansion into southern Russia, or toward the northwest to bring in the Turks living in Greece. Both of these ideologies had powerful adherents who could mobilize mass support for their causes. Proponents of expansion were powerful elements in the Provisional Assembly, and seemed likely to be influential once the war with Greece was concluded.

In fact, from certain perspectives, even those who backed Kemal and his more limited vision of Turkey might have been radicalized. Kemal's position was firmly based on Turkish nationalism, an ideology that was important to understanding the direction of RPP policy in the interwar period, and which provided Kemal with a foundation of legitimacy for his rule. Had nationalism become a tool for political competition rather than a source of political legitimacy, it is easy to imagine more widespread calls for the incorporation of ethnic Turks into the Turkish state as a way to win popular approval. In fact, many analysts see the combination of nationalism and bordering ethnic communities as a sufficient condition for a revisionist policy to expand the state and incorporate the entire ethnic community.[86]

Both the elites who favored Pan-Turkism and those who were Pan-Islamic had ideological advantages over Kemal's version of limited Turkish nationalism. Turks were quite comfortable thinking of themselves as Muslim, and as part of a larger Islamic community. Furthermore, there was extensive support for the notion of Turkey as the political capital of Islam, and also for the caliphate, as indicated by the outrage expressed by religious leaders throughout the Muslim world when Kemal abolished the caliphate. There was an enormous potential for Pan-Islamists in Turkey to mobilize mass support for Turkish expansion based on its role as political leader of the Muslim community.

Additionally, as was noted above, by the end of World War I Turkish nationalism and Pan-Turkism were nearly inseparable, and no real development of a limited Anatolian nationalism had been undertaken.

---

86. See, for example, Myron Weiner, "The Macedonian Syndrome: An Historical Model of International Relations and Political Development," *World Politics*, Vol. 23, No. 4 (July 1971), pp. 665–683.

Nationalist sentiments were most often expressed by Turkey's elite, though it seemed increasingly that there was a more mass-based audience for the nationalist message. Thus, a Pan-Turkic appeal might have resonated with a large segment of the population, and it certainly would have been more powerful than Kemal's novel and limited version of nationalism. Furthermore, the Pan-Turkic element was clearly more familiar to Turkey's nationalist elite and would have been a powerful magnet for most of them.

With such strong competition from other ideologies, the only way Kemal could hope to lead Turkey toward a peaceful foreign policy was by limiting the ability of his opponents to make ideological appeals; it is unlikely that he would have won an ideological competition against religious and Pan-Turkic messages. Thus for Kemal, the creation of the RPP as a dominant political institution was critical. By using the resources, such as organization, money, and personnel, that were afforded to him by the construction of the RPP from the CUP and self-defense organizations, Kemal forced more radical actors on foreign policy out of power, and kept them out through institutional mechanisms.[87] He denied advocates of these more aggressive policies access to political bodies, and to public fora such as the media. It was, therefore, Kemal's use of the RPP to dominate Turkish interwar politics that allowed him to demobilize these elements that would likely have led to a more aggressive foreign policy.[88]

Furthermore, the RPP created a situation in which an increasing competition around nationalist appeals, a nationalist spiral, was not likely. While the RPP was tied to Turkish nationalism, it could define "legitimate" political discourse and create strong incentives to stay within the limits of that discourse. That is, there was little gain in trying to compete through the use of nationalist symbols or ideology. RPP members had to express nationalist sentiment to be admitted to the party and to political office, but being too nationalistic did nothing for one's political career, and probably was a hindrance. What made for political success was carefully following the incentives provided by the RPP leadership.[89]

Thus, the RPP both eliminated from the political landscape those advocating an aggressive policy, and also made it unwise for political entrepreneurs to use nationalism for career advancement. Although

87. Lewis, *The Emergence of Modern Turkey*, pp. 382–383.
88. Rustow, "The Development of Parties in Turkey," pp. 120–121.
89. Frey, *The Turkish Political Elite*, p. 14.

Turkey was quite nationalistic, the RPP prevented the emergence of spirals of nationalist competition. Had the RPP not been dominant and had Turkey been a more open and democratic state, it appears quite likely that more aggressive ideologies with an expansionist element would have prevailed in interwar Turkish politics. These ideologies were more resonant with the Turkish population, could have mobilized more support than limited nationalism, and would have generated more belligerent policies in a more democratic setting. Contrary to the expectations of the monadic version of the democratic peace theory, democratic politics in interwar Turkey would have led to war, not peace.

Hungary in the Interwar Period

An interesting comparison to the Turkish interwar case is that of Hungary in the same period. Like Turkey, Hungary was a legal successor state to an empire that had been on the losing side (the Austro-Hungarian Empire), and was thus held responsible for World War I. Also like Turkey, Hungary was a much reduced state. As part of the Habsburg dual monarchy, in 1867 Hungary had gained autonomy and control over much of the Empire. When the war ended, much of the territory over which Hungary had exercised political control was made into new states that were meant to correspond to ethnic boundaries. However, given the patchwork of ethnicities in East Central Europe, such an enterprise was impossible. Where there were overlapping claims, decisions favored the new states, whose leaders had been allied with the West during World War I.[90] The Treaty of Trianon left Hungary a truncated state, with large groupings of Hungarians outside its borders. It also gave large areas to which Hungary made historical claim, such as Transylvania, to other states.[91] Thus, Hungary faced many of the same conditions as Turkey. However, their foreign policies were very different, particularly in the 1930s.

---

90. Nandor Dreisziger, *Hungary's Way to World War II* (Toronto: Weller Publishing, 1968), p. 19; and Stephen Kertesz, *Diplomacy in a Whirlpool: Hungary between Nazi Germany and Soviet Russia* (South Bend, Ind.: University of Notre Dame Press, 1953), pp. 14–19.

91. Andrew Janos, *The Politics of Backwardness in Hungary, 1825–1945* (Princeton, N.J.: Princeton University Press, 1982), p. 205. For a personal account of the negotiations for Trianon, see Albert Apponyi, *The Memoirs of Count Apponyi* (New York: MacMillan Press, 1935).

Hungarian politics in the first few years after the war were extremely unstable, with a succession of governments with radically different political perspectives and intentions. The governments ranged from the Western-oriented and liberal Michael Karolyi regime, to the communist government of Bela Kun, to finally the right-wing takeover led nominally by Admiral Horthy.[92] However, all of these governments relied on nationalist appeals, and they all promised to protect the territorial integrity of Hungary, promises that nobody could keep.[93]

HUNGARY IN THE 1920S: THE POWER OF THE PARTY

Once the right-wing came to power, Istvan Bethlen, who had been a prominent conservative politician during the prewar period, began building a political party that he intended to use to control Hungarian politics. Its core organization relied on the absorption of a prominent prewar agrarian party; conservative urban support was grafted onto it.[94] By 1922, the party had a much greater organizational capacity than its political competitors, particularly in the rural areas that composed the bulk of the society. Bethlen was able to use the party to control the Hungarian Parliament by engineering electoral majorities at elections. Much of the power of the government party was based on its ability to nominate candidates; nomination was almost the equivalent of electoral victory.[95] The remaining elements of parliament were to the left of Bethlen's party, and included a bourgeois liberal party and a socialist party that drew its strength from urban areas.

Thus, Bethlen's government party dominated the right and conservative portions of the political spectrum in the 1920s. Therefore, as in Turkey in the interwar period, the right-wing radicals

---

92. For a good account of this period, see C.A. MacArtney, *October Fifteenth: A History of Modern Hungary, 1929–1945* (Edinburgh: Edinburgh University Press, 1956), pp. 21–36. See also Jorg Hoensch, *A History of Modern Hungary, 1867–1986* (New York: Longman Press, 1988), pp. 86–99.

93. Tibor Hajdu, "Revolution, Counterrevolution, Consolidation," in Peter Sugar, ed., *A History of Hungary* (Bloomington: Indiana University Press, 1990), pp. 295–309.

94. Antony Polonsky, *The Little Dictators: The History of Eastern Europe since 1918* (Boston: Routledge and Kegan Paul, 1975), p. 53.

95. William Batkay, *Authoritarian Politics in a Transitional State: Istvan Bethlen and the Unified Party in Hungary, 1919–1926* (New York: Columbia University Press, 1983), pp. 35–36.

who were the most vocal advocates of an irredentist policy to expand Hungary by retaking areas in Czechoslovakia or Romania were excluded from the political process.[96] Bethlen viewed these right-wing radicals as the greatest threats to Hungary and took very active measures to suppress their activity. In 1923, Gyula Gömbös, the most prominent rightist in the party, was forced out, and thereafter the radical groups' activities were severely curtailed. Right-wing secret societies with irredentist goals were forced to shut down; the media was not accessible to these radical actors; and through its control over nominations to all political bodies for politicians from the right, Bethlen's party was able to ensure that irredentism, at least violent irredentism, was not a political force in Hungary in the 1920s despite widespread mass support for such a position.[97] Thus, like Turkey in the interwar period, a strong party and a moderate leader blocked Hungarian aggression in the 1920s.

The foreign policy that Bethlen pursued in the 1920s was one of improving relations with the West, and to some degree with the surrounding states that had formerly been subjects of the Austro-Hungarian Empire.[98] Hungary sought and received loans from the West in return for a renunciation of irredentism.[99] Thus, despite the preference by much of the population for an aggressive foreign policy, the conservative government party in Hungary was able to use its institutional power to exclude irredentist politicians, and effectively constrained the popular sentiment for aggression.

HUNGARY IN THE 1930S: RADICALISM AND AGGRESSION

In the early 1930s, the Bethlenite institutional structures began to break down, and more nationalistic politicians moved into positions of power as the government party lost its ability to remove radical politicians. Gyula Gömbös, who had been forced out of politics in

---

96. Istvan Mocsy, "Count Istvan Bethlen," in Pal Body, ed., *Hungarian Statesmen of Destiny, 1860–1960* (New York: Columbia University Press, 1989), pp. 129–133.

97. Support for revision of the Trianon cut across class boundaries and found an audience among the intelligentsia, bourgeois, peasants, and workers. See Gyorgy Ranki, "The Problem of Fascism in Hungary," in Peter Sugar, ed., *Native Fascism in the Successor States, 1918–1945* (Santa Barbara, Calif.: ABC-CLIO Press, 1971), pp. 67–68.

98. Mocsy, "Count Istvan Bethlen," pp. 138–139.

99. Gyula Juhasz, *Hungarian Foreign Policy, 1919–1945* (Budapest: Academiai Kiado, 1979), pp. 71–73.

1923 by Bethlen because he was too radical, became prime minister in 1932. His selection was based largely on his appeal to Hungarian nationalism, and on the idea that Hungary should be more assertive in its foreign policy in an attempt to recover its diaspora and expand back into the space that had been historically Hungarian.[100]

Gömbös's election marked a transition in Hungarian politics. While in the 1920s the government party had provided clear rules for political competition, in the 1930s political success was dependent upon proving that one was as, or more, nationalistic than other candidates. Even politicians who would have been inclined to follow the incentives of the 1920s, and who were not necessarily advocates of a more aggressive policy, found that in order to win or keep their constituencies, they had to appear more radical than others.[101] This created a spiral of nationalist appeal that even Gömbös had not foreseen or intended.

The most important of the extremists was Ferenc Szálasi, generally credited with being the father of the Arrow Cross, the clearest representatives of the Nazi movement in Hungary.[102] Until Szálasi, radicalism was expressed through the Government Party by Gömbös and through the patriotic associations that he sponsored.[103] Szálasi was able to band together the still disorganized elements of radicalism in Hungary, and moved the dialogue further to the right. The Arrow Cross offered no practical answers; its broad phrases and programs simply advocated purification of the Hungarian nation, and restoration of its previous boundaries, or even the extension of its rule over territories it never had controlled in the past. The thrust of Szálasi's ideas was purely nationalistic and mobilized disparate and widespread support because of their vagueness.[104] As one scholar

---

100. For the details on the breakdown of the party and the rise of Gömbös, see MacArtney, *October Fifteenth*, pp. 94–130.

101. For example, Pal Teleki, who became Hungary's prime minister at the beginning of World War II, was pro-revisionist, but of a conservative nature. Part of the reason that he continued courting Germany and pushing aggressive revision was to avoid a victory of the right-wing Hungarian fascists. L. Tilkovsky, *Pal Teleki: A Biographical Sketch* (Budapest: Academiai Kiado, 1974), p. 38.

102. For a very good analysis of the Arrow Cross, its support and effects, see M. Lacko, *Arrow Cross Men: National Socialists, 1935–1944* (Budapest: Academiai Kiado, 1969).

103. Ibid., p. 13.

104. MacArtney, *October Fifteenth*, p. 164; and Lacko, *Arrow Cross Men*, p. 14.

writes, "the very nebulosity of his ideas and his words . . . attracted a fair number of people tired to death of practical materialism which never seemed to bring any practical results."[105] Some officers even resigned their commissions in order to form paramilitary components of the Arrow Cross.[106]

Szálasi was hounded, thrown in jail, and effectively barred from power. But more important than Szálasi was the general nationalist trend that his movement perpetuated, a trend that had begun with Gömbös's rise to prominence and power.[107] Gömbös had changed the nature of politics from a system of deal-brokering among Hungarian aristocrats to a mass-based populism. Gömbös, however, had no monopoly on the use of radicalism; Szálasi and the Arrow Cross represented the next stage of radicalism and nationalism that replaced practicality as the basis for climbing to political power.

As this transformation in the way actors competed was taking place, Hungary was simultaneously becoming more democratic in some ways. Its parliament continued to function; political competition was quite open with no dominant group; and popular participation continued to expand, with new electoral laws late in the decade.[108] In many ways, Hungary was at least as democratic in the 1930s as in the 1920s, and its government better reflected the general preference for a more revisionist foreign policy than the governments of the 1920s. Gömbös and others became "champions of popular participation in politics."[109]

By the end of the 1930s, Hungary had become focused on border revisions. Throughout the decade it tied itself to Italy, with which it shared a common interest in territorial revisions in parts of the

---

105. MacArtney, *October Fifteenth*, p. 185. In fact, the rejection of practical material measures was responsible for the instability that brought Gömbös to power in the first place. See Dreisziger, *Hungary's Way*, p. 33.

106. Lacko, *Arrow Cross Men*, p. 36.

107. Ibid., p. 41.

108. In 1935, Gömbös proposed making the ballot secret in rural areas, and was blocked by Bethlen and Horthy. By 1938 the issue was raised again, and this time passed and allowed by Horthy. Bethlen still opposed it, realizing that becoming institutionally more democratic would give further power to the most radical elements in Hungary since the traditional, more moderate conservatives would be less able to influence outcomes. Thomas Sakmyster, *Hungary's Admiral on Horseback: Miklos Horthy, 1918–1944* (New York: Columbia University Press, 1994), pp. 178, 211; and MacArtney, *October Fifteenth*, p. 125.

109. Janos, *The Politics of Backwardness*, p. 257.

Balkans. Later it moved closer and closer to Germany, an obvious
source of support for violent revision of the status quo in the
region.[110] In 1938, Hungary participated in the destruction of
Czechoslovakia, which by most accounts was the most democratic
state of any in the region.[111] A year later, Hungary mobilized its military along the border with Romania, despite German pressure not to
do so. It forced German intervention and mediation, which resulted
in the awarding of part of Transylvania to Hungary.[112] Thus, benign
foreign policies did not accompany democratization. Contrary to the
monadic democratic peace argument, democratic politics did not
generate a less war-prone state. Moreover, the fact that democratization coincided with Hungary's participation in Germany's invasion
of Czechoslovakia also undermines the dyadic version of the democratic peace theory.

Hungary's foreign policies obviously contrast with those of Turkey.
Aside from the overt policy differences—that Hungary used its military for territorial expansion based on nationalist goals while Turkey
did not—the two states also responded differently to German overtures. While Hungary was aware of the risks of tying itself to
Germany and in some ways tried to balance the German ties with
others, such as ties to Italy, Hungary cannot be seen as an unwilling
participant in the German initiatives. Hungary actively sought
German assistance for its irredentism, and accepted German support
willingly.[113] In contrast, Turkey did not solicit German assistance
when it was clear that Germany was the great power that would support revision of the post–World War I arrangements, and it refused
repeated attempts by Germany to persuade it to move into the Axis
camp in return for promises of aid in securing areas in the Soviet
Union that contained ethnic Turks. Instead, Turkey remained neutral
for most of World War II, fearing German destruction of the coastal

110. Dreisziger, *Hungary's Way*, pp. 38–51; and Juhasz, *Hungarian Foreign Policy*,
pp. 108–135.

111. Dreisziger, *Hungary's Way*, p. 109.

112. Ibid., pp. 124–139.

113. Miklos Horthy, the regent of Hungary during the entire interwar period,
seems to have had serious misgivings about being tied closely to Germany, but
the draw of irredentism and the influence of the radical right were too strong for
Horthy or others to prevent Hungary's close relationship with Germany. See
Thomas Sakmyster, "Miklos Horthy," in Body, ed., *Hungarian Statesmen of
Destiny*, pp. 112–113.

areas that the British could not defend. When this danger had passed, Turkey entered the war on the Allied side.[114]

The story of Hungary in the interwar period is thus one in which a strong party advocating moderate foreign policies gave way to increasing political competition in which disparate groups vied for power through ever more radical nationalist appeals. The strong party built by Bethlen in the 1920s effectively excluded foreign policy radicals much as the RPP did in Turkey during the whole interwar period. However, once this party began to dissolve in the 1930s, ideological competition, particularly over nationalism and irredentism, increased and became the defining feature of political contests. Though Hungary remained an openly competitive system with universal voting rights, its foreign policy became more aggressive, including against democratic Czechoslovakia. Democratic institutions did not prevent Hungary from being aggressive; in fact, Hungary's aggression during the 1930s reflected mass sentiment far better than the foreign policy constraint shown during the more institutionalized, less democratic 1920s.

Conclusion

Neither the Turkish nor Hungarian cases conform to the expectations of the democratic peace theories. In Turkey, the strength of the RPP and its ability to exclude foreign policy radicals determined foreign policy outcomes and allowed Turkey to pursue a peaceful policy toward its neighbors and toward great powers with interests in the region. Had the RPP been a weaker party, and had Turkey been a more democratic and openly competitive political system, then foreign policy outcomes would likely have been aggressive rather than peaceful. There were many reasons that Turkey might have been more expansionist during the interwar period; the most important factor was that the most common conceptualizations of Turkish identity had international expansion as integral elements. If Turkey

---

114. Vere-Hodge, *Turkish Foreign Policy*, pp. 112–115. An interesting description of the German understanding of the Turkish position can be found in Franz Von Papen, *Memoirs* (London: Andre Deutsch, 1952). Papen writes that while he was ambassador to Turkey during the critical years prior to the war and during it, there was never any real question of Turkey's joining Germany. Rather, the best that Germany could hope for was that Turkey would not actively join the Allies; to this end, Germany made a series of threats and demonstrations, and offered carrots such as military hardware.

had been more democratic, these ideologies would have had a significant impact on policy, and would have led Turkey either to try to incorporate additional ethnic Turks in neighboring regions, or to try to expand to include a larger Muslim population from Arab-inhabited areas. In short, contrary to the monadic democratic peace argument, democracy would have made aggression more likely in this Turkey during the interwar period.[115]

A similar dynamic was at work in Hungary. During the 1920s, Bethlen's strong government party was able to prevent the radicalization of security policy by forcing right-wing politicians out of politics and marginalizing them. When this party broke apart in the 1930s, nationalist actors were able to move to the center of Hungarian politics largely because of weak institutions, Hungary's open competitive system, and its nationalist, irredentist population. This case indicates that democracies might be quite aggressive when a public is highly nationalistic and pushes leaders toward an aggressive nationalist policy.[116]

Consistent with the democratic peace theory, I suggest that domestic institutions are important for understanding war and peace; however, a more focused institutional approach is necessary to understand the outcomes in Hungary and Turkey. Regime type is too broad a category. Instead, we need to identify more specific institutions, such as parties, and the ways in which strong parties can regulate political competition by excluding certain actors who advocate international aggression. When parties are strong, they control politics and make it difficult for those seeking revision to gain power or mobilize support. When parties are weak, there are greater opportunities for successful appeals to ideological factors that lead to undesirable foreign policy consequences.

Thus, these cases suggest the need to reexamine the institutional relationships that some proponents have highlighted as the explanation for the democratic peace phenomenon. As critics have noted,

---

115. It also suggests a problem with a dyadic model, since Turkey would have been fighting Britain in areas such as Mosul.

116. An objection may be that Hungary was not actually a mature democracy; for example, it was not a liberal society. This criticism may be true, but it is also true that political competition was open and there were real political contests going on with direct elections and universal voting rights. In other words, Hungary had the key institutional features of a democracy. Rather than constraining aggressive leaders, these institutions created the conditions that led to an aggressive foreign policy.

democracies can be aggressive when a public is susceptible to nationalism or other aggressive rhetoric. These cases tend to confirm the validity of this critique. Furthermore, the cases, especially the Turkish case, demonstrate that an elite can be more peacefully inclined than the public that would pay the costs of aggression. That is, under certain conditions, nondemocratic states may be more peaceful than democracies precisely because they limit the influence of public opinion. Finally, this chapter may offer a useful starting point for re-specifying the institutional argument of the democratic peace theories: parties and related institutions that control access to the political system, and to some extent buffer political leaders from the direct influence of the public, are present in democratic states. These institutions tend to be well established and relatively strong in established democracies. It may be that these institutions, which exist in both democratic and nondemocratic states, partially account for peace between the stable mature democracies, and between some nondemocratic dyads as well.[117]

---

117. The potential policy implications of this are important, particularly for the United States, which has made democratization a foreign policy priority partly due to the belief that democratic states are more peaceful. Democratization as a way to peace is an expensive and potentially dangerous policy (see Mansfield and Snyder, "Democratization and the Danger of War"). If the argument in this chapter is correct, a less expensive and less risky way to accomplish the same goal would be to strengthen parties that support moderate leaders on foreign policy questions, rather than by insisting on the pursuit of rapid and full democratization.

Conclusion

Testing the Democratic Peace Theory

Miriam Fendius Elman

In contemporary international relations theory, a line has been drawn in the sand. On one side stand neorealists, who claim that the distribution of material capabilities in the international system drives state behavior, even among states that share democratic values. Neorealists argue that all war and peace decision making is a rational response to the constraints and opportunities generated by the anarchic international environment. Consequently, neorealists insist that democracies cannot create a lasting peace; while they may exhibit temporary peaceful relations, domestic regime type has little to do with this absence of war, and strategic considerations eventually outweigh ideological preferences.[1] On the other side of the line stand neoliberals, who insist that political ideologies and regime type determine states' threat perceptions and influence their propensity to wage war. According to democratic peace theorists, a world made up of democratic states would be a world with little or no war. Shared democratic institutions and values eliminate the motivation for war

The author thanks Colin Elman for helpful comments and suggestions.

1. See, for example, Kenneth N. Waltz, "Reflections on *Theory of International Politics*: A Response to My Critics," in Robert O. Keohane, ed., *Neorealism and Its Critics* (New York: Columbia University Press, 1986), p. 329; Stephen M. Walt, The Origins of Alliances (Ithaca, N.Y.: Cornell University Press, 1987), pp. 5, 263, 266–268; Ido Oren, "The Subjectivity of the 'Democratic' Peace: Changing U.S. Perceptions of Imperial Germany," in Michael E. Brown, Sean M. Lynn-Jones, and Steven E. Miller, eds., *Debating the Democratic Peace* (Cambridge, Mass.: MIT Press, 1996), pp. 263–300; and Christopher Layne, "Kant or Cant: The Myth of the Democratic Peace," *International Security*, Vol. 19, No. 2 (Fall 1994), pp. 5–49.

and make it more difficult for war-prone leaders to lead the state down the path to war.[2]

This book straddles the line. Unlike neorealists, we argue that domestic politics in general, and the democratic process in particular, crucially affect war and peace decision making, though not always in ways that are consistent with the democratic peace theory. We agree that the chief value of the democratic peace thesis is that it has helped to legitimize the study of domestic variables—that is, institutions and norms—to explain states' behavior. Contrary to democratic peace proponents, however, we argue that under certain conditions liberal peace can break down, especially when external threats are severe. Furthermore, our chapters collectively support a number of propositions that are inconsistent with the democratic peace theory: regime structure is frequently not the most important domestic political variable to influence war and peace decisions; the norms and institutions of democracy may not always prevent wars and ensure stable peace between democracies; the democratic process often generates aggressive foreign policies; and nondemocratic norms and institutions do not invariably increase the likelihood of war. Rather than reject the democratic peace theory as completely invalid or insist that it has universal explanatory power, in this book we try to identify the conditions under which it will apply best. We emphasize that some variants of the democratic peace proposition are more robust than others; that the democratic peace thesis may best account for U.S. foreign policy; and that it is easier for leaders to choose war in certain democratic systems than in others.

This book contributes to the contemporary debate over the democratic peace in three ways. First, we provide a qualitative, case-based assessment of the various arguments that might account for a democratic peace. In contrast, much of the recent debate has centered on quantitative studies that demonstrate the frequency with which democracy is associated with peace; such studies can neither explain the causal process that drives this correlation nor assess whether decision makers speak, write, and otherwise behave in a manner consistent with the theory's predictions.

The comparative case method offers several advantages. In the cases selected for this volume, the democratic peace theory frequently

---

2. See, for example, Bruce Russett, "Counterfactuals About War and Its Absence," in Philip E. Tetlock and Aaron Belkin, eds., *Counterfactual Thought Experiments in World Politics: Logical, Methodological, and Psychological Perspectives* (Princeton, N.J.: Princeton University Press, 1996), pp. 171–186.

predicts very different outcomes than neorealist theories, such as balance-of-power theory. By tracing the policy process and the motivations of policy makers, we can assess whether the predictions of the democratic peace theory are borne out by the cases examined, and how the democratic peace theory fares when pitted against rival neorealist theories. In addition, the comparative case method allows us to investigate a range of variables that are commonly said to explain the correlation identified by quantitative analysts. That is, with the case method we can further specify the causal steps between regime type (the independent variable) and peace (the dependent variable). By examining in detail how governments actually make war and peace decisions we can better assess whether democratic norms and institutions do indeed decrease the likelihood of international conflict. Moreover, we can identify the conditions that may sometimes produce democratic war. Case studies can tell us what conditions are likely to dampen democratic peace, and what kinds of democracies will be more likely to conform to the democratic peace theory's predictions. Statistical analyses of large numbers of historical episodes of war and peace leave us with the claim that democracies rarely fight each other; in-depth case study analysis enables us to delineate the contingencies under which democracies will be particularly vulnerable to war.[3]

Second, unlike much of the literature, which focuses on the behavior of democratic dyads, this book investigates international crises between democratic, democratic-nondemocratic, and nondemocratic pairs of states. We assess the extent to which domestic norms and institutions influence threat perceptions and the foreign policy making process in each type of dyad, thus testing both the dyadic and monadic versions of the democratic peace theory, as well as the theory's predictions regarding nondemocracies.[4] In short, this book provides a fairer treatment of the democratic peace thesis; by selecting

---

3. For a recent discussion of the merits of the comparative case method, see Stephen M. Walt, "Rethinking Revolution and War: A Reply to Jack Goldstone and Kurt Dassel," *Security Studies*, Vol. 6, No. 2 (Winter 1996/97), pp. 176–178.

4. The dyadic assertion is that democracies are as war-prone as other states, but do not wage war against one another: democracies will identify allies and enemies based on their regime type, and will be pacific only toward liberal democracies. The monadic assertion is that democracies are less likely to use force regardless of the regime type of their opponent: democracies choose war only as an option of last resort; do not base their foreign policy choices on the regime type of the other state; and will not pursue risky strategies that promise high costs.

case studies based on hypothesized causes (democracies versus non-democracies) instead of outcomes (peace or war), we can examine whether democratic norms and institutions made a difference, and whether the democratic peace theory is confirmed or disconfirmed.[5]

Finally, this book tests both normative and institutional explanations for the democratic peace phenomenon.[6] To date, proponents and critics of the democratic peace theory have tended to focus on the normative model. For example, proponent Bruce Russett suggests that the normative explanation is more robust than the institutional model and can better account for peace among democracies; critic Christopher Layne similarly finds the normative argument to be the theory's central causal claim, and investigates whether instances of democratic-democratic peace accord with this model's predictions.[7] By contrast, the contributors to this volume test both explanations. Different kinds of evidence should corroborate or challenge the models' central claims. The normative variant leads us to expect that democracies neither seek war nor threaten to use force against each other. This version of the democratic peace theory expects that democratic states will establish such warm and stable relations that the possibility of war is removed as a feasible foreign policy option. Consequently, a finding that democracies prepare for war against each other or make military threats would be inconsistent with the

---

5. Michael W. Doyle, "Reflections on the Liberal Peace and its Critics," in Brown, Lynn-Jones, and Miller, eds., *Debating the Democratic Peace*, p. 359. For example, Doyle faults Christopher Layne ("Kant or Cant") for selecting cases on the dependent variable; that is, all of his cases are instances of peace between democracies. For more on how selecting case studies on the dependent variable can produce misleading results, see Gary King, Robert O. Keohane, and Sidney Verba, *Designing Social Inquiry: Scientific Inference in Qualitative Research* (Princeton, N.J.: Princeton University Press, 1994), pp. 129–130.

6. According to the normative model, democratically elected leaders are biased against resolving international disputes violently because norms of peaceful conflict resolution are ingrained and reflect domestic experiences and values. Democracies know that other democracies share these norms and thus expect that conflicts will be resolved short of war. According to the institutional model, checks on the leader's ability to wage war without prior public approval and the need for public debate over foreign policy options slow the decision to go to war and provide sufficient time for crises to be resolved through negotiation. Because leaders in democracies know that fellow democratically elected leaders are similarly constrained, they are less likely to fear surprise attack.

7. Bruce Russett, *Grasping the Democratic Peace: Principles for a Post-Cold War World* (Princeton, N.J.: Princeton University Press, 1993), pp. 119–120; and Layne, "Kant or Cant," pp. 12–13.

normative model.[8] The institutional variant's main prediction is that democracies will not wage full-scale wars against each other; although threats to use force, militarized conflict, and preparations for war all challenge the normative model, they are not inconsistent with the institutional model.[9]

This chapter reviews our collective findings and develops the theoretical and policy implications of this book. I first discuss our conclusions regarding the democratic peace theory's challenge to neorealism; the extent to which the democratic peace theory adequately explains the domestic political process in democratic states; the democratic peace theory's claim for universal applicability; and the tendency for democratic peace proponents to treat nondemocracies as obstacles to international peace. I then offer some policy recommendations and suggest some promising avenues for future research.

Theoretical Implications for the Democratic Peace Theory

This book has implications for the way we study international relations in general, and the importance we should attach to the democratic peace theory in particular. It addresses the ongoing debate over the validity of neorealism; the extent to which the democratic peace theory adequately accounts for the domestic sources of foreign policy; whether we should treat the theory as universally applicable; and how well the theory explains the foreign policies of nondemocracies.

THE DEATH KNELL FOR NEOREALISM?

With the end of the Cold War and the breakup of the Soviet Union, leading scholars and policy makers are urging that neorealism—the paradigm that has long dominated the study of international politics—is obsolete. Critics assert that neorealism cannot explain the lack of a great power war since 1945; cannot explain the end of the Cold War; and distorts rather than illuminates international politics

---

8. See Russett, *Grasping the Democratic Peace*, pp. 42, 119–120.

9. Layne argues that the absence of wars between democracies sets the "threshold of proof too low." He insists that the democratic peace theory predicts that democracies should bend over backwards to accommodate each other in crises: "Ultimata, unbending hard-lines, and big stick diplomacy are the stuff of *Realpolitik*, not the 'democratic peace'." See "Kant or Cant," p. 14. While Layne is right that such evidence would be inconsistent with the normative model, the institutional model does not predict the absence of threats between democracies. In this book, Layne explicitly tests the normative variant (see Chapter 1).

for much of the Westphalian era.[10] These critics insist that domestic politics, cultural and normative frameworks, and leadership orientations affect states' behavior to a greater extent than relative material capabilities or external threats.

Democratic peace theorists ascribe to these variables the causal power that neorealists ascribe to the anarchic environment. Democratic peace proponents call into question neorealism's pessimism about the likelihood for a durable international peace. The existence of a permanent peace between democracies (the dyadic finding) and the fact that democracies appear to act in a more "peace-loving" manner than other types of states (the monadic finding) challenge the neorealist notion that conflict is always possible in an anarchic world order, so all states must vigilantly attend to relative capabilities and prepare for war. The democratic peace finding also undermines neorealist claims that anarchy and the current distribution of power are always the underlying causes of war and peace. Neorealists claim that anarchy causes all states to compete for security, form alliances, and fight wars. By contrast, the democratic peace thesis contends that a state's political system largely determines which states it will consider friends or foes, and whether it can easily wage war.[11]

The chapters in this volume provide mixed reviews for neorealism. Consistent with neorealism, many of the case studies show that democratic pairs of states prepared for war against each other, and threatened each other with force when vital interests were at stake. In

---

10. For more on these challenges to neorealism, see, for example, Richard Ned Lebow, "The Long Peace, the End of the Cold War, and the Failure of Realism," *International Organization*, Vol. 48, No. 2 (Spring 1994), pp. 249–277; Ted Hopf and John Lewis Gaddis, "Correspondence: Getting the End of the Cold War Wrong," *International Security*, Vol. 18, No. 2 (Fall 1993), pp. 202–215; and Paul W. Schroeder, "Historical Reality vs. Neo-realist Theory," *International Security*, Vol. 19, No. 1 (Summer 1994), pp. 108–148. For the counterargument that neorealism can account for both past and contemporary international events, see, for example, William C. Wohlforth, "Realism and the End of the Cold War," *International Security*, Vol. 19, No. 3 (Winter 1994/95), pp. 91–129; Christopher Layne, "The Unipolar Illusion: Why New Great Powers Will Arise," *International Security*, Vol. 17, No. 4 (Spring 1993), pp. 5–51; and Markus Fischer, "Feudal Europe, 880–1300: Communal Discourse and Conflictual Practices," *International Organization*, Vol. 46, No. 2 (Spring 1992), pp. 427–466.

11. Neorealism must be distinguished from realism. All neorealist theories assume that states weigh options and make decisions based on their strategic situation and an assessment of the external environment. By contrast, classical realists do not see states' behavior as primarily a response to structural causes. The

other chapters, strategic considerations mattered more than domestic regime type, and often outweighed ideological preferences. In some cases, democratic peace can be explained by neorealist factors outside of the purview of the democratic peace theory. Similarly, relations between nondemocracies and mixed dyads can be explained by international constraints, not domestic regime type.

Inconsistent with neorealism, however, are the arguments by several contributors to this volume which claim that states' behavior cannot be viewed as rational responses to international constraints and opportunities. These chapters show that domestic politics matters—but often in ways that do not support the democratic peace theory.

DEMOCRACIES PREPARE FOR WAR AGAINST EACH OTHER. Contrary to the normative model for peace among democracies, the contributors to this book find that democracies often threaten each other with force and prepare for war. In Chapter 1, Christopher Layne suggests that during the nineteenth century, while Britain and France were both liberal and shared democratic features, their relationship was characterized by intense rivalry; war loomed as a real possibility on several occasions. Contrary to what the normative model of the democratic peace theory would lead us to expect, Britain viewed France as a primary threat to its national interests, and was willing to go to war to compel France to withdraw from Belgium in 1831. Both countries also threatened each other with force and prepared for war in 1840 in order to protect vital interests in the Near East.

Similarly, Stephen R. Rock's analysis of Anglo-U.S. relations prior to the turn of the century (Chapter 2) indicates that the democratic peace

principal variables in classical realist writings include anarchy and the distribution of power, but also domestic politics. See, on this point, Jack Snyder, *Myths of Empire: Domestic Politics and International Ambition* (Ithaca, N.Y.: Cornell University Press, 1991), p. 19; and Colin Elman, "Horses for Courses: Why *Not* Neorealist Theories of Foreign Policy?" *Security Studies*, Vol. 6, No. 1 (Autumn 1996), pp. 20–21. Thus, the democratic peace theory competes with neorealism because the latter underemphasizes domestic-level variables and ideological and normative sources of state behavior. By contrast, the democratic peace theory competes with classical realism not because classical realism focuses on a different level of analysis, but because it emphasizes the material bases of state behavior instead of ideological and normative dimensions. For more on the relationship between realism, neorealism, and the democratic peace theory, see James Lee Ray, *Democracy and International Conflict: An Evaluation of the Democratic Peace Proposition* (Columbia: University of South Carolina Press, 1995), pp. 37–41; and John M. Owen, "How Liberalism Produces Democratic Peace," in Brown, Lynn-Jones, and Miller, eds., *Debating the Democratic Peace*, pp. 151–152.

theory's predictions are not fulfilled: though both countries were exemplars of liberal democracy, the United States and Britain saw each other as threats and frequently considered war to protect their national interests. For instance, in 1861, during the crisis over the *Trent Affair*, British foreign policy makers did not hesitate to threaten the use of force to compel the United States to meet their demands. Because the stakes were high and it was believed that national interests were at stake, Britain prepared for war against the United States, a country that all British decision makers recognized as democratic.

Finally, in Chapter 4, I suggest that the fact that Finnish and Allied troops did not fight on the battlefield does not mean that these democracies were at peace. The use of force was not ruled out as improbable, nor did Finland and the Allies settle their disagreements by mediation, negotiation, and diplomacy, as we would expect among liberal democracies: the United States broke off diplomatic relations and Britain declared war. Relations among these democracies during World War II does not fit into the category of stable peace, where the threat of force and serious conflict is nonexistent. Moreover, joint democracy did not prevent Finland's elected leaders from joining an alliance against the Western democracies, collaborating with their enemy, and pursuing policies that threatened the national interests of the democratic Allied forces.[12]

STRATEGIC CALCULATIONS OUTWEIGH IDEOLOGICAL PREFERENCES. Contrary to the dyadic democratic peace finding, many of the chapters in this book suggest that democracy is not the cause of peace among democracies. Furthermore, the cases demonstrate that ideological preferences typically do not determine democracies' relations with nondemocracies.

In Chapter 1, Layne proposes that domestic factors—particularly the impact of public opinion—pushed British and French leaders toward the brink of war. It was external strategic calculations that prevented war from breaking out: France backed down at the last moment because it realized that it could not win a war without allies or sufficient resources.

Like Layne, Rock (Chapter 2) argues that during the early period of Anglo-U.S. relations, conflict was often avoided due to strategic

---

12. This case suggests that conflicts between democracies may undermine the predictions of the democratic peace theory even in the absence of large-scale violence. A 1,000-casualty threshold eliminates many conflicts that satisfy our commonsense notion of war.

factors associated with neorealism. During the crisis over Oregon, for example, both the United States and Britain ultimately pulled back from the brink of war because both realized that the costs of battle were not worth the gains; during the *Trent* Crisis, the Lincoln administration gave in to British demands, calculating that the North could not afford a war with Britain while it was fighting the Confederacy. Similarly, British decision makers chose not to intervene in the U.S. Civil War not because the cabinet had liberal sympathy for the Union, but because they doubted whether intervention was feasible. In each of these instances, neorealism explains the peace.[13]

In Chapter 3, John M. Owen also suggests that the balance of power can outweigh ideological preferences. Owen argues that the liberal peace is generally robust, but that it can break down if liberal elites come to regard other liberal states as illiberal. Focusing on the Mexican-American and Spanish-American wars, he suggests that severe threats to territorial integrity and state sovereignty can undermine the liberal peace. Mexican liberals and Spanish liberals both began to perceive the United States as illiberal once U.S. aggressiveness posed a clear and present danger to Mexican and Spanish territory. Any value that these liberals had seen in good relations with their U.S. sister republic became outweighed by external threats—the United States, once a model to emulate, had become a menace to be feared. Similarly, in Chapter 4, I claim that Finnish foreign policy makers took direction from their strategic circumstances, not their ideological preferences. Finnish leaders viewed the Soviet Union as a threat not because it was a nondemocracy, but because it was nearby and very strong. By contrast, they viewed illiberal Germany as an ally.

Finally, Šumit Ganguly (Chapter 6) and Arie M. Kacowicz (Chapter 8) both maintain that war and peace decisions are often better explained by strategic imperatives. Ganguly contends that democratic India's decision to go to war against nondemocratic Pakistan in

---

13. Rock suggests that twentieth-century Anglo-U.S. relations are more consistent with the democratic peace theory; shared liberal values and democratic institutions do explain peace in this latter period, and especially account for U.S. foreign policy choices. Nevertheless, even here Rock suggests that neorealism remains relevant: twentieth-century peace between the United States and Britain is largely overdetermined, and strategic imperatives can equally account for the instances in which war was avoided. In particular, Rock suggests that in the early 1900s, Britain allied with the United States not because it deemed Germany illiberal, but because it perceived Germany to be the greater threat. Germany's material capabilities, geographic proximity, and aggressive intentions explain the "great rapprochement" between the United States and Britain.

1971 is better explained by neorealism; Pakistan's regime type was not paramount in India's decision making calculus. Furthermore, he argues that changes of regime type did not change the level of hostilities within the dyad as the democratic peace theory would lead us to expect: since 1971, India and Pakistan have remained at peace despite dramatic changes in the regime types of both countries. Ganguly points out that democratization does not explain the Indo-Pakistani peace from 1972–87, nor does it explain crisis resolution in the early 1990s. In the former instance, India possessed overwhelming conventional superiority over Pakistan, and war was avoided because Pakistan knew it could not prevail; in the latter instance, conflicts were resolved short of war because of fears of nuclear escalation. Similarly, Kacowicz argues that the peaceful resolution of serious crises can be explained without reference to the domestic political regimes of the countries involved. In accounting for the resolution of militarized crises between Peru and Colombia and between Senegal and Mauritania, Kacowicz highlights the importance of neorealist variables: the role of regional hegemons, geopolitical considerations, and the lack of material power to wage war.

WAR AND PEACE DECISIONS ARE OFTEN PRODUCTS OF DOMESTIC POLITICS. While we find that neorealism often provides more accurate predictions of, and more compelling explanations for, the behavior of democratic states than does the democratic peace theory, neorealism cannot account for all foreign policy outcomes. For example, in Chapter 4, I suggest that neorealism cannot account for Finland's foreign policy choices prior to the Winter War in 1939 or the Continuation War in 1940. On both occasions, Finnish decision makers chose actions that risked the high costs of war with a great power. Similarly, in Lawrence Freedman's analysis of British decision making prior to the Falklands War (Chapter 5), neorealism does not explain Britain's decision to use force. Britain initially sought a diplomatic solution because it had no adequate defense to a determined Argentine attack. In my case study of Israel's decision to invade Lebanon in 1982 (Chapter 7), I also argue that the external security environment cannot account for Israel's decision to launch a full-scale invasion of Lebanon. Israel faced fewer threats from the PLO than in the past; full-scale invasion was inconsistent with Israel's traditional military doctrine; and Israel's security environment would have equally supported a decision not to go to war. Finally, Kurt Dassel (Chapter 10) indicates that neorealism cannot explain Indonesia's violent confrontation with Malaysia in the 1960s, nor can it account for why Indonesia abandoned this aggressive policy. According to Dassel, the distribution of power remained constant, yet Indonesia initiated, then quickly ended, aggression against Malaysian forces.

As I suggest below, we can acknowledge that domestic politics matters in explaining war and peace decision making, but still question the explanatory power of the democratic peace theory. Neorealism and the democratic peace theory may both do poorly when pitted against alternative domestic-level and international-level arguments.

DOES THE THEORY GET DEMOCRATIC POLITICS RIGHT?

The democratic peace theory posits that domestic regime type matters more than other domestic level variables in explaining war and peace decision making. In this book, we argue that by focusing solely on types of government—democracy versus nondemocracy—the democratic peace theory conceals the fact that war and peace decision making transcends the independent effects of a single unit-level variable. We identify some of the factors that can affect the foreign policy process to a greater extent than whether a state is democratic or not.

In addition, our cumulative findings suggest that the democratic political process can lead to aggressive foreign policy behavior, an outcome that is inconsistent with the democratic peace theory. Contrary to the dyadic argument, we find that illiberal leaders can opt for war against a fellow liberal state, even though liberal elites reject this policy. Contrary to the monadic argument, we find that public opinion frequently does not generate benign foreign policies.

MISSING DOMESTIC-LEVEL VARIABLES. The democratic peace theory presents a truncated view of domestic politics in general, and democratic politics in particular. Specifically, the theory ignores the role of leaders; underemphasizes norms that are not associated with domestic political ideology; obscures the role of political parties; and discounts how civil-military relations can concentrate or disperse war powers.

First, the theory requires us to believe that it matters little who controls the state; that is, the democratic peace theory suggests that regime type predominates, hence the identity and beliefs of the governing coalition do not matter. We suggest that this is a very misleading and apolitical argument. For example, in Chapter 1, Layne argues that individual leaders made a difference in determining whether Anglo-French relations were conflictual or cooperative. The presence of Lord Palmerston in the British Foreign Office increased cross-Channel friction. Palmerston's replacement, Lord Aberdeen, had a more collegial diplomatic style. Thus, it is not surprising that in the 1840s Anglo-French relations shifted toward increasing conciliation and cooperation. Instead of changes of regime type, changes in foreign policy leadership made the difference.

Similarly, Kacowicz (Chapter 8) finds that domestic changes within regimes can bring to power new and moderate leaders, thus facilitating the resolution of militarized disputes. For example, leadership changes in Peru can explain why its conflict with Colombia was resolved short of war. In addition, in Chapter 7, I suggest that democracies will be more likely to initiate conflicts and use force if ruling coalitions favor the use of force to solve international conflicts. In Israel, since the two main political parties—Labor and the Likud— had different views regarding the legitimacy of using force, changes in leadership dramatically affected Israel's war-proneness. These intra-regime changes led to changes in Israel's foreign policy toward Lebanon even though Israel's regime type—democracy—remained constant.

In short, the important consideration may not be whether a country is democratic or not, but whether its ruling coalition is committed to peaceful methods of conflict resolution. By focusing solely on domestic regime type, the democratic peace theory obscures the extent to which hard-line leaders are often a prerequisite for war.[14]

Second, the democratic peace theory obscures the fact that war and peace decision making often reflects normative and cultural factors that have little to do with different political ideologies. For example, in Chapter 2, Rock suggests that beliefs in a common racial identity led Britain to retreat from the brink of war with the United States during the Venezuelan crisis. Anglo-Saxonism also explains the great rapprochement between the United States and Britain at the turn of the century; the British perceived the United States as less menacing than Germany because of the racial and cultural affinity they felt for Americans. Furthermore, public expressions of Anglo-Saxonist

---

14. This argument is consistent with classical realism, which focuses on how statesmen perceive and respond to international constraints. For more on the role of leaders in war and peace decision making, see Joe D. Hagan, "Domestic Political Systems and War Proneness," *Mershon International Studies Review*, Vol. 38, No. 2 (October 1994), pp. 183–207.

sentiment were loudest when diplomatic relations between the United States and Britain were at their worst, suggesting that Anglo-Saxonism was not merely a consequence of Anglo-U.S. reconciliation, as neorealists would argue. Ganguly (Chapter 6) also argues that the norms that drive foreign policy may only partly be related to political organization and regime type. In the war between Pakistan and India in 1971, political ideology—support for democracy and democratization—was less important than ensuring India's secular way of life.

Similarly, Freedman (Chapter 5) argues that while democratic peace theorists are right to emphasize the importance of norms in explaining a state's foreign policy choices, political ideology is not necessarily the most powerful normative justification for war or peace decisions. Consistent with the dyadic democratic peace argument, Freedman finds that support for democratic norms goes far in explaining Britain's decision to reoccupy the Falkland Islands by force. Argentina's regime type was a permissive condition for war: a military response was a more acceptable and feasible option than it might have been had Argentina been a liberal democracy. Nevertheless, Freedman points out that Britain justified its war decision on the grounds that it was upholding the international principle of self-determination, and not rewarding aggression. Instead of liberal ideology and the nature of the Argentine regime, these international rights were crucial in the British decision making calculus.

Third, the democratic peace theory discounts the fact that it is not regime type—democracy versus nondemocracy—that explains war and peace decisions, but particular attributes of democracy, such as the nature of political parties. According to John C. Matthews III (Chapter 11), the democratic peace is not a result of democracy, but of strong parties. Strong parties that favor the use of force only as a last resort can screen out more radical actors from the foreign policy making process.

Finally, the democratic peace theory ignores civil-military relations. The institutional argument for the democratic peace phenomenon asserts that democracies are less war-prone because the power to wage war is not concentrated in the hands of one person. But even democracies delegate war powers, increasing the chances that war and peace decisions will reflect the views of a small group of civilian and military figures. For example, in Chapter 7, I argue that due to the nature of civil-military relations in Israel, Defense Minister Sharon was able to direct and control the war in Lebanon. The cabinet was presented with faits accomplis that escalated actions in

Lebanon and incrementally led to the implementation of a far larger military initiative than the cabinet had originally approved. Similarly, Layne (Chapter 1) suggests that Britain's Lord Palmerston had a great deal of power to decide war and peace issues due to the way in which foreign policy was delegated.

In sum, like democratic peace proponents, we argue that internal characteristics of the state are relevant for predicting whether states will or will not fight each other. However, we reject the claim that crude attributes of states' domestic political systems—democracy versus nondemocracy—provide sufficient information about the domestic sources of foreign policy. While domestic politics matters, it is not regime type that crucially accounts for variations in foreign policies, but other variables that may be present or absent in democracies (and nondemocracies).

DEMOCRATIC AGGRESSION. In this book we find that democracies may act aggressively for two reasons. First, illiberal leaders can pursue hard-line policies against liberal states, including war. Second, the influence of public opinion on foreign policy making can increase the chances for war.

According to democratic peace proponents, liberal peace emerges because illiberal leaders are restrained from going to war against liberal states. Democratic structures give citizens leverage over the foreign policy process; consequently, institutions of free speech, and regular, competitive elections force illiberal leaders of democracies to follow liberal ideology. Illiberal leaders are restrained by liberal elites who "agitate against war."[15] By contrast, several authors in this volume suggest that illiberal leaders can pursue hard-line policies against liberal states, including war. For example, in Chapter 1, Layne argues that Lord Palmerston could implement a hard-line policy toward France despite substantial opposition from cabinet liberals: "Palmerston could brush aside francophile colleagues who argued that liberal solidarity required that London appease Paris." Similarly, according to Rock (Chapter 2), while some British liberal elites disagreed with the cabinet's hard-line policy toward the United States in the early 1860s, they had little influence over foreign policy and exerted little moderating influence on the cabinet; there were few mechanisms for liberals to affect policy, since they were outnumbered in Parliament and excluded from the cabinet. In short, democratic

---

15. See Owen, "How Liberalism Produces the Democratic Peace," pp. 118–119, 129–130, 149, 153.

peace theorists maintain that illiberal leaders can be constrained from fighting liberal states due to the intervention of liberal elites. However, while this causal argument may explain instances in which U.S. leaders were compelled to back down from the brink of war, it may have less explanatory power outside of the U.S. context.[16]

A cumulative finding of this book is that public opinion often is not a force for peace. For example, in Chapter 1, Layne argues that British and French public opinion pushed leaders toward war. In the 1830s, the British public demanded that the government take a hard line against France; in 1840, public opinion in France demanded war, while the illiberal monarch restrained the state from taking that path. Contrary to the dyadic argument, Layne shows that public opinion did not reduce the chances for war between these liberal states. Similarly, according to Rock (Chapter 2), the impact of public opinion did not ensure benign foreign policies, even among democracies. Rock explains that the Anglo-U.S. Oregon Crisis of 1845–46 was initiated by the United States largely because of domestic politics; President Polk's initial bellicose position was aimed at securing public approval. In Britain, public opinion and the Whig opposition in Parliament forced the cabinet to take a hard line even though cabinet members preferred compromise. Later, during the *Trent* Crisis, U.S. public opinion once again forced the Lincoln administration to take a hard-line position, while British public opinion supported Lord Palmerston's own uncompromising stance.

Like Layne and Rock, in Chapter 5, Freedman argues that the British war decision undermines the notion that public opinion in democracies restrains war-prone leaders. The British public pushed the Thatcher government in a hawkish direction, setting limits on the areas in which compromise with Argentina was possible. Specifically, the British government had to consider the prospect of defeat at the polls. Although the government preferred a negotiated settlement, it adopted a hard line due to British public opinion. Furthermore, contrary to the monadic variant of the democratic peace theory, Freedman argues that the British public was willing to support war

---

16. All of Owen's case studies involve U.S. decision making, where the legislative branch holds significant war powers. Acting through the U.S. Congress, liberal elites can often force an illiberal executive's hand. See, for example, ibid., p. 136. Thus, while Owen presents a persuasive explanation for U.S. war and peace decision making, his theoretical model may less successfully account for the foreign policies of other democracies, especially those that do not separate executive and legislative powers.

against Argentina despite reports that there would be a high number of British casualties. The notion that democratically elected leaders can only fight cheap wars that promise quick, decisive victories because the public will not condone wars with high costs in lives is not borne out in the Falklands case. Contrary to this monadic argument, Freedman writes that "a democratic foreign policy does not need to reflect a chronic fear of casualties and a desperate search for compromise."[17]

Finally, in Chapter 8, Kacowicz also finds that the influence of public opinion can encourage moderate leaders to adopt more aggressive policies. In 1932, the Colombian leadership did not want war with Peru but the voting public pushed in that direction. In 1989, Senegal's president initially adopted a conciliatory tone and insisted on negotiation to resolve the crisis with Mauritania, but was compelled to harden his position because an activist public and a militant political opposition pushed for war. In both instances, the influence of opposition parties made the escalation of international disputes a requirement for retaining domestic political power.

IS THE THEORY UNIVERSALLY APPLICABLE?

Many democratic peace proponents insist that the democratic peace proposition has the status of law; that is, democratic states have never fought interstate wars against each other. Furthermore, even those democratic peace theorists who view the theory as a probabilistic statement—democracies have rarely fought each other—attempt to show that instances of alleged democratic war were not true wars between true democracies.[18] Consequently, there have been few attempts to identify the conditions under which the democratic peace might break down.

In this book we suggest that, contrary to the dyadic version of the democratic peace theory, joint democracy is not always a sufficient condition for peace. Our cumulative findings suggest that the dyadic proposition has less explanatory power when democracies face

---

17. Also contrary to the monadic argument, Freedman argues that democracies are not necessarily deeply reluctant to go to war, and do not see force merely as a last resort. For a similar argument, see my analysis of Israel's invasion of Lebanon (Chapter 7). For an alternative argument see Ganguly (Chapter 6). He suggests that the 1947–48 war between India and Pakistan provides some support for the monadic thesis: democratic India did see war as an option of last resort, and tried to resolve the crisis over Kashmir through peaceful means.

18. See, for example, Ray, *Democracy and International Conflict*, pp. 86–130.

severe external threats. We also suggest that the dyadic proposition can account for U.S. foreign policy choices (especially in the twentieth century), but does less well in explaining the foreign policies of other democratic states. Finally, we argue that only certain democracies will display foreign policies that are consistent with the monadic variant of the democratic peace theory; some democracies are more war-prone than others.

SMALL STATES VERSUS GREAT POWERS. All other things being equal, the democratic peace theory will best explain the foreign policies of great powers. Great powers do not face severe security threats, their survival is rarely at stake, and they have more leeway for action. They can afford to give ideological preferences an important role in war and peace decision making. By contrast, small states do not have the luxury of basing foreign policy on norms and ideology; since the external environment is extremely threatening, they must vigilantly attend to relative material capabilities and external threats. In short, "states are more likely to follow their ideological preferences when they are already fairly secure."[19]

My analysis of Finnish decision making during World War II (Chapter 4) supports this claim. As a small democratic state that faced severe external pressures, regime affinity was irrelevant to Finland's alignment choices, and to the way leaders identified friends and foes. Finnish President Ryti viewed Germany as less of a threat despite its illiberal regime; he viewed Germany through the prism of Finland's national interests and its need for a counterbalance to the Soviet Union.

Similarly, according to Owen (Chapter 3), democracies that face extreme external threats are more likely to exhibit foreign policies that diverge from the expectations of the democratic peace theory. Due to overwhelming security threats, Mexican and Spanish liberals began to perceive the United States as illiberal, and they became willing to go to war against a state that they had long viewed as a model republic. Any lingering affinity for the United States was trumped by a very real threat that sovereign territory would be lost.

---

19. Walt, *The Origins of Alliances*, pp. 37–38. See also Randall L. Schweller, "Domestic Structure and Preventive War: Are Democracies More Pacific?" *World Politics,* Vol. 44 (January 1992), pp. 264–266; Robert Jervis, "Cooperation Under the Security Dilemma," *World Politics,* Vol. 30, No. 3 (1978), pp. 172–174; and Miriam Fendius Elman, "The Foreign Policies of Small States: Challenging Neorealism in Its Own Backyard," *British Journal of Political Science,* Vol. 25, No. 2 (April 1995), pp. 171–217.

In sum, while the dyadic variant of the democratic peace theory asserts that democracies view other democracies as natural allies and treat nondemocracies with suspicion, democratic states that face severe external threats are unlikely to act according to their ideological preferences.

THE UNITED STATES AND THE REST. More than other democracies, the United States has tended to identify friends and foes on the basis of regime type. We find that the dyadic version of the democratic peace can account well for U.S. foreign policy, but proves less robust in explaining the motivations of decision makers in other democracies. While the United States has consistently emphasized political ideological principles, other democracies do not seem to treat political ideology as central to their identity, and to the way in which allies are distinguished from potential enemies.

For example, Rock (Chapter 2) finds that U.S. war and peace decision making after the turn of the century is consistent with the predictions of the dyadic variant of the democratic peace theory. Perceptions of Britain's regime type played a crucial role in the U.S. decision making calculus. Indeed, Rock argues that political ideology mattered more to U.S. decision makers than it did to the British. In resolving crises peacefully, U.S. policy makers gave greater weight to shared liberal values and democratic institutions; by contrast, British leaders emphasized cultural connections.

Similarly, Owen (Chapter 3) suggests that U.S. liberals have tended to assess international threats through an ideological prism. For example, U.S. President Polk and the Jacksonians welcomed war against Mexico, which they perceived to be illiberal. The Jacksonian desire to "republicanize" Mexico made it easier to declare war when Mexico appeared on the verge of a monarchy. Later, U.S. liberal elites favored war with Spain in order to rescue the Cuban people from a country they considered to be a despotic monarchy.[20]

Finally, in Chapter 4, I point out that U.S. behavior toward Finland accords well with what the democratic peace theory would lead us to expect. U.S. decision makers were reluctant to break off relations or declare war on democratic Finland. Finland's regime type played an

---

20. Both Rock and Owen undermine the monadic proposition. Contrary to the monadic argument, both of their chapters find that the regime types of other states have played an important role in U.S. war and peace decisions. U.S. liberal elites acted belligerently toward states they regarded as illiberal; whether they were likely to view the use of force as a legitimate foreign policy option was dependent on their perceptions of the opponent's regime type.

important role in the U.S. decision making calculus, and U.S. decision makers referred to shared democratic institutions and liberal political ideology in justifying their positions.

Together, these chapters indicate that the dyadic variant of the democratic peace theory may be less a theory of international politics than it is a theory of U.S. foreign policy. U.S. foreign policy may conform more to the dyadic democratic peace argument for three reasons. First, the United States is "uniquely and self-consciously" founded on a set of political ideals.[21] Consequently, U.S. citizens have wanted their country's foreign policy to be based on principles and values, as well as on strategic interests. Second, for much of its history, the United States has been a great power. Decision makers have thus been able to give priority to ideological preferences. Significantly, U.S. foreign policy was most consistent with neorealism—and most inconsistent with the democratic peace theory—during the early years of its existence, when U.S. survival was by no means assured.[22] Finally, the U.S. Constitution, which separates executive and legislative powers, places both *ex ante* and *ex post* constraints on war-prone leaders. Liberal elites can agitate against war with fellow liberal states, and can prevent an illiberal president from acting on his or her preferences. U.S. presidents have faced far more constraints on their ability to lead the state to war than have executives in other democracies.[23]

CENTRALIZED AND DECENTRALIZED DEMOCRACIES. Our cumulative findings suggest that the monadic version of the democratic peace theory accounts for the war and peace decision making of some democracies better than others. In certain democratic institutions, war-prone leaders will find it easy to take the state down the path to war; in a different set of institutions, war-prone leaders will face an uphill battle and will be constrained from acting on their preferences. We argue that what matters in a crisis is the organization of foreign policy authority—the centralization of the executive and its autonomy from the legislature—not whether the state is democratic or not.

For example, my analysis of Finland's alignment policies during World War II (Chapter 4) suggests that centralized democratic institutions facilitate aggressive behavior when leaders prefer war. By

---

21. See Strobe Talbott, "Democracy and the National Interest," *Foreign Affairs*, Vol. 75, No. 6 (November/December 1996), pp. 49–50.

22. For more on this point, see Rock, Chapter 2 in this volume.

23. For more on this point, see below.

contrast, decentralized democracies are better able to constrain a leader bent on war. In Finland's semipresidential democratic system, the Parliament could exercise little direct influence over the executive in the area of foreign security policy; if it had been more involved in the policy making process, a pro-German policy might not have emerged. In Finland, the president has almost total *ex ante* control over the foreign policy process. Thus, by privileging a president who favored a pro-German policy and undermining the bargaining power of more moderate forces represented in Parliament, Finland's democratic regime type decreased the chances of a Soviet-Finnish peace in the aftermath of the Winter War, and put Finland on a collision course with the democratic Allies.

Similarly, my analysis of Israel's decision to invade Lebanon in 1982 (Chapter 7) indicates that the institutional model for the democratic peace overstates the capacity of the public to restrain an executive bent on war. In many democracies, such as Israel, the public and the legislative branch pose *ex post* constraints on the executive and can only force a change of leadership if the goals of war are not achieved; that is, military actions that have become costly and ineffective can be stopped, but the public and the legislature can do little to prevent an executive from choosing war in the first place.

In addition, Israel's foreign policy toward Lebanon in the period before and after the 1981 Israeli elections shows that intra-regime shifts matter. Prior to the 1981 elections, Israel's decentralized coalitional cabinet compelled parties with diverse foreign policy preferences to cooperate to sustain the government. Radical and risky foreign policies were avoided during this period. By contrast, following the 1981 elections, the Likud party formed a government with the sustained confidence of the legislature. It faced few *ex ante* constraints on its capacity to initiate war. In short, the Israeli case suggests that parliamentary systems have few institutional safeguards to restrain the war-propensity of a homogeneous executive that has majority support in the legislature.

In sum, rather than addressing how democratic states behave differently from other types of states, democratic peace theorists should also question why certain democratic states act differently than other democracies. The institutional variant of the democratic peace theory assumes that in democracies, leaders cannot act autonomously because they must enlist widespread public support before engaging in risky foreign policies that promise large-scale violence. But in many democracies, the public and the legislature do not exert a strong influence on the foreign policy making process; they have less influence on decisions to wage war than the democratic peace theory leads us to expect. Democratic systems that do not separate the powers of the executive and legislative branches, and provide few *ex ante* checks on the executive's foreign policy making authority, are unlikely to prevent war-prone leaders from taking the state down the path toward war.[24]

ARE NONDEMOCRACIES OBSTACLES TO PEACE?

The dyadic version of the democratic peace theory posits that democracy is a sufficient condition for peace, not a necessary requirement. That is, the theory does not claim that nondemocracies or democratic-nondemocratic pairs of states are in a constant state of war; shared democracy is not a necessary condition for avoiding war.[25] Nevertheless, the literature on the democratic peace is full of propositions suggesting that relations among democratic-nondemocratic and nondemocratic dyads are highly conflictual. First, democratic peace theorists claim that democracies treat nondemocracies with suspicion. Since nondemocatic leaders are not subject to institutional constraints, democracies must anticipate that they may become the targets of attack. Moreover, since nondemocratic leaders do not abide by norms of peaceful conflict resolution within their borders, democracies cannot expect them to act peacefully abroad.[26] Second, democratic peace theorists often argue that nondemocracies initiate wars because of domestic political variables associated with their flawed regimes, such as unconstrained leaders. The common strategy in the literature is to observe wars between nondemocracies or mixed regimes and then work backwards, attempting to find the nondemocratic feature that must have generated the aggression. Finally, democratic peace theorists imply that peace between nondemocracies or mixed regimes can only be the result of strategic calculations; that is, nondemocratic states refrain from initiating aggression if they perceive the costs of war to be greater than the potential benefits. In short, democratic peace theorists tend to treat nondemocracies as the

---

24. In addition to disaggregating democracies, democratic peace theorists should also differentiate among nondemocratic states. For example, Dassel (Chapter 10) and Matthews (Chapter 11) identify subsets of authoritarian states that will tend to be pacific outside of their borders. For more on this point, see below.

25. Russett, "Counterfactuals About War and Its Absence," p. 177.

26. Russett, *Grasping the Democratic Peace*, pp. 30–40.

bogeymen of international politics. In the literature on the democratic peace, nondemocracies are viewed as inherently dangerous—they
are bad states that act badly abroad.

This book challenges these assertions. Just as we differentiate
among democracies, noting the variables that lead them to act in disparate ways, we find that nondemocracies cannot be lumped together in one monolithic group. Many of the same variables that can lead
democracies to act peacefully or aggressively—relative material
capabilities, centralized governments, and shared norms and culture—can also affect nondemocracies in different ways. First, our
cumulative findings suggest that democracies often do not view nondemocracies with suspicion, and that nondemocratic institutions frequently do not keep them from cooperating with democracies.
Second, we find that two characteristics of nondemocracies—that
leaders are not constrained by public opinion and other decision
making bodies, and that norms of peaceful conflict resolution are not
ingrained domestically—can facilitate international conflict resolution and peace. Third, we suggest that some of the very mechanisms
that are posited to account for the democratic peace—normative consenses against the use of force—can also account for peace among
nondemocracies and mixed regimes. Finally, we find that the initiation of war by nondemocracies often cannot be easily traced back to
regime type.

DEMOCRACIES DO NOT TREAT NONDEMOCRACIES WITH SUSPICION.
Contrary to the claims of the dyadic democratic peace argument,
there is no reason to assume that democracies treat nondemocracies
with suspicion. For example, Freedman (Chapter 5) finds that despite
Argentina's authoritarianism, the British government was willing to
transfer the Falkland Islands to Argentina, a fact that belies the notion
that democracies find it difficult to cooperate with nondemocracies.
Similarly, in Chapter 7, I argue that democratic peace theorists over-
state the extent to which democracies prefer democratic neighbors.
Israel's foreign policy toward Lebanon shows that democratic states
do not necessarily treat democracies with the expectation of amity,
and nondemocracies with suspicion. Israel consistently acted to
undermine Lebanon's democratic system, preferring a Lebanese state
where the pro-Israeli Maronite minority would not have to share
power with the anti-Israeli majority. Indeed, Israeli leaders were not
concerned with Lebanon's domestic regime type, but with which
Lebanese made up the ruling coalition. In sum, contrary to the claims
of the dyadic version of the democratic peace theory, cooperative

relations are possible—and are often sought—with states that use domestic coercion.

NONDEMOCRATIC REGIME FEATURES HELP TO KEEP THE PEACE. Our cumulative findings show that nondemocracies do not necessarily apply their internal norms of political behavior to their foreign relations, and that such domestic norms do not necessarily reduce the chances for international cooperation. For example, Kacowicz (Chapter 8) notes that both Mauritania and Peru upheld norms of conflict resolution, compromise, and mediation at the international level, though they ignored similar norms at home. Our findings suggest that we should not assume that nondemocracies externalize domestic norms of conflict resolution when dealing with international actors. They frequently initiate international negotiations and see war as an option of last resort. Thus, aggressiveness or peacefulness cannot be readily inferred from the degree of violence in a state's domestic arena.

In addition, we note that the absence of institutional constraints on leaders can facilitate peace. Martin Malin (Chapter 9) points out that because of the absence of governmental and societal constraints on foreign policy, Iran and Iraq were able to resolve long standing disagreements in the 1970s. The freedom of both executives made the negotiation of a peaceful settlement easier than it might otherwise have been; neither government feared the domestic political consequences of an unpopular agreement. Similarly, in Chapter 11, Matthews argues that during the interwar period, nondemocratic Turkey was able to pursue a moderate foreign policy toward Greece because there were no institutional constraints on the leader's discretion. Had Turkey been more democratic, it would have been more aggressive internationally because hard-line elites would not have been excluded from the policy making process. Thus, Matthews argues that when leaders are moderate and prefer peaceful methods of international conflict resolution, nondemocracy—particularly the absence of checks on the leader's foreign policy choices—can be a force for peace instead of an obstacle.

Kurt Dassel (Chapter 10) also suggests that a sizeable subset of nondemocracies will usually adopt peaceful rather than aggressive foreign policies. Dassel argues that, in authoritarian states that have unstable regimes, if the military can use force domestically without jeopardizing its cohesiveness, it will favor repressing domestic opponents and refrain from international aggression. Thus, Dassel points out that regimes in which there are few checks on foreign policy decision makers, and in which domestic conflicts are resolved through massive violence, may be the very states that pursue pacific foreign policies; because force can be used at home, it will not be used abroad.

In short, democratic peace theorists wrongly assert that nondemocracies are predisposed to aggression because of the characteristics of their governments. In this book, we suggest that only some nondemocratic states will use force abroad; treating all nondemocracies as potential aggressors is misleading.

SHARED NORMS CAN EXPLAIN NONDEMOCRATIC PEACE. Several contributors to this book find that nondemocracies and mixed dyads can share a peace based on normative consensus. Consequently, peace among mixed dyads and nondemocracies is not merely a result of common interests or relative material capabilities. Like democracies, these states can also build a normative foundation for peace. For example, Kacowicz (Chapter 8) contends that joint democracy is necessary for the evolution and deepening of stable peace where there are no expectations of violence and where war has been deemed illegitimate; however, he points out that joint democracy is not necessary for forging a normative consensus based on the absence of war. Nondemocracies and democracies in South America and West Africa have been able to develop a regional normative consensus against the use of force.

Similarly, Malin (Chapter 9) argues that the absence of internal norms of peaceful conflict resolution does not preclude nondemocracies from establishing norm-governed international peace among themselves. Malin argues that the Iran-Iraq peace, forged in the 1970s and culminating in the 1975 Algiers Accord, is an example of how nondemocracies can establish a peace founded on shared norms of behavior. These states enjoyed peace not because it was backed up by coercive threats or calculations of strategic advantage, as democratic peace theorists would lead us to expect. The Accord did not merely reflect the absence of conflict due to stalemate, coercion, or coincidental interests. Instead, it constituted a warm, pacific relationship of the type expected only among democracies.[27]

NONDEMOCRATIC REGIME FEATURES DO NOT CAUSE NONDEMOCRATIC WAR. We suggest that, contrary to the claims of democratic peace theorists, nondemocracies' decisions for war often have little to do

27. For a recent study that suggests that nondemocracies can adhere to international norms, see Jeffrey W. Legro, "Which Norms Matter? Revisiting the 'Failure' of Internationalism," *International Organization*, Vol. 51, No. 1 (Winter 1997), pp. 31–63.

with the flaws of their regime type. For example, in Chapter 6 Ganguly argues that neorealist factors account for Pakistan's decision to use force against India in 1965: Pakistan had important strategic incentives to wage war at the time. Consequently, wars initiated by nondemocracies against democratic opponents do not necessarily provide conclusive evidence of the dyadic version of the democratic peace theory.[28]

Similarly, Malin (Chapter 9) argues that basing an explanation of Iraq's decision to go to war against Iran in 1980 solely on the domestic features of Iraq's nondemocratic regime is misleading. While Saddam Hussein was able to use force against Iran without being constrained by domestic considerations, he neither decided on war immediately after the Iranian revolution nor acted rapidly to exploit the domestic turmoil in Iran. Instead, Hussein made numerous attempts at diplomacy in hopes of maintaining cordial relations; he viewed war only as an option of last resort. Malin argues that a new set of international threats accounted for Iraq's war decision; the democratic peace theory's focus on regime type—nondemocracy—obscures a complex set of external constraints.[29]

Policy Implications for the Democratic Peace Theory

The democratic peace theory is an appealing and romantic vision. It is parsimonious and conceptually clear, and fits with our intuitive beliefs that nondemocracies are not to be trusted, and that democracy is a desirable form of political organization. Because it has the merit of simplicity and is palatable to our liberal sensitivities, international relations scholars and U.S. foreign policy makers treat the democratic peace theory as a reliable guide to foreign policy.

The insight that democracies do not fight each other currently serves as the basis for U.S. foreign policy making. President Bill Clinton and former National Security Adviser Anthony Lake have

---

28. Like Ganguly, I suggest in Chapter 4 that the Soviet Union's initiation of war against Finland in 1939 does not automatically vindicate the dyadic democratic peace proposition. Prior to the Winter War, the Soviet leadership was not averse to negotiation and compromise.

29. In addition, Malin argues that regime type cannot adequately account for the Iran-Iraq war because regime type remained constant while conflict between these states increased dramatically. Neither Iran nor Iraq became more autocratic—yet cordial relations established in the 1970s deteriorated to war in the early 1980s. Thus, by overemphasizing regime type, we neglect the domestic transformations that occur within nondemocratic states.

repeatedly invoked the absence of war among democracies as justifying the promotion of democracy abroad. In his 1994 State of the
Union message, President Clinton declared that "ultimately the best
strategy to ensure our security and to build a durable peace is to support the advance of democracies elsewhere. Democracies don't attack
each other."[30] Aid to Russia and military intervention in Bosnia and
Haiti have been justified on the grounds that democracies do not go
to war with one another. Democratic enlargement has replaced communist containment as the U.S. grand strategy, and as its new strategic vision for the post–Cold War era. The administration has firmly
grasped the notion that as free states grow in number and strength,
the international world order will become both more prosperous and
more secure.[31]

The idea of a world where democracy brings peace has a great deal
of intuitive appeal. We do not recommend that U.S. foreign policy
makers jettison a commitment to democracy; nor do we reject the
claim that domestic norms and institutions can affect both foreign
policy outcomes and the ways in which states identify external
threats. But the contributors to this book warn that the idea of a democratic peace should not be used as an excuse for aggression against
nondemocracies. Nor should it serve as a rationale for ignoring
domestic developments in, and challenges from, democratic allies.
Our discussion of war and peace decision making in democratic,
democratic-nondemocratic, and nondemocratic pairs of states has
four main implications for U.S. foreign policy.

DO NOT PUT DEMOCRATIC ALLIES ON AUTOMATIC PILOT
One of the implications of our analysis is that war among democratic
states is not impossible. Our case studies show that democracies prepare for war against each other, and threaten the use of force when
vital national interests are at stake. Furthermore, we show that strategic imperatives often outweigh ideological preferences, and can lead
to wars among democracies—even among those that perceive each
other as democracies.

Taken at face value, the democratic peace theory fosters a complacency about dangerous domestic developments within democratic
allies, and implies that the United States can be indifferent about great
power challenges from these states. For example, the democratic

---

30. "Transcript of Clinton's Address," *New York Times*, January 26, 1994, p. A17.

31. Douglas Brinkley, "Democratic Enlargement: The Clinton Doctrine," *Foreign
Policy*, No. 106 (Spring 1997), pp. 111–127.

peace theory implies that the United States need not be concerned about the emergence of Japan and Germany as great powers and need not worry about the relative distribution of material capabilities between itself and these states. But if history and the case studies presented in this book are to serve as a guide, the United States would be well advised not to develop a false sense of security toward its democratic allies. Treating today's democratic allies with complacency means that we may not be able to defend our interests against these states if we need to in the future.

In addition, we recommend that the United States closely monitor domestic developments within other democracies. One of the cumulative conclusions of this book is that domestic politics affect states' foreign policies, but that crude distinctions based on regime type—democracy versus nondemocracy—tell us little. Among democracies, the leadership's willingness to solve international conflicts through peaceful methods; how power over military operations is divided between civil and military leaders; the strength of political parties; and the extent to which war-prone leaders are constrained by the public and other decision making bodies can vary dramatically. Basing foreign policy on whether a country is democratic or not provides a simple metric, but is a poor formula for determining a state's war propensity. U.S. decision makers would be well advised to look beyond the democratic peace theory for a model of how domestic political processes influence war and peace decision making—it is an unreliable guide to the domestic sources of foreign policy.

REGIME TYPE IS NO EXCUSE FOR BELLIGERENCE AGAINST
NONDEMOCRACIES

By portraying international politics as a world in which democracies cooperate while democracies and nondemocracies are doomed to compete, the democratic peace theory robs policy makers of flexibility, and can turn states that might otherwise be neutral or friendly into enemies. The chapters in this volume show that cooperative foreign relations are possible with states that use domestic coercion. Furthermore, our findings suggest that not all nondemocratic states are inherently hostile; some nondemocracies eschew aggression outside of their borders, and the absence of democratic features can make it easier for nondemocracies to pursue benign foreign policies. The failure to uphold liberal values at home and the lack of institutional constraints on leaders' autonomy does not necessarily translate into aggression abroad.

Our findings suggest two guidelines for U.S. foreign policy. First, the United States should not base policy on the idea of the democratic peace if doing so needlessly antagonizes potential nondemocratic allies. For example, promoting the expansion of NATO on the grounds that democracies do not go to war with each other threatens Russia. The policy implies that Russia is not really a democracy, and therefore by its very nature poses a danger to the fledgling democracies of East and Central Europe. NATO expansion that is justified on the basis of promoting democracy in the former Soviet Union can thus have harmful unintended effects: it is a provocative threat to Russian security, and can potentially undermine Russian democracy while increasing friction between Russia and the West. Similarly, the democratic peace theory should not be read as removing the possibility for peaceful relations between the West and nondemocracies, such as China. A policy toward China based on the idea of democratic peace, which would treat nondemocratic China as intrinsically hostile, could drive it to forge anti-U.S. alliances solely out of a need for self-preservation. In short, instead of using regime type as a blueprint for dividing the world into good states and bad states, the United States should focus on states' foreign policy behavior, treating states that display malign behavior as enemies, and states that act peacefully as potential friends.

Second, the United States should dissuade its democratic allies from using the democratic peace theory as a convenient excuse for taking hard-line positions against nondemocratic neighbors. In the Middle East, Israeli opponents of the Arab-Israeli peace process have drawn on the democratic peace theory to justify their position: since stable peace can only be concluded among democratic states, Israel should postpone any peace settlement until Israel's Arab neighbors democratize.[32] The United States should remind its democratic allies that the democratic peace idea is no excuse for intransigence.

DO NOT ASSUME THAT NEW DEMOCRACIES WILL CONFORM

By the end of 1995, one hundred and seventeen countries—nearly two out of every three sovereign states—had chosen their leaders by the ballot. According to democratic peace theorists, this new wave of democratization will vindicate the democratic peace proposition: while critics have argued that in the past, the number of democracies

---

32. Raymond Cohen, "Pacific Unions: A Reappraisal of the Theory that 'Democracies Do Not Go to War With Each Other,'" *Review of International Studies*, Vol. 20, No. 3 (July 1994), p. 223.

in the international system has been so small that the absence of wars between them is statistically insignificant, proponents claim that a large number of democracies acting peacefully today will prove that the democratic peace is not merely the product of random chance.

This book presents a less sanguine view. U.S. policy makers should not assume that the foreign policy behavior of new democracies will be especially benign. First, most of the new democracies today share borders. As our case analyses demonstrate, when territorial integrity is at stake—as is likely to happen in the new Europe and elsewhere where democracies have common borders—shared liberal ideology and democratic institutions may not be enough to keep the peace. Second, many of these new democracies are weakly institutionalized, and do not have strong party systems. As the cases in this book show, under these conditions, nationalism becomes a convenient tool that politicians can use in competing for political power, making foreign aggression more likely—both against nondemocratic and democratic neighbors.[33] Finally, unlike in the past, virtually all of the new democracies that have recently emerged are small states, not great powers. Great powers are relatively secure, and have the luxury of defining their interests in terms of ideological principles. By contrast, small states that risk occupation or extinction cannot afford to make foreign policy mistakes, and are thus more likely to base foreign policies on the strategic environment. As our cumulative findings show, small states that face severe external threats are more likely to exhibit foreign policies that diverge from the expectations of the democratic peace theory.

DO NOT ASSUME THAT ALL DEMOCRACY IS U.S.-STYLE DEMOCRACY

We recommend that U.S. foreign policy makers recognize that promoting democracy abroad and exporting U.S.-style democracy are two separate agendas—the United States' policy of democratic enlargement may lead to more democracies, but not necessarily to more democracies that are like the United States. One of the central conclusions of this book is that democracies (and nondemocracies) need to be disaggregated. The democratic peace theory incorrectly

33. For more on these dynamics, see Edward D. Mansfield and Jack Snyder, "Democratization and the Danger of War," *International Security,* Vol. 20, No. 2 (Summer 1995), pp. 5–38; V.P. Gagnon, Jr., "Ethnic Nationalism and International Conflict: The Case of Serbia," *International Security,* Vol. 19, No. 3 (Winter 1994/95), pp. 130–166; and Alexander V. Kozhemiakin, "Democratization and Foreign Policy Change: The Case of the Russian Federation," *Review of International Studies,* Vol. 23, No. 1 (January 1997), pp. 49–74.

502 | PATHS TO PEACE

lumps disparate systems of government into a catch-all category. It also implies that all democracies will use political ideological principles as guides for identifying international friends and foes. This book challenges both claims.

Some democracies—those in which the executive is decentralized or lacks autonomy from the legislative branch—are more likely to exhibit foreign policies that conform to both the dyadic and the monadic versions of the democratic peace theory. It is partly for this reason that we find that U.S. foreign policy has been consistent with the theory's central predictions. By contrast, democracies that do not grant the legislature a significant *ex ante* role in the foreign policy making process provide fewer opportunities for liberal elites to prevent illiberal leaders from waging war. Most parliamentary democracies provide few *ex ante* constraints on an executive that commands a majority in the legislature—and when the ruling party favors war, leaders in these democracies may have even more foreign policy leeway than their nondemocratic counterparts.

In addition, some democracies—such as the United States—base their self-identity on their political ideologies, and tend to judge the threat that other states pose according to these beliefs. But as the case studies in this book show, most democratic states tend to base foreign policy choices on other international or domestic normative values. For example, we suggest that many democracies see religion and culture as the basis of self-identity.

In short, it is essential that U.S. policy makers who are contemplating the promotion of democracy be aware of differences among democracies, and recognize that liberalism is not necessarily the set of normative values and principles that will guide the foreign policies of other democracies.

A Final Word: The Future of the Democratic Peace

The central criticism of the democratic peace theory is that peace among democracies can be attributed to influences other than shared democratic institutions and liberal norms, primarily the relative distribution of power and the material capabilities for war-fighting. Many dissenters conclude that neorealist factors—power and strategic calculations—determine states' decisions to fight each other, and that the democratic peace theory should be jettisoned, since it offers only limited insights into war and peace decision making.

This book takes a different position. We do not deny that neorealism can often account for instances of democratic peace, as well as instances where democracies have chosen to fight or threaten one another. Power, geopolitical interests, and strategic calculations greatly influence the decision making calculus of all states, democratic or not. But we contend that there is a connection between democracy and foreign policy, and that much of international relations cannot be explained without reference to domestic-level variables. We suggest that the democratic peace theory is neither completely invalid nor universally applicable. Rather than jettison the theory or give it the status of a social science law, democratic peace theorists and their critics should identify the conditions under which the theory will be most and least applicable. This book starts to develop such a contingent theory of democratic peace, but much more work is needed to identify conditional generalizations linking regime type to war and peace. Our work points to four promising avenues of research on the democratic peace.

First, more research should test the democratic peace theory against alternative domestic-level and international-level theories. The democratic peace theory posits that one domestic factor—regime type—matters more than all other domestic variables in the explanation of war and peace. Consequently, it competes with other domestic-level theories that emphasize the role of leadership orientations, civil-military relations, political parties, or presidential versus parliamentary government. We can test the democratic peace theory against these alternative domestic-level theories to develop a more complete theory of the domestic sources of foreign policy.[34] In addition, the democratic peace theory competes not only with neorealism, but with other international-level approaches. For example, the democratic peace theory competes with neoliberal institutionalism, which explains international cooperation on the basis of institutionalized rules and decision making procedures; the nature of the interacting states' regime types is irrelevant to this conceptual

---

34. Testing the predictions of the democratic peace theory against those posited by competing domestic-level theories would also clarify the extent to which the democratic peace theory is compatible with classical realism. Many of the cases in this book support a classical realist reading of international politics; they focus on domestic politics, and on the role of foreign policy makers. But there remains a need to further specify how the democratic peace theory competes with, or complements, the writings of classical realists.

framework.[35] Testing the democratic peace theory against neoliberal institutionalism would allow us to develop a fuller theory of the ideational and institutional sources of international cooperation.

Second, few studies have attempted to distinguish different types of democracies and nondemocracies, and to assess the foreign policy implications of these differences. The case study analyses presented in this book suggest a need to examine the effects of different democratic institutions and different nondemocratic regime types. We find that the foreign policies of certain democracies and nondemocracies will be inconsistent with the predictions of the democratic peace theory. Studying the interactions among democracies and nondemocracies, and among nondemocracies themselves, will help to further specify the range of countries whose foreign policies will conform to the democratic peace theory's predictions. Such studies may also generate additional information about the sources of democratic peace.

Third, researchers should continue to test the various versions of the democratic peace theory against each other. For example, the case studies in this volume suggest that the dyadic version is more robust than the monadic argument: in many of the chapters, perceptions of the opponent's regime type were crucial to the decision making calculus; democracies did not see war only as an option of last resort; and democratic publics were not averse to the prospect of a war with high casualties. Yet, the jury is still out. Since many of today's democracies share borders with both democracies and nondemocracies, there are ample opportunities for proponents of both versions to test their competing claims. In addition, scholars should refine the causal logic that underlies the democratic peace by testing whether liberal norms or democratic institutions—or some combination of both— best account for the absence of war among democracies. In this book we test both institutional and normative models precisely because the empirical evidence that is inconsistent with one explanation may be perfectly accounted for by the other. More case studies might shed further light on this issue.

Finally, future research on the democratic peace theory should do more to assess whether liberal democracies behave differently from

35. For example, much work has applied the insights of neoliberal insitutionalism to the development of regional security organizations such as ASEAN, an international regime whose membership includes democracies and nondemocracies. See, for example, Sheldon W. Simon, "Realism and Neoliberalism: International Relations Theory and Southeast Asian Security," *Pacific Review*, Vol. 8, No. 1 (1995), pp. 5–24.

illiberal democracies. In this volume we point out that illiberal publics can push moderate leaders toward war when democratic institutions allow them access to the decision making arena. Since many democracies today do not view the world through a liberal lens, research on this issue is pressing.[36]

The democratic peace theory is not just a matter of abstract concern—it is a source of guidance for policy makers and challenges traditional ways of explaining international relations. The most popular version of the theory, the dyadic proposition, directs democratically elected foreign policy makers to make decisions on the basis of how democratic another government is. Another variant, the monadic proposition, posits that democracies are more pacific regardless of the regime types of other states; a world in which even some governments are democratic will be much less violent. Both arguments imply that nondemocratic governments are not to be trusted because they are illegitimate on normative grounds, and do not allow representative legislatures to restrain war-prone leaders. The contributors to this book, who disagree themselves on the existence of a democratic peace, find fault with each of these propositions, and urge democratic peace proponents and their critics to refine their arguments. We agree that the democratic peace thesis is an empirical phenomenon to be studied, not a matter of faith to be reaffirmed. We agree that it is important to continue to question the validity and limits of each democratic peace proposition. Most importantly, we concur that proponents and critics of the democratic peace thesis should forswear grand theories and simple dichotomies, and instead should develop contingent generalizations that identify the interactions among a greater number of domestic and international variables. Our book suggests that there are several paths that lead to war and several that lead to peace—and some that can lead to either. It may be a mistake to urge all states to follow a single path in their domestic politics, for the path that leads one state to pacific behavior may lead another to conflict within or abroad. In the final account, our analysis of democratic, democratic-nondemocratic, and nondemocratic war and peace decision making suggests that we may

---

36. Several democratic peace proponents recognize that illiberal democracies can act aggressively abroad, and that these democratic states are unlikely to enjoy a democratic peace. See Owen, "How Liberalism Produces Democratic Peace," pp. 127–128; and Michael W. Doyle, "Michael Doyle on the Democratic Peace— Again," in Brown, Lynn-Jones, and Miller, eds., *Debating the Democratic Peace,* p. 367. More statistical and case studies on this issue are needed.

need to go beyond the democratic peace. Since there are several paths to war and alternative routes to peace, democracy may not be the answer we are looking for.

Contributors

Miriam Fendius Elman is Assistant Professor in the Department of Political Science at Arizona State University. She received her Ph.D. from Columbia University, and was a research fellow at the Center for Science and International Affairs at Harvard University from 1995–96.

Kurt Dassel is a Post-Doctoral Research Fellow at the Olin Institute for Strategic Studies at Harvard University.

Lawrence Freedman is Professor of War Studies at King's College, London.

Šumit Ganguly is Professor of Political Science at Hunter College of the City University of New York and Adjunct Professor of Political Science at Columbia University. He is the author of *The Origins of War in South Asia: The Indo-Pakistani Conflicts Since 1947* (Westview, 2nd ed., 1994) and *The Crisis in Kashmir: Portents of War, Hopes of Peace* (Cambridge University Press and the Woodrow Wilson Center Press, 1997).

Arie M. Kacowicz is a Lecturer in International Relations at the Hebrew University of Jerusalem. For the academic year of 1997–98, he will be a Visiting Fellow at the Kroc Institute for International Peace Studies and the Kellogg Institute for International Studies at the University of Notre Dame. He is the author of *Peaceful Territorial Change* (University of South Carolina Press, 1994), and has recently completed a book on zones of peace in the Third World.

Christopher Layne is a Visiting Associate Professor at the Naval Postgraduate School in Monterey, California, and a resident consultant at the RAND Corporation. He is the author (with Sean M. Lynn-Jones) of *Should the United States Export Democracy? A Debate* (MIT Press, forthcoming 1998).

Martin Malin is Adjunct Assistant Professor at Columbia University.

John C. Matthews III has a Ph.D. in political science from Columbia University. He is a consultant for Monitor Company in London.

John M. Owen is Assistant Professor in the Department of Government and Foreign Affairs at the University of Virginia. From 1995–97, he was Assistant Professor in the Department of Government and Legal Studies at Bowdoin College.

Stephen R. Rock is Associate Professor of Political Science at Vassar College.

The Robert and Renée Belfer Center for Science and International Affairs

Graham T. Allison, Director
John F. Kennedy School of Government
Harvard University
79 JFK Street, Cambridge MA 02138
(617) 495-1400

The Belfer Center for Science and International Affairs (BCSIA) is the hub of research, teaching, and training in international security affairs, environmental and resource issues, and science and technology policy at Harvard's John F. Kennedy School of Government. The Center's mission is to provide leadership in advancing policy-relevant knowledge about the most important challenges of international security and other critical issues where science, technology and international affairs intersect.

BCSIA's leadership begins with the recognition of science and technology as driving forces transforming international affairs. The Center integrates insights of social scientists, natural scientists, technologists and practitioners with experience in government, diplomacy, the military, and business to address these challenges. The Center pursues its mission in four complementary research programs:

- The International Security Program (ISP) addresses the most pressing threats to U.S. national interests and international security.

- The Environment and Natural Resources Program (ENRP) is the locus of Harvard's interdisciplinary research on resource and environmental problems and policy responses.

- The Science, Technology, and Public Policy (STPP) program analyzes ways in which science and technology policy influence international security, resources, environment, and development and such cross-cutting issues as technological innovation and information infrastructure.

- The Strengthening Democratic Institutions (SDI) project catalyzes support for three great transformations in Russia, Ukraine, and the other republics of the former Soviet Union—to sustainable democracies, free market economies, and cooperative international relations.

The heart of the Center is its resident research community of more than one hundred scholars: Harvard faculty, analysts, practitioners, and each year a new, interdisciplinary group of research fellows. BCSIA sponsors frequent seminars, workshops and conferences, many open to the public; maintains a substantial specialized library; and publishes a monograph series and discussion papers. The Center's International Security Program, directed by Steven E. Miller, publishes the CSIA Studies in International Security, and sponsors and edits the quarterly journal International Security.

The Center is supported by an endowment established with funds from Robert and Renée Belfer, the Ford Foundation, and Harvard University, by foundation grants, by individual gifts, and by occasional government contracts.